STRANGE STORIES, AMAZING FACTS
of America's Past

Reader's Digest

STRANGE STORIES, AMAZING FACTS of America's Past

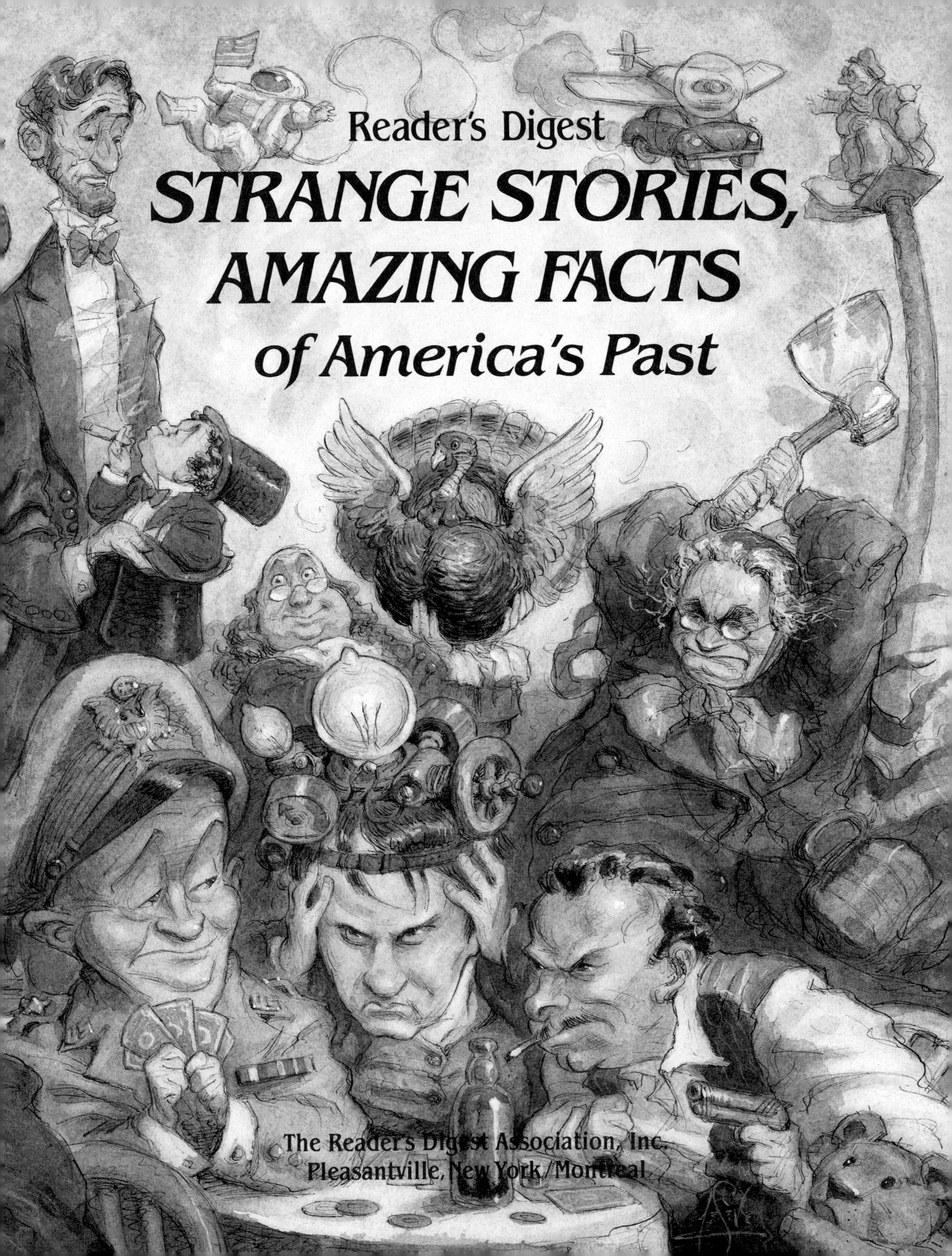

The Reader's Digest Association, Inc.
Pleasantville, New York/Montreal

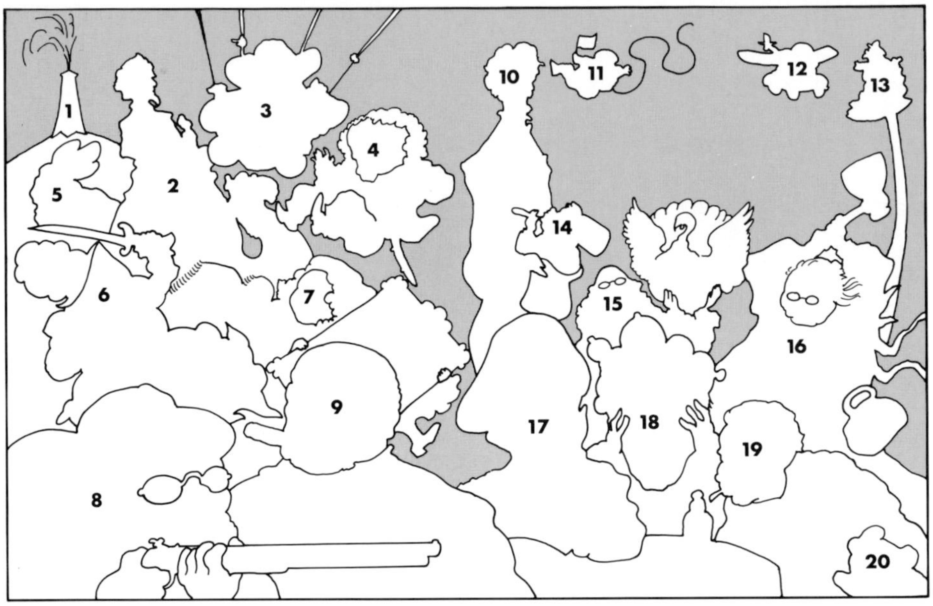

Guide to title page illustration

STRANGE STORIES, AMAZING FACTS
OF AMERICA'S PAST

The acknowledgments and credits that appear on pages 406–408 are hereby made a part of this copyright page.

The editors gratefully acknowledge their debt to the groundbreaking historical publications of *American Heritage,* which served as an inspiration and occasional model in the preparation of this book.

Library of Congress Cataloging in Publication Data

Strange stories, amazing facts of America's past.

At head of title: Reader's digest.
Includes index
1. United States—History—Anecdotes. I. Reader's digest.
E178.6.S896 1989 973 88-11515
ISBN 0-89577-307-4

Printed in the United States of America
Third Printing, October 1990

STRANGE STORIES, AMAZING FACTS of America's Past

Project Editor: Jim Dwyer
Art Editor: Kenneth Chaya
Associate Editor and Research Editor: David Palmer
Associate Editors: Noreen B. Church, W. Clotilde Lanig, Diana Marsh, Paula Pines
Art Associate: Nancy Mace
Research Associates: Barbara Guarino, Diane Zito
Library Research: Nettie Seaberry
Editorial Assistant: Vita Gardner
Editorial Intern: Melanie Williams

CONTRIBUTORS
General Consultant: Frank B. Latham
Business Consultant: The Winthrop Group, Inc.
Military Consultant: Col. John R. Elting, U.S. Army, Ret.
Editorial Research: Mary Hart, Madeleine Walker
Writers: Tom Callahan, David Caras, Rita Christopher, Ormonde de Kay, Josh Eppinger, Marjorie Flory, Signe Hammer, Jeanne Molli, Don O'Neill, Heinzdieter von Schoenermarck, David Sicilia, Robert Thurston, Terry Wells, Jeff Yablonka
Art Research: Mary Leverty, Lisa Barlow, Sybille Millard
Illustrators: Michael K. Conway, Peter de Sève, Gil Eisner, Gerry Gersten, Steve Gray, Gregg Hinlicky, Victor Lazzaro, Rick McCollum, Bill Shortridge, Ed Vebell, Richard Williams
Copy Editor: Eva Galan Salmieri
Indexer: Sydney Wolfe Cohen

READER'S DIGEST GENERAL BOOKS

Editor in Chief: John A. Pope, Jr.
Managing Editor: Jane Polley
Art Director: David Trooper
Group Editors: Norman B. Mack, Susan J. Wernert, Joseph L. Gardner (International), Joel Musler (Art)
Chief of Research: Monica Borrowman
Copy Chief: Edward W. Atkinson
Picture Editor: Robert J. Woodward
Rights and Permissions: Pat Colomban
Head Librarian: Jo Manning

"The past is a foreign country: they do things differently there."

Lesley Poles Hartley
The Go-Between (1953)

A traveler to the past is bound to encounter the strange and unusual, the odd and amazing, at every turn. That's a big part of the pleasure of travel, whether in time or space. And it's the underlying fun of history.

The "foreign countries" you'll visit in these pages go by such names as Jamestown 1644, where the young son of Princess Pocohontas and John Rolfe must choose whether to fight for his mother's people or his father's; Massachusetts Bay Colony 1660, where a young woman's life ends on a hanging tree because she won't renounce her religion; New York Harbor 1776, where a solitary hero in a hand-cranked submarine tries vainly to thwart a British invasion; Blennerhassett Island 1806, where a former vice president of the United States plots to claim much of North America as his private empire; the Missouri River 1819, where an intrepid explorer disguises his steamboat as a dragon to keep Indians at bay; the Sierra Nevada 1858, where an enterprising mail carrier uses a team of mongrels to pull his delivery sled through the snow; Bullfrog Mountain 1904, where a "single-blanket jackass prospector" called Shorty makes the biggest gold strike in Death Valley history, gets drunk, and sells his claim for $1,000.

Yes, they're all like foreign countries, and folks *do* do things differently there. And yet they're all America—this one-time wilderness, this vast raw opportunity, that grew into a nation because it was populated with people's dreams. The story of America is the sum total of those dreams: comic and serious, brilliant and deluded, grand and quietly personal, from the common moments of our greatest heroes to the heroic moments of the most common man. And those dreams are what this book is all about.

Here's history, warts and all: the scandal that ruined Alexander Hamilton's political career, the fistfights and gunplay in the Senate, the wheeling and dealing that built great fortunes. Here's the courage of Robert Peary and Matthew Henson trekking to the North Pole, and the chicanery of Dr. Cook pretending *he'd* done it first. Here's a flagpole sitter, a rainmaker who flooded whole counties, a tidal wave of molasses, and the last battle of the Civil War—in Alaska's Bering Strait.

There's plenty of laughter in this book, and perhaps a tear or two; but all of us who worked on it also found ourselves touched by wonder and awe—and a kind of joy in being American that goes far deeper than laughter. We hope you find that, too.

— *The Editors*

CONTENTS

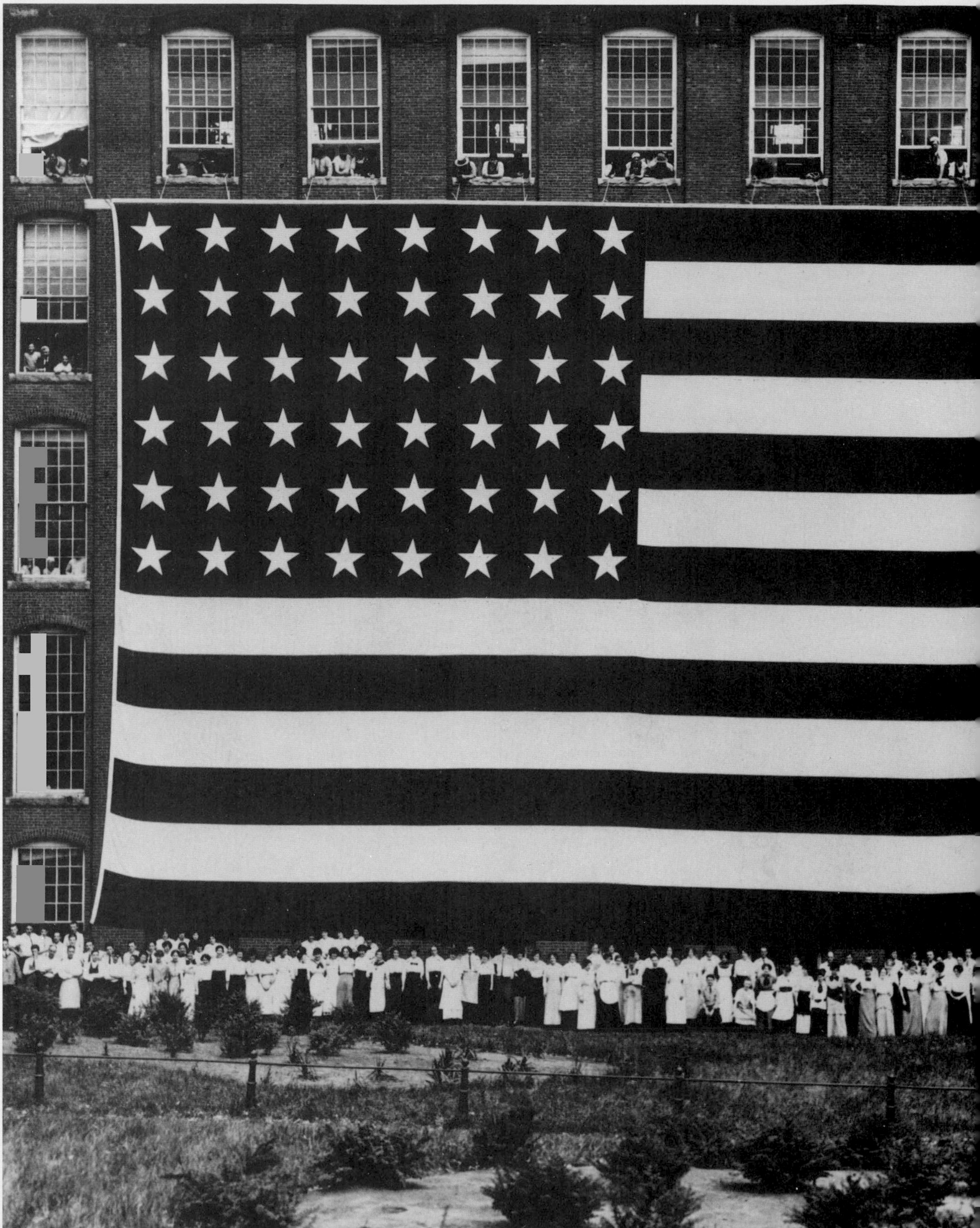

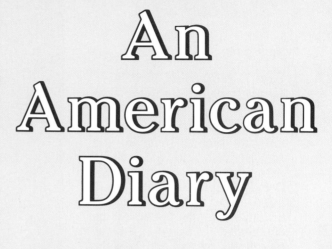

CHAPTER ONE

An American Diary

Hardly a day goes by that something strange and amazing doesn't happen somewhere in this wide and wonderful land of ours. So it has always been. In this chapter you'll find a kaleidoscopic selection, month by month, of a few of the oddities that have occurred in America over the years. And along with it, there's a calendar guide to some of the stories that are told elsewhere in the book.

200 pounds of patriotism, 95 feet by 50 feet (Manchester, New Hampshire, June 29, 1914)

January

A Free City

Jan. 7, 1861: Will New York secede with the Confederacy?

This 1862 cartoon portrayed President Lincoln, feebly armed with a gun swab and fettered to strict constitutionality by pro-Southern Tammany Hall Democrats, striving to crush the dragon of rebellion.

Civil war and the dissolution of the Union seemed imminent, and so Mayor Fernando Wood of New York, a powerful pro-Southern Democrat, made a startling proposal in his annual message to the city's Common Council: if the Southern states seceded, the city should do so too and become "equally independent." As a "free city," he argued, it would survive with the support of the South and the sizable income provided by import duties.

Attacking the Republican state legislature's tight control and taxation of the city, Wood asked: "Why may not New York disrupt the bands which bind her to a venal and corrupt master?"

Democrats in the council and a number of businessmen supported his idea, and secret plans were made to carry it out. But when the war's first shots were fired, New Yorkers proved to be staunchly pro-Union and Wood was voted out of office.

Later, as a leader of Northern antiwar Democrats, or Copperheads, Wood became a thorn in Abraham Lincoln's side.

Whither Will He Wander?

Jan. 9, 1793: President Washington watches man fly

George Washington had been intrigued by the idea of using balloons for transportation ever since the first manned flight in Paris in 1783, which Benjamin Franklin had recognized as portentous. And so, when the "greatest of the aeronauts," Jean Pierre Blanchard, crossed the Atlantic to give a demonstration, Washington was there.

The site chosen for the lift-off was the Walnut Street Prison courtyard in Philadelphia, the nation's capital. Arriving at 9:00 A.M., Washington thoughtfully presented Blanchard with a passport he himself had signed, not knowing how far the balloonist might travel.

When the 46-minute flight ended near Woodbury, New Jersey, 15 miles away, Blanchard was met by two astonished farmers, one carrying a gun. Blanchard, who didn't understand English, waved the paper with the presidential signature and produced a bottle of spirits. He was given a warm reception and passage back to Philadelphia.

At the end of his flight, Blanchard presented Washington with the first flag literally to fly over U.S. soil.

A Deadly, Sticky Disaster

Jan. 15, 1919: A tidal wave of molasses inundates Boston

Old-timers in Boston still talk about the molasses flood that engulfed the city's North End. It occurred on a warm winter day that had brought many Bostonians outdoors to bask in the unseasonable thaw. Some lunched in the shadow of the Purity Distilling Corporation's massive molasses tank. The steel-sided structure, 50 feet high and 90 feet in diameter, was filled nearly to the brim with 2,300,000 gallons of molasses intended for rum. And it was about to come apart.

First, molasses sweated through the tank's looser rivets—they popped out of their holes with a sound like machine-gun fire. Then, with a muffled roar, the weakened seams split, and tons of molasses spewed out in a sudden pitch-black flood.

The first wave, about 30 feet high, overpowered everything in its way, reducing buildings to rubble. Helpless men and animals were carried off like driftwood. A housewife died when her home collapsed around her. A boy buffeted by the surge was unable to call to his mother because his throat was clogged with molasses. A man was swept into Boston Harbor, which was fast becoming a brown, murky mess.

The tank wreaked havoc too, launching pieces of metal into the air like shrapnel. Flying shards sliced through a pillar of the Boston Elevated Railway, and an oncoming train braked just in time to avoid plunging into the ocean of goo.

After the flood had subsided, molasses clogged the streets, up to three feet deep in places. Victims continued to be found. A small girl still clutched firewood she had gathered. The corpse of a wagon driver was a molasses-coated statue. Survivors had to have their molasses-stiffened clothing cut off. Trapped horses had to be shot. The disaster left 21 dead (most of them drowned) and more than 50 injured.

In the ensuing weeks of cleanup, the citizens of Boston tracked molasses all over the city. People stuck to benches and sidewalks, or grappled with phone receivers glued to their ears. The molasses odor lingered for months—some say years. Even today people claim that on a hot afternoon there is a hint of it in the air.

Only hours before this picture was taken, a giant molasses tank stood here. At the left is the ruin of an elevated railroad track that collapsed in the flood.

It Happened on January . . .

1, 1802: *Thomas Jefferson gets a 1,235-pound cheese.–p.76*

1, 1889: *Wovoka, a Paiute, has a vision from God and begins the Ghost Dance religion.–p.388*

1, 1919: *Vladimir Zworykin, Russian immigrant who later invents television, lands in U.S.A.–p.350*

2, 1825: *George Rapp sells the entire town of Harmony, Ind., to Robert Owen.–p.277*

3, 1863: *Thomas Nast gives birth to Santa Claus as we now know him.–p.219*

3, 1914: *Pancho Villa signs a contract with Hollywood to film his battles live.–p.393*

4, 1493: *Christopher Columbus starts back to Spain.–p.260*

5, 1904: *Elizabeth Magie patents the Landlord Game, later to be called Monopoly.–p.151*

5, 1919: *Col. Luke Lea tries to kidnap the kaiser.–p.396*

6, 1853: *President-elect Franklin Pierce and his wife see their son die in a train wreck.–p.81*

6, 1969: *Gov. Jimmy Carter of Georgia spots a UFO visiting a Lions Club meeting.–p.256*

7, 1905: *Alfred Fuller sells his first brush.–p.133*

8, 1909: *Congress chastises Teddy Roosevelt for trying to blackmail its members.–p.95*

9, 1863: *Whaler George Weldon, stripped for a lashing, surprises the crew of the bark* America.*–p.276*

10, 1864: *Outlaw sheriff Henry Plummer is hanged from his own gallows.–p.172*

10, 1901: *The Spindletop gusher comes in with a roar; sets off the Texas oil boom.–p.130*

11, 1875: *Rev. Henry Ward Beecher goes on trial for dallying with one of his flock.–p.226*

Once Was More Than Enough

Jan. 19, 1896. *The congregation of St. Francis de Sales Church in Cincinnati gathered with pride for the consecration of their new bell. And with good reason. Seven feet high and weighing 35,000 pounds, it is one of the largest free-swinging bells in the world. People reckoned it would be heard for 15 miles. But when six men swung the huge clapper, an E-flat wasn't the big bell's only toll—buildings shook and windows shattered. Alarmed, the parish priests decided that the great clapper would never strike again. Instead, a small electrically operated hammer taps the bell's rim, producing a much more modest tone. No one expected such a ringing disaster when the giant was hoisted (above).*

Dr. James Naismith was looking for a game that students could play during the winter in the gym at Springfield College. He tried adapting soccer and lacrosse, but they proved too rough. When he made the goals smaller and hung them from the gym's balcony, the result was basketball.

It Happened on January . . .

13, 1957: *Wham-O Company creates the plastic Frisbee.**–p.254*

15, 1946: *The state of Georgia has three governors in office simultaneously.**–p.108*

18, 1896: *James Addison Reavis, self-proclaimed "Baron of Arizona," is indicted on 42 counts for an intricate land swindle involving some 13 million acres.**–p.182*

19, 1840: *Lt. Charles Wilkes sights Antarctica and claims the continent for the U.S.A.**–p.302*

19, 1854: *The* Deseret News *heralds the creation of a new Mormon alphabet.**–p.283*

20, 1892: *The first basketball game is played in Springfield, Mass., with peach baskets used as goals; a man has to climb a ladder in order to retrieve the ball after each score.*

21, 1893: *The awful Cherry Sisters make their professional debut in Marion, Iowa.**–p.184*

24, 1848: *On the unluckiest day of James Marshall's life, he finds a nugget and sets off the California gold rush.**–p.126*

25, 1848: *Nicholas P. Trist negotiates a treaty buying California from Mexico.**–p.372*

29, 1649: *Death warrant for King Charles I is signed by 59 people; 3 of them will flee to America, where they will be hunted for some 30 years.**–p.156*

30, 1835: *"Richard III" Lawrence fails to pull off the first presidential assassination.**–p.79*

30, 1925: *Spelunker Floyd Collins is trapped 125 feet down in Kentucky's Sand Cave, where he will die.**–p.244*

30, 1946: *The Roosevelt dime is issued on FDR's birthday (also the annual kickoff day for the March of Dimes) in honor of his fight against polio.**–p.107*

February

Hopping the Train

Feb. 3, 1898: Fortune smiles on piggyback locomotives

A blinding snowstorm had swirled across the frozen New England countryside since early evening. Now, around midnight, engineer Charles Eaton still struggled northward in his little Engine 684, pulling a two-car milk train on its daily run to Fitchburg, Massachusetts. Due in at 5:00 P.M., it was seven hours late.

Simultaneously, on this same stretch of New Haven Railroad track, the giant Mogul-type Engine 823 was pushing a huge snowplow southward. Dispatcher Perry White had decided that the snow wasn't yet deep enough to stop the important milk run, so he had given 684 the right of way and diverted the plow onto a siding. These instructions had been telegraphed to a dispatcher farther up the line, who was supposed to make the appropriate track switch. But that dispatcher had gone to dinner. A sign saying "Back in 10 Minutes" hung on the door of his empty office as the telegraph receiver clicked away.

By the time he came back, it was too late. When the two engines met head-on, the little milk train was going 40 miles an hour. Her engine ran right up the plow and came to rest on top of 823, whose startled engineer furiously exclaimed: "You've got a damned nerve to be on this track!" Nerve wasn't half of it.

Fortunately, the accident was more comic than catastrophic. No one was seriously hurt. Engineer Eaton broke his nose, and his fireman, who cut the back of his head, was drenched when the tender burst and the extra water supply gushed around him. Even the cleanup was convenient. Engine 823 just carried little 684 piggyback to the depot.

Immortal Amendments

Feb. 14, 1893. *Representative Lucas Miller of Wisconsin proposed amending the Constitution to change our nation's name to "the United States of the Earth [because] it is possible for this republic to grow through the admission of new states . . . until every nation on earth has become part of it."*

Twenty-seven years earlier, just after the Civil War, would-be amenders wanted to call the country simply America, "to indicate the real unity and destiny of the American people as the eventual, paramount power of the hemisphere."

Presidential election procedures have been another favorite topic in the more than 10,000 amendments proposed since 1789. One innovator suggested that we select the president from among retiring senators—by lot! And because four of our first five presidents were from just one state (Virginia), an amendment was introduced in the early 1820's to divide the country into regions, giving each a turn at electing the chief executive.

But it was Augustus Wilson who in 1876 went to the heart of presidential election complexities: he proposed we simply abolish the office altogether.

The morning after the crash, the snowplow, which had protected Engine 823 from extensive front-end damage, was towed away, leaving this astounding scene.

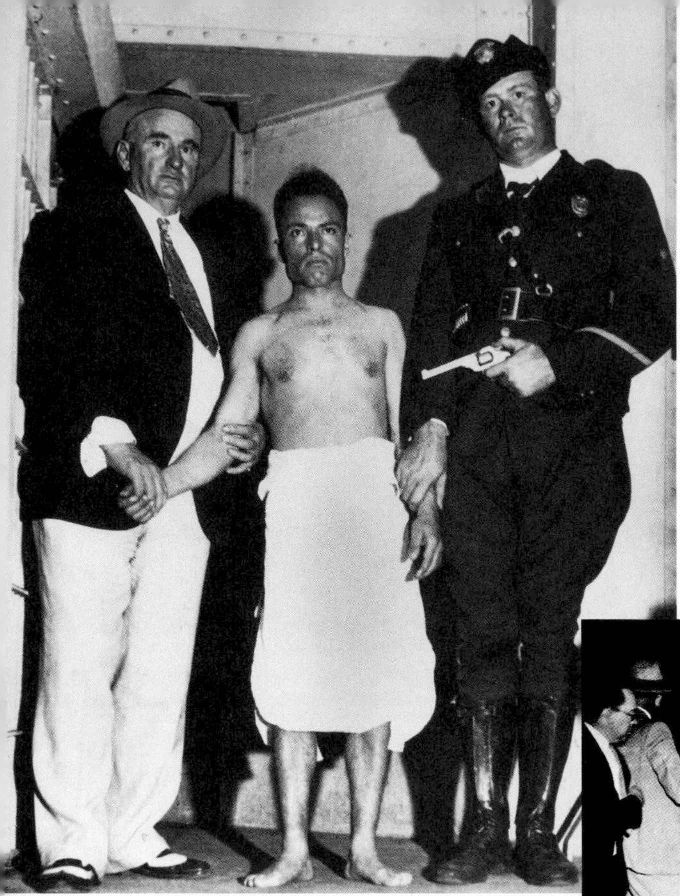

Left: Although sullen, 32-year-old assassin Giuseppe Zangara enjoyed the publicity he received after his arrest. Below: Mortally wounded, Mayor Cermak is helped from the scene of the attack. FDR himself cradled Cermak in his arms on the way to the hospital.

Ride for the Money

Feb. 18, 1855: Panic begins a California bank scare

The next time you hurry to the bank before it closes, think of rancher Louis Remme's ordeal.

From the day a steamer arrived in San Francisco with news that a major St. Louis bank had failed, financial panic swept central California. Remme couldn't withdraw his $6,000 from Adams & Company in Sacramento, but he could see one hope. Portland, Oregon, had no telegraph. If he could beat the steamer north, he might be able to get his money from the bank's Portland branch before its managers heard of the collapse.

The anxious cattleman headed into the teeth of a northern California winter. Some 6 days and 11 horses later, he had completed the 665-mile wilderness trek. When the steamer arrived in Portland, local banks quickly closed. But Remme already had his money.

An Assassin's Bullets for FDR

Feb. 15, 1933: The mayor of Chicago is shot in the attack

Giuseppe Zangara always had a stomachache. He blamed it (and everything else wrong with his life) on capitalists. But he was not a radical political activist. Rather, his discontent gave him an intense desire to kill someone in power.

Once, in his native Italy, he had planned to kill the king, but he couldn't get near enough. After moving to the United States, he considered killing our ever-placid president Calvin Coolidge.

Early in 1933 Zangara had targeted President Herbert Hoover but was dissuaded by the chilly Washington weather, which he feared might aggravate his stomach. Then he learned that President-elect Franklin D. Roosevelt would be speaking at Bayfront Park in Miami. It was near Zangara's home and seemed to offer a perfect opportunity. With an $8 revolver and 10 bullets, both newly purchased at a local pawnshop, he headed for the park.

At first he was frustrated. Stuck deep in the crowd, the five-foot assassin was too short to get off a shot when Roosevelt's open car rolled in. Five minutes later, however, at 9:35 P.M., FDR had finished delivering his brief speech from atop the backseat of the car. The crowd was beginning to disperse. Zangara lunged forward, leaped onto a vacant chair, and fired five shots. Each hit someone, but all of them missed Roosevelt entirely.

Four victims survived. One bullet, however, penetrated the right lung of Chicago mayor Anton Cermak. He died three weeks later, on March 6, two days after FDR's inauguration.

Within days of the attack Zangara was sentenced to 80 years in prison on four counts of deadly assault. After Cermak died, a new trial resulted in a new sentence: death. The assassin never pleaded insanity; he seemed proud of his guilt.

On March 20—just 33 days after the shooting and 14 days after Cermak's death—Zangara was electrocuted. Feeling slighted to the last, he complained that no photographers were present.

Davis's Successor

Feb. 25, 1870: The first black U.S. senator takes his seat

After the Civil War, former Confederate states faced the onerous task of gaining readmission to the Union. In January 1870 Mississippi impressed Congress by electing a U.S. senator who had helped organize Union regiments. His name was Hiram Revels. He was a graduate of Knox College in Ohio, an ordained minister, a respected educator, and a member of the Mississippi state senate. He was also black.

Mississippi was readmitted, but the New York *Herald* predicted that Revels would never be allowed to take his Senate seat—especially since Mississippi's most recent senator had been Jefferson Davis, who had walked out to become president of the Confederacy. In fact, political bickering did delay approval of the new senator's credentials. But finally he was seated. Even Davis gave him modest support: he hated to see Mississippi represented by a black man, he wrote, but if that had to be, he was glad the man was Hiram Revels.

The gallery was packed and emotions ran high when Hiram Revels took his oath of office on the Senate floor.

It Happened on February . . .

3, 1759: *Ben Lay, 4' 7" abolitionist caveman, dies at age 82.–p.200*

3, 1889: *Outlaw queen Belle Starr is murdered.–p.176*

3, 1943: *Four chaplains go down with the troopship* Dorchester *in the icy North Atlantic.–p.401*

5, 1785: *George Washington notes in his diary "the passing of two Acts by the Assemblies of Virginia & Maryland . . . for improving and extending the navigation of the river Potomac."–p.270*

5, 1895: *J. P. Morgan rescues the U.S. Treasury.–p.134*

5, 1960: *Ray Kroc buys out the McDonald brothers.–p.153*

6, 1858: *Rep. William Barksdale is "scalped" during a brawl on the House floor.–p.83*

9, 1824: *A "vote from God" makes John Quincy Adams president of the U.S.A.–p.78*

10, 1863: *P. T. Barnum's star midgets, Tom Thumb and Lavinia Warren, are married amid much ballyhoo.–p.218*

11, 1856: *President Franklin Pierce issues a proclamation requesting the citizens of all states to stop meddling in Kansas's affairs.–p.374*

14, 1870: *Esther Morris becomes the world's first female justice of the peace.–p.67*

14, 1876: *Rival inventors Elisha Gray and Alexander Graham Bell both apply for patents on the telephone.–p.330*

14, 1884: *Teddy Roosevelt's wife and mother die within hours of each other.–p.94*

15, 1798: *The first serious fist fight occurs in Congress.–p.82*

17, 1801: *Finally, after 36 ballots in the House of Representatives, Thomas Jefferson defeats his running mate, Aaron Burr, for the presidency.–p.76*

18, 1821: *Survivors of the* Essex, *sunk by a whale, are rescued after 83 days at sea.–p.276*

18, 1830: *S. Short and N. Bradford patent a submarine explorer (a large waterproof hose).–p.346*

19, 1796: *Dr. Elisha Perkins patents his medical marvel, the Metallic Tractors.–p.314*

21, 1828: *The first issue of the* Cherokee Phoenix *is printed, both in English and in the newly invented Cherokee alphabet.–p.315*

23, 1540: *Coronado, inspired by reports from the lost explorer Cabeza de Vaca, sets out to find the Seven Cities of Cíbola.–p.263*

23, 1846: *The Liberty Bell tolls for the last time, for George Washington's birthday.–p.49*

23, 1921: *First transcontinental airmail flight arrives in New York from San Francisco.–p.305*

24, 1803: *Chief Justice John Marshall, by refusing to rule on the case of* Marbury v. Madison, *gives the Supreme Court its greatest power.–p.73*

24, 1914: *Joshua Chamberlain dies of war wounds, the last Civil War soldier to do so.–p.385*

25, 1779: *The British surrender the Illinois country to George Rogers Clark at Vincennes.–p.362*

25, 1836: *Samuel Colt patents his revolver.–p.125*

25, 1862: *The ironclad* Monitor *is commissioned at the Brooklyn Navy Yard.–p.384*

25, 1872: *The beans are spilled about John D. Rockefeller's devious railroad scheme.–p.131*

27, 1891: *Robert Dyrenforth is named special agent for the Department of Agriculture; his task is to make rain.–p.350*

28, 1801: *Napoleon offers Robert Fulton a chance to demonstrate his new submarine.–p.313*

March

Too Mad a Poet?

March 6, 1831: West Point bounces Edgar Allan Poe

Poe, one of the first American writers to win international acclaim, failed to survive his first year at West Point. "Too mad a poet to like mathematics," was the judgment of a classmate.

Orphaned at the age of three, Poe had been well raised by John Allan and his wife, a friend of the child's mother. But when Edgar was 15, he and his guardian quarreled. It was traumatic for both. Although Allan was wealthy, he sent Poe off to the University of Virginia with hardly a penny. When the youth finished the first term with good grades but $2,500 in debt, Allan withdrew him. In despair, Poe joined the army. After two years Allan relented enough to help his ward get into West Point—but again almost penniless.

Entering the military academy at the age of 21, the new cadet won high marks with little effort, but again accumulated debts. Writing to a creditor, he excused his failure to get money from home with the remark, "Mr. A is not very often sober." The letter was forwarded to Allan. Outraged and hurt, he sent Poe the money to pay off the debt and then disowned him.

Frantic, Poe wrote to Allan on January 3, 1831, pouring out the bitterness that had prompted the insult. Adding that his poverty now forced him to leave West Point, he asked his guardian for written permission to do so. Contemptuous, Allan did not answer. With no alternative but to seek expulsion, Poe began skipping classes and meals. When he also refused to attend chapel, he was arrested and court-martialed. Finally, he was officially dismissed from West Point for disobedience and gross neglect of duty.

At West Point the precocious Edgar Allan Poe became a living legend, discoursing on English literature, writing poetry (including verse that lampooned officers), and creating an aura of mystery about himself. His later breakdowns, blamed on alcoholism and drug abuse, may have been due to a brain lesion. He died in 1849 at the age of 40.

Mutiny, Murder, and Trickery

March 9, 1841: The Supreme Court frees the Amistad *slaves*

The case had begun on the stormy night of July 1, 1839, while the *Amistad* wallowed through rough seas off Cuba. In the hold of the Spanish vessel were 49 men and 4 children, all chained together by their neck, hands, and feet. They had been kidnapped from Mende, in West Africa, and sold in the Havana slave market. In a topside cabin of the *Amistad* were their owners, Cuban planters Don José Ruiz and Pedro Montez. Ruiz had just paid $450 a head for the men; Montez owned the children. Now they were taking their slaves to another port in Cuba.

Escaping fate

Belowdecks, Cinqué, the tall, proud son of a chief, spoke forcefully: There was only one way to escape their fate. Mutiny! Tonight!

Quietly they pried off their chains and broke open a shipment of machetes. First Cinqué killed the cook, who had suggested the slaves would be eaten; then the captain. He was about to cleave Montez in two when the other Africans stopped him. Several of the crew had jumped overboard, and the blacks would need someone to guide the boat back to Africa. In terror, the Cubans agreed to cooperate with them.

But Montez was determined to reach America. By day, when Cinqué could check the position of the sun, he pointed the ship eastward; but by night he sailed northwest. After zigzagging for seven weeks, the vessel reached the eastern tip of Long Island, where a navy patrol ship approached it. The slaves were taken to New Haven, Connecticut, and jailed to await trial for murder and piracy.

Under the bold and determined leadership of Cinqué (left), the Africans chained aboard the Amistad *mutinied (above). His legend lived on; 133 years later, Donald De Freeze, leader of the Symbionese Liberation Army that kidnapped heiress Patty Hearst, would call himself Cinque.*

The language barrier

Given wide publicity in the newspapers, the plight of the Africans soon became a *cause célèbre* in the North, but no one could get *their* side of the story because of the language barrier. A linguistic expert, Dr. Josiah Gibbs, went to the prison and learned to count from 1 to 10 in Mende; he then scoured the New York City waterfront, repeating the words over and over. Finally he met a black from Sierra Leone who understood—an interpreter had been found.

Meanwhile, the Spanish government claimed that the slaves belonged to Montez and Ruiz and demanded they be turned over to Spain's minister. Eager to appease the proslavery South, President Van Buren was willing to comply. In January 1840 the case came before a federal judge, who was a Van Buren appointee.

Unexpectedly, he declared the Africans free, under an 1817 treaty in which Spain had outlawed importing slaves to her colonies. The abolitionists rejoiced—but only briefly. At the behest of the president, the U.S. attorney appealed the case to the Supreme Court, insisting that the blacks be returned to Spanish jurisdiction; the defense demanded their freedom.

A secret letter

Then Congressman John Quincy Adams, former president of the United States, rose to address the Court. Weeks earlier he had asked Congress for a full disclosure of all official documents touching on the case, and—lo and behold—a "confidential" letter had surfaced. Written by the secretary of state to the U.S. attorney in Connecticut, it contained Van Buren's instructions that the slaves be denied the right of appeal should the lower court decide against them. The 73-year-old Adams read the letter to a stunned audience and then scathingly attacked the president, asking: "Was ever such a scene of Lilliputian trickery enacted by the rulers of a great, magnanimous, and Christian nation?"

The blacks, who had spent 17 months in jail, were freed, given a year of Christian training, and then returned home. Many, including Cinqué, found that their families had been sold into slavery. Cinqué later became a slave trader.

It Happened on March . . .

2, 1877: *Rutherford B. Hayes is declared president by one vote the day before inauguration.–p.64*

2, 1939: *Massachusetts finally ratifies the Bill of Rights, 150 years after its adoption.–p.54*

3, 1855: *Congress appropriates $30,000 for a camel corps.–p.372*

3, 1917: *German Foreign Secretary Zimmermann admits plans to conquer the U.S.A. and return the Southwest to Mexico.–p.394*

3, 1931: *President Herbert Hoover signs a bill making "The Star-Spangled Banner" the national anthem.–p.51*

4, 1789: *Only 11 states are in attendance as the first Congress meets.–p.54*

4, 1849: *Sen. David Rice Atchison serves as U.S. president for one day.–p.80*

5, 1770: *British troops fire on demonstrators in Boston, killing black patriot Crispus Attucks, the first casualty of the Revolution.*

5, 1806: *Frederic Tudor lands in Martinique with a boatload of New England ice.–p.123*

5, 1879: *First group of black "Exodusters," en route to Kansas, arrives in St. Louis aboard the steamer* Colorado.*–p.295*

5, 1963: *Members of the Society for Indecency to Naked Animals picket the White House, demanding that Mrs. Kennedy put clothes on her horse.–p.256*

6, 1836: *The Alamo falls.–p.370*

6, 1854: *Know-Nothings steal the papal stone from the Washington Monument.–p.62*

6, 1857: *The Supreme Court decrees that no black person can be a U.S. citizen.–p.53*

7, 1935: *The frozen body of "silver queen" Baby Doe Tabor is found in her shack.–p.132*

Thundering torrents and swirling mist, shot through with vivid rainbows—Niagara Falls was America's foremost early tourist attraction. But building a bridge across it was a challenge that taxed both the skill and imagination of the best engineers of the time.

And a Little Child Shall Lead Them

March 7, 1848: A kite is the key to bridging the great Niagara

Charles Ellet had a problem. He had a contract to build an engineering marvel—a suspension bridge over the Niagara River—but no way of stretching his first cable between the shores. Any boat that tried to cross near the falls would be swept over. Then Ellet thought of kites; you could fly one to the opposite side and use its cord to pull larger cables across. So he announced a kite-flying contest.

Eighteen-year-old Homan Walsh decided to give it a try. Appropriately, he named his kite "The Union." On his first attempt the kite cord broke when it caught in the river's ice, but his next venture was successful. The first bridge—only 7½ feet wide—opened for business on August 1, and $5,000 in tolls was collected in 10 months. It seems that Walsh, however, got no more than $50 for his invaluable service.

The Pittsfield, Massachusetts, Pussycats

March 28, 1903. *The F. C. Bostock Animal Show had finished its performance, and crews were gingerly lowering two caged lionesses, Sappho and Victoria, from the third-floor stage entrance. Suddenly a rope snapped; the cage plummeted to the ground and the two angry beasts emerged. Immediately they rushed the helpless draft horses tethered nearby and mangled them viciously.*

Victoria was pregnant, which made her normally mean disposition even more foul. A trainer, Signor Arnoldo, fearing further carnage, fired a pistol at her but missed. Victoria took cover under a wagon and continued to menace anyone who came near her. Arnoldo fired again, and Victoria was dead.

Meanwhile, Sappho had trotted calmly down the street into the foggy night. Mr. and Mrs. Patrick McCarty were returning from grocery shopping when their path was blocked by what they thought in the mist was a neighborhood dog. An enormous paw swung at their bag of fresh meat. Outraged, Mrs. McCarty hit the animal between the eyes with her umbrella. It yelped and fled. Not until the next morning did the McCartys discover that they had met Sappho.

The lion was soon trapped in a garage and peacefully captured by Arnoldo, who patted her on the head as if she were a kitten.

It Happened on March . . .

9, 1862: *Two ironclad warships battle for the first time; the outcome is inconclusive.**–p.384*

10, 1876: *Spilled acid prompts the first telephone message.**–p.331*

12, 1889: *Kansas City undertaker Almon Brown Strowger, who blames the telephone operator for diverting business to his competitor, patents the automatic telephone exchange.**–p.331*

12, 1940: *Gerald Ford appears as a fashion model.**–p.112*

16, 1966: *Stephen Dennison is awarded $115,000 after serving 34 years in prison for stealing a $5 box of candy.**–p.192*

17, 1856: *New York* Herald *gloats over P. T. Barnum's ruin.**–p.124*

18, 1939: *Georgia finally ratifies the Bill of Rights.**–p.54*

19, 1687: *The explorer La Salle is killed by his own men.**–p.267*

20, 1866: *Horatio Alger, charged with shameful crimes, flees Brewster, Mass.**–p.125*

20, 1902: *Nathan Stubblefield demonstrates his invention, radio, in Washington, D.C.**–p.339*

23, 1857: *Elisha Otis installs the first modern passenger elevator in a public building, at the corner of Broome Street and Broadway in New York City.**–p.322*

25, 1865: *Confederate Capt. Robert C. Kennedy hangs for trying to burn New York City.**–p.382*

30, 1867: *U.S.A. buys Alaska from Russia for $7.2 million (about two cents an acre).**–p.324*

30, 1888: *Charles Lummis photographs the torturous rituals of Los Hermanos Penitentes.**–p.280*

31, 1776: *Abigail Adams writes to John that women are "determined to foment a Rebelion" if the new Declaration of Independence fails to guarantee their rights.**–p.66*

April

World Without End

April 3, 1843: Judgment Day for Miller's millenarians

All over the Northeast, some half a million Adventists—disciples of New York Baptist evangelist William Miller—piously awaited the end of the world. Journalists had a field day, but their reports are so rife with tall tales that it is hard to get at the facts.

Reportedly some disciples were on mountaintops, hoping for a head start to heaven. Others were in graveyards, planning to ascend in reunion with their departed loved ones. Philadelphia society ladies clustered together outside town to avoid entering God's holy kingdom amid the common herd.

Hearing loud trumpet blasts, the faithful in Westford, Massachusetts, fell to their knees. But it was only Crazy Amos, the village idiot. "You fools!" he said. "Go dig your potatoes. Angel Gabriel won't go a-digging 'em for you."

When April 4 dawned as usual, the Millerites were disillusioned, but they took heart. Their leader had predicted a range of dates for Armageddon. They still had until March 21, 1844.

The devout continued to make ready; but again they were disappointed. And again there was an adjustment: October 22, 1844, was now the projected Day of Doom. Amazingly, many followers were still committed. One shrewd Vermont farmer had sacred white robes made for six of his cows. "It's a very long trip, and the kids will want milk," he explained.

Again—no cataclysm.

Miller never abandoned his belief that the end of the world was near—though he stopped predicting dates. His followers broke into factions, and in 1863 a union of diverse Adventist sects was organized as the Seventh-day Adventists. Today there are several million followers worldwide.

A cartoon showed Miller, the Millerites, and even their tabernacles ascending wholesale to heaven.

Who Killed George Washington Ostrich?

April 9, 1926. *George Washington was found strangled at the birdhouse in Boston's Franklin Park Zoo. There were signs of a terrible struggle—Washington had a reputation as a fierce fighter—and one major clue: a torn raincoat. The coat led to William C. McIntyre, who pleaded self-defense as a victim of "fowl play."*

McIntyre said he'd been sneaking home after binging on Prohibition booze when he climbed over a fence and "right away something started hitting me on the head. All I did was grab hold of the thing and hold on for my life." The court was convinced and only fined him $20 for trespassing. But is his tale true? He was a wobbling 120-pound drunk. Could he really have throttled the angry 250-pound bird?

It Happened on April . . .

3, 1793: *America's first circus opens in Philadelphia.–p.206*

3, 1860: *First Pony Express rider leaves St. Joseph, Mo.–p.290*

3, 1954: *Lyndon Johnson keeps America out of Vietnam.–p.111*

5, 1892: *Johnson County Range War begins in Wyoming.–p.233*

5, 1976: *Billionaire Howard Hughes dies a recluse.–p.146*

6, 1896: *James Connolly wins the first modern Olympic event.–p.229*

6, 1909: *Peary and Henson reach the North Pole.–pp.236, 303*

8, 1981: *Ronald Reagan gets a goldfish.–p.113*

9, 1865: *Robert E. Lee surrenders to Ulysses S. Grant in Wilmer McLean's parlor.–p.385*

9, 1867: *Senate approves Alaska purchase by one vote.–p.79*

11, 1827: *Pawnee Indians prepare to sacrifice a woman to the morning star.–p.275*

11, 1916: *Louis Enricht demonstrates his gasoline substitute; Henry Ford buys it.–p.345*

11, 1917: *Allen Dulles snubs Lenin.–p.393*

11, 1951: *President Truman fires General MacArthur.–p.405*

12, 1826: *Stedman Whitwell renames everyplace.–p.277*

12, 1955: *Dr. Jonas Salk announces development of his polio vaccine on 10th anniversary of FDR's death.–p.107*

14, 1614: *Indian princess Pocahontas marries Jamestown planter John Rolfe.–p.116*

14, 1865: *Abraham Lincoln is assassinated; U.S. flag is raised at Fort Sumter.–pp.168, 375*

16, 1889: *Charlie Chaplin is born in England; Thomas Edison patents the movies.–p.332*

The First Round-the-World Phone Call

April 25, 1935. *At 9:30 in the morning, AT&T president Walter S. Gifford placed a call to his vice president, T. G. Miller, from company headquarters in New York City.*

The call was routed by underground and aerial wires via San Francisco to the shortwave transmitter at Dixon, California, where it was amplified and hurled 9,000 miles across the Pacific Ocean to Java. A second shortwave radio circuit took the call 7,000 miles to Amsterdam. Then land wires and underground cables sped it across the North Sea to London and on to the radio station at Rugby, England. From there, shortwave zapped the call across the Atlantic Ocean to Netcong, New Jersey, from whence a cable took it back to the AT&T Long Distance Building. A quarter of a second after Gifford placed the 23,000-mile globe-circling call, Miller's phone rang—about 50 feet away, in the next office.

What a way to celebrate AT&T's 50th anniversary!

The *Sultana* Explodes

April 27, 1865: The worst steamboat disaster in U.S. history

Thousands of ex-prisoners (some from the infamous Confederate prison at Andersonville) were sent north after the Civil War. When the Mississippi riverboat *Sultana,* carrying some 2,000 of them, pulled into Vicksburg, a repairman said that a leaky boiler should be fixed by replacing two sheets of metal, but the hurried captain settled for a thin patch.

Its decks crowded with homebound veterans and other passengers, the *Sultana* pushed upstream on a

Rite of Passage

April 28: Annual burial day for Georgia's Irish horse traders

Old Mattie Sherlock, proud patriarch of the Irish horse traders who roamed the byways of the South, died on March 8, 1944, in Brownsville, Tennessee. But he wasn't laid to rest until April 28—and then in Atlanta, Georgia.

No matter where or when members of Sherlock's fabled clan died, their remains were usually packed up and shipped to a funeral home on Peachtree Street in Atlanta to await Funeral Day, when horse-trader caravans from all over Dixie gathered for a family reunion. (When clan members enlisted in the army during World War I, many of them gave the funeral parlor as a permanent address.)

The eight immigrant families that formed the original horse-trader bands—they'd fled Ireland during the Potato Famine in the 1840's—had tired of city life in Washington, D.C., and taken to the open road in brightly painted wagons. Trailing behind them were the strings of horses and ponies they sold for a livelihood. When the group found a priest at Atlanta's Church of the Immaculate Conception who was willing to minister to them despite their nomadic lifestyle, they began the custom of gathering there once a year to bury their dead.

But Mattie Sherlock was one of the last to be laid to rest in the old way. In 1966, after more than 100 years as vagabonds, many of the horse-trader families settled permanently in a mobile-home village in North Augusta, South Carolina.

flood-swollen river. Three days later, a blast tore through the midsection. Steam and hot water shot into the night sky. The boilers had exploded and the boat was afire!

As wind-whipped flames swept toward the stern, hundreds of people clung to the bow. When the current swung the *Sultana* around, those who didn't jump were instantly incinerated.

Scalded survivors threw anything that would float into the dark water. The flooded riverbanks were a mile or more away; clinging to their bits of debris, victims were swept downstream by the current. Some grabbed onto trees jutting above the flood. Many more drowned.

The southbound *Bostonia* rescued some victims. And a flotilla of boats at Memphis pulled survivors from the water. Still, some 1,500 died; the exact figure will never be known. Sadly, many veterans who had managed to survive untold battlefield and prison horrors never made it home.

The doomed Mississippi riverboat, carrying an estimated 2,400 passengers (she was licensed to carry 376), passed Helena, Arkansas, on April 25.

It Happened on April . . .

17, 1850: *Henry S. Foote pulls a gun on Thomas Hart Benton during a Senate debate.–p.82*

17, 1906: *San Francisco is cursed by cult leader Joshua II.–p.239*

18, 1861: *Robert E. Lee refuses command of Union Army.–p.376*

18, 1906: *San Francisco is destroyed by an earthquake; Giannini saves his little bank.–p.144*

18, 1945: *Japanese machine-gun fire kills Ernie Pyle.–p.251*

18, 1955: *Albert Einstein dies; his brain is preserved for study.–p.353*

19, 1536: *First tourist cruise to America leaves England.–p.264*

19, 1939: *Connecticut finally ratifies the Bill of Rights.–p.54*

20, 1864: *Reuel Colt Gridley auctions off a flour sack.–p.383*

21, 1910: *Mark Twain, fulfilling his prediction, dies as Halley's Comet passes perihelion.–p.24*

22, 1889: *The Oklahoma land rush begins at noon; some people start out sooner.–p.299*

23, 1949: *Gov. Adlai Stevenson of Illinois vetoes a bill to protect birds from cats.–p.195*

24, 1775: *Israel Bissel spreads the word of the battles at Lexington and Concord.–p.361*

24, 1907: *Alferd Packer, the Colorado cannibal, dies.–p.166*

26, 1865: *John Wilkes Booth dies in a burning barn; Boston Corbett claims the kill.–p.169*

27, 1908: *The farmhouse of mass murderess Belle Gunness burns, revealing evidence of her ghastly crimes.–p.183*

28, 1834: *Naturalists John Townsend and Thomas Nuttall set out to explore the West.–p.280*

29, 1942: *Naval intelligence asks Lucky Luciano for help with the invasion of Sicily.–p.401*

May

The Actors' War

May 10, 1849: 31 killed in a theater riot on Astor Place

Macbeth himself was never more beleaguered than William Macready, the sophisticated British thespian, performing at the Astor Place Opera House in New York. Just three days earlier, his portrayal of Shakespeare's famous Scot had been routed in a barrage of eggs, foul-smelling asafetida, rotten potatoes, and chairs thrown from the audience. Outraged, the city's more dignified gentry had promised protection if the star would continue his engagement; the mayor had even called out the National Guard. But the performance on May 10 was an even greater disaster. Some 200 policemen were inside the opera house and another 125 were outside—facing a crowd of 15,000. When police moved to oust hecklers from the theater, the mob in the street began hurling cobblestones. Desperate, the sheriff ordered his troops to fire.

When it was over, 22 people lay dead (9 more later died of wounds), and 50 others were seriously injured. Miraculously, Macready finished the show; but he had to leave the theater in disguise, and that night he fled to Boston.

Edwin Forrest, America's foremost tragedian, thought the mayhem was just tit for tat. Critics had hooted his *King Lear* in London four years earlier, and Forrest was certain Macready's jealousy had been behind the scathing reviews. The American star had filled U.S. newspapers with reports of his shabby treatment in London and then had gone out of his way to schedule performances in competition with Macready's tour. The public took sides in the rivalry, resulting in the chaos on Astor Place. It was merely one more explosion in a cold war of national pride that had its roots as far back as the American Revolution.

Barrel-chested American tragedian Edwin Forrest (above, costumed as Shakespeare's Coriolanus) was so sure that William Macready had instigated his bad London reviews that he rose from the audience and hissed during his rival's performance of Hamlet *in Edinburgh, Scotland. Their feud led to a bloody riot (left) outside the New York theater where Macready later performed.*

Before Rosa Parks

May 11, 1871: Triumph for the first freedom riders

On Sunday, October 30, 1870, Horace Pearce and the brothers Robert and Samuel Fox boarded a nearly empty "whites only" trolley car in Louisville, Kentucky, paid their fares, and sat down. A white passenger quickly ordered them to leave. When the three blacks quietly refused, the driver abusively forced them from the car. The next day the case came before a local judge. Pearce and the Fox brothers were fined $5 each for disorderly conduct.

Robert Fox took the case to federal court, suing the trolley company for segregation that violated his civil rights. On May 11, 1871, a U.S. district court upheld his suit, awarding him $15. But three days of near riots followed, as city streetcar operators continued to refuse to carry blacks in white cars. Finally the companies gave in, fearing federal enforcement and further financial loss.

Eighty-four years later, blacks in Montgomery, Alabama, still endured segregated city buses. On December 1, 1955, Rosa Parks, a middle-aged seamstress on her way home from work, refused to give up her seat and started a bus boycott that helped launch another civil rights movement. This time the victory, spearheaded by Dr. Martin Luther King, Jr., would have national impact.

Inverted Jenny

May 14, 1918. *William T. Robey paid $24 for a sheet of 100 commemorative stamps at his local post office in Washington, D.C. The stamps depicted the Curtiss JN-4H airplane (nicknamed the Jenny) that was to be used the next day in the first airmail flight. On Robey's sheet each Jenny was flying upside down.*

Eight other inverted sheets had been produced, probably when the printer accidentally reversed the plate that printed the planes. All of these had been intercepted by the post office. But Robey didn't know this and wanted to make a quick sale before any more inverts could hit the market and devalue his prize. Six days later he sold the sheet to a stamp dealer for $15,000. The dealer already had an offer of $20,000 from a collector. Prices rose to more than $300 for each stamp. That was just the beginning.

In 1933 a block of four inverted Jennys fetched $15,000. By 1959 a single invert was worth $6,400. In 1982 the price reached $198,000.

(Ironically, the first airmail flight had ended with the real Jenny, bearing the same number as the one on the stamp, upside down in a field–p.305.)

"Reverence for the Mothers"

May 14, 1905: Anna Jarvis's mother dies

Anna Jarvis of Grafton, West Virginia, was devoted to her mother. Seven of her 11 siblings had died young, and the mother had clung to the survivors—especially Anna. After her mother's death, Jarvis began an impassioned crusade for a day to honor all mothers. Eventually she devoted herself exclusively (and obsessively) to her cause.

She began in her hometown with a special church service on the anniversary of her mother's death, and subsequently embarked upon a sweeping letter-writing campaign. Finally, on May 9, 1914, President Woodrow Wilson proclaimed the second Sunday in May as Mother's Day, urging citizens to fly the American flag "as a public expression of our love and reverence for the mothers of our country." It is the only national observance that commemorates someone's death.

Until her death in 1948, Jarvis fought commercialization, decrying the greeting cards that replaced handwritten notes, and the florists' huge profits from Mother's Day sales. Ironically, a group of grateful florists supported the impoverished crusader at the end of her life.

But not everyone credited the holiday to Anna Jarvis. Kentuckians claimed the honor for Mary Towles Sasseen, a teacher who, in 1887, celebrated her mother's birthday in her classroom. Other schools followed suit, and after Sasseen died, her family promoted her idea.

It Happened on May . . .

1, 1893: *Columbian Exposition opens in Chicago; a beam of starlight leaves Arcturus.–pp. 228, 247*

2, 1863: *Stonewall Jackson is shot by his own troops.–p.379*

3, 1866: *The clipper ship* Hornet *burns, giving Mark Twain his big break.–p.221*

4, 1819: *Stephen Long sets out in his dragon steamboat.–p.213*

5, 1945: *A Japanese balloon bomb kills six in Oregon.–p.399*

6, 1626: *Some Indians who don't own Manhattan sell it to the Dutch anyway.–p.199*

6, 1896: *Samuel P. Langley's steam airplane makes the first heavier-than-air flight.–p.340*

7, 1896: *Herman W. Mudgett, proprietor of Chicago's "Murder Castle," is hanged.–p.185*

8, 1541: *De Soto and a herd of pigs cross the Mississippi.–p.262*

8, 1886: *Cocaine-laced Coca-Cola is first sold in Atlanta.–p.231*

9, 1754: *Benjamin Franklin publishes America's first political cartoon.–p.53*

10, 1775: *Ethan Allen and Benedict Arnold capture Fort Ticonderoga from the British without firing a shot.–p.360*

10, 1869: *Golden spike is driven at Promontory Point, Utah.–p.136*

10, 1872: *Free love candidate Victoria Woodhull begins her presidential campaign.–p.89*

10, 1876: *America's 100th birthday party begins.–p.222*

11, 1829: *Murderess Patty Cannon poisons herself in jail.–p.165*

13, 1867: *Jefferson Davis is released after almost two years' detention without trial.–p.386*

15, 1923: *Author Upton Sinclair is jailed for reading the Bill of Rights aloud.–p.55*

Tale of a Comet

May 18, 1910: With only seconds to spare, a posse prevents a human sacrifice to Halley's comet

The Select Followers, a small group of fanatics in Oklahoma, were led by Henry Heinman, who said he'd received a revelation from God: on May 18, because of the poisonous gases in the tail of Halley's comet, the world would come to an end and the heavens would roll up like a scroll. Only a blood sacrifice, Heinman declared, would avert disaster.

On the fateful day a teenager from a farm in western Oklahoma, one Jane Warfield, was chosen by the religious leader. She was tied to a stake, where she was to be knifed and allowed to bleed to death. The Select Followers were doing a ritual dance around the stake when, just in the nick of time, a sheriff's posse arrived. They rescued Jane and arrested Heinman.

Accounts of the incident differ in several details. Was the intended victim nude or clad in virginal white? Did she have a wreath of roses atop her head? Was she really Heinman's stepdaughter? One local newspaper branded the whole thing a hoax perpetrated by the former editor of another paper. Hoax or not, newspapers from coast to coast covered the story, accurately reflecting the often hysterical mood of a comet-mad nation.

The comet named for astronomer Edmund Halley reappears regularly—most recently (and disappointingly) in 1986. In 1910 its arrival was heralded by an avalanche of advertisements and postcards (below) and by elegant comet parties featuring exotic drinks with such names as the Comet Cocktail, Halley's Highball, and the Nucleus Brandy Cocktail (so called because the comet consisted of a nucleus and a flaming tail) that promised "a sunbeam in every sip." But gripping fear and wide-eyed terror were as common as celebrations: in addition to predictions about the end of the world, there were dire warnings to "look out for earthquakes"; believers knelt in earnest prayer, and many were convinced that the comet would "cause diseases or fill our atmosphere with deadly gas."

It Happened on May . . .

16, 1868: *Impeached president Andrew Johnson is acquitted by one vote in the Senate.–p.87*

16, 1977: *Arthur D. Little Company floats a lead balloon.–p.352*

17, 1792: *N.Y. Stock Exchange is founded by 24 brokers.–p.139*

17, 1856: *Andrew Carnegie borrows $500 to get started.–p.135*

17, 1933: *Light from Arcturus arrives on earth and opens the Chicago World's Fair.–p.247*

18, 1904: *Arab terrorist Raisuli kidnaps Ion Perdicaris.–p.392*

19, 1841: *First wagon train leaves for California.–p.284*

19, 1896: *Martin Goetze patents a dimple maker.–p.349*

20, 1782: *Deborah Sampson joins the Continental Army.–p.364*

22, 1782: *George Washington refuses to become king.–p.71*

22, 1856: *Rep. Preston Brooks almost murders Sen. Charles Sumner on the Senate floor.–p.82*

22, 1957: *U.S. Air Force nearly nukes New Mexico.–p.405*

23, 1900: *Frances Hiller gets her wish, a fancy funeral.–p.145*

24, 1843: *Samuel F. B. Morse demonstrates his telegraph for Congress.–p.316*

25, 1855: *The Society of Bethel leaves Missouri for Oregon, led by a preserved corpse.–p.285*

29, 1839: *Hiram Ulysses Grant enrolls at West Point; becomes Ulysses Simpson Grant.–p.378*

29, 1866: *Asa Mercer's boatload of brides reaches Seattle.–p.288*

29, 1943: *Norman Rockwell's Rosie the Riveter is born.–p.249*

30, 1806: *Andrew Jackson kills Charles Dickinson.–p.164*

31, 1913: *Americans get the right to vote for senators.–p.64*

June

The Case of the Costly Comma

June 6, 1872: Congress passes a tariff act, error and all

A small punctuation mistake in legislation designed to reduce import duties nearly cost the federal government millions of dollars.

Congress intended that "fruit plants, tropical and semi-tropical for the purpose of propagation and cultivation" were to be tariff-free. But the clerk who copied the bill misplaced the comma, so the clause read: "Fruit, plants tropical and semi-tropical. . . ."

Revolving refunds

Importers took this to mean that *all* tropical and semitropical plants and *all* fruit were free of tariff. And a group of them joined forces to petition the Treasury Department for the refund that they felt was due them. At first, Secretary of the Treasury William A. Richardson agreed with the importers and on December 3, 1873, ordered hundreds of thousands of dollars worth of refunds.

But on December 10 Richardson changed his mind and suspended the refund. He reversed himself again the next day, ordering a settlement. And seven weeks after *that,* on January 31, 1874, the flip-flopping Cabinet member once more directed that the refunds be "revoked and cancelled."

Repayments revoked

On May 9, 1874, Congress finally enacted legislation suspending, once and for all, repayments to importers. The bill corrected the errant comma, thus preventing the mistake from becoming one of the costliest typographical errors in history.

Among those injured during the mishaps that marked the memorial service was Capt. Robert Wilbur (left). When his platoon was unexpectedly fired upon, his underwear was set aflame by a piece of shrapnel. And he was convinced that another piece would have pierced his heart had it not been stopped by a gold watch awarded to him by Queen Victoria.

The Civil War Recalled—and Refought?

June 13, 1883: Everything goes wrong at a dedication

The scene was repeated in towns and villages throughout New England. Veterans, other citizens, and perhaps a celebrity or two would gather to honor the Civil War dead and dedicate a monument to them. But when the town of Mystic, Connecticut, saw fit to pay tribute to those who fought so courageously, it became a day with a difference.

High on a pedestal, a dignified statue of a rifle-bearing Union soldier awaited unveiling. Gov. Thomas Waller and a beloved senator and former general, Joseph R. Hawley, had been invited. But the festive crowd of 2,000 was gravely disappointed to find that the VIP's were delayed, and as the expectant audience shifted impatiently in their seats, the stands on which the spectators were sitting—hastily and perhaps flimsily erected for the occasion—collapsed. And that, as it turned out, was just the beginning.

One of the features of the festivities was the mustering of local troops and those from nearby Norwich. As the aging ex-soldiers marched toward town, however, shots rang out, for the officer who was to give the order to fire the 38-gun salute (one for each of the 38 states of the Union) to herald the unveiling thought it might be nice to welcome the governor with it instead. The veterans, moving smartly up the street near the riflemen at that precise moment, suddenly faced the unexpected gunfire. Many were severely hurt; one officer's body was lacerated, the leg of another one was gushing blood. Despite these injuries, no fatalities were reported.

As the sounds of gunfire and moaning faded, General Hawley delivered a stirring 40-minute speech. Then the women of Mystic served up a delicious luncheon to the deserving crowd.

It was, perhaps, altogether fitting and proper that the celebration came to an end when a drenching downpour suddenly fell upon the assembled patriots.

Hello, Frisco!

June 17, 1914: A telephone pole goes up in Utah

It was the last of 130,000 telephone poles installed across the nation to carry two circuits, each of which utilized 6,780 miles of copper wire. The linemen felt justifiable pride.

It had been decided in 1913 that transcontinental telephone service should be in operation by January 1915, when the Panama-Pacific Exposition in San Francisco was to open. The workmen had no time to waste in meeting their deadline; their job was to "nurse and coax" a tiny current of electricity across 3,400 miles.

Not only did the lines between the East and Denver have to be rehabilitated, but west of Denver there were many gaps to close. The most difficult of all was the 475-mile stretch beyond Salt Lake City, an expanse of salt basins and snow-capped mountains.

First the surveyors, camping in tents or boxcars and working despite extremes of weather, plotted a route. Having no topographical maps, they used compasses and the stars to fix their position. On their heels came the line gangs. Roads were built and chasms bridged for hauling the telephone poles, wire, and other equipment on horse-drawn wagons or sleds. Following a beeline course across shallow lakes and mud flats, the linemen propped the poles to keep them upright in the wet earth. Where the ground was rock-hard, special machinery with an augur-like drill was brought in to bore pole-holes. Contending with blistering heat, record snows, and springtime floods, the crews regularly worked 11-hour days, with every third Sunday off.

January 25, 1915, found Alexander Graham Bell sitting with telephone company officials in New York while his assistant Thomas A. Watson waited in San Francisco. (Only 40 years earlier they had exchanged the first words conveyed by wire.–p.330.) At 4:30 P.M. New York time, Bell lifted the receiver. "Ahoy! Ahoy! Mr. Watson! Are you there? Do you hear me?"

"Yes, Dr. Bell," came the reply. "I hear you perfectly."

Officials at the Nevada-Utah border look on while linemen place and wire the final pole for America's first cross-country telephone line.

It Happened on June . . .

1, 1660: *Puritans hang Mary Dyer for being a Quaker.–p.157*

1, 1908: *John Albert Krohn starts his wheelbarrow tour of the U.S.A.–p.237*

2, 1944: *The answer to "11 across" in the London* Times *crossword puzzle panics the planners of D-Day.–p.403*

3, 1861: *Adah Isaacs Menken "bares it all" at the Green Street Theatre in Albany, N.Y.–p.219*

3, 1965: *Astronaut Ed White walks in space and refuses to come back inside.–p.306*

4, 1781: *Jack Jouett rides to save Thomas Jefferson from the British.–p.361*

6, 1816: *First of three summer blizzards hits the Northeast.–p.211*

6, 1822: *Alexis St. Martin gets a wound in his left side that makes medical history.–p.320*

6, 1866: *Charles Goodnight drives his herd of cattle westward toward Colorado.–p.296*

6, 1944: *Secret DD tanks sink off Omaha Beach on D-Day.–p.402*

7, 1913: *Mountaineers Rev. Hudson Stuck, Walter Harper, Harry P. Karstens, and Robert G. Tatum reach the South Peak of Mount McKinley–and see a flagpole on the North Peak.–p.303*

10, 1900: *Herbert Hoover and his wife are caught up in China's Boxer Rebellion.–p.105*

11, 1917: *Photographer Arthur S. Mole arranges 10,000 servicemen into a living flag.–p.236*

13, 1983: Pioneer 10 *leaves the solar system.–p.307*

14, 1798: *Eli Whitney lies to get a government contract.–p.316*

14, 1940: *Dr. Martin Couney presents diplomas to incubator babies he displayed at the 1939 New York World's Fair.–p.347*

"Unless you see 'Blondin walk' you don't see Niagara," gushed a correspondent of *The Times* of London in 1860.

Niagara's Greatest Drawing Card

June 30, 1859: Blondin makes first ropewalk across Niagara

When Jean François Gravelot first saw Niagara, he knew he had to cross it—on a rope. That was in 1858, and the French aerialist (who called himself The Great Blondin to play up his fair hair) was touring America with P. T. Barnum. The next year he returned and stretched a 1,300-foot length of manila rope, 2 inches thick, between the steep cliffs walling the rapids below the falls. Then, as 10,000 spectators held their collective breath, the 35-year-old Blondin stepped onto the rope from the U.S. side. Stopping midway, he lowered a line to a waiting steamer 190 feet below, drew up a bottle of wine, drank it, and then continued to the Canadian side.

For two summers Blondin performed above the Niagara. He crossed it on a bicycle, on stilts, and at night. He swung by one arm, turned somersaults, and stood on his head on a chair. Once he pushed a stove in a wheelbarrow and cooked an omelet.

But his greatest feat was to carry a man across on his back. With his passenger secured by a harness with foot hooks, Blondin grasped his 35-foot balancing pole and ventured down the steep incline of the rope. Several times his brave companion dismounted to give Blondin a rest and then climbed on his back again. A gust of wind caused them to sway, and spectators quaked with terror. (According to reporters, gamblers had loosened some guylines.) Blondin sprinted the last few yards and plunged with his human cargo headlong into the crowd.

In 1860 the Prince of Wales (later King Edward VII) was among the spectators. Politely refusing an invitation to be carried across, the prince persuaded Blondin to come to London's Crystal Palace. The aerialist performed in London and Europe until 1896. The next year, at the age of 71, he died in bed.

It Happened on June . . .

15, 1859: *The Pig War begins on San Juan Island.–p.375*

16, 1806: *Tecumseh's brother, the Prophet, blots out the sun.–p.366*

17, 1775: *Battle of Bunker Hill is fought on Breed's Hill.–p.360*

17, 1776: *Counterfeiter Issac Ketcham gets out of prison by revealing a plot to poison George Washington.–p.160*

17, 1862: *C. M. French and W. H. Fancher patent a combined plow and gun.–p.327*

18, 1812: *The U.S.A. declares war on Great Britain.–p.368*

19, 1827: *Three-Legged Willie arrives in Texas.–p.173*

19, 1864: *U.S.S.* Kearsarge *sinks the Confederate warship* Alabama *off the French coast.–p.384*

20, 1782: *Congress approves the Great Seal of the U.S.–p.56*

23, 1803: *The first horse sets foot in Hawaii.–p.300*

24, 1763: *British use germ warfare against Indians.–p.358*

25, 1976: *Missouri's governor finally rescinds an 1838 order to exterminate all Mormons.–p.283*

26, 1844: *President John Tyler is secretly married.–p.80*

26, 1873: *The first Russian Mennonite buys Kansas land.–p.295*

27, 1921: *The American Stock Exchange moves indoors.–p.139*

28, 1865: *The Confederate clipper ship* Shenandoah *fires the last shot of the Civil War off the Alaska coast.–p.384*

28, 1941: *LBJ loses an election to Pappy O'Daniel.–p.105*

29, 1776: *Mission San Francisco de Assisi is founded.–p.269*

29, 1871: *Explorer Charles Hall leaves for the North Pole on the ship* Polaris.*–p.301*

July

The Fatal Pursuit

July 28, 1852: A steamboat race ends in disaster

It was early morning when two sleek white steamers carrying New York–bound passengers swung out from the Hudson River docks in Albany—first the *Henry Clay* and then, in her wake, the *Armenia.* Prostrated by food poisoning, the captain of the *Henry Clay,* John Tallman, lay in his cabin; Thomas Collyer, builder and part owner of the boat, was in charge.

Collyer, who had earlier built the *Armenia,* had sold her to Capt. Isaac Smith with the agreement that the two boats would never race each other and that the *Henry Clay* would make her departures well in advance. And so, when the *Henry Clay* docked at Hudson, the first scheduled stop, Collyer was outraged to see the *Armenia* race past. He rushed the *Henry Clay* back into the channel, but the *Armenia* was a good mile ahead.

Determined not to be outdone, Collyer and the crew increased the pressure on the two boilers to 350 pounds per square inch. The blowers hummed, the boat trembled, and coal dust drifted onto the decks. Frightened, the passengers pleaded with the officers to stop the race, but the crew was too exhilarated.

After a speedy docking at Catskill, the *Henry Clay* closed the gap. Her pilot, Jim Elmendorf, nosed in beside the *Armenia.* Prow to prow, the two boats swept on. Then, as the *Henry Clay* shot a few feet ahead, Elmendorf rammed the *Armenia,* splintering her bow.

"To larboard," the passengers of the *Henry Clay* were ordered. Shrieking with fear, they ran to the far side, lifting the boat's starboard guard above the larboard of the *Armenia*. Then, crashing down, the *Henry Clay* drove the *Armenia* toward shore. To avoid being run aground, the *Armenia*'s captain quickly cut his engines, and the boat drifted clear.

Racing furiously now, with red-hot embers from the smokestacks showering her decks, the *Henry Clay* forged on. At Poughkeepsie, 20 protesting passengers debarked. At Newburgh the *Armenia* was so far behind that new passengers, including architect Andrew Jackson Downing, gladly boarded rather than wait.

It was 3:00 P.M. and the *Henry Clay,* still at top speed, had just passed Yonkers (only a few miles from her destination) when a stoker staggered up on deck. A human torch, his clothes aflame, he jumped into the river. Within seconds, the boat was ablaze.

Collyer stood dumbstruck while Elmendorf swung the boat into the east bank. She ran a full 25 feet up the embankment, with an impact that toppled a smokestack and hurled many people, including Collyer, onto land and safety. Others were pitched into the water; some—trapped on the stern by a sheet of flame—had to jump into the river. Within 20 minutes the wooden boat had burned down to water level.

Throughout the hot afternoon and the moonlit night, men dredged for bodies. The next morning it was reported that of the 300 or so passengers, 80 had died—among them Maria Hawthorne, sister of the novelist Nathaniel Hawthorne, and Downing.

Collyer and the officers of the *Henry Clay* were acquitted of manslaughter. The New York State legislature later outlawed steamboat racing on the Hudson.

As flames consumed the steamboat, Collyer and others frenziedly worked to rescue victims, throwing them wooden chairs and fence boards. A train stopped abruptly and passengers rushed to help. A Newfoundland dog joined the effort and dragged a child out of the water. Meanwhile, river pirates tried to rob the drowning of their valuables. Contrary to this rendition of the disaster, the steamboat was beached.

President Franklin D. Roosevelt ordered a search for downed flying great Amelia Earhart (left). For two weeks seven navy ships scoured 250,000 square miles of the vast Pacific —but found nothing. Even today, rumors persist that Earhart was captured by the Japanese and executed as a spy.

Lost Landfall

July 2, 1937: Amelia Earhart sends her last message

In 1932 Amelia Earhart became the first woman to fly solo across the Atlantic. Now she and navigator Fred Noonan were on the longest leg of a round-the-world flight. As they neared tiny Howland Island in the Pacific, fuel was precariously low and stormy weather made radio communication difficult. But Earhart was not broadcasting her position. Her husband, George Palmer Putnam, had sold exclusive rights to the story of her flight to the New York *Herald Tribune,* and she may have wanted to keep other newspapers from getting the scoop. Just before 8:00 A.M. local time, Earhart radioed Howland: "We are circling but cannot see the island. Cannot hear you." Her last message 45 minutes later was unclear. She and Noonan were never seen again. Ironically, the aviatrix had said that the round-the-world trip would be her last long-distance flight.

The Agonies of April Began in July

July 1, 1862. *Until the Civil War there was no federal income tax. The government was supported largely by bonds, excise taxes, and "external revenue" from tariffs on imported goods. The expensive war, however, led legislators to explore new sources of "internal revenue" from citizens at home. On August 5, 1861, a 3-percent tax on annual incomes over $800 was adopted—but no one bothered to collect it, perhaps because it met such a small part of government needs. On July 1 of the following year, a new tax law was signed, giving America its first operable federal income tax. This was repealed in 1872—it had just been a temporary way of funding the war debt—and no new income tax was proposed until 1894, when the government needed money to meet financial crises caused by a monetary panic. But on May 20, 1895, the Supreme Court ruled that the whole idea of an income tax was unconstitutional, since the tax would not be distributed among the states in proportion to their populations. It took the 16th Amendment (ratified on February 3, 1913) to make income tax legal.*

It Happened on July . . .

1, 1893: *President Grover Cleveland loses part of his jaw in secret cancer surgery.* –p.92

1, 1946: *First peacetime atom bomb test blasts Bikini.* –p.252

2, 1776: *America's real birthday.* –p.48

2, 1881: *Abraham Lincoln's son is present as President Garfield is assassinated.* –p.91

3, 1776: *The Declaration of Independence is approved by one vote.* –p.48

3, 1916: *The Witch of Wall Street dies, leaving more money than J. P. Morgan.* –p.139

4, 1776: *Not much happened, Britain's King George III writes in his diary.* –p.48

4, 1826: *Both Thomas Jefferson and John Adams die.* –p.75

4, 1839: *Rent war is declared against Van Rensselaers.* –p.369

8, 1869: *John Wesley Powell is saved by longjohns.* –p.288

10, 1787: *While the Founding Fathers debate the Constitution in Philadelphia, an old woman is beaten to death as a witch.* –p.53

11, 1804: *Aaron Burr kills Alexander Hamilton in a duel.* –p.162

12, 1856: *American filibuster William Walker becomes the president of Nicaragua.* –p.373

13, 1805: *Oliver Evans drives his brand-new steam automobile through Philadelphia.* –p.315

13, 1876: *"There's lots of humanity in Calamity," reports the Deadwood* Pioneer. –p.292

13, 1897: *John Sievers patents a cow-shaped hunting decoy.* –p.339

14, 1881: *Pat Garrett guns down Billy the Kid.* –p.171

14, 1965: Mariner 4 *flies by Mars; finds no canals.* –p.328

"Wrong Way" Corrigan was an experienced pilot who was denied official permission for a transatlantic flight. So he hopped into his antiquated single-engine "crate" and headed home to California. But, he claimed, his compass was stuck, so he "got mixed up in the clouds" and crossed the Atlantic anyway. His dramatic feat made him an international hero—and a movie star.

"Many Moons Ago I Lived"

July 8, 1913: Pearl Curran first contacts Patience Worth

For almost a year Pearl Curran, a St. Louis housewife with little education and no literary ambitions, had been playing with a Ouija board. Suddenly, on a hot summer evening, some words appeared that changed her life: "Many moons ago I lived. Again I come—Patience Worth my name." Patience claimed to be the spirit of a 17th-century woman who had come to the New World late in life and had been murdered by Indians.

Over the next quarter-century, letters, short stories, books, poems, and plays flowed from Patience, via Pearl. Hundreds of people visited the Curran household to participate in the séances during which Patience produced her voluminous correspondence. Two of her books, and numerous poems, were published to critical acclaim. One reviewer commented that she had "a sense of humor that is rare in ghosts or secondary personalities." An expert in the field of psychic phenomena found Patience's intellect "keen, swift, subtle, and profound." And, at her insistence, the Currans adopted a child, whom the spirit considered to be "mine own bairn [baby]."

Pearl continued to record communications from Patience until shortly before her own death in 1937. The material filled 29 volumes.

It Happened on July . . .

15, 1742: *After the War of Jenkins' Ear, Spain cedes the colony of Georgia to the British.–p.358*

17, 1871: *Lawyer Clement Vallandigham shoots himself to defend a client.–p.182*

17, 1934: *Gov. Bill Langer of North Dakota issues that state's Declaration of Independence from the U.S.A.–p.102*

18, 1846: *America's first plank road opens to traffic.–p.213*

18, 1938: *Douglas Corrigan earns his nickname by landing in Ireland instead of California.*

19, 1945: *Harry S Truman plays Paderewski's* Minuet *for Stalin at Potsdam Conference.–p.108*

19, 1952: *UFO's are spotted over the White House.–p.252*

20, 1676: *King Philip's family is imprisoned by Puritans.–p.356*

21, 1619: *Jamestown's Polish immigrants win the vote.–p.266*

21, 1861: *The First Battle of Bull Run overruns Wilmer McLean's Virginia plantation.–p.385*

21, 1884: *Reports of Grover Cleveland's illegitimate child lead to a dirty campaign.–p.101*

21, 1925: *John Scopes is fined $100 for teaching evolution.–p.241*

21, 1969: *At 1:54 P.M. EDT, man leaves the surface of the moon for the first time, after a visit of 21 hours and 37 minutes.–p.257*

22, 1934: *The FBI says it killed John Dillinger.–p.192*

28, 1932: *Bonus marchers are driven from Washington, D.C.–p.246*

28, 1945: *The B-24* Lonesome Lady *is shot down near Hiroshima; crew are prisoners there when the U.S. drops the A-bomb.–p.404*

30, 1888: *Harold P. Brown tortures a dog; later invents the electric chair.–p.334*

When Julia Holmes wanted to take her turn on night guard duty, the expedition leader, "conservative up to his eyes," would not permit it.

August

Trailblazer

Aug. 5, 1858: A woman scales 14,110-foot Pikes Peak

The "Pikes Peak or Bust" frenzy was a year away when Julia Archibald Holmes and her husband joined the first group of Kansas gold-seekers to head for Colorado. The 20-year-old Julia—much to the consternation of the men in the party—wore bloomers on the trail, for "comfort and convenience."

A pioneer in every sense, she enjoyed her travels thoroughly, walking beside the wagon (though women were supposed to ride *in* it), peering at an Indian village in defiance of orders to stay hidden, camping in the Garden of the Gods at the foot of Pikes Peak—and climbing the majestic mountain.

As the Holmeses scaled Pikes Peak, they discovered Amphitheater Canyon, where they rolled stones down to hear a "thundering sound from the hidden depths below." At the top, they marked their arrival by inscribing their names on a rock. Julia later wrote to her mother: "In all probability I am the first woman who has ever stood upon the summit of this mountain and gazed upon this wondrous scene." And indeed she was.

Notorious Outlaws, Model Prisoners

Aug. 10, 1887: Headliner badmen start a prison newspaper

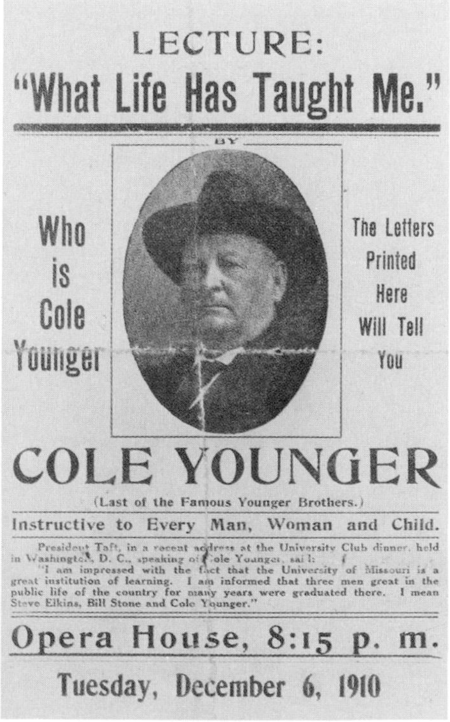
LECTURE:
"What Life Has Taught Me."
BY
Who is Cole Younger
The Letters Printed Here Will Tell You
COLE YOUNGER
(Last of the Famous Younger Brothers.)
Instructive to Every Man, Woman and Child.
President Taft, in a recent address at the University Club dinner, held in Washington, D. C., speaking of Cole Younger, said:
"I am impressed with the fact that the University of Missouri is a great institution of learning. I am informed that three men great in the public life of the country for many years were graduated there. I mean Steve Elkins, Bill Stone and Cole Younger."
Opera House, 8:15 p. m.
Tuesday, December 6, 1910

Cole Younger eventually took to the lucrative lecture circuit, where he gave inspirational talks like the one advertised in this handbill.

Not only was the concept of an inmate-run newspaper a novel idea in the 19th century, but having convicts put up money to get it started was even more innovative. When 15 convicts at the Minnesota state prison in Stillwater contributed $200, among the "stockholders" listed on the front page of the first edition were the Younger brothers. Notorious killers, bank robbers, and cohorts of the infamous Jesse James Gang, the trio had often been headlined in national newspapers.

Convinced that *The Prison Mirror* was a worthy enterprise, Jim Younger and his brother Cole invested $20 each; their brother Bob donated $10. And on the masthead of that first edition Cole, the prison librarian, appeared as printer's devil (a minor editorial position, but listed no doubt in recognition of his exceptional notoriety as a murderer and thief). The front page carried the maxim "God helps those who help themselves"—a motto that was later changed to "It's never too late to mend."

Published biweekly by and for inmates, *The Mirror* is today the oldest continuously published prison paper in the United States. It boasts awards as the "Best Printed Prison Newspaper," and its subscriber list eventually was extended far beyond the prison walls. But what of some of its famous founders?

Two years after the newspaper appeared, Bob Younger died at the penitentiary, a victim of tuberculosis. Cole and Jim were paroled in 1901. A year later Jim committed suicide in a St. Paul hotel because, under the terms of his parole, he could not marry the woman he loved. His surviving brother, who achieved legitimate renown with his autobiography *The Story of Cole Younger, by Himself*, died in 1916 in his hometown of Lee's Summit, Missouri, of natural causes.

Washington and the Moonshiners

Aug. 7, 1794: The president defends the government's authority

The farmers along the Monongahela River in southwestern Pennsylvania were a mere one-seventieth of the new nation's population, but they owned a quarter of its stills. They weren't drunkards, just good businessmen who had found that a jug of liquor was cheaper to transport and more profitable to sell than the grain it took to produce it. Not surprisingly, these wily frontiersmen were furious when Secretary of the Treasury Alexander Hamilton pushed Congress to adopt an excise tax on spirits in 1791. Hadn't Americans fought the Revolution to get out from under such taxes imposed by the British?

Hamilton argued that the whiskey makers wouldn't lose any money; they would just pass the tax on to buyers as higher prices. Nonetheless, in the best Sons of Liberty tradition, the Pennsylvania farmers responded to tax collectors with tar and feathers.

One moonshiner tried a different approach. When revenue men arrived, he hospitably offered them ginger cakes—laced with whiskey. After a few generous helpings the officials passed out. The farmer then stepped outside, hid his still, and was a paragon of innocence when the tax collectors awoke.

By the summer of 1794, however, the Whiskey Rebellion, as the frontiersmen's resistance was called, had gotten ugly. After two days of siege, the home of the district excise inspector had been overrun by a mob of 500 and burned to the ground. Terror gripped Pittsburgh shortly thereafter when 5,000 armed protesters occupied the city. There was even serious talk of secession.

On August 7, President George Washington declared that southwestern Pennsylvania was in a state of insurrection. By October a force of 13,000 militiamen from four states was marching to put down the rebellion. Among the commanders was Alexander Hamilton, who now was also acting secretary of war. As the army advanced, the whiskey makers' resistance collapsed. By mid-November their movement was finished. A few leaders were arrested but were ultimately pardoned. Historians have called this one of the greatest threats to the stability of the Union prior to the Civil War.

Tar and feathers often greeted tax collectors during the Whiskey Rebellion, one of the earliest challenges to the power of the young federal government.

It Happened on August . . .

1, 1861: *General Beauregard orders blackout in response to night flights of Union balloons.–p.376*

1, 1911: *Harriet Quimby becomes the first American woman to get a pilot's license.–p.304*

2, 1776: *The Declaration of Independence is finally signed.–p.48*

2, 1790: *Counting begins for the first U.S. census.–p.204*

4, 1913: *Joe Knowles strips and goes back to nature.–p.236*

4, 1943: *James Wright's lab experiment unexpectedly yields Silly Putty.–p.352*

5, 1924: *Little Orphan Annie debuts as a female.–p.241*

6, 1727: *Eleven Ursuline nuns land in New Orleans.–p.289*

6, 1774: *Mother Ann Lee and eight fellow Shakers land in New York City.–p.209*

6, 1867: *A group of Cheyenne braves derail a Union Pacific train near Plum Creek, Nebr.; they are the first Indians ever to engineer a train wreck.–p.291*

7, 1782: *Sgts. Elijah Churchill, William Brown, and Daniel Bissel are awarded the first Purple Hearts.–p.365*

8, 1867: *William Thompson asks Dr. Richard Moore of Omaha to sew his scalp back on.–p.292*

9, 1904: *Shorty Harris makes Death Valley's biggest gold strike.–p.127*

10, 1680: *Pueblo Indians revolt against Spanish rule.–p.202*

10, 1927: *Gutzon Borglum starts sculpting Mount Rushmore.–p.58*

11, 1895: *George Loher heads across U.S.A. on a bicycle.–p.232*

12, 1869: *Norton I, Emperor of the U.S., abolishes the Democratic and Republican parties.–p.225*

12, 1886: *Dr. McLean dies before his "peace makers" end war.–p.326*

Lounging at lagoons was reportedly a popular lunar pastime.

The *Sun* and the Moon

Aug. 25, 1835: A great lunar hoax peddles papers

The weather was steamy, and the news was even hotter. According to the New York *Sun*, Sir John Herschel, a noted British astronomer, had discovered life on the moon: blue unicorns, tailless beavers walking on two legs, and—most spectacular of all—batlike, four-foot-tall moon people covered with copper-colored fur! Males and females supposedly had animated conversations, leaving no doubt about their rationality. More intimate moonfolk relations were said to have been observed; but good taste prohibited detailed reports, for they "would ill comport with our terrestrial notions of decorum."

Further revelations halted abruptly when reporter Richard Adams Locke confessed he had made the whole thing up. Luckily for Locke, Herschel burst out laughing when he heard that his name had been taken in vain. The *Sun* had the last laugh though: thanks to its inspired lunacy, daily circulation rose from 8,000 to 19,360, making it the most widely read paper in the world.

WALTER
LIBERACE
Wisconsin's foremost young pianist is back again in the Red Room bar and cocktail lounge with his songs at the piano in his own inimitable way.
RED ROOM
PLANKINTON ARCADE

For an encore in La Crosse, Wisconsin, Walter Liberace departed from his classical repertoire and played Kay Kyser's hit "Three Little Fishies" ("and they swam, and they swam, all over the dam"). "I was trying to tell the people that you could have fun... without sacrificing the greatness of the music," he later said. The audience got the message, and their rousing ovation gave the young virtuoso a new "idea on how to make money playing the piano."

It Happened on August . . .

14, 1889: *Supreme Court justice Stephen J. Field is arrested for murder.–p.181*

15, 1915: *New York* World *blabs on German spies.–p.394*

17, 1955: *Top Ford executives gather to view a full-scale mock-up of the Edsel.–p.255*

18, 1920: *Harry Burn's mother gives women the vote.–p.67*

19, 1877: *"Lemonade Lucy" Hayes dries out the White House.–p.90*

19, 1909: *The Indianapolis Speedway opens with a disastrous 300-mile race.–p.148*

23, 1784: *A convention opens to request recognition of the new state of Franklin.–p.270*

23, 1861: *Allan Pinkerton arrests Rose O'Neal Greenhow, leader of a Confederate spy ring.–p.380*

24, 1814: *Dolley Madison saves George Washington's portrait from the British.–p.368*

27, 1587: *Gov. John White of Roanoke sails to England for badly needed supplies.–p.264*

27, 1896: *The first dial telephone is installed (in the Milwaukee city hall).–p.331*

27, 1906: *Teddy Roosevelt tries to reform American spelling.–p.94*

28, 1859: *Edwin Drake strikes oil in Pennsylvania.–p.129*

28, 1948: *"Landslide Lyndon" Johnson wins by 87 highly questionable votes.–p.111*

30, 1862: *The Second Battle of Bull Run overruns Wilmer McLean's Virginia plantation.–p.385*

31, 1911: *At age 19, Cromwell Dixon becomes America's youngest licensed aviator.–p.304*

31, 1939: *A young concert pianist plays a pop tune; grinning and winking at the audience, he discovers the rewards of showmanship.*

September

The Big Break Begins

Sept. 5, 1774: First Continental Congress meets

In response to the Boston Tea Party in December 1773, Parliament imposed the Coercive Acts, which closed Boston's port and tried to crush colonial resistance. But the harsh acts had just the opposite effect; they rallied Americans to the cause of liberty.

In early September 1774, 56 delegates from every colony but Georgia (whose governor prohibited representatives from attending) met in Philadelphia. Joseph Galloway of Pennsylvania urged preserving America's place in the British Empire. Many delegates agreed, and his proposal—calling for a colonial legislature whose acts could be vetoed by the king's appointed president-general—was defeated by only one vote. By mid-October the congress was committed to aggressive retaliation, in the form of a boycott of British goods. A revolution was about to begin.

Delegates to the First Continental Congress prayed for guidance as they deliberated about the colonies' role in the empire. The question often divided friends. Loyalist Joseph Galloway had been a protégé of rebel Benjamin Franklin.

A Texas-Size Train Wreck

Sept. 15, 1896: The "Crash at Crush" draws thousands

Amazed that people would turn up in droves to gawk at train wrecks, William Crush, a passenger agent for the Missouri, Kansas & Texas Railroad, proposed that the line stage a crash for publicity and profit. Officials agreed, and thus was born what one reporter called "the event of the year."

Billing it as the "Monster Head-end Collision," Crush had two old steam locomotives freshly painted, and arranged for each to pull six cars. A site near Waco, Texas, was chosen and named in honor of the energetic promoter. Hundreds of workmen descended and set up an instant city: a railroad depot and telegraph office appeared, as well as a restaurant in a circus tent. Statewide ballyhoo brought huge crowds; 10,000 people had arrived at Crush by 10:00 A.M.; by afternoon there were 40,000. As they jostled for a good view of the action, one newspaperman noted that "a wonderful recklessness marked the conduct of many." One man warned Crush that the people were too close for safety, but was pooh-poohed.

At 5:20 the trains thundered down the track, meeting head-on with a roaring crash. Then the boilers exploded. Debris flew through the air, killing two men; many more were injured as people ran for their lives.

Crush was fired by the railroad that night. Ever resourceful, he convinced his employers that they could turn the disaster into publicity for railroad safety—and they rehired him the next day.

A split-second after this picture was taken the two locomotives met. The photographer lost an eye in the ensuing explosion. Scott Joplin honored the event in his "Great Collision March."

Who Planted the Bomb?

Sept. 16, 1920: Mystery explosion rocks Wall Street

It was a boom day on Wall Street, but the results were fatal. Parked next to the new U.S. Assay Office and right across the street from the handsome J. P. Morgan Building was a horse-drawn cart loaded with metal sash weights—and TNT. Around noontime, when the streets were filled with lunchtime crowds, the bomb went off, hurling shrapnel into the crowd and through windows. Thirty-five died, and hundreds were wounded; many bodies were mangled beyond recognition. The blast was widely suspected to be an anarchist attempt on the life of J. P. Morgan, Jr., but the tycoon was in Europe. (His son Junius Spencer Morgan was slightly injured by flying glass.)

Finding the culprit would prove impossible. As dogged investigators sifted through the debris, they discovered a horseshoe that they finally traced to a blacksmith's shop on the Lower East Side. But the blacksmith wasn't much help, and the person who sent Wall Street skyrocketing was never found.

Flying metal dug holes in the limestone of the Morgan Building; the scars can still be seen on the dignified edifice at the corner of Wall and Broad Streets.

The city's papers were published as one for a week until pressmen negotiated a settlement. The first edition was small, but not the masthead!

The Combined New York Morning Newspapers

New York American
THE NEW YORK HERALD
The Journal of Commerce
DAILY NEWS
The Morning Telegraph

The New York Times.
New York Tribune
The World.
New-Yorker Staats-Zeitung
IL PROGRESSO ITALO-AMERICANO

Vol. LXXXIII No. 28,066 — Wednesday, September 19, 1923

Peters Not in Gunman Car, Ward Admits
Mills Asserts Statement to Sheriff Was False, as Slain Man Was Not in Westchester County

Visit by Lloyd George Expected by Coolidge

Oklahoma's Legislators Defy Walton
Continue Plans for Extra Session Despite Threats of Jail; Claim Majority Required to Impeach

White Star and Cunard Merge Winter Service

Wilson Ready To Run Again, Say Friends
Canvasses 1924 'Timber' With Illinois Leader, Implying He Would Heed Call if Deadlock Came

Pressmen's Chief Orders End to Walk-Out at Once

Press Strike Is Denounced As 'Outlaw'
International President Repudiates Action of Local Pressmen, and Orders Them to Work

It Happened on September . . .

1, 1871: *Mark Twain patents a self-pasting scrapbook.–p.329*

2, 1858: *"The Yellow Rose of Texas" is copyrighted.–p.370*

2, 1890: *First automated census counts 62,622,250 Americans.–p.336*

3, 1908: *The Wright brothers give their first public demonstration at Ft. Myer, Va., almost five years after having made their historic initial flight.–p.340*

6, 1776: *The* Turtle, *making the world's first submarine attack, fails to sink the British* Eagle.*–p.312*

6, 1901: *Abraham Lincoln's son is present as President McKinley is assassinated.–p.91*

7, 1921: *Margaret Gorman wins the first Miss America contest.–p.242*

7, 1982: *In answer to a "prayer," Stanton Lee Powers's bank balance jumps to over $5 million.–p.152*

8, 1861: *Lincoln asks Italian revolutionary Giuseppe Garibaldi to head the Union Army.–p.376*

8, 1892: *"The Pledge of Allegiance to the Flag" is published in* Youth's Companion; *probably written by staff members Francis Bellamy or James Upham.*

13, 1961: *Congress declares "Uncle Sam" Wilson of Troy, N.Y., the "progenitor of America's national symbol."–p.59*

14, 1814: *Francis Scott Key starts "The Star-Spangled Banner."–p.51*

16, 1908: *William C. Durant founds General Motors without J. P. Morgan's help.–p.344*

17, 1630: *Puritan magistrates at Plymouth sentence Thomas Morton to the stocks; his possessions are seized, his house is burned, and he is exiled.–p.265*

17, 1908: *First fatal air crash kills Orville Wright's passenger.–p.341*

19, 1923: *New York printers go on strike; newspapers join forces.*

After the Civil War, Capt. John Lea (below) organized Ku Klux Klan dens throughout his home county in North Carolina. Often donning masks and robes to hide their identity (left), Klansmen terrorized newly freed blacks to keep them in submission.

"Wait Till I Die"

Sept. 29, 1935: Death brings revelation of a murder

When Capt. John Lea, a respected tobacco man, died at 92, the nation discovered he had gotten away with murder. He was the last of the perpetrators of a Klan execution that had taken place 65 years earlier in Caswell County, North Carolina. The victim was a state senator and justice of the peace named John Walter Stephens.

Lea, the scion of a slaveholding family, was a Confederate veteran of the Civil War and an organizer of the Ku Klux Klan in Caswell County. Stephens was a scalawag, working to deliver the black vote for the Republican Party. In his fervor, he intimidated white Democrats.

On Sunday morning, May 22, 1870, Stephens was found in a storeroom of the county courthouse, brutally murdered. The killing created a furor. It was widely believed that Stephens's death was a Klan execution, and numbers of white men, including Lea, were arrested and questioned. But all remained silent, and all were released.

As time passed, the various suspects died, until only Captain Lea was left. Asked repeatedly what had happened, he would cagily reply, "You all can wait till I die." In 1919 he secretly gave three state officials a statement about the murder, to be read posthumously.

Made public upon his death, the affidavit stated that Stephens had been "tried" for arson and extortion, found guilty, and sentenced to death by the Klan. Naming the Klansmen involved, Lea then described how Stephens had been lured to his execution chamber, disarmed, strangled with a rope, and stabbed "in the breast and also in the neck." Stephens "had a fair trial before a jury of twelve men," Lea commented with no indication of remorse.

It Happened on September . . .

20, 1919: *Women trolley conductorettes are fired as the men come back from World War I.–p.397*

20, 1956: *A year before Sputnik, Wernher von Braun is denied permission to launch a missile with orbital capability.–p.252*

23, 1861: *Acting Secretary of War Thomas A. Scott asks Gov. Oliver Morton not to dress Indiana's troops in gray, "the color generally worn by the enemy."–p.380*

23, 1897: *The world's first professional rodeo is held in Cheyenne, Wyo.–p.232*

24, 1861: *Leontine Lowe sees her balloonist husband shot down behind Confederate lines and leads Union troops to the rescue.–p.376*

24, 1869: *Black Friday; the price of gold plummets as President Grant bursts Jay Gould's overinflated bubble.–p.138*

25, 1780: *Peggy Arnold stages a mad scene for General Washington after her husband's treason is discovered.–p.362*

25, 1846: *Juan Flaco rides for California's independence.–p.371*

25, 1919: *President Wilson collapses in Pueblo, Colo.–p.99*

26, 1820: *Daniel Boone dies from eating too many sweet potatoes.–p.271*

26, 1918: *Final Allied offensive of World War I begins; more explosives are used on the first day than all the cannon ammunition fired by the Union Army during the entire Civil War.–p.395*

26, 1933: *Machine Gun Kelly coins the term* G-men.*–p.193*

27, 1852: Uncle Tom's Cabin *opens in Troy, N.Y.–p.216*

30, 1780: *As General Washington offers to trade spy John André for traitor Benedict Arnold, a two-faced effigy of Arnold is burned in Philadelphia.–p.362*

October

Two Is an Unlucky Number

Oct. 5, 1892: The Dalton Gang bites the dust

Five men on horseback rode slowly into the bustling boomtown of Coffeyville, Kansas. Three of them wore false mustaches. They were the notorious Dalton brothers—Bob, Emmett, and Grat—and Coffeyville was their hometown. The other two were their henchmen, Bill Powers and Dick Broadwell. Bob, the leader, decided they would make history by robbing *two* banks in one raid.

The outlaws had reached the middle of town before a storekeeper recognized them and quietly spread the news. Unaware, Bob took Emmett into the First National Bank while Grat and his two chums strode into the private bank of C. M. Condon & Co.

Emerging with more than $20,000 stuffed into a grain sack, Bob and Emmett killed three townspeople and would have escaped if the other bank heist hadn't gone sour. Grat had been delayed by the Condon's bank officers long enough for gun-toting citizenry to get into position outside. When the three finally ran out, their guns blazing, rifle fire and shotgun blasts swept the street. As bullets slammed Grat backward, he managed to kill a town marshal. Powers and Broadwell were shot dead in their saddles.

Bob and Emmett rushed to help Grat. Reunited for the final time, the three shot futilely at their attackers. Grat was killed, then Bob. Emmett was riddled with bullets. Only 15 minutes had passed since the Dalton Gang first entered the banks.

Emmett recovered and was sent to prison. After his parole, he became a respected businessman in Los Angeles. Years later he was an adviser for the romanticized movie *When the Daltons Rode*.

After the shootout, the two dead Daltons (still with their false mustaches) and their companions were put on display in Coffeyville. People poured into town from miles around to view them and take their picture.

A Dim Forecast

Oct. 7, 1819: First American visits Saigon, Vietnam

A true Yankee trader, Capt. John White sailed his brig out of Salem, Massachusetts, in January 1819, determined to reach a new market: Saigon. Six months later he touched the coast of present-day Vietnam near the mouth of the Donnai River. His destination lay some 60 miles upstream.

Needing a river guide and permits to proceed to the royal city, White contacted a local potentate. While putting on a show of hospitality, the chief detained him for weeks and demanded as presents just about everything on the ship. White finally bought "peace and goodwill at the expense of a pair of pistols . . . 25 cartridges, 12 flints, one six-pound canister of powder, some shoes, much liquor, and a Dutch cheese." Impatient, White sent his own delegates to Saigon and secured permission to proceed. He and his crew reached the city on October 7.

First impressions

The American was impressed by the fortifications and armaments of the walled inner city. Near one of its four great gates he noticed "two hundred and fifty pieces of cannons . . . principally of European manufacture" (evidence of Indochina's already long and stormy association with France).

But in business transactions he found the capital's government officials even more rapacious than their rural counterparts. The price of the most desirable commodity, sugar, soared from "eighty to one hundred percent" after his arrival. White concluded that unless the local people shaped up, the civilized world would find nothing in that country but "a source of deep regret and commiseration."

It Happened on October . . .

1, 1867: *Credit Mobilier finagles a scandalous contract.–p.136*

1, 1907: *The Aerial Experiment Association is formed by Alexander Graham Bell, Thomas Selfridge, and three others to further research in manned flight.–pp.330, 341*

2, 1919: *Woodrow Wilson has a massive stroke; his wife becomes, in effect, acting president.–p.99*

6, 1777: *George Washington returns General Howe's dog.–p.206*

6, 1897: *Hearst reporter Karl Decker breaks the "Cuban Joan of Arc" out of prison.–p.390*

7, 1935: *The Supreme Court meets in its own building for the first time.–p.73*

7, 1952: *Al Capone's brother, a federal law officer, dies.–p.191*

9, 1924: *Ezra Meeker travels the Oregon Trail for the fourth and final time, by airplane.–p.285*

10, 1792: *Welshman John Evans arrives in America in search of Welsh-speaking Indians.–p.260*

11, 1809: *Meriwether Lewis dies mysteriously at Grinder's Stand, on the Natchez Trace.–p.273*

13, 1792: *The cornerstone is laid for the White House.–p.60*

13, 1805: *Capt. William Clark writes in his journal that "a woman with a party of men is a token of peace."–p.272*

13, 1863: *Lloyd Magruder is killed with an ax, leading to Idaho's first murder trial.–p.172*

13, 1939: *Shipwreck Kelly stands on his head all day atop a 56-story building.–p.247*

14, 1912: *A thick speech saves Teddy Roosevelt from an assassin's bullet.–p.96*

15, 1860: *Eleven-year-old Grace Bedell advises presidential hopeful Abraham Lincoln to grow a beard.–p.84*

The Great Peshtigo Fire

Oct. 8, 1871: Chicago got all the headlines

For three days the nation's newspapers were black with headlines about the horror of the Chicago fire. Almost unnoticed was the fierce firestorm that began in northern Wisconsin the same evening and went on to devastate Peshtigo and neighboring lumber towns in Wisconsin and upper Michigan.

No soaking rain had fallen for 14 weeks, and the pine forests, piles of sawdust, stacks of raw timber, even the swamps around Peshtigo were as dry as matchsticks. Small fires, many the result of carelessness or slash-and-burn land clearing that had been done to build a railroad, gnawed at forest debris and the roots of towering pines. When the wind rose, the trees crashed to the ground, showering sparks through the underbrush. And now surging autumn breezes were fanning the flames into a conflagration.

The widespread smaller blazes in the forest surrounding the town had created a great vacuum into which winds of hurricane force rushed. The sky became a shower of flames as fireballs burst in the treetops. Within minutes every building was ablaze. The huge woodworking factory exploded. Families who sought refuge in open fields were roasted as they lay on the ground. Those sheltered in wells were scalded. The lucky ones made it to the river, but even here they had to dunk their heads to prevent their hair from catching fire. The blaze was equivalent to the energy in a 20-kiloton bomb.

TR Says He'll Ban the Brutal Sport of Football

Oct. 9, 1905. *Theodore Roosevelt held a tense meeting at the White House with the coaches from the three reigning football powers: Harvard, Princeton, and Yale. After seeing a horrifying photograph of Bob Maxwell, a Swarthmore College lineman who had been savagely beaten during a game, he had decided to take action. If football couldn't put an end to on-field brutality, he would abolish the game by executive decree. His concern was justified. Players wore little padding (even helmets were optional), and such popular plays as the flying wedge—in which an entire team formed a V and swept down the field like a tank—led to slugfests. During the 1905 season alone, 18 college players died and another 159 were badly injured. The coaches agreed that new rules should stress speed rather than brute force; among the innovations for 1906 was the forward pass. Only six players were killed that year, including three Ivy Leaguers who died in fistfights.*

Panic at Peshtigo was far beyond that depicted by Harper's Weekly *(above). The fire's swiftness left no time for either boats or belongings.*

More than a million acres (2,400 square miles) of forest were destroyed and some 1,200 people perished. It was the worst forest fire in American history. But for days few people knew about it—the one telegraph wire into town had melted almost as soon as the fire struck. By the time word did get out, Chicago (where some 300 people died) was the fire story that had grabbed the headlines.

Aloys Peters had a great act. Diving from a platform with a noose around his neck, he grabbed the specially made rope seconds before it tightened, absorbing the deadly shock with his arms and the rope's elasticity. He'd been doing the act for more than a dozen years. But the night of his 75-foot leap at the Firemen's Wild West Rodeo and Thrill Circus in St. Louis, tragedy struck. Perhaps he misjudged the distance. Perhaps the cables in the new rope tangled. It tightened before Peters grasped it, breaking his neck instantly. More than 5,600 spectators witnessed his death—but not his pregnant wife, Catherine. It was the first performance she had missed in their three years of marriage.

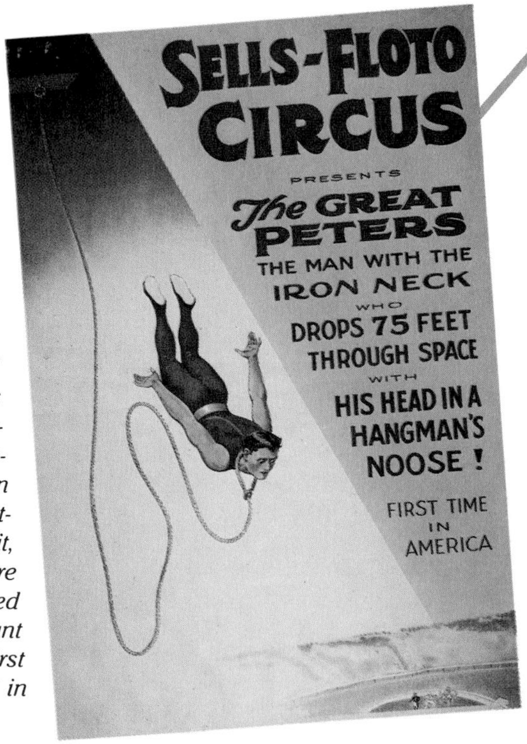

It Happened on October . . .

15, 1899: *Frankie Baker shoots her lover, Albert (not Johnny) Britt, in St. Louis.–p.188*

16, 1846: *William Morton uses ether for painless surgery.–p.319*

16, 1891: *Sarah Winnemucca, the first female Paiute chief, dies at the age of 47.–p.286*

19, 1864: *Confederate soldiers rob a Vermont bank.–p.382*

21, 1929: *Thomas Alva Edison collapses at the Golden Jubilee of Light.–p.245*

21, 1951: *Cathedral of St. John the Divine unveils a stained-glass window devoted to sports.–p.243*

22, 1919: *Nan Britton bears a baby girl; blames future president Warren Harding.–p.100*

22, 1921: *Four unknown American soldiers are exhumed in France; one will lie in Arlington National Cemetery.–p.397*

22, 1943: *The Great Peters reaches the end of his rope.*

23, 1781: *Tench Tilghman brings news to Philadelphia of the surrender at Yorktown.–p.361*

23, 1918: *Influenza kills 851 people in New York City.–p.235*

26, 1825: *The Erie Canal is completed.–p.210*

27, 1873: *Joseph Glidden patents improved barbed wire.–p.255*

28, 1789: *British spy George Beckwith assigns code number 7 to his best American contact, Secretary of the Treasury Alexander Hamilton.–p.205*

28, 1886: *The Statue of Liberty is dedicated.–p.62*

28, 1914: *The first true zipper, Hookless No. 2, is sold.–p.323*

31, 1936: The Literary Digest *confidently predicts Alf Landon will defeat Franklin Delano Roosevelt for the presidency.–p.109*

November

A Royal Refuge?

Nov. 9, 1793: An aristocratic haven is called Azilum

If the guillotine had not nixed the plan, the backwoods of Pennsylvania might have become home to King Louis XVI and Queen Marie Antoinette of France.

When the French Revolution exploded in 1789, thousands of aristocrats fled to America, congregating in Philadelphia, the U.S. capital. Several of these exiles hoped to create a haven for the royal family and other French refugees. Their supporters included Vicomte Louis-Marie de Noailles, a brother-in-law of General Lafayette, who used his clout to acquire the land: 2,400 acres on the Susquehanna River near present-day Towanda. Lots up to 400 acres were offered to the French for two or three dollars an acre.

The queen's house

The king was guillotined in January 1793, just as the project was launched, but the French exiles still hoped to save their queen. One of the first houses to be built was for her—a grand two-storied structure with 16 fireplaces. Wishing to see the colony, Noailles arrived on November 9 and gave the town its name, Azilum (as the French pronounced the word "asylum"), to reflect its purpose.

The colony soon had some 50 houses and about 250 residents. But Queen Marie Antoinette was not among them. Unbeknownst to them, she had been beheaded.

Preferring a more elegant life than the rustic frontier offered, the French ached to go home. When, after a few years, they learned that they could obtain pardons, the exodus from Azilum began. By 1803 only three Frenchmen remained.

"The Great Descender, mighty PATCH/ Spurner of heights—great Nature's overmatch!" eulogized the poet Dr. Thomas Ward of New Jersey about Jumping Sam.

Jumping Sam Patch

Nov. 13, 1829: He makes his final leap

Sam Patch's love of leaping started early. At six months, he claimed, he was leaping into a basin of bubbles from his nanny's arms. As a youngster, leapfrog was his favorite game. Soon he was leaping from boat masts into the waters below.

At the age of 20, Sam gave up his job as a cotton spinner in Paterson, New Jersey, and took to traveling from town to town, diving off bridges and other high places into bodies of water. "There's no mistake in Sam Patch," he'd tell the throng before a jump. "Some things can be done as well as others." His apothegm became a national catchphrase.

Friday, November 13, found Sam preparing to make his second leap of 125 feet over the Genesee Falls. After a practice dive, he had boasted to admirers: "I'll show you how it's done." From the scaffold at the brink of the falls he bragged to the crowd: Napoleon couldn't make the jump, "but I can do it—and I will." He swayed as he spoke, and onlookers realized with a shock that he was drunk. Sam jumped, but his usually graceful headfirst dive turned into a fall. He hit the water sideways and never reappeared. Some thought the stunt a hoax. But the following March a farmer discovered Sam's broken body frozen in a block of ice.

Yet so beloved was Sam Patch that his legend grew after his death. The "doing Sam Patch" craze swept the country; clerks jumped counters, and farmers jumped fences. A touring comedian made his fame playing the part of Jumping Sam. Poems were written about him, and Nathaniel Hawthorne pondered: "Was the leaper of cataracts more mad or foolish than other men who throw away life, or misspend it in pursuit of empty fame and seldom so triumphantly as he?"

Double Trouble

Nov. 23, 1889: Montana's first legislature holds twin sessions

For sheer outrageousness, the first session of the Montana legislature is hard to beat. The voters had split the new state house of representatives between Democrats and Republicans, with five seats in dispute. To protect its party's claim to victory, each set of representatives met independently, in separate locations, for the entire 90-day session. Thus, Montana had *two* houses of representatives.

The state senate also was evenly split. Since the lieutenant governor, a Republican, held the tie-breaking vote, the Democrats refused to attend. In retaliation, the Republicans passed a resolution subjecting the absentees to arrest and stiff fines. The Democrats took it on the lam, eluding the law by fleeing the state.

In the end, Montana's fractious first legislature failed to pass a single law, not even a "feed bill" to pay expenses and keep itself going. For which, no doubt, Montanans breathed a sigh of relief.

Leadville's Magnificent Ice Palace

Nov. 25, 1895. *A cornerstone of ice was laid in Leadville, Colorado—the beginning of the largest ice palace ever built in America.*

The town was in the doldrums: the repeal of the Sherman Silver Purchase Act in 1893 had ended its glory days as a silver-mining center. In an effort to keep their city alive, the citizens staged a winter carnival.

On New Year's Day, 1896, the town turned out for the grand opening. The palace, costing more than $40,000 and measuring 450 feet long by 320 feet deep, covered more than three acres. The towers that flanked the entrance were 90 feet high. Inside was a 16,000-square-foot skating rink. Colored lights embedded in the walls and columns produced a radiant glow, and the ceiling glistened like diamonds.

A woman viewing fireworks reflecting off the palace walls finally looked away, saying it was "too unearthly a vision" to gaze upon. But by the end of March the vision was melting away.

There was no pot of gold at the end of this rainbow; the thousands of visitors spent very little. Still, most felt it was all worthwhile. And, as Frank Vaughn, the town's poet laureate, observed:

"Chances are they won't have
No ice palace in hell."

It Happened on November . . .

2, 1872: *Victoria Woodhull, free-love candidate for president, goes to jail for sending obscene material through the mail.–p.89*

2, 1920: *Federal prisoner Eugene V. Debs, serving a 10-year sentence, receives almost a million votes for president.–p.98*

2, 1948: *Thomas E. Dewey fails to oust President Harry S Truman from the White House.–p.109*

5, 1781: *John Hanson is elected President of the United States in Congress Assembled.–p.70*

6, 1878: *Grave robbers steal the body of merchant king A. T. Stewart and hold it for ransom.–p.142*

7, 1775: *The loyalist governor of Virginia declares martial law and frees any slaves who will join the fight against American revolutionaries.–p.362*

7, 1811: *Tecumseh's brother, the prophet Tenskwatawa, loses badly to William Henry Harrison at Tippecanoe.–p.366*

7, 1876: *Secret Service agent Lewis Swegles foils grave robbers in their attempt to steal the body of Abraham Lincoln.–p.169*

7, 1916: *Montana elects Jeannette Rankin to be America's first congresswoman.–p.98*

7, 1917: *The Russian Revolution costs Citibank millions.–p.149*

7, 1918: *World War I ends the first time.–p.396*

11, 1833: *Cornelius Vanderbilt is seriously injured in America's first fatal train wreck.–p.137*

11, 1918: *World War I ends again.–p.396*

13, 1902: *Train robber Al Jennings gets out of jail; later runs for county attorney in Oklahoma.–p.177*

14, 1854: *Alpheus Myers of Logansport, Ind., patents a tapeworm trap.–p.325*

Supership Is Sunk on Her First Night at Sea

Nov. 29, 1944. *The submarine* Archer-Fish *(her crew, above, is shown with her symbol, designed by Walt Disney) was assigned to "life-guarding" off Tokyo Bay; her mission on November 28 had been to pick up downed U.S. airmen. But it was a quiet day, and skipper Joseph Enright ordered the radar disassembled for repair. By 8:30 P.M. the radar was in working order; immediately, it picked up a target. Since the only thing in sight was an island, Enright assumed that the radar was still broken and reprimanded its operator. Within minutes, the sailor returned. "Captain," he reported. "Your island is moving . . ."*

What the radar screen had detected was a supership built in such secrecy that the mere mention of her was punishable by death. She was Japan's powerful aircraft carrier Shinano, *on her maiden voyage. For seven hours the* Archer-Fish *pursued her zigzagging quarry, but could never position herself for an attack. Then the* Shinano's *captain made a fatal mistake: he headed straight at the sub.*

Four torpedos hit home, and by 11:00 A.M. the 72,000-ton Shinano *had sunk, taking the captain and 1,400 crew members to their watery graves. It was the end of what the Japanese had proudly called their "unperishable castle of the sea."*

Slipping out of town: Before the redcoats finally evacuated New York City, they greased their flagpole. One American soldier after another slid off the pole trying to lower the Union Jack. Finally a resourceful sailor managed to scale the slippery flagstaff (right), Old Glory was triumphantly raised, and the last of the British departed. Only then did George Washington feel that the Revolution was truly over.

It Happened on November . . .

15, 1577: *Sir Francis Drake sets sail around the world from England; during the journey, he claims California in the name of Queen Elizabeth I.–p.268*

15, 1902: *Teddy Roosevelt's sportsmanship brings about the first teddy bear.–p.95*

16, 1800: *Abigail Adams, arriving in Washington, D.C., finds she must hang her laundry in the East Room of the White House.–p.60*

16, 1807: *The women of New Jersey lose the right to vote.–p.66*

17, 1896: *Mysterious UFO's visit Sacramento, Calif.–p.229*

18, 1872: *Susan B. Anthony is arrested for voting.–p.89*

18, 1883: *Railroads invent time zones.–p.223*

19, 1863: *Abraham Lincoln, suffering from smallpox, delivers the Gettysburg Address.–p.85*

19, 1915: *Joe Hill tells the firing squad: "Go on and fire!"–p.186*

20, 1903: *Professional killer Tom Horn is hanged by a rope he may have made himself.–p.180*

25, 1783: *The British, who have held New York City throughout the Revolutionary War, go home at last. Evacuation Day is celebrated in New York until 1916.*

26, 1883: *On the day after the 100th anniversary of Evacuation Day, a statue of George Washington is dedicated at Federal Hall, where he took the oath of office.*

29, 1847: *Cayuse Indians kill missionary Narcissa Whitman, one of the first two white women to cross the continent.–p.282*

29, 1872: *Horace Greeley dies insane, three weeks after losing the presidency to U. S. Grant.–p.88*

30, 1776: *Tories imprison Richard Stockton, the only signer of the Declaration of Independence who later recanted his signature.–p.48*

December

Paper Chase

Dec. 30, 1842: The Archive War of Texas begins

It was a bloodless two-day battle over three wagonloads of paper, in which the only shots were fired by a middle-aged woman, but they called it the Archive War.

When Austin became the capital of Texas in 1839, state documents were moved there. Sam Houston, however, wanted these archives in his namesake city; after he was elected president of Texas in 1841, he decided to get the papers. Using recent Mexican Army incursions into Texas as his excuse, he dispatched Col. Thomas Smith with 20 men and three wagons to steal the archives from the Austin Land Office.

Arriving on the morning of December 30, the paper pilferers had the wagons almost filled when they were discovered by Angelina Eberly, a local innkeeper out for a stroll. Arousing the citizenry, she positioned herself at a howitzer (originally in place to fight Indians) in front of the land office. Turning it toward the building, she lit its fuse.

The subsequent fusillade persuaded Smith and his men to leave the remaining archives and get out of town. The posse that followed had few weapons—but they *did* have the howitzer.

The chase ended the next day. The thieves, camped only 18 miles from Austin, woke up surrounded by the posse. With the cannon pointed straight at them, they prudently gave up without a fight.

Houston failed in other efforts to retrieve the archives. And it was the location of the state documents that helped determine where the state capital finally would be.

Elvita Adams Is Saved by a Stiff Breeze

Dec. 2, 1979. *The 86th-floor observation deck of the Empire State Building is surrounded by a seven-foot-high steel fence topped by curved spikes, but determined jumpers are often able to scale this obstacle. One was Elvita Adams, who managed to climb over without attracting the attention of some 50 tourists on the deck with her. Leaping off the edge, she fell about 20 feet before a 30-m.p.h. gust of wind blew her back onto a ledge $2\frac{1}{2}$ feet wide. A guard, hearing her cries of pain (she'd broken her hip), rescued her.*

Thus Adams joined the list of other ledge-landers like Thomas Helms, who in 1977 suffered only shock and lacerations and succeeded in crawling through an open window of NBC's transmitter room, startling an engineer. But one jumper who landed on the ledge refused to accept his fate; he got right up and leapt again.

One Last Wave From a Dying Pilot

Dec. 8, 1942: Ghost plane appears in the clouds over China

When radar picked up a plane coming from the direction of Japan, officials knew something was amiss. It was dusk, the sky was overcast, and the enemy never attacked in that kind of weather or at that time of day. Then two American pilots spotted a P-40 bearing markings that hadn't been used since Pearl Harbor, a year earlier. A close look revealed a bullet-riddled plane without wheels. Slumped over the controls was a blood-soaked pilot who turned his head and waved weakly. A few seconds later, the plane hit the ground and exploded. Little remained to identify the flier, but there *was* a diary.

The diary traced the mystery flight back to Mindanao, an island some 1,300 miles from the crash site. Possibly the pilot was one of 19 Americans and 7 Filipinos who refused to surrender, but took to the jungle with the last P-40 on the island. Cannibalizing parts from downed planes, they readied the fighter for one final attack on the Japanese.

None of this, however, was officially confirmed. What *is* certain is that somehow a forgotten American plane made it through more than 1,000 miles of hostile airspace to once again touch friendly soil. But its pilot and his mission remain one of the mysteries of World War II.

The P-40 must have used bamboo skids during takeoff; it had no wheels.

Frozen Alive

Dec. 22, 1850: Defrosted lovers survive shipwreck in Maine

The cold was bitter; the winds and snow, violent. Towering waves walloped Maine's rocky coast in showers of spray that quickly froze into shrouds of ice more than a foot thick. When the storm hit, mate Richard Ingraham and his fiancée, Lydia Dyer, were safe and dry on a schooner anchored near Rockland. The only other person on board was seaman Roger Elliott.

Shortly before midnight both anchor cables snapped. Like a twig in a torrent, the boat shot out of the harbor and crashed on the ledges beyond Owl's Head. As icy water cascaded into the vessel, the three passengers grabbed their blankets and struggled to the deck. The blinding blizzard made it impossible to signal for help. Standing exposed to the full fury of the wind and sea, Ingraham proposed a desperate plan. Dyer wrapped herself in blankets and lay down on the deck. Her fiancé then wrapped his body and blanket around her, and Elliott did the same next to him. The seaman carried a sheath knife so that he could chip a breathing hole through the protective ice that would form over them.

Hours later, as the storm began to subside, Elliott punched and chiseled his way to freedom. The two lovers lay motionless. Fighting fatigue and frostbite, the seaman torturously made his way across the slippery ledges and up onto the point, where he was rescued by a passerby. Before he collapsed, he managed to whisper the message, "Others—on the wreck."

When a rescue party arrived, they found a grim sight: two bodies entombed in a block of ice frozen to the deck. Racing against the rising tide, the rescuers carefully removed the ice block and carried it to a nearby house. Through delicate thawing and chipping they peeled the ice from the lovers' bodies. Then they poured cold water over them, gradually increasing the temperature to 55 degrees, and began softly massaging the seemingly lifeless victims. After two hours, Dyer opened her eyes. An hour later, Ingraham stirred. "What is all this?" he asked. "Where are we?" He looked over at his fiancée and saw her smile. Recovery was slow but complete. Six months later, in June 1851, the pair were married. Elliott, however, the true hero of the saga, never fully recovered.

After their apparent death off Owl's Head, Richard Ingraham and Lydia Dyer married and had four children.

It Happened on December . . .

1, 1718: *Blackbeard the Pirate dies fighting.–p.159*

3, 1941: *"Pearl Harbor will never be attacked from the air," predicts Adm. Charles McMorris.–p.398*

4, 1619: *The first annual Thanksgiving Day observance in America is ordained at Berkeley Hundred, Va.–p.198*

4, 1945: *Capt. Charles McVay, commander of the* Indianapolis, *is court-martialed for losing his vessel to enemy action.–p.403*

5, 1784: *Phillis Wheatley, the black "poetess laureate" of Boston, dies young.–p.205*

5, 1916: *Ben Kuhl pulls off America's last stagecoach robbery; he is convicted because of a bloody palm print.–p.174*

5, 1933: *Prohibition ends.–p.240*

6, 1877: *Thomas Edison sings "Mary Had a Little Lamb" to his new phonograph, cutting the world's first record.–p.332*

6, 1884: *The Washington Monument is finally completed, after 105 years.–p.62*

7, 1941: *Pearl Harbor is attacked from the air. Dr. Lytle Adams has a brainstorm: send bats to firebomb Japan.–pp.398, 399*

10, 1869: *Women win the vote in Wyoming.–p.67*

13, 1809: *An angry mob gathers as Dr. Ephraim McDowell removes a 22½-pound ovarian tumor without anesthetics.–p.317*

13, 1898: *Frank M. Archer of New York City patents an electrical bedbug exterminator.–p.335*

13, 1904: *Cassie Chadwick, Andrew Carnegie's "daughter," is indicted.–p.134*

14, 1799: *George Washington's doctors bleed him to death.–p.72*

15, 1781: *Benedict and Peggy Arnold flee to England.–p.363*

Albert Goodwill Spalding (below) was the premier pitcher of the 1870's and, despite the fact that he threw underhand, the first hurler to win 200 games. He went on to found the sporting goods firm that still bears his name. In 1888–89 he took two American baseball teams on a worldwide promotional tour that included Cairo, Egypt (left).

Inventing the Inventor of Baseball

Dec. 30, 1907. *Abner Doubleday became the father of our national pastime 68 years after the game was supposedly born. His paternity was proclaimed by a commission that A. G. Spalding had started in response to the suggestion that the sport wasn't American but had evolved from a British game called rounders. The search for American roots led to testimony by Abner Graves, who claimed to have played in the first baseball game when Doubleday marked a rough diamond in the dirt at Cooperstown, New York, in 1839. The only trouble with Graves's story was that Doubleday had been a cadet at West Point that year, and the witness himself had been only five years old. Unfortunately, Doubleday (a heroic Civil War general–p.375) could not address the commission; he was already dead and had never mentioned the game in his letters or memoirs. Almost no one believes Graves's story today.*

It Happened on December . . .

15, 1791: *The Bill of Rights is adopted.–p.54*

15, 1890: *Chief Sitting Bull is shot down.–p.389*

16, 1938: *With the feds at the door, master swindler Philip Musica shoots himself.–p.147*

17, 1641: *Pocahontas's son, Thomas Rolfe, asks permission to visit his Indian relatives.–p.356*

17, 1959: *Confederate infantryman Walter W. Williams, at age 117 the last Civil War veteran, is laid to rest in Franklin, Tex.*

19, 1799: *Robert E. Lee's father, "Light-Horse Harry," eulogizes George Washington as "first in war, first in peace, and first in the hearts of his countrymen."–p.72*

19, 1986: *A first edition of John Eliot's 1663 Algonquian Bible is sold for $220,000.–p.199*

22, 1791: *Alexander Hamilton pays James Reynolds $600 hush money and continues his affair with Mrs. Reynolds.–p.161*

24, 1918: *Maj. Gen. Clarence Edwards bestows the Medal of Honor on Maj. Charles Whittlesey, commander of the Lost Battalion in World War I.–p.395*

24, 1931: *The first Rockefeller Center Christmas tree is decorated with tin cans and paper.–p.248*

27, 1769: *The Grand Ohio Company is formed to create the colony of Vandalia.–p.118*

28, 1917: *H. L. Mencken fibs about Millard Fillmore and his White House bathtub.–p.61*

31, 1823: *Citizens of Hamilton and Rossville, Ohio, after hearing John Symmes's lecture, pass a resolution that the earth is indeed hollow.–p.302*

31, 1879: *Thomas Edison demonstrates his incandescent light bulb for guests at his "invention factory" in Menlo Park, N.J.–p.333*

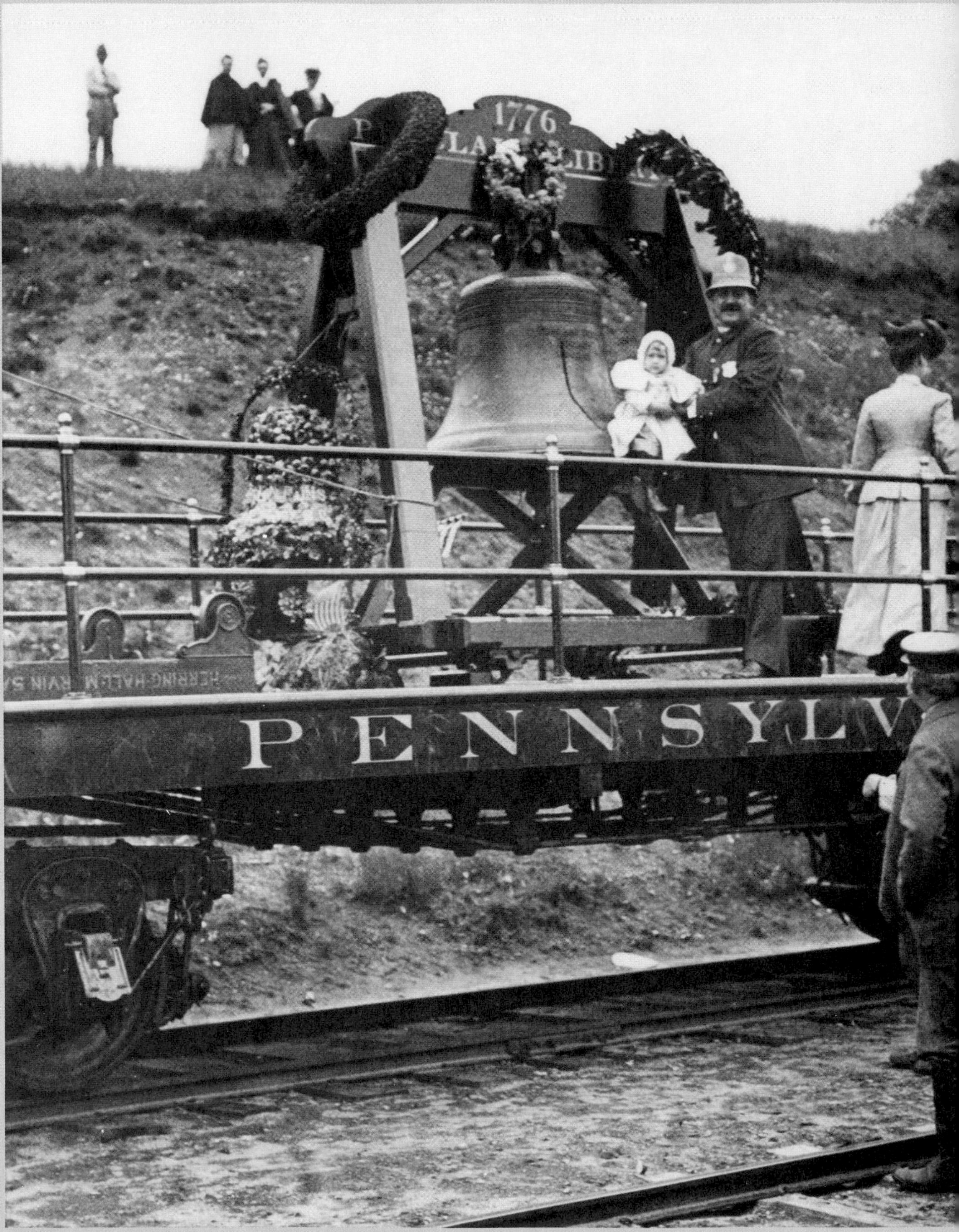
1776
PENNSYLV

The Liberty Bell on tour (Plainfield, Connecticut, 1903)

CHAPTER TWO

Symbols of a Nation

Here's a collection of stories that your history teacher probably never told you about some of our revered national treasures.

July 2—America's Real Birthday

That was the day Congress declared independence

On July 3, 1776, John Adams made the following prophesy in a letter to his wife, Abigail: "The Second Day of July 1776 will be the most memorable Epocha, in the History of America. I am apt to believe that it will be celebrated, by succeeding Generations, as the great anniversary Festival. It ought to be commemorated as the Day of Deliverance."

By the time the letter was published in the 19th century, July 4 had become the traditional day of celebration, and so an editor (a nephew of Abigail's) redated the letter July 5 and changed the first line to read "The Fourth Day" rather than "The Second."

What *did* happen on July 4? Legend has it that the delegates gathered at Independence Hall in Philadelphia to sign the Declaration of Independence. In fact, they met that day to approve the final version of the Declaration, which they had scrutinized. Only two people—John Hancock, the president of Congress, and Charles Thomson, the secretary—signed anything then, and their signatures went on the draft copy. The order for the formal document to be printed on parchment wasn't placed until July 19. It was signed by 50 delegates on August 2. Six others signed later.

The crucial vote

The resolution "that these United Colonies are, and of right ought to be, free and independent States" had first been proposed on June 7 by Richard Henry Lee of Virginia. By July 1, when the Continental Congress finally prepared to vote on Lee's resolution, only 9 of the 13 colonies were firmly in favor. New York was abstaining, South Carolina and Pennsylvania were opposed, and Delaware was on the fence. Two of Delaware's delegates were in opposing camps and the third, Caesar Rodney, was on business 80 miles away. To break the tie, the pro-independence delegate sent for Rodney. Setting out in the predawn of July 2, Rodney rode furiously north through a driving rain and arrived at Independence Hall just in time to cast Delaware's deciding vote.

In the meantime, Adams and others had won the support of South Carolina and Pennsylvania. Thus the tally for independence, which inspired Adams's letter to his wife, was 12 to 0. The following week New York made the Declaration unanimous.

The reluctant author

The most famous of Thomas Jefferson's many achievements is the authorship of the Declaration of Independence. Yet he had to be cajoled into writing it. Adams, who refused to write the document himself, told Jefferson why *he* should undertake the task:

"Reason first—you are a Virginian, and a Virginian ought to appear at the head of this business. Reason second—I am obnoxious, suspected, and unpopular. You are very much otherwise. Reason third—you can write ten times better than I can." "Well," Jefferson replied, "if you are decided, I will do as well as I can."

The Ordeal of Richard Stockton

The only signer to recant

Only months after he had signed the Declaration of Independence, Richard Stockton of New Jersey recanted and swore allegiance to King George III. Born in 1730 of a wealthy family, Stockton became a prominent lawyer and served on the provincial council of New Jersey under its Royal governor, William Franklin (the illegitimate son of Benjamin Franklin). At first in favor of conciliation with Britain, Stockton was won over to the cause of independence, and he became a delegate to the Continental Congress in June 1776.

That fall, after signing the Declaration, Stockton was seized by New Jersey Tories. He was taken to New York, where he was imprisoned as a common criminal and subjected to cruel treatment. When his colleagues in the Continental Congress heard about it, they asked General Washington to intercede. Whether he did so is unknown, but in March 1777 Stockton was back home in Princeton, freed because he had defected.

The British command had offered to pardon all Patriots who would recant the call for independence and take a pledge of neutrality. By spring 4,800 people, most of them from New Jersey, had accepted British amnesty.

Washington countered by ordering the defectors to "take the oath of allegiance to the United States of America." Those who refused were to be treated as common enemies. Stockton, ill in health and broken in spirit, finally complied. The unhappy man, shunned by his former friends, died four years later of cancer.

The Liberty Bell

Its cherished crack has nothing to do with Independence Day

According to the well-known story, on July 4, 1776, a small boy brought the glad tidings that independence had just been declared to a feeble, white-haired bell ringer in the steeple of Philadelphia's Independence Hall. Rejuvenated by the news, the old man rang the bell so vigorously that it cracked.

In fact, the bell never rang out independence—news of the Declaration was not proclaimed until July 8, and the crack had occurred years before. The great bronze bell, inscribed with the words *Proclaim Liberty Throughout All The Land Unto All The Inhabitants Thereof,* had been ordered from London in 1751 to commemorate the 50th anniversary of Pennsylvania's democratic constitution. On arrival, the bell was hung in the belfry of the State House (later known as Independence Hall). It cracked while being tested. The bell was melted down, recast, and rehung. In 1835 it cracked again, possibly when it was tolled on the death of John Marshall. The clappers would have been muffled, however, which makes it unlikely. It pealed for the last time on Washington's birthday in 1846, after which it was taken down.

It was not until 1839—when it was used as a symbol by abolitionists because of its inscription—that the State House bell came to be called the Liberty Bell. The popular story linking the crack with the first Independence Day was fabricated in 1847 by George Lippard in a book called *Washington and His Generals, or Legends of the American Revolution.* Thus the Liberty Bell was launched as one of the nation's most potent—and profitable—symbols of patriotism, depicted on every conceivable item from neckties and coffee cups to Liberty Bonds.

On the first minute of the bicentennial year, 1976, the bell with its revered crack was removed from Independence Hall and enshrined in a glass-walled pavilion nearby.

"Ring!" cried the lad to the old man. The Liberty Bell story and the above engraving appeared in Graham's Magazine *in 1854.*

The Liberty Bell Slot Machine

When San Francisco entrepreneur Charles Fey invented a new, improved three-reel slot machine in 1898, he chose the Liberty Bell for both its name and its jackpot symbol. The wide-open seaport city went wild for the Liberty Bell machine, even though the odds against a payoff were 10 times steeper than with the single-disc type that was then popular. The Liberty Bell machine should have earned Fey millions, but he stubbornly refused to have it patented. Finally, a rival slot machine mogul stole the design. During the fire that followed the 1906 San Francisco earthquake, Fey rescued the first Liberty Bell machine from his offices. It wound up as an exhibit in a Reno restaurant and saloon.

Legends of Old Glory

Betsy and George

Mrs. Ross did not design the Stars and Stripes

The Legend: *In 1776 George Washington and two other patriots called on Betsy Ross, a Philadelphia seamstress, to ask her to stitch up the new American flag. She examined the design they produced, recommended a five-pointed star, and went to work.*

The Facts: The story originated in 1870, when Betsy's grandson, William J. Canby, passed it on to the Pennsylvania Historical Society, saying he had heard it from Betsy herself when he was a child. Years later the legend appeared in a book on the flag, the Betsy Ross Memorial Association was formed, Betsy's house was purchased, and a painting was produced of Betsy meeting the committee. Thus Betsy Ross became enshrined. The records of her time reveal no foundation for the legend, but they show that she was paid for making flags for the Pennsylvania Navy in 1777.

At the outset of the Revolution, the regiments of the 13 colonies flew their own colorful banners. The first flag to symbolize unity (raised by Washington on New Year's Day, 1776) was actually a modification of a British naval flag. The colonists imposed 6 white stripes upon its red field—thus creating 13 stripes to represent the 13 colonies—but kept the crosses of St. George and St. Andrew in the top corner. The Grand (or Great) Union flag, as it was known, became obsolete with the Declaration of Independence, because the two crosses symbolized loyalty to Britain.

On June 14, 1777, the Continental Congress resolved that the national flag should have "13 stripes, alternate red and white," and that the crosses be replaced by "13 stars, white in a blue field, representing a new constellation." Quite possibly the Stars and Stripes was intended for the navy. Washington and the Board of War wanted a different standard for the army. It was not until March 1783, a month before Congress proclaimed an end to hostilities, that Washington received the first shipment of colors. What design the flags bore and what he did with them remains unknown.

"The Spirit of '76"

The flag that nobody flew

The Legend: *The familiar banner, with its 13 red and white stripes and its circle of 13 five-pointed stars, flew proudly over American troops throughout the Revolution.*

The Facts: Americans fought under many banners, but rarely the Stars and Stripes. Its earliest versions had various combinations of blue, red, and white stripes, with the stars usually set in rows. There is no documentation for the flag depicted in Archibald Willard's famous painting "The Spirit of '76," shown above.

The pine tree flag was carried in the Battle of Bunker Hill, June 1775.

The Moultrie flag flew over the defenders of Charleston in June 1776.

The Rhode Island was flown at the Battle of Trenton, Christmas 1776.

Frocks for Flags

Did John Paul Jones fly a flag of ladies' finery?

The Legend: *On July 4, 1777, Capt. John Paul Jones urgently needed a battle flag for his ship, the* Ranger. *To make him one, five ladies of Portsmouth, Maine, sacrificed their best silk dresses, including a fine wedding gown.*

The Facts: Pure fiction, the story was concocted by Augustus C. Buell in a book about the great naval hero published in 1900. The ladies (to whom Buell gave names) would not have had time to learn about the new flag, decided upon by Congress in mid-June, let alone to make one by the Fourth. Moreover, Jones had not yet assumed his command.

The *Ranger* was the first warship to fly the Stars and Stripes, however, and Jones was the first to obtain foreign recognition of the American flag. At Quiberon Bay, France, in 1778, he induced the French fleet to exchange salutes, an act signifying official recognition of the new national standard. Continuing on, Jones defeated a British sloop and raised the Stars and Stripes above it.

In the next year Jones again invaded British waters. Seizing the gunboat *Serapis,* he boarded it, raised the American flag, and sailed for Holland. The British wanted Jones arrested for piracy because he sailed under an unrecognized banner. The Dutch refused and had documentary paintings made of two of the flags flown. Both were clearly Stars and Stripes, but they were remarkably dissimilar in design. The *Serapis* flag had blue stripes combined with the red and white; of its 13 raggedy stars, 12 were eight-pointed and 1 seven-pointed. The ladies of Portsmouth would have done better!

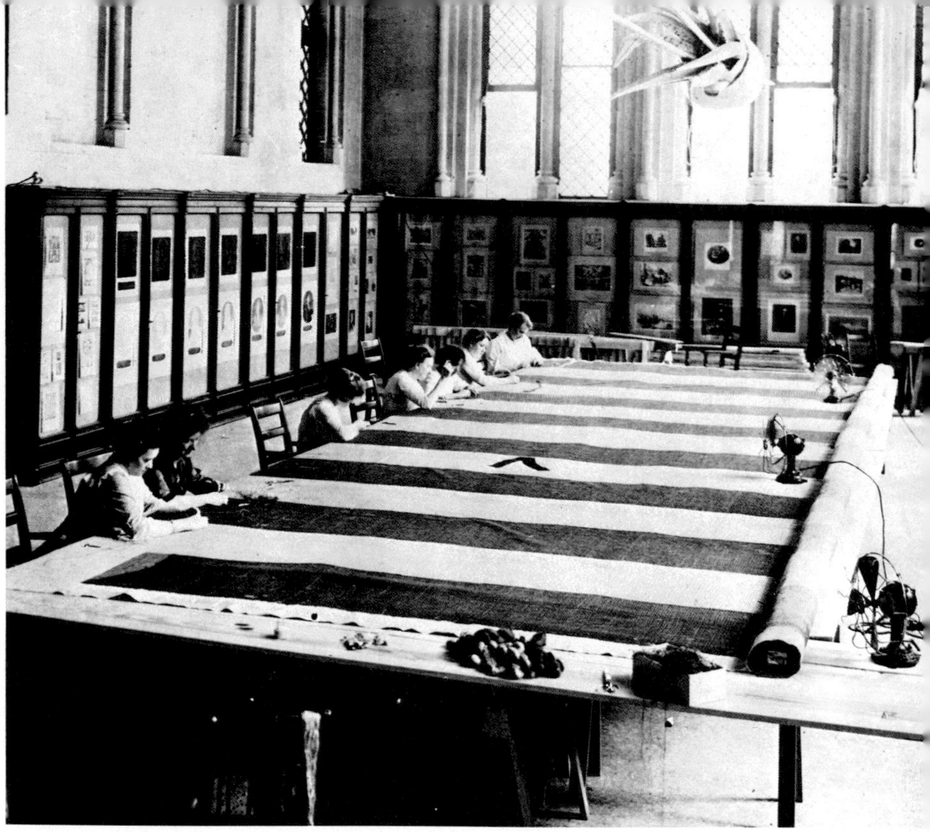

In 1914 a volunteer group of women salvaged the flag Key had seen billowing over Fort McHenry a century earlier, sewing it to a linen backing. It now hangs at the Smithsonian Institution in Washington, D.C.

"The Star-Spangled Banner"

The true circumstances that inspired the national anthem

The Legend: *Francis Scott Key wrote "The Star-Spangled Banner" while a prisoner of the British fleet during a 25-hour siege of Fort McHenry that ended on the morning of September 14, 1814.*

The Facts: Key, a Georgetown lawyer, was actually the head of a peace mission sent to the British fleet in Chesapeake Bay to secure the release of Dr. William Beanes, a physician. The British received Key courteously and agreed to release Dr. Beanes. But there was a snag. Inadvertently, Key had caught them preparing to launch an attack. Fearing that he would alert the Americans, the British detained Key and his party on their sloop, the *Minden,* until after the attack.

It was from the vantage point of the *Minden* that Key watched the bombardment. After the guns fell silent, Key saw in "the dawn's early light . . . that our flag was still there." Inspired, he began the lyrics of "The Star-Spangled Banner" on the back of a letter he had in his pocket. The tune he used, popular in America for years, was that of a bawdy British drinking song called "To Anacreon in Heaven." It had been composed by John Stafford Smith around 1775 as an anthem for the Anacreontic Society, a London gentleman's club named for a Greek poet who worshiped "the Muses, Wine, and Love." Key's song was an instant hit. It grew in popularity, competing with "America the Beautiful" for first place among patriotic songs until 1931, when it was officially designated the national anthem.

The Constitution of 1787

Why Was It Written?

The choice: Build anew or repair the roof

The Constitution of the United States is actually the *second* governing document in the nation's history. The first, the Articles of Confederation, was in effect from 1781 to 1789. (Oddly enough, one of the document's provisions, set forth in Article 11, was that the colony of Canada could join the Union at any time, although no other colony could be admitted without the agreement of 9 of the original 13 states.)

Government under the Articles failed because, as George Washington said, it was "little more than the shadow without the substance." There was no true central authority. Although Congress could declare war and enact treaties, it lacked the power to collect taxes, to regulate commerce, to maintain order, or even to enforce its own decisions. Interstate disputes proliferated, worthless money flooded the country, discontented people rioted, and foreign nations refused to deal with a government so powerless at home. Anarchy, rebellion, and chaos threatened the land.

The Continental Congress called for a committee to amend the Articles, but when the delegates met in Philadelphia in May 1787, they boldly decided to ignore the directive and write a *new* constitution that would establish a strong federal government. "We are razing the foundations of the building, when we need only repair the roof," protested Oliver Ellsworth of Connecticut.

After a long summer of contention and compromise, their task was miraculously completed.

Ben Franklin and the Iroquois

The American Indian influence on the Constitution

Benjamin Franklin, that wise and witty elder statesman of Revolutionary times, helped to work out the Constitution's system of representative government. Franklin was himself inspired by the Iroquois Indians, whose League of Five Nations functioned as a representative democracy for two centuries before the Constitution was written.

The five nations of the Iroquois Confederacy—Onondaga, Mohawk, Seneca, Cayuga, and Oneida—were united under the Law of the Great Peace. An unwritten constitution with 117 sections, it detailed the makeup of the ruling council, its methods of reaching decisions, the duties and qualifications of its members, the limitations of its power, and the rights of the people. The council, made up of 50 sachems, or chiefs, had no power over the inner workings of any tribe, but dealt only with such mutual concerns as war and treaties. Decisions were reached through a precisely outlined procedure, with the sachems of the Mohawks and Senecas forming one deliberating body, those of the Oneidas and Cayugas another, and the Onondaga sachems wielding a kind of veto power. (A sixth nation, the Tuscarora, joined the confederacy in 1722 but did not take an active part in league councils.) All decisions had to be unanimous.

The sachems were appointed by the senior women of the communities, who themselves formed a Council of Women of the Five Nations. This women's council oversaw the deliberations of the sachems, and if it deemed that the will of the people was not being followed, it could remove any or all of the sachems from office.

In 1744 Franklin's Philadelphia press published an article about the Lancaster Treaty between the Iroquois and the British. It contained the advice of Canasatego, an Onondaga sachem: "Union and amity between the five nations have made us formidable. We are a powerful confederacy, and by your observing the same methods . . . you will acquire fresh strength and power. . . . Whatever befalls you, never fall out with one another."

Franklin was apparently impressed, for he studied the system of the Iroquois Confederacy. Seven years later he himself wrote, "It would be a very strange thing if six Nations of ignorant Savages should be capable of forming a Scheme for such a Union," and yet the English colonies should find it "impracticable."

In 1754, when war with the French and their Indian allies seemed imminent, delegates of the seven northern colonies met in Albany, New York, to draw up a plan of defense. Franklin, the Pennsylvania delegate, proposed a confederacy much like that of the Iroquois. The Albany Plan failed, but it paved the way for the Articles of Confederation. The Articles in turn led to the formation of a new, stronger federal government under the Constitution, reflecting Iroquois concepts of liberty and democratic organization.

When the Constitution was submitted for a vote of approval, Franklin pleaded that anyone who still had objections would, with him, "doubt a little of his own infallibility" and agree to it.

Benjamin Franklin (wearing a fur cap in this portrait by John Trumbull) dramatized his call for a united front against France with the design at right. America's first editorial cartoon, it appeared in Franklin's newspaper, the Pennsylvania Gazette, *in May 1754.*

JOIN, or DIE.

A Witch Hunt as Democracy Is Born

Barbarous deeds on the streets of Philadelphia

It was Tuesday, July 10, 1787, and the great statesmen at the Constitutional Convention in Philadelphia were concentrating on the crucial question of representation. While they labored, a barbarous mob in the New Market area pelted a poor, haggish old woman thought to be a witch, shouting that she had caused a child to sicken and die. The child's mother was indicted for assault and several citizens volunteered to testify on behalf of the beaten woman, known as Korbmacher. But she died of her injuries eight days later.

During another attack two months earlier, Korbmacher's forehead had been cut as an antidote to any evil spells she may have cast. Decrying such "worm-eaten prejudices," the *Pennsylvania Packet* had observed that belief in sorcery and witchcraft belonged to the Old World, not "in the free and civilized parts of independent America."

Merely Three-fifths of a Person

A foundation of compromise that was slow to crumble

Slavery: Without it there would be no America, no nation dedicated to liberty and equality. This was the paradox faced by delegates to the Constitutional Convention. The southern states had made it clear that they would not join the Union if slavery was not accepted. And although abolitionist sentiment was strong in the North, pragmatism and politics dictated brutal compromise. As a result, it would take a civil war and 175 years to correct the injustices incorporated into the new Constitution.

The very language of the Constitution reflects the convention's spirit of compromise. Nowhere in the document is the word *slavery* found. But the continuation of the system was provided for in three separate passages.

Article I, Section 2, spelled out the formula for determining each state's popular representation in the lower house of Congress: Count all free persons, exclude Indians not taxed, then add "three fifths of all other Persons." Thus a compromise was struck between the South, which wanted slaves counted for the sake of representation, and the North, which wanted them excluded.

Article I, Section 9, stated that the importation "of such Persons as any of the States now existing shall think proper to admit" would be permitted until 1808. Thus the South conceded in return that the slave trade would end in 20 years—as it did.

Article IV, Section 2, prevented a "Person held to Service or Labour in one State" from escaping his bondage by moving to another state. Known as the fugitive slave clause, this was the Constitution's

most effective protection of the institution of slavery.

In the first half of the 19th century what rights the black slave had, if any, were at the discretion of local authority. As to the small population of free blacks, who lived mostly in the North, the situation varied from state to state. In New York, New Jersey, Pennsylvania, and most of New England some even had the right to vote before 1820, but gradually the status of free blacks degenerated to that of noncitizen. The Supreme Court made this official with the Dred Scott decision in 1857.

Scott was a slave whose suit to gain freedom went to the nation's highest court. In delivering the majority opinion, Chief Justice Roger Taney not only rejected Scott's plea but stated that the Constitution was written only for whites and that blacks, even free blacks, could never be citizens.

The decision was met with cries of protest from the North and of approval from the South. The foundation of compromise upon which the Constitution had been built began to crumble and civil war ensued. The Emancipation Proclamation of 1863 freed slaves in the seceding states only; until the war was over, it had no practical effect. In 1865 the 13th Amendment ended slavery once and for all in the United States.

In 1868 Justice Taney's interpretation of the Constitution was nullified by the 14th Amendment, which ensured full rights of citizenship to "All persons born or naturalized in the United States." The right of citizens to vote regardless of "race, color, or previous condition of servitude" was guaranteed in 1870 by the 15th Amendment.

Finally, in 1964, the 24th Amendment abolished the poll tax, making it clear that "WE THE PEOPLE" means *all* the people.

The Bill of Rights

The Fight for the Bill of Rights

Wanted: The blessings of liberty

More concerned with the need for a strong central government than with the protection of people's rights, the delegates to the Constitutional Convention didn't officially discuss the idea of a bill of rights until the last week. A resolution to draft such safeguards was defeated, and on September 28, 1787, the Constitution was submitted to the states for ratification. It met strong opposition.

In one state convention after another the issue of a bill of rights was central to the fight for ratification. The Federalists claimed that a bill of rights was unnecessary: most state constitutions already had such provisos, and Congress under the new Constitution had been given no power to override them. The anti-Federalists, joining forces with those advocating a bill of rights, contended that the new federal government would be more powerful than any state and that a constitution that did not specifically restrict that power was an invitation to tyranny.

The battle became intense. In Pennsylvania the opposition tried to block ratification by absenteeism, to prevent a quorum, and were literally dragged from their homes for a vote. Riots occurred, and the Pennsylvania framer of the Constitution, James Wilson, was burned in effigy.

By June 21, nine states had ratified, although Massachusetts and New Hampshire demanded a bill of rights. The Constitution was adopted, but Virginia and New York had not approved it. They were vital. Virginia was the richest and most populous state; New York was second, and without it the nation would be physically divided into north and south.

More than two-thirds of the New York delegates opposed ratification, and 31-year-old Alexander Hamilton fought alone to stem the tide. Day after day he spoke for hours on end, arguing the Federalist cause and preventing a final ballot in the hopes of good news from Virginia. There the debates were heated, with Patrick Henry leading the opposition.

"The plot thickens fast," Washington wrote to his friend the Marquis de Lafayette. "A few short weeks will determine the political fate of America." On June 25, by a vote of 89 to 79, Virginia backed the Constitution, calling for a long bill of rights. A month later New York followed, 30 to 27, with similar recommendations.

North Carolina and Rhode Island held out, and so the Union included only 11 states when Congress convened for the first time on March 4, 1789. Under Madison's lead, a bill of rights became the main order of business, and in September Congress submitted to the states for approval a series of amendments guaranteeing individual freedoms and property rights. A few months later the two holdouts voted to accept the Constitution. The 10 amendments became law on December 15, 1791, upon approval by three-fourths of the states. Curiously, Massachusetts, Georgia, and Connecticut did not ratify the Bill of Rights until 1939, the 150th anniversary of the new government.

"I Would Rather Have a King"

Patrick Henry, foe of the Constitution

In his stand against British tyranny in 1775, Patrick Henry had thundered, "Give me liberty or give me death!" Thirteen years later the perceived threat to American liberty was the proposed new government, which in his view would substitute American despotism for the British variety. "I would rather have a King, a House of Lords and Commons than the new government," he told the Virginia state convention during its long debate over ratification of the Constitution.

"Who had the effrontery to insert the opening phrase 'We the People' instead of 'We the States'?" he angrily demanded, predicting that states' rights would be destroyed. Under the new "consolidated" government, he warned, "other rights, too—the rights of conscience, liberty of the press, all your communities and franchises, all pretensions to human rights and privileges, are rendered insecure, if not lost."

Denouncing British tyranny before the Virginia Assembly in 1775, Patrick Henry cried, "Give me liberty or give me death!"

Upton Sinclair ran for governor of California in 1934.

High Crime

Upton Sinclair went to jail for reading the Bill of Rights

In 1923 Upton Sinclair, the well-known muckraker and novelist, was arrested while addressing a group of striking transport workers. His crime? Reading aloud the Bill of Rights. He had uttered part of the First Amendment—guaranteeing freedom of religion, of speech, and of the press, and the right of "the people peaceably to assemble"—when the Los Angeles police nabbed him.

Charged with expressing ideas "calculated to cause hatred and contempt" of the U.S. government, he was held incommunicado for 22 hours before he finally reached a courtroom. The police chief planned to hold him longer, but a subordinate informed Sinclair's wife, who called a lawyer. Later the police chief got an ignominious comeuppance. He was dismissed after being caught one night in a parked car with a woman and a bottle of whiskey.

The Great Seal

If Benjamin Franklin had had his way, the symbol of sovereignty for the United States would have been a turkey. "For my part, I wish the bald eagle had not been chosen as the representative of our country," he wrote his daughter in 1784. "He is a bird of bad moral character."

Maybe a Turkey?

Moses, a pillar of fire, and Hercules were suggested

Over a period of six years, three separate committees tried to come up with an acceptable design for the Great Seal of the United States, the national coat of arms that was needed in order to authenticate official documents.

The first committee—Thomas Jefferson, Benjamin Franklin, and John Adams—was appointed by the Continental Congress only hours after the formal adoption of the Declaration of Independence. The three turned to the Bible and to classical mythology for inspiration. Jefferson proposed that the seal depict the Israelites' passage through the wilderness, led by a divine cloud and a pillar of fire. Adams suggested the mythical hero Hercules choosing between the paths of virtue and self-indulgence. Franklin wanted to show Moses commanding the Red Sea to close over the pharaoh.

In a quandary, they called in a consultant, a Swiss-born Philadelphia artist named Pierre Eugène Du Simitière. He pointed out that the greatest thing about the United States was that it was a new nation forged out of many. To illustrate this, his design featured an escutcheon, or shield, showing the emblems of the six European homelands from which most early immigrants had come. Around the shield were 13 smaller ones representing the new states,

The creation of one new nation from many was the theme of Du Simitière's design for the obverse of the seal.

Franklin's proposal, showing Moses closing the Red Sea over the pharaoh, was an indictment of tyranny.

Charles Thomson's sketch of an American eagle "on the wing and rising" led to the designs finally adopted.

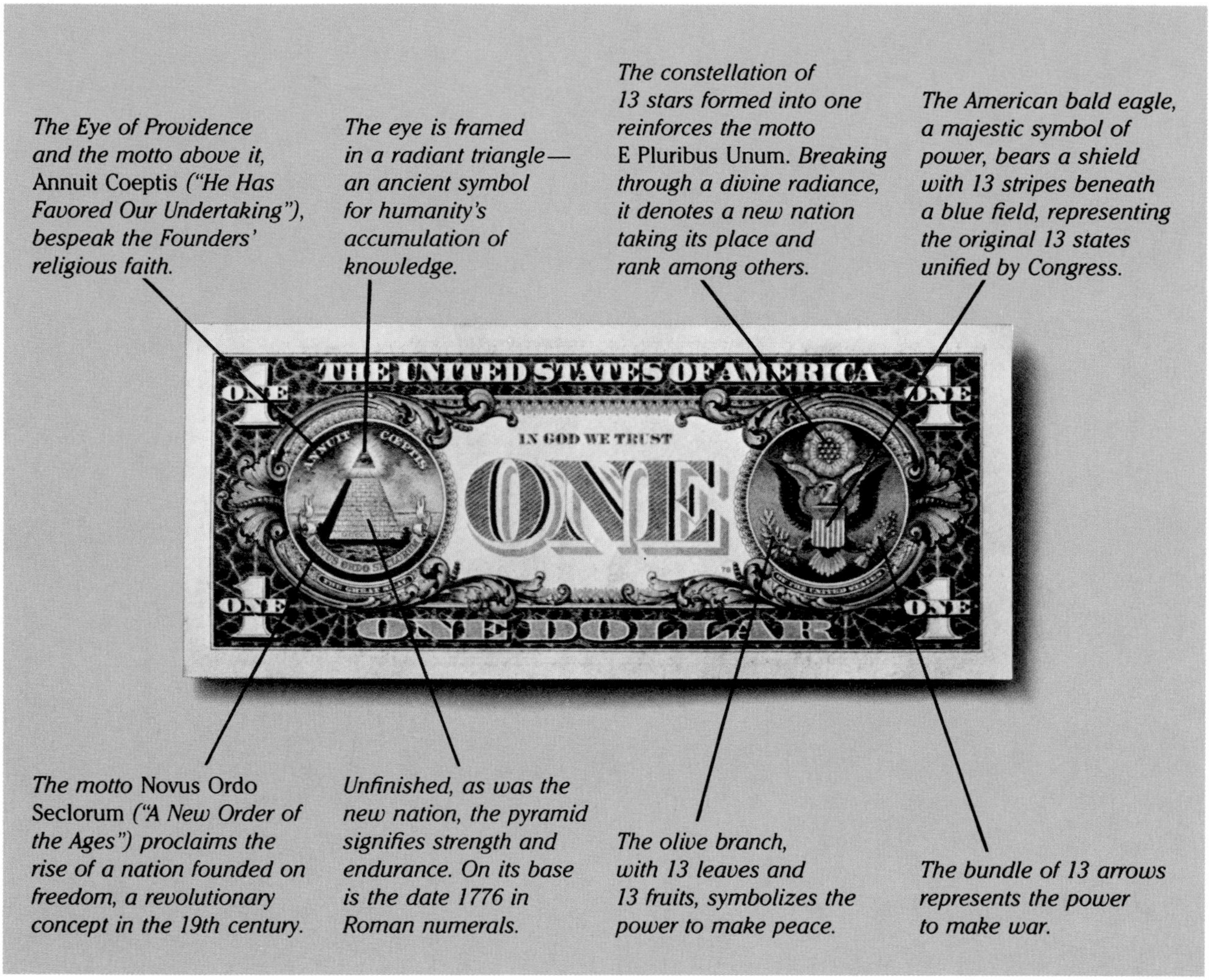

linked by a gold chain. Supporting the shield were the goddesses of Liberty and Justice. Above was the Eye of Providence and below was the motto *E Pluribus Unum,* "Out of Many, One."

The Eye of Providence and the motto above it, Annuit Coeptis *("He Has Favored Our Undertaking"), bespeak the Founders' religious faith.*
The eye is framed in a radiant triangle—an ancient symbol for humanity's accumulation of knowledge.
The constellation of 13 stars formed into one reinforces the motto E Pluribus Unum. *Breaking through a divine radiance, it denotes a new nation taking its place and rank among others.*
The American bald eagle, a majestic symbol of power, bears a shield with 13 stripes beneath a blue field, representing the original 13 states unified by Congress.
THE UNITED STATES OF AMERICA
IN GOD WE TRUST
ONE
ONE DOLLAR
The motto Novus Ordo Seclorum *("A New Order of the Ages") proclaims the rise of a nation founded on freedom, a revolutionary concept in the 19th century.*
Unfinished, as was the new nation, the pyramid signifies strength and endurance. On its base is the date 1776 in Roman numerals.
The olive branch, with 13 leaves and 13 fruits, symbolizes the power to make peace.
The bundle of 13 arrows represents the power to make war.

The committee chose Du Simitière's design for the obverse, or front, and Franklin's for the reverse and submitted them to Congress. But Congress, preoccupied with the Revolutionary War, tabled the project.

A second committee, appointed in 1780, proposed a design for the obverse featuring a shield with 13 stripes, supported by a sword-bearing soldier and a woman holding the olive branch of peace. A radiant constellation of 13 stars was the crest. The reverse featured the goddess of Liberty. The designs were rejected.

A third committee, named in 1782, called upon William Barton, a Philadelphia authority on heraldry. For the obverse he introduced the European eagle, placing it in the crest, and for the reverse he conceived an unfinished 13-stepped pyramid.

Congress then turned the accumulation of designs over to Charles Thomson, secretary of Congress. Synthesizing and simplifying them, he retained the first committee's motto, *E Pluribus Unum,* the second committee's shield and olive branch, and the third's eagle and pyramid. However, he substituted a rising American bald eagle for the European heraldic eagle, making it the centerpiece, placed the shield upon the eagle's breast, and put a clutch of arrows in its talons. He handed the designs over to Barton, who arranged the stripes vertically on the shield and gave the eagle upswept wings. The results of their joint effort were instantly approved by the Continental Congress. Seven years later the seal was adopted by the first federal Congress and put in the custody of the first secretary of state, Thomas Jefferson.

Mount Rushmore

Sculpting mighty faces with jackhammers and dynamite

"American history shall march along that skyline," announced Gutzon Borglum in 1924, gazing at the Black Hills of South Dakota. The great sculptor had been invited there by a local official familiar with his work in Georgia: a colossal bas-relief on the face of Stone Mountain, depicting Confederate heroes. Hoping to draw tourists to his state, the South Dakotan envisioned a parade of famous frontiersmen carved in rock.

But Borglum felt the memorial should represent the nation as a whole and proposed portraits of Washington, Lincoln, Jefferson, and Theodore Roosevelt. Eleanor Roosevelt later suggested including the suffragist leader Susan B. Anthony, but she was overridden.

The site the artist chose—the nearly perpendicular face of 6,000-foot Mount Rushmore—offered a solid expanse of granite beneath its fissured surface. Facing generally southeast, it caught the sun most of the day.

Work began in the summer of 1927. Using models on a scale of one inch to a foot, Borglum plotted the presidential features, transferred his measurements to the mountainside, and instructed his crew where to cut away rock.

Most of the sculpting was done by experienced miners. Working with jackhammers and dynamite, they removed some 400,000 tons of outer rock, cutting to within three inches of the final surface. So skilled were they with the tools of their trade, even in contouring the eyes and lips, that the sculptor's traditional mallet and chisel were used very little.

As each face took shape, Borglum studied it with binoculars from several miles away and made minor adjustments. Working errors and hidden flaws in the rock repeatedly forced him to rethink the composition and alter the arrangement of figures. One mistake in cutting rock, for example, ruined Jefferson's head, which was to have been on the right side of Washington's. It was blasted away and recarved on the left. The project dragged on for 14

Only Washington's head was completed when this photograph was taken of Mount Rushmore in 1932. The date 1776 was to have been the start of an ambitious 500-word inscription summarizing American history but it was blasted away and replaced by the head of Lincoln.

years, its cost escalating to $1 million. When Borglum died in 1941, his dream—the creation of the world's most gigantic sculpture—was near completion; his son oversaw the final work.

The monument has evoked mixed feelings. Some see it as a desecration of nature. Others, like President Franklin Delano Roosevelt, are overawed not only by its magnitude, but by "its permanent beauty and its importance."

The Two Uncle Sams

Which Sam Wilson inspired the beloved figure?

Few people realize there was a *real* Uncle Sam—in fact, *two* of them. Both were named Samuel Wilson and both lived for many years in Troy, New York. One is buried there; the other lies in Merriam, Indiana. Although a congressional resolution honored Troy's Sam Wilson in 1961 "as the progenitor of America's national symbol of Uncle Sam," the people of Indiana stand by *their* Sam Wilson as the real thing.

Troy's Sam, born in 1766 in Massachusetts, settled in Troy and opened a meat-packing plant. A stocky, clean-shaven fellow, he was a kindly employer who became affectionately known as Uncle Sam. During the War of 1812 he sold 300 barrels of beef and pork in brine to Elbert Anderson, a food wholesaler with an army contract. Each barrel was stamped top and bottom "EA-US," the initials standing for Elbert Anderson and the United States. However, when a workman was asked what the letters stood for, he jokingly replied, "Uncle Sam Wilson," and the name stuck. Troy's Sam lived to be 87.

Merriam's Sam Wilson, born in Delaware in 1778, also moved to Troy. He took a job clerking in a general store owned by Ebenezer Anderson. During the War of 1812 Anderson's store became a war supply headquarters, and Sam oversaw the handling of government orders. Again, boxes were marked for shipment with the letters "EA-US" (the "EA" being for Ebenezer Anderson), and again someone identified the "US" as Uncle Sam. This second Sam later moved to Indiana, where he died at the age of 100.

Whichever Uncle Sam was the original, the nickname spread like wildfire, and in 1813 it began to appear in the newspapers as a synonym for the United States government.

The first known cartoon of Uncle Sam (1832) shows him as an invalid surrounded by quack doctors Thomas Hart Benton, Amos Kendall, Andrew Jackson, and Martin Van Buren, all in the political forefront then.

The White House

Washington's Folly

From a presidential palace to the White House

Wilson's White House Sheep

During World War I, in order to save manpower and set a good example for the nation, President Wilson had sheep crop the White House lawns. The flock numbered 18 at its peak. The wool was shorn and auctioned for a total of $52,823, which was donated to the Red Cross.

If George Washington had had his way, the president's house would have been a palace nearly five times the size of the existing mansion. At least, that was what he and the French architect Pierre Charles L'Enfant envisioned in the spring of 1791. But when the building commissioners had their first view of L'Enfant's plan, they were apparently alarmed by its extravagance and grandeur.

Arrogantly assuming he needed only Washington's authority, L'Enfant commenced work at once. When Secretary of State Jefferson dismissed him in February 1792, the grounds had been staked out, the cellars dug, and some of the foundation stone delivered.

Eager to take charge, Jefferson proposed a competition for plans for the president's house and the Capitol. With Washington's consent, he drafted an announcement, offering a prize of $500. The winner was James Hoban, an Irish architect. His plan for a typical 18th-century English mansion struck Washington and the commissioners as "convenient, elegant, and within moderate expence."

In October 1792 the cornerstone was laid. But the Capitol and other government buildings took priority, and so work on the president's house was delayed.

Abigail Adams's laundry

Finally, in the gray month of November 1800 John Adams and his wife, Abigail, moved in. She found "a castle of a House" clearly "built for ages to come," but only half the rooms were plastered. Shabby government furniture had been brought from Philadelphia and set about. Outdoors were tree stumps, hacked weeds, piles of rubble, and—in full view—a presidential privy.

"Not one room or chamber is finished of the whole," she complained. "It is habitable by fires in every part, thirteen of which we are obliged to keep daily. . . ." She needed "about thirty servants to attend," but had only six, and there were no bells with which to summon them. Worse, she wrote her daughter, "We have not the least fence, yard, or other convenience without, and the great unfinished audience-room [the East Room] I make a drying-room of, to hang up the clothes in."

Abigail had to endure her miseries only briefly. Her husband lost the presidency to Thomas Jefferson, and by March she was back home in Quincy, Massachusetts. Jefferson, challenged by a house he considered Washington's folly, quickly set to work changing it inside and out.

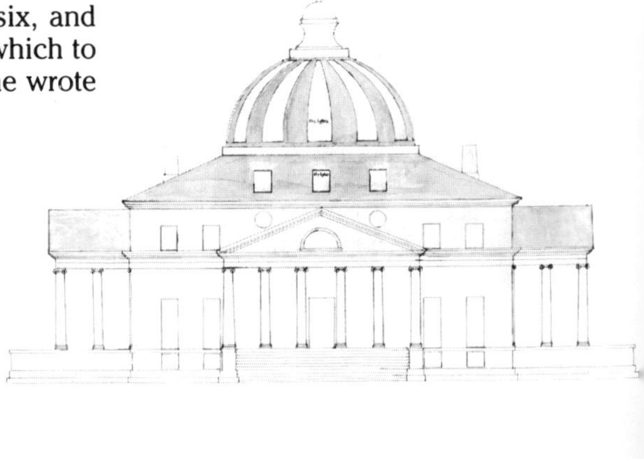

Of the nine entries in the competition for the design of the White House, the sketch at right, a modification of the Villa Rotunda in Vicenza, Italy, by Andrea Palladio, placed second. Mysteriously signed A.Z., it has been ascribed by some to Thomas Jefferson.

Millard Didn't Do It

The White House bathtub: A hoax that won't die

In the works of several scholars and historians, you will find the claim that Millard Fillmore gave the White House its first bathtub in 1851. It would be an interesting bit of presidential trivia if it were true—but it isn't.

The story began in 1917, in a column written for the New York *Evening Mail* by that irrepressible author, editor, and iconoclast H. L. Mencken. Hoping to divert his readers from the gloomy news of World War I, he concocted a spoof on the history of the bathtub in America—and in the process he perpetrated a hoax that will not die.

The first stateside bathtub, an elegant mahogany contraption, he wrote, had been installed in the home of a Cincinnati businessman in 1842, and the odd practice of bathing soon caught on among the wealthy. When word of the fad got out, it set off a public outcry against the "epicurean and obnoxious toy from England, designed to corrupt the democratic simplicity of the republic." By bravely installing a bathtub in the White House, Mencken went on, Fillmore had helped gain public acceptance for the habit of regular bathing.

In 1926, alarmed that his fabrication had entered history in the guise of gospel truth, Mencken wrote a confession of his hoax. But despite his efforts to set the record straight, the story endures to this day.

(The fact is that a bathing room with copper tubs and a shower was established on the first floor of the White House in 1833 or 1834; the first permanent bathtub on the second floor was installed by President Pierce in 1853.)

Rebuilding the White House

How Harry Truman nearly dropped in on the DAR

Nobody would have blamed Harry Truman in 1947 if he thought he was living in the House of Usher. Like Poe's doomed mansion, the White House was beginning to collapse.

One day while the president was bathing, he felt the tub settle. Below him, his wife, Bess, was holding a reception for the Daughters of the American Revolution. Afterwards, he suggested to her the comic possibility of his unannounced appearance in his birthday suit. During a concert in the Blue Room, attended by several hundred people, the president was warned that the chains holding the two-ton chandeliers could break at any time. After another event, in the East Room, the servants discovered a large pile of ceiling plaster on the floor. Finally, when a leg of daughter Margaret's piano broke through the first-floor ceiling, Truman decided that something had to be done.

An investigation showed that the second floor was on the verge of collapse and, according to one expert, the first-floor ceiling stayed in place only by "force of habit." The outer walls were solidly constructed, but the supports of the inner walls rested only on clay, thanks to hasty reconstruction after the British had burned the building in 1814. During the next 100 years, supporting walls and beams were drilled and cut through to put in running water, gas lighting, central heating, and electricity, and a fireproof floor was installed in the third story.

Congress finally approved funds to salvage the mansion. Begun in late 1949, the job cost nearly $7 million to complete. In March 1952 the First Family returned to a modernized Executive Mansion that architects assured them would stand for the next 500 years.

A $20 bill printed before 1948 shows the White House without a balcony. It was added to the front portico during renovations.

Because of the alteration, a new plate had to be engraved. A post-1948 $20 bill shows the present facade.

The Statue of Liberty

From a 4-foot model to a 150-foot symbol

Given by the people of France to the people of the United States as a symbol of enduring friendship and mutual love of freedom, the Statue of Liberty is the largest freestanding sculpture ever created. Towering 151 feet above her pedestal, Miss Liberty weighs 225 tons and has a girth of more than 100 feet. Her nose is 4½ feet long, her eyes each 2½ feet wide, and her mouth 3 feet wide. Her upraised right arm extends 42 feet, while her hand is 16 feet 5 inches long and her index finger is 8 feet.

Incredible as it seems, the starting point for the mammoth work was a miniature 4-foot plaster model the artist Frédéric Auguste Bartholdi had submitted for the approval of the Franco-American Union, founded by the French in 1875 for the creation of the memorial. First he translated it into a 9-foot reproduction and then into a 36-foot quarter-size model. Next, taking thousands of measurements, he enlarged each section to its final dimensions. Full-size lathwork and plaster forms were then made, over which hundreds of plates of pure copper (hammered to a thickness of 3/32 inch) were fitted and shaped. The project kept a large staff of craftsmen busy for five years.

To keep the enormous copper shell from toppling over, the famous engineer Gustave Eiffel designed an interior framework of iron. Completed and assembled in Paris in May 1884, the glistening lady was formally presented to "the people of the United States" on July 4. Then she was dismantled and packed. Some 200 huge wooden crates were hauled on a 70-car train to Rouen and shipped to Bedloe's Island in New York harbor. Reassembled on her concrete pedestal and unveiled on October 28, 1886, Miss Liberty has been a welcoming beacon ever since.

The face behind the statue's face is that of the sculptor's mother, who lived under German domination in Alsace, his birthplace. Ironically, Madame Bartholdi was a domineering bigot, who frowned on the sculptor's marriage and contributed to her other son's eventual madness—he was afraid to tell her of his love for a Jewish woman.

The Washington Monument

Bigotry almost botched it

It stands as a symbol of George Washington's strength and vision. A marble obelisk soaring more than 555 feet from its base, the Washington National Monument pierces the sky above the nation's capital, inspiring all who see it with the purity of its design. But it sheathes a turbulent history.

The memorial was 105 years in the making, from its proposal by the Continental Congress in 1783 to its public opening in 1888. The first idea, much to General Washington's pleasure, had been to erect an equestrian statue, but the plan went awry. One of the problems was money—or the lack of it. The other was congressional disagreement about an appropriate tribute. In 1833 a group of citizens organized the Washington National Monument Society to raise funds, commission a suitable design, and oversee construction.

The marble cornerstone of the monument was laid on July 4, 1848, with a ceremony that generated enthusiastic financial response, not only from individuals but from organizations, banks, and various states. Alabama donated a commemorative plaque for the interior, and other states followed suit—as did fire companies, social clubs, Indian tribes, and even foreign countries, including the Vatican.

By 1854 the obelisk was 152 feet high. But the marble plaque given by Pope Pius IX, taken from the Temple of Concord in Rome, indirectly brought work to a halt. At dawn on March 6, 1854, some members of the super-patriotic American Party (who were known as the Know-Nothings) broke into the monument grounds, removed the papal stone, and presumably

In 1879, when Mathew Brady took this photo of the Washington Monument, it was 150 feet tall. Plans for a building at the base were dropped.

The above design, submitted by Robert Mills, an eminent architect, won the Washington Monument contest in 1836. The exotic design shown above right was among the entries considered.

dumped it into the Potomac. It was never recovered. Then, as the result of a rigged election in 1855, the Know-Nothings took charge of the monument society. In turn, Congress, which had planned to allocate $200,000 for the project, withdrew its funding, and public support withered.

Over the next three years, the Know-Nothings (who succeeded in raising all of $285.09) added four feet of inferior marble to the monument, which later had to be removed. Work stopped during the Civil War and little was done for more than a decade afterward. The Washington Monument remained a pitiful stub in the heart of the capital city.

On the centennial of independence in 1876, Congress gave funds for the monument's completion. Then another problem surfaced: the U.S. Army Corps of Engineers discovered that the obelisk's foundation was inadequate to support its proposed height. Some 70 percent of the ground under the shaft had to be removed in order to strengthen the base with additional concrete footings. As an extra precaution, the target height of the obelisk was lowered from 600 to 555 feet 5 1/8 inches. Work was resumed on the shaft in 1880, and the monument rose an average of 80 feet annually until its completion on December 6, 1884.

Today 190 commemorative plaques can be viewed from the Washington Monument's interior staircase. Among them is a replacement for the stolen plaque, sent by the Vatican in 1982.

Who Were the Know-Nothings?

In the 1840's a good many so-called native Americans felt menaced by the influx of Irish and German immigrants (most of whom were Catholic and poor), and so they formed a secret society, swearing to vote only for American-born Protestants and to oppose the Catholic Church. If asked about the politics of their order, members uniformly answered, "I know nothing." Hence they were called the Know-Nothings. Organized nationally as the American Party in 1854, they became powerful.

Alarmed by this flood of bigotry, Abraham Lincoln wrote: "As a nation, we began by declaring that 'all men are created equal.' . . . When the Know-Nothings obtain control, it will read: 'All men are created equal except Negroes, foreigners and Catholics.' " But the American Party rapidly withered away.

The Ballot Box

Voting for President

The constitutional right that doesn't exist

Ask Americans which constitutional right they most treasure, and the chances are that voting for president will be high on the list. In fact, the Constitution gives no such right.

Although Benjamin Franklin and a few others favored popular election of the chief executive, most of the framers of the Constitution feared that less educated Americans might elect corrupt or incompetent men to the powerful office, and so they decided that the president and vice president would be chosen by a special body of electors. The Electoral College would, they felt, exercise superior judgment. The Constitution allotted each state as many electors as it has senators and representatives, and left the manner of their selection to the states.

In the early years the electors were usually appointed by the state legislatures. But by 1832 the choosing of electors by popular vote had become the rule except in South Carolina. With the steady growth of population, and hence the number of electors, the lists of individual electors became long and unwieldy, and in 1892 a trend began to group the electors by political party, requiring only a single vote.

The names of the presidential candidates did not begin to appear on ballots along with those of the electoral candidates until 1897. The voting machines introduced a few years later lacked space for long ballots, and so Iowa and Nebraska began to list *only* the names of the presidential and vice presidential candidates, dropping the names of the electors altogether. A vote for a party's candidate was taken as a vote for the electors of that party. Gradually the rest of the states followed suit and adopted the short ballot.

Despite the directive of the ballot, and despite party loyalty oaths, electors are constitutionally free to vote as their judgment dictates when they meet in their state capitals in December. In the elections of 1948, 1956, and 1960, several electors ignored the voters' wishes.

Traditionally, the electors of a state vote as a bloc for the candidate receiving the most votes in that state. As a result of this strange practice, two presidents—Rutherford B. Hayes in 1876 and Benjamin Harrison in 1888—won with a majority of the Electoral College while losing the popular vote to their opponents.

Voting for Senator

Because the Founding Fathers created the Senate to represent the states rather than the people, the Constitution stipulated that senators would be elected by state legislatures, not by popular vote. It was not until 1913, when the 17th Amendment was ratified (after nearly a century of pressure), that citizens were granted the right to vote for senators.

Who Really Won?

The election of 1876 almost rekindled the Civil War

Little more than a decade after Lee's surrender at Appomattox, civil war almost broke out anew over the rival claims of Samuel J. Tilden and Rutherford B. Hayes to the presidency. The election returns gave Tilden, the Democrat, almost 51 percent of the popular vote, and he seemed to have won in the Electoral College as well.

Hayes was ready to concede defeat until a top editor of *The New York Times* alerted the Republicans that Democratic leaders were unsure of the electoral votes in Florida, Louisiana, and South Carolina—the last southern states to remain under Republican domination in the Reconstruction era following the Civil War.

In these states the northern politicians in control (supported by federal troops in South Carolina and Louisiana) had encouraged former slaves to vote Republican, while white southern Democrats had tried to keep blacks from the polls by force and intimidation. At the same time, Republican election officials had thrown out or invalidated thousands of Democratic ballots. Each side accused the other of corruption, and rival sets of certified electoral returns were submitted to Congress.

To unravel the tangle, Congress created a special Electoral Commission of 15 men—five each from the Senate, the House of Representatives, and the Supreme Court. Seven were Republicans, and seven Democrats. The 15th member was to have been Justice David Davis, an Independent who was considered nonpartisan. The reluctant Davis escaped this onerous task by resigning from the Court when the Illinois legislature elected him to the U.S. Senate.

The remaining four justices then chose Justice Joseph P. Bradley, a Republican.

While the commission members studied the rival claims, the date for the presidential inauguration neared—and with it the specter of a vacant Oval Office.

Right up until the final hours the outcome was in question. In February, just a day before the decision on the Florida contest was announced, Bradley prepared an opinion supporting the Democrats in that state. The next day, he switched sides and supported the Republicans. He later attributed his change of mind to further reflection, but he was helped in this decision by a late-night visit from two Republican Party leaders. Behind the scenes a compromise was worked out: In exchange for Democratic support, the Republicans promised that the new president would withdraw all federal troops from the South.

By straight partisan votes of eight Republicans to seven Democrats the commission awarded the electoral votes of the three contested states to Hayes. Oregon's vote, disputed when the state's Democratic governor replaced a Republican elector with a Democrat, also went to Hayes, giving him a one-vote majority—185 to 184. At 4:10 A.M. on March 2 the president of the Senate announced Hayes's election.

Since Inauguration Day, March 4, fell on a Sunday, Hayes privately took his oath of office in the Red Room of the White House on Saturday, March 3. On Monday he was publicly inaugurated amid cries of "Fraud," "Eight to seven," and "President Rutherfraud." Tempers gradually cooled, however, as thoughtful men of both parties realized that there was no truly just way to settle the dispute.

President Hayes lived up to his part of the "Compromise of 1877" by promptly withdrawing all federal troops from Louisiana and South Carolina and ending Reconstruction. But peace was won at the price of curtailing federal protection for the rights of blacks.

Celebrating the Popular Vote

For well over a century and a half, the citizens of Sussex County, Delaware, have celebrated election returns. It began in 1828, when Delaware gave the people the right to vote for delegates to the Electoral College. Previously, the electors had been chosen by the legislature.

Polling places were established in the towns and the marked ballots were returned to Georgetown, the county seat, for tabulation. Families poured into Georgetown on the Thursday after Election Day to hear the sheriff announce the results. Over the years Return Day became a colorful local festival, complete with an ox roast on the village green.

Cartoonist Thomas Nast conjured up the specter of violence during the months of tension before the Hayes-Tilden electoral vote was resolved; some Democratic governors and editors had threatened the use of troops to ensure Tilden's election. Bowing to the decision of the electoral commission, Tilden's manager said, "I prefer four years of Hayes' administration to four years of civil war."

The Ballot Box (continued)

Stolen Suffrage

New Jersey women had the vote, but it was taken away

According to the state constitution drawn up by the Provincial Congress of New Jersey in 1776, women had the right to vote in that state. It may have been an oversight, but the document nonetheless stipulated that "all inhabitants" meeting age and residency requirements and worth at least £50 could vote. It made no reference to sex.

The women of the state had not petitioned for suffrage and, oddly enough, they seemed quite indifferent to it. There is no record of a New Jersey woman voting before 1790. But activism appeared in 1797, when John Condict of Newark ran against William Crane of Elizabeth for a seat in the state legislature. Condict barely won in a tight race—and he nearly lost when, at the last minute, a group of some 75 Elizabeth women turned out to cast their ballots for their hometown candidate.

After that eye-opening election, women of all ages—including some who were underage—were literally hauled to the polls in carriages and wagons by political candidates and party leaders who were eager for votes.

At an election held in 1807, the people of Newark and Elizabeth battled over the location of a new courthouse. Women were thrown into the fight by both towns in a contest that was virtually a carnival of skulduggery. Boys even dressed as women to cast ballots. Shocked by this "saturnalia of corruption and abuse," the New Jersey lawmakers quickly passed new voting laws and barred women from the polls.

Abigail Adams, portrayed by Gilbert Stuart in 1812, a few years before her death, was known for her spunky independence of mind, a quality that endeared her to her husband if not to others. Her strongly expressed views during Adams's term of office won her the title Mrs. President.

Abigail's Insurrection

Mrs. John Adams wanted more than the vote for women

If Abigail Adams had gone to the Continental Congress in 1776 instead of her husband, John, the status of American women might have been quite different. As a female she couldn't go, but she did what she could to—in the words of a later century—raise her husband's consciousness as he helped shape a new nation.

On March 31, 1776, she wrote to him: "I long to hear that you have declared an independency—and by the way in the new Code of Laws which I suppose it will be necessary for you to make I desire you would Remember the Ladies, and be more generous and favourable to them than your ancestors. Do not put such unlimited power into the hands of the Husbands. Remember all Men would be tyrants if they could. If perticular care and attention is not paid to the Laidies we are determined to foment a Rebelion, and will not hold ourselves bound by any Laws in which we have no voice, or Representation."

He replied on April 14: "As to your extraordinary Code of Laws, I cannot but laugh. . . . Depend upon it, We know better than to repeal our Masculine systems. . . . in Practice you know We are the subjects. We have only the Name of Masters, and rather than give up this, which would compleatly subject Us to the Despotism of the Peticoat, I hope General Washington, and all our brave Heroes would fight."

Abigail retorted on May 7: ". . . whilst you are proclaiming peace and good will to Men, Emancipating all Nations, you insist upon retaining an absolute power over Wives. But you must remember that Arbitrary power is like most other things which are very hard, very liable to be broken—and . . . we have it in our power not only to free ourselves but to subdue our Masters, and . . . throw both your natural and legal authority at our feet."

"Entirely Indebted to Men"

How women won the vote in Wyoming

Some said that from the day in 1869 when 54-year-old Esther Morris rode into South Pass City to join her husband and sons, life in Wyoming Territory changed. For Mrs. Morris, a tall, strapping woman who had had her share of hard knocks, is credited with winning the fight for suffrage in the territory that year. According to one H. G. Nickerson, she invited him and his political opponent, William Bright, to a tea party before the election for the new territorial legislature and exacted promises from both that the victor would introduce a bill granting women the vote. Bright won and kept his word.

But as Mrs. Morris acknowledged, the Wyoming women were "entirely indebted to men" for their new status. In Wyoming, males outnumbered females by about 6 to 1, and the legislators hoped their bold step would attract more women. Democrats supported the measure lightheartedly, counting on the Republican governor, John Campbell, to veto it and thus politically hang himself and his party. The bill passed and Campbell, who was young but no fool, promptly signed it into law. (Two years later the Democrats tried to have the law repealed and offered Campbell $2,000 to cooperate. The governor firmly refused.)

Wyoming chose to honor Esther Morris (pictured above) by placing her statue in the U.S. Capitol's Statuary Hall.

Mother's Rose Was Yellow

One vote passed the woman suffrage amendment

Some called it the War of the Roses. At issue was the ratification of the 19th Amendment, guaranteeing women the right to vote. The symbol of the suffragists, or "Suffs," who supported it was a yellow rose. Their opponents, the "Antis," rallied to a red rose.

By the summer of 1920, 35 states had ratified it, one short of the three-fourths needed. The rest were very much in doubt. The Suffs pinned their hopes on Tennessee; while they tucked yellow roses into legislative lapels and pleaded their case, the Antis kept money and liquor flowing freely among the state's lawmakers.

When the legislature assembled on Wednesday, August 18, Suff campaign workers, counting roses from the gallery, were dismayed to see young Harry Burn, from heavily Anti McMinn County, wearing a red rose. Earlier, Burn had told them, "My vote will never hurt you."

The first ballot ended in a tie. Then, on the second, Harry Burn changed his vote to aye. The crowd went wild—Tennessee had ratified the 19th Amendment! The next day Burn attributed his dramatic switch to a letter received from his mother. "I know that a mother's advice is always safest for her boy to follow," he said, "and my mother wanted me to vote for ratification."

THE END OF THE CLIMB

A drawing by Rollin Kirby in 1920 celebrated the passage of the 19th Amendment. The loudest voices on both sides of the suffrage debate were women's.

OFFICIAL
15535
NO.
I
CIAL

CHAPTER THREE

The Campaign Trail

Although they say that baseball is our national pastime, politics has always really been America's favorite spectator sport. We take pride and sometimes gleeful pleasure in the fact that our leaders have feet of clay. And so the triumphs, travails, transgressions, travesties, and tragedies of office seekers and office holders—from presidents right on down—are the basic stuff of American headlines and legends.

Wendell Willkie in his hometown minutes before accepting the Republican presidential nomination (Elwood, Indiana, August 17, 1940)

Presidential Trivia

- ***The only president who . . .***

was unanimously elected—Washington
was both vice president and president without being elected to either office—Ford
joined the Confederate government—Tyler
was impeached—A. Johnson
resigned—Nixon
received a patent—Lincoln
could simultaneously write Greek with one hand and Latin with the other—Garfield
earned a Ph.D.—Wilson
received the Pulitzer Prize—Kennedy
was the father of another—J. Adams
was the grandfather of another—W. Harrison
was born on July 4—Coolidge
was a licensed pilot—Eisenhower
was sworn in by a woman—L. Johnson
commanded a submarine—Carter

- ***The first president who . . .***

shook hands rather than bowing at White House receptions—Jefferson
rode on a train—Jackson
was born an American citizen—Van Buren
married while in office—Tyler
ate White House meals prepared on a cookstove rather than a fireplace—Fillmore
had a White House Christmas tree—Pierce
was a bachelor—Buchanan
was born outside the 13 original states—Lincoln
received royalty—A. Johnson *(Queen Emma of Hawaii in 1866)*
had a White House telephone—Hayes
visited the West Coast—Hayes
had a child born in the White House—Cleveland *(The Baby Ruth candy bar was named for the child.)*
had electricity in the White House—B. Harrison *(He didn't trust it; so servants switched the lights on and off.)*
left the U.S. while in office—T. Roosevelt
rode in an automobile—T. Roosevelt
flew in an airplane—T. Roosevelt (*as ex-president*; F. Roosevelt *while in office*)
had a car at the White House—Taft
rode in a car to his inauguration—Harding
crossed the Atlantic—Wilson
appeared on TV—F. Roosevelt
hit a hole-in-one—Eisenhower
named a woman to the Cabinet—F. Roosevelt
named a black to the Cabinet—L. Johnson
visited China—Nixon

During John Hanson's year-long term as president (1781–82), the nation adopted its Great Seal, which has remained virtually unchanged since then. (Both sides of the seal appear on the dollar bill.) A charter for the first centralized U.S. bank, the Bank of North America, was also approved during his tenure.

The Man From Maryland

Was he really our first president?

Bells pealed, cannons boomed, and fireworks lit up the sky. It was March 1, 1781, and citizens were celebrating "the final ratification in Congress of the Articles of Confederation and perpetual union between these states." With the passage of this legislation a man from Maryland became the first person to serve the one-year term as president. His name was John Hanson.

Born into a politically active family in 1715, Hanson served in the pre-Revolutionary Maryland assembly, helping choose delegates for the First Continental Congress, approving funds for beleaguered Boston in 1775, and helping raise the first southern troops to join the Continental Army under George Washington. In 1779 Hanson was elected to the Continental Congress in Philadelphia. It was a hardship to be a congressman; for one thing the pay was poor (and in any case the city didn't recognize Maryland's money). But Hanson went, and on March 1, 1781, he and his fellow Maryland delegate, Daniel Carroll, were the last two signers of the Articles of Confederation. Thus the United States of America was born, and Hanson—perhaps in appreciation for his signature, since Maryland had been a holdout—was elected "President of The United States in Congress Assembled." He served the term despite failing health and the death of his last surviving daughter.

Soon after Hanson's election, Washington delivered General Cornwallis's sword to Congress, and Hanson presided over the ceremony celebrating Britain's defeat at Yorktown. On behalf of the Congress, the president congratulated the man who was to become our first president under the Constitution.

King George? Never!

No crown or scepter upon these shores, vowed Washington

At best, it was a preposterous suggestion. In a long letter received in late May 1782 by George Washington, Col. Lewis Nicola—a respected officer who had served ably in the Revolutionary War as a writer of military manuals—complained about the inadequacy of Congress. The nation's treasury lacked the funds to pay off foreign loans and support the government, let alone pay the soldiers.

"The experience of the war," Nicola argued at one point, "must have shown to all, but to military men in particular, the weakness of republics."

To forestall complete chaos, he suggested that America become a monarchy, with the commander in chief as king. Washington's proposed title? George I of the United States.

From his headquarters in Newburgh, New York, Washington responded at once: "Be assured, sir, no occurrence in the course of the war has given me more painful sensations than your information of there being such ideas existing in the army as you have expressed and I must view [them] with abhorrence, and reprehend with severity. . . .

"Let me conjure you then," Washington continued, "if you have any regard for your Country, concern for yourself or posterity, or respect for me, to banish these thoughts from your Mind, and never communicate, as from yourself, or any one else, a sentiment of the like Nature."

And thus the great hero of the American Revolution summarily dismissed any thought of a reign of royalty in the nation that had fought so hard under his leadership to win its independence.

Washington's Herculean Chef

An 18th-century tale in which a mysterious nighttime disappearance was never solved

The president of the United States faced a personal dilemma with political overtones. When the nation's capital was moved from New York to Philadelphia, George Washington, unimpressed with the taste and quality of the food that was served to him, brought his own black chef, Hercules, from Mount Vernon to spice up his daily fare. The arrival of Hercules, however, and the length of his stay, posed a problem: Pennsylvania law stipulated that slaves be given their freedom after six months of residency. To get around this provision, Washington found various pretexts for returning his household slaves—including the talented chef—to Virginia just short of the six-month deadline. Then, after several weeks, the president would bring them all back to Philadelphia.

But Hercules, a rather dapper man who had gained a fine reputation of his own in the capital, was quick to resist this sleight-of-hand. He had no intention of remaining a slave, and so one night he simply disappeared.

After months of disappointing dining, Washington, who had vowed "never again to become the master of another slave by purchase," was faced with the prospect of buying a new black chef. The quandary was happily resolved, however, when he found a white housekeeper who also knew her way around in the kitchen.

And what of the fabled Hercules? Although Washington made several attempts to have him apprehended, the chef with the magic touch was never ever heard from again.

Washington confers with an overseer during the harvest at Mount Vernon. Gathering in the crops of the flourishing farmland required all help available, in addition to the slaves who worked as field hands.

Too Much Blood

Was Washington bled to death by the best doctors of his time?

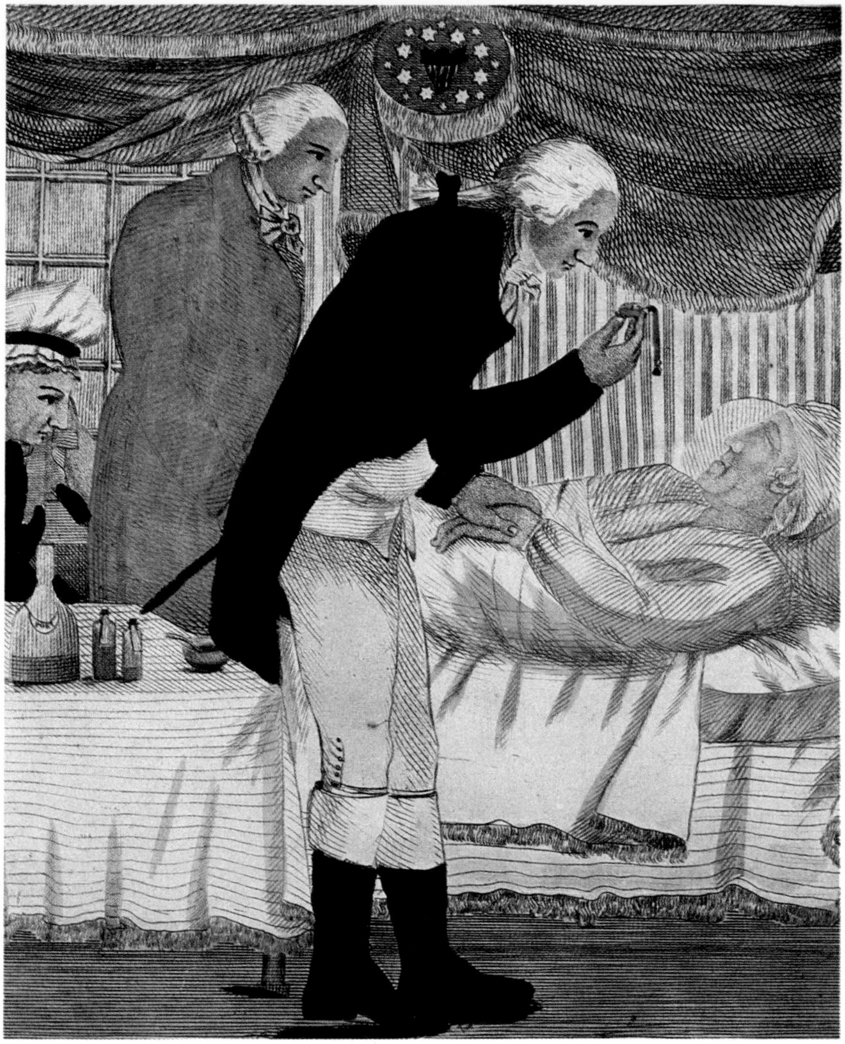

George Washington's death on December 14, 1799, may have been hastened by the three physicians who attended him.

In the bleak dawn of a December day in 1799, George Washington lay ill and weak in his Mount Vernon bedroom, his throat swollen, scarcely able to breathe. Speaking with difficulty, the 67-year-old ex-president summoned the overseer of his estate and asked the man to draw blood from his arm.

Bleeding, a standard medical practice of the time, was based on the theory that removing diseased blood would speed the development of fresh, healthy blood. It was commonly done by opening a vein with a sharp instrument called a lancet.

"Don't be afraid," Washington told the trembling man, and the incision was made. "The orifice is not large enough," he whispered, and it was enlarged.

Martha Washington, who had been awakened by her stricken husband earlier that morning, appealed to Washington's aide Tobias Lear that too much blood was being taken. Lear tried to intervene, but Washington gestured for yet more blood to be drawn. After half a pint had been taken, the bleeding was halted.

At 9 A.M. the patient's longtime physician, James Craik, arrived. He made a preliminary diagnosis of inflammatory quinsy, an extreme form of tonsillitis, and ordered a second bleeding. There was no improvement—Washington was still unable to swallow or even to cough—and so a third bleeding was conducted.

Later that afternoon, two more physicians were summoned. After agreeing on the diagnosis, Dr. Elisha Dick urged a tracheotomy, to cut an opening in the windpipe below the obstruction. His older colleagues felt that the move was too radical. Dr. Dick also argued against further bleeding. "He needs all his strength," he said. "Bleeding will diminish it." He was overruled and Washington was bled yet once more. We don't know how much blood was taken altogether, but this time alone a whole quart was removed. (The human body contains only five quarts of blood.)

Although he was in considerable pain, Washington never complained. Gradually suffocating, he expressed his thanks to the doctors for their attention and then advised them to ". . . let me go off quietly; I cannot last long."

He didn't. Hours later, he summoned Lear to his bedside and whispered: "I am just going. Have me decently buried, and do not let my body be put into the vault in less than three days after I am dead." Lear nodded and Washington asked, "Do you understand me?"

"Yes, sir," said Lear.

"'Tis well," said Washington. They were his last words.

In retrospect, Dr. Craik wrote to one of the associates, had they "taken no more blood from him, our good friend might have been alive now. But we were governed by the best light we had."

Parson Weems, Mythmaker

"I cannot tell a lie," said little Georgie Washington. "I chopped down the cherry tree with my hatchet." Everyone knows the heart-warming tale, and most people know that it never happened. The story first appeared in 1806 in a book called The Life and Memorable Actions of George Washington.

The author, Mason Locke Weems, was an Episcopalian minister whose fiddle-playing, bawdy sense of humor, and opposition to slavery had cost him his church. He went on the road, becoming a popular guest preacher, book peddler, and writer. After a rousing sermon, he'd step from the pulpit to sell Bibles—he sold thousands along with his own moral tracts and inspirational biographies.

In 1800 Weems wrote his publisher that he had nearly finished a new book about Washington "... enlivened with anecdotes apropos, interesting and entertaining."

The first editions sold like hotcakes. In 1806 the best-selling author decided to add several "new and valuable anecdotes," among them the famous story of the cherry tree; he also doubled the price, to 50 cents a copy. The 82nd (and last) edition appeared in 1927.

The Homeless Supreme Court

No power, no prestige, and (for 145 years) no home of its own

John Jay, first chief justice of the United States, resigned in 1795. Five years later, when John Adams asked him to return, he refused because the Supreme Court lacked "energy, weight, and dignity."

Of the government's three branches, the Supreme Court was shortchanged by the Constitution. "The judicial power of the United States shall be vested in one Supreme Court," the document said, but it gave only a vague description of what that power meant. One thing it did *not* say was that the Court should rule on the constitutionality of acts of Congress. That power, clearly establishing the Court as the equal of the president and Congress, came in 1803, when the fourth chief justice, John Marshall, simply ruled that the Court had it.

The wandering Court

The Supreme Court shared its first quarters with the House of Assembly of New York, the nation's capital. After Philadelphia became the capital in 1790, it met in an unheated room in Independence Hall. When new space was found in City Hall, the Court had to share it with the Mayor's Court. And later, when the new Capitol was constructed in Washington, D.C., nobody thought to give the Court a building, and so beginning in 1801, it sat in a 24- by 30-foot office of the Senate clerk. In 1809 it moved to a larger room in the Capitol basement. Then it began sharing chambers with the U.S. Circuit Court and the District of Columbia's Orphans' Court. After the British sacked the Capitol in 1814, the Court sat in a local tavern; by 1819 it had moved to a semicircular room below the Senate chamber.

In 1860, when new wings were added to the Capitol, the Supreme Court inherited the Senate's former chamber. Not until 1925—after furious lobbying by Chief Justice William Howard Taft (an ex-president)—did Congress authorize construction of a building solely for the tribunal. Ten years later, on October 7, 1935, the Court finally moved into its long overdue home.

John Marshall takes charge

Chief Justice Marshall's historic ruling that "a law repugnant to the Constitution is void" was almost accidental. The case, *Marbury* v. *Madison,* involved a judicial appointment—one of 42—that John Adams had made in the closing hours of his presidency. Because of a slipup by the secretary of state (*also* Marshall, who held both jobs simultaneously for a time), some of the commissions were not sent out until Adams's term had expired. Now the new president, Thomas Jefferson, and his secretary of state, James Madison, refused to honor them. One of the appointees, William Marbury, appealed to the Court to force Madison to grant his commission. Marshall knew that Madison would ignore such an order, further weakening the Court. But he felt that Marbury had a case. His solution was to castigate Madison and Jefferson for withholding Marbury's commission and then to declare that he could do nothing about it: the section of the Judiciary Act of 1789 conferring such power upon the Supreme Court was unconstitutional. Although Jefferson denounced Marshall's "twistifications" of logic, he and his successors accepted the Court's right of judicial review.

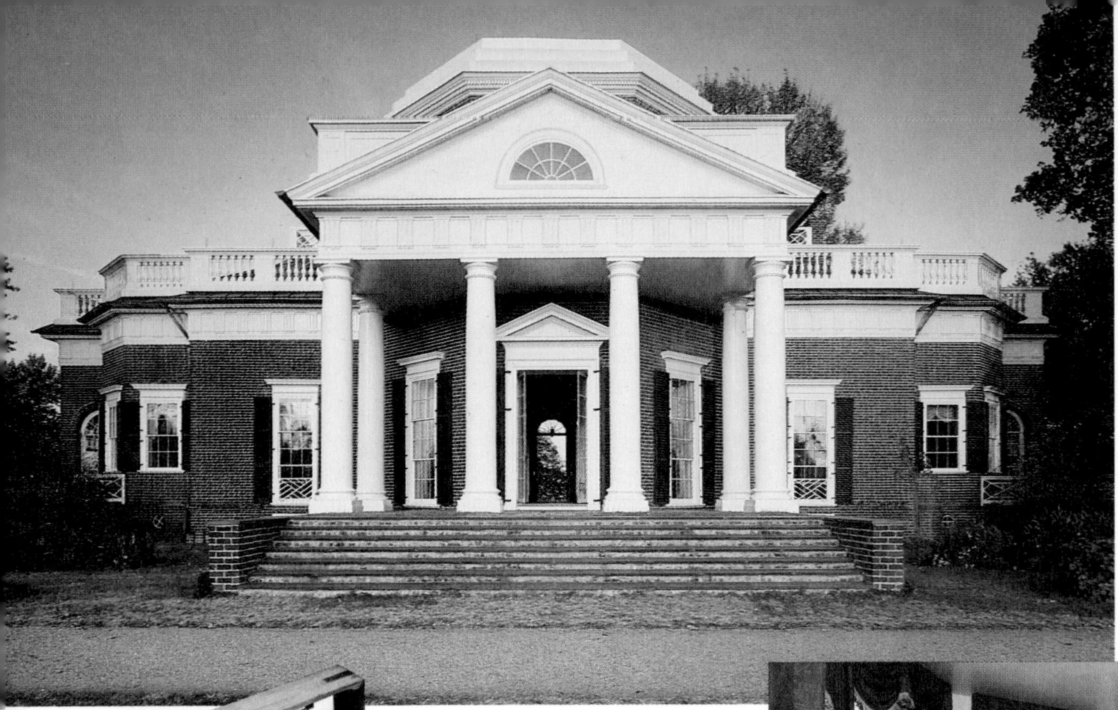

Jefferson (as architect) designed every detail of Monticello, his home in Virginia (left). By building his bed (below) between the bedroom and the study, he could arise in either room. The chair is fitted with candlesticks; the table surface revolves.

Jefferson (as inventor) improved the polygraph, a device with two simultaneously operated pens, so that he could make copies of his letters while he wrote them.

The Man From Monticello

Thomas Jefferson: Statesman, inventor, architect, and authentic genius

At a White House dinner for Nobel Prize winners, John F. Kennedy called his guests "the most extraordinary collection of talents . . . that has ever been gathered at the White House, with the possible exception of when Thomas Jefferson dined alone."

Among America's great statesmen, Jefferson stands out as a Renaissance man with an incredible range of interests, knowledge, and abilities. In the thick of politics for 40 years, he still found time for other pursuits—farming, architecture, law, geography, botany, natural history, his violin, and fine food and wine. With an inquiring mind and an incisive intellect, he wrote prodigiously and insightfully about anything that interested him. His writings on agriculture alone fill a 704-page book. An avid reader, he amassed a personal library of 6,487 volumes that became the nucleus of the Library of Congress in 1815.

More than an armchair genius, Jefferson found practical application for his talents. A dedicated farmer, he was the first person in North America to raise tomatoes for food (they were considered poisonous), and his experiments with rice made the nation a leading producer of that crop. He also invented a new moldboard for the plow. Among his other inventions—many for personal convenience—were a swivel chair, a pedometer to measure his walks, a chair that folded into a walking stick, a dumbwaiter, a revolving music stand, and a calendar clock. (So that others could have free use of his inventions, he patented nothing.) A talented architect, he adapted Roman classicism to native materials, developing a distinctive American style for the University of Virginia in Charlottesville. Not only did he design its buildings; he was also its general contractor, bookkeeper, overseer during construction, and landscapist.

Perhaps Jefferson is best summed up in his own words: "Determine never to be idle. . . . It is wonderful how much may be done if we are always doing."

"Thomas Jefferson Survives" *An old friend's final words*

About 6 P.M. on July 4, 1826, John Adams, second president of the United States, died at the age of 90 at his home in Quincy, Massachusetts. His final words were: "Thomas Jefferson still survives."

But unknown to Adams, the 83-year-old Jefferson, the nation's third president, had died several hours earlier at Monticello. An astonishing coincidence, since these two friends-turned-enemies-turned-friends-again were the only signers of the Declaration of Independence to become presidents of the republic they had helped to forge . . . and both died on the 50th anniversary of America's independence.

That Jefferson should be on Adams's mind during his last moments was not surprising. Their lives had been intertwined ever since the days when they worked together to produce the historic document—Adams had suggested that Jefferson write the Declaration and then had defended it. Both men emerged from that experience with profound respect for each other. "Laboring always at the same oar . . . we rode through the storm with heart and hand, and made a happy port," Jefferson wrote to Adams.

But after independence was won, the two followed different political paths. For a while both served in the diplomatic corps, Adams as minister to England and Jefferson as envoy to France. When they returned, each was accused by the other's supporters of harboring unhealthy ties to the nation in which he had served. Jefferson was called a sympathizer of the French Revolutionists (he was in Paris when the Bastille was stormed), while Adams was accused of trying to impose a British-style monarchy on the United States. By the end of Washington's second term as president, Adams and Jefferson were the leaders of the two factions that would become the nation's first political parties.

The Jeffersonian Republicans, suspicious of big cities and banks, believed that America should look to its vast land resources for growth. Adams's Federalists, representing the emerging capitalist urban class, favored a strong central government.

In the election of 1796, these two candidates and philosophies clashed in what is *still* considered one of the most venomous campaigns in U.S. history. A blizzard of pamphlets castigated each man. The Federalists denounced Jefferson as a rabble-rousing atheist, a coward, and a tool of France, while the Republicans lambasted Adams as a monarchist and an enemy of liberty. When the dust finally settled, Adams had won by three electoral votes. Four years later Jefferson ousted Adams by eight votes.

A mutual friend and fellow signer of the Declaration of Independence, Dr. Benjamin Rush of Pennsylvania, finally brought the two rivals together in 1811. Then began a voluminous correspondence—a rich exchange of letters that would continue the rest of their lives. "Refusing to be gladiators," one historian commented, "they conversed as sages."

Although more than 160 years have passed since the historic day when Thomas Jefferson and John Adams went to their graves, the spirit of the two great men indeed survives.

Sad Footnote for a Founding Father

It was a situation filled with irony. Thomas Jefferson, who as president had opened abundant land to settlement, found himself deeply in debt at the end of his life; the farms of his beloved Virginia were unable to compete with the fertile western plains and valleys. Just months before his death in 1826, Jefferson obtained permission from the Virginia legislature to sell off his property by a state lottery. But ticket sales faltered because of an economic depression. In desperation, his grandson canvassed in the North and raised $16,500. The former president gratefully accepted this "offering of love," although in the end it was scarcely enough to save Monticello. (The magnificent estate was eventually auctioned off, and generations passed before 20th-century admirers rescued it from decay and restored it to its original grace and splendor.)

Jefferson *v.* Burr: The Tied Election

How a constitutional loophole turned running mates into rivals for the presidency of the United States

"The Person having the greatest Number of Votes shall be the President," says Article II, Section 1, of the Constitution, referring to the votes cast by each state's electors. It goes on to say that the next highest vote-getter would become the vice president. Thus the framers of this historic document left a loophole that allowed Thomas Jefferson and Aaron Burr, candidates on the Republican ticket for president and vice president, respectively, to wind up with the same number of electoral votes.

The deadlock threw the election of 1800 into the House of Representatives, where many ballots and much political maneuvering were needed to resolve it. With President John Adams's term of office due to expire in a few months, some politicians and journalists foresaw the astonishing possibility of anarchy.

By the time the votes were cast in December, there were 73 Republican and 65 Federalist electors. As it turned out, although there appeared to be a rift in the Federalist ranks, every Republican elector had voted for both Jefferson *and* Burr. (Burr, while declaring that he was not in competion with Jefferson, never actually renounced the presidency.)

Balloting began in the House on February 11, 1801. Each of the 16 states had one vote; a simple majority, or nine votes, was needed to win. On the first ballot, Jefferson got eight and Burr six. Two states were undecided. The count had not changed by midnight, when the 19th ballot was cast. For six more intriguing, scheming, rumor-filled days, voting continued. Alexander Hamilton, though a Federalist, urged fellow Federalists to support Jefferson, on the grounds that—although Jefferson was "a contemptible hypocrite"—he *did* have some "pretensions to character," whereas Burr's "public principles have no other spring or aim than his own aggrandisement. His elevation can only promote the purposes of the desperate and profligate."

Most Federalist representatives regarded Jefferson as a dangerous radical, so they ignored Hamilton. They did not have enough votes to elect Burr, but as March 4—the end of Adams's term—loomed, they thought their support might swing a number of the Republican votes.

As the lobbying grew more intense, there was talk of civil war. Some accused the Federalists of planning to usurp the presidency. The Virginia militia was even reportedly prepared to march on Washington, D.C., if it became necessary.

Finally Delaware's representative decided that Burr could never be elected. The only reason to go on supporting him was "to exclude Jefferson at the expense of the Constitution," and this he would not do. Thus, after an astounding 36 ballots, the acrimonious deadlock was broken and Jefferson was finally declared the third president of the United States, with Burr as his vice president.

By the time the next presidential election rolled around, the 12th Amendment, specifying that the electors vote separately for president and vice president, had been ratified.

Thomas Jefferson and the Big Cheese

The 1,235-pound cheese was 4 feet across and 15 inches thick. It arrived at the White House on New Year's Day, 1802, in a cart drawn by six horses and bearing a sign: "The greatest cheese in America for the greatest man in America."

The gift to Thomas Jefferson

Anne Royall, Scold

She may not have caught the president skinny-dipping, but it's almost all she didn't do

President Harry Truman once told novelist John Hersey a tale about a "shrew of a newspaperwoman" named Anne Royall. It seems that she followed John Quincy Adams to the Potomac River, where he customarily took an early morning swim in the nude. She sat on his clothes, trapping him in the water until he agreed to an interview. Later, Truman said, "she was tried in a court in Washington and caught a big fine as a common scold."

Truman had the story partly right. Anne Newport Royall *was* a newspaper editor, perhaps America's first woman editor, and she *was* fined $10 at the age of 60 for being a common scold—she is the only American ever convicted of the charge.

But the story of her coerced interview is dubious. Not that she would have been daunted at trapping the president in the buff—she wouldn't have had to. Adams was a longtime friend of this courageous woman, whom he called *was the inspiration of a Baptist minister, John Leland of Cheshire, Massachusetts. That summer, he and his congregation had milked some 900 cows at one time, processing the result in a giant ciderpress. Jefferson, who quipped that the cows were all Republican, gave Leland $200 rather than accept a gift from poor farmers. They say that the cheese was served at the White House until 1805.*

in his journal "a virago errant in enchanted armor."

Forced at the age of 55 to earn her own living, Royall produced 10 travel books, a novel, and a play, and ran two newspapers before she died 30 years later.

When she was a teenager, she and her widowed mother had become servants in the house of Maj. William Royall. He took an interest in her and educated her. In 1797 they married; he was 47, she 28. He died in 1813, making her his heir, but 10 years later his family broke the will and Anne was left penniless.

With Adams's help, she tried to get a pension as a veteran's widow. When it was refused, she turned to her pen. For eight years she traveled through settled and frontier America by stagecoach, steamer, and on foot, collecting material for the volumes of travel sketches that made her nationally known. Royall signed up subscribers as she went, and she always carried a trunkful of her many books to sell.

She was an outspoken foe of the evangelical, anti-Masonic Protestants who wanted to make their church a political force. In 1827, in Vermont, one such "blueskin" (as she called them) threw her down the steps of his store, breaking her leg. In 1829 a local congregation came to her Washington home to convert her. She drove off the hymn-singing rock throwers, who then took her to court as a scold. Royall was convicted, and newspapermen paid her fine.

In 1831 she launched her first newspaper, *Paul Pry*. A voice of conscience, it exposed graft and supported free speech. When it failed, she launched *The Huntress*, which ran for 18 years, until just before her death, at 85, in 1854. Truly, she earned the title later bestowed upon her, Grandma of the Muckrakers.

John Quincy Adams did enjoy early morning nude swims, but this vision of his entrapment by a fashion-plate Anne Royall is pure fancy.

Thank Heaven, Mr. Adams

How a "sign from God" gave the presidency to John Quincy Adams

When John Quincy Adams won the presidency in 1824, he did it without a majority of electoral votes. In fact, Andrew Jackson beat him in both the popular vote and the Electoral College. But because Jackson did not have an outright majority, the issue was decided in the House of Representatives, and the outcome finally hung on a single vote, cast by an aging patroon from upstate New York.

The election was odd from the start. The two-party system had collapsed, and all the principal candidates claimed to be Republicans. Various state legislatures nominated their own favorites, and in all some 17 candidates were in the running. By Election Day the field had narrowed to four:

Tennessee Senator **Andrew Jackson,** hero of the Battle of New Orleans, was the people's choice. His opponents regarded him as a semiliterate hothead, good in a fight but ill-prepared for national leadership.

John Quincy Adams, secretary of state and son of a president, came in second. Though highly qualified by education and experience, he was viewed as a cold fish lacking in human warmth.

Third was **William H. Crawford** of Georgia. He owed much of his support to a bulging pocketful of political debts that he had collected during his term as secretary of the treasury. (So flagrant was his abuse of patronage that, in the course of a discussion on the subject, the outgoing president, James Monroe, had threatened him with a pair of fire tongs.)

Kentuckian **Henry Clay,** speaker of the House, was fourth. Since the 12th Amendment specified that the choice be made among the top three vote-getters, he was eliminated from the race. After a private meeting with Adams, during which Clay reportedly was offered the post of secretary of state, he threw his substantial support to the New Englander.

On February 9, voting day in the House, Adams knew that he had to win on the first ballot or be overwhelmed by Jackson's popular support. Each state had one vote, to be decided by the majority of its representatives. Adams was sure of 12 states—one short of the majority he needed—and the New York delegation was tied.

Clay felt that one of the New York representatives, the immensely rich and pious old landholder Stephen Van Rensselaer III, could be swayed, although his vote was supposedly committed to Crawford. As the delegation arrived, Clay ushered Van Rensselaer into the speaker's room, where he and Daniel Webster exercised their considerable powers of persuasion on Adams's behalf.

They failed. But the encounter flustered the old aristocrat. Before casting his vote, Van Rensselaer bowed his head in prayer, and the first thing he saw when he opened his eyes was a slip of paper marked with Adams's name—possibly a discarded ballot. Taking it as a sign of God's will, he put the slip in the ballot box and made John Quincy Adams the sixth president of the United States.

Another Vote Lost

Presidential candidates did not openly campaign for themselves during most of America's first century (it was felt that the office should seek the man), but they generally made it a point to appear congenial in public. When a proud mother once handed Andrew Jackson her particularly dirty baby, however, Old Hickory's political grace was strained to the limits. "Here is a beautiful specimen of young American childhood," he said. "Note the brightness of that eye, the great strength of those limbs, and the sweetness of those lips." Then he looked again at the filthy face and handed the baby to his friend John Eaton. "Kiss him, Eaton," he said.

On January 30, 1835, Richard Lawrence fired two pistols at Andrew Jackson at point-blank range, and became the first person to attempt to assassinate a president of the United States. Both weapons misfired.

The First Would-be Assassin

Andrew Jackson's life was saved by the weather

On a raw January day in 1835, the aged and infirm President Andrew Jackson leaned on the arm of a Cabinet member as he emerged from the Hall of the House of Representatives, where he had attended a funeral service for Congressman Warren Davis. Waiting behind a column in the Capitol's eastern portico was his would-be killer, a handsome young man named Richard Lawrence. Concealed in the folds of Lawrence's long, dark cloak was a pair of single-shot pistols.

When Jackson was some eight feet away, Lawrence sprang out, a pistol in each hand. Raising his right hand, he drew a bead on the president's chest and confidently pulled the trigger. The explosion of the percussion cup echoed through the chamber, and chaos ensued. But Jackson did not fall. The gun had misfired.

Jackson, ever the fighter, raised his cane and charged the assassin, shouting in fury. With the old man almost upon him, Lawrence shot again. Incredibly, the second gun also misfired. The gunman was quickly wrestled to the ground and spirited away.

Two clear shots—two misfires; the odds have been calculated at 125,000 to 1. Both weapons were properly loaded and both functioned perfectly in later tests. Lawrence blamed the dampness.

A host of conspiracy theories blossomed, but it became clear at Lawrence's trial that his was an act of lunacy. He had lived a normal life until 1832, when he suddenly became obsessed with delusions. One was that he was King Richard III of England and that Jackson had killed his father and was withholding royal funds in U.S. banks.

No precedent existed for trying a failed assassin, and so the crime was treated as a simple assault, a misdemeanor at the time. The prosecutor, Washington District Attorney Francis Scott Key (writer of "The Star-Spangled Banner"), agreed that the defendant should be treated as a madman, and Lawrence was freed on a plea of insanity. He spent the rest of his life in asylums and died in 1861.

One Vote Decided . . .

Texas. *The 28th state squeaked into the Union in 1845 by one vote in the Senate. Because of Texas's size, the lawmakers stipulated that four more states could be carved out of its territory.*

Alaska. *The vote of just one senator also approved "Seward's Folly," the 1867 deal by which Secretary of State William Seward purchased the vast territory of Alaska from Russia for over $7 million.*

President Smith. *In a caucus at the 1864 Republican Convention, Kentucky Congressman Green Clay Smith was reportedly one vote shy of becoming Abraham Lincoln's running mate. Andrew Johnson got the nod and became president after Lincoln's death. Smith later ran for president on the Prohibition Party ticket.*

The Secret Wedding of John Tyler

Twice-married, the 10th president fathered 15 children

The 54-year-old groom slipped into New York incognito to marry a well-born, well-heeled beauty of 24. Thus John Tyler became the first president to wed while in office—and the only one to do so secretly—when he married Julia Gardiner on June 26, 1844. As news of the wedding spread, eyebrows rose and tongues wagged. But Washingtonians weren't surprised: they had taken note of the budding romance between the lonely chief executive and the lively belle ever since the two had begun to see each other just months after the death of Letitia, Tyler's wife of 29 years and the mother of his first seven children. And they knew the wedding had been quiet to assure privacy for the Gardiners, in mourning for the bride's father, who had died in an explosion in February.

Julia Tyler relished being mistress of the White House, but after only eight months she and her husband had to make way for the new president, James K. Polk. The pair took up residence at Sherwood Forest, Tyler's Virginia plantation, and before the year was out she was pregnant. The busybodies who had forecast frustration for the aging president's young bride were proven wrong: Julia bore her husband seven children. Tyler, in fact, was by far the most prolific of presidents, fathering eight sons and seven daughters (one of Letitia's died in infancy). His first child, born in 1815, was five years older than his second wife—and 45 years older than his last child, born in 1860.

In 1861 Tyler presided over a conference seeking a last-ditch formula to avert civil war. Later elected to the Confederate House of Representatives, he died in 1862, at age 71, before taking his seat. The Confederates buried him at Richmond with honors, but the federal government pointedly ignored the passing of the only president who ever subsequently became a sworn enemy of the United States.

Chaos followed the explosion of the navy's huge gun aboard the Princeton *in 1844. When the smoke cleared, David Gardiner, former New York senator and father of President Tyler's future wife, was among those found dead on deck.*

President for a Day

There has been only one 24-hour chief executive

A dedicated proponent of westward expansion and a leading advocate of states' rights, David Rice Atchison served ably as a senator from Missouri from 1843 to 1855. But perhaps his chief distinction was the day he served as president of the United States.

The Constitution provides that the vice president serves as the official president of the Senate, but in his absence from the chamber a president pro tem ("for the time being") is elected. According to a congressional act passed in 1792, the president pro tem of the Senate would become the nation's acting president in the event that both the president and vice president were unable to fill their offices.

During his 12 years in the Senate, Atchison was elected president pro tem 16 times. One of these occasions was on March 2, 1849, just before Zachary Taylor was to take the oath of office as the nation's 12th chief executive. Since Inauguration Day fell on Sunday, Taylor decided to postpone the swearing-in ceremony until the following day. And so for 24 hours, from noon on Sunday—when President James K. Polk and his vice president left office—until noon on Monday, Atchison was the acting president of the United States.

It seems that he was not unduly excited by the honor, however; having worked extremely hard during the previous week, he slept through most of his one-day tenure as chief executive.

(A geographic footnote: Atchison County, Missouri, and the city of Atchison, Kansas, were both named for this not-quite-forgotten president.)

The youngest—and probably the handsomest—president up to that time, Pierce fell far short of expectations, and his personal life was dealt a crushing blow when his young son (shown above with Mrs. Pierce) died in a train wreck.

Franklin Pierce: A Heartbroken President

A family stalked by political and personal tragedy

Only one elected president—Franklin Pierce in 1856—has ever been denied renomination by his own party. He had tried, through compromise, to unite a nation that was bitterly divided over the slavery issue, and he had failed miserably.

But the tragedy of Pierce's administration was as much personal as political. A popular, hard-drinking extrovert, he had, as a young representative from New Hampshire, married a shy, puritanical woman. Jane Pierce, in poor health, hated partying, the damp Washington climate, and public life of any kind. Throughout Pierce's early political career his wife spent much of her time at their New Hampshire home.

Two sons died in infancy, and when a third son, Benjamin, was born in 1842, Pierce heeded his wife's pleas and retired from national politics. He virtually stopped drinking, devoted himself to his family and his successful law practice, and limited his political activities to the state level.

In June 1852, however, after service in the Mexican War, Pierce allowed himself to be nominated at the deadlocked Democratic convention, and on the 49th ballot he became the party's dark-horse presidential candidate. When news reached the Pierces, Jane, who had lived in dread of the moment, fainted.

Pierce persuaded her that to be president would create a fine legacy for Bennie, then a bright 11-year-old. To everyone's surprise, he won. Then, shortly before the inauguration, the family was involved in a train wreck. Neither parent was hurt, but their beloved son was thrown from the car and crushed to death before their eyes. Despondent, the newly elected president went to Washington alone. At first he virtually camped out in the chilly White House, sleeping on the floor. He resumed drinking and contracted chronic bronchitis. (As a result, he installed a greatly improved heating system in the White House.) When Jane finally joined him in Washington, she kept to her room, writing notes to their dead son.

Pierce was elected in the same year that Harriet Beecher Stowe's book *Uncle Tom's Cabin* was published and the nation was nearly aflame over slavery, but he seems never to have understood the intensity of the conflict. A series of calamitous decisions led to administrative disaster and bloody violence, and he was refused his party's renomination.

The Pierces retired to their New England home, where Jane died in 1863. Six years later, at 65, the former president passed away, a lonely and obscure man among the White Mountains of New Hampshire.

Matthew Lyon, shown above defending himself with fire tongs, later spent four months in jail for violating the short-lived Alien and Sedition Acts. His crime: publishing a criticism of President John Adams.

Representative Preston Smith Brooks was never censured by Congress for the beating he gave Senator Charles Sumner; he got off in court with a $300 fine.

Congressional Violence

Dignity and decorum have not always prevailed in the Senate and the House

When Vice President Martin Van Buren presided over the Senate in the mid-1830's, he occasionally wore sidearms to help keep order. It is a wonder that others have not followed his example, considering how many lawmakers in both houses of Congress have resorted to fists, guns, or clubs.

The spitting Lyon
One of the first was Representative Roger Griswold of Connecticut. On January 30, 1798, when Matthew Lyon of Vermont slighted Griswold's home state, he retaliated by insulting Lyon's war record. Lyon promptly spit in Griswold's face. Two weeks later Griswold attacked Lyon at his desk with a stout stick. Lyon counterattacked with a pair of fire tongs snatched from the fireplace behind the speaker. House members finally separated them.

"Let the assassin fire!"
Mississippi Senator Henry S. ("Hangman") Foote and Missouri's Thomas Hart Benton were already bitter enemies in 1850, when, during a rancorous speech by Foote, Benton kicked back his chair and moved menacingly forward. Foote drew a gun and aimed it at the advancing Benton. "Stand out of the way!" Benton shouted to others. "Let the assassin fire!" Foote, who was quickly disarmed, later claimed that he thought Benton, too, had a gun.

A brutal clubbing
In May 1856 abolitionist Senator Charles Sumner of Massachusetts insulted Senator Andrew P. Butler of South Carolina in a tirade against slavery. Later, while Sumner was writing at his desk, Butler's nephew, Representative Preston Smith Brooks, entered the Senate chamber with a fellow South Carolinian and bludgeoned Sumner with a heavy cane. Sumner tried to rise but was trapped under his desk. With blood flowing from his head, he managed to rip the desk loose from the floor, then fell back, unconscious. His injuries kept him away from the Senate for three years.

A modern wrestling match
In 1964 Strom Thurmond of South Carolina and Ralph Yarborough of Texas took off their coats in a Senate corridor and thrashed out a dispute over a civil rights appointment. Thurmond pinned Yarborough but could not get him to cry "Uncle." The two later reconciled at a picture-taking session.

The War of Barksdale's Wig

The biggest congressional donnybrook of all

On the night of February 5, 1858, the House was tied up by a filibuster over admitting Kansas to the Union, a bitter issue fraught with all the emotional tension that would soon lead to civil war. About 1:30 in the morning, with many members of the chamber showing signs of having nipped at too much alcohol, an argument erupted between Galusha Grow of Pennsylvania and Laurence Keitt of South Carolina. Keitt called Grow "a black Republican puppy."

"No Negro-driver shall crack his whip over me," Grow responded. Keitt promptly went for Grow's throat, whereupon Grow decked Keitt. In a twinkling—"a very slow twinkling," according to one newspaper account—congressmen from both sides waded into the fray. Bodies writhed on the floor and fists found their mark in a wild and bruising battle. At one point a spittoon flew through the air. As the sergeant at arms enthusiastically wielded his ceremonial mace, the speaker, in utter futility, pounded his gavel for order.

Mississippi's William Barksdale was wrestling with Grow when Cadwallader Washburn of Wisconsin, getting ready to hit Barksdale in the mouth, seized him by the hair and drew back to deliver a haymaker. The blow never landed, however, for Barksdale's wig came off in Washburn's hand, and the angry brawl ended in gales of raucous laughter.

William Barksdale of Mississippi inadvertently ended Congress's biggest brawl by losing his wig. Soon John "Bowie-knife" Potter of Wisconsin was racing about with it, screaming, "Hooray, boys, I've got his scalp!"

Bob La Follette, Filibuster Champion

Neither pistols nor poison could stop him

Filibustering—the parliamentary delaying tactic of refusing to give up the floor—has long been a favored weapon of stalwart congressional orators. One of the best was Robert La Follette, Sr., a Wisconsin senator from 1905 to 1925. His feats of endurance provoked threats of violence and even attempted murder.

In her biography of her husband, Belle La Follette told how, during a record-breaking 1908 filibuster, he braced himself with occasional glasses of an eggnoglike concoction. One of these drinks was so bitter that after a sip he had it taken away. (Analysis showed that it contained enough ptomaine bacteria to kill him.)

He became ill but kept on talking and set a one-man filibuster record of 18 hours, 23 minutes. His record held until 1953, when Senator Wayne Morse spoke for more than 22 hours. (In 1957 Senator Strom Thurmond set a new record of 24 hours, 18 minutes.)

Another filibuster, in 1917, brought La Follette dangerously close to a shootout with Senator Ollie James of Kentucky. An argument escalated to a confrontation between the two, both of whom were known to carry guns. La Follette's friend Senator Harry Lane of Oregon armed himself with a sharp file, vowing to stab James if he moved toward his weapon. No gun was drawn, and it was just as well, for La Follette's pistol, which he thought was in a handy traveling bag, had been surreptitously removed by his son, the future Senator Bob La Follette, Jr.

Blazing the Campaign Trail

They said Stephen A. Douglas peddled ideas "as a tin man peddles his wares"

Until Stephen A. Douglas ran against Abraham Lincoln and two others in 1860, no American had ever declared his own candidacy, openly sought nomination, or publicly campaigned for the presidency. When Douglas hit the road on his own behalf, orating to crowds from railroad coaches, hotel balconies, and city park speaking stands, many were offended by his brash behavior.

Although Douglas carried his message far and wide, his stumping was a pale version of today's barnstorming. In fact, when he set out to spread his message eastward, he announced the trip as a visit to his mother in Clifton Springs, New York. It took him almost a month of stopovers to get there. One Republican handbill taunted: "A Boy Lost! Left Washington D.C. some time in July . . . has been seen in Philadelphia, New York City, Hartford, Conn., at a clambake in Rhode Island. He has been heard from at Boston, Portland, Augusta, and Bangor, Me. . . . He has an idea that he is a candidate for President."

While the final vote confirmed Lincoln's popularity, Douglas nevertheless made an admirable showing. As for high-visibility presidential candidates campaigning for themselves, he started it all.

Dubbed "The Little Giant," Stephen A. Douglas was about a foot shorter than the rangy Lincoln.

The Many Beards of Abraham Lincoln

Abraham Lincoln said he grew a beard because a young girl, Grace Bedell, wrote to him that "All the ladies like whiskers, and they will tease their husbands to vote for you and then you would be president." Perhaps, but he didn't start the famous fringe until after the election. The news that he would arrive be-whiskered posed problems for printers planning to sell his photograph at the inauguration: no one knew exactly what the beard would look like. They simply added beards to existing engravings, and proceeded to conduct a brisk business in fancifully festooned presidential portraits.

Gettysburg Address

Haunting, memorable words from an ailing president

"A few appropriate remarks" were requested of President Abraham Lincoln for the dedication of the cemetery on the Civil War battlefield in Pennsylvania, set for November 19, 1863. In fact, Lincoln was not the featured speaker. That honor went to the eminent orator Edward Everett—a Massachusetts clergyman, journalist, academician, and, later, a congressman and statesman. While Everett had been given two months to prepare his speech, Lincoln was not even invited to speak until two weeks before the event.

At intervals during a photographic session on November 15 he began making notes. On the 17th, the day before his departure for Gettysburg, he wrote his first draft on a sheet of White House stationery. During the train trip, the president gave his speech more thought, and on the eve of the ceremony he completed its final draft, adding another nine lines in pencil on a piece of lined foolscap.

True to form, the eloquent Everett delivered a dramatic two-hour oration. Lincoln, suffering from what was later diagnosed as smallpox, rose with his mismatched sheets in hand and in less than three minutes delivered a ten-sentence speech of some 270 words. A smattering of applause followed from an audience unsure he was finished.

The press reaction was mixed. One paper wrote that "the cheeks of every American must tingle with shame as he reads the silly, flat and dishwatery utterances." But another accurately prophesied that "the dedicatory remarks of President Lincoln will live among the annals of man."

Was Mary Todd Lincoln a Spy?

During the Civil War, Washington was a hotbed of gossip

Mrs. Lincoln's family was deeply involved in the Confederate cause, a fact not lost on gossip-mongers. A half-brother was accused of brutalizing Union prisoners, her half-sisters were married to Confederate officers, and her brother thought Lincoln was "one of the greatest scoundrels unhung." It didn't help that she badgered her husband about political appointments and called Secretary of State William Seward "a dirty abolitionist sneak." Her secretary later wrote that rumors flew about Mrs. Lincoln's "constant correspondence, as a spy, with the chiefs of the Rebellion. Through her they obtained the secrets of the Cabinet and plans of generals."

Finally a Senate committee convened in secrecy to consider the accusations. According to a member, the meeting had just begun when the officer posted at the door opened it. The senators were "almost overwhelmed by astonishment," for there stood Lincoln, alone. Pathos was written upon his face and an "almost unhuman sadness" filled his eyes. Speaking "with infinite sorrow," he said: "I, Abraham Lincoln, President of the United States, appear of my own volition before this Committee of the Senate to say that, I, of my own knowledge, know that it is untrue that any of my family hold treasonable communication with the enemy."

Lincoln turned and left. Overcome, the committee dropped all consideration of rumors that Mrs. Lincoln was a Confederate spy.

In a wartime capital rife with rumor, the president's wife was a continual target: her alleged frugality, mistreatment of servants, and meddling in state matters were topics of constant comment. Further tales concerned séances she held at the White House after young Willie Lincoln died. During one, a confused message was supposedly received from George Washington, Benjamin Franklin, and Napoleon. It was described by the president as "a good deal like the talk of my Cabinet."

Andrew Johnson, Battler

When the president was acquitted by one vote, it climaxed a career in the eye of a storm

In 1824, 15-year-old Andrew Johnson and his brother ran away from the North Carolina tailor to whom they had been indentured in childhood as slavelike apprentices. The tailor posted a $10 reward for their return, warning "all persons . . . against harboring or employing said apprentices." Johnson eventually fled to Tennessee and three years later opened his own tailor shop.

He soon married his 16-year-old sweetheart, Eliza McCardle. Unlike her husband, who could read only a few simple words, she had some education. Sitting by his side as he sewed, she shared it with him. He learned to read well, to write, and to figure. An exciting world was opened to him; he began to read voraciously and to involve himself in the issues of the day.

The proud mechanic

The Age of the Common Man was rushing in, impelled by Andrew Jackson of Tennessee, and the young tailor rode its crest. Proudly labeling himself a "mechanic," or craftsman, he battled what he was later to call "an illegitimate, swaggering, bastard, scrub aristocracy," and rose from local to state office. In 1843 he went to Congress, where his speeches, according to *The New York Times,* "cut and slashed right and left, tore big wounds and left something behind to fester and remember."

Elected governor of Tennessee in 1853, he was soon the focal point of a number of issues that would lead to civil war. Once, after a placard was posted urging that "Andie Johnson" be shot on sight, some friends wanted to act as his bodyguards. Saying that he wanted "no man to be in the way of the bullet" meant for him, Johnson walked alone to the Capitol.

He carried a gun while running for reelection. At one point, in defiance of death threats, he put it on the rostrum at a meeting and said, "If any man has come here tonight for the purpose [of assassination] . . . let him shoot." No one did.

Traitor to the South

"If Johnson were a snake," one Southern leader said, "he would hide himself in the grass and bite the heels of the children of rich people." He was a senator by then, fighting against the fast-growing secessionist movement. After Lincoln's inauguration in 1861, Johnson hurriedly left for home, hoping to keep Tennessee in the Union.

After the Senate failed to remove Andrew Johnson from office, a hostile press pictured him as a drunken monarch, wearing spurs with which to ride a defeated Congress. The scissors at his belt refer to his early career as a tailor. Even after he became president, Johnson often visited tailor shops to chat.

At Liberty, Virginia, his train was boarded by an armed mob. "Are you Andy Johnson?" a man demanded. Johnson said he was. "Then I'm going to pull your nose!" the man said, reaching for that large, often caricatured feature. Drawing his pistol, Johnson protected his nose and cleared the car.

At Lynchburg, Virginia, he was dragged from the train, kicked, spit upon, and almost hanged. The angry mob finally let him go on the grounds that his fellow Tennesseans should not be denied the privilege of killing him.

Wearing his pistol, he stumped his home state. He was hanged and shot in effigy in Nashville, Knoxville, and Memphis, but the cool courage with which he argued his cause kept would-be attackers at bay. When Tennessee joined the Confederacy in June 1861, Johnson kept his Senate seat—the only Southern senator to do so.

Appointed military governor of Tennessee by Lincoln in 1862, he persuaded the legislature to renounce secession and end slavery in the state. In 1864, because of Johnson's unique value as a loyal Southern Democrat, Lincoln chose him as his running mate on the National Union Ticket.

Andy the Sot

Ill and exhausted on Inauguration Day in 1865, Johnson braced himself with brandy. Tipsy, he slurred his speech, and from then on the newspapers called him Andy the Sot.

Only 41 days later, on April 15, 1865, Lincoln was dead and Andy the Sot was president. Proposing to follow Lincoln's lenient Reconstruction policy, he supported an amnesty for Southerners who would swear allegiance to the federal government, and did not insist that the former rebel states give blacks the vote. Opposing Johnson in Congress were the Radical Republicans, who wanted to impose military rule on the South, enforce the black vote, and disenfranchise ex-rebels and confiscate their land. Johnson repeatedly vetoed such legislation. Calling him an "insolent, drunken brute," the radical press accused him of having plotted Lincoln's assassination.

The impeachment

Sweeping the congressional elections in 1866, the radicals gained the strength not only to overide Johnson's vetoes, but to pass laws that limited his power. One of these, the Tenure of Office Act, forbade him to dismiss any official without prior Senate approval. Ignoring it, he proceeded to fire Secretary of War Edwin M. Stanton, replacing him with Ulysses S. Grant. But at the Senate's insistence, the office was restored to Stanton. When Johnson fired him a second time, the House voted 126 to 47 to impeach.

"Let them impeach and be damned," Johnson said. He did not attend the Senate trial, a sold-out, two-and-a-half-month show, presided over by Chief Justice Salmon P. Chase. The charges were flimsy (the Tenure of Office Act was later declared unconstitutional) and the conduct of the trial was scandalous. No Cabinet member was allowed to testify for Johnson, and the Senate overruled 17 of Chase's decisions to admit evidence on his behalf. The final vote was 35 to 19 for conviction, 1 short of the two-thirds needed, and Andy the Sot remained president of the United States.

The Crucial Vote

Edmund Ross's political career was ruined because he voted for acquittal

On May 11, 1868, Senate Republicans caucused to see how the vote would go in Andrew Johnson's trial. Thirty-five votes were firm for conviction. Six seemed assured for acquittal. One man remained silent: Edmund Gibson Ross, the 42-year-old freshman senator from Kansas.

A newspaper publisher and editor, Ross had been appointed in 1866 to finish the term of Senator James H. Lane, who had shot himself over criticism of his support of President Johnson. Later that year Ross won election on his own. A staunch Republican since the party's formation in 1856, he had voted consistently against Johnson, but after the House impeachment he told a colleague that "so far as I am concerned . . . he shall have as fair a trial as an accused man ever had on this earth."

Word went out that Ross was "shaky." Letters and telegrams poured in from Kansas, demanding that he vote to convict. "I have taken an oath to do impartial justice," he replied to one telegram. ". . . I shall have the courage and the honesty to vote according to the dictates of my judgement."

On May 16, the day of the Senate vote, all six "renegade" Republicans were sure to vote with the Democrats for acquittal. All eyes turned to Ross.

"I almost literally looked into my open grave," he was later to write. "Friends, position, fortune, everything that makes life desirable to an ambitious man, were about to be swept away by the breath of my mouth, perhaps forever."

The breath of his mouth was at first so thin that his vote could not be heard. The second time, they heard him in the gallery: "Not guilty."

A justice of the Kansas Supreme Court sent a telegram: "Unfortunately, the rope with which Judas hung himself is mislaid, but the pistol with which Jim Lane killed himself is at your service."

None of the seven ever served in the Senate again. Ross finished his term as an Independent and returned to Kansas, where he resumed his newspaper career and became a Democrat. Badly beaten in a later race for governor, he moved to New Mexico. President Grover Cleveland appointed him governor of the territory.

Just before Ross's death at 80, the state of Kansas sent him a message of appreciation for his courageous conduct during Johnson's impeachment trial nearly 40 years before.

The Strange Presidential Election of 1872

Grant* v. *Greeley: A choice between "hemlock and strychnine"

It was clearly a Hobson's choice between two men almost equally unfit for the presidency. It reduced both major parties to squabbling shambles, and it opened the way for a bizarre parade of minor candidates to espouse a wide range of causes, from the noble to the lunatic. Among America's many strange presidential races, few have been stranger than the election of 1872.

The incumbent was Ulysses S. Grant, whose administration had been fraught with corruption and incompetence. The prospect of his renomination split the Republican Party, giving birth to the Liberal Republicans. After a near-riotous convention they nominated Horace Greeley, founder and editor of the *New York Tribune* and champion of nearly every social reform that came his way. Greeley was a brilliant journalist, but as a statesman he was impractical and inconsistent—a gullible idealist whose public demeanor was clownish at best. "Success with such a candidate is out of the question," sighed Charles Francis Adams, the son and grandson of presidents, who lost the nod to Greeley on the sixth ballot.

The regular Republicans renominated Grant. A month later the Democrats, in a surprise move, selected the man who once said, "All Democrats may not be rascals, but all rascals are Democrats." It was none other than Horace Greeley. (Southern Democrats, it seemed, would vote for anyone who favored amnesty for former Confederates and the withdrawal of federal troops from the South. As one of them said: "If the party puts Greeley into our hymn book we'll sing him through if it kills us.")

Grant spent a quiet seaside summer while Republican speakers, editorialists, and cartoonists recalled his Civil War heroism and ridiculed Greeley's baby face, chin whiskers, and rumpled clothes. They jeered at the editor's support of vegetarianism, prohibition, and communal living schemes. (*The Phrenological Journal,* however, having measured Greeley's cranium, wrote glowingly of his natural qualifications for office.) Meeting ridicule everywhere, Greeley grew more frenetic and morose. He said later that he didn't know whether he was running for the presidency or the penitentiary.

Personal grief compounded his public ordeal. In September he returned to New York to sit at the bedside of his dying wife. Grief-stricken, he slept little until her death on October 30. A week later he was massacred at the polls, capturing only 6 states while Grant swept 30.

Editor-turned-candidate Greeley, as depicted by cartoonist Thomas Nast.

The Pitiful End of Horace Greeley

A poignant footnote to an odd election

Few serious candidates before Horace Greeley had ever been so thoroughly repudiated at the polls; none before or since has been so totally destroyed by defeat. Crushed by the loss of his beloved wife, he saw himself as "the worst beaten man who ever ran for high office." But further humiliation was to come. When Greeley tried to resume control of his beloved *Tribune,* he was rebuffed by acting editor Whitelaw Reid. Instead of welcoming Greeley back, Reid ran a front-page box mocking the Republican office seekers who had sought the old editor's help, then refused to print Greeley's response. Greeley's mind snapped and his health broke. He died, insane, in a physician friend's suburban retreat only three weeks after the election.

An Odd Couple in Pursuit of the Presidency

Two colorful candidates who ran for office

Among the minor-party candidates in that strange campaign of 1872, two of the most fascinating, by all odds, were Victoria Woodhull, whose Equal Rights Party spoke for "the unenfranchised women of the country," and George Francis Train, self-proclaimed "Champion Crank of America."

Woodhull and her sister had already invaded traditional male preserves by becoming Wall Street brokers and by publishing a political journal, *Woodhull & Claflin's Weekly*. Free-thinking reformers, they spoke out for free love, abortion, divorce, legalized prostitution, and women's voting rights. In an address to a meeting of the National Woman Suffrage Association, Woodhull delivered the clarion call that was her campaign theme: "We mean treason; we mean secession . . . we will [overthrow] this bogus Republic." On Election Day she and her sister were in jail, charged with sending obscene literature through the mail—the offensive material was an article congratulating the popular preacher Henry Ward Beecher for having the good sense to dally with a married lady parishioner but chiding him for his failure to openly advocate the free love he clearly practiced. Reports about Woodhull's personal life, including the ménage à trois in which she lived, did not help her at the polls.

Train was controversial in a different way. An eccentric and flamboyant self-made millionaire with a flair for publicity, he was obsessed with speed and drawn to struggles for freedom. Jules Verne modeled *Around the World in 80 Days* on a journey Train had made in 1870. In the course of the trip, Train became embroiled in a revolution against the Third Republic in France and avoided the firing squad by wrapping himself in both the French and American flags—it was one of 15 sojourns in foreign jails in the course of his long life. (He deducted the enforced stopover from the 80-day count.) He was later to break his own record by circling the globe in 67½ days. During the 1872 campaign he became a political rarity: a losing candidate who made a *profit*. Charging admission for his orations, he barnstormed the country, delivering an amazing 1,000 speeches to a total of 2 million people. Calling himself "your modest, diffident, unassuming friend, the future President of America," he held forth on his own magnificence. Finally, he became involved in the Victoria Woodhull controversy. In response to the charges against her, Train published a collection of biblical quotations that were, he said, more obscene than anything his opponent had written. He, too, was clapped in jail.

Eccentric millionaire George Francis Train ran for president in 1872.

Victoria Woodhull, a most unconventional 19th-century candidate, was pictured by Nast as Satan.

"Is It a Crime for a United States Citizen to Vote?"

This was the well-publicized query voiced many times by suffragette Susan B. Anthony, who was arrested during the 1872 election—for the crime of voting. At her trial in Canandaigua, New York, Supreme Court Justice Ward Hunt flouted legal procedure, capping his conduct by ordering the jury to find her guilty. Sentenced to a token fine of $100 plus court costs, Anthony vowed, "I will never pay a dollar of your unjust fine"—and she never did. Justice Hunt refused to have her imprisoned, thus denying her right to appeal. (She'd have been mortified to know that the 19th Amendment granting woman suffrage was not ratified until nearly 50 years later.)

Lemonade Lucy and the Roman Punch

During the Hayes administration, "water flowed like champagne at the White House"

Rutherford B. Hayes was no teetotaler; he'd been known to lift a glass or two, though never to excess. But soon after taking office in 1877, he declared the White House alcohol-free. In part, the decision was because his wife, Lucy, believed in temperance, then gaining a following as a moral crusade. Moreover, Hayes, whose administration followed the scandal-ridden, whiskey-soaked White House years of Ulysses S. Grant, wanted to set a wholesome example for the nation. (Besides banning booze, Hayes began the cheery tradition of Easter egg hunts on the White House lawn.)

One Washington wit said that "water flowed like champagne at the White House," and among thirsty dignitaries, Mrs. Hayes became known as Lemonade Lucy.

The White House staff, however, found a way around the prohibition. The chef instituted a regular course, Roman Punch. Served midway through dinner, it was a hollowed-out, frozen orange filled with a sherbetlike concoction into which, according to one thankful senator, "as much rum was crowded as it could contain without being altogether liquid." It was up to the waiters to ensure that the heaviest drinkers got the most potent punch.

The president had the last laugh, although no one knew it until after he died. "The joke of the Roman Punch oranges was not on us," read an entry in his diary, "but on the drinking people. My orders were to flavor them *rather strongly* with the same flavor that is found in Jamaica rum. . . . There was not a drop of spirits in them!"

Lucy Hayes, shown with two of her eight children and a playmate (in white), was the first president's wife to be called First Lady of the Land.

Garfield's Ordeal

Did the bullet kill him—or was it the doctors?

It took James A. Garfield 11 weeks to die after being shot in the back by assassin Charles Guiteau on July 2, 1881. The bullet nicked an artery, and it was this wound that eventually killed the president; but the earnest efforts of the best physicians of his day would have finished him off anyway.

Since it was believed that the bullet itself would cause infection, the first concern was to find it. This was done by poking into the wound, trying to follow the bullet's channel with a metal probe or a finger. And because most American doctors were still skeptical about Louis Pasteur's 20-year-old theory of bacterial infection, the probes were not sterilized and some of the fingers were not even washed.

Smith Townshend, District of Columbia health officer, was the first doctor to stick his finger into Garfield's wound. He didn't find the bullet, but reported that the president complained of heaviness, numbness, and pain in his legs, and that he declared himself to be "a dead man."

Next D. W. Bliss, a prominent Washington surgeon and Garfield's boyhood friend, succeeded in getting his heavy Nélaton probe (one tipped with rough porcelain) stuck in the fragments of a shattered rib. Removal was quite painful. Undaunted, he tried again with his little finger, then with a long, thin, flexible silver probe.

Over the next few days, the list of famous doctors who poked into Garfield's wound was impressive. So was the depth to which they probed; upon withdrawing his finger, the surgeon general of the navy reported feeling a perforated liver seven inch-

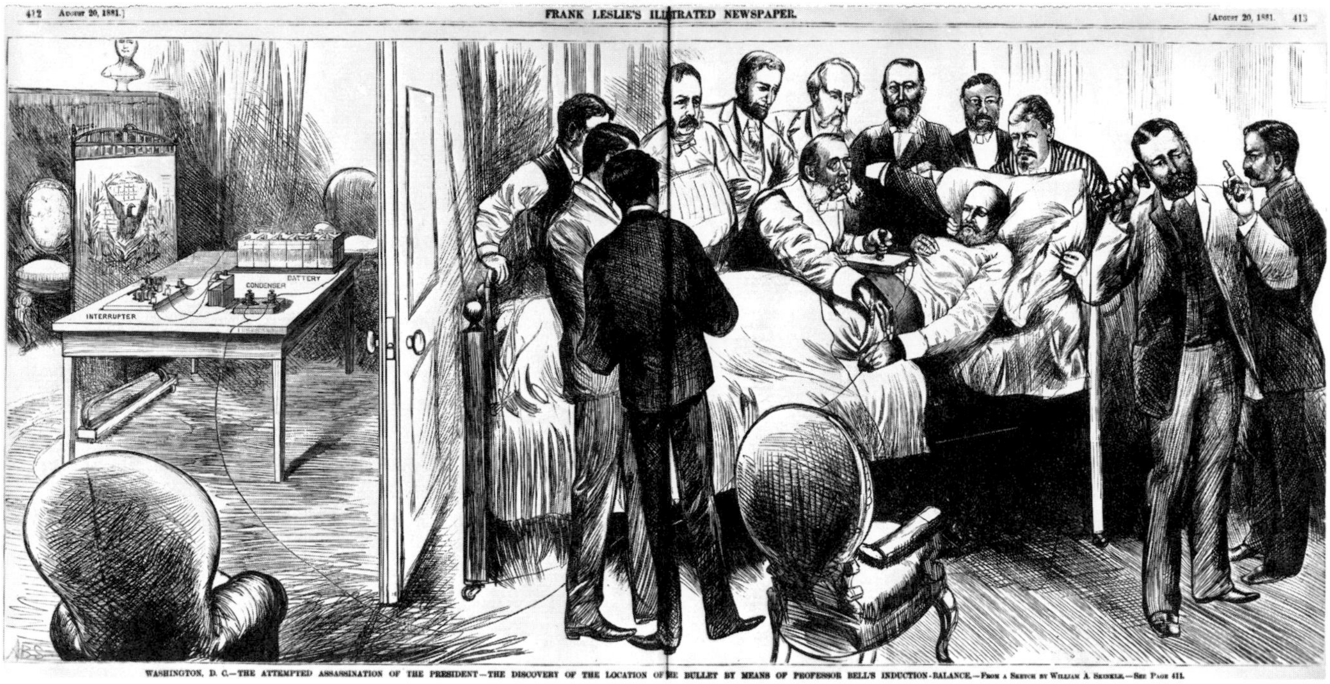

While the stricken president watched, Alexander Graham Bell used a device similar to a modern mine detector in a vain attempt to locate the bullet.

es from the bullet's entry point.

To relieve the president's discomfort in the muggy Washington heat, a Baltimore engineer improvised an air-conditioning scheme using an exhaust fan and 3,000 feet of turkish toweling saturated with iced saltwater. It brought the temperature in the room down from 99 degrees to the mid-70's.

On July 22 the wound began to suppurate. To enlarge and drain it, Dr. Hayes Agnew of Philadelphia performed two operations—one without anesthesia. Garfield was given "nutritional enemas" of eggs, beef extract, and whiskey, which did no good at all. Inexorably, the infection spread. By August 18 the president showed signs of blood poisoning. His face was paralyzed, his mind was wandering, and he had lost 80 pounds. Again the doctors operated without anesthesia.

Resigned to death, the president begged to be taken to the New Jersey shore. On September 6 his bed was mounted on springs in a railroad car cooled with iceboxes and, by way of a specially built spur line, he was taken to his cottage door. He rallied briefly, but on September 19, when the nicked artery finally burst, he died. At his autopsy, the bullet was found safely encapsulated in scar tissue far from any of the doctors' probings, doing no harm.

Today, of course, X-rays would find the bullet, the artery would be surgically repaired, and intravenous feeding would keep up Garfield's strength. Given such modern care, he might well have lived to a ripe old age.

Robert Todd Lincoln—Presidential Jinx?

Abraham Lincoln's eldest son, Robert Todd, was not at Ford's Theatre when his father was shot in April 1865, but he was at the president's side when he died, and was traumatized by the event.

Sixteen years later, he was secretary of war when James A. Garfield called him in to discuss the assassination. Two days after that meeting, Garfield was shot in Washington's Baltimore & Potomac Railroad Station just as Lincoln was entering to meet him.

And 20 years after that, on September 6, 1901, Lincoln was invited to attend the Pan-American exposition in Buffalo. As he came into the Exposition Hall, shots rang out, and William McKinley slumped to the floor, mortally wounded.

Lincoln became a recluse. "There is a certain fatality about presidential functions when I am present," he lamented.

Even in death, presidential tragedy remains close to him. He lies in Arlington National Cemetery, scant yards from the grave of yet another assassinated president—John F. Kennedy.

A Well-Kept Secret

The nation didn't know about Grover Cleveland's bout with cancer

Early in his second term as president, Grover Cleveland had a battle to win in Congress—one that he viewed as immensely important to the economic health of the nation. But before he could fight and win in the public arena, he had to conquer a terrifying personal foe: cancer of the jaw.

The public battle is well documented. The nation in 1893 was on the edge of a depression, which Cleveland blamed in part on the inflationary Sherman Silver Purchase Act (passed in 1890 during Benjamin Harrison's administration). It required the Treasury to buy 4.5 million ounces of silver each month and to issue notes against it redeemable in silver *or* gold. A firm believer in the gold standard, Cleveland vowed to use the full power of his office and his considerable oratorical skill to force the repeal of the act at a special session of Congress, scheduled for August 7, 1893.

Former President Cleveland and his wife, Frances, at home in Princeton, New Jersey, in 1907. The next year he died of a heart condition.

A grim diagnosis

Cleveland's private battle, less well known, did not become public knowledge until 1917, nine years after his death. The ordeal began on May 27, 1893—while brushing his teeth, he discovered a small rough area on the roof of his mouth. Tissue tests revealed malignancy: the cigar-loving chief executive had cancer of the jaw. Surgery was clearly necessary.

The 56-year-old president accepted the news stoically. To avert public panic, he ordered elaborate measures to ensure that word of his coming operation would not leak out. Not even his pregnant young wife was told about his illness or his imminent surgery.

While preparations for the operation were made with the deviousness of a spy mission, a cover story was issued that Cleveland was vacationing at his summer home. The surgery was to take place not in a hospital, but on the *Oneida,* a friend's yacht anchored in New York's East River. He was smuggled aboard under cover of darkness; the doctors arrived separately to avoid arousing suspicion.

Secret surgery

Just after noon on July 1 Cleveland settled his massive bulk into a chair that had been specially adapted to allow his head to tilt back. With five eminent medical men clustered around the operating chair, a dentist administered nitrous oxide—a new anesthetic later nicknamed laughing gas—and extracted two bicuspids to give access to the diseased area. Ether was then successfully administered, to the relief of the doctors, who had worried about its effect on their corpulent patient.

To avoid telltale facial scars, all work was done *inside* Cleveland's mouth, using two new instruments: a special retractor designed to push aside his heavy jowls and a battery-operated electric knife for cauterizing the wounds. Discovering a more advanced cancer than expected, the chief surgeon was forced to cut away most of the upper left jaw.

Although the president recuperated splendidly, the battle was not yet won. Lacking much of his upper jaw, he could barely communicate. His face was lopsided, and his speech was like that of a man with a cleft palate. But because rumors about his health had begun to spread, he could not postpone his appearance at the crucial congressional session—only a month away. A prosthetic device was quickly created of vulcanized rubber, which gave him an artificial jawline and made it possible for him to speak again. For hours each day he labored to improve his diction. Meanwhile, the device was refined and refitted. In the midst of these hardships, a second operation was performed to remove further malignant growth.

Cleveland kept his appointment with Congress and, speaking slowly but articulately, successfully urged the repeal of the Sherman Act. At the same time he allayed growing suspicions that he was ill. An account of the operation *did* appear in a newspaper (the dentist had spilled the beans), but the administration denied the report, saying that only routine dental surgery had been done. When the truth was finally revealed, it was no longer a sensational story and, in the midst of World War I, it received little public attention.

Did Every Pocket Have a Silver Lining?

A pack of thieves rode Bryan's campaign bandwagon

When William Jennings Bryan carried his 1896 presidential campaign across the country by train, sometimes delivering as many as 30 speeches a day, he unwittingly attracted a band of faithful followers he hadn't counted on: pickpockets.

The candidate of the Democratic, Populist, and National Silver parties, Bryan advocated the free coinage of silver, at a ratio to gold of 16 to 1. His chief purpose in stumping the country was to reach the farmers of the Midwest, who would benefit from the freer supply of money the silver standard would bring about. A gifted orator, the energetic 36-year-old nominee addressed huge crowds at every stop, assailing Wall Street and extolling the virtues of silver. To make the point that silver was as widely accepted as gold, he would ask his listeners to raise their hands if they carried gold in their pockets, and then ask the same of those who had silver.

What Bryan didn't realize, however, was that in doing so, he was aiding some 50 pickpockets who would hop on the train at the beginning of the day, blend in with the others on board, and then pile out at each whistlestop to work the tightly packed crowd that had assembled. The thievery became such a serious problem that Bryan finally had to hire a Pinkerton detective. On one occasion, he even interrupted a speech to point out a fast-fingered operator.

Meanwhile, his Republican opponent, William McKinley, conducted his entire campaign from his front porch in Canton, Ohio. Special railway excursion fares were offered, and between June and November 1896, close to 750,000 people visited him, arriving by the thousands from 30 states. McKinley and gold triumphed.

In Bryan's third and last campaign for the presidency in 1908, he was defeated by William Howard Taft. Still popular and influential in 1912, Bryan threw his support to fellow Democrat Woodrow Wilson and helped him win the election. In return, Wilson appointed him secretary of state. Above, Baltimore citizens crowd around Bryan after a speech, hoping to shake hands.

"A Grief Too Deep"

. . . drove TR to seek a new life in the Wild West

"There is a curse on this house," Theodore Roosevelt's brother told him. "Mother is dying and Alice is dying too." This was the news that greeted the future president on a foggy evening in 1884 as he burst into the family's New York mansion in anticipation of seeing his new daughter for the first time. By the next day he had lost his young wife—who had just given birth to their first child—and his mother. Both of them died on Valentine's Day, Teddy and Alice's fourth wedding anniversary. "The light has gone out of my life," TR later wrote in his diary.

Leaving the baby in his sister's care, the 25-year-old politician soon resumed his seat in the state legislature, but he was no longer the same man. "You could not talk to him about it," a fellow assemblyman noted sympathetically. "You could see at once that it was a grief too deep."

After the legislative session, Roosevelt headed west to the Dakota Badlands, where he had part interest in a cattle ranch. He bought another and ran it himself, planning to stay. The vigorous frontier life agreed with him, but in 1886, after a disastrous winter, he returned east. There he remarried and in time fathered five more children.

Although he mourned Alice, oddly enough she is not mentioned in his autobiography. But while out west, he *did* write movingly of her as "beautiful in face and form, and lovelier still in spirit; as a flower she grew, and as a fair young flower she died." And with these touching words, he laid to rest his grieving sadness and deep despair.

Describing himself as a "cowboy dandy," TR posed in the fringed frontier splendor that recalled his days in the Badlands. Ridiculed at first for his affected eastern speech—a favorite expletive was "By Godfrey!"—he gained instant respectability in the Dakota Territory by knocking out a cowpoke who'd called him four-eyes. Soon "Hasten forward quickly there!" (one of his early roundup orders) had entered the local slanguage. Later capturing a gang of rustlers, TR went on to become a deputy sheriff.

"Mr. Rucevelt's" New Word List

Teddy Roosevelt was "surprized" at the ruckus "razed" in response to his 1906 order to the public printer. In it he listed 300 words that henceforth would be spelled according to the Simplified Spelling Board guidelines.

Funded by millionaire industrialist and philanthropist Andrew Carnegie, the organization crusaded for deleting the u *in "honour" and "parlour," changes that eventually came into general usage. (More radical ideas, like* kist *for* kissed *and* tho *for* though *have not endured.)*

The press reacted to TR's order with sarcasm. One editor wrote that "nuthing escapes Mr. Rucevelt. No subject is tu hi fr him to takl, nor tu lo for him tu notis."

Questioning the president's power to change American orthography, Congress instructed the printing office that all the material sent to its chambers contain standard spellings.

Roosevelt regretfully withdrew his order in response to the general outcry. Yet he later wrote that he was glad he "did the thing anyhow."

DRAWING THE LINE IN MISSISSIPPI

Leading the Teddy Bear Parade . . .

While hunting on the Mississippi Delta in 1902, TR refused to shoot a bear that had been run down by hounds, knocked unconscious, and tied to a tree. In depicting the scene, cartoonist Clifford Berryman inadvertently spawned a sensation: the Teddy Bear. There are two versions of how the stuffed bears came to be sold. In one, Brooklyn storeowners Rose and Morris Michtom asked Roosevelt for permission to use his nickname, and he agreed. In the other, a German woman, Margarete Steiff, made a cute bear that was an instant international hit. In any case, the results were impressive: between 1903 and 1911 millions were sold, and what began as a fad survives as a classic.

A White House First

Guess who came to dinner

When Booker T. Washington joined Theodore Roosevelt for dinner in 1901, he was aware of the political danger. But it was the first time that a black man had been invited to dine at the White House, and the head of the Tuskegee Institute felt obliged to accept as a representative of his people.

Southern papers, charging that Roosevelt's action declared the "Negro . . . the social equal of the white man," shocked the ex-Rough Rider. When the same papers attacked Washington for betraying his stated philosophy of blacks and whites being "separate as the fingers" socially, but "one as the hand in all things essential to mutual progress," the black leader hoped the furor would not erode white support for his cause.

Neither man ever commented on the incident. Roosevelt, however, was embarrassed by his political clumsiness. But Washington, often attacked for accommodating segregation, became a hero among blacks for his "courage" in accepting the invitation.

Cloak-and-dagger Government?

How members of Congress chastised TR for spying on them

In a controversy spawned by Capitol Hill rumors and political maneuvers, Washington in 1908 was alive with speculation that President Theodore Roosevelt had used the Secret Service to compile dossiers on the private lives of congressmen—and that he meant to use them. Congress was looking for a way to strike back.

The Secret Service, the Treasury Department's investigative branch, was at the core of the dispute. During his administration TR had made liberal use of it in his anticorruption crusades. The defenders of the service argued that, as the federal government's only corps of trained investigators, its survival was vital. Its detractors compared the service to Napoleon's secret police—perhaps inspired by the fact that Attorney General Charles Bonaparte was a great-nephew of Napoleon I. In a carefully worded bill, Congress moved to restrict the Secret Service's power. Roosevelt fought back with his major weapon: eloquence.

A war of words

In verbal and written attacks, legislators claimed that the president sought despotic powers and a secret police force. Roosevelt declared that he only wanted the tools to fight corruption, even if his inquiries brought him right up to the halls of Congress. Charges and countercharges in the press and on the Hill flew thick and fast. Finally, on January 8, 1909, Congress officially defended its "maligned integrity." By an overwhelming vote of 212 to 36, the House tabled (that is, formally ignored) the section of Roosevelt's annual message that criticized the restriction of the Secret Service. Not since Andrew Jackson's administration in the 1830's had a chief executive suffered this insulting form of congressional rebuke.

In a way both sides won. As a result of Roosevelt's maneuvering, a bureau of investigation (later the FBI) was formed in the Justice Department. And Congress, sensitive to the slightest hint of domestic governmental spying, had sent a clear signal that such tactics would not be tolerated.

The President Who Created His Own Political Party

A 20th-century tale: The short, sassy story of a lively Bull Moose

Teddy Roosevelt's campaign song, "There'll Be a Hot Time in the Old Town Tonight," befit his oratorical style.

The Bull Moose Party charged into the political arena with all the energy of its colorful, dynamic standard-bearer, Theodore Roosevelt. TR was denied the Republican presidential nomination in 1912 despite his contention that he was "as fit as a bull moose," so he left the Republicans to run under the banner of the Progressive Party. It was promptly renamed the Bull Moose Party in his honor.

While the new party's platform called for liberal reform, its true impetus stemmed from Roosevelt's desire to defeat the portly man who had succeeded him as president in 1908, William Howard Taft. They had once been friends and allies, but their political differences and personal animosity had changed that. Taft characterized TR as a "dangerous egotist" and a "demagogue," and Roosevelt countered by calling Taft a "fathead" and a "puzzlewit." Although the ever-crusading TR claimed that "we stand at Armageddon and we battle for the Lord," Senator Robert La Follette, Sr., of Wisconsin, saw his candidacy as an "overmastering craving for a third term."

Attempted murder

On October 14, while campaigning in Milwaukee, Roosevelt had a close brush with death, which he dramatically turned to his advantage as only he could. He was leaving his hotel, having stuffed a copy of his long speech into his breast pocket, when he was confronted by a gun-wielding bartender who fired at him at point-blank range. (The assailant was driven to the deed because he had dreamed that McKinley's ghost demanded TR's death.) The bullet penetrated Roosevelt's coat, vest, eyeglass case, and the sheaf of heavy paper in his pocket, finally cracking a rib. TR insisted on going ahead with the speech, but his announcement of the assassination attempt was met with cries of "Fake." Baring his bloody shirt, he bellowed, "It takes more than one bullet to kill a bull moose."

Off the campaign trail for two weeks recovering from the incident, Roosevelt made a spectacular comeback at Madison Square Garden in New York. With an enthusiastic crowd of 16,000 cheering supporters responding to his energetic arm-waving and powerful rhetoric, he made one of his finest speeches.

And the winner is . . .

The election resulted in a Woodrow Wilson landslide, but Roosevelt's showing brought him in second with 88 electoral votes. He thus achieved his sought-after personal triumph over Taft, who was humiliated with a mere 8 votes. Although the Bull Moose Party was soon dissolved, briefly resurfacing in 1924 to sponsor La Follette for president, its platform foreshadowed Franklin Delano Roosevelt's New Deal.

A Bathtub for Big Bill

The ability of the White House staff to supply creature comforts was severely tested in 1909. There wasn't a tub big enough for the new president, William ("Big Bill") Howard Taft, who carried well over 300 pounds on a 6-foot 2-inch frame. The solution came from the captain of the battleship North Carolina. *Told of an approaching presidential visit, the fast-thinking officer had a special tub constructed. Satisfied with his soak at sea, Taft had the tub installed in the White House. Seven feet long and 41 inches wide, the bathtub could (as proven by the White House workmen posing here) accommodate four normal-size men.*

A Parade of Political Animals

Cartoonists invented the popular party symbols

The Democratic donkey and the Republican elephant were introduced more than a century ago. Both proud symbols were born in a spirit of mockery. Although the first cartoon picturing the Democratic Party as a donkey actually appeared in 1837, with outgoing President Andrew Jackson astride the beast, true credit for popularizing the Democratic animal goes to cartoonist Thomas Nast. Drawn in 1870, the creature was labeled "The Copperhead Press," a reference to Democratic newspapers that sympathized with the South. Nast used other animals, too, to represent Democrats—notably New York's Tammany tiger. But his comic donkey struck the public's fancy and became the party symbol.

The Republican elephant, a Nast creation, appeared in 1874. With midterm elections approaching, the New York *Herald* suggested that Ulysses S. Grant planned to run for an unprecedented third term in 1876. The paper dubbed this Caesarism, after the Roman emperors. Weeks later, the *Herald* reported (falsely) that New York City's zoo animals had escaped and were roaming Central Park. On November 7, just before elections, *Harper's Weekly* published a Nast cartoon showing a donkey clad in a lion's skin marked "Caesarism" scaring other beasts—including an elephant labeled "The Republican Vote." The elephant quickly emerged as the Republican symbol.

The donkey, representing Democrats, first appeared in an 1837 cartoon (top); Thomas Nast's cartoon version of the Republican elephant (above) was published in 1874.

Boston Curtis Runs for Office

In this case, the candidate was a mule

In 1936 the Democratic mayor of Milton, Washington, the Honorable Kenneth Simmons, placed a candidate named Boston Curtis on the ballot for Republican precinct committeeman. Curtis, who ran as a "dark horse," delivered no speeches and made no promises. Astonishingly, his unusual political campaign proved successful at the polls; he won by a unanimous vote of 52 to 0. But Curtis, being a mule, was different from other candidates for public office, and he became famous. As "the people's choice," he was featured in national magazines and a major film studio tried to place him under contract. His election even momentarily upstaged FDR's victory over Republican Alfred M. Landon in the presidential race that year.

Simmons claimed that he sponsored the mule's candidacy to demonstrate the carelessness of the voters. Perhaps he was also demonstrating a wry humor, for he had succeeded in running the offspring of a donkey—symbol of the Democrats—for a Republican office.

Jeannette Rankin poses for photographers as she leaves Washington to lobby for world peace at the Republican and Democratic conventions in Chicago in 1932.

The First Congresswoman

A pacifist who voted against world war—twice

Elected as a representative from Montana in 1916 and again in 1940, Jeannette Rankin, the first woman to serve in Congress, is best recalled as the only member of either house to vote against the nation's entry into both world wars. She was born in the Montana Territory, where women, as recent pioneers, commanded more political respect than did their eastern counterparts. In 1911, at 31, she began a campaign that gave Montana's women the right to vote. On April 2, 1917, Rankin took her seat in the House and four days later was considering the resolution to enter World War I. When her name was called, she said, "I want to stand by my country, but I cannot vote for war." She was not alone; the resolution passed, but there were 50 nays.

In 1919 Rankin became a lobbyist for social justice and world peace. Then, with Europe again at war in 1940, she ran for Congress once more—and won. When President Roosevelt asked for a declaration of war following Japan's attack on Pearl Harbor, she again voted nay, saying, "As a woman I can't go to war, and I refuse to send anyone else." This time she was alone; the vote was 388 to 1.

After World War II she continued to crusade for peace. In 1968, at 87, she led the 5,000-woman Jeannette Rankin Brigade up Capitol Hill to protest U.S. involvement in Vietnam. She died five years later, at age 92.

As the Candle Flickered

Campaigning from a prison cell, he got almost a million votes for president

Labor leader Eugene V. Debs ran for president five times as the standard-bearer of the Socialist Party, but his best showing was in 1920, when he campaigned from a cell in the Atlanta Federal Penitentiary. He was serving time for speaking out in 1918 against the Espionage Act—by its own terms, to criticize the law was to break it. In the final weeks of the campaign, Debs was allowed to issue one press bulletin a week. On Election Eve he wrote: "The result will be as it should be. The people will vote for what they think they want, to the extent that they think at all, and they, too, will not be disappointed."

The election, in which he received 919,799 votes (about 5.7 percent of Warren Harding's showing) marked the end of socialism as a third-party movement. It was, according to one Socialist leader, "the last flicker of the dying candle."

Combining rural native populism with the class-conscious concerns of foreign-born urban workers, the dynamic Debs rose to fame as a railway union leader.

To the delight of his devoted wife (seated at his right), President Woodrow Wilson carries on a tradition begun by his predecessor in office, William Howard Taft, as he opens the 1916 baseball season. Three and a half years later he was incapacitated by a stroke.

Was There Once a Woman President?

Not according to history books, but there was Mrs. Wilson

The Iron Queen. The Presidentress. The Regent. These were some of the names they called Edith Wilson after her husband suffered a massive stroke while speaking in Pueblo, Colorado, in 1919. The First Lady came to dominate the White House. A senator coined the phrase that was on everyone's lips: Petticoat Government.

Although she barred everyone, Cabinet officers and trusted aides alike, from the president, Mrs. Wilson insisted that she had no role in executive decisions. "The only decision that was mine was what was important and . . . when to present matters to my husband." Daily bulletins assured the country that the president was recovering, but, in fact, he was partially paralyzed and nearly blind. When Wilson was scheduled to address Congress, the message sent to Capitol Hill was instead a patchwork of reports by Cabinet members, with penciled corrections by Edith herself. Some lawmakers observed that Wilson knew nothing about the message, and the government limped along, grimly controlled by the First Lady.

A descendant of Indian princess Pocahontas, Edith was a strange match for this president. Shrewd, with little formal education (while Wilson held a Ph.D.), she was a political innocent who, though a 20-year resident of Washington, had never visited the White House. Indeed, initially she could not even recall who she had favored in the 1912 election—which Wilson, a Democrat, had won. But after their marriage she rapidly became his confidante in all matters, enabling her to assert her influence during his illness.

After his death in 1924 she was as protective of his memory as she had been of him, preserving memorabilia and tirelessly attending the dedication of any public building named in his honor. And 44 years after she stood at her husband's side as he took the oath of office, Edith Wilson appeared at the inauguration of another Democratic president, John F. Kennedy. Less than a year later she died at the age of 89. In her obituary *The New York Times* noted that "some went so far as to characterize her as the first woman President of the United States." And, indeed, many still agree.

Take This Job and . . .

Although twice elected vice president, Thomas Riley Marshall was determined never to be president; he said it would be "a tragedy for the country." Long before Woodrow Wilson's incapacitating stroke, Marshall stopped going to Cabinet meetings and took to the lecture circuit to supplement his income. So remote did he become from affairs of state that, at first, no one at the White House thought it necessary to tell him how serious the president's illness was.

But Marshall did achieve immortality of a sort. Once, while presiding over a dull Senate debate, the vice president—who was seldom seen without a stogie clamped between his teeth—uttered the unforgettable line: "What this country needs is a good five-cent cigar."

The Harding Scandals

Revelations private and presidential marked a short, sensational administration

Nominated by "15 men in a smoke-filled room," the handsome and popular Warren G. Harding was elected in 1920. By the time he died in 1923—amid rumors of suicide or murder—his administration had been "responsible in its short two years and five months for more concentrated robbery and rascality than any other in the whole history of the Federal Government," according to a historian writing in 1931. His busy love life also became grist for scandal mills.

Political chicanery

Easygoing and malleable, Harding hadn't wanted the presidency. Put up to running by his domineering wife and by a political boss, he won by a wide margin.

Shortly after the inauguration, Secretary of the Interior Albert Fall leased naval oil reserves, including some in Teapot Dome, Wyoming, to business cronies, becoming some $300,000 richer in the process. When the deal was made public, Fall's leases were declared fraudulent, and he eventually went to jail. Others of the president's "Ohio gang" (he was from Marion, Ohio) also got rich through his free-wheeling patronage.

In July 1923, on a trip west, Harding was diagnosed as having food poisoning, then suffered a heart attack. He died on August 2. There was no autopsy, and many insiders came to believe the rumor that Mrs. Harding had poisoned her husband to save him from disgrace.

Personal peccadillos

In 1927 a sensational book appeared, *The President's Daughter,* in which a woman named Nan Britton told the story of her long love affair with Harding and claimed that she had borne his only child. According to her tale—440 pages of it—she fell in love with Harding at 14 when he, age 45, was running for governor of Ohio. By 1917 Nan was in New York, writing to Harding for help in getting a job. He came to see her and "tucked $30 in my brand new silk stocking." Between their ensuing meetings in hotel rooms around the country, he wrote her long love letters—all of which Nan claimed to have destroyed by agreement with Harding. She said he had destroyed her letters, too, but after his death Mrs. Harding burned most of his personal correspondence, and so the truth may never be known. Tantalizingly, one empty folder, labeled "Heart-Throb Letters," survived.

Harding's letters to Nan could yet turn up. Another cache of love letters really *did* turn up—in the house of an elderly Ohio recluse named Carrie Phillips, the wife of one of Harding's best friends. They show that Carrie "was the love of Harding's life." Their torrid 10-year affair apparently began when the two couples toured Europe together in 1909. Between meetings, Harding wrote Mrs. Phillips sexually explicit 40-page love letters and even verse, posthumously revealing an unexpectedly lyrical side of his personality.

Harding had many other affairs—he even maintained a room next to the Oval Office for quick liaisons—and seemed to be insatiable, perhaps a victim of satyriasis, an excessive, unmanageable need for sex. The long, graphic love letters he wrote may have been another symptom of the disease.

At his death, Harding was still popular and respected. In the years that followed, however, his reputation was badly tarnished by scandals that continued to surface long after he was in his grave.

At home in Ohio in 1920 (above), the year he won the election, the personable president posed with Mrs. Harding, five years his senior. He called her the Duchess. The beauty Nan Britton (right) claimed in a sensational book that Harding had fathered her daughter, Elizabeth Ann.

The Spotlight of Scandal . . .

has caught many a politician in its glare

Americans have always loved a scandal. Through the years some have wrought great changes on the political scene.

• Consider **Andrew Jackson.** His Cabinet became ensnarled in a bitter dispute over the marriage of Jackson's close friend Secretary of War John Eaton to Peggy O'Neale, a tavern-keeper's daughter whose first husband had died at sea. Because of Peggy's questionable past, the Eatons were ostracized by most of Washington society, including Vice President John C. Calhoun. When Jackson's temper came to a boil in 1831, Secretary of State Martin Van Buren, an Eaton defender, resigned to, as he said, enable Jackson to get rid of his quarrelsome Cabinet. When Eaton also resigned, Jackson was able to force the resignation of three pro-Calhoun Cabinet members, thus dampening Calhoun's presidential hopes. Van Buren, not Calhoun, became Jackson's vice president in 1832 and won the presidency in 1836. (That same year Jackson appointed Eaton ambassador to Spain, where Mrs. Eaton, cavorting at the court of Queen Maria Cristina, became known as "Pompadour Peggy.")

A cartoon that appeared in 1884 called the presidential candidate's illegitimate son "another voice for Cleveland."

• In 1884, during **Grover Cleveland's** first run for the presidency, it was revealed that he had fathered the child of a young widow who lived in Buffalo, New York. Determined to face the scandal head-on, Cleveland, then a bachelor, admitted paternity and went on to win the election. His honesty did much to defuse the issue despite a popular campaign chant that his detractors enjoyed: "Ma, Ma, where's my Pa? Gone to the White House, Ha, Ha, Ha!"

• Even though the spotlight is harsh on a president, it often takes time for scandal to emerge from the shadows. Years after his assassination, women came forward who claimed to have known **John F. Kennedy** intimately. The most sensational was Judith Campbell Exner, who readily detailed her two-year relationship with the chief executive. Records show that the FBI was onto their liaison and that she was reputed to be the mistress of a Chicago crime boss as well. To many, it seemed inconceivable that one woman could have had simultaneous affairs with the president of the United States and a Mafia leader.

• For other politicians, the spotlight of scandal can be glaring and instant. **Wilbur Mills,** 65 years old and longtime chairman of the powerful House Ways and Means Committee, was photographed in 1974 cavorting on the stage of a seedy Boston nightclub with stripper Fanne Fox. Two months earlier, the duo had burst into the headlines when she bolted from a car she was sharing with Mills and dove into Washington's Tidal Basin at 2 A.M. Although Mills was reelected that year, the incidents essentially ended his long political career.

This 1974 photo reveals the friendship of a stripper, Fanne Foxe, and Representative Wilbur Mills of Arkansas. He publicly acknowledged that he suffered from alcoholism and did not seek reelection in 1976.

Musical Chairs in the Governor's Office

A case of "overenthusiastic" fund-raising leads to turnstile politics

North Dakota politics were turbulent during the Depression, and at the center of the turmoil was Gov. William "Fighting Bill" Langer, a cigar-chomping maverick Republican who took office in 1933.

The new governor delighted his constituents with fiery rhetoric and folksy humor, but in his fund-raising zeal—he demanded that state employees contribute a percentage of their salaries to his political organization—he ran afoul of the law. Since some state workers were paid in part by federal agencies, Langer was charged with conspiring to defraud the U.S. government. His trial, headlined "Uncle Sam Versus Bill Langer," ended in conviction in June 1934, but he refused to step down.

Confusion ensued. Having barricaded himself in the governor's office, Langer issued a state declaration of independence and proclaimed martial law. At one point he even hurled a cuspidor through a window. Only after the state supreme court ruled him ineligible to serve as governor, in July 1934, did he eventually resign in favor of Lt. Gov. Ole H. Olson.

Still, Fighting Bill kept battling. He campaigned vigorously for his wife, who replaced him as his party's nominee for governor but lost to Democrat Thomas Moodie. Inaugurated in January 1935, Moodie served just four days. The relentless Langer revealed that the victor had voted in another state within the past five years, which made him ineligible, and so *again* the state's high court disqualified a governor. Moodie resigned and Lt. Gov. Walter Welford was sworn in—North Dakota's fourth governor in a mere seven months.

A tireless campaigner and inveterate handshaker, the charismatic Huey Long poses with a group of staunch supporters (left) who, when they heard that he had greeted a foreign delegation in gaudy pajamas, added to his collection of colorful sleepwear. The politician wielded such power that in later years many viewed him as a rival to FDR; one cartoonist even depicted multiple images of the pajama-clad Kingfish haunting the president's sleep (below).

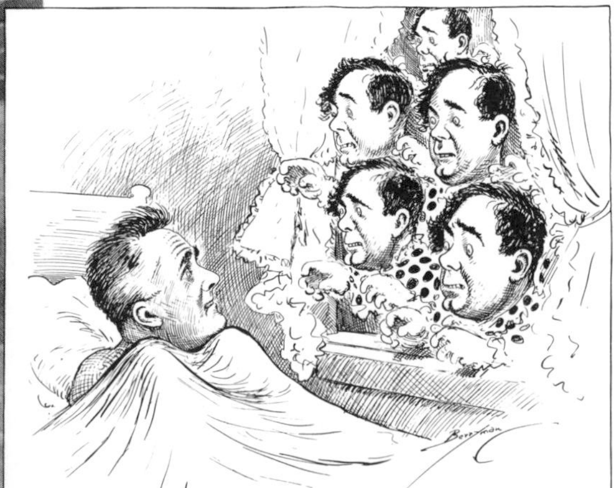

The Dynasty Continues

Earl K. Long: The governor who was declared sane

Huey's younger brother Earl carried a political tradition into the late 1950's as Louisiana's three-term governor. But in his last term he had to have himself declared sane to keep his job.

When "Ol' Earl's" wild behavior caused his family to have him committed to a Texas institution, he objected violently, saying he was a "governor in exile, by force and kidnapping." Later he agreed to be treated at a New Orleans clinic. But it was a short stay; after a day he simply drove off to the capitol at Baton Rouge. Promptly recommitted, he protested that his hospitalization was unlawful imprisonment. When the state hospital board agreed to hear his case, he fired the hospital superintendent, replacing him with an old friend who declared him sane. Earl died in 1960, just months after completing his term.

Calling himself the Last of the Red-Hot Papas, Ol' Earl Long—always fiery, often profane—warms up for one of his political harangues.

Clothes Make the Man?

A splash of color for the colorful Kingfish

When the German consul and the commander of a German cruiser paid a courtesy call on Gov. Huey P. Long of Louisiana in 1930, they were hardly prepared for his sartorial splendor. For there was the Kingfish in green silk pajamas, a red and blue robe, and blue slippers, looking, as one reporter put it, like "an explosion in a paint factory." Seeing that the consul was flustered, the irrepressible Long returned the visit the next day dressed in pin-striped pants borrowed from a hotel manager, a waiter's boiled shirt, a swallowtail coat, and a collar "so high I had to stand on a stool to spit over it." Received cordially amid military pomp and splendor, Governor Long impressed the commander as "a very interesting, intelligent and unusual person."

This colorful, freewheeling behavior was typical of the man who had become the state's youngest governor in 1928. Sailing into office on the campaign slogan "Every man a king, but no man wears a crown," he made himself the virtual dictator of Louisiana. He provided free school textbooks, raised funds for a university, built a modern highway system, and expanded hospitals and other institutions—largely financed by the taxes imposed on utilities and oil companies. He also used every means to stifle his political enemies. When, in his habitually high-handed manner, he imposed a new, heavy tax on the oil industry, Long incurred the wrath of a hostile legislature, which promptly impeached him on 19 counts. But he wiggled off the hook by forcing 15 state senators to pledge allegiance to him, no matter what the evidence revealed.

Cleared of the charges, Long rallied his supporters and got himself elected to the U.S. Senate in 1930—yet he continued to serve as governor for two more years. Arriving in Washington in 1932, he took on bigger game: FDR and his New Deal. In short order Long was proposing a radical plan to redistribute the nation's wealth through a tax-the-rich scheme and demanding that the federal government furnish every family with an allowance, an annual income, and benefits. He called it the Share Our Wealth program.

By 1935, as a possible third-party presidential candidate, he was considered a real threat to Roosevelt's reelection. But on September 8, 1935, while preparing to curtail New Deal programs in Louisiana, the indomitable Long was shot down by an assassin in the state capitol. Although he died two days later, his spirit lives on, for the Louisiana Pied Piper left as his legacy a powerful political dynasty.

Goat Gland Brinkley's Run for Governor

Sexual rejuvenation and other roads to success

The desperation of the Great Depression gave rise to a new breed of populist politician. But none was stranger than John Romulus Brinkley, the so-called Goat Gland Doctor of Kansas. Brinkley—whose questionable medical certification came from several diploma mills, including the Eclectic Medical University in Kansas City, Missouri—had gained a considerable following in the 1920's with his claims of sexual rejuvenation for aging or "tired" men. Brinkley's cure: A transplant of young buck goat sex glands into the gonads of human beings.

Brinkley owned a radio station, KFKB—"Kansas First, Kansas Best"—and used it to advertise his services. Men flocked to the Brinkley Gland Clinic in Milford, Kansas, where they paid a minimum of $750 for the surgery. By 1928 Goat Gland Brinkley was performing from 20 to 40 operations a week. He was reputed to be a millionaire, having implanted perhaps 5,000 pairs of goat glands.

Brinkley's activities also attracted the attention of the American Medical Association, which quickly branded him a "blatant quack of unsavory professional antecedents." In 1930 the Kansas medical board finally stripped him of his license. (A year later the Federal Communications Commission shut down his radio station.)

To "avenge his reputation and save his business," Goat Gland Brinkley announced himself as a write-in candidate for governor of Kansas in 1930. His slogan: "Clean out, clean up and keep Kansas clean." The political joke proved to be a serious threat. He received one of the largest write-in votes in American history, finishing a close third in the race. Two years later he tried again, using his powerful, newly purchased radio station just over the Mexican border to blow his political horn. But the voters were unimpressed, and he lost to incumbent Alfred M. Landon, who would soon be a presidential candidate. On his third try, in 1934, he was trounced.

Brinkley turned again to the business of sexual rejuvenation, but this time without the use of goat glands. Establishing a practice in Del Rio, Texas, and another in Little Rock, Arkansas, he promised sexual restoration through prostate surgery and a cure-all made of a little hydrochloric acid and some blue dye. Over the years, his political views drifted far right to a growing fascist movement. By the late 1930's expensive lawsuits had stripped him of much of his wealth, and he died poor in 1942. While the political impact of the Goat Gland Doctor was slight, his nefarious medical career had social value: it led to significant reforming legislation to protect patients.

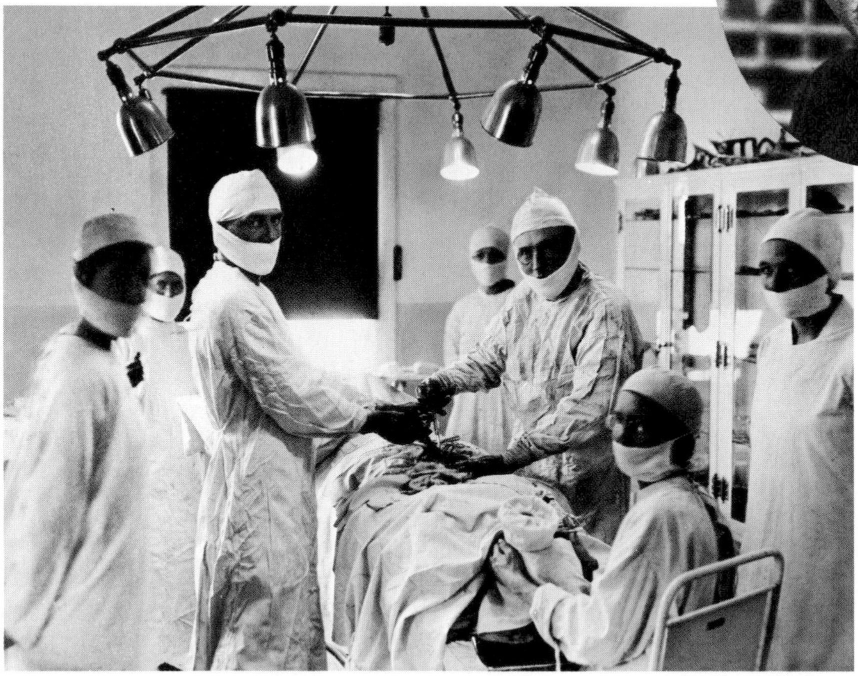

By surgically implanting glands of selected billy goats, "Dr." Brinkley promised a rekindled sex life to all the men who traveled to his Kansas clinic.

The Hillbilly Politician

They all laughed when Pappy O'Daniel ran for governor of Texas

In 1938 the Democrats nominated a man for governor of Texas who was so uninterested in politics that he had never voted. He was W. Lee O'Daniel, a Fort Worth radio entertainer known as Pappy, no doubt from the flour advertisement that opened his daily program: "Please pass the biscuits, Pappy."

Born in Ohio in 1890 and raised on a Kansas farm, O'Daniel had gone into the flour business; in 1935 he formed his own company to market Hillbilly Flour. By then he had an army of loyal listeners and was broadcasting hillbilly, religious, and historical programs. Fans urged Pappy to run for governor, and in 1938 he agreed. His platform was the Ten Commandments.

O'Daniel's candidacy was widely regarded as laughable, but when he stumped the state, he drew big crowds. They listened when he railed against politicians and demanded $30 a month for everyone over 65. On July 23 he garnered 51 percent of the vote.

Reelected governor in 1940, O'Daniel left the office in 1941 to run for the U.S. Senate. He won, defeating an ambitious young representative, Lyndon B. Johnson.

Pappy literally sang his own praises during the 1938 campaign. Accompanying him were his two sons: Mike was the fiddler, and Pat played the banjo.

A Bit of Chinese Chatter in the White House

President Hoover, will you repeat that please?

When Herbert Hoover and his wife, Lou, wanted to speak privately in the presence of White House guests, they spoke Chinese. They had learned the language during their postwedding years in China, which had climaxed in the nightmare of the Boxer Rebellion of 1900.

In 1899 Hoover, then a young mining engineer, became a consultant to the Chinese director of the Ministry of Mines, who hoped to locate gold in the interior. The quest sent Hoover far afield.

While on a trip in May 1900 he heard alarming reports of the ominous antiforeign movement spearheaded by the *I Ho Tuan,* known as the Boxers, and so he returned to Peking. There he found Lou seriously ill. The Hoovers took a train to nearby Tientsin, where there was an able physician, and returned to their home in the city's foreign compound, a settlement about a quarter-mile wide and a mile long, edging the Peiho River.

On June 10 "there exploded in the faces of two 26-year-old peaceful Americans," Hoover later wrote in his memoirs, "an event that was to modify their lives, and also give them something to talk about 'for the rest of their born days.' " That morning they and the 300 other foreigners in the compound were awakened by shells bursting overhead. They were under attack by some 25,000 well-armed Chinese troops led by the fanatic Boxers. While men, women, and children prepared to defend themselves, Hoover supervised the task of barricading the exposed sides of the settlement, using sacks of grain to build walls.

The anticipated mass attack never came, but as Hoover described it, some 60,000 shells were fired into the compound during the month-long siege and at times the cross streets were "simply canals of moving lead." Miraculously, there were few civilian casualties. Toward mid-July relief forces reached the settlement and freed those inside. After a brief trip to London, the Hoovers returned to the Orient, and by early 1901 the future president was back in Tientsin attempting to rebuild the mining operation.

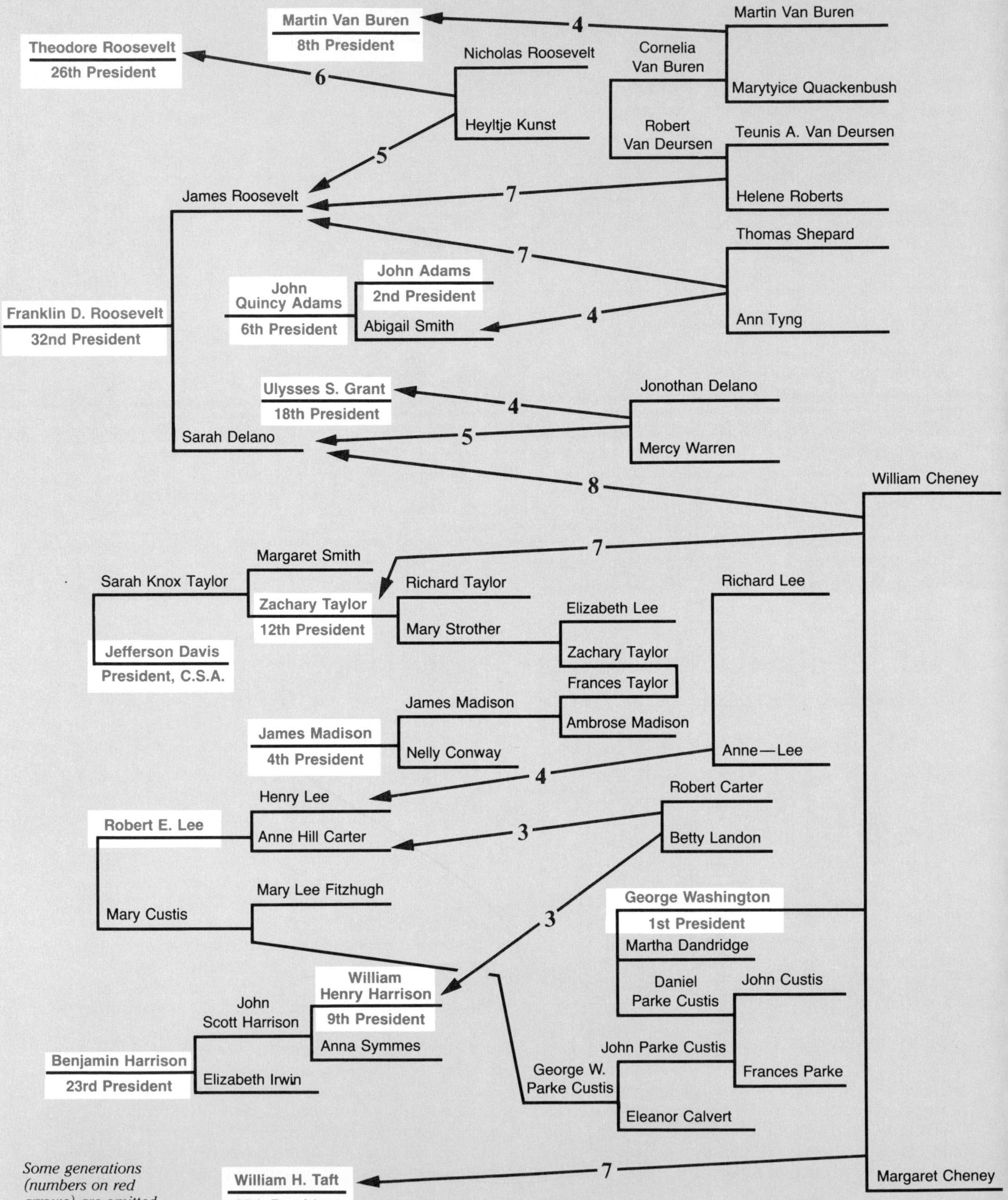

Some generations (numbers on red arrows) are omitted because of space considerations.

A Dozen Presidents on the Family Tree

Assiduously tracing the Roosevelt roots, genealogists discovered that FDR was related to no fewer than 11 previous presidents of the United States. Although he did not seem to attach great significance to this distinguished lineage (sometimes dubbed the Royal Family of America), FDR's mother relished recalling antecedents who included "half the aristocracy of Europe and all that of the Hudson River Valley."

1924: His polio attack behind him, the dynamic FDR met with politicians after the Democratic Convention.

The FDR Dime

Why is Roosevelt's picture on the 10-cent coin?

Today polio is just one of several ailments American children must be immunized against before attending school. But in 1921, when Franklin D. Roosevelt contracted polio, it inspired more fear than any other childhood disease.

Although 75 percent of its victims were youngsters (hence the name infantile paralysis), FDR was 39 when polio struck him. At first the attack was pronounced a bad cold, then a spinal blood clot; finally Roosevelt's high fever and paralyzed legs persuaded his doctors that he had polio. Beyond the diagnosis, physicians could do little—there was no cure.

Fighting back

Determined not to let his infirmity end his political career, FDR took charge of his own rehabilitation, exercising his upper body so strenuously that he bragged, "Maybe my legs aren't so good, but look at those shoulders." His burly torso created such an air of overall well-being, in fact, that many people were unaware of the extent of his disabilities.

But if something happened to the braces and crutches that supported him when he stood, he was helpless. In front of 100,000 people gathered at Franklin Field in Philadelphia to hear him accept the nomination for a second presidential term in 1936, one brace snapped. Roosevelt fell forward, unable to move until a bodyguard righted him and refastened the support. "It was the most frightful five minutes of my life," he later admitted.

Warm Springs

The only freedom the chief executive had from braces, canes, and crutches came when he swam; he was especially invigorated by the mineral waters at Warm Springs, Georgia. In 1926, wanting other polio victims to have the same opportunity, he donated a substantial portion of his personal wealth to the establishment of a foundation at Warm Springs.

Despite his generosity, however, Roosevelt's ambitious plans meant that Warm Springs operated in the red. Various fund-raising campaigns had failed to erase the deficit when entertainer Eddie Cantor suggested a more effective approach in 1937: Why not ask everybody in the country to send a dime for polio research to the president at the White House? Cantor even suggested a catchy name—the March of Dimes.

The response was overwhelming; sometimes as many as 150,000 dime-laden letters a day arrived at the White House. Beginning with that first campaign, contributions were used not only to pay for treatment of polio victims, but for the research necessary to triumph over the disease.

The dimes

FDR didn't live to see that victory. But he and the March of Dimes had become so closely identified that, after his death in 1945, Congress voted to honor his memory by depicting him on the coin. The first Roosevelt dimes were released on January 30, 1946, FDR's birthday *and* the annual kick-off day of the March of Dimes appeal.

Millions of the Roosevelt coins had been contributed to the March of Dimes by April 12, 1955. On that day—exactly ten years after Roosevelt died of a stroke at his cottage, the "Little White House," in his beloved Warm Springs—Dr. Jonas Salk's discovery of the first polio vaccine was announced.

No Room at the Top

A tale of three governors—and only one office

Surrounded by supporters, Herman Talmadge learns that a judge has dismissed a lawsuit seeking to oust him from the governorship. But his jubilation was short-lived, for Georgia's highest court overruled the decision.

When Eugene Talmadge died in 1946, before he could be sworn in as governor of Georgia, the state legislature appointed his 33-year-old son, Herman, to the job. But two other men also claimed the governorship, and the ensuing political chaos resembled what one magazine called "something conceived at night by three unemployed radio writers."

Ellis Arnall, still the incumbent governor, asserted that since Herman Talmadge had not been an announced gubernatorial candidate, he could not assume the office. Undaunted, Talmadge moved into Arnall's outer office anyway, saying, "I do not object to Ellis Arnall hanging around as long as he wants to." Arnall countered that the "pretender" was welcome to visit.

Chaos prevailed as Talmadge men switched the office locks, forcing Arnall to camp out in the capitol lobby. Lawsuits were initiated; countersuits were filed. At one point a whiff of tear gas and a firecracker, mistaken for a gunshot, enlivened the scene.

The standoff became triangular when M. E. Thompson, the newly elected lieutenant governor, was sworn in to that office. He immediately declared himself acting governor and started appointing his *own* officials. The enraged Talmadge wouldn't budge, on the grounds that since his father had died *before* taking office, Thompson had absolutely no claim to succeed him. Thus, until Arnall resigned in Thompson's favor, Georgia could boast that it indeed had three governors.

The stalemate was finally broken after two months, when the Georgia Supreme Court ruled that Thompson was the lawful governor. Talmadge did not appeal the decision. Instead, he vowed that he'd "take this to the court of last resort—the people." And when the 1948 election rolled around, he won the governorship easily in his own right.

The Piano-Playing President

Harry S Truman (shown at right as painted by Ben Shahn) took piano lessons as a child, and he was good. His instructor, who had studied with the great Paderewski's teacher, took him to a Paderewski concert in Kansas City. It "was a wonder," Truman recalled. "I was studying [his] minuet," and afterward "we went back behind the scenes. . . . She told him I didn't know how to make 'the turn' in his minuet, and he said, 'Sit down,' and he showed me how to do it. I played it at Potsdam for old Stalin. I think he was quite impressed." Truman considered a musical career, but gave it up after his father went broke speculating on the grain market. "A good music-hall piano player is about the best I'd have ever been," Truman said. "So I went into politics and became president of the United States."

Truman: The Loser Who Won

They called him "Give 'em hell Harry." And he did

When the Democrats nominated Harry S Truman for the presidency in 1948, a flock of white pigeons was released over the Philadelphia convention hall to symbolize peace. But more symbolic to observers was that one bird crashed into the ceiling and fell to the floor. Experts said that Truman had about as much chance of winning as that bird. Indeed, he had been a compromise vice presidential candidate in 1944, and when Franklin Roosevelt died the next year, Truman wasn't alone in feeling that "the moon, the stars, and all the planets had fallen on me." Many agreed that the job might overwhelm him. "To err is Truman" became a popular saying.

Meanwhile, the Republicans nominated Gov. Thomas E. Dewey of New York, who had made a surprisingly strong showing against Roosevelt in 1944. Although he didn't exactly set crowds on fire, he was an efficient administrator with a rich speaking voice perfect for radio. And the icing on Dewey's presidential cake came when two wings of the Democratic Party bolted from the Truman ticket. With FDR's coalition in tatters, it seemed impossible for Truman to win (an opinion reflected in the polls). Dewey reacted by avoiding issues whenever possible. He even took time out during the campaign to plan his inauguration. But the president forged ahead. From June on, he made 556 speeches as his campaign train whistle-stopped some 31,700 miles across the nation. "I'm going to fight hard," he declared, "and I'm going to give 'em hell."

On election night pollsters, political pundits, and professional Republicans—along with a fair amount of the populace—were stunned, for Dewey's cautious campaign had managed to snatch defeat "out of the jaws of victory." And Truman, the feisty man from Missouri, had handily won both the popular and electoral votes to pull off what has been called the greatest upset in American political history.

The Sun.
HUGHES ELECTED BY NARROW MARGIN; SWEEPS WEST; HAS 291 ELECTORAL VOTES; CONGRESS TO BE SPLIT; WHITMAN AND CALDER CHOSEN BY HUGE MAJORITIES

The Literary Digest
NEW YORK
OCTOBER 31, 1936
Topics of the day
LANDON, 1,293,669; ROOSEVELT, 972,897
Final Returns in The Digest's Poll of Ten Million Voters

Many Happy Returns?

The Chicago Tribune*'s "Dewey Defeats Truman" wasn't the only postelection newspaper boner in U.S. history. The New York* Sun *headlined the 1916 election of Charles Evans Hughes as the nation's 29th president; the victory, of course, went to Woodrow Wilson. Twenty years later* The Literary Digest *poll, which had an excellent track record for presidential predictions, asked 10 million Americans "to settle November's election in October." The results showed Alf Landon defeating Franklin Roosevelt by a comfortable margin. But on Election Day the only poll that counted told a different story: Roosevelt trounced Landon, sweeping all but two states.*

A premature headline in the Chicago Daily Tribune *delights Harry Truman. Ten days before the election,* Life *magazine called Thomas E. Dewey "the next President." When a reader queried, "How does it feel to be out on that limb?"* Life *replied, "Crowded."*

Merchandising the Presidency

How the "television election" of 1952 changed politics forever

A nation that had been hooked on radio for a generation was switching to television in 1952, buying seven million sets that year. Thus, for the first time, voters could *see* Republican Dwight D. Eisenhower and Democrat Adlai E. Stevenson vie for the nation's highest office—and major networks could vie for viewers' time. (During the conventions, stations paired familiar long-time radio commentators with newcomers on the screen. A happy result was the broadcaster selected to appear with Edward R. Murrow; the newcomer—who was a natural—was Walter Cronkite.)

Eisenhower's strategists, recognizing the potential of projecting his famous grin into millions of living rooms, used the small screen throughout the campaign. And as it drew to a close, they blitzed the airwaves with 60-second spots. The most effective one showed Eisenhower giving this response to a question about inflation: "My wife, Mamie, worries about the same thing."

Adlai Stevenson, on the other hand, didn't even *own* a TV set. What he liked was delivering a witty, carefully crafted speech to a live audience, and he was a master of the art. But he was stiff and unnatural on television, and did not make use of electronic campaigning. It was "selling the presidency like cereal," he complained. "How can you talk seriously about issues with one-minute spots?" Ironically, Stevenson's most effective television appearance was his speech conceding defeat. Comforting his crestfallen supporters, he confessed that he felt like a little boy who had stubbed his toe in the dark—it hurt too much to laugh and he was too old to cry.

Despite the power of TV, buttons and slogans were still a part of the 1952 political hoopla. Lampooning Eisenhower's "I Like Ike" slogan, cartoonist Walt Kelly proposed his famous 'possum for president with the rallying cry "I Go Pogo." And Pogo even snared some write-in votes.

JFK's Health: A Medical Question With Political Overtones

"I have never had Addison's disease," said John F. Kennedy after winning the presidency in 1960. "I have been through a long campaign and my health is very good today." According to one of his many doctors, however, "Jack had been diagnosed as having Addison's disease."

It was a potentially explosive issue. Until the 1940's the incurable adrenal disorder was always debilitating and often fatal. By the election year of 1960 it was controllable with cortisone—but merely having to explain that fact would surely have cost Kennedy votes.

Perhaps it was simple curiosity that precipitated three known break-ins or attempted break-ins (one merely a lock-tampering job) of JFK's doctors' offices. We will probably never know. The young candidate's medical files were marked with assumed names or kept in secure places, and so his privacy was protected and the issue of his "killer" disease—if, indeed, he had it—was never raised beyond the level of rumor.

Only 87 Votes Got Him on the Ballot

So they dubbed him Landslide Lyndon

Lyndon Johnson was a young representative and his opponent was a seasoned former governor, Coke Stevenson. In the rough-and-tumble arena of Texas politics, the two fought hard for the Democratic Party's senatorial nomination in 1948.

The primary was odd from the start. A block of votes "turned up" in Duval County after the polls had closed. Then, because of a "mix-up" in nearby Jim Wells County (which routinely boasted high voter turnout—sometimes well in excess of distributed ballots), the lead kept changing. Each side promptly accused the other of fraud. When the smoke cleared, Johnson seemed to be 87 votes ahead, finally nailing down the nomination at the state convention. But Stevenson wouldn't quit. He demanded an inquiry, and months of maneuvering led to a direct appeal to Supreme Court Justice Hugo Black. Just weeks before the election, LBJ's name was finally printed on the ballot.

As a result, the Jim Wells County investigation was halted (with voting lists "lost" or stolen), the Duval County ballots were burned by the courthouse janitor, and Johnson went on to win the Senate seat by a 2-to-1 margin—and with it, a stepping-stone to the White House.

The Man Who Kept Us Out of Vietnam

A powerful Senate minority leader asks a vital question

"The President has asked me to call this meeting." With those words Secretary of State John Foster Dulles called to order a secret Saturday morning gathering of eight congressional leaders. It was April 1954, and France was about to lose its war in Indochina. Eisenhower wanted Congress to grant him the power to send American air and naval support to aid the French. If the United States did not act quickly, the administration reasoned, the Western powers might well lose their influence in Asia.

The legislators began to raise a flurry of questions. Would this mean war? If the first single strike failed, would ground troops be used? Then the Senate minority leader asked Dulles what proved to be the crucial question of the meeting: Could other allies be depended upon to join America in supporting the French? When the group finally adjourned, one point was clear—without allied support, there would be no congressional approval. At all costs the United States should avoid another Korea.

A few weeks earlier, National Security Council members had expressed the same hesitancy about the plan that the minority leader had voiced. And, though the NSC was safe to ignore politically, the powerful minority leader certainly was not. Without his approval, the plan was doomed. Dulles searched for two weeks, but could find no allies to join the project, and thus the United States avoided entanglement in Vietnam.

The senator was, of course, Lyndon B. Johnson. And though he kept us out of war in 1954, 10 years later, as president, he would enmesh the country in it. Ultimately, public and political opposition to U.S. military involvement in Vietnam would cause him to give up the presidency after only one term.

A David Levine cartoon combines LBJ's famous postsurgery pose with a map of Vietnam.

"You Won't Have Nixon to Kick Around Anymore"

A famous news conference was hardly prophetic

It seemed to be the end of the political road for Richard Nixon, who had just lost the 1962 election for governor of California to the incumbent, Pat Brown. Appearing unexpectedly at a press conference, Nixon rambled on about a number of subjects, finally focusing on the media. "As I leave you I want you to know . . . how much you're going to be missing," he said, his voice edged with bitterness. "You won't have Nixon to kick around anymore."

In fact, it was neither the last press conference for Nixon nor the end of his political career. He licked his wounds, campaigned hard for Republican candidates in 1964, and by 1968 was back in charge of the party. Snaring the presidential nomination, he was elected by more than 500,000 votes.

It was quite a comeback for a man whose career had been marked by controversy. Nixon's 1950 senatorial race against Helen Gahagan Douglas was called the "dirtiest campaign on record." Later, as Eisenhower's running mate in 1952, he made his emotional "Checkers" speech, defending himself against charges of accepting improper campaign contributions. But he and Ike won the election easily (at 40, Nixon became the nation's second-youngest vice president) and were reelected in 1956. Then in 1960 Nixon ran for president, losing to John F. Kennedy by only about 100,000 votes out of the nearly 69 million cast.

It was a mere two years later that the gubernatorial defeat seemed to end Nixon's career. But he bounced back as a two-term president, in the process giving rise to the Watergate scandal—and once again there was ample opportunity "to kick Nixon around."

1962: "This is my last press conference" was one Nixon prediction that did not come true.

A Model President

"A New York Girl and Her Yale Boy Friend Spend a Hilarious Holiday on Skis" was the title of a six-page article in a 1940 issue of Look *magazine. It featured a handsome law student, who was also an assistant football coach and a partner in a New York modeling agency. His girlfriend, Phyllis Brown, who arranged the partnership, appears as the "New York Girl" in this photo from the magazine, now a collector's item. The "Yale Boy Friend" became the nation's 38th president—Gerald Ford.*

Jimmy Carter to the Rescue

A radioactive repair job

1952: Lt. Jimmy Carter checks equipment aboard a submarine during his seven-year tour of duty in the navy.

After graduation from the U.S. Naval Academy, Jimmy Carter was fascinated by nuclear power, and particularly by the potential of atomic submarines. Both his expertise in nuclear theory and his practical experience in building the first nuclear propulsion components were unexpectedly put to the test in 1953, when a nuclear reactor in Chalk River, Canada, developed a leak, releasing radioactive material into the atmosphere.

Carter, who was then studying reactor technology and nuclear physics as a graduate student at Union College in Schenectady, New York, was called in along with two other naval officers to help disassemble the damaged nuclear reactor core. Because of the extreme danger posed by exposure to radiation, Carter and his team had only 90 seconds to retrieve the damaged pieces of the underground reactor core.

The trio first practiced on an exact mock-up of the equipment, which had been constructed on a tennis court close by. They became familiar with the damaged pieces and the tools that would be used to remove them. When they finally descended into the core, each wearing a suit of white protective clothing, they worked frantically—and accomplished the task in 89 seconds.

It has been estimated that in those few seconds each man absorbed a year's maximum dosage of radiation. Carter, later to become our 39th president, wrote in his book *Why Not the Best?*: "There were no apparent aftereffects from this exposure—just a lot of doubtful jokes among ourselves about death versus sterility."

"Honey, I Forgot to Duck"

This was Ronald Reagan's much-publicized comment to his wife, Nancy, after would-be assassin John Hinckley shot him on March 30, 1981. The chief executive may well have recalled the remark from a story about boxer Jack Dempsey, who after losing the heavyweight championship to Gene Tunney in 1926, used exactly the same words to explain his battered appearance to his wife. That bit of lore could hardly have been lost on former sportscaster Dutch Reagan.

While the president was recovering from his gunshot wound, well-wishers showered him with cards and gifts, including 500 bouquets, a music box, a 55-pound glass pig filled with jelly beans, a 10-pound box of chocolates, and a photograph of Bob Hope and Jill St. John wearing bunny costumes. One get-well gift was outstanding, however, especially in its manner of delivery: it was a goldfish that survived a trip through the mail from Albany, New York, in a water-filled plastic bag. Barney Bullard, the 10-year-old who sent it, explained in a note that he was enclosing "a companion, a goldfish named Ronald Reagan II. I hope you like him. Just feed him daily every morning and he will be fine." Dubbed the First Fish, Ronald Reagan II was promptly placed in a tank emblazoned with the presidential seal, where he lived happily for more than three years.

CHAPTER FOUR

Rags to Riches

Whatever else there is to say about the American Dream, it has usually involved getting rich. And right from the beginning, Americans have found odd, imaginative, and sometimes slippery ways to go about it—along with some weird and wonderful ways to spend their money once they had it. Even so, you might be surprised at the modest ways in which some of the nation's corporations—whose names are household words today—got started.

Celebrating success (New York City, circa 1901)

When Pocahontas made her debut at the court of King James, she probably wore the costume she later donned for this portrait—a gold-stitched red brocaded mantle over a rich but subdued dress with starched lace collar and cuffs, a red-trimmed hat, and a white plume fan. The unsigned oil, thought to be by the Dutch artist Simon Van de Passe, hangs in the National Portrait Gallery in Washington, D.C.

The Business of Jamestown

An American princess goes to King James's court to raise money

Jamestown, the first permanent English settlement in America, became a crown colony in 1624, but it didn't start that way. It was founded in 1607 as a business venture by the Virginia Company of London. The company's many investors, of both upper and lower classes, pooled their shares in a common stock to finance the enterprise, hoping to reap profits from the abundant gold and silver the New World was expected to yield.

But the shareholders were in for a disappointment. The gold and silver failed to materialize, and the small colony barely survived starvation, malaria, and Indian attacks. By 1616 the Virginia Company was in serious trouble, with no saleable products except cedar board for wainscoting and a small tobacco crop, which John Rolfe had begun cultivating in 1613. Stockholders abandoned the company in droves, leaving it on the verge of bankruptcy.

Casting about for a way to raise money, Jamestown's governor, Thomas Dale, hit upon a brilliant idea: the company would send Pocahontas across the Atlantic and have her presented at court. The 21-year-old Indian princess was already a celebrity in England, thanks to Capt. John Smith, who had written glowingly of her intercession with her father, Chief Powhatan, to save his life in 1608.

From the first, Pocahontas had seemed spellbound by the colonists—she emulated them, learned their language, adopted their dress, converted to Christianity (taking the name Rebecca), married the planter John Rolfe, and bore him a son, Thomas. She was the perfect model to show what the English could achieve in the New World.

In late June 1616 Pocahontas debarked at London, accompanied by her husband, her small son, and a retinue of 10 or 12 Indians—including her half-sister Matachanna (who served as the infant's nursemaid) and Matachanna's husband, Tomocomo, an agent for Powhatan. Received with fanfare, they were lodged at the Bell Savage Inn, which was famous for its exotic occupants and bizarre sideshows. (The inn was later called La Belle Sauvage in honor of Pocahontas.)

John Smith, who was in England, wrote to Queen

Anne, extolling the American princess and hinting that if she were not well received it would bode ill for the English overseas. Meanwhile, Pocahontas was fashionably outfitted and instructed in court deportment.

Finally, the regally poised little princess was escorted to the palace and presented to Queen Anne and King James I. (Her husband was excluded as a commoner—in fact, he was nearly imprisoned for his audacity in marrying royalty.) The aging monarch was impressed by the Indian girl. In his eyes she was surrounded by a divine aura, a sign of royal blood, and he asked his Privy Council to check whether her son might inherit America.

Pocahontas became the darling of the upper classes. When not being honored at some gala affair, she received such distinguished visitors as Sir Walter Raleigh and the poet and dramatist Ben Jonson. So successful was she in winning publicity for the Virginia Company that its management gave her a salary of £4 a week, although the sum strained its reserves.

Tomocomo, however, detested the English and their ways and made no bones about it. He wore his native dress—an ornamented breechcloth, a fur mantle, and face and body paint—and scorned the white men's food. Serving as eyes and ears for Powhatan, who had told him to count Englishmen in order to judge the threat they posed, he began by cutting notches in his staff, but quickly gave that up. Through an interpreter he argued religion with the bishop of London and other church officials, vigorously defending his own god. Before assemblies of scholars he discoursed about his homeland and social traditions and even demonstrated ritual songs and dances.

The fast pace and the damp London climate took their toll on the Indians. Several died, and Pocahontas fell ill. On a foggy March day in 1617 she boarded a ship at Gravesend, at the mouth of the Thames, for the long voyage home. As it prepared to sail she quietly died, probably of pneumonia. She was buried in an unmarked spot beneath a church floor; her remains have never been found.

Pocahontas had done her job well. So many wanted to go to the New World that the firm reorganized as a land company, giving each shareholder a 50-acre plot. The tobacco industry was flourishing and the Virginia Company was on the brink of prosperity in 1622, when a massacre led by Pocahontas's uncle took the lives of 347 colonists. Future plans were abandoned and the king had the company charter annulled.

How They Got Started . . .

Tobacco. *From its beginning in Jamestown, the tobacco business flourished despite fierce opposition. King James I called smoking "a custome lothsome to the eye, hatefull to the Nose, harmefull to the braine, [and] dangerous to the Lungs" and did all he could to stop it. But men smoked on, and Virginia grew wealthy on their addiction. Tobacco was even legal tender in the colony; until the 1750's the salaries of clergymen were paid in it. (Later the tobacco industry featured its Virginia origin: the 1860's tobacco label below shows the rescue of John Smith by Pocahontas.)*

In 1760 a Huguenot named Pierre Lorillard began selling highly flavored pipe and chewing tobacco and snuff concocted in his New York City plant. His success brought tobacco new popularity—and new condemnation. For a century P. Lorillard and Sons dominated the market with imaginative sales devices, such as the wooden cigar store Indian. On its 100th anniversary, the company stuffed $100 bills into random packages of Century cigarette tobacco.

Ready-made cigarettes were hand-rolled and costly until 1881, when James Duke introduced machines that could roll 200 a minute. At five cents a pack, sales skyrocketed. In 1890 Duke merged America's five largest cigarette companies into the American Tobacco Company.

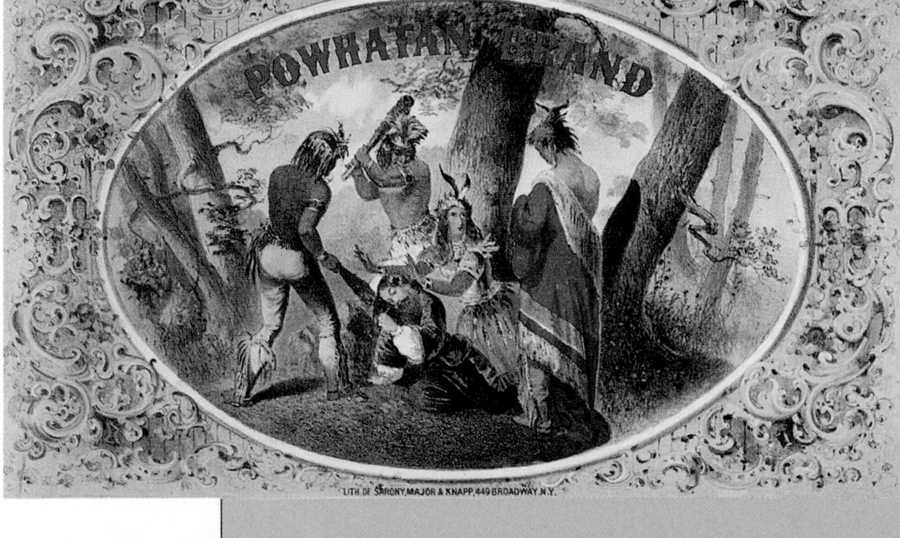

The Land-grab 14th Colony

Only the Revolution thwarted the scheme

Land speculation was among the most enticing investments for fast-track 18th-century financial players. As new settlers arrived and land prices soared, huge profits could be made.

In the late 1760's Samuel Wharton, a Philadelphia merchant, joined with a group of colonial businessmen who had suffered financial losses during the French and Indian War. They sought reparations for their losses in the form of land grants from the Crown. Striving to overcome British resistance, their consortium grew to become the Grand Ohio Company. Franklins, Washingtons, Galloways, and Lees were among its distinguished members.

Officially, the company sought to create a 14th colony: Vandalia, in present-day West Virginia and Kentucky. In fact, the company was engaged in a spectacular land grab, in which its shareholders would *own* 20 million acres of prime frontier land.

Their scheme almost worked. The Crown approved the colony in the spring of 1775, but withheld the grant while quelling a seemingly minor disturbance caused by a few rebellious farmers at Lexington and Concord. No one involved in the deal realized that the American Revolution had begun.

Years of careful financial maneuvering had vanished in a volley of musket fire. Wharton continued to press his claim with the new American government, but the grant was never recognized. He died in 1800, impoverished.

Making Money in Maine

Taber bills became a bane to their maker

Who hasn't dreamed of printing his own money? In 1804 the dream became a reality that soon turned into a nightmare for John Taber.

Taber was a merchant in Portland, Maine, with a successful import-export business. Maine, then part of Massachusetts, was suffering a severe currency shortage because a state law forbade banks from issuing paper currency in denominations lower than $5. To help alleviate the shortage, John Taber & Son decided to use the equity of the firm to back its own notes in denominations of $1, $2, $3, and $4. The firm's reputation was so solid that the Taber bills became popular currency in Portland. But fate conspired against the well-intentioned merchant-turned-banker.

When Congress declared a trade embargo in 1807, during the struggle between England and Napoleonic France, it caused many New England shipping businesses to fail. Among them was John Taber & Son. Sadly, Taber's son Daniel added to the problem. Whenever he wanted extra money, he had signed a new lot of bills, without his father's knowledge and without sufficient gold reserves to back it up. Unable to redeem the bills, the company was ruined.

Sometime later, Taber went to collect a debt of $60 from a former associate, a Quaker. When the man paid him in Taber bills, Taber protested that the money was now worthless. His ex-partner replied, "Well, well, that is not my fault. Thee ought to have made it better."

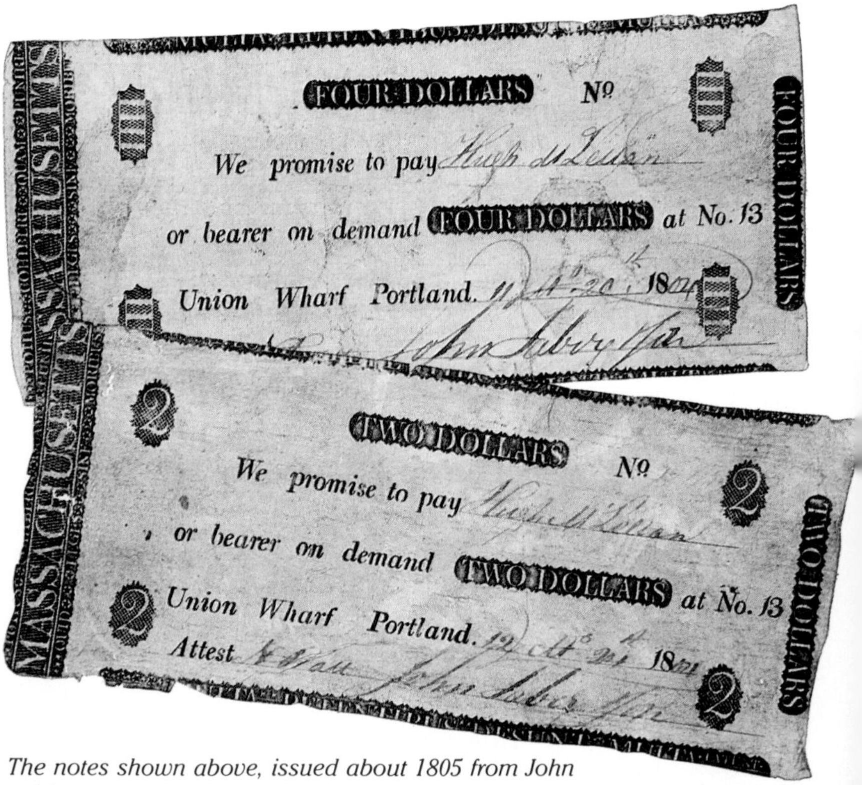

The notes shown above, issued about 1805 from John Taber's "private mint," promised the bearer $2 and $4.

Convicted of Making a Profit

Price-fixing in colonial Massachusetts

A prominent Boston merchant named Robert Keayne was brought before the General Court in Massachusetts in 1639, accused of making an excessive profit. Keayne's background paralleled that of many New England merchants. On completing an apprenticeship as a merchant tailor in London, he sailed to Massachusetts in 1635 and opened a shop in the heart of Boston to sell English imports. It was a time of rampant inflation and Keayne did well, selling a variety of goods for whatever prices they could command.

The trouble began four years later, when Keayne was challenged by local officials for selling a bag of nails at what they considered to be an exorbitant price. He was brought to trial, and during the proceedings his profits on gold buttons, thread, a bridle, and other sundries were also scrutinized. "He was charged," Gov. John Winthrop explained, "with many particulars; in some, for taking above six-pence in the shilling profit; in some above eight-pence; and, in some small things, above two for one."

Keayne was fined £200, but his troubles were hardly over. The church summarily took its turn, subjecting his affairs to "exquisite search." Although he was not excommunicated, he was declared a sinner in the eyes of God and the public and was required to acknowledge his sins before he could regain full church membership. Keayne's conduct seemed to have struck a chord in a community torn between the rising tide of mercantile capitalism, with its profit motive, and more traditional Christian values, such as the idea of a "just price" above which it was usurious to charge. Church authorities pointed out the "false principles" that other merchants would do well to resist—especially the notion that "a man might sell as dear as he can, and buy as cheap as he can."

Years later Keayne composed a 50,000-word "Last Will and Testament," in which he fumed over his profit-making censure: "these were the great mattrs in which I had offended, when my selfe have offten seene & heard offences, complaynts & crymes of a high nature against God & men such as . . . fornications, drunckenes, fearefull oathes quareling, mutines sabboth breakings thefts fforgeries & such like which hath passed with fynes or censures so smale or easy as hath not beene worth the nameing."

But it was his public denunciation as a sinner that most goaded and haunted Keayne, who agonized: "the newnes and straingnes of the thing, to be brought forth into an open Court as a publique malefactor, was both a shame and an amazement to me."

How They Got Started . . .

Salt. *Selling salt to American consumers in the early 1900's was no easy shake. The common container was a large barrel. But in 1911 Joy Morton developed free-running salt and a round asphalt-laminated paper canister with an aluminum pouring spout, which eventually became the industry standard. Then he decided to advertise nationwide. One ad prepared for* Good Housekeeping *magazine caught the fancy of company executives. It featured a little girl under an umbrella, with a container of salt pouring out behind her. The slogan read: "Even in rainy weather it flows freely." Nice idea, but it needed work. Finally they boiled it down to "When It Rains It Pours," and one of America's most familiar advertising logos was born.*

Jell-O. *"America's Most Famous Dessert" did not take shape quickly. Its patent goes back to 1845 and Peter Cooper, a New York industrialist and philanthropist. But not until 1897—when Pearl B. Wait, a successful building contractor, entered the young packaged-food business—did the dessert go into production. Wait's wife, May, coined the name Jell-O. The company was a bust, so Wait sold it to his neighbor Orator F. Woodward for $450. At first Woodward fared no better than Wait had done. One day, in despair, he offered to sell the whole kit and kaboodle to his plant superintendent for $35. The superintendent refused.*

By 1906 sales had soared to just under the $1 million level, and Jell-O, after a shaky start, was well on its way to being a molder of American cuisine.

Piercing the Adobe Curtain

Brave entrepreneurs blazed a trail to Santa Fe for Spanish silver dollars

Santa Fe, capital of New Spain's northernmost province of New Mexico, was long closed to American traders. The Spanish, alarmed at America's westward expansion, forbade them under penalty of imprisonment.

The small adobe town was a potentially rich market, the commercial center for thousands of Spanish and Mexican ranchers and landowners. Dependent for much-needed goods upon the annual wagon train that would make the 600-mile journey from Chihuahua in north-central Mexico, by way of the tortuous El Camino Real ("The King's Highway"), they were hungry for manufactured items—and they could pay in gold or silver bullion.

In 1807 Jacques Philippe Clamorgan, an old-timer in the fur trade, thought he could get around the Spanish by befriending the Pawnee Indians east of Santa Fe. Using their camps as distribution centers, he would lure the Santa Feans out for trading. He and a small party left St. Louis in August with four pack mules loaded with dry goods and housewares. Four months later they were in Santa Fe. But the plan went awry, and the Americans were hustled south to Chihuahua to be questioned by the Spanish authorities. They allowed Clamorgan to sell his goods there and go back to Missouri via Texas. He thus became the first American trader to return from Santa Fe with a profit—even though his trading was done in Chihuahua.

Santa Fe stayed closed until 1821, when the Mexicans overthrew Spanish rule. But William Becknell was unaware of the change when he left Franklin, Missouri, in September of that year to trade with the Plains Indians. At the Raton Pass near the Colorado–New Mexico border he and his party met some Spanish-speaking soldiers, who told them the news. The Americans rushed to Santa Fe. They returned home with bags of silver dollars.

In June 1822 Becknell set forth again, taking 21 men and three wagons piled with $150 worth of goods. Unable to take the vehicles through the Raton Pass, they ventured south and blundered into the 60-mile-wide Cimarron Desert. Running out of water, they were forced to drink the blood of their mules. Then they killed a stray bison for the liquids in its stomach.

A bison in the desert? It meant there was water nearby! The strongest of the men staggered on, discovered the Cimarron River, and returned with water in the nick of time. It was November before the party reached Santa Fe, where they sold their goods at an enormous profit.

For two decades wagon caravans plied the 800-mile Santa Fe Trail. Annual sales averaged as much as $130,000, with profits of 10 to 40 percent. Finally, in 1846, the Mexican War ended the golden era of the Santa Fe trader.

"Brown Gold" and the Mountain Men

Jim Bridger was only 18 in 1822, when he was recruited by Ashley Expeditions to search the wilds for furs. Jedediah Smith was 23. They were to become the most celebrated of that dauntless and hardy breed called mountain men. Along with Hugh Glass, John Colter, Joe Walker, and others, they opened the West, blazing trails through wilderness, finding passes over mountain ranges, and seeing fresh the wonders of the continent.

But they were no mere adventurers. They were in business—the fur business—and they endured hardship and risked their lives to get their stock in trade: "brown gold," or beaver pelts, to satisfy the vogue for beaver tophats back east

Jim Bridger, left, discovered Utah's Great Salt Lake in 1825. He thought it was a branch of the Pacific Ocean.

and in Europe. In 1826, when William H. Ashley, founder of the Rocky Mountains Fur Company, retired with his gains of $80,000, Smith and two other mountain men, David Jackson and William Sublette, bought him out.

Seasoned and savvy, the trio led the search for new trapping lands and gave the British-owned Hudson's Bay Company and the American Fur Company, owned by that ruthless merchant John Jacob Astor, some stiff competition. In the quest, Smith and a party of two blazed a trail across the Sierra Nevada and became the first Americans to reach California, then part of Mexico, by an overland route. Satisfied with their earnings after four years, Smith and his partners sold the company to Jim Bridger and four others in 1830. Smith retired to St. Louis; the following year he was killed by Comanches on the Santa Fe Trail.

Astor's American Fur Company waged an all-out war to destroy the enterprise with bribes, threats, and shipments of liquor to ply the Indians. The mountain men finally sold out to him, and in 1836 the Rocky Mountains Fur Company was dissolved. During its 14-year career it had sent to St. Louis, its home base, about 1,000 packs of beaver pelts, netting $500,000 at a cost of 100 lives. Bridger, only 37, went on to become a legendary guide and an army scout. Forced into retirement in 1867 by arthritis and failing eyesight, he died in Missouri in 1881.

Firewater for Furs

Astor built a steamboat for smuggling whiskey to the Indians

Whiskey! John Jacob Astor's success in the western fur trade depended upon it, and he didn't accumulate America's first eight-figure fortune by doing less than was needed. The Indians who supplied the pelts gladly took such trade items as guns, knives, blankets, and fabrics—but the trader who also had whiskey was the one they preferred to deal with. The Hudson's Bay Company, operating from Canada, could give them whiskey openly; Astor, constrained by U.S. law, could not. A steamboat, however, was allowed an allotment of whiskey for each crew member and passenger.

And so, in mid-April 1831, the *Yellow Stone*, a 120-foot-long sidewheeler that Astor commissioned at a cost of $8,000, started up the Missouri River from St. Louis for Fort Union, his trading post near the Canadian border. In its hold, along with the usual trade goods, were more than 1,000 gallons of whiskey—some of it legal.

Its three boilers roaring as they consumed 10 cords of firewood a day, the vessel worked its way past tree-sized snags and over sandbars. (One effective method of getting across a bar was to have the crew and passengers march in unison from side to side, rocking the boat free.) It got only as far as Fort Tecumseh, near present-day Pierre, South Dakota, on that first trip. But that was farther than a steamboat had ever gone before, and the trading was successful. The next year, the *Yellow Stone* left earlier to take advantage of high water from the spring thaw; it reached Fort Union in mid-June.

On the way back, the boat's master learned of a new law—no liquor could be taken into Indian country under *any* pretext, and all cargo was to be searched. Stopping just long enough to load up another 1,000 gallons of whiskey, he turned around and made the trip again before enforcement began. From then on, new ways had to be found to get whiskey upriver, including carrying it in wagons past the inspection point at Fort Leavenworth, Kansas. Eventually, a still, made of parts shipped on the *Yellow Stone*, was built at Fort Union.

Astor founded Fort Astoria (below), the first permanent U.S. settlement on the West Coast, in 1811. He gave up fur trading in 1835 to concentrate on Manhattan real estate.

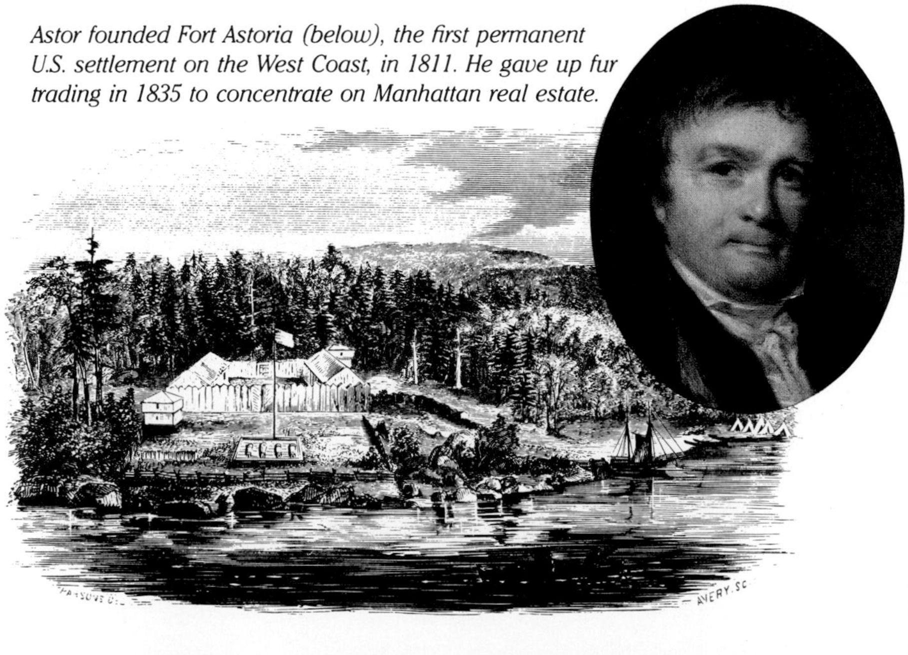

French, American, British, and Dutch flags fly over rented trading marts near the Canton harbor in the 1830's.

"I Have a China History"

Did FDR know that his inheritance came from smuggling opium?

"I do not pretend to justify the prosecution of the opium trade in a moral and philanthropic point of view," wrote Warren Delano, Franklin Delano Roosevelt's grandfather, in a letter home from China, "but as a merchant I insist that it has been a fair, honorable and legitimate trade; and to say the worst of it, liable to no further or weightier objections than is the importation of wines, Brandies & spirits into the U. States, England, &c."

The China trade

Only 24 years old when he arrived in China in 1833, Delano soon became the head of Russell & Company, the biggest American trading firm there. He was directly involved in what was euphemistically called the China trade. Bringing Chinese tea, silk, and porcelain to the West was an important part of that trade, but the most lucrative part was smuggling opium into China from India and Turkey.

Between 1821 and 1839 the opium trade rose from 5,000 chests per year (each weighing 133.5 pounds) to 30,000 chests, paid for by 100 million ounces of Chinese silver. Called "foreign mud" by Chinese officials, who were powerless to stop its spread, the drug had created more than two million Chinese addicts by 1835.

First million

In 1839 the emperor named a new and incorruptible high commissioner of Canton, who tried to end the trade. The first of a series of Opium Wars broke out between China and British traders. Delano's boat, flying a flag of truce, was ambushed from shore, and Delano was taken prisoner, though he was held only briefly.

Undeterred, he and other Yankee traders enthusiastically resumed the opium trade at the end of the war in 1842. Delano did so well that he sailed home that autumn, married, and returned with his bride to China, where he stayed for three more years. Then he retired to New York and invested in western railroads. Sara, the future mother of President Roosevelt, was born into the family in 1854.

Delano was a millionaire by 1857, but his fortune was wiped out overnight in that year's financial panic. Not one to be easily defeated, he returned to the Orient and reentered the China trade; within five years he made a second fortune, again trading in opium.

The heritage

How much FDR knew about his grandfather's career as an opium smuggler is a mystery. But the president did acquire from him a feeling of kinship for China. "You know, I have a China history," Roosevelt once told Gen. Joe Stilwell, who was in command of U.S. forces in China during World War II. "My grandfather went out there . . . he made a million dollars; and when he came back he put it into western railroads. And in 8 years he lost every dollar. Then . . . he went out again . . . and made another million. This time he put it into coal mines, and they didn't pay a dividend till 2 years after he died. Ha! Ha! Ha!"

The Ice King Cometh

Frederic Tudor made a fortune refreshing the Tropics

Ice was unknown in the Caribbean until 1806. That year a 22-year-old Bostonian named Frederic Tudor took a boatload of it to Martinique. Insulated with hay, it didn't melt on the way, as laughing skeptics had predicted. Tudor persuaded the owner of the Tivoli Garden to let him make ice cream. The man had never heard of the stuff, but after selling $300 worth in one night, he clamored for more. There was no more. The young entrepreneur had failed to provide insulated storage, and his exotic cargo dissolved at the docks.

Personal debts and the War of 1812 prevented another try for nine years. Then Tudor went to Havana—this time taking lumber for an icehouse. He earned a tidy sum. "Drink, Spaniards and be cool," he wrote in his Ice House Diary, "that I, who have suffered so much in the cause, may be able to go home and keep myself warm." He returned by way of Martinique, where he obtained a 10-year monopoly.

By the 1820's Tudor also had icehouses in Charleston and New Orleans. He invented the refrigerating jar, a precursor of the Thermos, and his agents gave them to bartenders—and even gave away free ice until the public was hooked. One happy result was the frosted mint julep. Without plenty of Yankee ice, that quintessential Southern drink could never have been born.

As Tudor developed better ways to store ice, his business became worldwide. In 1833, after a four-month voyage, his ship docked at Calcutta, India, with almost two-thirds of its 180-ton cargo intact. An astounded Parsee asked how ice grew in America: Was it on trees?

The Ice King lived to be 80. The business he founded flourished for another quarter of a century, managed by one of his sons, until manufactured ice made it obsolete.

At first, Frederic Tudor cut ice from his father's pond near Boston. Later he bought cutting rights to others, including Thoreau's retreat, Walden Pond.

How They Got Started . . .

Frozen Food. *When Clarence Birdseye (above) went fishing in Labrador, it was so cold that the fish froze as they came through the ice. Thawed in water, they began to swim. This led Birdseye to try quick-freezing food to retain its fresh flavor. His experiments worked, and in 1924 Birdseye launched a seafood company in Gloucester, Massachusetts. Five years later he sold it—for $22 million.*

Heinz 57. *As businessman Henry J. Heinz rode the elevated train through New York City in the early 1890's, his imagination was sparked by an advertisement touting "21 Styles" of shoes. He felt 57 had a catchy cadence and greater "psychological influence"; so—even though his company was marketing over 60 products at the time—*Heinz 57 *became its symbol.*

P. T. Barnum's Lost Fortune

The great showman never said, "There's a sucker born every minute," but he proved it was true

They say you can't kid a kidder. Put another way: You can't con a con man. But in the case of Phineas T. Barnum, master of hyperbole and hoax, the adage did not hold true. The flamboyant promoter was the victim of several scams throughout his life, none more notorious than the Jerome Clock Company episode.

In 1851 the immensely successful 41-year-old Barnum was looking for a "profitable philanthropy"—something to ensure a comfortable income and help transform his reputation from that of huckster to social benefactor. With William H. Noble, a wealthy Bridgeport investor, he laid plans to create East Bridgeport, a pleasant, well-designed community that would include factories, stores, and housing for hundreds of workers and their families.

The two began buying up land along the Pequonnock River in Connecticut. After securing 224 acres, they parceled and sold scores of home lots, and constructed bridges and a spacious park. To attract industry, they offered incentives, from cheap land to easy credit, and a few manufacturers set up operations at the site.

In 1855 a representative of the Jerome Clock Company of New Haven, then perhaps the nation's largest such business, approached Barnum with a proposition. If he would agree to lend his name as security to a $110,000 note, thus helping the company through a hard season, Chauncey Jerome would relocate the firm in East Bridgeport. Barnum jumped at the chance to save jobs and at the same time move most of the 700 or more employees into his pet development.

Barnum stipulated that he would lend up to $50,000 and would back promissory notes for a maximum total of $60,000. "I was willing that my notes," he later explained, "when taken up, should be renewed, I cared not how often, provided the stipulated maximum of $110,000 should never be exceeded."

Over several months, Barnum endorsed a series of $3,000, $5,000, and $10,000 notes. The payment periods were to range from 5 to 60 days, but he left the dates blank to ease transactions. For a time he renewed notes only as earlier ones were paid off, but eventually, he admitted, "my confidence in the company became so established that I did not ask to see the notes that had been taken up, but furnished new accommodation paper as it was called for."

When the banks began to refuse his notes, Barnum became alarmed and sent a man to investigate. It turned out that, rather than cancel earlier notes, Jerome had dated them as long as two years into the future, while taking new paper from Barnum. "Further investigation revealed the fact that I had endorsed the clock company to the extent of more than half a million dollars. . . . My agent who made these startling discoveries came back to me with the refreshing intelligence that I was a ruined man!"

Ballerina Ernestine de Faiber was an attraction at P. T. Barnum's Museum in New York City in the 1850's, some 20 years before he founded the circus that still bears his name. Gossips said she attracted him more than the public.

Public reaction to the scandal broke like a thunderclap. "Barnum and the Jerome Clock Bubble" was transformed—by many who had recently been touting Barnum's promotional genius—into a great moral lesson about the "instability of ill-gotten gains."

But not everyone rejoiced at the showman's dilemma; an impressive list of friends offered loans and gifts. Refusing to accept their help, Barnum liquidated assets to pay off most of his debts and began rebuilding his fortune. Reflecting on the Jerome Clock debacle, he later wrote, in typical fashion: "When the blow fell upon me, I thought I could never recover; the event has shown, however, that I have gained both in character and fortune, and what threatened, for years, to be my ruin, has proved one of the most fortunate happenings of my career."

The Gun That Almost Wasn't

Saved by the Texas Rangers

Samuel Colt's six-shooter—often called the Gun That Won the West—played a vital role in American history. But it almost missed its entrance because of its creator's early business failure.

Born in Connecticut in 1814, Colt was a restless boy. He conceived the idea of a revolving pistol at the age of 16, while sailing to India. When he was 22, he secured his first U.S. patent for the gun and soon became a partner in an arms manufacturing company in Paterson, New Jersey.

After initial success, demand for the company's guns languished—some early models had a tendency to blow up. The factory closed in 1842, and by 1846 Colt was near financial ruin.

That same year America went to war with Mexico after the annexation of Texas. The Texas Rangers had been using Colt's handguns for years in their battles against the Comanches and were impressed with the weapon. At their leaders' urging, the secretary of war ordered 1,000 revolvers for $25,000.

Colt began to search for one of his guns to use as a prototype. Then the crisis occurred: none could be had. He advertised in newspapers but couldn't afford the prices people asked. Finally, in January 1847 Colt approached Orison Blunt, a New York gunsmith, to make a prototype based on another Colt pistol and incorporating suggestions made by Texas Ranger Sam Walker. Eli Whitney, Jr., the son of the inventor of the cotton gin, was engaged to produce this .44-caliber six-shooter. Other orders followed, and before Colt's death in 1862 his revolvers were standard equipment for soldiers and pioneers alike.

Horatio Alger's Lifelong Repentance

The sins and sorrows of the rags-to-riches man

Horatio Alger's best-selling novels told of young boys rising from the depths of poverty to the heights of great wealth through hard work, punctuality, honesty, and virtue. But early in his life, the author brought several Cape Cod boys to disgrace. He spent the rest of his life and much of his money trying to atone.

A Harvard Divinity School graduate descended from the Pilgrims, Alger certainly seemed to embody all that was right and good. In 1864, at the age of 30, he became minister of a small parish in Brewster, Massachusetts. His flock accepted him with enthusiasm and especially appreciated his efforts on behalf of the young, such as organizing Cadets for Temperance.

These efforts soon came under the scrutiny of the town gossips, however. Why wasn't the bachelor clergyman interested in the congregation's single women? Why did he devote so much time and energy to young boys? The questions came up during a regular meeting of the parish committee, after which Thomas Crocker questioned his own son. The boy reported that he had been sexually molested by the minister. Alger did not deny the charges. He immediately resigned and left town. It was a good thing, too, because the townspeople wanted blood.

Racked by shame, he devoted his life to the betterment of impoverished boys. Settling in New York City in 1866, he became associated with Charles Loring Brace and the Newsboys' Lodging House, a shelter for street kids. His experiences there inspired many of his books. He was also involved in the Fresh Air Fund, which took underprivileged children to the country for two summer weeks, and continues to do so to this day. And he gave most of the royalties of his best-selling works to scores of disadvantaged young men. But Alger's greatest legacy is the novels themselves, a statement of the American dream that shaped the values and lives of generations.

Horatio Alger's lingering guilt over the Brewster incident is apparent in a poem he wrote in 1872 about Friar Anselmo, who wanted to die for committing a deadly sin but found new life in helping others:

Courage, Anselmo, though
 thy sin be great,
God grants thee life that
 thou may'st expiate.
Thy guilty stains shall be
 washed white again,
By noble service done
 thy fellow-men.

Alger's life was a singular expression of the poem's theme of redemption.

The Man Who Began the California Gold Rush

"Yankeedom $600,000,000 . . . Myself Individually $000,000,000"

At about 7:30 on Monday morning, January 24, 1848, James Marshall reached down through six inches of icy water and picked up a nugget of gold worth perhaps 50 cents. Over the next half century some $2½ billion of the glittering metal would be mined in California. But Marshall never profited from it, never struck gold again, and died broke.

Born in 1810, the son of a New Jersey wheelwright, Marshall traveled west in his mid-twenties, eventually settling in 1845 at John Sutter's remote outpost in the Sacramento Valley. Eighty-five miles to the southwest, the quiet seaport of Yerba Buena (soon to be renamed San Francisco) had only a few hundred residents. Gold would change all that.

In 1847 Sutter and Marshall became partners in a sawmill. It was during Marshall's inspection of the mill's tailrace that he discovered the gold. Rumors of the strike spread quickly, but people remained skeptical—until Sam Brannan came on the scene.

Brannan ran the store at Sutter's Fort. In early May, while one local newspaper was still calling gold rumors "all sham . . . got up to guzzle the gullible," Brannan arrived in San Francisco waving a bottle full of gold dust. He had bought every iron pan in town for 20 cents each and was selling them at his new store near the gold fields for as much as $16, the price of an ounce of gold.

When President Polk mentioned the strike in a December speech, California was suddenly a national mania. Gold-hungry miners destroyed Sutter's lands and livestock. During the first year of the rush, one Sacramento meat company made $60,000 on stolen Sutter cattle alone.

Marshall could have made a fortune at the sawmill, for lumber in the gold fields sold at $500 per 1,000 board feet. But he was an inept businessman. Becoming entangled in a dispute between the miners and the Indians, he feared for his life and fled the area.

When he returned a few weeks later, he gave up trying to protect his land claims and began prospecting himself. But many miners believed he had a gift for finding gold, and he was followed wherever he went. On one occasion miners even threatened to hang him if he would not lead them to a strike. Failing as a prospector, Marshall worked at odd jobs, became increasingly eccentric, and began to drink heavily.

He once estimated that his discovery had profited "Yankeedom $600,000,000 . . . Myself Individually $000,000,000." Petitioning California for compensation, he was granted a $100-a-month pension in 1872; but it was revoked six years later, after he wandered into the state assembly drunk. He remained impoverished until his death in 1885, his total estate valued at $218.82.

His grave overlooks the site of the discovery that made him famous and ruined his life. In 1890 a $9,000 statue of Marshall was dedicated at the grave. The caretaker was paid $75 a month.

The Temple of Gum Shun

When the "miners forty-niners" descended on California in the early 1850's, "darlin' Clementine" wasn't the only one in pigtails. The gold rush attracted many middle-class Chinese, such as the prospector at left, who sought their fortunes in the land of Gum Shun ("Gold Mountain") and were among its most diligent miners. By 1852 there were 2,500 Chinese working in or around Weaverville, and the temple they built there in 1874 still stands. It is called a joss house, a term that probably entered Chinese in the early days of European contact as a corruption of the Portuguese word for God. Patterned after similar temples in China, the Weaverville joss house was built to honor Taoist deities.

Shorty Harris (left, with three friends) on cars: "These flivver prospectors have never made a strike. If any more good stuff is found in this country, it will be the jackass men who turn the trick."

The Tall Tale of Shorty Harris

"A single-blanket jackass prospector"

Shorty Harris was buried standing up, 282 feet below sea level at the bottom of Death Valley, so that he "could be ready to step into heaven." Five times during his life he had stepped into gold. It made him famous, but never rich.

Born in Providence, Rhode Island, in 1857, he was orphaned at 7, a mill hand at 11, and on the road by 14. Before he was 20 he was prospecting in the West. Scarcely 5 feet tall, Shorty once proposed marriage to Bessie Hart, a 6-foot, 210-pound cook in the mining camp at Ballarat, California. She turned him down . . . gently.

Unlucky in love, his luck as a prospector was renowned—and so was his failure to make any money from his strikes. Once he sent his partner to file a claim. But the man got sidetracked in a saloon before he made it to the record office. Another time, Shorty, who had a love for the "Oh Be Joyful" himself, sold a claim for $1,000 and three cases of whiskey. His partner held on and got $40,000 for his share, but Shorty didn't care. He was still working on the whiskey when his partner lost everything at the gaming tables in Ballarat.

His biggest strike, at Bullfrog Mountain in 1904, set off the greatest gold rush in Death Valley history. Fortune hunters were near tears because burros couldn't be had for as much as $500. After the pack animals were gone, they loaded handcarts. When the carts were gone, they set off with wheelbarrows on the 75-mile trek to the gold fields. Shorty had a prime claim—but he went on a six-day drunk and sold his rights for $1,000.

Shorty died in 1934. Because he was so short, the grave diggers dug a short hole. But his coffin was standard length, and as it was lowered, it became wedged at an angle in the grave. When the grave diggers tried to lengthen the hole, sand slid back in, propping the casket practically upright. Then they remembered—that's the way Shorty wanted it anyway. Once again, he had been lucky. The plaque marking his grave bears the epitaph he wrote for himself: "Here lies Shorty Harris, a single-blanket jackass prospector."

What, No Tuba?

In 1918 a saloonkeeper in Nevada City, California, sent to Germany for the world's largest mechanical organ. The Popper Felix—11 feet tall and 20 wide—could imitate a piano, xylophone, piccolo, violin, kettle drum, triangle, and Chinese cymbals. It also gave a light show, featuring the picture of a buxom woman who seemed to throw roses. Silent for some 60 years since Nevada City's mines played out, the organ today graces the home of a Michigan antiques collector.

A 20-mule team had only 18 mules. Two horses were at the wagon's tongue; the smartest mules led.

How to Get a Fortune out of Hell

It wasn't gold. Or silver. It was . . . borax!

F. M. Smith quit looking for gold in 1872, when he found huge deposits of white crystalline "cottonballs" in the Nevada desert. The stuff was valuable and he knew it. He bought out rivals and even held some of them off at gunpoint. Soon he monopolized the bonanza, earning the nickname "Borax" Smith.

Eight years later a chance encounter abruptly changed the scenario. Aaron Winters had spent most of his 60 years prospecting for gold. But his efforts never panned out, and by 1880 he was resigned to spending his twilight years with his wife, Rosie, in a shack just east of California's Death Valley. Then an itinerant prospector told Winters how folks in Nevada were making a fortune from borax and described how it was tested to make sure it wasn't salt. Winters suppressed his excitement. So *that* was the white stuff littering acres of Death Valley.

As soon as the prospector left, Winters and his wife got some sulphuric acid and alcohol and hightailed it to Furnace Creek. When it was dark Winters poured the chemicals over a saucer of the white crystals and, with a trembling hand, struck a match. "She burns green, Rosie!" he whooped. "We're rich!"

Reality set in. Death Valley was one hell of a place to make your fortune—130° in the shade some days, and no water. Winters knew he'd never get the borax across 165 miles of desert to the nearest railroad junction. And so, when San Francisco entrepreneur William Coleman offered him $20,000, he grabbed it and moved on.

Coleman had carried cargo with multiple mule teams before. Now one of his superintendents suggested hitching a pair of teams to two wagons at a time. The wagons he designed, with rear wheels 7 feet in diameter, could haul 36½ tons—not only borax but enough water, food, and fodder to supply the crew and 20 animals throughout the 10-day trek.

So successful were these spectacular desert freight trains that the product became known as 20-mule-team borax. But because of the great new supply, prices plummeted, and in 1890 Coleman went broke. Who bought him out? None other than Borax Smith. Adopting the 20-mule-team name as a trademark, Smith promoted borax into a household panacea for aiding digestion, softening water, keeping milk sweet, and curing epilepsy and bunions.

Doctor, Lawyer, Banker, Dupe

Drake struck oil—but didn't strike it rich

"I bot by Townsend's advice without investigating," Edwin Laurentine Drake reminisced, "and a few months afterwards when I did try to investigate I made up my mind my friend had pulled me in, in trying to get out himself."

Drake, who had retired as a railroad conductor in 1858 because of a bad back, lived with his wife and child at the Tontine Hotel in New Haven, Connecticut. Money was scarce, and so he was interested when a fellow boarder named James Townsend talked about the potential commercial value of Seneca oil. Indians had long used the stuff—found in creeks and salt wells—to soothe aching joints. Townsend thought it might sell as a substitute for whale oil in lamps or even as a lubricant. But so far no one had found a way to extract it from the ground in quantity.

It happened that Townsend, a bank president, was one of a trio of New Englanders—the others were Dr. Francis Brewer and lawyer George Bissell—who had formed the Seneca Oil Company and bought a tract of 100 acres on aptly named Oil Creek, near Titusville in western Pennsylvania. They needed a "general agent" for their wild venture. Who better than Drake, an innocent who resembled a deacon with his black clothes, dark beard, and sorrowful eyes.

Drake was made president of the company, awarded a huge block of stock (which he was quickly relieved of), and promised a year's salary of $1,000 for operating expenses. He was also gulled into sinking his entire savings of $200 into the project. Drake and his family took the train to Titusville.

Having no idea how to get oil out of the ground, he employed men for a dollar a day to dig with picks and shovels. They failed, and so he turned to drilling. Keeping precise records of his expenses, he bought lumber to build a derrick and a $500 nautical engine for power. Searching for a dependable helper, he met and hired "Uncle Billy" Smith, a blacksmith with salt-boring experience.

By then it was spring 1859, and the directors had lost interest. But Drake doggedly persisted. Thwarted by sand and clay clogging the drill hole, he had a brainstorm: he would drive pipe down to bedrock to form a shaft for the drill. Drake's brilliant innovation made oil wells possible, but it never occurred to him to patent it.

On Sunday, August 28, he saw something glistening in the hole, 69½ feet down. "What's that?" he asked. "That is your fortune," replied Uncle Billy. Soon gushing oil filled all the barrels they could find. Drake had drilled the world's first commercial oil well.

Overnight Titusville became a boomtown; Brewer, Bissell, and Townsend scrambled to buy up all the shares of Seneca Oil. Men were on their way to becoming millionaires—except Drake. Inept in money matters, he hung around for four years as an agent and justice of the peace and saved a measly $16,000. Then he lost it all speculating on Wall Street.

Years later, when he and his family were found living in destitution, the state of Pennsylvania granted him an annual $1,500 pension. After his death in 1880, the citizens of Titusville erected a monument to honor him as the man who launched the oil industry.

When Edwin L. Drake arrived in Titusville in 1858 to raise oil from the ground, local people felt sorry for him, wondering how such a nice fellow could have been so badly gulled by the "fancy stock company." Several years later the unlikely hero of the oil industry (in top hat) revisited the well that changed their lives. In the background is the derrick he built.

The First Texas Oilman

Most people in Melrose, Texas, thought the land around Oil Springs was worthless. But not storekeeper Talliaferro "Tol" Barret; in 1859 he leased 279 acres there. Had he been able to get the right machinery then, Barret would have drilled the first producing oil well in America. But the Civil War intervened and it was 1866 before he got started. Just as he struck oil—at 106 feet—the price of crude took a sharp drop. His savings gone, Tol abandoned his oil field and returned to the store. Before he died in 1913, there had been so much drilling at Oil Springs that he could no longer locate the site of his original well.

The Day Spindletop Roared

America's first gusher—and no one knew how to stop it!

Back in 1900 there wasn't much excitement in Beaumont, Texas, a modest lumber and rice marketing town. And so the youngsters loved it when Pattillo Higgins, their Sunday school teacher, took them out to Spindletop, a knoll south of town named for a cone-shaped tree. They would watch the eerie way the natural gas burned when he poked a small hole in the ground and lit a match.

Higgins, a brick maker and real estate promoter, had a passion for geology and he was sure that where there was gas there was oil. The adults of Beaumont scoffed, especially after four shallow wells were drilled on Spindletop without success.

But Anthony F. Lucas, an Austrian-born mining engineer, shared Higgins's view. Answering the promoter's ad in a trade journal, Lucas leased land for exploration and got the backing of banker Andrew Mellon and two Pittsburgh oilmen. The investors hired Al, Jim, and Curt Hamill, who had drilled at Corsicana, the first major oil field in Texas. In October the Hamill brothers started drilling. The going was slow. First they hit quicksand, then rock. But they worked around the clock, stopping only for a Christmas break.

They'd gone down 1,020 feet on January 10, 1901, when the drill stuck. They pulled it out, replaced the bit, and began to lower it. Suddenly mud started boiling up from the hole, pushing the drill pipe with it. Then, with an explosive roar, mud and debris shot into the air, followed by a geyser of oil more than twice the height of the derrick. The men, backing off in alarm, were drenched.

The explosion was heard miles away. Awestruck farmers rushed to the scene. No one in America had ever seen such a gusher before. Oil spewed out at a record 80,000 barrels a day and fire was a deadly threat, but no one knew how to stop the flow. The well roared and gushed for nine days, hurling nearly a million barrels of crude into the air, before the Hamills devised a way to cap it. Fashioning a T-shaped pipe fitted with valves, they risked their lives against the tremendous power that steadily burst from the earth and screwed the device to the drill pipe.

Spindletop was transformed. A forest of oil derricks sprouted near the first well, so dense that their supports overlapped. An acre of land sold for $1 million. Shantytowns sprang up, including Gladys City, named for one of Higgins's young pupils. Wildcatters lured by the boom lived in tents, or rented pool tables or barber chairs for the night. Saloons, gambling parlors, and brothels prospered. So did crime. Con men sold so much worthless stock that the hill became known as Swindletop.

But overproduction quickly drove oil prices down to three cents a barrel, while scarce water cost $6 a barrel. Spindletop's boom was over by 1903, but it spawned the first of many Texas millionaires.

Visiting Spindletop in 1901, a Standard Oil official shrugged: "Too big, too big; more oil here than will supply the world for the next century—not for us!" But the age of liquid fuel soon ensued.

"Between Me and My God"

Rockefeller's railroad skulduggery

"Don't buy new clothes and fast horses," John D. Rockefeller (above, in 1872) advised his Standard Oil partners. "Let your wife wear her last year's bonnet. You can't find anyplace where money will earn what it does here."

"I am opposed to the whole scheme of rebates and drawbacks—without I'm in it," declared John D. Rockefeller, quoting another oil baron. Rockefeller, the powerful founder of Standard Oil, was accused in the early 1870's of a practice that was then industry-wide.

Actually, it was Henry Flagler, a partner of Rockefeller's, who negotiated Standard Oil's first railroad rebates, or partial refunds of shipping fees, from the Atlantic & Great Western and several other railroads. But he soon learned a hard fact about the business: other refiners were receiving similar favors. The system dated back to at least 1856. By the time Rockefeller started Standard Oil in 1867, it was widespread.

Rockefeller became so obsessed with ending this cutthroat competition and bringing order to the industry—with himself on top—that he was receptive to an even *more* cutthroat plan. Through a Pennsylvania corporation called the South Improvement Company (SIC), Standard and a few other oil refiners agreed to divide their rail shipments as follows: 45 percent for the Pennsylvania Railroad and 27.5 percent each for the Erie and the New York Central.

In return, member oil companies were to receive not only substantial rebates on their *own* oil shipments, but also a percentage of the higher shipping fees paid by their *competitors.* The railroads were to provide SIC with confidential information on shipments made by nonmembers.

In practice, the scheme meant that the cost of shipping a barrel of refined oil from western Pennsylvania to New York would be $1.44½ for nonmembers but only 80 cents for insiders. Thus, SIC members would earn an additional $5 million to $6 million a year.

Rockefeller, a religious man, considered the maneuver ethical and even thought it would act as a helpful "evener" of railroad traffic. "I had our plan clearly in mind," he reflected. "I knew it was a matter of conscience. It was right between me and my God."

The public felt otherwise. News leaked out when a railroad manager jumped the gun in putting the new rates into effect. Newspapers launched an onslaught of criticism. Crude oil producers and refiners who had not joined the organization formed an embargo against SIC, which crippled the scheme. In April 1872 the Pennsylvania legislature revoked SIC's charter. So ended the ingenious plan by which business rivals would unknowingly have financed their own downfall.

What's in a Name?

Phillips 66. *When Frank and L. E. Phillips, founders of a new oil company, needed a catchy sign for their first gas station in 1917, the combination of a number and a name was quite fashionable. For them the answer seemed ordained: "high gravity" was a buzzword for quality gas then, and theirs was 66. On top of that, their first oil refinery was located on Texas State Route 66. Still, they weren't sure.*

Then a Phillips official, road-testing the new gas on Route 66, remarked, "This car goes like 60." "Sixty, nothing," his driver replied. "We're doing 66!" The combination of coincidences was too much to resist, and the Phillips 66 logo was born.

Shell Oil. *Back in the 1830's Marcus Samuel ran a curio shop. During a seaside vacation, his children began decorating their lunchboxes with shells, and Samuel, aware of the Victorian craze for decorative knickknacks, immediately recognized a potential best-seller. He began making and selling shell boxes. People loved them, and his place became widely known as The Shell Shop.*

Years later his son Marcus Jr. built up an oil business. By 1897 it had become so big that he formed a new company and named it after his father's shop. A few years later he adopted the Shell symbol. The rest, as they say, is history.

Nobody's Baby Now

The silver queen who ended her days in squalor

Among America's most poignant and scandalous love stories is that of Horace Tabor and Elizabeth Bonduel McCourt Doe (known as Baby Doe), who met in Leadville, Colorado, in 1880.

Tabor, 50 years old at the time, was a prominent silver king and the state's lieutenant governor. While he enjoyed his newfound wealth and position, Augusta, his wife of some 20 years, remained haunted by past poverty and nagged him constantly about money.

Love strikes

Then Baby Doe, a young divorcée, came to town. Five feet two with eyes of blue, a headful of golden curls, and a curvaceous figure, she was an eyeful and a charmer. Tabor fell wildly in love. In short order he arranged for a secret divorce in the remote town of Durango, and in September 1882 he and Baby Doe were clandestinely married in St. Louis.

On March 1, 1883, they were remarried by a priest in Washington, D.C., where Tabor was serving as an interim U.S. senator. A week before the ceremony, Tabor wrote to his "Darling Babe": "I love you to death and we will be so happy. Nothing shall mar our happiness for you are all my very own and I am yours from hair to toes and back again. I love you I love you Kiss Kiss for ever and ever."

Snobbery and scandal

Government wives shunned the wedding, described as "picturesquely vulgar," but many notables attended, among them President Chester A. Arthur. The nationwide attention given the event stirred up gossip, and before long news of the Tabors' St. Louis marriage surfaced. The priest was outraged by the deception. The public gasped as one delicious revelation after another circulated, including the illegality of the Durango divorce.

*Baby Doe Tabor, the beauty who had scandalized Denver society (above), revisited the town in 1931 dressed in rags (right). The reclusive widow greeted unwanted visitors with a shotgun, but became more amiable after a film and an opera—*The Ballad of Baby Doe*—were based on the Tabors' life.*

The Tabors returned to Denver. Snubbed and sneered at by society, they lived in ostentatious style until 1893, the year Tabor's financial empire collapsed. He had to go back to pushing a slag-heap wheelbarrow. Political friends got him appointed Denver postmaster—in a building on land that he himself had originally given to the city. To everyone's surprise, Baby stuck with him.

Tabor died in 1899, leaving his love an unintentionally cruel legacy. "Hold on to the Matchless," he had advised her, referring to a once-great Leadville mine that he still owned. Baby Doe obediently took her two lovely daughters to Leadville. When they finally left her—one to renounce the family forever and the other to die in a Chicago slum—she became a recluse, living in a shack close by the defunct Matchless Mine, which she claimed was "her mission and her life." For 35 years she struggled in poverty, working the mine by day and tormented at night by visions of her beloved Tabor, her daughters, the devil, and Jesus Christ.

On March 7, 1935, after a three-day blizzard, her frozen body was found on the floor of the shack, her arms outstretched in the form of a cross. Baby Doe Tabor's mission had finally ended.

Make a Million—Bet a Million

For John Gates, business was a game of roulette

John W. "Bet-a-Million" Gates loved to gamble—on anything. He earned his nickname by plunking down $1 million on a horse at the Saratoga racetrack. They wouldn't take the bet.

It was the love for taking chances that earned him millions. An Illinois country boy with a high-school education, he had saved enough money at 19 to buy a half-share in a small hardware store. That same year, 1874, he gambled on barbed wire, a new invention. Maneuvering a partnership with a manufacturer, Gates took to the road selling the product. To convince skeptical Texans, he built a barbed-wire corral in a San Antonio plaza and penned up 30 snorting longhorns for an afternoon. Before long Gates owned the American Steel and Wire Company, the nation's largest such concern.

Described by his secretary as "a great boy with an extraordinary money sense annexed," Gates outraged Wall Street financiers with his ability to best them. When J. P. Morgan sought the Louisville & Nashville Railroad, Gates grabbed control of the line and made Morgan pay through the nose. But the day came when Gates's luck ran out and he went begging to Morgan. Morgan told him to get out.

His finances still somewhat shaky, Gates went to Texas in 1901, right after Spindletop, one of the great gushers in petroleum history, had been struck. Gambling again, he formed an oil company on the spot. In a few years he had at least $50 million. In 1911 Bet-a-Million sent Morgan a copy of his firm's financial statement, just to rub it in. He died later that year.

A compulsive gambler, John W. Gates would happily bet $1,000 a race on which of two raindrops would reach the bottom of a windowpane first. Confident that he would always recover his losses and then some, he was ready to lose $250,000 in a poker game. Gates, who viewed business in the same way, was regarded as unprincipled by such buccaneers of business as Andrew Carnegie and J. P. Morgan.

Knock, Knock. Who's there? Your Fuller Brush Man. The breed was lampooned in a 1948 movie starring Red Skelton (above).

How They Got Started . . .

Fuller Brush Man. *"I washed babies with a back brush," related the original Fuller brush man, "swept stairs, cleaned radiators and milk bottles, dusted floors—anything that would prove the worth of what I had to sell."*

Born in January 1885 on a Nova Scotia farm, Alfred G. Fuller left home at 18 to find work in the Boston area. The shy youth eventually began selling brushes. On the eve of his 21st birthday, in response to his customers' complaints and suggestions, he invested $65 in equipment and began modifying stock items—and also making a few brushes of his own design. Within a few years Fuller had salesmen all over the country, trained in the high art of opening doors. When he died in 1973, saleswomen called Fullerettes outnumbered the men.

J. P. Morgan to the Rescue

The day America almost went broke

In January 1895 a crisis at the U.S. Treasury threatened to make American currency worthless. A severe depression stifled the economy, and large financial institutions, fearing that paper money would be devalued, were nervously cashing in their greenback dollars for Treasury gold. Gold reserves were draining out at the rate of $3 million a day. Experts, especially those who supported the gold standard, feared that public confidence in paper money would collapse and greenbacks would become worthless. Desperately, the government needed to replenish the gold supply—but how?

For political reasons, President Grover Cleveland wanted Congress to take the initiative with a bill authorizing a public sale of bonds, the money to be used to buy gold. Financier John Pierpont Morgan was certain the scheme would lead to disaster. Not only was there too little time, but the announcement of the sale—acknowledging the Treasury's weakness—would in itself cause a rush to cash in greenbacks.

On Tuesday morning, February 5, Morgan met with the president, who was still committed to the idea of a congressionally mandated public bond sale. Toward noon they received a report that the New York subtreasury had only $9 million in gold left. Morgan personally knew of a man who might present more than $10 million in drafts that very afternoon. Collapse could be only hours away.

Morgan presented a workable solution. A forgotten Civil War law already existed, allowing the Treasury to buy gold coins directly with bonds. This law gave Cleveland the authorized bonds he wanted, while at the same time allowing him to sell them privately—and quickly—to Morgan's syndicate without a public announcement.

There remained one problem: Morgan must guarantee that large financial institutions would stop cashing in greenbacks for the very gold that the scheme would provide. It was an astounding request: the president was asking Morgan to control the entire international financial community and to ensure its support of American paper money. Fully realizing the difficult manipulations that this would require, Morgan gave the president a promise that no one else *could* have made—and he kept it. The gold was delivered to the Treasury and the gold drain was stopped. For all his efforts, Morgan's company made less than one percent profit on the deal.

Looking into J. P. Morgan's black eyes, said famed photographer Edward Steichen, "was like confronting the headlights of an express train bearing down on you."

Carnegie's "Daughter"

A sweet-talking swindler bilked banks of millions

Elizabeth "Cassie" Bigley was born beautiful, but not rich. To remedy this oversight, she took up the art of the con, first passing herself off as an heiress in Toronto, then as Mme. Lydia De Vere, Clairvoyant, in Toledo. In that guise, she persuaded one gentleman to obtain $10,000 in cash for her forged notes, and wound up in jail for her trouble. In 1893 she was pardoned by Gov. William McKinley.

Settling in Cleveland, she met Dr. Leroy Chadwick in a bordello. They married and soon became one of the city's most celebrated couples. Their large, ornate home bespoke Cassie Chadwick's fondness for spending huge sums, and so did their lavish entertaining and extravagant gifts. To support this lifestyle, she pulled her biggest con—persuading bankers that she was Andrew Carnegie's illegitimate daughter.

Cleverly convincing, she once took some Ohio

"The Goose That Lays the Golden Eggs"

How Andrew Carnegie learned the secret of investing others' money

He was regarded as a brilliant and aggressive steel magnate, and was one of the nation's great success stories. But long before Andrew Carnegie earned millions in metals, he made his first fortune through investments—and he never used a penny of his own money.

The poverty-stricken Carnegie family arrived in America from Scotland in 1848, and 12-year-old Andrew took a factory job for $1.20 a week. Four years later, when he was earning $4 a week as a telegrapher, Tom Scott of the Pennsylvania Railroad hired him as his personal secretary. Carnegie idolized Scott, who apprenticed the ambitious youngster in this fast-growing business. But Scott taught Carnegie about more than railroads; he introduced him to the wonders of investment.

The first lesson came in 1856. "Fortunatus knocked at our door," Carnegie later wrote. "Mr. Scott asked me if I had $500 . . . to make an investment for me. Five hundred cents was much nearer my capital." Scott advised him to buy 10 shares in the Adams Express Company, about which the older man had inside information. (At that time, trading on the basis of inside information was a common—and still legal—practice.)

Curiously, Carnegie later wrote that his mother had borrowed the $500 from his uncle, but his own papers contain an IOU to Scott, who clearly lent the young man the funds himself. Nearly six months later, when the note came due, Carnegie had saved $200 and borrowed the rest from another man, offering his Adams shares as security. Thus began Carnegie's method of using dividends from stock to make payments against loans; when the loans were paid off, the dividends were his. This was a system he would use repeatedly to build his assets and income without having to invest his own capital.

The canny Carnegie went on to amass a staggering fortune in the steel business. (J. P. Morgan once called him "the richest man in the world.") But for the rest of his life, he would recall vividly the envelope that contained his first monthly dividend of $10. "It gave me the first penny of revenue from capital—something that I had not worked for with the sweat of my brow. 'Eureka!' I cried. 'Here's the goose that lays the golden eggs.' "

---

lawyers to Carnegie's New York mansion. Asking them to wait in the carriage, she entered the mansion, talked to the maid, then left, waving a friendly farewell. Once outside, she showed the lawyers notes for almost $1 million signed "Andrew Carnegie." The signatures were impressive—but bogus. In another scam, Cassie claimed that Carnegie had given her $7 million in securities and got a bank receipt for the tidy sum; the securities, of course, were more of her artful forgeries.

Using the credit inspired by her receipt and the Carnegie name, Cassie continued to litter banks with forged paper, managing to spend about $1 million a year. Finally one lender sued, and when Carnegie disavowed any knowledge of his "daughter," the banks immediately panicked. One banker, having lent Cassie four times his institution's entire capitalization *and* quite a bit of his own money, begged her for repayment. When she refused, he fainted.

Cassie was arrested and brought to trial. But despite her powers of persuasion, she couldn't con her way out of prison, where she died, penniless, in 1907.

Cassie Chadwick loved to spend money, and the hoax that allowed her to indulge her luxurious ways—she claimed to be Andrew Carnegie's illegitimate daughter—lasted seven years. When the steel magnate publicly stated that he did "not know Mrs. Chadwick," her glittering world crumbled.

May 10, 1869: A golden spike was driven at Promontory Point, Utah, to signal the completion of the first transcontinental railroad. After the momentous meeting of eastbound and westbound locomotives, a crowd of workers and owners looked on as the two chief engineers, C. P. Montágue of the Central Pacific (left) and Grenville M. Dodge (right) of the Union Pacific, shook hands.

Famous Achievement—Infamous Scandal

The "unmitigated frauds" that helped to drive the golden spike

One of America's greatest achievements—stretching a railroad track from coast to coast—was also one of our greatest scandals.

The owners of the Central Pacific and the Union Pacific railroads had devised a clever scheme to reap enormous profits. They created their own construction companies and charged the railroads exorbitant rates to lay tracks. Thus they made money two ways: by pocketing the extra fees and by inflating the price of the railroads' stock with padded holdings.

The Central Pacific's owners, including the well-known Charles Crocker and Collis P. Huntington, set up a construction arm called the Contract and Finance Company. Similarly, the Union Pacific, headed by Thomas C. Durant and Oakes Ames, created the Credit Mobilier Construction Company. The Central Pacific, building eastward from Sacramento, California, completed 742 miles at an expense of about $120 million (actual cost: some $58 million). The Union Pacific, building westward from Omaha, Nebraska, paid $94 million for 1,038 miles of track (true value: only about $50 million).

To ensure the success of the scheme, the plotters bribed congressmen and government officials—including future President James Garfield and Speaker of the House Schuyler Colfax (a future vice president). Almost $500,000 went for the purpose, including 343 shares of railroad stock.

Scandal erupted after a series of articles in the New York *Sun,* beginning in September 1872, revealed that the owners of Credit Mobilier held more than 367,000 shares of Union Pacific stock that had not cost them a cent. Congress created the Poland Committee to investigate. But because many of the central figures of the plan had used dummies for their activities, few of them could be identified. Moreover, so convoluted and secretive were their dealings that the investigators were unable to sort out much of what had really happened.

A few ringleaders, principally Oakes Ames, were censured. Congress enacted legislation in 1873 directing the attorney general to sue Union Pacific stockholders for illegal profits from contracts the owners had made with themselves.

The Supreme Court ruled on the suit in 1878, saying that "more unmitigated frauds were never perpetrated on a helpless corporation by its managing directors." But, it further stated, since "the government has received all the advantages for which it has bargained," it could collect nothing.

A Reluctant Rider on the Money Train

Commodore Vanderbilt hated railroads—until he made a fortune from them

When Cornelius Vanderbilt died on January 4, 1877, at the age of 83, he was probably the richest man in the world. He left an estate of some $104 million—$2 million more than the entire U.S. Treasury. About 90 percent of his fortune came from railroads, and yet Vanderbilt hated railroads and refused to have anything to do with them until the last 15 years of his life.

His antipathy dated from November 1833, when he was a passenger, along with former President John Quincy Adams, on the Camden and Amboy Railroad. The train, bound for Perth Amboy, New Jersey, broke an axle and jumped the track, killing two people—it was the first fatal train wreck in U.S. history—and critically injuring Vanderbilt.

Not until the early 1860's, when the railroad boom had begun, did the lure of high profits help Vanderbilt surmount his deep aversion. He was worth some $11 million by then, earned from his large fleet of steamships (hence the title commodore). He reasoned that, if he could gain control of the railroads, he would be able to extend his freight-carrying capacity from the coastal docks into the heart of the country.

First, he secretly bought the New York & Harlem Railroad, which ran 52 miles from 42nd Street in Manhattan to Brewster, New York. The stock cost him $9 per share; it soon reached $50, earning millions. His acquisition of a Broadway streetcar franchise, extending his rail service all the way down to the Battery seaport, made the Harlem stock even more valuable.

Vanderbilt's rivals tried to have the streetcar franchise annulled while they sold Harlem stock short; but the shrewd commodore bought up all the available Harlem stock until it was cornered.

Now fully launched, Vanderbilt began to expand vigorously. Despite outcries of "monopoly," he acquired the Hudson River Railroad, which ran parallel to his own Harlem line but continued on to Albany. He then set his sights on the New York Central going from Albany to Buffalo, and in less than a year he had amassed a controlling interest of $2.5 million in shares.

He was dissatisfied, however, with the comparatively small amount of freight that was being transferred from the Central to his southbound Hudson River line, which turned over most of its westbound freight to the Central. And so, waiting until midwinter, when boats could not ply the frozen Hudson River, Vanderbilt informed the Central's management that the Hudson would no longer accept its freight. In addition, he directed his trains to stop some two miles short of a bridge near Albany, forcing the Central's passengers to make the connection on foot. The railroad's stock plummeted, and Vanderbilt snatched up the shares—about $6 million worth. The Central caved in. When its stockholders later asked him to become president, the commodore accepted with aplomb.

Vanderbilt merged the Central and Hudson lines, thinking that the move would make both more valuable. Yet, much to his disgust, freight rates were on the decline. He tried to get the Pennsylvania and the Erie lines to agree on higher rates; but the Erie, a trunk line of nearly 500 miles, was a "guerilla": it blocked his every move to establish connections to the Midwest. So Vanderbilt attempted an age-old solution: buy out your rival.

The Erie was not easily bought. It was run by a trio of unscrupulous rascals: sinister Daniel Drew, flamboyant Jim Fisk, and taciturn Jay Gould. As fast as Vanderbilt could buy Erie stock, they kept selling. They converted Erie bonds into stock, sometimes illegally; and when an old printing press was found, they churned out some 100,000 counterfeit shares to sell him. The four-year war of the Erie, after entertaining the dismayed public with its combination of comedy, burlesque, and lawlessness, reached its peak in 1868.

The enraged Vanderbilt called on one of his "tame" New York State judges to order the arrest of Drew, Fisk, and Gould. But they had been warned. Hurriedly gathering all incriminating evidence and $6 million in illegal profits, the trio fled across the river to the safety of New Jersey.

This defeat was one of the darkest occasions in the commodore's life. His opponents had cheated him—worse, they had outwitted him! Their dispute almost plunged the railroad industry into financial disaster. Vanderbilt relented, however, and agreed to settle with his enemies.

Vanderbilt emerged triumphant in 1875. After conquering the Lake Shore & Michigan Southern, the Canada Southern, and the Michigan Central railroads, he was finally able to link them with the New York Central line, thus creating one of the world's greatest systems of rail transport, stretching all the way from the eastern seaboard to the industrial heart of the country.

Jay Gould's Black Friday

A golden scheme of ruinous proportions

Modern stockbrokers and speculators still shudder at the thought of Black Tuesday—October 29, 1929, when the market's spectacular nosedive set off the Great Depression. That's how their great-grandfathers felt about Black Friday—September 24, 1869, when a scheme to corner the nation's gold market brought about a near-ruinous collapse.

The mastermind of the plan was the brilliant and cagey Jay Gould, recently victorious against Commodore Cornelius Vanderbilt in the fight for control of the Erie Railroad. His plan hinged on the fact that gold was constantly required by businessmen for foreign trade. If Gould could corner the market, the needs of international merchants would drive the price of gold upward. And since there was only some $15 million to $20 million in gold in New York, a corner seemed easy—if the U.S. Treasury's holdings of $80 million could be kept off the market.

Inside connections were vital to the plan; so Gould contacted Abel Corbin, brother-in-law of President Ulysses S. Grant, who often bragged of his influence, and had him arrange for Daniel Butterfield to be appointed assistant U.S. treasurer in New York. He even met with the president, to convince him that a higher gold price would avert a national currency crisis. But Grant, a "sound money man," was noncommital.

The scheme went into full swing that September, with Gould buying gold contracts secretly through various brokers. And to secure the alliance of his henchmen, he also bought millions in gold contracts for *them*—without demanding payment.

But rumors about Gould's gold corner soon leaked out, and a counterattack to force down the price stalled the market. Gould enlisted the help of Jim Fisk, an old cohort who had previously backed out of the scheme. Fisk was to openly purchase gold, building confidence and driving up the price. He complied, loudly predicting that gold would soon hit $200. It worked—the price of gold climbed steadily.

But Gould had stacked the deck: while Fisk bought furiously at ever-inflated prices, Gould secretly sold through dozens of brokers. Gold finally reached $162, and that's when the secretary of the treasury put $4 million in government gold on the market. Instantly gold fell $27. Black Friday had come!

In the ensuing pandemonium some brokers fainted, others were taken to hospitals, and one, Solomon Mahler, committed suicide. Fisk saved himself from financial ruin by repudiating his contracts. Gould had "tame" judges issue injunctions halting the payoffs of various financing agreements.

Estimates of Gould's profits ranged from $11 to $40 million—some claimed that he later shared the bonanza with Fisk.

Unscrupulous financier Jay Gould, depicted below by Thomas Nast, began his fortune by selling an "improved" mousetrap invented by his grandfather. It was stolen from him, but later retrieved. The story was the first of many scurrilous tales featuring Gould.

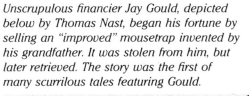

HONOR AMONG —.

JAY GOULD. "For the Sake of Peace!"

The Witch of Wall Street

With riches aplenty, she still wore rags

Hetty Green could read the financial pages by the age of six. At 30, in 1864, she inherited her father's fortune of about $1 million and began trading on Wall Street with a bold audacity that became legend. She bought Civil War bonds when others spurned them, and they paid off. Hetty made ailing businesses profitable by driving stocks up and down. But it was her personal style as much as her skill against such fierce competitors as Jay Gould that earned her the title the Witch of Wall Street.

For while her peers lived in opulence, Hetty lived like a pauper. She worked alone on the floor of a bank—where she had coerced free space—and for lunch she'd pull a ham sandwich from her grubby pocket.

She married so her inheritance would go to her children rather than other relatives. But the children, Ned and Sylvia, were subjected to her brutal thrift. They ate and traveled as cheaply as possible, shuttling to and from dingy hotels to avoid paying property taxes. When Ned was injured in a sledding accident, Hetty took him to a charity ward, but was recognized and charged. Refusing to pay, she treated the wound herself. It festered, and Ned's leg later had to be amputated.

Hetty Green died in 1916 of a stroke suffered while arguing with a maid over the price of milk. She left her children about $50 million each.

Hetty Green was a well-known figure on Wall Street in the black dress she always wore. To save the cost of soap, she seldom washed it—except the hem that dragged on the ground. Her petticoats had many pockets that bulged with stocks, bonds, and wads of cash as she made her rounds.

How They Got Started . . .

Wall Street. *Two of the world's foremost financial institutions, the New York and the American stock exchanges, can trace their beginnings to a colorful and chaotic open marketplace in lower Manhattan. In this curb market, bankers, brokers, and investors traded stocks on street corners.*

On May 17, 1792, a group of 24 brokers each paid $200 to form the Tontine Coffee House Company, forerunner of the New York Stock Exchange, on Wall Street. Rival groups later formed, such as the Mining Exchange, which flourished briefly during the gold and silver rush years. Like private clubs, they regulated membership, procedures, and listings.

But the curb market—open to anyone wishing to trade—continued to be the scene of the most exciting action. When telephones came along, clerks made hand signals from windows to their brokers on the street, who wore distinctive identifying apparel. Visits from such unusual characters as Hetty Green were common.

Eventually the curb market standardized its operations and formed the New York Curb Market Agency, predecessor of the American Stock Exchange. Finally, on June 27, 1921, it moved indoors and opened for trading in a grand new edifice on Trinity Place.

"You've Got to Look Like Money"

Diamonds were always Jim Brady's best friend

Jim Brady owned a set of diamonds for each day of the month, complete with stickpin, shirt studs, cuff links, vest buttons, and belt buckle.

Jim Brady bought his first diamond, a one-carat sparkler for his little finger, in 1879, when he was 23. It cost $90, nearly half of his savings; he blew the rest on clothes. He'd just landed a job selling railroad supplies, and he knew that impressions were important. "If you're going to make money—you've got to look like money" was his credo.

Diamond jewelry was common among traveling salesmen; it impressed clients and hotel clerks. But Brady made the gems his trademark. He won them in card games, bought them in pawnshops, and traded for them. Soon he was called Diamond Jim. He even gave away sparklers to special customers—skeptics were silenced when he scratched his name on the nearest window.

Real wealth began when Brady became the exclusive agent for a steel undercarriage for railroad cars, then built mostly of wood. Eventually he introduced steel cars and formed his own company.

By the time he turned 32, Diamond Jim was a celebrity. He reveled in the role. He was a regular at Harry Hill's, a night spot frequented by the likes of Thomas Edison, P. T. Barnum, and John L. Sullivan. Often accompanied by his lifelong friend Lillian Russell, he was a conspicuous first-nighter, sitting in the front row, resplendent in his black cutaway and flashing diamonds. His parties were legendary, with unlimited food, wine, cigars, and chorus girls, and his restaurant bills were astronomical. He himself would tuck away three dozen oysters, half a dozen crabs, six or seven lobsters, two ducks, steak, vegetables, pastries, and chocolates. Surprisingly, however, his favorite drink was orange juice.

Diamond Jim was the first to be seen in a horseless carriage in New York, streaking down Madison Avenue at 11 miles an hour. When bicycles became fashionable, he ordered several—gold-plated with silver-plated spokes. For Lillian Russell he had a special cycle made, studded with diamond chips and gemstones and sporting mother-of-pearl handlebars. When they went cycling, traffic halted and throngs gathered; the police had to clear their way.

In 1912 Diamond Jim underwent a chancy operation for kidney stones. Doctors found that his stomach was six times the normal size. Recovering, the ever-generous Brady presented 50 two-carat diamond rings to the nurses. When he died in 1917, crowds gathered at his house on East 86th Street to pay their last respects as he lay in his coffin, decked out in diamonds. And they fought to get into the chapel for his funeral. Most of them, from the famous on down to newsboys, wept openly.

The Paperback Shopping Mall

Mail order changed the lifestyle of Middle America

Traveling in the South as a salesman in 1870, Aaron Montgomery Ward saw how local merchants exploited rural people by selling at heavily marked-up prices. If he could pay cash for goods in large quantities, he could sell them for much less.

Ward's first one-page mailing listed 163 items, but business mushroomed so rapidly that he was soon sending out bound catalogs. In 1875 Chicago-based Montgomery Ward was the first company to offer its customers a money-back guarantee—a revolutionary move at a time when the warning "Let the buyer beware" was customary. Because of federal weight restrictions on packages, the company had to be resourceful: heavy coats, for example, were shipped in two halves, with a needle and thread included, so that they could be sewn back together.

Ward's customers often requested more than the catalog listed. Hundreds of letters came from men seeking wives; some wanted a particular female model shown on one of the pages. Others asked for summer boarders, good lawyers, and babies to adopt. Troubled correspondents wanted marital advice.

Occasionally the company tried retail areas beyond its capabilities. It marketed a stylish automobile, called the Modoc, but the venture failed because no one had foreseen the need to have Modoc dealers and service garages.

When Rural Free Delivery was initiated, merchants—angry because customers would not have to come to town to pick up their mail—staged catalog-burnings in the town squares, but to no avail. Over the years Montgomery Ward & Co. grew from its small mail-order origins into a chain of hundreds of retail stores. The story of Rudolph the Red-nosed Reindeer originated as a Ward's sales promotion. The company discontinued the catalog in 1985.

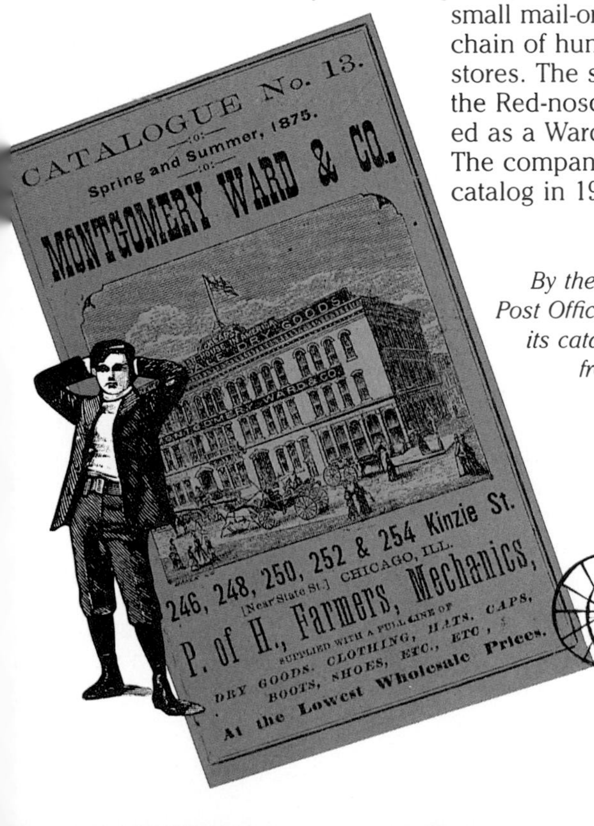

By the 1890's Ward's was the Post Office's largest patron, with its catalog offering everything from bicycle suits to this "sports buggy."

How They Got Started . . .

Sears, Roebuck. *Managing a railroad and express office in North Redwood, Minnesota, a town with three houses in 1886, left Richard Warren Sears plenty of time to free-lance. In those days wholesalers would often ship goods on consignment; if the shipment was unclaimed, the freight agent could have it at a reduced price so he could resell the wares at a profit.*

When Sears acquired a box of $25 gold-filled watches this way, he offered them at bargain rates to other agents. In six months, he made $5,000. Quitting his job, he set up a watch company and advertised for a watchmaker. Alvah Curtis Roebuck responded. Before long the pair branched out; in 1893 they formed Sears, Roebuck and Co. and began issuing their catalog—soon known as the Wish Book and the Farmer's Bible. But customers had to be wary. One Sears ad offered a "sewing machine" for $1. It was a needle and thread.

Avon. *David H. McConnell, an itinerant book salesman in 1886, found that the best way to get his foot in the door was to offer housewives free cologne. Before long it became even clearer that the fragrances were more popular than the books. McConnell began manufacturing a line of colognes and hired housewives to ring doorbells. Years later, he named his expanded enterprise, headquartered near Suffern, New York, after the Avon River in Shakespeare's England because of the similarity of the countryside.*

The Merchant Prince Mystery

An empty grave—a baffling puzzle

Along with William Astor and Cornelius Vanderbilt, Alexander Turney Stewart was one of the three richest Americans of his time. A millionaire by 1837, he made his fortune in the New York retail trade. His elegant emporium on lower Broadway became the model for modern department stores, and by the 1860's his shops were earning more than $50 million a year. When Stewart died childless on April 10, 1876, the executors of his estate included his widow and Henry Hilton, his attorney and longtime confidant.

Two years later, in a shocking turn of events, grave robbers spirited away Stewart's corpse. Hilton, at the widow's behest, offered a $25,000 reward. He later doubled the offer, but there was no response. Soon newspaper reports began to appear, among them a story that the body awaited reburial at a cathedral that had been built with Stewart money in Garden City, Long Island. This proved false, as did other stories. Tales of the corpse's safe return circulated until 1886, when Mrs. Stewart died. Since she left no provision in her will for the search to continue, speculation increased. Had the body been reburied?

Subsequently, the memoirs of a retired policeman claimed that the body had been ransomed, but several dubious details were never verified. And to this day nobody really knows where the remains of New York's first great merchant prince now rest.

A. T. Stewart's body was stolen from the churchyard of St. Mark's-in-the-Bowery, New York City.

Kellogg, Dietary Crusader

The idea for wheat flakes came in a dream

When young John Harvey Kellogg attended the Bellevue Hospital Medical College in New York, he sustained himself on breakfasts of seven Graham crackers, supplemented by an occasional coconut, potato, or bowl of oatmeal. He'd been sent to medical school by the Western Health Reform Institute of Battle Creek, Michigan, a retreat whose founder, Ellen G. White, followed literally the advice of Genesis: "Behold, I have given you every herb-bearing seed . . . to you it shall be for meat."

Offering only the blandest of foods—largely whole-grain cereals without flavoring—and no entertainment, the institute had difficulty competing with more posh spas. It needed, at the very least, a staff physician. "Hustle young men off to some doctor-mill," advised Mrs. White's husband.

Early efforts

Medical degree in hand, Kellogg returned in 1876 to take his place as the institute's medical superintendent. Renaming it the Medical and Surgical Sanitarium, he introduced such amenities as wheelchair socials and string orchestra concerts.

The spa expanded and thrived. Remembering his difficulty in maintaining "dietary correctness" in New York, Kellogg set to work developing a precooked, ready-to-eat health food, which he called Granula. In 1881, after finding that the name had already been used by James C. Jackson of Dansville, New York—who sued—Kellogg renamed his product Granola.

By then he had married Ella Eaton, a fellow dietary activist, and had hired his younger brother, William K., as an assistant. Together, they ran the Sanitas Food Company and the Sanitas Nut Food Company. These tiny concerns produced not only health foods but such exercise equipment as muscle beaters and flesh brushes.

Broken teeth and inspiration

Kellogg's biggest breakthrough came as a result of an old lady's false teeth: she broke them on some zwieback he had prescribed and she sued, collecting $10. He began to think about softer ready-cooked food. Then he was awakened one night in the midst of what he would later call "a most important dream . . . a way to make flaked foods. The next morning I boiled some wheat, and, while it was soft, I ran it through a machine Mrs. Kellogg had for rolling dough out thin. This made the wheat into thin films, and I scraped it off with a case knife and baked it in the oven."

John Harvey Kellogg (above, age 85) and his wife, Ella, took in and raised 42 children over the years. His brother, William, built the family fortune; the main competitor was an ex-patient named C. W. Post. Right: an early Post Toasties advertisement.

These first wheat flakes were christened Granose. Distribution was limited, for Kellogg was adamantly noncommercial, and he guarded his secrets. But potential profits were great, and dozens of imitators flocked to Battle Creek to produce their own nutritious brands. One of Kellogg's patients, C. W. Post, created thicker flakes with crispy bubbles, which he called Elijah's Manna. The biblical name created a storm of protest among religious groups, so he renamed the cereal Post Toasties. He was a millionaire within seven years.

When, after decades of subservience, William Kellogg bought his brother's corn flake company, he leaped on the commercial bandwagon. "The Genuine Bears This Signature—W. K. Kellogg," read the legend on each box of cereal he sold.

How They Got Started . . .

Betty Crocker. *"How do you make a one-crust pie?" "What's a good recipe for apple dumplings?" In 1921, when the Washburn Crosby Company, makers of Gold Medal Flour, needed a name to sign replies to the questions contained in an avalanche of customer mail, they invented Betty Crocker. The surname belonged to William Crocker, a director of the company, and Betty was a popular nickname. Today, as the General Mills spokesperson, Betty Crocker still stands for the positive attitude in homemaking. Indeed, she became "the eternal and supreme housewife, all-wise, generous of time, advice, sympathy."*

Fannie Farmer. *Born in Boston in 1857, Fannie Merritt Farmer suffered a childhood illness that left her with a limp. Doctors forbade college, so in 1887 she entered the Boston Cooking School. By 1891 she was running it.*

In those days, cooking was hit-or-miss: a pinch of this, a dab of that. But Farmer believed in scientific cookery. In 1896, for the first edition of The Boston Cooking-School Cook-book*—predecessor of the best-selling* Fannie Farmer Cookbook*—she standardized measurements (we owe the level teaspoon to her). She also offered the reassurance of firm authority. "It is the duty of every housekeeper to learn the art of soupmaking," she wrote. Then she taught it.*

Giannini's Bank of America *The banker who invested in people*

Amadeo Peter Giannini was a banker who disliked banks. To him, the world's most precious commodity was not money, but people. Yet though he cared little for riches, he created one of America's most powerful financial institutions, the Bank of America.

Giannini's impeccable business sense was recognized very early by his stepfather, for whom he worked in a produce market in San Francisco. He became a full partner in the business at 19. Young Giannini, a tireless worker, invested in real estate, and at the age of 31 he announced his retirement. He explained that the $250 a month he earned on his investments was enough for him and his family. "I don't want to be rich," he stated. "No man actually owns a fortune; it owns him."

His "retirement" ended a year later, in 1902, when he was made a director of a small bank in San Francisco's Italian section, North Beach. Banking interested him, but he disliked its practices; they ignored the needs of the common man. So in 1904 Giannini organized his own bank, the Bank of Italy. Made up of small shareholders, it would change banking practices in America.

Giannini did what was then unheard of for a banker: he solicited business. Through advertisements and personal persuasion, he convinced people that their money was safer in his bank than hidden under mattresses. He then recycled this newfound capital back into the community by giving small loans to individuals with only their wages as collateral. Soon recognizing that local banks could distribute capital more efficiently, he became the pioneer of branch banking.

When the great earthquake of 1906 struck San Francisco, he quickly removed all the bank's cash and hid it. The day after the disaster, his was the only institution open for business—dispensing loans over a wooden plank. Again in 1907, when unbridled financial speculation ruined many banks, Giannini had foreseen the crash and had hoarded gold. He stacked it in his tellers' windows in plain sight—a display of confidence that convinced customers that their money was safe with him.

By the time he retired in 1934, Giannini had built the world's largest commercial bank, with more than $5 billion in assets. Yet he remained true to his principles about personal wealth: at his death in 1949, his estate was no larger than it had been in 1904.

Amadeo Peter Giannini (left) saved his tiny bank during the San Francisco earthquake by hiding its $80,000 in a produce wagon and driving it to safety.

The Obsessive

Frederick Taylor's systems still rule the lives of many workers

As giant factories revolutionized American industry during the late 1800's, work patterns were drastically changed. Much of this was due to the obsessive, controlling personality of Frederick W. Taylor, nicknamed the Father of Scientific Management.

Taylor was born in Philadelphia in 1856. As a boy, he tested various strides when walking, to see which one yielded the greatest distance with the least effort. Other children disliked playing with him—his games were more efficient than fun. Before a party, he made lists of pretty and plain girls so that he could spend equal time with those in each category. As an adult, he continued to live by a rigidly precise pattern of counted steps and measured gestures. Neither a smoker nor a drinker, he worked compulsively and slept little.

He became a pattern maker and machinist at the Midvale Steel Company, but soon rose in station by imposing his precision on others. Studying time and motion, he defined strict work standards.

Taylor's rules were ruthlessly enforced. There were fines for broken parts (which in one case amounted to more than two months' pay), carelessness, tardiness, and unexplained absences. Some workers resisted by staging slowdowns, sabotaging equipment—even threatening physical violence.

By the time Taylor published *The Principles of Scientific Management* in 1911, his methods had been instituted in several major factories. Even the Bolshevik leader V. I. Lenin was a strong advocate of the system. Perhaps only Taylor could have thrived for long under his own regimen.

Mrs. Hiller's huge funeral carriage had to be cut down to pass under the town's trolley wires.

Mrs. Hiller's Dream

All she wanted from life was a glorious funeral

During the 1890's Mrs. Frances Hiller displayed her own $30,000 coffin in her front parlor in Wilmington, Massachusetts. She frequently climbed into it to show visitors how she would look when she was finally laid out. Later she added a life-sized wax dummy of herself, dressed in a $20,000 funeral robe. Her fascination with funerals may have derived from the fact that all 23 of her children (including seven sets of twins) died in infancy. At any rate, her husband, Dr. Henry Hiller, had hired a renowned wood carver to fashion ornate caskets for the couple.

Dr. Hiller, whose fortune came from a patent medicine he had invented, had always indulged his wife's eccentric tastes. She owned hundreds of hats and wore costly jewelry while gardening. When he died in 1888, the first coffin—which Frances had intended for herself—was only half-finished. Henry's body was kept in a vault until the funerary masterpiece was ready. It sported hand-carved ivy vines, angels, cupids, dragons, bats, and a lizard crawling out of a skull's eye socket. It was borne to a resplendent tomb in a procession that included a military band and 2,000 people carrying lighted torches.

Five years later, Frances married her chauffeur, on the provision that he change his name to Henry Hiller. When she died in 1900, she was placed in her casket—a duplicate of the first Henry's—which was so heavy that it took 10 men to carry it. The funeral car, drawn by four coal-black horses covered with black netting, sagged and almost capsized under the weight. A journalist described the ceremonies as matching the excitement of the local cattle fair.

In 1935 the ostentatious Hiller mausoleum was declared an eyesore and destroyed. The magnificent coffins were buried. Only a pair of urns and simple bronze plaques now mark their location.

The Spruce Goose, *an eight-engine plywood flying boat designed by Hughes, cost $18 million to build. With Hughes at the controls, it flew one mile, skimming the water, in 1947.*

The Inmate Who Owned the Asylum

The dark legacy of billionaire Howard Hughes

On any given day in the 1930's and 1940's, Howard Robard Hughes cut a dashing figure—as a white-scarfed aviator, as a tuxedoed film producer escorting a screen goddess, or as an aggressive industrialist. But the private Howard Hughes was a man sick with phobias. In the 1950's, as his wealth grew, he began a slow descent into a personal hell.

Born in Texas in 1905, Hughes was the son of a rich industrialist and an obsessive mother, who dosed him with mineral oil and kept him from playing with other children lest he be exposed to germs. She died when he was 16; his father, two years later.

In 1924 the youth became head of the Hughes Tool Company. He was to prove an able businessman—some said a genius. Becoming restless, Hughes went to Hollywood and became a movie producer. Among his best efforts were *Scarface,* with Paul Muni, and *Hell's Angels,* in which Jean Harlow was launched. In 1941 he produced *The Outlaw,* starring the buxom Jane Russell, for whom he designed a clever push-up bra.

In the meantime, Hughes, who loved flying, formed the Hughes Aircraft Company and test-piloted his own planes. By 1938 he was a national hero, having set three world speed records. He also crashed several times; his injuries resulted in lifelong pain and dependence on codeine.

After a series of mental breakdowns in the 1950's, the public idol insulated himself from the world and conducted all his business through intermediaries. Most of his staff were Mormons, whom Hughes considered pure of body and spirit. Visitors had to perform bizarre cleansing procedures and wear white cotton gloves. He himself dispensed with clothes for sanitary reasons.

Finally, the reclusive billionaire became an inmate in his own asylum (a Las Vegas hotel that he bought so he wouldn't have to move), his every whim catered to, his needs neglected. Lying naked in a darkened penthouse room, Hughes watched old movies around the clock. When he complained that a local TV station didn't show late-night movies, his aides arranged to buy it. When he developed a passion for Baskin-Robbins banana-nut ice cream, a flavor about to be discontinued, they special-ordered 350 gallons of it. Undernourished, the 6'4" Texan weighed scarcely 90 pounds when he died at the age of 70. Fittingly, death came to him in an airplane as it approached Houston, the city of his birth.

Honest in Spite of Himself

The giant drug company that was built by a master swindler's scam

McKesson Corp., today one of the world's largest and most respected pharmaceutical companies, was floundering in 1926, when a man named F. Donald Coster bought the century-old business (then known as McKesson & Robbins) for $1 million. Within 12 years, through aggressive mergers with 66 wholesale drug distributors throughout the United States, Coster had built it into the third-largest drug concern in the world, worth $87 million. Drawing only a modest salary for himself, he remarked, with an air of dedication, "I live for this company."

He was hailed as a financial genius for his wizardry in the buying and selling of crude drugs in international markets. The company books showed supplies and monies moving smoothly through Canadian warehouses, banks, and holding companies—turning an average profit of 10 percent on each exchange.

The only problem was that these transactions were bogus, camouflaged by the creative accounting practices of Coster and his three closest associates, who were later discovered to be his real-life brothers, Arthur, George, and Robert. Since inventories were never checked, the scam enabled Coster and his family to steal millions from McKesson & Robbins before a suspicious employee brought the whole house of cards crashing down in 1938.

But the real shock came with the revelation that the man named Coster was actually Philip Musica, called one of the master swindlers of the century, and that he and his brothers had been using the company as a front to buy raw alcohol. This they turned into ersatz Scotch, which they sold to bootleggers.

Musica, whose earlier scams had landed him in jail twice, had emerged from his second stint during Prohibition, and quickly found a way to profit from the nation's "great experiment." Under the name of Frank Costa he obtained federal permits to manufacture drugs and other such alcohol-laced products as dandruff remover. Before long, having made some $8 million from bootleggers, his true customers, he decided to expand. That was when he became F. Donald Coster and bought McKesson & Robbins.

Amazingly enough, after the scandal had passed, accountants found that the structure Musica had built was basically sound: his swindles had been only in crude drugs. The company survived and prospered. The same cannot be said for Musica. He shot himself in his Connecticut home just as federal men arrived to arrest him. His brothers landed in jail.

SMITH BROTHERS'
S. B.
COUGH DROPS.
POUGHKEEPSIE, N.Y., U.S.A.
TRADE
MARK
S.B.COUGH DROPS
A COUGH is a social blunder. It shows lack of consideration for others. There is no excuse for it. For coughing is *unnecessary*. S-B Cough Drops relieve it. Pure. No drugs. Just enough charcoal to sweeten the stomach.
Drop that Cough
SMITH BROTHERS of Poughkeepsie
Famous since 1847

How They Got Started . . .

Smith Brothers. *James Smith, a restaurant owner in Poughkeepsie, New York, got the formula from a roving peddler, mixed it up on his stove, and sold it as James Smith & Sons Compound of Wild Cherry Cough Candy "for the Cure of Coughs, Colds, Hoarseness, Sore Throats, Whooping Cough, Asthma, &C, &C." After James died in 1866, his sons, William and Andrew—not Trade and Mark—shortened the name and the claim, built the country's first cough-drop factory, and in 1872 put their own pictures on one of the first uniform "factory filled" packages.*

Dr. Pepper. *Dr. Pepper lived in Rural Retreat, Virginia. When Wade B. Morrison wooed his daughter, Pepper discouraged the match. Morrison later opened Morrison's Old Corner Drug Store in Waco, Texas. In 1885 his pharmacist, Charles Alderton, began experimenting with fruit flavors at the store's soda fountain and came up with a mixture that became a local favorite. People asked what it was called, and the father of Morrison's fondly remembered lost love became immortalized.*

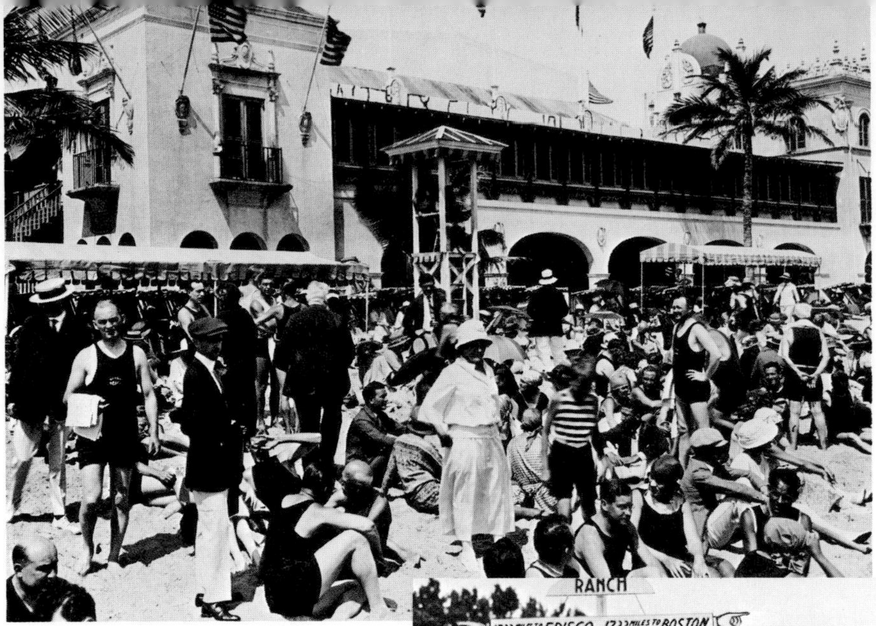

Dauntless Carl Fisher left his mark on America by launching Miami Beach, the Indianapolis Speedway (shown far right in 1909), and the transcontinental Lincoln Highway. A halfway sign in 1915 extended the road beyond its New York terminus.

The Man Who "Rehearsed the Mosquitoes"

He had poor eyesight, but his vision revolutionized America's travel and leisure

Born semiblind in rural Indiana in 1874, Carl Graham Fisher didn't discover his disability until he was 31. It certainly never cramped his style. As a young man, he promoted his bicycle business by riding on a tightrope, and his auto dealership by floating over Indianapolis in a car suspended from a balloon. In 1904, the same year he went into the headlight business and started to get really rich, he set a world auto speed record of nearly 60 miles per hour.

Prest-O-Lite

Undependable carriage lamps lent fear to night driving then. Selling $6,000 in stock, Fisher and two partners started the Prest-O-Lite Company and began experimenting with compressed carbide gas as lamp fuel. The experiments were dangerous—tanks often exploded, sometimes taking entire factories with them. Finally, asbestos linings made them safe. In 1912 the partners sold out to Union Carbide for $9 million.

Speedway and highway

Hoping to help Indianapolis outstrip Detroit as the hub of the emerging auto industry, Fisher spent part of his Prest-O-Lite fortune to develop the Indianapolis Motor Speedway. It opened on August 19, 1909, with a three-day, 300-mile race—and tragedy. Drivers were blinded by dust from the gravel track, and five people died. Fisher aborted the race. Undiscouraged, he resurfaced the 2½-mile oval with brick and in 1911 launched the Indianapolis 500.

The next year found Fisher raising funds for another dream: the first coast-to-coast road. The 3,389-mile Lincoln Highway, named for his favorite hero, was finally completed with federal money in 1923.

Miami Beach

Vacationing in Florida in 1913, Fisher peered at a forlorn island off Miami and envisioned a tropical playground. Buying an interest in Miami Beach, he cleared out the mangroves, filled the swamps, and completed a bridge to the mainland. Few lots sold for five years, but the end of World War I brought a boom, and at its peak Fisher's holdings were said to be worth up to $100 million. He "rehearsed the mosquitoes," quipped Will Rogers, "till they wouldn't bite you until after you'd bought."

By 1926 the boom was a bust; land speculators ruined the market and a hurricane did much the same to the city. Fisher suffered again in the Wall Street crash of 1929. He died 10 years later, leaving an estate of only $40,000.

Comes the Revolution!

Why Citibank has no branches in the Soviet Union

As the 20th century dawned, the Russian economy flourished. Both its rate of industrialization and its grain exports were among the highest in the world. As early as 1902 Frank A. Vanderlip, president of National City Bank (renamed Citibank in 1976), had thought of opening several branches in Russia. So in 1916, two years after the outbreak of World War I, the bank initiated an aggressive investment program there.

The United States supported Russia in the war against Germany, and National City, which underwrote the bonds of the czarist government, still held Russian funds on deposit for the purchase of arms and supplies. The bank's managers believed that if they could establish a strong base in Russia, they could capitalize on the country's expected growth during the postwar period, beating out the competition on the international banking scene.

The plan was wholeheartedly endorsed by the administration of President Woodrow Wilson. As the U.S. ambassador to Russia, David R. Francis, put it, that country offered "a better field for the investment of American ingenuity and enterprise" than any other.

The bank's idea was to open 11 branches, spanning the vast country from Warsaw in the west to Vladivostock on the Sea of Japan. The first branch opened in Petrograd in January 1917—just two months before the overthrow of the czarist government by the Socialists. It would be some time before the full impact of the revolution would become clear to the capitalist world.

Meanwhile, Vanderlip and other American businessmen remained optimistic. The U.S. government continued to provide credit to the Russian government, and even National City's branch representative in Petrograd seemed untroubled—he was making plans to open a second branch in Moscow.

But on November 7, 1917, Petrograd became the scene of yet another uprising as the Bolsheviks, led by Leon Trotsky and V. I. Lenin, took control. Five weeks later Lenin proclaimed banking to be a state-controlled monopoly. The immediate impact on National City was its loss of $7 million in loans and assets.

There was a more devastating problem, however: depositors, many of them American-based companies such as International Harvester and Standard Oil, had entrusted some $26 million to National City's Russian operation. This sum represented 40 percent of the bank's total capital. Its loss would be a crushing blow.

The legal and political problems took years to resolve. In the end, National City Bank settled some claims in Russia by paying depositors in rubles, and others in New York by paying in dollars. The bank ultimately lost only $10 million—much less than feared. Still, the experience proved to be an expensive lesson in the changing fortunes of international banking.

How They Got Started . . .

Chewing gum. *When Antonio López de Santa Anna, the Mexican leader of the Alamo attack, was in exile on Staten Island, New York, in 1869, he brought with him a large lump of chicle, the elastic sap of the sapodilla tree, which Mayan Indians had been chewing for centuries. He hoped that Thomas Adams, an inventor, could refine the chicle for a rubber substitute. Adams experimented with the stuff, but it remained lifeless.*

By chance, he saw a little girl buying paraffin—a "pretty poor gum"—at a drugstore. Adams asked the druggist if he would be willing to try a new kind of gum. He agreed. Rushing home, Adams soaked and kneaded the chicle into small, grayish balls. The druggist sold them all the next day. With $55, Adams went into business making Adams New York Gum No. 1—and set the world to snapping and chewing.

Hershey Chocolate. *Milton Hershey began his fortune by producing caramels. Thinking they were a fad, he started making such novelties as chocolate cigarettes and dominoes as a sideline. Soon he decided to concentrate on chocolate because it would retain the impress of his name in hot weather, which caramel would not. Inspired by Swiss milk chocolate bars in 1893, he hit on the idea of mass-producing a five-cent bar from his own recipe, using fresh milk. The Hershey Bar was an instant success, as was his 1907 creation, the Hershey Kiss.*

Mme. Walker's Dream Came True

Selling beauty door-to-door—the success story of a sharecropper's daughter

She was born to poverty in 1867, but she had a dream. Literally. One night she dreamed of making and selling a formula to straighten and improve the quality of black women's hair. Few success stories can compare with that of Sarah Breedlove, better known as Mme. C. J. Walker.

Orphaned at an early age, married at 14, widowed at 20, Sarah took her daughter to St. Louis, where for 18 years she struggled to make ends meet as a washerwoman. Then in 1905 she decided to go into business for herself. Investing $2, she mixed up shampoos and ointments and used heated iron combs to develop a treatment that later became famous as the Walker Method, or Walker System: it made hair smooth and lustrous.

The business caught on and she moved to Denver, where she soon established her reputation as the hard-working Mme. C. J. Walker, traveling widely to demonstrate and sell her products. She extolled "cleanliness and loveliness," hoping it would not only prove good business, but also encourage self-respect and advancement among black women.

At its peak, her company employed thousands of Walker Agents who touted more than a dozen beauty products. All packages were adorned with Mme. Walker's picture, making her one of the nation's best-known women, and, eventually, its wealthiest black woman. When she died in 1919, an editorial noted that Mme. Walker had "revolutionized the personal habits and appearance of millions." And in the process she had *made* millions as well.

In the driver's seat: Mme. C. J. Walker, whose million-dollar cosmetics empire, augmented by real estate investments, allowed her to support many philanthropies.

Who Invented Monopoly?

The murky origins of a favorite game

In the history of board games, Monopoly wins the popularity prize hands down. Since it was patented, millions of sets have been sold, bringing riches to Parker Brothers, which bought the rights to it in 1935, and to Charles B. Darrow, who invented it. Or did he?

For years it was believed that Darrow, an unemployed salesman, sketched the original version of Monopoly on a piece of oilcloth. Lacking the means to produce and distribute it, he offered it to Parker Brothers. But the company decided that the game was too complicated and turned it down. Undaunted, Darrow teamed up with a friend and sold several sets in the Philadelphia area. The game caught on and Parker Brothers reconsidered.

Then in 1971 along came the game Anti-Monopoly, drawing scornful attention from Parker Brothers' attorneys. Litigation followed, and courtroom testimony revealed differing stories about Monopoly. Witnesses claimed that it was patented in 1904 by Elizabeth J. Magie, a follower of economist Henry George, to portray the "evils" of real estate monopolies. In this early version, called the Landlord Game, spaces had names like Poverty Place and Lord Blueblood's Estate (no trespassing—go to jail). By the 1920's it was being played as a left-wing game by students at top eastern colleges and universities. A 1924 Haverford yearbook referred to it as Monopoly.

In 1929 a Quaker teacher in the Atlantic City Friends School introduced the game to her colleagues and students. They gave the spaces familiar Atlantic City place names, such as Park Place, assigned property values, and painted the playing board as it is known today.

A visitor took the game back to Philadelphia and introduced it to a Quaker hotel manager named Charles Todd, who in turn introduced the game to Darrow. "He took a long time catching on to how it was played," said Todd. "He asked me to write up the rules and make him some copies and copy the game board for him. . . . He stole the game and took it from there." Todd pointed out that, in copying the game for Darrow, he had misspelled Marven Gardens as Marvin Gardens, the spelling that still persists.

Charles B. Darrow may not have invented the game, but he certainly got into its spirit: he was the first entrepreneur to succeed in getting a monopoly on Monopoly.

How They Got Started . . .

Leo the Lion. *Bitten by the show-biz bug, Sam Goldfish knew the importance of a name. So when he formed his own film production company, he combined his name with that of his partner, Edgar Selwyn.*

Eager for an image to enhance the name, Sam Goldwyn hired a promoter who found inspiration at a football game: as Columbia University fans sang "Roar, Lion, Roar," their team's mascot ran onto the field. Success! The king of beasts was a natural trademark. And when a merger created Metro-Goldwyn-Mayer, Leo won out over Metro's parrot.

A real lion—all 350 pounds of him—was acquired by MGM in 1927. Charles Lindbergh's transatlantic flight dominated the headlines then, so MGM cashed in on the excitement of the day by arranging for Leo to embark on a well-publicized cross-country jaunt. When his plane went down near the Grand Canyon, a bring-him-back-alive lion hunt resulted, generating enough headlines to warm the heart of the stoniest press agent. Leo survived to roar on as the enduring symbol of MGM.

Praying for Dollars

The wondrous story of a miraculous machine and a blessed bank balance

In Santa Cruz, California, an arthritic 40-year-old artist named Stanton Lee Powers eked out an existence on Social Security disability payments and the odd pen-and-ink drawing he managed to sell. But, God willing, his life would change dramatically over the course of a few days in 1982.

The miracle

One fall evening, Powers went to a branch of the County Bank, where he had a grand total of $1.17 in his account. He paused in front of the automatic teller machine and began to pray. And lo, as he later told it, a miracle occurred. His balance had grown to $1,600. He returned to the machine two days later and once again bowed his head in supplication. Again his prayers were answered—the balance shown was in excess of $5 million.

Powers—who promptly made a withdrawal—then did what many devout but desperate Americans might do when confronted by such a test of faith. He got himself a lawyer. And, after reviewing the facts of the case, the attorney felt that some research was in order. There were at least five million priorities he wanted to check out.

First he had the artist sign a document giving him one-third of the book, movie, and TV rights to the Miracle of the Automated Teller; then he and his client went to a County Bank cash machine. There they again witnessed the Miracle: the $5 million-plus sum appeared in response to a balance inquiry. The lawyer had Powers withdraw some money, then took him to another machine. Within a few days, a bit more than $2,000 was taken.

The letdown

But good fortune did not continue to shine upon Powers, for the bank froze his account, and the next time he tried to withdraw some money, the machine "ate" his card. In the eyes of Powers's legal counsel, the bank's action was akin to blasphemy. He demanded empirical proof that the fortune wasn't God's handiwork. If the Almighty could turn water into wine and bread into fish, he argued, He should be able to put $5 million into a bank account.

Bank officials didn't take Powers's account of his account on faith. "It's the first time I've heard of God being active in this type of thing," said one. Another noted that the Divine Deposit was invalid if it wasn't accompanied by a check from God.

And so it came to pass that Stanton Lee Powers was charged with grand theft and brought to trial. And lo, when it was time for him to take the witness stand, he changed his story.

The havingness machine

Powers told of being given a reading by a psychic—appropriately named Fortune—who, he said, "told me things about my past I've never told anyone." Fortune offered to rid his life of obstacles. "I visualized the color green flowing into my aura. 'That's the color of self-love,' she said." Now that Powers was fully in touch with his personal aura, Fortune told him to "turn up your shock roots . . . to experience a havingness machine."

This state of transcendence was abetted, no doubt, by some 16 Ritalin (antidepressant) pills, several codeine tablets, and the 10 or 12 wine coolers Powers had recently consumed. He then went to the cash machine, his havingness machine turned up to 100 percent. He stopped and meditated. And then it happened.

Powers recalled discussing his enriching meditation with a couple of people. And one of them had offered a recommendation: "The public won't understand it if you say meditation. . . . Tell everybody God did it." So Powers did just that.

The unbelievers

Obviously Powers's trial lawyer (not the same one who had led him from machine to machine) thought that once the jury heard the defendant's testimony, it couldn't hold him responsible for anything, much less masterminding a $5-million scam. But the prosecutor argued otherwise by showing that Powers had punched in large deposits on the automatic teller keyboard—without putting in a great deal of money. Because of a bank holiday, the institution did not immediately reconcile the very impressive keyed-in sums with Powers's very small deposit. And because of a programming tic, the bank's computer credited and deposited over $5 million at once, so withdrawing a mere $2,000 or so was certainly no problem.

Powers was found guilty. But in view of his precarious mental state, his sentence was lenient: pay back the money and perform 750 hours of community service. (He gave art classes in a senior citizens' home.) Of the episode, Powers complained: "I lost everything I had—my money, my friends. *And* I was rear-ended four times by hit-and-run drivers." Yes, the Lord does work in strange ways.

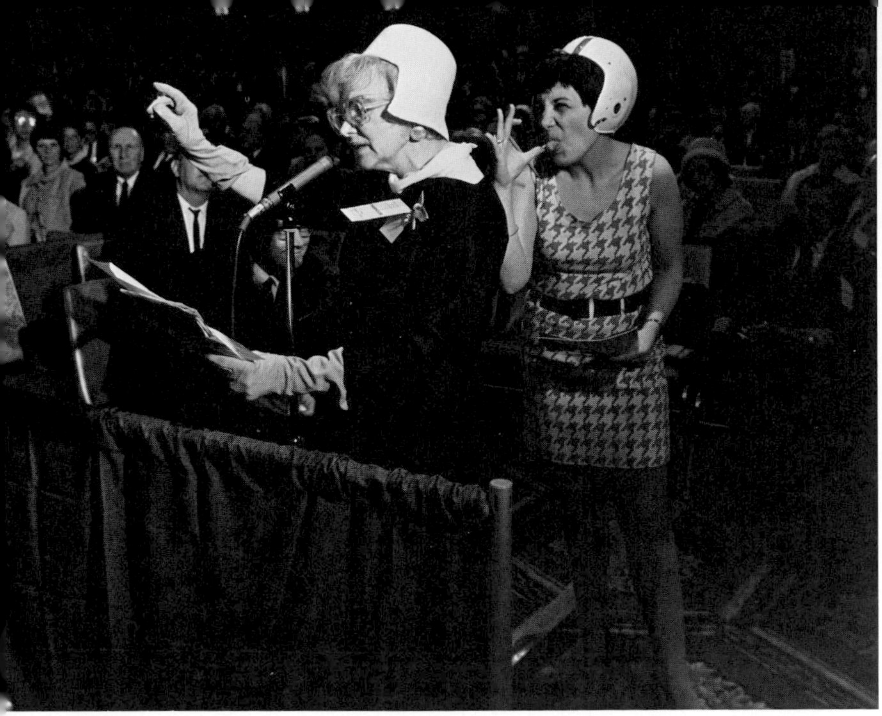

Wilma Soss's outrageous costumes—this one was inspired by COMSAT's space technology in 1965—and outraged diatribes often brought derision, but she did much to protect the interests of individual shareowners.

Speaking Up for Small Stockholders

Champion corporate gadfly

Wilma Soss never controlled a large corporation. She owned a few shares of this, a couple of that—but she always made sure her voice was heard by the powers in charge. She once attended a U.S. Steel stockholders' meeting in a Gay '90's costume to dramatize the company's antiquated business procedures. The next year, she wore a Roaring '20's outfit to show that it *still* had a way to go.

The steel giant wasn't her only target. For nearly 40 years this unlikely crusader attended annual meetings armed with sharp questions—and attired for the occasion. When quiz-show scandals rocked television, Soss personified the need for a cleanup by carrying a mop and broom to a CBS meeting. And when financial woes forced the N.Y. Central Railroad to cancel a dividend, she wore widow's weeds. (Asked why she tormented the company, Soss said, "Because I love the N.Y. Central," causing an executive to plead: "Couldn't you . . . find some other railroad to love?")

Soss could make a point just as easily with her wit as with her wardrobe. U.S. Steel once held an annual meeting on the day before Thanksgiving. When Soss complained that she had a big dinner to cook, the chairman suggested she go home and start basting her turkey. "I'm here to *talk* turkey," she retorted, "not to baste turkey."

Despite her antics, Soss was more than a comedian. When she died in 1986 at age 86, *New York Times* Chairman Arthur Ochs Sulzberger, whose company had been subjected to her barbs, noted that Soss "represented the small shareholders with dignity, pride, and courtesy." Ahead of her time, she demanded sensitivity to stockholders' interests, condemned excessive stock options for executives, and campaigned for more women board members. Her maxim was simple: "The truth is, we shareholders own the corporations."

How They Got Started . . .

McDonald's. *The golden arches that virtually span America date from a day in 1954 when Ray Kroc, a 52-year-old milkshake-mixer salesman, walked into a busy drive-in restaurant in San Bernardino, California. The McDonald brothers, the owners of the eatery, were selling milkshakes, fries, and 15-cent hamburgers through a "speedy system." They owned eight of his multimixers, each of which could make five shakes at once. Impressed by the cleanliness, efficiency, and volume of their operation, Kroc convinced them to let him create a franchise chain. Part of the agreement was that they would keep the original McDonald's. Kroc opened the first franchise in Des Plaines, Illinois, in 1955. Within five years he had 228 stores that were grossing some $40 million annually.*

That's when Kroc decided to buy the original site. But the brothers wouldn't sell and negotiations grew bitter. Kroc finally built one of his red, white, and gold structures a block from the old store (below) and drove the original McDonald's out of business.

CHAPTER FIVE

Laws and Outlaws

We are proud to be a nation ruled by law. But there are always those who behave as though laws are made to be broken. And so America's past is studded with the stories of outrageous lawbreakers—and some pretty strange law enforcers as well. Then there are the laws themselves: you'll find that some amazing ones actually got passed in various places from time to time.

The long arm of the law (New York City, circa 1897)

Hiding the King Killers

Accused of regicide for Charles I's execution, they found refuge in New England

A long, futile manhunt in 17th-century New England involved three men who were no ordinary criminals. John Dixwell, William Goffe, and Edward Whalley were wanted by British authorities; officers in the army of Whalley's cousin Oliver Cromwell, they were among the 59 signers of the death warrant for King Charles I, who was executed in 1649.

When the Stuart monarchy was restored in 1660, Charles II declared amnesty for all except those who had helped behead his father. Just before the new king was crowned, Goffe and Whalley sailed for Boston. Dixwell eventually took off for Prussia.

New World welcome

Warmly received in New England, Goffe and Whalley—who did little to hide their true identities—remained proud and unrepentant for the rest of their lives. The king, not about to let them mock him by living freely in the colonies, posted a handsome reward for their capture. By the time an arrest warrant was issued, however, the men had left Massachusetts.

Fleeing to New Haven, they were again welcomed and given shelter. But the refuge was temporary, for they were being sought by two royalist zealots. The hunters had difficulty convincing the deputy governor of the need for speed and secrecy, and the delay gave the pair time to escape to a nearby cave, where a sympathetic farmer left food for them daily.

Royal troops search Boston

Strangers all along the way took grave risks for Goffe and Whalley, but when they offered to surrender, their new friends objected vehemently. By 1664 the enraged Charles II sent troops to Boston to snare the elusive men, who promptly fled to Hadley, Massachusetts. There they lived in freedom, secretly communicating with their families back home, and enjoying a visit from Dixwell, who had settled in Connecticut. Disguised as a retired merchant, he lived there until his death in 1688.

The bearded savior

The hunt for Whalley failed; he died peacefully in Hadley in 1674. But Goffe made one more appearance—one that helped save the community. Legend has it that while the townsfolk, including some of the king's men, were at church, Indians attacked. Seemingly out of nowhere an elderly bearded man appeared. He rallied the town's defenses and then just as suddenly disappeared. Later, he was spotted in Hartford and reported to local officials—who refused to arrest him. Goffe died of natural causes in 1679.

The Eccentric Governor

He was often seen "wearing a hoop skirt and headdress"

Queen Anne appointed her cousin Edward Hyde, Viscount Cornbury, to be governor-general of New York and New Jersey in 1702. At his welcoming banquet he paid tribute to his wife's ears, inviting the men present to feel them. One evening not long afterward, a woman rushed up to a watchman and pulled *his* ears. "She" turned out to be the royal governor. Thereafter Cornbury would often parade in his wife's dresses and, shrieking with laughter, pounce on other men's ears. He even wore a dress to his wife's funeral.

In 1708 the queen finally relieved her luxury-loving cousin of his post. He was promptly thrown into debtors' prison, but his father's timely death made him an earl, immune to prosecution. The man credited with doing more harm to the English cause in America than anyone else immediately sailed for London.

All the time, Cornbury had claimed that he was simply trying to represent the queen by resembling her "as faithfully as I can."

The elegantly attired governor (right) was "a frivolous spendthrift, an impudent cheat and a detestable bigot." A crony of his named Hyde Park (later the site of FDR's home) after him.

The first time Mary Dyer was sentenced to death, she stood with a noose around her neck and watched her two companions hang before she was spared. One by one the Quakers climbed the ladder and—as a corps of drummers drowned out their attempts to speak—were "turned off" it. Mary later became the first woman to die on the hanging tree.

The Martyrdom of Mary Dyer

Puritan persecution of "a cursed sect of heretics"

Although the Puritan founders of the Massachusetts Bay Colony fled from persecution in England, it didn't stop them from passing strict laws in the very place where they sought religious freedom. Thus in 1656, as members of England's scorned Society of Friends (Quakers) arrived in Boston, some were whipped, jailed, and hanged. When it became a capital crime for them even to *visit* the colony, the Quakers saw themselves as God's instruments, sent to strike down injustice. Members of the pacifist sect—among them Mary Dyer—fought with their only weapon: their lives.

Neither prison nor torture imposed by the legislature were deterrents as protesters from other colonies flooded into Massachusetts worship services. Then in 1659 Quaker activists William Robinson and Marmaduke Stephenson, jailed in Boston, were offered their lives if they would leave the colony. The men refused and, by staying, dared the authorities to impose full punishment. It was then that Mary Dyer, a Rhode Island mother of seven who'd been exiled twice for her activism, returned to Boston to support these two. Such audacity forced the court to detain her as well.

The three were found guilty and banished, but since they remained in Boston, they were rearrested and sentenced to death. The men were hanged, but Dyer was spared. Banished again, Dyer defiantly returned to Boston and was arrested yet again. On June 1, 1660, right at the hanging tree, a judge offered to spare her life if she swore to stay away. "Nay I cannot," were the proud martyr's last words. "For in obedience to the will of the Lord God I came and in His will I abide faithful to the death."

It was a crime in Puritan New England

for ministers to perform wedding ceremonies (marriages, considered to be secular, were conducted by magistrates until the law was changed in 1692)
to dance in a tavern or at a wedding
to celebrate Christmas
for theatrical performances or sports events to occur
to practice blasphemy, idolatry, or witchcraft
to question the word of God
for religious music to be performed
to smite your parents if you were over 16—or simply to be a rebellious son above the same age
for the poor to adopt "excessive dress" such as lace, frills, or shoe buckles.

The Fool of Fortune

Captain Kidd's evil reputation was largely unearned

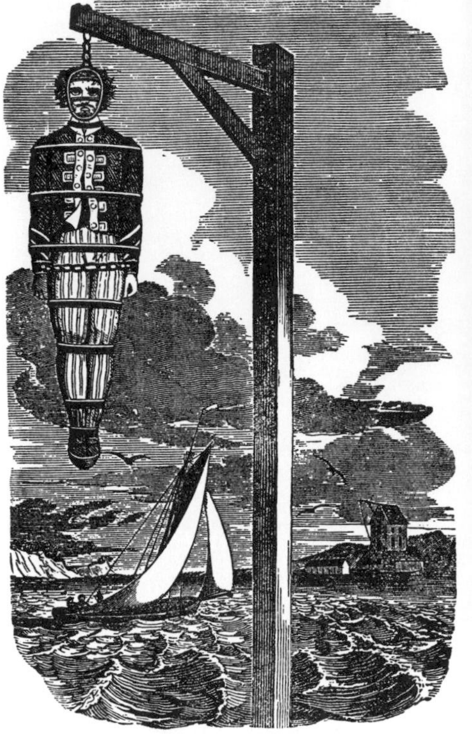

Kidd was hanged on May 23, 1701, in London. His body was left to rot near the Thames River as a grim warning to passing sailors who might contemplate a life of piracy.

Perhaps he did commit an act or two of piracy, but Capt. William Kidd was never the bloodthirsty buccaneer created by legend. In the late 1680's he was a British privateer, licensed by the government to prey on enemy merchant ships. (A pirate, on the other hand, was licensed only by his cannon and cutlass.)

By 1691 Kidd had moved to New York, where he settled down to married life, became a reputable trader, and even helped to build Trinity Church. Privateering lured him back, however, and 1695 found him hunting pirates for William III. But since there were no encounters with treasure-laden enemy vessels, his crew—who shared the plunder—advocated piracy. Kidd concurred, so they took a couple of small ships as prizes. As he sailed from port to port, Kidd's drunken speeches rang more of pirating than pirate hunting. Finally, when he took the one great prize of the voyage, Kidd thought his luck had changed. And it had, but for the worse. Though the captured ship was a legitimate privateer's prize, her influential owners protested to the king. In addition, Kidd's backers worried about their involvement with the privateer-turned-pirate—no matter how briefly—and denounced the captain.

Meanwhile, Kidd, after a brief stop at Gardiners Island to bury a treasure (possibly *still* interred on that dot of land in Long Island Sound), returned to New York. There the governor trapped him into turning himself in. He was sent to England to stand trial, and it went badly: evidence was withheld that might have proven him innocent, and members of his crew testified against him. And so Kidd went to the gallows, "a man neither very good nor very bad, the fool of fortune and the tool of politicians."

From New Providence in the Bahamas, two pirates—both of them women—set out to plunder ship after ship. Praising their boldness, one witness noted that nobody "was more resolute, or ready to board or undertake any Thing that was hazardous, than she [Mary Read, far right] or Anne Bonny [right]." In 1720 they were caught, tried, and convicted, but they avoided execution by "pleading their bellies." Both of the women were pregnant.

The Contest in Hell

How a tough, mean pirate tested his crew's mettle

When the ferocious Blackbeard died at the hands of a naval officer off the coast of Virginia in 1718, gone was the formidable buccaneer who grew a beard so thick and long that he could twist it into braids intertwined with ribbons.

Tall and powerful, Capt. Edward Teach—known as Blackbeard—was proud of his savage reputation. His smoldering eyes, glinting above his huge beard, inspired fear. He nurtured his swashbuckling image by wearing daggers in his red silk sash and by slipping slow-burning matches under his hat so that smoke would billow, demonlike, around his face.

One day Blackbeard bellowed to his crew: "Let us make a Hell of [our] own and try how long we can bear it." With several men he went below deck, closed the hatches, and filled the hold with burning brimstone. All the men emerged long before the terrible Teach, who bragged how he'd outlasted his gasping shipmates. When a crewman said he looked like he'd been at a hanging, Blackbeard roared: "Next time we shall play at gallows and see who can swing longest . . . without being throttled."

A Fierce Pair of Females . . .

were among the boldest pirates to ply the seas

Anne Bonny, the daughter of a prominent attorney in Charleston, South Carolina, was married and living in the Bahamas when she met up with Calico Jack Rackam. Smitten, she left her husband, helped Rackam steal a merchant sloop, and put to sea with him as his devoted mistress and eager comrade in arms.

One day Jack flew into a jealous rage when he saw Anne whispering with a young sailor. Just in time to avert murder, Anne revealed that the sailor was no rival, but another woman, Mary Read.

Reared as a boy in England, Mary was serving as a seaman on a Dutch ship when it was seized by Rackam's pirates. Forced to join the crew, she proved willing and courageous. Only Anne and Jack knew her true sex until the day she "accidentally" showed her breasts to a handsome sailor who had also been pressed into piracy from a plundered ship. The pair became secret lovers; on one occasion Mary picked a fight with and killed one of Rackam's veteran pirates to keep him from dispatching the youth in a duel.

When Rackam's ship was captured by the law in 1720, all of the male pirates lay drunk below deck. The redoubtable Anne and Mary fought furiously to the end, to no avail. Anne, allowed to see Calico Jack before his execution, taunted him: "Had you fought like a man, you need not have been hanged like a dog."

Warned his peas were poisoned, Washington tossed them out a window. Chickens ate them and fell dead.

The Plot to Kill Washington

How a plate of poisoned peas might have changed American history

Suppose that George Washington had not led the Continental Army in the Revolution? There might never have *been* a United States. It could have happened that way—and probably would have if it hadn't been for Phoebe Fraunces, daughter of New York City tavernkeeper Samuel Fraunces.

Phoebe was a housekeeper for Washington when Thomas Hickey, a member of his guard, enlisted her help in killing the general. Phoebe's role was to serve Washington a plate of poisoned peas, and she agreed to play it. But as she presented the dish, she whispered a warning, and Washington flipped the peas out the window.

The failed plot came to light on June 17, 1776. By then Hickey, in jail for passing counterfeit money, was hatching another, wider plot. A fellow prisoner said that he was trying to enroll prisoners in a secret Tory corps within the rebel army; some 700 soldiers, Hickey boasted, were on the payroll of the Tory governor of New York, William Tryon, and the mayor of New York City, David Matthews. They apparently planned to support a British invasion by turning their guns on their comrades. New York City would be set ablaze while a drummer in Washington's guard would stab the general.

An investigation was launched. Mayor Matthews surrendered without protest and was jailed; he later escaped to England. Hickey was hanged in New York City on June 28, 1776, before a crowd of 20,000—the first U.S. soldier to be executed.

In reporting to Congress, Washington wrote: "I am hopeful this example will produce many salutary consequences and deter others from entering into like traitorous practices."

"How Sharper Than a Serpent's Tooth . . ."

Benjamin Franklin's son, William, fought for the British during the Revolution

About 1730, in what he later described as the "hard-to-be-govern'd passions of youth," Ben Franklin sired an illegitimate son, William. Ben later married and had two legitimate children—a son, Francis Folger, who died of smallpox at the age of four, and a daughter, Sarah, who survived.

William was never slighted in his upbringing. Ben gave the boy love and an education. He took him along in 1757, when he went to England to present the colonists' grievances, and even managed to have him appointed colonial governor of New Jersey.

But the Revolution changed their relationship dramatically. The father championed American independence; the son remained loyal to the Crown. When the Revolutionary War began, William refused to give up his office and was imprisoned.

Upon his release two years later, William organized a band of Loyalist guerrillas. But the group so embarrassed the British with its wanton pillage, arson, rape, torture, and murder that it was disbanded in 1782.

His cause lost, William fled to England, where he spent the rest of his life. He also lost the love of his father, who wrote him that "nothing has ever hurt me so much . . . as to find myself deserted in my old age by my only son."

Alexander Hamilton and the Blackmailer

Was the philandering secretary of the treasury also a forger?

Despite his diminutive stature, Alexander Hamilton, with his red hair and his deep blue eyes, had a well-deserved reputation as a ladies' man. But, of his many romantic liaisons, none was as embarrassing to him as his affair with Maria Reynolds.

The relationship began in 1791, when Mrs. Reynolds appeared at Hamilton's doorstep in Philadelphia begging for a loan. Though she did not know Hamilton, then secretary of the treasury, the comely Mrs. Reynolds explained that she and her child had been abandoned by a wastrel husband and needed money to return to New York. Hamilton agreed to help. Instead of giving her cash on the spot, however, he visited her boardinghouse with $30 that evening. Ushered into her bedroom, he quickly took advantage of the opportunity.

The amorous meetings with Maria Reynolds continued, often taking place at Hamilton's own home while his wife and children were away. But then *Mister* Reynolds appeared and demanded cash satisfaction for his wife's favors.

Hamilton paid $1,000 in blackmail, yet he did not stop meeting Maria Reynolds. Her husband, his wounded pride apparently forgotten, begged the secretary not to curtail his visits because, he claimed: "I find when ever you have been with her she is Chearful and kind, but when you have not in some time she is Quite to Reverse."

Wearying of Reynolds's escalating requests (which by now included demands for a government job), Hamilton sought to bring the affair to a close. But things got ugly after Reynolds was arrested for a swindle involving fake veterans' claims. Attempting to trade for his freedom, he broadly hinted that the secretary of the treasury had, himself, secretly participated in the fraudulent scheme.

As rumors began to circulate, three congressmen (James Monroe, Frederick Muhlenberg, and Abraham Venable) confronted Hamilton and demanded an explanation. In his defense, he produced the blackmail letters—20 in all—that he said he had received from James and Maria Reynolds, and denied any wrongdoing beyond a foolish dalliance. So convincing was Hamilton that the matter was dropped.

The sordid tale resurfaced several years later when James Callender, a notorious drunk with a venomous pen and a distaste for Alexander Hamilton, told it in a widely circulated pamphlet. In response, the outraged Hamilton published the embarrassing letters. "My real crime," he said, "is an amorous connection with his wife."

Rather than end the scandal, publication of the letters raised a question that scholars debate to this day. Did Hamilton forge the blackmail demands to clear himself of the more serious charge of fiscal misconduct? Suspicious inconsistencies were apparent: Reynolds was poorly educated, but the letters contained some highly elevated language; and although simple words were misspelled, the complex vocabulary was without error.

It is impossible to resolve whether Alexander Hamilton turned forger to squash allegations of corruption. All the letters were apparently burned by Mrs. Hamilton after his death.

Alexander Hamilton and his wife, Elizabeth, had eight children; his dalliance with other women never seemed to have affected their relationship.

In an artist's rendering of the famous duel, Burr aims his fatal shot at Hamilton, whose gun discharged a bullet that became embedded in a tree branch. Ironically, Hamilton's pair of 54-caliber pistols (below) had been used in a duel between Burr and Hamilton's brother-in-law and, later, in a duel in which Philip Hamilton, his son, was killed at the age of 19.

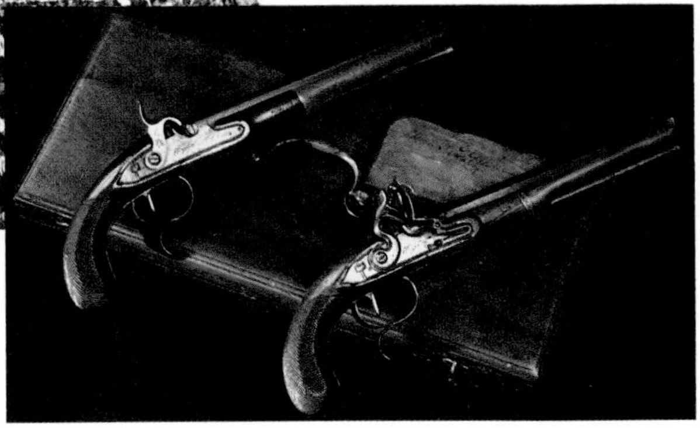

A Duel to the Death

Only one vice president was ever indicted for murder

Sunrise on July 11, 1804, found Vice President Aaron Burr and former Secretary of the Treasury Alexander Hamilton standing 10 paces apart, each holding a loaded, cocked pistol. They were on a bluff overlooking the Hudson River at Weehawken, New Jersey, a popular dueling ground beyond the reach of New York law. Their seconds had measured off the distance. Raising his gun, Hamilton turned it this way and that, and then, apologizing for the delay, he put on his spectacles. This suggested that Hamilton intended to shoot to kill.

On the signal to fire, two shots rang out. Hamilton's bullet embedded itself in an overhead branch, but Burr's slammed into Hamilton's side, sliced through his liver, and lodged in his spine. He died the next day, and the nation he had helped to found reeled in shock.

Former friends

In the absence of laws making dueling illegal during the early days of the Republic, it remained a common way for gentlemen to settle differences. Those who refused a challenge were branded cowards, a disgrace to avoid even at the cost of life.

Oddly enough, Hamilton and Burr had once been friends: Both had served in the Continental Army and, after the Revolution, had established successful law practices in New York, occasionally working on cases together. They both also became involved in politics, Hamilton a Federalist to the core, and Burr favoring a looser coalition of states. Clashing head on, they became implacable foes, with incident upon incident fueling the fire of resentment.

Burr unseated Hamilton's father-in-law, General Schuyler, as the U.S. senator from New York. Six years later, as the result of a public scandal that undermined his political career, Hamilton challenged James Monroe to a duel. The duel never took place, but the fact that Monroe had named Burr as his second increased the enmity between the two. When Senator Burr was up for reelection, Hamilton engineered his defeat. Another incident led to a duel between Burr and Hamilton's brother-in-law, John B. Church, in which neither was harmed. Hamilton's involvement in Burr's losing the 1800 presidential election further widened the rift. And the last straw occurred in 1804, when Burr made a bid for the governorship of New York and Hamilton blocked him.

In April of that year, the Albany *Register* published some letters claiming that Hamilton had called Burr "a dangerous man," regarded him as unfit to govern, and had privately expressed "a still more despicable opinion" of him. Burr called Hamilton to account, but the reply was evasive. Then, on June 27, after futile exchanges of letters, Burr forwarded his challenge.

Did Hamilton hold his fire?
Although Hamilton deplored dueling, he feared that a refusal to meet the challenge would discredit him. Both men put their affairs in order, with Hamilton writing an explanation of his actions, admitting he might have wronged Burr. He wrote that he planned to hold his fire—a statement friends would cite to brand Burr a cold-blooded killer.

Speculation on the outcome of the duel abounded: Had Hamilton secretly set his pistol's hair trigger—capable of providing a split-second advantage—and then accidentally fired before he had Burr in his sights? Did Hamilton suicidally withhold his fire, pulling the trigger inadvertently from the impact of Burr's bullet? There were many questions and few answers.

Thousands mourned
On July 14 a great public funeral was held for the 47-year-old politician; thousands of angry citizens mourned. Burr was bewildered by their reaction—the duel had been conducted honorably—and he remained in seclusion. Despite murder indictments in New York and New Jersey, he was able to slip away, heading south to Philadelphia and beyond. Eventually he returned to Washington, taking up his duties as vice president. The next year he completed his term and, after an eloquent farewell speech, left for dubious adventures in the Mississippi Valley. Hamilton's death had knelled his own political demise.

Empire, Power, and Glory

The ambitious dreams and grand schemes of Aaron Burr

After his farewell speech to the Senate in March 1805, Vice President Aaron Burr was unemployed. The duel with Hamilton had made him a political pariah, and now his former colleagues waited to see how a man of such intellect, energy, and ego would repair his fortunes. "Considering how little restraint laws human or divine have on his mind, it is impossible to say what he will attempt—or what he may obtain," wrote Senator William Plumer of New Hampshire.

Even Plumer could not have imagined the bizarre lengths to which Burr's ambition would drive him: He proposed carving a personal domain from the American West—greatly enlarged by the recent Louisiana Purchase. Burr found a willing ally in the commanding general of the U.S. Army, James Wilkinson, an unscrupulous soul who supplemented his salary by informing for Spain. Calling himself "the Washington of the West," Wilkinson had visions as grandiose as those of Burr himself—who dreamed of conquering Mexico, uniting it with the frontier states, and apparently ruling his own empire.

Traveling down the Ohio and Mississippi rivers to New Orleans, buying supplies and recruiting followers, Burr talked in glowing terms of the future of the area. Chief among his converts was Harman Blennerhassett, who lived in splendor on a private island in the Ohio River in what is now West Virginia. Described as having every kind of sense but common, he fell under Burr's spell and bankrolled the plan, offering his island as its home base. Burr's small, loosely organized force—fewer than 100 strong—stored food and ammunition there, waiting for the call to action. Finally Burr sent Wilkinson the long-awaited message that on August 1, 1806, he would embark on his western expedition "never to return. . . . The gods invite us to glory and fortune."

But Wilkinson saw that the plans had no chance of success and, turning informer, wrote Thomas Jefferson a full account of the proceedings. The president, who called Burr's scheme "the most extraordinary quest since the days of Don Quixote," decided he had to act. When Burr was apprehended in February 1807 he was brought to Richmond to be tried for treason. But Wilkinson's testimony proved unimpressive, the prosecution could not produce witnesses to support the charges, and Burr was acquitted.

Even so, Burr thought it prudent to leave the country—though not before he had the audacity to ask the ruined Blennerhassett for introductions to Britons who might be interested in his plans for empire. In France he also wrote to Napoleon Bonaparte, proposing to reconquer Louisiana and Canada if the French emperor provided the money. Both England and France turned him down flat.

In 1812 he returned to New York, but misfortune followed him. His grandson died in South Carolina, and when his grieving daughter—the apple of his eye—sailed for New York to seek her father's solace, her ship disappeared in a storm. She was presumed drowned.

Burr died in 1836 at the age of 80, and contemporary accounts confirm that his ego remained intact to the end. Told of his deteriorating condition he cried, "I can't die!" But his doctor replied, "Mr. Burr, you are already dying."

DREADFUL FRACAS ATWEEN THE GINERAL AND THE BENTONS AT NASHVIL

Andrew Jackson, Gunfighter *Feisty Old Hickory was never one to back down*

By the time Andrew Jackson made his successful run for the presidency in 1828, the 60-year-old general had been involved in 103 duels and altercations, 14 times as a principal. As a legacy from two of these jousts, bullets lodged near his heart and in his left arm gave him decades of agony. For one of his antagonists, however, the legacy was death.

The Dickinson duel

A snarl of insinuations over a bet on a forfeited horse race led to his 1806 duel with Charles Dickinson, a 27-year-old lawyer. The day before the affair of honor, as Jackson and his second, Gen. Thomas Overton, rode toward the dueling field at Harrison's Mills, Kentucky, they discussed strategy. Not only was Dickinson 12 years younger than Jackson, but he was known to be a superior marksman. A snapshooter, he was called, for his speed and accuracy in leveling and firing his weapon without taking deliberate aim. The two generals agreed to risk letting Dickinson fire first, so that Jackson (if he was lucky) could take time to aim carefully.

Traveling with friends via a different route, Dickinson showed a cheery confidence. At a tavern along the way he stopped to practice his marksmanship and severed a string at a dueling distance of 24 feet. "If General Jackson comes along this road, show him that," he called to the proprietor.

Face to face

The next morning the two parties met, Dickinson properly clad in a close-fitting waistcoat and snug trousers, Jackson sporting a loose frock coat that concealed his thin frame. At the signal, Dickinson whipped up his pistol and fired.

Unflinching, Jackson pressed his left arm against his chest and raised his gun. Reeling back in disbelief, Dickinson cried out, "Great God! Have I missed him?"

Fatal shot

Returning to his mark, he waited, eyes averted. Jackson coolly squeezed the trigger, but the gun stuck at half-cock. Recocking, he carefully aimed again and fired. The bullet tore into Dickinson's abdomen, fatally wounding him.

Overton, startled to see blood filling one of Jackson's shoes, asked if he had been hit. "Oh, I believe he has pinked me a little," he replied, determined that Dickinson not have the satisfaction of knowing. In fact, Dickinson's bullet had broken some ribs and lodged within an inch of his heart—too close for removal. Because of the

Jackson holds center stage in an old caricature of the Benton brawl (left). When Old Hickory became president, Senator Tom Benton, then called Old Bullion, was his staunch supporter.

loose coat, Dickinson had slightly misjudged. Back at the inn, Jackson ordered that a bottle of wine be sent to his dying antagonist.

The Benton brawl

A very different chain of circumstances led to a shootout in 1813 between Jackson and Thomas Hart Benton, his close friend and personal attorney. It began because, in a duel fought by Benton's younger brother, Jesse, Jackson had acted as his opponent's second. This disloyalty outraged Tom.

The confrontation between Jackson and the Benton brothers was more of a free-for-all than a duel. It took place at Nashville's City Hotel. Andy, backing Tom onto a rear porch, shouted, "Defend yourself!" As Tom edged away, Jesse sneaked up on Old Hickory and shot him, shattering his left shoulder and leaving a ball embedded in his left arm. Falling, Jackson fired twice at Tom, singeing the cloth of his sleeve.

While Jackson was being ministered to, two of his friends carried on the battle with the Bentons. Jesse just missed being killed, and Tom took a nasty fall down the porch stairs. Jackson, carried into the hotel, bled profusely and the doctors advised amputation. "I'll keep my arm," he snapped.

The lucky baby

At least one bullet went through the wall into a nearby room, narrowly missing a young couple and their baby. The infant was John Charles Frémont, future presidential candidate and husband of Jessie Benton, Tom's daughter.

Patty Cannon, Mass Murderess

The heinous crimes that shook Delaware

On an April day in 1829, the town crier of Seaford, Delaware, called out: "Three o'clock and Patty Cannon taken."

The arrest of the woman, then in her sixties, followed a discovery made by a tenant on her farm at Johnson's Cross Roads (renamed Reliance in 1882 to escape its infamous past). He had been plowing "when his horse sunk in a grave, and on digging, he found a blue-painted chest" containing the bones of a man missing for about 12 years. The victim, a slave trader from Georgia, had been carrying $15,000 on his person, too much money for Patty and her son-in-law, Joe Johnson, to resist. They had murdered him at the supper table in her house.

It was no accident that the Georgian was there. Patty, a widow accused by some of having poisoned her husband, was in the business of kidnapping free blacks in her region and selling them into slavery for as much as $1,100 a head. It was rumored that she and Johnson kept them chained in the attic until they could be shipped south.

But that wasn't all. Digging around the farm, authorities found the remains of other victims, including children. A servant claimed that Patty had murdered at least one black child she thought unsalable and had bludgeoned to death another, about seven years old, with a thick stick of wood.

Patty Cannon was never brought to trial: she poisoned herself in jail. Her body was exhumed in the early 1900's, and before it was reburied, her skull fell into the hands of a Delaware resident, whose nephew lent it to the Dover public library. Every Halloween, to this day, it is put on display there.

NARRATIVE AND CONFESSIONS
OF
LUCRETIA P. CANNON,
WHO WAS TRIED, CONVICTED, AND SENTENCED TO BE HUNG AT GEORGETOWN, DELAWARE, WITH TWO OF HER ACCOMPLICES.
CONTAINING
AN ACCOUNT OF SOME OF THE MOST HORRIBLE AND SHOCKING MURDERS AND DARING ROBBERIES EVER COMMITTED BY ONE OF THE FEMALE SEX.
Page 16.
NEW YORK:
PRINTED FOR THE PUBLISHERS.
1841.

A sensational 1841 book purported to tell the story of Patty Cannon in her own words. It was filled with hearsay accounts of numerous villainous deeds. The illustration on the title page (right) shows Patty holding a black child in the fire until death stops its crying.

Colorado Cannibal

He was a miner named Alferd (not Alfred) Packer

The snow was deep and the weather bitter when 21 hopeful miners arrived in Colorado in January 1874. Despite the advice of a local Indian that they delay their quest for silver, Alferd Packer convinced five of the men to follow him into the San Juan Mountains. Foolhardy from the start, the expedition became lost and ended in a crime so bizarre as to boggle the mind; for Packer was convicted of murdering his companions and living off their remains.

A likely story

Some 65 days after starting out, Packer strolled into an Indian agency alone, with an extraordinary tale about being abandoned by the others. When he later displayed a large wad of cash and a gun belonging to one of the miners, suspicion flared. Finally he said that the members of his party had killed and eaten each other, one by one, until only two remained: Packer and Wilson Bell. One night, he claimed, after a tense stand-off, Bell attacked him with a rifle butt, but Packer prevailed and Bell became his meal.

Jailed at once, Packer escaped. The bodies were soon found, and it was clear Packer had killed and eaten them all. It was nine years

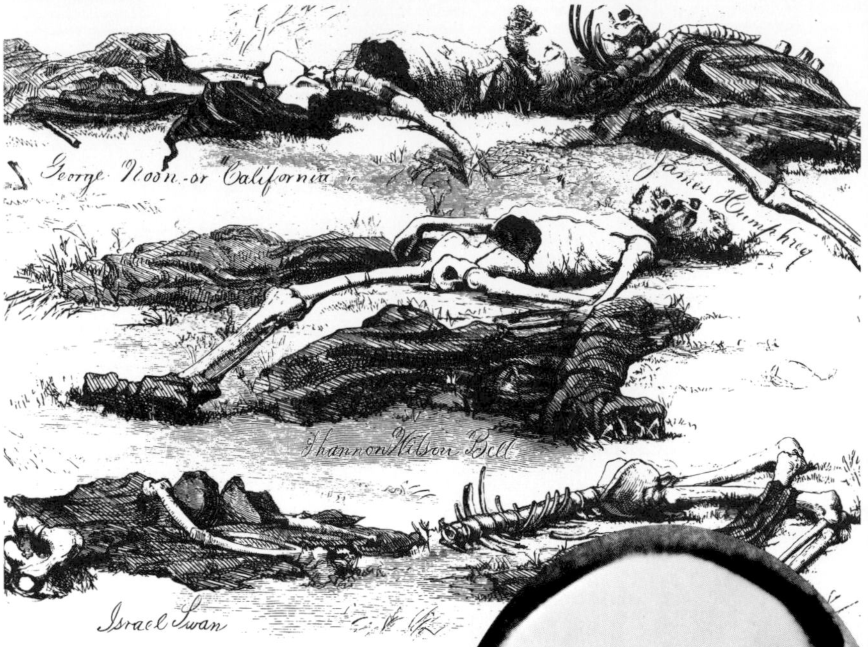

This grisly 1874 sketch by John A. Randolph, showing the remains of Packer's companions near Lake Cristobal, disproved the cannibal's story. Packer (right) claimed that the others, not he, had done all but the last killing and feasting.

before he was nabbed, found guilty of murder, and sentenced to hang—the first person accused of cannibalism under Colorado law.

"They was seven dimmycrats in Hinsdale County," the judge is alleged to have complained, "and ye ate five of 'em." Packer avoided the gallows when the law under which he was sentenced was declared unconstitutional.

The verdict

Three years later, in 1886, Packer was retried and sentenced to 40 years. He left behind several memorials to his dubious claim to fame. His victims' remains are buried on Cannibal Plateau, just above Dead Man's Gulch, and a snack shop at the University of Colorado is called the Alferd A. Packer Memorial Grill. Its most popular item? The Packerburger.

For the Donner Party: A Trail of Lies, a Trail of Death

America's best-known case of cannibalism involved the Donner Party, a California-bound wagon train of 82 souls that was snowbound in the High Sierras in the winter of 1846–47. Less well known is the fact that they were led to their tragic fate by a lie told by Jim Bridger, the famed mountain man.

Bridger owned a supply post along a new route known as the Hastings Cutoff, and he wanted the route used. He told the Donners it was "a fine, level road." They set out on July 31. By October—after struggling across boulder-strewn terrain and trackless desert—they were snowed in. It was six months before help reached them. Thirty-three perished; many of the rest survived by eating the dead. Jacob Donner was eaten by his children. James Reed, the only leader who survived, later wrote that, at Bridger's post, letters had been withheld advising "by no means to go the Hastings Cutoff."

The Original Private Eye

The founder of Pinkerton's once had a price on his head

Allan Pinkerton, born in a tough section of Glasgow, Scotland, in 1819, grew up amid poverty and crime. Forced to leave school at the age of eight after his father's death, he eventually became apprenticed to a pattern maker. By the time he was 20, he was a militant member of the Chartists, a radical reform movement striving to make the government more democratic.

As the Chartists became more aggressive, warrants were issued for their arrests, and in the winter of 1842 Pinkerton found himself "an outlaw with a price on my head," dependent on friends to hide him from the police. Not until April was he able to escape, smuggled out at night aboard a ship bound for America, taking with him the sweetheart who just weeks before had become his bride. The ship was wrecked by ice off the Nova Scotia coast, and they had to abandon it in lifeboats. Eventually they made their way to Dundee, a settlement of Scottish immigrants 50 miles northeast of Chicago, where Pinkerton throve as a cooper, and by chance discovered a new career.

One day in 1847, while cutting wood for barrels on a deserted island, Pinkerton found evidence that men had camped there. Becoming suspicious, he informed the local sheriff. After a long stakeout, the pair captured a counterfeiting gang that used the spot as a rendezvous. As a result Pinkerton was made a deputy. He then moved to Chicago, joined the sheriff's department, and by 1849 had become the city's first detective—performing so well that hoodlums attempted to assassinate him.

Chicago in 1850 was a burgeoning frontier metropolis bursting with opportunity, and Pinkerton fit right in. He soon started his own company of professional private detectives, who became famous for their use of disguise. Their office has been compared to backstage at a theater, with a large costume closet and agents carefully rehearsing for their undercover roles. Much of Pinkerton's business involved protecting railroads. While working for the Illinois Central, he met with the line's attorney and later saved his life. The attorney was Abraham Lincoln.

In the early months of 1861, Pinkerton, a staunch abolitionist, uncovered a plot to assassinate Lincoln as he changed trains in Baltimore en route to his inauguration. Infiltrating rebel groups, Pinkerton and his agents were able to thwart the assassins and sneak the president-elect through the city at night. The next morning Pinkerton sent a message announcing Lincoln's safe arrival in Washington: "Plums arrived with Nuts this morning." The unfortunate code, in which "Nuts" referred to Lincoln, led to Pinkerton's ridicule, and even today many people doubt that the plot really existed. However, one of Pinkerton's loudest detractors was a man who himself had offered Lincoln a gun and bowie knife for the trip. Lincoln had smilingly declined.

The Pinkerton logo, the open eye, is the origin of the term private eye. *Tales of Allan Pinkerton's exploits were contained in the detective's detailed memoirs, an 18-volume extravaganza that enjoyed the tremendous success of popular novels.*

Mary Surratt (above) died on the gallows on July 7, 1865, along with Lewis Paine, who had attempted to kill Secretary of State William H. Seward; David Herold, who had helped Booth to escape; and George Atzerodt, who was supposed to have ambushed Vice President Andrew Johnson. The other defendants—Samuel Arnold, Michael O'Laughlin, Edward Spangler, and Dr. Samuel Mudd—were given varying prison sentences. Mudd, whose only crime was to set Booth's broken leg, served three years, and as a prisoner was instrumental in the fight against yellow fever. He was pardoned in 1868.

The Lincoln Assassination Conspiracy

Did Mary Surratt hang for her son's guilt?

Eight people were convicted by a military court of helping John Wilkes Booth murder President Abraham Lincoln on April 14, 1865. Four were put to death—one of them, Mary Surratt, becoming the first woman ever hanged by the U.S. government. The evidence against the 45-year-old widow was inconclusive at best, and her guilt has been debated ever since.

Booth had enlisted the aid of Mary's son, John, who had been a spy for the Confederacy, and so Mary's boardinghouse in Washington, D.C., had been a meeting place for the plotters.

They were such a motley group that many doubted they could have carried out the assassination. It was even rumored that they were the agents of a more powerful conspiracy, headed by Secretary of War Edwin M. Stanton. No evidence of a larger plot, however, has ever been produced.

Mary may have suspected what the group was up to. Their plotting was open enough to arouse the suspicions of another boarder, Louis Weichmann, who later became a chief witness against her. Yet no other testimony suggested that Mrs. Surratt knew any details of the scheme.

As it turned out, Weichmann may have testified to save himself. For it was he who drove Mary Surratt into town on the day Lincoln was shot. Booth had asked her to deliver a package. It contained binoculars that he used in his escape; Mrs. Surratt later denied all knowledge of its contents.

By the time the trial began, less than a month after the assassination, John Wilkes Booth was dead. John Surratt, considered by prosecutors to be the second most important figure in the case, was a fugitive in Canada. By default, Mary Surratt became the focal point. The prosecutors may well have hoped that, by bringing her to trial, they would shame her son into turning himself in. But not even the urgent threat of his mother's execution impelled John Surratt to return.

There was no surprise when three of the conspirators—Lewis Paine, George Atzerodt, and David Herold—were condemned to die. But shock followed Mary Surratt's death sentence. Five of the nine military judges signed a petition asking President Andrew Johnson for clemency. The execution was delayed in hopes of a reprieve. But none came. (Johnson later denied receiving the request.) And so, mounting the scaffold, Mary Surratt took her pitiful place in history.

Epilogue

Two years after the execution, it was discovered that the prosecutors had suppressed vital evidence, a diary that had been found on Booth's body at the time of his death. It revealed that the original plan had been to kidnap Lincoln, not to kill him, and that Booth had not decided to assassinate the president until the very day he committed the act. Hence, it was unlikely that Mary Surratt could have known about it.

John Surratt, meanwhile, had gone from Canada to England, and then to Italy. There, under an assumed name, he joined the Papal Zouaves, a short-lived corps of colorfully costumed, fez-wearing volunteers who fought in the Papal Army. He was arrested but escaped. Soon recaptured, he was brought home to stand trial, arriving in Washington on June 10, 1867. The trial ended in a hung jury, and later that year Surratt was included in a general presidential amnesty. His mother had already paid the price for his part in the murder of Abraham Lincoln.

Who Shot John Wilkes Booth?

Was it Boston Corbett?

Boston Corbett (above) claimed he shot Booth, but the reward was equally divided among the men of the 16th New York Cavalry, each getting $1,653.

"Providence directed me to shoot John Wilkes Booth," claimed Thomas "Boston" Corbett, a sergeant in the 16th New York Cavalry. The unit had tracked the fugitive to a tobacco barn near Fort Royal, Virginia, and Corbett fired, despite orders that Booth was to be taken alive.

Corbett, who called himself Boston after the city in which he'd received a spiritual revelation, avowed that he took orders only from God. When the Almighty had ordered him to avoid sexual temptation in 1858, he had castrated himself with a pair of scissors.

Did Corbett actually inflict the mortal wound? He later testified that he fired a carbine. But an autopsy showed that Booth was killed by a pistol bullet, and after the body was dragged from the barn the commanding officer flatly stated, "He shot himself."

Nonetheless, Corbett continued to claim the credit for the assassin's death and became something of a national hero. Appointed doorkeeper for the Kansas state legislature, he threatened the lawmakers with a gun in 1887 and was committed to an insane asylum. He escaped and was never heard from again.

Lincoln's Restless Repose

On the night of November 7, 1876, John Hughes, Terrence Mullen, and Lewis Swegles broke into the National Lincoln Monument in Oak Ridge Cemetery, Springfield, Illinois, and pried open the marble sarcophagus containing Lincoln's coffin. The men, operators of a counterfeiting ring, planned to ransom the body for $200,000 and the release of a fellow counterfeiter from prison.

Unknown to the rest of the gang, Swegles was a Secret Service agent; he was to signal police captain P. D. Tyrrell when the coffin was removed. Although Swegles was kept busy holding the lantern and fetching the getaway wagon, he still managed to double back and alert Tyrrell, who ordered Hughes and Mullen to give themselves up. They escaped that night, but were later arrested. They could be tried only for stealing a coffin worth $75.

Soon after, the Lincoln Guard of Honor was formed to protect the president's remains, and the coffin was taken to a memorial hall. Later, it was buried in the ground. There were at least a dozen more moves before Lincoln's body was finally sealed in 1901 in a steel and concrete vault beneath the burial chamber in Springfield.

Tom Smith's he-man methods were effective against rollicking cowboys, but failed in a serious land dispute.

Abilene's Two-fisted Lawman

Tom Smith faced down gunslinging cowboys barehanded

When tall, good-looking Marshal Tom Smith came to Abilene, Kansas, in 1870, it was a wide-open town—the end of the Chisholm Trail for cattle drovers who'd been riding herd for months from Texas and were ready for a good time. The cowhands, who got their pay in a lump sum after the cattle were sold, were welcome for the money they had to spend; but their general disregard for law and order was a problem. It was Tom Smith's job to come up with a solution.

Smith, a New Yorker by birth, had been a successful marshal in Kit Carson, Colorado, when he applied for the same job in Abilene. Known for his cool courage under fire, he resolved to enforce the town's standing ban on firearms. A posted notice already proclaimed this rule, but it had been riddled with bullet holes.

Smith's first challenge came from a rowdy known as Big Hank. Hank refused to hand over his gun, so Smith dropped him with a punch to the jaw, took his gun, and ordered him to leave town. Hank obeyed. Word of the tough new marshal's action spread quickly, prompting another challenge from a braggart called Wyoming Frank. Again, Smith's fists upheld the law. The marshal's quiet but effective methods brought a massive turn-in of weapons, and—as he patrolled his town astride a big, iron-gray horse named Silverheels—calm returned to Abilene.

Months later, Smith was promoted to deputy U.S. marshal for the entire Abilene district and hired a sheriff as an assistant. Soon after, a defiant homesteader named Andrew McConnell shot and killed his neighbor in a land dispute. When the marshal and his assistant rode out to arrest him, McConnell opened fire. Smith was gunned down, and the frightened sheriff fled. Left behind, the marshal was nearly decapitated with an ax.

Abilene, in shock over the loss of its lawman, gave him a hero's funeral. "Women wept," wrote the brother of the mayor. "Men stirred and batted their eyelids hard, to hide emotion."

A monument, erected 34 years later, proclaims Smith a "fearless hero of frontier days who in cowboy chaos established the supremacy of the law."

Justice From a Medical Book

The druggist's prescriptions included time on a chain gang

Dr. Charles Meyer, a German druggist and an educated man, was often called upon to settle disputes in the lawless town of Tucson, Arizona. He owned two books—perhaps the only two in town. Both were in German. One was about setting broken bones; the other was a materia medica, dealing with medicinal drugs.

Becoming justice of the peace, Meyer set up court in his drugstore. When confronted with a difficult case, he would open his materia medica and study it solemnly. Then he would declare something like, "I find here a case quite similar to the one we face. It says that the plaintiff is correct and the defendant is guilty and owes him $10. Case dismissed."

People seldom challenged Meyer's decisions. If they did, he doubled the fine. A lawyer once demanded a trial by jury. "What is a jury?" Meyer asked. When told, he sentenced the client to two weeks on a chain gang, cleaning the streets and removing sewage. The lawyer got one week. "Now, how do you like that trial by jury?"

Another time, after Meyer and a friend had been stopped by the town marshal for exceeding the five-mile-an-hour speed limit behind a team of spirited horses, he fined his friend $15, then doffed his robe, stood before the bench, and fined himself $25.

Pat Garrett (above) wrote a biography of Billy the Kid; even that was a financial failure.

The Hard-Luck Gunman

When Pat Garrett shot Billy the Kid in 1881, his luck changed—for the worse

The public demanded the capture of Billy the Kid. The governor of New Mexico offered a $500 reward for the trigger-happy youth, said to have killed 21 men by his 21st birthday, and Pat Garrett, the sheriff of Lincoln County, went after it.

He tracked the Kid to the old Maxwell ranch near Fort Sumner. Garrett went into one bedroom; Billy backed in from a front porch. Pat fired, and the Kid died young. "You didn't have the nerve to kill him face to face," sobbed the girl who had hidden Billy.

Everything Pat Garrett did from then on seemed to go wrong. Many said he'd murdered the Kid, and he couldn't collect his $500 reward until the state legislature passed a special act. He later invested in a system to irrigate the Pecos Valley, but his partners forced him out of business, leaving him high and dry.

In 1901 Theodore Roosevelt appointed Garrett customs collector in El Paso, and later invited him to a convention of the Rough Riders. Unfortunately, Garrett brought along a gambler friend incognito. The deception displeased Roosevelt, and the customs appointment was not renewed.

Destitute, the ex-sheriff tried to sell his ranch. When he rode out to clinch the deal, the buyer started a quarrel, and as Garrett turned away, a bullet struck the back of his head. No one was ever convicted of Pat Garrett's murder.

Billy the Kid didn't die in a showdown, as depicted below and often since in film and fiction. Garrett shot him in the dark, and the Kid never knew what hit him.

A Bandit Who Was Sheriff *They strung him up on his own gallows*

Henry Plummer was a handsome young easterner with a glib tongue and an affable manner. Soon after arriving in the booming California gold-rush town of Nevada City in 1852, he won the job of town marshal. He also won the love of a woman whose husband he proceeded to murder, and he was sentenced to 10 years in jail.

Later pardoned, he moved on to rowdy Lewiston in Idaho's gold-mining territory, where he organized a gang devoted to murdering and robbing successful miners. When one of his henchmen was strung up, Plummer left town.

Arriving in Bannack, Montana, he killed the one man in town who knew of his past. Not only was Plummer acquitted of this crime, but the locals took to him and elected him sheriff. By day, he tended to his business as the chief law enforcer in the gold-rich region; by night, he and his band robbed and killed the unwary. Misleadingly called the Innocents (their password was "I am innocent"), they worked a stretch of road between Bannack and Virginia City.

But a member of Plummer's gang killed one man too many, and an outraged mob arrested him and hanged him on the main street. The vigilante action inspired other groups; two more of Plummer's pals were caught and strung up, and one of them, in the shadow of the scaffold, spilled the beans about the double-dealing sheriff. To his surprise and horror, Plummer found that his own neck was in danger of being stretched.

With evidence mounting, angry citizens nabbed Plummer and two of his accomplices. And as arctic winds whistled through town on a fierce winter day in 1864, the three men were hanged, their bodies left to swing from a gallows that, in an ironic twist of fate, had been erected by none other than Sheriff Henry Plummer.

A Nightmare Comes True *Murder and the chase to nab the killers*

"Murder is becoming a mere pastime in Idaho Territory," an 1870's editorial proclaimed. It was hardly news, however, for a murder had taken place in 1863 that was noted both for its gruesomeness and for the sensational way in which the killers were discovered.

The victim was Lloyd Magruder, who had set out from Lewiston to sell supplies to miners some 90 miles away. His good pal Hill Beachy feared for his safety; in a nightmare he saw Magruder being hacked to death with an ax.

Just after his friend departed, Beachy noticed three strangers leaving town. They overtook the tradesman, struck up a friendship, and accompanied him to Virginia City, where he sold his goods profitably. The return trip proved Beachy's premonition: Magruder's skull was smashed with an ax, and his body, along with those of other members of his party, was dumped off a cliff.

When the gang returned alone, Beachy, remembering his dream, became suspicious. And when he heard the news of Magruder's brutal death, he went after the killers. He was indefatigable. He followed them by coach, on horseback, and by boat to Portland, Oregon; and then, after a 700-mile cross-country trek, he tracked them down in San Francisco. The killers were returned to face the hangman's noose in Lewiston.

Luna House Hotel was owned by Hill Beachy (far left), whose painstaking detective work brought the killers of his good friend Lloyd Magruder to justice. When they were returned to Lewiston, Idaho, they were held under guard at the hotel until their trial.

Justice, Texas Style

Law and order come to the Lone Star State

In a frontier land where disputes were often settled with guns, and where judges and lawyers were generally looked upon with deep suspicion, few lawmen were as colorful or distinguished as Robert "Three-Legged Willie" Williamson. Polished and well educated, as befitted a young man descended from a long line of respected Georgia lawyers, he could have remained in that genteel Southern society. Instead, he chose the rough-and-tumble world of Texas, where he settled in 1827 at the age of 23.

As an early circuit judge, he had the tough task of bringing the law to a territory that preferred more direct methods. But Three-Legged Willie could be as direct as the rudest frontiersman in his own way, which was usually spiced with humor. A contemporary writer remembered him as "one of the leading spirits . . . equally at home conducting a revival meeting or a minstrel show. In the latter performances his wooden leg played an important part, said member being utilized to beat time to his singing."

The story told of his first Texas court session is typical of the man who, with a velvet-gloved iron fist, helped to bring law and order to the Lone Star State. When he arrived to set up court in the town of Shelbyville, Williamson had to use a general store as his courtroom and a dry goods box as his bench. A local resident greeted the judge by throwing a bowie knife down on the box and shouting: "This, sir, is the law of Shelby County." Three-Legged Willie promptly pulled out his pistol, placed it next to the knife, and declared, "This is the constitution which overrides all law!"

Williamson had a serious side as well. As a leader of the war party and the first major in the Texas Rangers, he battled relentlessly for independence from Mexico, and is still honored as a hero of the Texas Republic. (So fervent was his fight that he actually named one of his sons Annexus.) One Texan said that he "did more than any one man to nerve our people to strike for liberty."

After independence was won in 1836, Three-Legged Willie was elected by the first Texas Congress as a district judge. Unlike many frontier jurists, who arbitrarily dealt out cruelty, he brought people around with his courage, quick wit, and knowledge of the law.

Judge Robert Williamson was nicknamed Three-Legged Willie because he walked on a peg leg attached to his right knee. His own withered limb, probably the result of a teenage bout with infantile paralysis, was bent behind him.

*It's a Crime . . . **

to go to church in Georgia without a loaded rifle.
to enter Urbana, Ill., if you are a monster.
to carry bees in your hat in Lawrence, Kans.
to let a cat run loose in Sterling, Colo., without a taillight.
to give your sweetheart in Idaho a box of candy weighing less than 50 pounds.
to sing the song "It Ain't Goin' to Rain No Mo' " in Oneida, Tex.
to wear cowboy boots in Blyth, Calif., unless you own two cows.
to divorce your wife in Tennessee without giving her 10 pounds of dried beans, 5 pounds of dried apples, a side of meat, and enough yarn to knit her own stockings for a year.
to kiss in Riverside, Calif., without wiping your lips with carbolized rose water.
to eat a snake on Sunday anywhere in Kansas.

And: *Whenever two trains meet at a crossing in Texas, both of them must come to a full stop; then neither one may proceed until the other has gone.*

** All are—or were once—real laws.*

After every robbery, dapper "Po-8" Black Bart (above) left a rhyme in the empty strongbox. One read:

Blame me not for what I've done,
I don't deserve your curses;
and if for some cause I must be hung
Let it be for my verses.

Verse and Reverse

Black Bart rhymed his way to ruin

Riding home from school one evening, so the story goes, Charles E. Boles, a teacher in California's northern mine country, heard a stagecoach approaching. He knew the driver and decided to play a practical joke. Tying a scarf over his face and holding a pistol-size stick, he commanded the driver to halt. The driver, having no shotgun rider, threw out the strongbox and, laying whip to the horses, dashed off. Boles was left with a fortune in gold coins and bullion. This, he decided, was a good way to make a living.

He went to San Francisco and deposited his haul in a bank, claiming to be in the mining business. From then on, Boles lived a life of leisure in San Francisco, occasionally taking a few days to roam the countryside, listening for news of a sizable shipment. Then, brandishing an empty shotgun and wearing a sack over his head, he would rob the stage, leaving behind a bit of verse signed "Black Bart, Po-8."

Between 1875 and 1883 Black Bart robbed a total of 28 stagecoaches. His "po-8-ry" entertained everyone except the Wells Fargo detectives—especially unamused was J. B. Hume, whose job was dogging Black Bart's trail.

Bart's luck ran out when he dropped a handkerchief, which bore the laundry mark FX07. Hume traced the kerchief to a San Francisco laundry, and then to C. E. Bolton (Black Bart's banking name). The teacher-bandit spent four years in San Quentin.

A few weeks after his release, they say, the robberies began again. There was no signature or "po-8-ry" this time, but the Wells Fargo men recognized the style. They called Boles in and supposedly struck a deal: in return for giving up the robbery business, Black Bart was to get a lifelong pension of $200 a month.

The Last Stagecoach Robbery

Out of one era and into another

On the blustery day of December 5, 1916, the postmaster of the remote village of Jarbidge, Nevada, became worried when the horse-drawn mail stage was three hours overdue. Searchers found the empty coach about 11 P.M. The driver was dead from a bullet wound. A bloodstained overcoat found nearby led police to Ben Kuhl, a drifter.

Kuhl was charged with murder and convicted. In addition to a pistol, which was found in his tent, an envelope picked up near the coach bore a bloody palm print—it matched an impression of Kuhl's. This marked the first time such a print was admitted as evidence in court. Of the $3,000 stolen in the nation's last stage robbery, only $182 was recovered.

How Mattie Silks Got Her Man

She did it with a gun

Upon discovering one of his infidelities, Mattie Silks publicly thrashed her "solid man," Cort Thompson. Worse yet, he had used her *money for his jaunt.*

During the silver boom years of the 1870's, Mattie Silks ran such a successful brothel that she became known as the Queen of the Denver Tenderloin. And she looked the part in her elaborate French-styled gowns, complete with cloaks and trains. Her skirts, though, had two hidden pockets: in one she carried gold coins; in the other, a pearl-handled pistol.

Mattie was madly in love with her "solid man," a drinking, gambling, two-timing dude named Cort Thompson. Trouble erupted when another "working girl" named Katie Fulton tried to win him away from Mattie. Katie's fiery temper clashed with Mattie's indomitable pride, and the two rivals agreed that pistols would be the only way to decide who got Cort.

Much of Denver, including Cort himself, turned out to witness the duel. At the count, the two women whirled and fired. Both were still standing when the smoke cleared, but Cort Thompson was on the ground, with blood spurting from his neck.

Mattie rushed to his side and tried to stanch the bleeding with her lace kerchief. She took Cort home and thereafter spent a fortune supporting his vices until he died in 1900. To this day, no one is sure who shot Cort, or whether it was done on purpose.

The Two Will Wests: Fingertips Tell the Difference

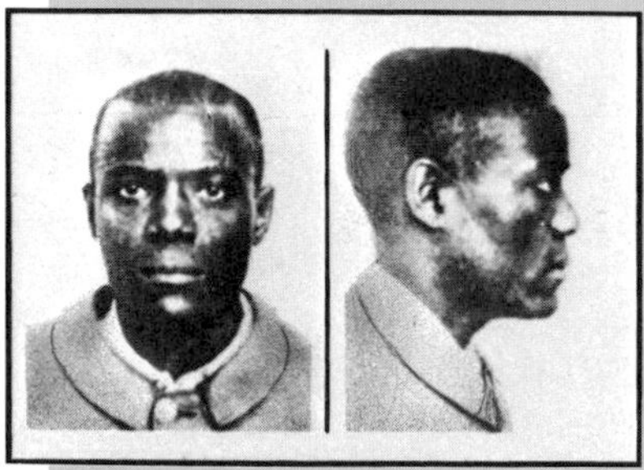

Will West (above)

The first Americans identified by their fingerprints were both named Will West. One was already in the Leavenworth penitentiary when the other arrived in 1903. Confused officials at first thought their prisoner had escaped and been returned. The two denied kinship, but they looked so much alike that, according to the then current Bertillion System of identification based on bone measurements, they were the same person. Fingerprinting, recently perfected by Scotland Yard in England, resolved the dilemma, and a precedent was set.

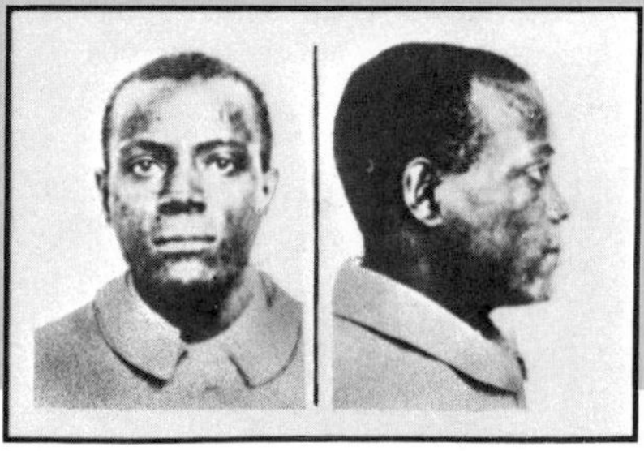

Will West (right)

It's a Crime . . . *

to ride in a baby carriage in Roderfield, W. Va., unless you are a baby.
to carry an uncaged bear down a highway in Missouri.
to drive buffalo through the streets of Newton, Kans.
to whistle or sing "After the Ball" between 6 A.M. and 10 P.M. in Mankato, Kans.
to eat in a place that is on fire in Chicago.
to drive a mule through Lang, Kans., in August unless it is wearing a straw hat.
to throw an onion in Princeton, Tex.
to carry an ice cream cone in your pocket in Lexington, Ky.
to mistreat rats in Denver.
to go to bed with your boots on in North Dakota.
to practice knife-throwing at a man wearing a striped suit in Natoma, Kans.

** All are—or were once—real laws.*

Belle Starr's Children

The murder and legacy of the Belle of the West

That Sunday in February 1889 when the saddled but riderless horse galloped up to the house, Pearl Starr ran for her half-brother, Eddie Reed. A little later she found her mother lying dead in the road a mile from their home at Younger's Bend, near Fort Smith, Arkansas. The 41-year-old Belle Starr, known as the Bandit Queen, had been shot in the back.

At her funeral three days later, Jim July, Belle's last "husband," accused a neighbor, the villainous outlaw Edgar Watson, of having murdered Belle to settle an old quarrel. Watson was taken to Fort Smith under arrest, but the federal marshals discharged him for lack of evidence. Eddie, Belle's son by her first husband, Jim Reed, was also questioned because he had threatened his mother after she gave him a severe beating for mistreating her horse. But Eddie was able to account for himself. Several others were suspected as well, including Jim July, but Belle's assassin was never identified. Most writers on the subject believe it was Watson.

Pearl was Belle's firstborn, an illegitimate child who used the last name of Belle's second husband, Sam Starr. Devoted to her mother, she ordered a white marble tombstone with a touching inscription. After her brief marriage ended, all Pearl had left was Eddie, in prison for horse theft.

Entering a brothel, she saved enough money to hire two attorneys. They got the attention of President Grover Cleveland, and in 1893 Eddie was pardoned. Pearl then opened her own "house" at Fort Smith. Appalled to find her living in shame, Eddie told her he would rather have stayed in jail. After another brush with the law, he married a Cherokee schoolteacher, settled down, and became a deputy marshal. In December 1896 Eddie was shot and killed when he attempted to arrest two men for the illegal sale of whiskey. Pearl, who went from bad to worse, died in Douglas, Arizona, in 1925.

A legend in her own time, Belle Starr lives on, her reputation as a notorious outlaw magnified by lurid fiction and the silver screen.

Sharpshooter Belle Starr (left), an attention-getter in her black velvet gown and plumed white hat, was a well-known horse thief. She rode bucking broncos, played saloon piano, and, when provoked, could swear like an angry mule skinner.

The Incompetent Train Robber

For Al Jennings crime paid, but in odd ways

In his brief career as a train robber, Al Jennings was a dismal failure. But he turned the experience into a real advantage.

Al, whose father was a judge, began practicing law in Oklahoma in 1889. Eventually he joined his brothers Ed and John in their law firm in the cowtown of Woodward. In October 1895 Ed was shot dead by a noted lawyer named Temple Houston in a barroom fight that had begun as a courtroom argument. When Houston got off scot-free, Al and another brother, Frank, vowed to avenge the murder. "I reverted to the primitive man that was within me," said Al, but he never caught up with Houston.

He and Frank then joined a gang of outlaws. In August 1897 they held up a Santa Fe train to rob the mail car, but the man in charge refused to open it and the conductor chased them away. Two weeks later the bandits piled ties on the tracks to stop a train, but the engineer opened his throttle and barreled right through. In October they flagged down a Rock Island passenger train and tried to blow open its two safes. The safes stayed shut, but the box car exploded. They *did* manage to collect $300 from the passengers.

The outlaws were soon caught and sentenced to five years, except for Al, who got a life sentence for robbery with intent to kill. But President William McKinley commuted his sentence and by late 1902 he was free.

Jennings went back to the law, married, and in 1907 got a "full citizenship" pardon from President Theodore Roosevelt. By 1912 he was making $5,000 a year as a lawyer in Oklahoma City. He ran for county attorney, promising: "When I was a train robber I was a good train robber, and if you choose me, I will be a good prosecuting attorney." He won the nomination but lost the election. When he ran for governor in 1914, newspapers editorialized against him, and he came in third.

"It takes the same sort of nerve to be an honest governor as to rob a train or bank," said Al Jennings in 1914, alluding to his past as an outlaw.

Jennings, whose urge to write had been encouraged by the writer O. Henry, a former cellmate, went to California in 1915. There he worked on a novel and ghost-wrote movies based on his life, and soon became a literary figure. He died in 1961 at the age of 98.

Who Was That Woman?

Like other frontier families, the Plummers, who lived in Muscotah, Kansas, in the 1870's, kept a candle in the window at night to guide luckless travelers in need of shelter. But such hospitality could be chancy. One evening "a tall, ungainly-looking woman, queerly dressed, carrying a heavy satchel," appeared. Mrs. Plummer, alone just then, let her come in. The woman went to bed soon, keeping her satchel within easy reach, and left the next morning before the Plummers awoke. Afterward they learned that their guest was none other than the killer-bandit Jesse James, on the run from the law.

Gang Rule

When armies of thugs openly terrorized New York

They called themselves by such names as the Roach Guards, the Dead Rabbits, the Shirt Tails, and the Plug Uglies, and in the 1840's and 1850's the sidewalks of New York were their unchallenged domain. The police were powerless as the huge street gangs, each claiming a spot of urban turf, took what they wanted and occasionally battled each other to the death.

Uniforms and banners

The Plug Uglies, a fierce mob of six-foot Irishmen, wore plug hats stuffed with wool and leather to serve as helmets. Heavy stomping boots added to their wardrobe. Each man went into battle with a brickbat in one hand, a bludgeon in the other, and a pistol in his pocket. The toughest rival gang member feared a Plug Ugly.

The Dead Rabbits adopted their name when a foe threw a rabbit corpse at them during a stormy meeting. From then on, the gang marched into battle behind a dead rabbit hanging from a pole. So good were they at the art of "persuasion" that in 1856 they helped reelect Mayor Fernando Wood, who won by 9,000 votes in an election that featured at least 10,000 fraudulent ballots.

Blood in the street

Occasionally, various gangs would join forces against the infamous Bowery Boys. Not typical street criminals, all of the Bowery Boys held day jobs; the fact that they were also volunteer firemen ensured their influence with the politicians of Tammany Hall.

Open warfare erupted on July 4, 1857, when the Plug Uglies and the Dead Rabbits invaded the Bowery. As 1,000 gang members fought, reported one newspaper, "brick-bats, stones and clubs were flying thickly around." A cop who tried to break up the fight was knocked down, stripped, and beaten with his own nightstick. Wearing only his cotton drawers, he managed to crawl back to the police station. After two days of pitched battle, and with the help of the National Guard, order was finally restored.

A melee of mayhem and bloodshed: During the long hot summer of 1857, gangs battled (top) on New York's Lower East Side. A member of the Dead Rabbits gang glowers above.

Stickup men

The Molasses Gang was named for its *modus operandi.* Members would ask a store clerk to fill a hat with molasses—to settle a bet. Then they'd jam it on his head and rob the store while the victim wrestled with the sticky mess.

The First American Police Force

Although not the "Finest," it set a precedent

The sensational murder of Mary Cecilia Rogers, a young New York woman whose body was found floating in the Hudson River in 1841, had two unexpected results: it inspired Edgar Allan Poe's gruesome tale "The Murder of Marie Rogêt"; and it spurred New Yorkers, alarmed at a rapid rise in violent crime, to demand the establishment of a regular police force.

With a population of some 350,000, New York City had grown too large to depend on its traditional but informal combination of constables and night watchmen for protection. Criminals of all kinds operated openly, and the recent influx of immigrants had turned many of the city's neighborhoods into ethnic battlegrounds.

In 1845 New York formed a peacekeeping force of 800 men. Each wore a copper star, giving rise to the inevitable nickname "cops." But the new police were an embarrassingly haphazard lot. An English visitor described them as "of all ages and sizes, including little withered old men, five feet nothing high."

At first the robbers and thugs regularly got the better of the cops, who were unable to stop the bloody gang fights. Yet it was corruption, not crime-fighting, that proved to be their greatest weakness. With local aldermen in charge of nominating recruits, all too often the officers were no more than graft collectors for their political patrons. And since a change in party power meant that an officer could lose his job, most were not above knocking a few heads together on Election Day to ensure a favorable result.

Corruption remained rampant in the police department until the turn of the century, when civil service reform was instituted and the force in New York City, as well as those in other eastern cities, became regulated.

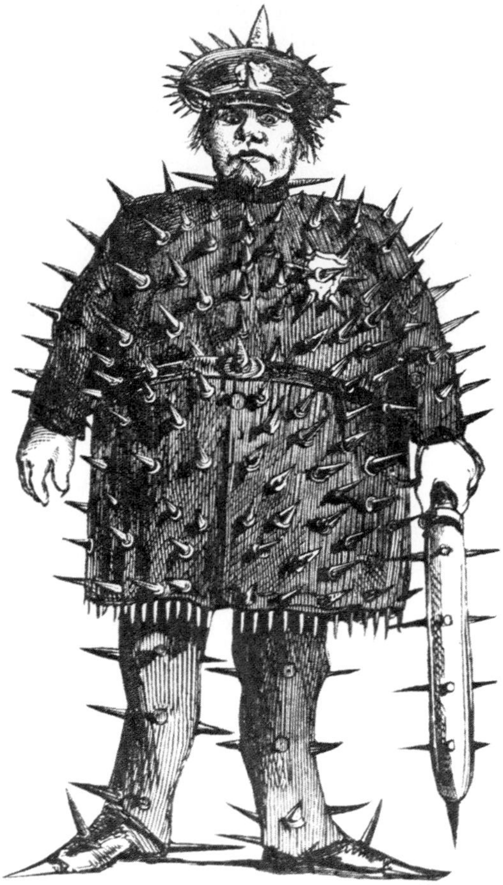

This 1858 cartoon suggests what might be suitable attire for the police in gang-ruled New York City.

Teddy Tries to Clean Things Up

When Theodore Roosevelt became police commissioner of New York City in 1895, he tackled corruption in a characteristically flamboyant manner, by making all-night forays to observe the conduct of patrolmen on the beat. He found that some cops were away from their posts; others were caught drinking on duty. Reporters dubbed him Haroun al Roosevelt, for the legendary caliph who roamed Baghdad's streets after dark.

Another notable TR maneuver was an attempt to enforce an old law prohibiting the sale of liquor on Sunday—he thought it would help break the power of the city's crooked political bosses. Needless to say, it failed. At left is a poster advertising one of a series of magazine articles Teddy wrote about his job.

Murder Was His Business

Working for the law or against it, Tom Horn was the best at what he did

He was no Jesse James or Billy the Kid. Unlike those legendary desperadoes, Tom Horn did not kill for robbery or revenge; he was a hired assassin who saw himself as a businessman. "Killing is my specialty," he boasted. "I look at it as a business proposition, and I think I have a corner on the market."

From lawman . . .

Horn believed that when men in authority (including the government) had use for a murderer, they would keep him from the clutches of the law. And, for the most part, that's just the way it worked out.

At various times in his career, he worked as a scout for the U.S. Army, as a deputy sheriff in Colorado, and as a detective for the noted Pinkerton Agency. When Gen. Nelson A. Miles needed a super-scout to track down Geronimo, the renegade Apache chief, he turned to Tom Horn. Some even credit Horn with arranging the Indian's surrender.

With his piercing eyes and serious manner, Horn wasn't taken lightly. While working for Pinkerton, he reputedly killed 17 men. He was so effective, so the story goes, that once he simply walked up to a man accused of murder and robbery, announced that he had come for him, and the man surrendered. "I had little trouble with him," Horn recalled.

. . . to hired killer

After four years of detective work, he quit. "It was too tame for me," he claimed. He wasn't out of a job for long. In 1894 Horn was hired as a range detective by an association of Wyoming cattle barons who wanted to make use of his special skills in fighting a range war against small ranchers and homesteaders. Ostensibly, he was to find rustlers and turn them over to the authorities.

But, in fact, Tom Horn was the cattlemen's law, judge, jury, and executioner. His price per hit ranged from $300 to $600. He never engaged in gunfights or fancy fast draws. His style was simple: he waited in ambush and killed his target. Then, as a calling card, he would place a rock beneath the victim's head.

In 1902 Horn was arrested for killing the 14-year-old son of a settler. The trial created a sensation in Cheyenne. Many townspeople expected the killer to get off—the cattle barons were paying for Horn's defense, after all, and he had enough information to bring them all down with him.

To nearly everyone's surprise, Horn was found guilty. (He had confessed to the crime while drinking with a sheriff.) He broke out of jail but was quickly recaptured, and the National Guard was called out to prevent another escape. On November 20, 1903, Tom Horn went to the gallows. According to onlookers, he died without a whimper.

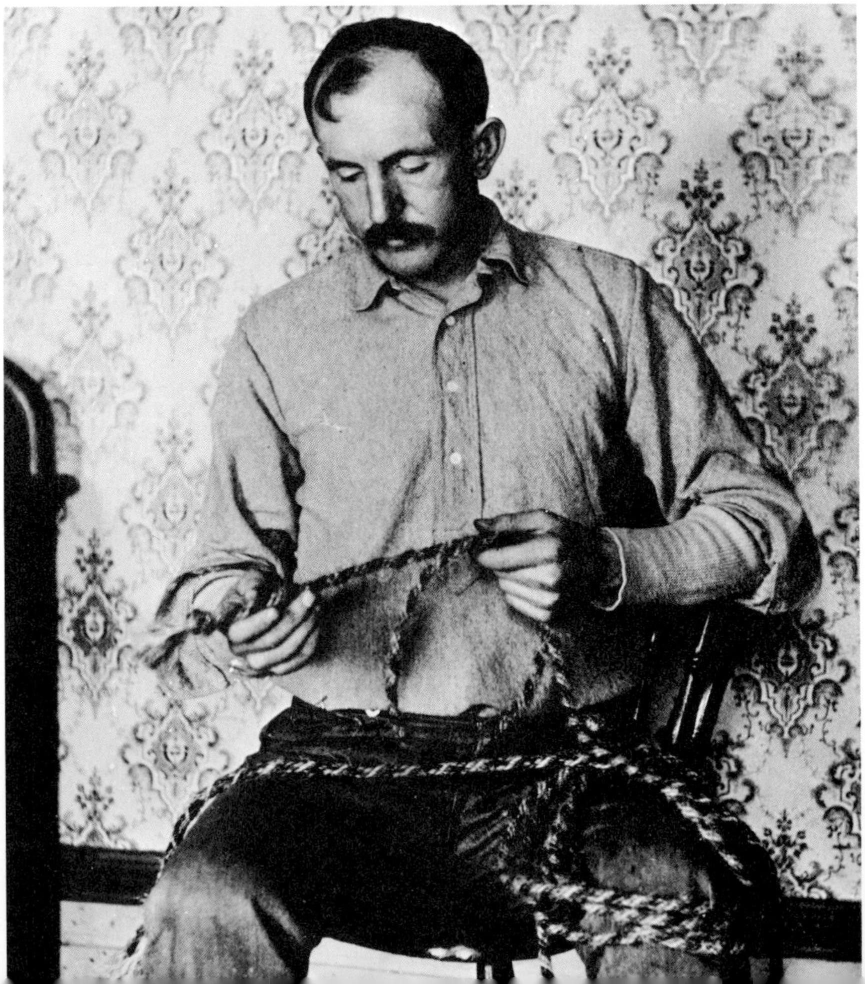

Tom Horn (right), hired gunman, spent his time in jail braiding ropes out of horsehair. Legend has it—but it's probably untrue—that he was hanged with one of them.

The lynching of Cattle Kate Watson and Jim Averill brought national attention to the war between the cattle barons and small ranchers of Wyoming. Witnesses were killed or simply disappeared, preventing legal action against those behind the lynching. The case led to the "Johnson County War" of 1892, in which the U.S. Cavalry was called in to restore order.

Cattle Kate Watson

Her "story is an awful one . . ."

Born in 1866 with far too restless a spirit for the Kansas plains, Ella Watson ran away from home to become a dance-hall girl and changed her name to Kate. According to her father, she was "a fine girl of handsome form" and "robust physique" who weighed "between 160 and 180 pounds."

In 1888 she received a business proposition from Jim Averill to come to Sweetwater Valley, Wyoming. There she set up a homestead about a mile from Jim's saloon and went into the business of "entertaining" his customers. Now, Averill was no ordinary saloonkeeper. An articulate man, he was the leader of the area's small ranchers and homesteaders and had written to the local newspapers denouncing the greed of the cattle barons.

A savage winter had intensified the bitter range war that raged around Sweetwater Valley. As small ranchers struggled to survive, they openly rustled cattle from the barons' vast herds to feed their families. Kate made it known that she would accept livestock in return for her favors, thus earning the nickname Cattle Kate. More than a few of her growing herd bore a baron's brand.

When an angry cattleman confronted Kate, claiming that 20 of his stolen steers were in her pen, she insisted she had bought them. He demanded proof. She produced a rifle, and the mere sight of it concluded the argument. Then a spy was sent to watch Kate's ranch; he reported that she had at least 50 stolen steers.

On July 20, 1889, a vigilante party of 20 men abducted Kate and Jim Averill, took them to a nearby canyon, and hanged them from a cottonwood tree. Although four prominent barons were charged with the murders, they never stood trial. "We didn't mean to hang 'em," said one, "only scare 'em a little."

Justice Field Beats the Rap

The gun wasn't even in his hand

In 1861, when Stephen J. Field was chief justice of the California Supreme Court, he sent President Abraham Lincoln the first transcontinental telegram. Lincoln later appointed him to the U.S. Supreme Court, and in 1889 he became the only member of that body ever to be arrested for murder.

The arrest grew out of a divorce appeal: In September 1888 Field ruled that the marriage contract between Sarah Althea Hill and a wealthy mine owner was invalid and that she had no claim to his money. The ruling angered her attorney and current husband, Judge David Terry (also a former chief justice of the California Supreme Court). A courtroom brawl erupted, and Field jailed them both for contempt. They publicly vowed revenge.

The following summer Field and his bodyguard, U.S. Marshal David Neagle, were on the same train as the Terrys, bound for San Francisco. At a stop near Stockton, the Terrys entered the station dining room and saw Field. Sarah rushed back to the train. Judge Terry slapped Field's face. Neagle, pulling a gun, shouted, "Stop! I am an officer!" When Terry began fumbling in his coat, Neagle fired, and Terry slumped to the floor. Then Sarah returned, carrying a satchel with a loaded revolver in it.

Field and Neagle were arrested for murder. Unruffled, Field said: "I recognize your authority, sir, and submit to the arrest."

The governor of California ordered Justice Field freed. Neagle's case led to a landmark decision: the Supreme Court ruled in 1890 that because he was acting under federal authority, he was not subject to the laws of California.

Beyond the Call of Duty

The lawyer who gave his life to defend a client

Clement Vallandigham, banished during the Civil War, inspired Edward Everett Hale's story "The Man Without a Country."

As a congressman, Clement L. Vallandigham led the Copperheads (Northerners who were vociferously opposed to the Civil War) and was banished to the Confederacy as a traitor. But by 1871, back in his native Ohio, he had built an outstanding reputation as a defense lawyer.

One of his clients, the raffish Thomas McGehan, was accused of murder, though he swore he'd never fired his pistol. Vallandigham thought he had a way to clear him by showing how the victim could have shot himself while drawing his own gun.

In his hotel room the day before the trial, the attorney demonstrated his dramatic ploy for colleagues. Taking a presumably empty pistol from atop a dresser and pressing it to his chest, he pulled the trigger. Unfortunately, there had been *two* guns on the dresser and he'd picked up the wrong one—the loaded one.

"My God, I've shot myself!" he shouted, staggering backward. Twelve hours later he was dead. No one knows how the gambit might have influenced a jury, but McGehan was acquitted at a subsequent trial.

The Bogus Baron of Arizona

An accomplished forger almost swindled his way into a fabulous empire

For about a decade a man named James Addison Reavis laid personal claim to some 17,000 square miles of what is now Arizona and New Mexico. It was a bold and clever swindle, and—but for a sharp-eyed newspaperman—he might have gotten away with it.

While in the Confederate Army, Reavis had developed a talent for forging officers' signatures onto passes. After his discharge, he refined his skill by forging deeds in a real estate office in St. Louis. Thus he was ready when, in 1871, another swindler, Dr. George M. Willing, Jr., broached a grandiose scheme to him. Willing died three years later (probably of poison), and Reavis went on with the plan alone.

First he got a job in the federal land records office in Santa Fe, New Mexico, and spent years studying treaties between the U.S. and Mexico. He was especially interested in the Gadsden Purchase, which pledged to honor Spanish land grants. He also made a study of the Spanish idiom, the penmanship, and the special parchments used in 18th-century documents. Traveling to Mexico (and possibly to Spain), he forged new names on ancient documents, sometimes inserting whole pages of text, and obtained notarized copies from Mexican officials.

In 1883 he finally filed a claim, based on the following intricately fabricated story: In 1748, in return for services rendered to the king of Spain, Don Miguel de Peralta de la Cordoba was made baron of the Colorados and received 300 leagues (about 1.3 million acres) of territory. The childless second baron deeded the land to George M. Willing, whose widow sold it to Reavis.

The claim brought panic to the territory and an outpouring of riches to the new baron Peralta-Reavis. The Southern Pacific paid $50,000 for its right-of-way. And with promises of more to follow, the Silver King Mine paid $25,000 for the right to stay open. Thousands of ranchers and businesses paid dearly for quitclaim deeds to their property. When Reavis married an "heiress" (an innocent girl he had groomed for the job), more than doubling his claim, the money burgeoned.

Then disaster struck. A newspaper publisher noticed that the type on one of the documents was of recent origin and that the watermark on the paper belonged to a fairly new Wisconsin paper mill. State Department agents were dispatched to Mexico and Spain. With chemical and microscopic tests, they found that the final pages of the Peralta grants were written in the wrong kind of ink on 10-year-old parchment.

Reavis was convicted in 1896 and sentenced to six years in jail. He died a pauper in 1908.

A Queen-size Killer *Unlike Bluebeard, Belle killed for big bucks*

Belle Gunness and her first husband adopted a daughter, then had some children of their own; the first two died in infancy of severe intestinal inflammation—or strychnine. Both were insured. So were the couple's candy store and house, which burned down.

The husband died in 1900; his death certificate gave the cause as an enlarged heart—also a symptom of strychnine poisoning. He was insured for $8,500.

Belle moved on, buying a farm in La Porte, Indiana, and marrying Peter Gunness, a hog butcher. He lasted less than a year, but his death was declared accidental. According to his widow, he jarred the stove, overturning a pot of boiling water on himself and dislodging a meat grinder, which hit him between the eyes. Belle collected $2,500 in insurance.

She hired several handymen, but they kept "leaving" suddenly. Then in 1905 she advertised for a new husband, using her farm as bait. A number of suitors showed up. They, too, disappeared.

In April 1908 Belle's farmhouse burned down. In the cellar were found the charred remains of a headless woman and three children. Soon a South Dakota farmer, Asle Helgelein, came looking for his brother Andrew, who had left to woo Belle that January. Andrew's body was found in a rubbish pit, his limbs, torso, and head in separate sacks. He had withdrawn $2,900 from his bank just before disappearing.

Diggers unearthed the skeleton of Belle's adopted daughter, who had supposedly left for California in 1906. Eight more butchered bodies eventually turned up, presumably those of suitors and hired men. There were watches and razors belonging to 11 men. But the great mystery was: What happened to Belle? The headless body was small; Belle weighed 250 pounds. A head was found in the cesspool and, later, Belle's bridgework, but identification was uncertain.

One hired man, Ray Lamphere, who had hung around after being fired (perhaps he had no insurance), was convicted of arson, but not of murder. Although Belle Gunness's remains were never clearly identified, she was declared dead.

The gory story of Belle Gunness inspired sensational literature, including the book shown at right, and proved a bonanza for the town of La Porte, Indiana. Thousands of tourists flocked there to watch the excavations and buy a sort of chili called Gunness Stew.

Typhoid Mary

She was an innocent killer

Mary Mallon was no criminal. She was a cook, and a pretty good one. But her body was the incubator of a deadly disease to which she, herself, was immune, and so she was tracked down, arrested, and locked up for life.

Not long after Mary had been hired as a summer cook by a wealthy New York family in 1906, six people in the household came down with typhoid fever. George A. Soper, a sanitary engineer with the New York City Department of Health, was called in to find the cause. Upon learning that Mary had left the household three weeks after the onset of the illness, Soper, who knew of the new German theory of disease "carriers," traced her working history: she had fled after typhoid outbreaks in at least five other homes.

When the tenacious medical detective finally tracked Mary down, she attacked him with a serving fork. It took five burly policemen to subdue her. Although she declared herself innocent of any crime, her body was found to be continually breeding and discharging the deadly bacteria *Salmonella typhosa*. She was confined for two years to an isolated hospital in New York's East River. Legal battles were waged on her behalf, and she was released on the condition that she keep away from food services.

But Mary went right back to cooking and eluded detectives for another five years. When recaptured, she was confined to the hospital for the rest of her life. She had her own cottage and worked in the laboratory, but she always ate alone. Mary died as the result of a stroke in 1938 at the age of 70. She had infected at least 57 people and caused 3 known deaths.

The World's Worst Entertainers

They lost their case, but set a lasting legal precedent

The Cherry Sisters first burst upon an unsuspecting public in 1893, performing an act that was so awful it became a smash hit. People flocked to theaters to hurl abuse and refuse at them. They finally made it to Broadway, under the auspices of the famed impresario Flo Ziegfeld himself, but they won their place in history when they sued a newspaper—and lost.

The sisters made their debut in Marion, Iowa, with an hour of songs that netted them $250 and their only good review. They moved on to Cedar Rapids, where the *Gazette* called their performance "unlimited gall" and mentioned the overshoes that were thrown at them. In Dubuque, the act was met by a fire extinguisher, a volley of turnips, and a tin wash boiler. And a Davenport paper heralded their arrival with a notice that rocks larger than two inches would not be allowed in the theater.

But it was the Des Moines *Leader* that carried the fateful review: "Effie is an old jade of 50 summers," Addie was a "capering monstrosity of 35," and the sounds from the other sisters "were like the wailings of damned souls."

Addie sued; and after the sisters performed in court, the *Leader* won. "Freedom of discussion is guaranteed by our fundamental law," was the Iowa Supreme Court's verdict. Today the standard textbooks on First Amendment law cite the Cherry Sisters' case.

When the Cherry Sisters opened on Broadway in 1896, a fishnet was stretched across the stage to protect them from hurled objects.

Murder Castle

Grisly revelations of a house of horrors in Chicago

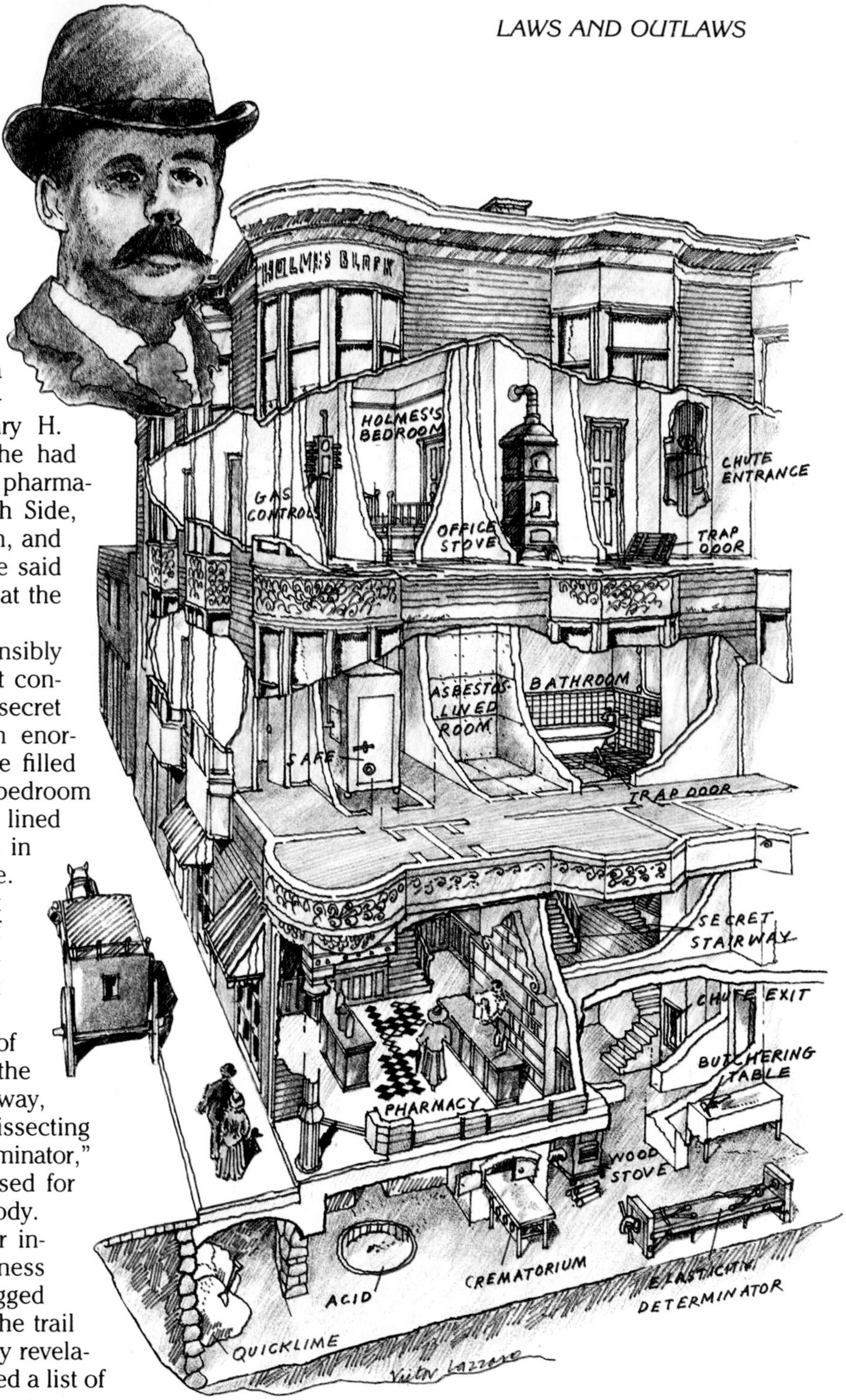

Herman W. Mudgett was a handsome, charming, intelligent man. He was also one of the most monstrous criminals America has ever produced. Trained as a doctor, he moved to Chicago in the mid-1880's and changed his name to Henry H. Holmes to avoid creditors and a wife he had abandoned. He established himself as a pharmacist and entrepreneur on the city's South Side, near the site of the Columbian Exposition, and by 1893 had finished a large building (he said he planned to rent rooms to fairgoers) that the press would later call Murder Castle.

The imposing three-story structure, ostensibly containing apartments and shops, in fact concealed a labyrinth of windowless rooms, secret passageways, and torture chambers. An enormous safe on the second floor could be filled with gas from a set of valves in Holmes's bedroom closet. One room had sheet-iron walls lined with asbestos; human bones were found in the oversized stove of the third-floor office.

It was in the basement that the most ghastly evidence was found. Vaults of quicklime, a barrel of acid, a huge wood-burning stove, and a zinc-lined cedar vat connected to a tangle of oil pipes—all provided for the discreet, efficient disposal of bodies. A system of trap doors connected the upper floors to the cellar via a secret stairway, and a chute ran from the third floor to a dissecting room in the basement. The "Elasticity Determinator," a rack with pulleys at both ends, was used for "experiments" in stretching the human body.

Holmes was arrested late in 1894—for insurance fraud and the murder of a business partner in Philadelphia. Only through dogged police work and a few lucky breaks did the trail slowly lead back to Chicago and the grisly revelations of Murder Castle. Authorities compiled a list of at least 50 missing persons (including a long succession of young secretaries to whom Holmes had promised marriage) who had last been seen about the time that they took up residence in the building. But the complete story—how many people he actually killed, and why—will never be known.

Convicted of the single Philadelphia murder, Holmes was hanged in 1896 and buried (at his own expense) in a reinforced coffin beneath two feet of concrete.

Herman W. Mudgett (top) achieved infamy as the fiendish killer Henry H. Holmes. In the course of less than two years, while running his pharmacy near the 1893 Columbian Exhibition in Chicago, he is presumed to have killed at least 50 people. The bodies of his victims, including tourists, customers, business associates, and employees, were efficiently disposed of in the elaborately diabolical house that he built (above).

The Legend of Joe Hill

Framed for murder, he gave the order for his own execution

In the early morning of November 19, 1915, Joe Hill, the Hobo Poet, was led to the execution yard of the Salt Lake City prison. He had been convicted of having killed a grocer and his son, perhaps in an attempted holdup, even though the bullets were not from Hill's revolver and no one had identified him as the murderer. The only evidence against him was that he himself had been shot in the chest at about the same time, under circumstances he refused to explain—it had to do with a woman, he said. Also, he was labeled a dangerous left-wing agitator.

Hill, born Joel Hägglund in Sweden in 1879, had emigrated to America in 1902 and Americanized his name. Failing to find a land of golden opportunities, he had toiled in the mines, on ranches, and on the docks, and joined the radical Industrial Workers of the World (also known as the Wobblies). Although a loner, he became well known for his songs about the down-and-out. One, "The Preacher and the Slave," sung to the tune of "In the Sweet Bye and Bye," satirized religious leaders who urged pious resignation: "Work and pray, live on hay; / You'll get pie in the sky when you die."

Following Hill's death sentence, the governor of Utah turned down thousands of demands for clemency and a request from President Woodrow Wilson for a stay of execution. Hill, who had chosen to be shot rather than hanged, reportedly refused a blindfold. After declaring his innocence, he added, "I die fighting, not like a coward." Then he shouted to the squad of five men poised with their guns, "Fire—go on and fire!" And they did.

A decade later the poet Alfred Hays wrote a ballad in Hill's memory: "I dreamed I saw Joe Hill last night, / Alive as you and me. / Says I, 'But Joe you're ten years dead,' / 'I never died,' says he."

Militant in its stance against capitalism, the Industrial Workers of the World (established in 1905) was also a singing union, striving to attract farm, textile, and mine workers to its ranks. The songs of Joe Hill, published in The Little Red Song Book, *were especially successful. Among them was the widely sung "Hallelujah, I'm a Bum."*

Dead at Last

They had to hang Wild Bill Longley three times

The 27-year-old gunman cheerily mounted the scaffold at Giddings, Texas, in October 1878. He was smoking a cigar and joking with the crowd. A few days earlier he had written, "Hanging's my favorite way of dying." Wild Bill Longley had, after all, been hanged once already.

A few years before, a group of vigilantes had mistaken Longley for a horse thief, strung him up from a limb, and fired a departing volley at him. A bullet split the rope above his head and he dropped to the ground, unscathed.

A ruthless murderer with a short fuse, the tall, handsome, slim-hipped Longley killed men at the drop of an insult. He especially enjoyed gunning down freed blacks during the post–Civil War years. Altogether, between 1867 and his execution in 1878, he killed 32 people—more than most other gunfighters—but he never achieved the notoriety of such fabled outlaws as Billy the Kid.

This time he was convicted in Giddings, near his father's hometown of Evergreen, for the murder of a man he believed had killed his cousin. Before he put his head in the noose, he addressed the crowd of more than 4,000 spectators on the virtues of a Christian life. Then he kissed the sheriff and a priest, and waved farewell.

The trap was sprung, and Wild Bill dropped through it—all the way to the ground, falling on his knees. He may have thought he was saved again, but the hangman had other ideas. The rope was adjusted and Longley was properly hanged. The wary authorities let him swing for more than 11 minutes, and then had three doctors pronounce Wild Bill dead.

During excavations for a new store in 1950, a whiskey barrel was found, containing the bottom part of George's skull and other remains (below), now in the Carbon County Museum in Rawlins. The skull is an exact fit for the skullcap in Omaha. Somehow George (left) never got himself together.

Big Nose George Parrott

How a small-time bandit went to pieces

The outlaw George Francis Warden, a "tiny, squeaky man," was known as Big Nose George Parrott because of his proboscis. In 1878 he led a Wyoming gang in an attempt to hold up a Union Pacific train by prying the spikes off the railbed. Foiled, they took off. Pursued by two deputy sheriffs who had tried to join the gang as undercover agents, the bandits waited to ambush them. They killed their men and got away. Two years later Big Nose bragged about the killings in a Montana saloon and was arrested.

Awaiting trial in Rawlins, Wyoming, George nearly escaped, but the jailer's wife grabbed a rifle and said, "George, get back into your cell or I'll kill you." She was later awarded a watch.

That night, March 22, 1881, a masked lynch mob dragged George out and stood him on a barrel under a telegraph pole to hang him. Something went wrong, so they tried again, propping a ladder against the pole. In the meantime, George worked his hands free. When someone kicked the ladder away, George grabbed the pole and screamed: "For God's sake, someone shoot me. Don't let me choke to death." He finally slipped and, weighted by leg irons, slowly strangled.

The undertaker had a problem with George, whose nose "was so large it interfered with the lid of the coffin and much pressure had to be exerted in nailing it down." George's body was exhumed for dissection by a local doctor, John E. Osborne, who tanned the skin from George's chest and thighs and had it made into a medicine bag and a pair of two-toned shoes he wore around town. He cut off the skullcap—to see whether the brain would show why George was so mean—and gave it to his young assistant, Lillian Heath, who filled it with rocks and used it as a doorstop.

Osborne, who later served as governor of Wyoming, a congressman, and an assistant secretary of state, donated the skin shoes and George's death mask to the Rawlins National Bank. Heath, who became the first woman doctor west of the Mississippi, chose to donate her bit of George to the Union Pacific museum in Omaha.

He Was Her Man, But the Song Was Wrong

"Frankie and Johnny were lovers, oh lordy how they could love . . ."

The ballad tells a poignant tale of two-timing love. And nothing made Frances Baker—the "Frankie" of the familiar lyrics—angrier than hearing "Frankie and Johnny." Especially since her St. Louis neighbors identified her as the female immortalized in it.

Frances never denied that, as an emotional 22-year-old in 1899, she shot her 17-year-old boyfriend (who was named Allen, but was called Albert, *not* Johnny). What really got her dander up was the song's description of her as a woman of easy virtue.

Even after she was acquitted of murder on the grounds of self-defense, there seemed no escaping the song, with its lyric calling her a "queen sport" who killed her boyfriend when she found him with another woman. "I just did not care for that humiliation—having me in front of the public all the time," she'd complain.

Two years after the incident, Frankie thought she could end the unwelcome serenading by moving first to Omaha and then to Portland, where she ran a shoeshine stand. But the song followed her. "I was pointed out as the worst woman in the world," she lamented. "You'd think it happened yesterday."

Nor did matters end there: a play and then a movie, released in 1936, celebrated the song's love triangle. In 1942 Frankie decided she had suffered enough and sued Republic Pictures for $200,000 for defamation of character. At last, 42 years after the shooting, Frankie had a chance to tell her side of the story.

She wasn't anything like the girl celebrated in the ballad, she testified. "If I was a 'queen sport,' they did not call me that to my face," she said. Nor did she wear big diamonds or fancy clothes. Her dresses were "just plain ordinary cotton ones." A neighbor pointed out that Frankie's income was not derived from loose morals at all, but from "washing and ironing and scrubbing steps."

Frankie even claimed she hadn't been upset when she learned that Albert was also seeing Alice Pryor. "I never fussed with her about it," she told the court. Moreover, she was at home in bed in her own apartment when Al came by. In fact, it seems it was Al who had designs on Frankie's life.

Al threatened Frankie, first with a lamp and then with a knife. "He ran a hand into his pocket . . . opened his knife and started to cut me," Frankie said. But she was well-prepared: she had a silver-plated pistol at her bedside. "Just run my hand under the pillow and shot him and he says, 'Oh, you have me,' " Frankie recounted. And, unlike the song, she *never* shot root-a-toot-toot-toot three times. "Didn't shoot him but one time," she testified, "standing by the bed."

The more convincing Frankie's story became, the less convinced the court was that the song was about her *at all.* Although one witness claimed that a St. Louis songwriter, Jim Dooley, had penned the ballad after hearing about the shooting, others pointed out that versions of it, with heroines whose names ranged from Annie to Lilly, had been in existence in at least 11 other states long before Frankie had shot Al.

In the end, Frankie lost the suit. She returned to Portland and in 1950 was committed to a mental institution, where she died two years later at the age of 75. Her long crusade never stopped St. Louis from billing itself as the birthplace of "Frankie and Johnny." Nor did it deter several generations of singers from belting out that classic refrain, "He was her man, but he done her wrong."

Frances "Frankie" Baker in 1899 (right), when she shot her lover. In 1942 (far right), she sued a film studio for defamation of character.

His megaphone at the ready, director D. W. Griffith prepares to shoot a scene for Intolerance (1916), with stars Dorothy Gish and Blanche Sweet.

Hooray for Hollywood—And Its South-of-the-Border Escape Route

In the early 1900's the weather in Hollywood was sunny and agreeable, the labor affordable, and the local business interests cooperative. But a big lure for a number of moviemakers was its proximity to Mexico.

At the start, motion picture moguls were working under a monopolistic cloud: the Motion Picture Patents Company, an international consortium formed by Thomas Edison in 1909, controlled virtually every phase of production, from supplying film to licensing exhibitors. Since this trust made it unlawful to produce a movie without the company's permission, from time to time it was expedient to get out of the country in a hurry. Mexico was indeed handy for dodging subpoenas and injunctions.

Finally a group of strong-minded producers encouraged dozens of other independents to join them in the glorious climate of southern California. Together, they effectively beat the system. Though it was several years until the trust was ordered by the courts to disband, by 1913 moviemaking was *Hollywood.*

And there were no more sudden trips south.

The Complete Con Man

He perfected the art of separating suckers from their money

"I never cheated an honest man, only rascals." Thus spoke Joseph "Yellow Kid" Weil, the con man who brought good old American ingenuity to the art of swindling.

In one of his favorite cons, he'd take a dog into a bar, show the bartender its well-forged pedigree, and ask him to mind the canine. Another man would enter, admire the dog, and offer to buy it for an outrageous sum. Later, when Weil returned and the greedy bartender offered him a few hundred for the dog, he'd reluctantly accept. The second man would never return, of course, and the bartender would be stuck with a costly mutt of dubious descent.

The drama of a Weil scam could also rival grand opera. Once he set up shop in a vacant bank; staffing it with tellers, guards, and customers—all fellow con artists—he relieved an "investor" of $50,000.

Sporting a trim beard and impeccably tailored suits, the dapper Weil raked in some $8 million with his scams. In later years, after he'd spent time in prison, he continued to proclaim his rob-the-rich Robin Hood views: "Our victims were mostly big industrialists and bankers," he boasted. "We never picked on poor people."

Swindler Joseph "Yellow Kid" Weil often wore yellow gloves. His nickname came from a popular comic strip of the 1890's.

King of the Bootleggers *George Remus did things his way*

During his short reign as King of the Bootleggers, George Remus lived very, very well. At his Cincinnati housewarming in 1920, the party favors were jewelry for the men and a new Pontiac sedan for each lady guest (the vehicle's title was tastefully left under her dinner plate). He swam in a marble pool and collected rare books and fine art.

A German immigrant and former pharmacist, Remus was a respected lawyer who quickly saw the income potential of Prohibition. Selling his law practice and some property to raise $100,000 for his scheme, he purchased Death Valley Farm near Cincinnati, the hub of the American liquor industry. Then he bought up a number of distilleries that the government allowed to remain in operation for the production of medicinal alcohol.

Next, Remus hired some 3,000 men to go around with trucks to steal alcohol from the plants he now owned. At Death Valley Farm the stuff was converted into booze, bottled, stored, sold, and shipped. For a time Remus had an inventory of 3 million gallons of liquor hidden in barns and chicken coops; his gross profits were between $60 million and $75 million.

Bragging that he had cornered the market, Remus bribed public officials to the tune of $20 million. But the law caught up with him anyway, and he was sentenced to two years in the federal penitentiary in Atlanta. After a huge send-off party, locally called the social event of 1924, he traveled to Atlanta in a luxurious railroad car he had rented, accompanied by a number of his friends and the federal marshals. While they wined and dined at his expense, he retired to his compartment and read Dante's *Inferno.* In jail Remus got the cushy job of prison librarian, arranged for maid service and fresh flowers in his cell, and secured permission to dine regularly with the chaplain.

By the time he got out, gangsters had muscled in on the bootlegging business and dethroned him. But Remus made the headlines once more. In 1927 he shot and killed his wife, claiming she had been having an affair with the federal agent whose evidence had convicted him. The jury found him insane, and he was sent to an asylum. But he soon convinced the Ohio Court of Appeals that he was sane after all, and he was released. He retired to an obscure life in Covington, Kentucky, where he died in 1952, at the age of 78.

Bootlegging enabled George Remus (right) to live in high style; his immense mansion held a marble Grecian pool, a golden piano, and a lush profusion of plant life.

Bing Croons From a Cell

After leaving a Hollywood bash one night in 1930, during the filming of The King of Jazz *(right), Bing Crosby had a minor car accident. A policeman smelled liquor on the crooner's breath and took him in. In court two weeks later the judge asked: "Don't you know that there's a Prohibition law in the United States and liquor is forbidden?"*

"Yes," Bing replied, "but nobody pays any attention to that!"

"Well," said the judge, "you'll have 30 days to pay some attention to it!" Bing went to the clink.

Al Capone's Brother

Not quite the white sheep of the family

Almost no one knows that the gangster Al Capone, who made a fortune from bootleg whiskey in the 1920's, had a brother, Jim, who was a law-enforcement officer—specializing in Prohibition violations.

As a boy, Jim Capone ran away from home to become a circus roustabout. After traveling around the United States and Central America, he arrived in Homer, Nebraska, on a freight train and decided to stay. At some point he had changed his name to Richard Joseph Hart. During a flash flood he saved a grocer and his daughter, and then married the daughter. Inventing a war record for himself, he became commander of the local American Legion post.

Known as Two-Gun Hart in Homer because he carried a pistol on each hip, he was a crack shot who could hit a bottle cap 100 feet away—shooting with either hand. He became town marshal and then sheriff, busting stills statewide. As a Prohibition investigator for the Indian Service, Hart earned a reputation among the Indians for brutality. In Sioux City, Iowa, he killed an Indian in a barroom brawl but was acquitted when the victim turned out to be a bootlegger.

Reappointed Homer's town marshal, Hart was suspected of petty thievery while on night patrol and relieved of his duties. Broke, he appealed to his family for help in 1940, and one of his brothers, Ralph, began sending a monthly check. Only then did Richard Hart tell his wife that he was Scarface Al Capone's brother. He died in 1952.

It's a Crime . . . *

- *to buy a beer in the state of Maine unless you are standing up at the time.*
- *to drink a beer in Cartersville, Ga., unless you're sitting down in your house.*
- *to drink beer in your underwear in Cushing, Okla.*
- *to own or sell anything that tastes like, smells like, or looks like beer anywhere in the state of Alabama.*
- *to buy whiskey in Greenville, S.C., if the sun isn't shining.*
- *to sell liquor to a married man in Cold Springs, Pa., unless you have his wife's written consent.*
- *to own a copy of the* Encyclopaedia Britannica *in Texas (it contains a liquor recipe).*
- *to tap your foot, nod your head, or otherwise keep time to music anywhere that liquor is sold in New Hampshire.*
- *to do a fan dance in a bar in Montana while wearing a costume that weighs less than 3 pounds, 2 ounces.*
- *to wiggle while dancing in a bar in Stockton, Calif.*
- *to operate a still in Kentucky unless you blow a whistle.*
- *to play baseball or climb a tree while intoxicated in Council Bluffs, Iowa.*
- *to wear trousers with a hip pocket (in which a flask might be carried) in Lexington, Ky.*
- *to get a fish drunk anywhere in the state of Oklahoma.*

However: *A Missouri court once ruled that "it is the inalienable right of the citizen to get drunk."*

** All are—or were once—real laws.*

The Legend Lives

Did the FBI really kill Dillinger?

The FBI files say that John Dillinger died in a hail of bullets on a hot July night in 1934 in front of the Biograph Theater in Chicago. Perhaps he did. But according to Jay Robert Nash, an authority on the history of American crime, the Bureau was duped into killing the wrong man and, ashamed to admit the mistake, falsified evidence in an elaborate cover-up.

John Dillinger, Public Enemy

John Dillinger (center) and prosecutor Robert Estill (left) are surrounded by guards in the Crown Point, Indiana, jail. The gangster escaped on March 3, 1934, using a wooden gun.

---

34 Years for a Box of Candy

Stephen Dennison, a 16-year-old from a broken home near Salem, New York, stole a $5 box of candy from a roadside stand in 1925. He pleaded guilty and was given a 10-year suspended sentence. But because he failed to report monthly to a minister in his home town, Stephen was sent to the Elmira Reformatory in 1926. He remained imprisoned for the next 34 years.

In 1927 Stephen was classified as a "low-grade moron" and transferred to the Institution for Male Defective Delinquents. Only six months before the 10-year term was up, he was sent—without a court hearing or judicial review—to Dannemora, a state hospital for the criminally insane, on a certificate of lunacy.

It took his half-brother, George, 24 years to win his release on a writ of habeas corpus *in 1960. Stephen, who was by then 51 years old, sued the state over his illegal incarceration and was awarded $115,000. But according to Judge Richard Heller, "No sum of money would be adequate to compensate the claimant."*

A certificate of lunacy sent Stephen Dennison (right) to jail without trial. Later these certificates were declared unconstitutional.

Number One, became more myth than man despite his very real career of crime. During the early 1930's a desperate and disillusioned public applauded his ruthless exploits along with those of Bonnie and Clyde, Ma Barker, Baby Face Nelson, and other bandits who seemed to be beating the system. Newspapers catered to the public hunger for heroes with banner headlines and exciting copy.

FBI Director J. Edgar Hoover—no slouch himself when it came to publicity—vowed to get the man who had mocked law-enforcement officials by breaking out of jails and holding up police stations. But he wanted to do more than arrest Dillinger; he wanted to squash his legendary invincibility.

The Bureau got a tip from a madam, Anna Sage, who ran a brothel in Gary, Indiana. About to be deported to her native Romania on a morals charge, she promised to divulge the gangster's whereabouts and to set him up for the G-men. In exchange, they would put in a good word to the Immigration Department.

Sage was the notorious Woman in Red, and she *did* attend the Biograph Theater on July 22, 1934, with a man who died in a hail of bullets. But Nash claims that the man was an impostor—James Lawrence, a minor underworld character—and that a cover story about Dillinger having had plastic surgery was concocted to support the hoax. He says that Sage and her lover, a crooked Indiana detective, designed the scam to help Dillinger escape, and he backs up his allegations with the following details from an autopsy report that was supposedly missing from the Cook County coroner's office for some 30 years:

- The man shot that night was neither the same height nor weight as Dillinger. His eyes were brown; Dillinger's were blue.
- A birthmark was missing from the bullet-riddled body. In addition, the corpse had more teeth than the bank robber did.
- There was evidence of a rheumatic heart in the man, which would have prevented Dillinger from serving in the U.S. Navy.

The FBI has denied Nash's allegations, claiming that the record (including their own fingerprint file) speaks for itself. But whether John Dillinger died that night or disappeared, the legend of his invincibility survives.

Mrs. Machine Gun Kelly

The woman behind the man behind the gun

Kathryn Shannon might have been a good wife for a corporation executive. She knew how to help her man's career. In 1929, soon after she married George Kelly—a big, broad-shouldered bruiser who had often bragged, "No copper will ever take me alive"—she bought him a machine gun from a pawnshop. Then, though he hated guns, she told him to learn how to use it.

After much practice, George got the hang of the thing. At his wife's urging, he organized a gang and started robbing and killing. Kathryn phoned newspapers regularly to brag about Machine Gun Kelly's exploits, and the band was soon known as "the most dangerous ever encountered." But bank takes were low during the Depression, so Kathryn pressed for a more profitable venture: kidnapping.

The Kelly Gang snatched an Oklahoma businessman, netting $200,000 in ransom. But even though the victim had been blindfolded, he was able to lead the police to the farm of Kathryn's parents, where most of the gang was arrested—all except the Kellys, who were on a spending spree with their share of the loot.

When the FBI finally cornered them in a Memphis hideout, George reportedly hollered out, "Don't shoot, G-men," thus coining a lasting nickname for J. Edgar Hoover's gangbusting brigade. As they were dragged into custody, Kathryn shouted at her husband, "You rat! You've brought disgrace to my family."

In 1933 the Kellys were among the first to be sentenced to life imprisonment under the new Lindbergh kidnapping law. Ironically, the amiable George died in prison in 1954, while his glamorous wife (above), the instigator of the crimes, was released in 1958.

Like most swindles, the Ponzi Scheme—named after the man who invented it (above)—depends on its victims' greed and gullibility. The 5-foot, 2-inch Charles Ponzi understood that, but he didn't take his own greedy dreams into account.

Get-Rich-Quick Ponzi

The super-swindler who conned himself

Charles Ponzi saw himself as a man of substance, a mover and a shaker on the order of J. P. Morgan and John D. Rockefeller. The jaunty Italian immigrant felt confident that, if he could only amass enough capital, he could buy his way into the rarefied world of high finance, and then nothing could stop him from taking his rightful position on top of the heap.

In the summer of 1919 he discovered international reply coupons, issued to compensate for erratic rates of foreign exchange. You could buy a coupon in Spain for a penny and redeem it for a six-cent stamp in the U.S. "Why can't I buy hundreds, thousands, millions of these coupons?" he wondered. So he borrowed money and invested. Then he learned that postal regulations forbade his plan.

Still, the coupons *looked* impressive and the plan *sounded* good. Setting up shop in Boston, he printed an investment prospectus that promised a 50-percent return in 90 days. When he paid off on time, the word spread. Soon cash was pouring in—as it *had* to, because he was using the money from the front of the line to pay off those few at the end who didn't reinvest.

In eight months Ponzi took in $15 million. He was negotiating to merge with the Bank of America when the bubble burst and he came up $5 million short. He tried to recoup at the Saratoga gaming tables, but three days later, broke, returned to Boston to face the music.

Jailed in Massachusetts, then deported to Italy, he ended up in Rio de Janeiro. There, in 1949, he died in a charity ward, leaving behind his unfinished autobiography. He'd named it *The Fall of Mister Ponzi.*

Go Directly to Jail—At Home

Credit a comic strip with a novel approach to law enforcement. A New Mexico judge, inspired by a Spiderman villain who tracked his victim by attaching an electronic monitor to his wrist, thought of applying the idea to prisoners and parolees. The device—a bracelet or an anklet—is equipped with a transmitter. The signals it emits stop if the wearer strays beyond a certain distance from his home; it is programmed to allow for trips to work and other specific errands. By 1987 some 12 companies were producing the gadgets.

Electronic house arrest for those convicted of minor nonviolent crimes is one remedy for overcrowded jails. The device monitors movements, but can't eavesdrop on conversations. And prisoners welcome the chance to live at home and to keep their jobs while serving time. (Penologists say this may be a long-term benefit.)

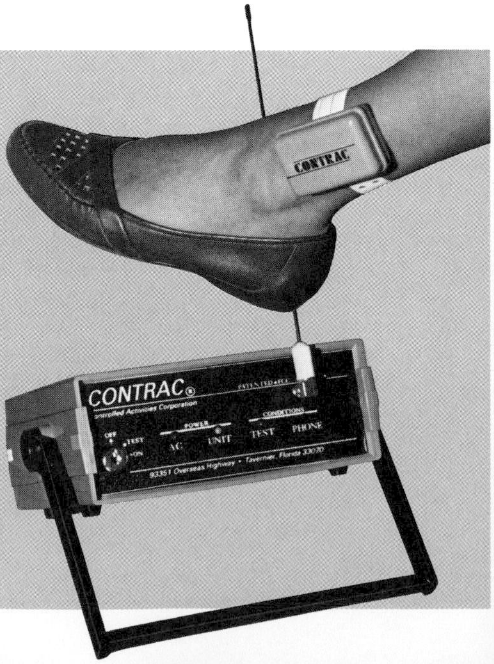

It's a Crime . . . *

to bathe less than once a year in Kentucky, and more than once a week in Boston.
to carry fishing tackle into a cemetery in Muncie, Ind.
to insert a penny in your ear in Hawaii.
to go to a public dance without a corset on if you are a girl in Norfolk, Va.
to shoot off a policeman's tie in Frankfort, Ky.
to catch mice in Cleveland without a hunting license.
to tie a giraffe to a telephone pole in Atlanta.
to throw a reptile at someone in Toledo, Ohio.
to carry a corpse in a taxi in Hartford.
to walk across a Kansas highway at night without a taillight.
to whistle underwater in Vermont.
to put a skunk in your boss's desk in Michigan.
to bowl at ninepins in Connecticut. (The 10th pin was added to get around this 1841 antigambling law.)

However: *In 1949 Gov. Adlai Stevenson of Illinois vetoed a bill to protect birds by restraining cats. "We may be called upon to take sides as well in the age old problems of dog versus cat . . . ," he feared, "even bird versus worm. [We] already have enough to do without trying to control feline delinquency."*

** All are—or were once—real laws.*

A Decade of Counterfeiting

Were crimebusters really seeking this mild-mannered man?

He was no master criminal, just a former building superintendent who passed phony $1 bills. Yet the nation's most-hunted counterfeiter eluded detection for some 10 years.

A cheerful little white-haired man, 63-year-old Edward Mueller moved into a New York City tenement in 1938. Fiercely independent, he told his children he was comfortably well-off, but in fact he had little money. As his savings dwindled, he began turning out $1 bills. The results were terrible; using ordinary paper, he made no attempt to reproduce the fine details of a real bill. And his spending style was as modest as his means: Mueller would pass a bill or two each day—just enough to support himself and his dog. He never passed more than one to any given person, in time branching out from his own neighborhood.

The least greedy counterfeiter on record was caught only by chance: His apartment burned, and some boys who were exploring the rubble found a cache of "stage money." One boy's father recognized the bills and turned the money in.

It wasn't easy for authorities to believe that the charming old man was their quarry. Freely admitting his crime, Mueller was sentenced to a year and a day and was ordered to pay a fine. The amount? One dollar—the genuine article, of course.

Creating cash in the kitchen: Edmund Gwenn (right) played the title role of Mr. 880 in the 1950 movie version of Edward Mueller's life as a counterfeiter. (The case was open for so long that Mueller became known by its number, 880.) After photographing a $1 bill, Mueller made zinc plates for a small press that sat on a sink-side counter. Retouching the plates by hand, he produced thoroughly unconvincing singles. (He spelled the name of the first president "Wahsington.")

MISS BAY RIDGE
MISS READING
LOUISVILLE
CHICAGO

CHAPTER SIX

The Passing Parade

Presenting a panorama of America's past, era by era—the fashions and fads, headlines and heroes, that people were talking about back then.

Contestants in the Miss America Pageant (Atlantic City, New Jersey, 1924)

Strangers on a Foreign Shore

The First Thanksgiving

The Puritan Saints would not be happy to know what we do in their name

Thanksgiving: Turkey and stuffing and cranberry sauce . . . mashed potatoes and gravy . . . hot rolls and butter and corn on the cob . . . and, of course, a big slice of pumpkin pie. Bow your head, think about the *Mayflower* and Plymouth Rock, fill your face, and watch a football game.

If there's one thing that all Americans know about—or *think* they know about—it's the first thanksgiving: how, in the fall of 1621, the Pilgrims, wearing their funny hats and bonnets, sat down with the friendly Indians and, as a way of giving thanks to God, shared a mighty feast.

Prayer in Virginia

In fact, the first recorded American thanksgiving took place in Virginia more than 11 years earlier, and it wasn't a feast. The spring of 1610 at Jamestown ended a winter that came to be called "the starving time." The original contingent of 409 colonists had been reduced to 60 survivors. They prayed for help, with no way of knowing if or when any might come. When help did arrive, in the form of a ship filled with food and supplies from England, they held a prayer service to give thanks.

Although, in years to come, the Jamestown colonists surely thought back on that heartfelt thanksgiving, they never commemorated it. Another Virginia group did that, also before the Pilgrims. On December 4, 1619, 38 colonists landed at a place they called Berkeley Hundred. "Wee ordaine," read an instruction in their charter, "that the day of our ships arrival . . . in the land of Virginia shall be yearly and perpetually keept holy as a day of Thanksgiving to Almighty god." On the first anniversary they fasted and prayed. But before the December holiday rolled around again, the entire colony had been massacred by Indians.

Harvest Home

The Puritans in Plymouth (who called themselves Saints, not Pilgrims—that term didn't become popular until the 1790's) also observed thanksgiving days. But the 1621 feast we commemorate with full bellies and football wasn't one of them. A Puritan thanksgiving day was one of fasting and solemn prayer; it might be declared when a drought broke or a battle was won. Failure to observe it was a crime (as was participation in a sporting event on the Sabbath).

The first Jamestown colonists (above, being welcomed by enthusiastic Indians) had to endure a disastrous winter. When help arrived in the spring, the survivors held the first recorded American thanksgiving service.

The famous feast was not a thanksgiving but a three-day Harvest Home celebration, an ancient tradition—the best way to preserve food for the winter was in the form of body fat. Gov. William Bradford invited the Indian chief Massasoit and his brother to join the feast, not because they'd helped grow the food, but because he still deemed it wise to stay friendly with them. To his surprise, they showed up with some 90 tribesmen.

If turkey was eaten (and there is no proof that it was), it wasn't the main course—venison was. There were no potatoes; although the Spanish had brought the tubers to Europe from South America, they were still considered poisonous. There was no grain, and so no rolls; no cattle, and so no butter. There *was* corn, but not on the cob; the tough kernels were boiled, mashed, kneaded, and fried into flat cakes. There were cranberries, to be sure, and other wild fruits; but no oranges or apples (hence, no apple cider). There were squash and pumpkins aplenty, but, alas—lacking flour—no pumpkin pie.

Harvard's Indian College

A grand dream of conversion that came to naught

When the Massachusetts Bay Colony founded America's first college in 1636, a major purpose was to educate Puritan ministers. Two years later the school was named for John Harvard, a clergyman who had left it his library of 400 books and half his estate.

Harvard's first president, Henry Dunster, had a dream: to train Indians to preach Puritanism to their people. In 1653 the English Society for the Propagation of the Gospel in New England sponsored "one Intyre Rome att the College for the Conveniencye of six hopfull Indians youthes." Dunster put up a two-story brick building to house 20 Indians and 2 tutors. On the ground floor was the college press.

Four youths are known to have attended Harvard's Indian College; others were chosen, but died of "hecktick fevers" or other diseases before entering. Only one, Caleb Cheeshahteaumuck—who could speak Latin and Greek—graduated. He died of tuberculosis the following spring. Another, Joel Iacoomis, was shipwrecked on the Nantucket shoals while returning from a visit to Martha's Vineyard and was "murthered by some wicked Indians of that place." A third, Eleazer, wrote a Latin and Greek elegy before he died. The sole survivor, John Wompas, "a towardly lad and apt witt for a scholler," left Harvard after a year and bought a house on Boston Common. Jailed for debt, he escaped to become a real estate agent, of sorts—he sold an entire township he didn't own. For years, the Indian College housed only the press, on which, in 1663, was printed the first American Bible—an Algonquian translation. The building was torn down in 1698.

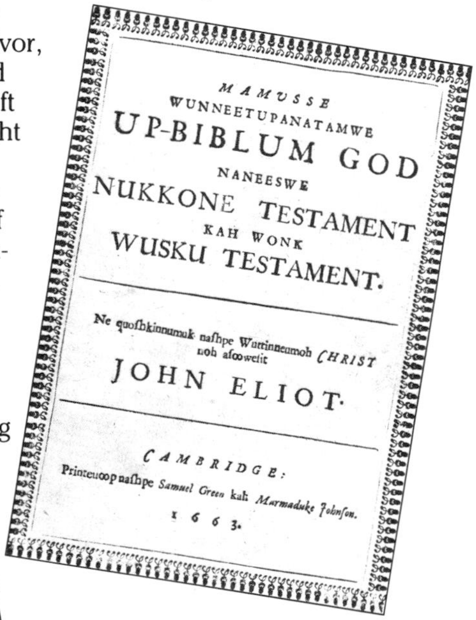
MAMUSSE
WUNNEETUPANATAMWE
UP-BIBLUM GOD
NANEESWE
NUKKONE TESTAMENT
KAH WONK
WUSKU TESTAMENT.
Ne quoshkinnumuk nashpe Wuttinneumoh CHRIST noh asoowesit
JOHN ELIOT.
CAMBRIDGE:
Printeuoop nashpe Samuel Green kah Marmaduke Johnson.
1 6 6 3.

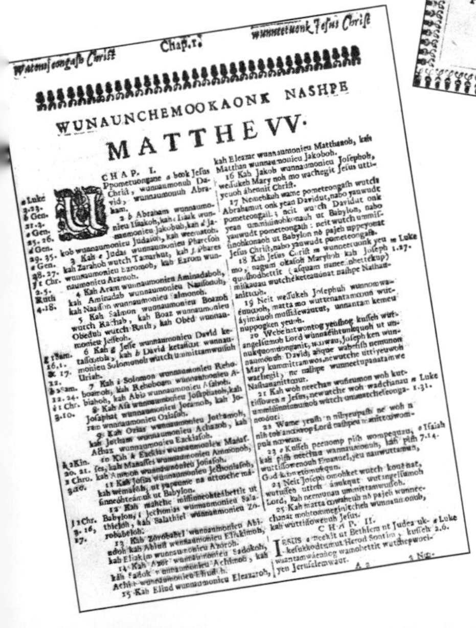
Wutinnieongash Christ Chap. I. wunneetuonk Jesus Christ
WUNAUNCHEMOOKAONK NASHPE
MATTHEVV.
CHAP. I.

John Eliot's 1,200-page Algonquian Bible, called "probably as good as any first version that has been made . . . in a previously unwritten and so-called barbarous language," took three years to print on Harvard's college press. On the page at left, from the Gospel According to Matthew, the word wunnaumonieu *means "begat." In 1986 a rare first edition was auctioned for $220,000.*

Buying Manhattan

Did Peter Minuit swindle the Indians? Or vice versa?

Manahatin ("Hill Island" in Algonquian) was a rich land occupied by two Indian tribes. The Weckquaesgeeks ranged over the northern three-quarters of the island, hunting beaver, deer, bear, and even bison. They fished for sturgeon in the Hudson River and harvested oysters from its huge beds. The Canarsees, from what is now Brooklyn, made forays to the southern tip of the island.

Neither tribe owned Manahatin or even recognized ownership in the European sense, but the Canarsees certainly had less claim to it than the Weckquaesgeeks.

Yet when Peter Minuit, the new director-general of the Dutch colony, arrived on May 4, 1626, the Canarsees were the Indians he met. His instructions from Holland were that "in case the said Island is inhabited by some Indians . . . these should not be driven away by force or threats, but should be persuaded by kind words or otherwise by giving them something, to let us live amongst them."

Mindful of powerful English settlements to the north and south, and anxious to establish a legal claim, Minuit didn't quibble. Nor did Seyseys, the Canarsee chief. Happily accepting—in return for real estate he didn't own—60 guilders, or about $24, worth of beads, knives, axes, clothes, and (perhaps) rum, he paddled back to Brooklyn, where his tribe was to leave its name on the landscape.

If there had been banks in Brooklyn back then, and if the Canarsees had invested their $24 windfall at six-percent interest, compounded annually, by 1988 they would have amassed nearly $35 billion—and almost double that by the year 2000.

The Conscientious Caveman

Benjamin Lay (right) was a gnome of a man—4 feet 7 inches tall, with a hunched back and sticklike legs—who inhabited a cave near Philadelphia. Appalled that his fellow Quakers condoned slavery, he and his dwarf wife, Sarah, refused to live among them, although he made forays into town to disrupt meetings. Among his friends was Benjamin Franklin, who once dined in the cave. Later called by the poet John Greenleaf Whittier the community's "pertinacious gad-fly on the sore places of its conscience," Lay eventually won. In 1758, a year before his death at the age of 82, the Quakers finally denounced slavery.

Salem's Psychedelic Witchcraft

In December 1691 some girls in Salem Village, Massachusetts, began to twitch, convulse, and scream that devils were pinching them. After they were fed special "witch cakes," they began accusing women of consorting with Satan. Before history's most famous witch hunt (below) was over a year later, 19 citizens had been hanged and 1 pressed to death beneath heavy weights. Of the many theories offered to explain what happened, perhaps the most intriguing is that the girls had eaten grain contaminated with the poisonous fungus ergot; its principal component, an alkaloid called lysergic acid amide, is closely related to lysergic acid diethylamide—or LSD.

Lost and Found

So common was slavery throughout the American colonies that most newspapers featured classified advertisements offering slaves for sale, want ads seeking slaves with specific skills, and lost-and-found ads asking for the return of escaped slaves. Escapes were so routine that printers kept woodcuts in stock, such as those at left, to accompany the ads; the owner supplied a specific description of the escapee and often offered a reward.

Counterfeit Wampum

Few early colonists brought much money with them to the New World. They didn't think they'd need it. And they were right; the natives had their own currency—wampum. Made of shell beads by coastal Indians, the six-foot "fathoms" (right, above) and seven-inch "hands" (below) were accepted by such inland tribes as the Iroquois (center) in exchange for furs. Wampum was declared legal currency in many English and Dutch colonies.

Before long the Indians began dyeing white beads (from conch shells) with huckleberry juice and passing them off to the unsophisticated settlers as the more valuable dark ones (made from the hearts of quahog clamshells). Eventually the colonists learned to spit on the beads to test them, as Indians did. Then a man named William Pynchon turned the tables. Having acquired bushels of loose wampum beads, he hired the women and children of the Massachusetts Bay Colony to string them together and flooded the market, inflating the currency. Finally, glass beads, fabricated at first in England and later in the colonies, brought about the collapse of the wampum economy.

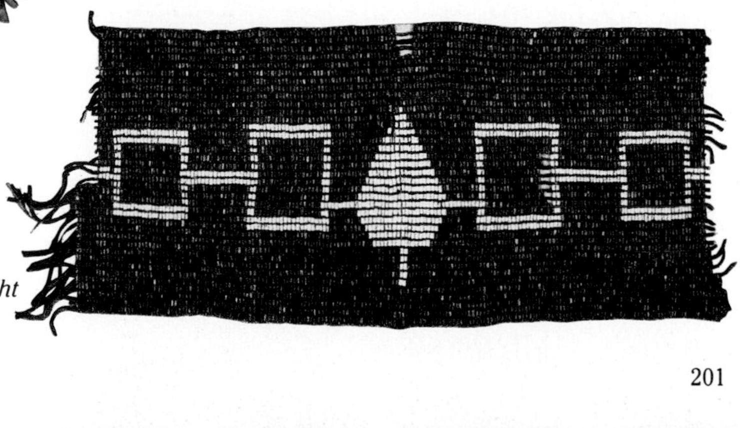

Pueblo Popé's Rebellion

He led a peaceful people to revolt against Spanish rule

The Pueblo Indians of New Mexico had been living under the Spanish colonial government for nearly a century. Although there had been sporadic, easily subdued uprisings from time to time, on the surface things seemed peaceful enough.

A docile, agricultural people, the Pueblos fought for defense, not conquest. Their villages, multistoried adobe structures, had high walls to keep out their enemies, the Apaches. But the muskets of Spanish soldiers offered better protection than their walls and weapons, just as European plowshares yielded richer harvests than the Pueblos could get with their own tools, and so there seemed little reason to resist. The Indians obligingly attended the Spanish Franciscan missions, sang in choirs, and served their masters as best they could without giving up their own ways entirely.

But in 1675 officials of the church, who had long deplored the fact that civil authorities tolerated the continuing observance of ancient Indian religions, enlisted the aid of the colonial governor in a campaign to stamp out pagan practices. A kiva, or underground prayer room, was raided and 47 men were arrested for participating in a traditional ceremony wherein masks were worn in imitation of the gods. Three were hanged; the others were whipped, imprisoned, and warned against further blasphemy.

From their ranks rose the man who would unite his people, lead them in a bloody revolt, and drive their oppressors from the land. His name was Popé, and he came from the village of Ohke.

Retreating to a kiva at Taos, which became his headquarters, he and his counselor, a yellow-eyed ebony giant said to be a messenger from the war god (in fact, an escaped mulatto slave from Mexico), spent the next five years weaving careful plans for rebellion. When, in 1680, Popé finally sent Indian leaders knotted skeins, telling them in code the date of the uprising, many agreed to participate. Others, however, informed the Spanish, and so the date of the attack was moved up.

At 7 A.M. on August 10, 1680, Popé's warriors struck. Their victory was swift, sure, and brutal. They murdered men, women, and children all over the territory, taking special care to kill all priests. Despite a valiant effort by an outnumbered garrison at Santa Fe, by August 21 the Indians had succeeded in driving the Spanish into Mexico. It was the only totally successful Indian revolt in American history.

But Popé, inspirational in war, became tyrannical in victory. He decreed that every trace of the Spanish occupation be destroyed; only the governor's mansion and carriage in Santa Fe were spared—Popé kept them for himself. The speaking of Spanish was forbidden under cruel penalty. Churches were burned. People were whipped for using plows.

Popé died in 1688. His harsh, oppressive rule had left his people so destitute and bitter that when Diego de Vargas and a force of some 200 soldiers besieged the capital at Santa Fe in 1692, the defending Pueblos not only surrendered but greeted their conquerors with open arms.

The Rogerenes

John Rogers and his followers fought for religious freedom

Many American colonies were founded for the sake of religious freedom, but most were concerned only with their *own* freedom. Few tolerated dissenters. But John Rogers, born into a wealthy Connecticut merchant family in 1648, was one early American who took a stand for the basic principle of religious freedom. As a result, he spent years in jail, endured public whippings, and lost most of his property through fines.

Believing that Christians were answerable to God alone, Rogers opposed salaried clergy, meetinghouses, and formal prayers. He freed his slaves and refused to take medicines, trusting in prayer and anointment with oil. Above all, he held that state-enforced religious laws were invalid and advocated passive resistance to them.

But he and his followers, the Rogerenes, weren't always passive. They had a knack for dramatic public protest. Sometimes they would simply enter a meetinghouse and sit through the service with their hats on. On other occasions, they became more extreme.

"The madness, immodesty and tumultuous conduct of Rogers and those who followed him, at this day, is hardly conceivable," fumed the flagrantly biased historian Benjamin Trumbull a century later, in his *A Complete History of Connecticut.* "It seemed to be their study and delight to violate the sabbath, insult magistrates and ministers, and to trample on all law and authority, human and divine. They would come, on the Lord's day, into the most public assemblies nearly or quite naked, and . . . behave in a wild and tumultuous manner, crying out, and charging the most venerable ministers with lies and false doctrines."

Trumbull's outrage was based on exaggeration, but the fact remains that Rogers was tried and convicted of everything from entertaining two Quakers in his home to burning a New London meetinghouse. He was imprisoned seven times, for a total of 15 years, and once received 76 stripes, or lashes, for blasphemy. Many of his followers, men and women alike, were publicly stripped and whipped or tarred and feathered. In 1677 a court ordered that Rogers be fined £5 every month no matter *what* he did.

When his first wife divorced him, Rogers declared that neither marriage nor divorce laws had any validity. Later, since he considered himself still married in the eyes of God, he tried, unsuccessfully, to kidnap his wife from the bed of her new husband.

He eventually took a second wife, without the formality of a wedding. She was more to his liking, as she demonstrated by dumping a pot of scalding water from a second-story window onto a constable who had come around to collect some fees. But when she was convicted of bearing Rogers's child out of wedlock and was given the choice of leaving him or receiving 40 stripes for the offense, she left him.

Rogers eventually pushed his belief in God's protection too far. In 1721, at the age of 72, he traveled to Boston during a smallpox epidemic and visited the sick, as was his habit. Returning home to New London, he died of the disease within a few days.

Long after Rogers's death, the Rogerenes persisted with his war to separate church and state. The group petered out in the 19th century, but by then their efforts in Connecticut had long since borne fruit in the First Amendment to the U.S. Constitution.

Mary Burton's wild accusations of a slave uprising in New York City brought about an orgy of persecution. In the course of six months, some 20 people were hanged, 13 burned at the stake, and 70 deported. Mary collected a reward and disappeared. The engraving at left, depicting the events, was actually made many years later.

The Black "Conspiracy" in New York

Mary Burton was only 17 years old, a not-too-bright indentured servant to a New York tavernkeeper, when she became the center of public attention in 1741. Before she was done, she had set off a wave of persecution that swept the city like a disease.

It began with a burglary in a tobacco shop. Mary led the auorities to a hoard of silver coins that she said two slaves had stolen on behalf of her master. While the three were being held, a series of fires broke out, rumored to have been set by slaves.

Of New York City's 12,000 inhabitants, some 2,000 were black slaves, and tensions ran high. The busy seaport was no southern plantation; slaves mixed with free blacks as well as with merchant seamen, privateers, and others considered unsavory by the proper citizenry. Many New Yorkers still remembered an abortive 1712 uprising that had resulted in some 21 executions by fire, hanging, and torture, and anxious rumors of new slave revolts circulated regularly. And so, when Mary began embellishing her story, people were ready to listen. The tavernkeeper, she said, was the center of a plot in which slaves would burn the city, slaughter the whites, and divide the surviving women among them.

Two more slaves were arrested, tried without counsel—no lawyer would defend them—and burned alive. Flushed by her newfound celebrity, Mary kept coming up with fresh, grandiose accusations. Her targets, to save their skins, accused others, and hysteria spread. Only when Mary pointed the finger at leading citizens did the attorney general come to doubt her word.

A Nation of Our Own

The 1790 Census

Counting heads was an arduous job

Making his way in all weather on dirt roads and wilderness trails, the deputy marshal of the U.S. District Court combed the area assigned him. He stopped at farms, plantations, country stores, and backwoods cabins—wherever he could find people. Swinging off his horse, he drew some loose sheets of paper, a pen, and a bottle of ink from his saddlebag (he had no pad with printed forms) and began quizzing those around him. The year was 1790 and he was participating in the new nation's first census.

His questions were simple and straightforward: How many free persons in the family? What sex and color? How many free white males over 16? How many under 16? How many slaves? The name and address of the head of family? He didn't ask about age (except to separate the men from the boys), religion, place of birth, occupation, income, or the quality of life. He was simply counting heads, to learn how many people lived in the United States. Even so, many folk were suspicious that the census had to do with their taxes. Others just didn't like being counted.

It took 18 months to complete the census. The final tally? A mere 3,929,214. Of this number, 19.3 percent were blacks, most of whom were enslaved (hence, according to Article I, Section 2, of the Constitution, each was counted as three-fifths of a person).

The tabulation was needed primarily to determine the number of delegates each state could send to the House of Representatives. (The Constitution stipulated one representative for every 30,000 people.) The count was also necessary for apportioning taxes among the states.

Some Americans, expecting the first census to show a population topping 4 million, thought the final count was a bit on the anemic side. They feared that the unimpressive statistic might weaken the fledgling country's influence in Europe. But President Washington reassured them that "our *real* numbers will exceed, greatly, the official returns."

James Madison had hoped that the census would obtain other useful information for study. In subsequent years it did, and in 1830 printed questionnaires were introduced. Among the most unwieldy schedules of all time was the 1890 form, asking for 13,000 bits of information. An innovation, the world's first punch-card tabulation, made it possible to process all the data gathered.

America's 10 Largest Communities in 1790

1.	New York	33,131
2.	Philadelphia	28,522
3.	Boston	18,320
4.	Charleston, S.C.	16,359
5.	Baltimore	13,503
6.	Northern Liberty, Pa.	9,913
7.	Salem, Mass.	7,921
8.	Watervliet, N.Y.	7,419
9.	Ballstown, N.Y.	7,333
10.	Stephentown, N.Y.	6,795

Although Virginia, with nearly a fifth of the nation's inhabitants, was the most populous state, New Yorkers could boast that 4 of the 10 largest communities were in their state.

The Buck Stops Where? *What did Washington know, and when did he know it?*

With war clouds gathering over Europe, President George Washington proclaimed that U.S. policy was to remain neutral: no entangling alliances and no commercial treaties. But Alexander Hamilton, his secretary of the treasury, had other ideas.

Convinced that the nation should favor Britain, Hamilton met in secret with a British spy, Maj. George Beckwith, in New York City. In October 1789 Hamilton told the agent: "I have always preferred a Connexion with you, to that of any other Country. . . . We wish to form a commercial treaty with you." His ideas, Hamilton claimed, "are those of General Washington, I can confidently assure you, as well as of a majority in the Senate." But, he prudently added, "I should not chuse to have this go any further in America." Meanwhile, he told Washington nothing of his intrigue.

Again, in the summer of 1790, when war between Spain and Britain seemed imminent, Beckwith returned to New York to tap Hamilton (known to the British ministry by the code number 7) about America's position. And again Hamilton overstepped the bounds of his office and of presidential policy, all but promising a military alliance and disparaging the judgment of Gouverneur Morris, Washington's official emissary to London.

Maneuvering behind the scenes, lying and deceiving as necessary, Hamilton worked to implement his policy over that of his chief. How much Washington suspected is unclear, but had Hamilton's machinations been uncovered, his political career certainly would have been aborted. As it was, his secret meddling threw Thomas Jefferson's State Department into confusion and frustrated efforts to pursue a coherent foreign policy throughout Washington's administration. Eventually he brought about the Jay's Treaty of 1794, strongly favoring Britain. Although officially negotiated by John Jay, its terms had been largely shaped by Hamilton and Beckwith during their clandestine meetings.

Boston's Slave Poetess Laureate

The triumph and tragedy of Phillis Wheatley

Kidnapped in Africa, the child was shipped to Boston in 1761. She was probably about seven. Put on the auction block naked, she stood shivering until she was bought by John Wheatley, a prosperous tailor, to be a servant for his wife, Susannah.

Mrs. Wheatley named the girl Phillis. Impressed by her precocity, she decided the child should learn to read and write. Phillis soon could translate Ovid's poetry from Latin and began writing English verse in imitation of Alexander Pope. When, at about 17, she wrote an elegy on the death of a popular preacher and it was published, skeptical Bostonians came to call. They were won over by her articulate conversation and unassuming manner. Becoming known as Boston's poetess laureate, she was invited to literary banquets—but, fully aware of the prejudice against her "sable race," she always chose to sit at a separate table.

In 1773 Phillis went to England, where she met aristocrats and writers. They, too, were captivated. She was about to meet King George III when Mrs. Wheatley fell ill. Returning home, Phillis stayed with her mistress until her death. Then she was set free.

Phillis Wheatley moved out on her own. During the Revolution, she dedicated a poem to George Washington, who expressed gratitude to "a person so favored by the muses" and invited her to visit his headquarters. But she found it hard to make a living. In 1778 she married John Peters, a black grocery-store manager and a deadbeat. Her three children died young. Her own health failed and, in her early thirties, she died in poverty in a rooming house.

A portrait of Phillis Wheatley (above) appeared in a volume of her work, Poems on Various Subjects, Religious and Moral.

Ne'er shall look upon his like again
The celebrated Cornplanter taking a flying leap over Silva a Horse of his own height

For Children of All Ages—The First Circus!

Marvel at his "surprising feats of horsemanship!" Cheer as he mounts his speeding horse and rides "with one foot on the saddle in a pleasing attitude!" Gasp at his amazing leap over 10 spirited horses!

The spectacular showman was John Bill Ricketts, and when he and his small troupe presented America's first complete circus performance in 1793, he dazzled the Philadelphia audience with his derring-do. The circus delighted George Washington, and soon the performer and the president became friends. When Washington's handsome white steed Jack was put out to pasture, Ricketts offered Washington $150 for him, and Jack became a favorite circus attraction. Soon Ricketts introduced his trained horse Cornplanter (above), and added fireworks and a dwarf called the Warsaw Wonder to the circus. (He already had a clown.) Then he took his show on the road.

The circus was hailed as "a place to dispel the gloom of the thoughtful, exercise the lively activity of the young and gay, and to relax the mind of the sedentary and industrious trader." And for a time it did just that. Then disaster struck: in 1799 Ricketts's amphitheaters in Philadelphia and New York both burned to the ground. The staggering losses brought bankruptcy. Distraught and discouraged, the enterprising Scot decided to return to Britain, but somewhere at sea his ship and all aboard were lost. And so the glitter and glow of the nation's first circus were extinguished.

A President's Best Friend

George Washington, who boasted a fine pack of hounds, enjoyed nothing more than an exciting hunt deep in the Virginia woods (above). In fact, it seems he was devoted to all breeds, on the battlefield and off. So it came as no surprise during the Revolutionary War, when a dog wandered into his camp wearing a collar with the name of Britain's Gen. William Howe on it, that Washington promptly returned the pooch—under a flag of truce.

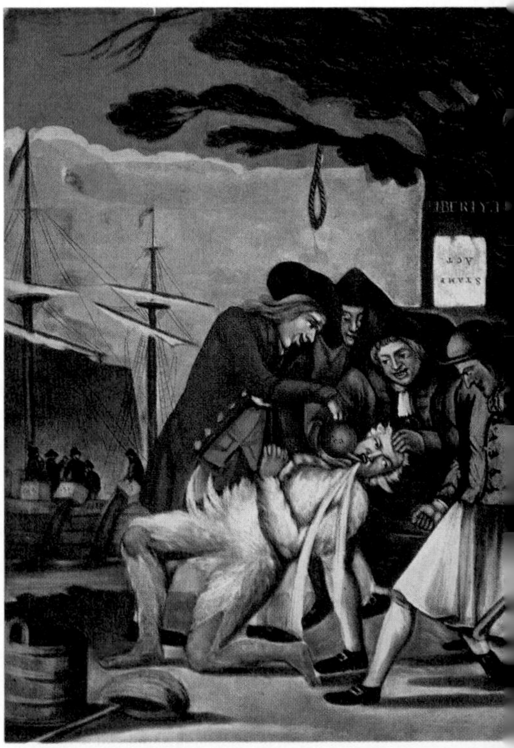

Portrait Painter and Practical Joker

A 1795 portrait by Charles Willson Peale shows two of his sons climbing stairs. To enhance the realism, Peale mounted the painting in a doorway, a wooden step at its base. The illusion was so successful that George Washington actually bowed to the sons. Over the course of 59 years and 3 wives, the famed portraitist sired 17 children, naming many of them for classical artists. Titian and Raphaelle Peale appear at the right.

How to Tar and Feather Someone

First strip a Person naked, then heat the Tar until it is thin, & pour it upon naked Flesh, or rub it over with a Tar brush. After which, sprinkle decently upon the Tar, whilst it is yet warm, as many Feathers as will stick to it.
Then hold a lighted Candle to the Feathers, & try to set it all on Fire.

Tarring and Feathering

The angry 18th-century Bostonians (left) who set upon a tax collector may well have read the detailed directions published in 1770 (above). Just before and during the Revolutionary War, tarring and feathering was a mob ritual. In the 19th century con men, wife beaters, and others who offended community standards were liable to this horrible punishment.

A Lady of Louisiana

Born into slavery, she freed herself and her children and built a great estate

She was baptized Marie Thérèze, but she preferred the African name her slave parents gave her, Coincoin. Born a slave in 1742 at Natchitoches, Louisiana, she faced a life of bondage, but through luck, hard work, determination, courage, and extraordinary intelligence, she achieved the impossible for a black woman in that time and place.

Plantation life

Unlike most slave children, Coincoin enjoyed a solid family life. Although the "law of the plantation" was a perfectly acceptable means of marriage in the region, her parents were wed in the Catholic Church because their owners were deeply religious; like all of their slaves' children, Coincoin was baptized. Circumstances changed, however, when the owners died and Coincoin was inherited by their daughter. By the time she was 25, the unmarried slave had borne four children.

Then in 1767 she caught the eye of a newly arrived merchant, the worldly, city-bred Claude Metoyer. He soon arranged to lease the young house servant, and thus began a liaison that would last for nearly 20 years and produce 10 children.

A slave mistress

Coincoin might have ended her days as a concubine had it not been for the arrival of a Spanish priest, Father Luis de Quintanilla. Deploring the fact that a shortage of marriageable women in the colony had led many young men to take up with slaves, the priest set out to make an example of Metoyer and Coincoin, who were very open about their relationship.

Though interracial marriage was illegal, Metoyer managed to maintain the status quo for eight years by arranging, on paper, for Coincoin to be freed.

A plot of land

In 1786 the union came to an end. Metoyer deeded to the mother of his children some 70 acres of land and a modest annuity.

Though she was now in her forties and had been a house and bedroom slave all her life, Coincoin set up housekeeping in her own small cabin and began to farm her own fields. It was a meager start, but her courage, resolve, and hard work began to pay off; year by year her tobacco crop became bigger and better.

Coincoin ran her plantation with great skill and efficiency, and she invested her growing income in the best possible way—one by one, for cash or for barter, this remarkable woman bought her own 14 children out of slavery.

Successful landowner

In 1793 she increased her holdings by applying for and receiving a land grant, and later acquired another tract of 912 acres, which became a profitable cotton operation. (This is today Melrose Plantation, a National Historic Landmark and popular tourist attraction.) In addition to tobacco and cotton, Coincoin sold bear grease (in great demand as an emollient and a lubricant) and pelts. So successful did she become that at one time she herself owned 16 slaves.

Coincoin, who had moved from slave mistress to successful matriarchal planter, died in 1816 or 1817. To her free children and grandchildren she bequeathed not only her property, but the inspiration of her grit and her wisdom, which, between them, produced one of the richest plantation systems in antebellum Louisiana.

The Bible According to Jefferson

Another facet of a multitalented man

His enemies called him an atheist, and he never publicly denied the label. His religion, he felt, was his own affair. If he became president, they shrilled, America's Bibles would be burned.

In fact, according to a respected 20th-century clergyman, Thomas Jefferson's "knowledge of and admiration for the teachings of Jesus have never been equaled by any other president." So deep was his admiration that he compiled his own New Testament, consisting of extracts from the Gospels that he regarded as the actual words of Jesus. It was originally meant for the benefit of the Indians, but later versions, titled *The Life and Morals of Jesus of Nazareth,* were published in Greek, Latin, French, and English.

Although Jefferson claimed to have spent only two or three nights on the project while he was president, he wrote in a letter to a friend that reading the volume every night before bedtime had become part of his daily routine. "A more precious morsel of ethics was never seen," he said.

Mother Ann Lee, the Second Coming

Dancing was an important part of a Shaker worship service. This painting was made by a visitor to the Shaker community at New Lebanon, New York.

She founded a strict religious sect that flourished for more than a century

In 1774 Mother Ann Lee, who proclaimed herself the female incarnation of Christ, arrived in New York with a band of eight followers. Two years later, after much hardship, she founded a small communal settlement at Watervliet, near Albany.

Born in 1736 in the smoke-blackened industrial city of Manchester, England, Ann Lee had joined a radical Quaker sect at the age of 23. Called Shaking Quakers, or Shakers, for their practice of jumping and jerking as the spirit moved them while at worship, the sect was millenarian, believing that the second coming of Christ was at hand. In 1770, while serving a jail term for her beliefs, Ann Lee experienced a series of visions which persuaded her that she herself was the reborn Messiah.

Sexual relations, she said, were the root of humanity's problems; only strict celibacy could make up for past sins. (She herself had endured a late and unhappy marriage, and all four of her children had died in infancy.) Her doctrine not only split the sect; it also increased the persecution of her remaining followers in England. In response to another vision, she brought them to America.

By 1780 Mother Ann's Shaker community was beginning to thrive, but suspicions of its English origin led to her arrest and brief imprisonment as a suspected spy. Upon her release, she spent two years on a pilgrimage throughout New England, gaining a wide reputation as a faith healer.

Her death in 1784 at the age of 48 might have ended the Shaker experiment, but new leaders emerged and the sect survived and spread. To keep in touch with Mother Ann, spiritualism—already a Shaker practice—became increasingly important. At the height of Shaker popularity, in the 1840's, there were 19 communities from Maine to Kentucky and Indiana and about 6,000 adherents.

The Shakers, believing in segregated equality of the sexes (many of the leaders were women), housed males and females in separate wings of huge dormitories. They did not procreate, of course, but increased their numbers with converts and, later, by adopting orphans. Holding to the sanctity of honest, simple labor, they earned a reputation as fine craftspeople and farmers. Their meticulous villages attracted tourists from around the world, and Shaker furniture is still prized for its quality and for its blend of function and form.

Reaching Westward

The Erie Canal *Building it was "a little short of madness," said Thomas Jefferson*

Some 363 miles of deep forest and swampland separated Albany, New York, from Buffalo. The rise in elevation was 675 feet. Yet DeWitt Clinton staked his political career on the promise of digging a canal through that wilderness. When he became governor of New York in 1817 with nearly 97 percent of the vote (43,310 to 1,479), he took it as a mandate to get the job done.

The idea of linking the Great Lakes with the Hudson River had been around since 1784. The young nation *had* to find a way over or around the Appalachian Mountains or it could lose its frontier to France or England. But no project of this size and scope had ever been attempted before, and the controversy was fierce.

In 1810 Clinton had served on a New York State commission to study the question. Chaired by Gouverneur Morris, an early proponent of the canal, the group deemed the job beyond the state's means and called for federal funding. Other states objected: since New York State would benefit, let New York build the thing.

Building the thing became Clinton's crusade, and in March 1817 the state legislature passed his funding bill. But the approval of a five-man Council of Revision was still necessary. Two were in favor, two opposed. The swing man, Chief Justice James Kent of the New York Supreme Court, was preparing to vote *No* when the vice president of the United States, Daniel Tompkins, paid a surprise visit.

Another war with England was imminent, Tompkins told the com-

The Erie Canal opened the West and changed the destiny of the nation. Among the devices created to clear the land was a 16-foot-high stump-puller (right); a team of horses, hauling a rope coiled on the center wheel, wound the chain around the axle. In the lock at West Troy, near the eastern terminus (below, painted by John Hill about 1835), boatmen and passengers socialized or did chores while waiting for the water level to rise.

mittee. New York should not waste its time and money on such foolishness. Kent, deeply offended at this saber-rattling intrusion, spoke up: "If we must have war, or have a canal, I am in favor of the canal."

No American engineers had expertise in building such a canal, and so two lawyers, Benjamin Wright and James Geddes, were chosen to head the project. "A brace of country lawyers with a compass and a spirit level," one newspaper mockingly called them.

They started in the middle in July 1817. The land west of Frankfort, in Oneida County, was soft and level—a good place to begin on-the-job training.

The canal was to be 4 feet deep and 40 feet wide, tapering to 28 feet at the bottom. Before it could be dug, underbrush had to be cut, trees chopped down, stumps uprooted. The work was done in sections, some only a quarter-mile long, by farmers and local contractors. Muscle, human and animal, was the only source of power, but devices were invented to help.

Cement was needed that would harden underwater. A young man named Canvass White found suitable limestone and created the new substance. Aqueducts were built over rivers, streams diverted through pipelines. When, in the marshes of western New York, malaria became a threat, men wore small, necklacelike smudgepots to keep mosquitoes at bay.

In all, 83 locks were constructed, including 5 blasted from solid rock at the future site of Lockport. Designed by Nathan S. Roberts, they lifted the canal 76 feet over the Niagara Escarpment.

In November 1825 the *Seneca Chief* brought a keg of Lake Erie water to New York Harbor for a symbolic Wedding of the Waters. The canal's cost, $7 million, was repaid by tolls, averaging only pennies a mile, in 12 years.

The Year Without a Summer

They called it "eighteen hundred and froze-to-death"

Mount Tambora, a volcano in the Dutch East Indies, blew up in 1815, sending a cloud of dust, ash, and cinders into the upper atmosphere. As a result, snow fell on the northeastern United States throughout the summer of 1816, killing newly planted crops and dooming the region to a winter of hunger and a desperate spring.

May had been cold, but a warm spell in early June encouraged farmers to plant. Then a bitter wind arose, and on June 6 and 7 snow fell, drifting to 20 inches in Danville, Vermont. Four weeks of good weather encouraged replanting, but by July 4 another cold wave wiped out corn, beans, and squash. Farmers burned their hay to try to save their corn; preachers told them the killing cold was God's punishment. Again warmth returned, and again farmers replanted. And on August 21 snow fell that would last all winter. Over the next year, farming families left their land in record numbers to move south or to work in factories and on the Erie Canal.

Sawing Off Manhattan

Big ideas were rampant in 1824

The southern tip of Manhattan Island, weighed down by buildings, was about to break off and sink into the ocean. So said a retired carpenter named Lozier, the acknowledged expert among the retirees and unemployed who solved the world's problems while idling away the hours at the old Centre Market. He'd been talking to Mayor Stephen Allen, he said, who'd asked him to deal with the situation. His solution: saw the island off at Kingsbridge, on the northern end, row it out to sea, turn it around, and reattach it. The Centre Market gang scoffed. They'd scoffed at the Erie Canal, too, said Lozier and his accomplice, "Uncle John" DeVoe, and wasn't it nearly finished?

Word spread, and before long, the hoaxers were signing up hundreds of hopeful laborers, offering triple wages to anyone who volunteered to saw underwater. They arranged for 500 cattle, 500 hogs, and 3,000 chickens to feed their work force, and wagonloads of lumber for barracks. Prices skyrocketed. They set blacksmiths and carpenters to work designing 100-foot-long saws with 3-foot teeth to dismember the island, 250-foot oars to propel it, and huge anchors and chains to secure it in case of a storm.

Finally, in August, after almost two months of planning, the big day arrived. Sawyers and oarsmen, butchers with their various animals, contractors and craftsmen, and hordes of wives and children assembled at Spring Street and the Bowery, along with a fife and drum corps that would lead them to their glorious labors. But where were Lozier and Uncle John? A delegation sent to find them came back with a message: they'd left town on account of their health.

In fact, they were hiding in Brooklyn. Although they were eventually located, no one would press charges, and so the perpetrators of one of America's grandest hoaxes got off scot-free.

The Divine Fanny

They called it Elssler Mania. During her two-year tour in the early 1840's, the Viennese ballerina Fanny Elssler (left, in La Gypsy*), a true superstar, took America by storm. Wherever she went, the Divine Fanny drew vast hordes of admirers. They rioted outside her hotel in New York and mobbed her carriage in Baltimore (below). In Washington, Congress adjourned so lawmakers wouldn't miss her performance. Poems and songs were written about her. (One said the whole city of New Orleans had "got Elssler fever.") Parasols, garters, shaving soaps, and cigars bore her name—as did the boiler of a railroad engine that was dedicated to her. Philosopher Ralph Waldo Emerson found her performance transcendental, and novelist Nathaniel Hawthorne placed her portrait between his pictures of saints Ignatius Loyola and Francis Xavier.*

Showboat's A-Comin'

The first American showboat, a 120-foot barge called the Floating Theatre *(left), was built in Pittsburgh in 1831 by the British actor William Chapman. Floating down the Ohio and Mississippi rivers during summer and fall, Chapman tied up at towns to present plays with most of his family in the cast. Then, having sold the boat in New Orleans, he would return to Pittsburgh and build another one. Finally, he bought a small steamboat so he could travel upstream; he remained a fixture on major waterways until 1847.*

Fire-breather

Maj. Stephen H. Long was worried about Indians and so, to explore the Missouri River in 1819–20, he designed a steamboat that looked like a dragon (left). "The bow of this vessel exhibits the form of a huge serpent," wrote a newspaperman, "black and scaly . . . his mouth open, vomiting smoke, and apparently carrying the boat on his back." The Western Engineer *completed its explorations without Indian interference to the vicinity of present-day Omaha.*

The Wooden Road Craze

America's first plank road (below), running southward from the tip of New York's Lake Oneida to the Erie Canal at Syracuse, was opened to traffic on July 18, 1846. Made of four-inch-thick hemlock planks eight feet long, it set off a rash of road building; over the next decade, thousands of miles of wooden roads were laid in several states. Then, as the early roads began to rot away, the public became disenchanted and macadam roads (layered and rolled gravel) came back into favor. Nonetheless, particularly in such dry areas as the deserts of the Southwest (right) where wood is slower to decompose, plank roads continued to be used well into the 20th century.

Power to the Beard

Joseph Palmer, a hard-working husband and father, never intended to start a protest movement. The feisty Fitchburg, Massachusetts, farmer just wanted to keep his flowing beard. But the community frowned upon it, and Palmer found himself an object of contempt and ridicule, snubbed by neighbors and local merchants, stoned by angry gangs, and denounced from the pulpit.

One day in 1830, Palmer was ambushed by a group of men intent on trimming his whiskers. He fought them off but was fined for assault and—upon his refusal to pay—jailed. His case gained national attention; such figures as Ralph Waldo Emerson and Henry David Thoreau gave him support. After a year in jail, he was offered his freedom, but he refused to leave until his right to a beard was acknowledged. Finally, he was forcibly removed.

By the time Joseph Palmer died in 1875, beards were commonplace. His tombstone (below) stands as a memorial to his stubborn integrity.

Two Unorthodox Utopians

Mix-and-match mating in Free Love Valley and the Oneida community

The great religious revival that swept the United States in the 1830's inspired two extraordinary New Englanders, Theophilus Ransom Gates and John Humphrey Noyes, to set up unique utopian communities.

Gates, a descendant of Connecticut clergymen, was an itinerant schoolteacher who wended his way southward in the course of pursuing his profession. Religion was revealed to the frail and melancholy misfit during a night of agonized prayer in the Virginia woods. A local minister, told of Gates's mystical experience, welcomed him as a guest preacher.

No more marriage

Moving to Philadelphia, Gates kept busy preaching and publishing religious tracts. He attacked existing churches and foretold worldwide destruction, followed by a new order in which everyone would live together in "primitive love and affection." Marriage, he prophesied, would disappear. His newsletter, the *Battle-Axe,* cited Jeremiah: "Thou art my battle-axe and weapons of war: for with thee will I break in pieces the nations."

Gates's first convert was a prostitute, who readily embraced his notion that women could be chosen by God as "brides in Christ" of unhappily married men. One father of 10 to whom she proposed such a union became so distraught that he committed suicide.

Free Love Valley

Gates soon left town and, with some 30 followers, formed a community called Free Love Valley on the Schuylkill River. Neighbors were shocked by such practices as communal nude bathing and expressions of free love during ecstatic revival meetings. At least two illegitimate babies were born, each hailed as Christ. (Both died young, but were expected to rise again.) Gates reportedly shunned sex, and was not among the four disciples tried for flouting Pennsylvania's marriage laws. After his death in 1846, the group disbanded.

Meanwhile, along came Noyes, a member of a prominent Vermont family. Younger and more practical than Gates, Noyes—a Dartmouth graduate who had studied theology at Yale—became a devotee of perfectionism. He believed that A.D. 70 had marked the second coming of Christ. Since the kingdom of heaven was literally at hand, those who lived pure, perfect lives could enjoy it on earth, and in 1834 he declared that he himself had achieved perfection. His license to preach was revoked, but he nevertheless attracted disciples. He shared some views with Gates, whom he once visited to express friendship while "correcting" the older man's excesses. Noyes, too, disavowed marriage. But when his letter on the subject was printed anonymously in Gates's *Battle-Axe*, the two evangelists became bitter enemies.

Noyes founded his own religious community in Putney, Vermont, and, despite his antimarriage views, managed to wed a contributor, Harriet Holton. Perhaps inspired by her four painful stillbirths, he decided that "it is as foolish and cruel to expend one's seed on a wife merely for the sake of getting rid of it, as it would be to fire a gun at one's best friend merely for the sake of unloading it." Thus began his doctrine of male continence, or nonejaculatory sex. Later, when Noyes was attracted to a disciple and convinced her husband and Harriet to agree to marriage "in quartette form," he proclaimed the doctrine of complex marriage. This he soon expanded to include the marriage of all men to all women in the community.

Arrested for adultery, Noyes jumped bail and fled to Oneida, New York. His disciples followed. An able administrator, he established the manufacture of steel traps, canned goods, silk, and silverware as the economic base of the Oneida community, which eventually numbered 300 people. Men and women were considered equals and worked side by side. A committee of elders ruled on their requests for various sexual partners. Anyone had the right to refuse (one man who resisted a woman's "No" was thrown into a snowdrift to cool off). To perpetuate the community—which included some disillusioned Battle Axes—Noyes later introduced "scientific breeding." About 100 chosen men and women took part; Noyes himself fathered 9 of the 58 resulting children.

Like Free Love Valley, Oneida aroused antagonism. Eventually Noyes fled to Canada, where he died in 1886. After he left, his disciples paired off in conventional marriages. Unlike Gates's community, Oneida survived—as a joint stock corporation. In time, it became America's leading producer of stainless-steel flatware.

Members of the Oneida community viewed themselves as belonging to one big family, with prophet-founder John Humphrey Noyes as its father figure. An important part of their unique way of life was the ballot box (right), used to decide a variety of issues, both personal and public. The community cooperated in all endeavors, including the care of its offspring (below), who seemed to thrive in the Children's House, away from their unmarried parents.

A House Divided

The Spark That Lit a Fire

Harriet Beecher Stowe and Uncle Tom's Cabin

After Abraham Lincoln issued the Emancipation Proclamation in September 1862, he was visited by the author of *Uncle Tom's Cabin,* Harriet Beecher Stowe. Shaking her hand, he reportedly said, "So this is the little woman who made this big war." It was not much of an overstatement. Her book had been the first American novel to take black people seriously and the first to have a black hero. Its vivid portrait of slavery's evils had polarized the nation.

The first *Uncle Tom*

Eleven years earlier, Stowe—daughter of a Congregational minister, wife of a religion professor, and mother of seven—had written a sketch for the *National Era,* an abolitionist newspaper in Washington, D.C. She had published other stories, but this one, about the death of a slave named Uncle Tom, got a lot of attention. Abolition, an impassioned cause since colonial days, had become a fiery crusade in the North. Two of Stowe's brothers, the preachers Edward and Henry Ward Beecher, were deeply involved. She herself taught black children in a Cincinnati Sunday school, and she had once helped a black mother and child evade a slave hunter.

Yet Stowe saw herself as a reformer, not a radical abolitionist. Writing, to her, was holy work.

Edward's wife wrote: "Hattie, if I could use the pen as you can, I would write something which would make this whole nation feel what an accursed thing slavery is." Stowe replied, "I will write that thing if I live." And she did.

"God wrote it"

When she finished expanding the sketch into a novel, she said it had come to her in a vision—that "God wrote it." Although John P. Jewett thought it was a long book on an unpopular subject, he published it in two volumes in 1852. Stowe feared that abolitionists would find the book mild, but it sold 10,000 copies the first week and 300,000 the first year.

Everywhere reaction was intense. Within three years, almost 30 anti-*Uncle Tom* novels were published. Stowe received mountains of threatening mail (one package included the severed ear of a slave), and her Georgian cousin asked her not to put her name on the outside of letters. Critics hooted at her inaccura-

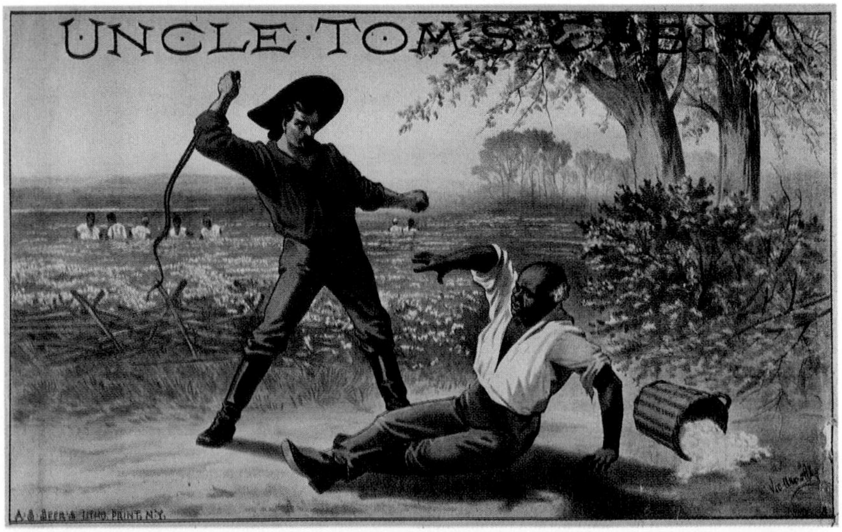

In theatrical productions based on Mrs. Stowe's novel, Uncle Tom (left, being whipped by the infamous Simon Legree) and Topsy (above, left), who "jest growed," were reduced to pathetic racial caricatures. Nonetheless, the plays, like the book that inspired them, increased the nation's awareness of the cruelty inherent in the institution of human slavery.

Harriet Beecher Stowe (above) never dreamed that Uncle Tom's Cabin *would be published worldwide in 37 languages.*

cies; she had seen a plantation only once and had asked Frederick Douglass, the prominent black abolitionist, for help in learning many details of slave life.

Yet in Boston, Stowe was idolized, receiving a standing ovation while attending a concert on the day the Emancipation Proclamation took effect. Virtually every Northern intellectual read her book; the poet Longfellow wrote, "How she is shaking the world."

Caricatures on stage

Although Stowe's own dramatization of *Uncle Tom's Cabin* was unsuccessful, nine unauthorized stage versions appeared and were performed well into this century—the first, by actor George L. Aiken, opened in Troy, N.Y., on September 27, 1852, and ran for 100 performances. Most of these plays distorted Stowe's original heroic view of the characters and added stagy dramatic effects, such as bloodhounds chasing Eliza and choruses of angels welcoming Little Eva to heaven. The character of Uncle Tom, a strong, Christlike figure in the novel, was debased into a shuffling, subservient old man, the source for our disparaging use of "Uncle Tom" today.

The Abolitionist Who Hated Blacks

His rabidly racist book helped elect Lincoln

Politics creates strange bedfellows, and certainly Hinton Rowan Helper was among the strangest that humanitarian Republicans could have embraced, despite his antislavery views. Helper was the son of an illiterate North Carolina backwoods farmer. Orphaned early, he came to hate blacks; he saw them as the foundation of an economic system that enriched slave owners while impoverishing the South's white working class. In 1857 he published *The Impending Crisis of the South: How to Meet It,* a raging polemic in which he castigated slavery not for exploiting blacks but for causing "unparalleled illiteracy and degradation" among the white Southern masses. His solution: form a political party to bring about abolition.

The book ignited a controversy even more sensational than the one *Uncle Tom's Cabin* had caused five years earlier. Four ministers were banished from North Carolina for owning copies, and three men were lynched in Arkansas merely for possessing the book. Congressman John Sherman of Ohio lost the speakership of the House of Representatives because he supposedly supported Helper's views. But Republicans, embracing the book as an endorsement of their fledgling party's bid for power, distributed more than 100,000 abridged copies during the 1860 campaign. In 1861 President Lincoln appointed Helper to a diplomatic post in Argentina—perhaps to remove him from the capital's political turmoil.

After the war Helper returned to America, continued his racist writings, and went broke in a scheme to build a railroad from Hudson Bay to the tip of South America. Insane and impoverished, he killed himself in a Washington boardinghouse in 1909.

"Way down upon the Yazoo River"

When many Americans hear the phrase "Way down upon the Swanee River," they believe it's a line from a black folk song. In fact, the lyric was written by Stephen Foster, a man of Anglo-Irish ancestry who never visited the South. He wrote the song "Old Folks at Home" in 1851 for the minstrel shows that were popular at the time. Foster, who hoped to be recognized for his serious music, thought little of what became his most famous work and allowed the leader of the Christy Minstrels to publish it under his own name.

The words for "Old Folks at Home" were chosen casually. Foster asked his brother Morrison to think of a Southern river with a two-syllable name to fit a tune he was writing. Morrison proposed the Yazoo, but Stephen rejected this suggestion. Running his finger down a U.S. map, Morrison stopped at the Suwannee in Florida. "That's it!" Stephen said. And so it was almost by chance that the song did not start, "Way down upon the Yazoo River"—and become the state song of Mississippi instead of Florida.

A New Fashion Blooms

"At the outset, I had no idea of fully adopting the style; no thought of setting a fashion. . . . I stood amazed at the furor I had unwittingly caused." Thus Amelia Jenks Bloomer, suffragist and temperance reformer, recalled the outfit that she made famous.

As editor of The Lily, *one of the rare newspapers owned and published by a woman, Bloomer wrote enthusiastically of the innovative garb—an adaptation of Turkish pantaloons worn under a knee-length dress—meant to replace the cumbersome skirts of the time. Feminist awareness was blossoming, and* The Lily *exerted considerable influence. The pantaloons became known as bloomers.*

The comfortable, unrestricted clothing suited the feminists' ideal, and it caught on quickly. "For some six or eight years," Bloomer later reminisced, "I wore no other costume." The style even provided inspiration for a song (right), as well as many bitter jokes and cartoons about who was to wear the pants in the family.

The feminist struggle continued, but by 1860 the garb had faded into obscurity, given up by women who believed that the attention paid to clothes distracted from more substantial issues. And, although Bloomer vowed that she never thought her support "would create an excitement throughout the civilized world," her name will forever identify the outfit she popularized.

A Big Wedding for the Little People

In the dark days of the Civil War, the wedding of 35-inch-tall Tom Thumb and 32-inch Lavinia Warren was an entertaining diversion indeed. Global tours under the guidance of P. T. Barnum had made Tom a millionaire at 25. When he retired, Barnum found another attraction—and, as it turned out, a wife for Thumb. The wedding on February 10, 1863, boasted a guest list of 2,000, including "the élite, the crème de la crème." New York's streets were filled with crowds eager for a glimpse of the well-publicized tiny wedding carriage. The ceremony (left) and reception were smashing successes. Gifts were lavish, and the couple met with President Lincoln during their honeymoon tour. For a while, the nation forgot the horrors of war.

Santa Claus Comes to Town

The solemn Saint Nicholas who first arrived in America with the 17th-century Dutch settlers bore little resemblance to today's Jolly Old Saint Nick. It wasn't until cartoonist Thomas Nast drew him in 1863 that he became the rotund, red-cheeked man with the white beard whom we know and love as Santa Claus (left).

Every Christmas, Nast, famous for his illustrations of the Civil War, depicted buoyant scenes as a respite from the clever and often biting cartoons that had made his reputation. It was with these forays into the land of make-believe that Nast did a lot to popularize Santa Claus and his beloved world of holiday merriment, North Pole workshops, and a gift-filled sleigh pulled by obliging reindeer—everything to delight children during the Christmas season.

The "Naked Lady" Wore Tights

In 1861 Adah Isaacs Menken transformed a tired old melodrama into one of the most successful theatrical spectacles of its day. Mazeppa, *penned in 1830 by Henry M. Milner (based on a poem by Lord Byron), was the swashbuckling tale of a Polish prince. For 30 years a stunt by a live horse had been the play's main appeal. But when an Albany theater owner cast buxom young Adah in the leading role, and lashed her—clad in a loose-fitting tunic and flesh-colored tights—to the horse (right), a star was born.*

Adah, whose acting career had gotten off to a slow start due to lack of talent, found herself completely at home in the role of a celebrity. She took Mazeppa *to New York, where she opened to rave reviews, then went on to wow 'em out west. Adah's curvaceous calves did the trick. Neophyte journalist Mark Twain was smitten. Mormon leader Brigham Young, though expressing shock, managed to sit through the whole show. And souvenirs of the risqué performance (above, right) sold like hotcakes.*

Lusty Adah divorced one husband, married another, then shed him too before leaving for Europe. There she repeated her successes, both theatrical and amorous. The girl from New Orleans fancied herself a poet, and the literary lights of the Continent were charmed, if not always by her verse. She was at the height of her fame in 1868 when she collapsed onstage in Paris. Within a month the theater's "Naked Lady" was dead of tuberculosis in her early thirties.

At Bat: Baseball's First Pro Player

In 1864 hard-hitting second baseman Al Reach left the Brooklyn Atlantics for the Philadelphia Athletics so that he could earn $25 a week. Fans, vociferous from the start, objected to a player taking money for the privilege of batting a horsehide sphere with a wooden stick. But Reach set a precedent: he became the first salaried baseball player, thereby transforming an amateur sport into a professional one.

Before Reach joined the A's, outstanding athletes had been given money under the table—shares of gate receipts, gifts, and promises of political favor. By the end of the decade, baseball players were openly earning as much as $1,400 a year.

Brattle Street Bard

Why a great American poet grew his flowing beard

Henry Wadsworth Longfellow's impressive beard was more than a reflection of 19th-century fashion. It was a painful reminder of the bizarre and heartrending circumstances of his second wife's death.

A summer breeze

In the summer of 1861, as Fanny Longfellow was using hot wax to seal locks of her two youngest daughters' hair in paper packets, a wayward spark ignited her dress. Whipped by a breeze from an open window, the flames quickly enveloped Fanny, who fled in panic to her husband in his study. Seeing his wife ablaze, Longfellow smothered the flames by wrapping a rug around her.

Terribly burned, Fanny survived the night, but died the next day. Longfellow's intense grief was all the more painful because, in his valiant attempt to save her, he himself had suffered severe burns on his face and hands.

So badly burned was the poet that he could not even attend Fanny's funeral, though it was held right in the library of their home in Cambridge, Massachusetts. To hide the disfiguring scars left on his face by the flames, Longfellow let his beard grow.

"The village smithy"

Along Brattle Street, the thoroughfare on which Longfellow lived,

A poster (above)—appropriately illustrated with the insect for which the ship was named—announced the departure of the Hornet *for its fateful trip around Cape Horn. Mark Twain (left) finally won the recognition he craved with his moving account of the vessel's survivors.*

he was not the only noted literary figure. One of his neighbors was Dexter Pratt, immortalized in the poem "The Village Blacksmith."

The poet's words had made a celebrity not only of the "mighty man . . . with large and sinewy hands" but of the tree that guarded his shop. Visitors to the tranquil neighborhood regularly stopped by to visit Pratt and to pause for just a moment beneath the "spreading chestnut tree."

Slaughter on Brattle Street

The popularity of the site, however, evidently did not impress the city fathers, who in the mid-1870's decided to widen the street. Even though Longfellow himself implored them to spare the landmark, the tree came down. "There was a slaughter on Brattle Street today," Longfellow wrote when he heard the news.

A chestnut chair

Nonetheless, the tree remained a part of Longfellow's life. With money raised by the schoolchildren of Boston, a chair, decorated with carved chestnut leaves, was made from its wood and presented to the poet on his 72nd birthday, February 27, 1879. His verse "From My Arm-chair" was a thank-you note for the gift.

Longfellow died three years later, but the chair still remains where he placed it in his study. The handsome mansion, which is now open to the public, is a reminder of the poet's long life and enduring works.

The death of Longfellow's wife inspired a sonnet, "The Cross of Snow," found among his papers after he died.

"A Literary Person" *How a disaster at sea led to Mark Twain's magazine debut*

When the 30-year-old Mark Twain went to Hawaii in 1866 as the correspondent for a California newspaper, he had already won journalistic acclaim for his story "The Jumping Frog of Calaveras County." But Twain had bigger dreams. "In my view," the writer later confessed, "a person who published things in a mere newspaper could not properly claim recognition as a Literary Person; he must rise above that; he must appear in a magazine."

The disaster that struck the clipper ship *Hornet* gave Twain the raw material he needed. Her sails filled with the winds of a stiff January breeze, the three-master left New York for San Francisco with a highly flammable cargo of kerosene and candles. But 108 days later, after a careless sailor ignited a barrel of kerosene, she burned like a torch. All 33 people aboard safely abandoned the doomed vessel in three small boats.

The survivors, adrift more than 1,000 miles from land, had enough supplies for only 10 days. Two lifeboats were never heard from again. And in the end, it was 43 days before Capt. Josiah Mitchell, in an act of astounding seamanship, piloted his longboat to Hawaii. Incredibly, after the 4,000-mile ordeal, all the men in the open boat were still alive.

An embarrassing affliction nearly kept Twain from getting the story of the *Hornet* survivors: he was suffering so badly from saddle sores that he had to be carried on a stretcher to their hospital and was forced to take notes lying down. Still, after working on his article all night, he dramatically tossed it on a California-bound ship at the last minute. It was a scoop—the first detailed report to reach the mainland—for which he requested and was paid an extraordinary $300 bonus.

On his return to California several months later, Twain found that his shipmates included Captain Mitchell and two brothers, 18-year-old Henry and 28-year-old Samuel Ferguson, who had been passengers on the *Hornet*. Twain persuaded the Fergusons to let him copy the diaries both had kept throughout their harrowing experience. He also copied entries from the captain's log.

To his delight, the resultant, more detailed narrative was accepted by *Harper's New Monthly Magazine*. It appeared in the December 1866 issue. Still, Twain's debut as a Literary Person was far from perfect. Unable to decipher his handwriting, the editors listed the author of "Forty-Three Days in an Open Boat" as Mike Swain.

Expanding Horizons

The Centennial *The reunited nation's 100th birthday party featured American know-how*

It was hailed as "an international exhibition of arts, manufactures, and products of the soil and mine"—but in the wake of a financial panic and the ensuing depression, it nearly didn't get off the ground. And while critics said that European royalty wouldn't celebrate a democracy's birth, others wondered whether Americans themselves, still recovering from a bitter civil war, would attend.

Fairest of fairs

The Old World *did* help the New World mark America's 100th birthday. Fifty nations sent displays to the Centennial Exposition in Philadelphia in 1876, and before it was over 8 million people had paid 50 cents each to see the fair.

Landscaped gardens and lawns laced with roads and spanned by bridges transformed West Fairmount Park into a 285-acre wonderland. The exhibit boasted 249 buildings and its own railroad. Amid speeches, music, and hoopla, President Ulysses S. Grant opened the fair on May 10, and visitors streamed in. Foreigners were impressed, and Americans took time out to sample life as tourists. They were shocked by nudity in French paintings, delighted by a graceful Japanese teahouse, fascinated by the exotic taste of Russia's reindeer meat, and intrigued by Austrian bath shoes.

Science and industry

The fair was also a setting for the exchange of technical information, and visitors to these shores were awed by America's industry and inventiveness. Thomas Edison's multiple telegraph was displayed, as was Alexander Graham Bell's telephone. And the typewriter on exhibit no doubt inspired Mark Twain to buy one. (He was the first U.S. author to switch from a pen.) As an English observer reported: "The American invents as the Greek sculptured and the Italian painted: it is genius."

July 4, 1876: Not far from the Centennial Exposition, as cheering crowds celebrated the nation's birthday, bands played and fireworks lit up the sky over Philadelphia's Independence Square.

The invention of agribusiness by railroadmen opened North Dakota's fertile Red River valley to one of the biggest land rushes in history.

Amber Waves of Grain

A railroad created an American breadbasket

In 1873 the Northern Pacific built a railroad to Bismarck, North Dakota, but it produced absolutely no business. Its major assets were tremendous land holdings on both sides of the track. Since northern Plains land was considered worthless, something had to be done to prevent bankruptcy, and railroad agent James Power did it.

Inspired by the appearance in Fargo of a farmer with 1,600 bushels of wheat that sold for an unheard-of $1.25 a bushel, Power convinced two railroad officers to put up money for a 13,400-acre farm. "Minnesota Wheat King" Oliver Dalrymple came on board to manage it, and when his first harvest netted $1 a bushel, the boom was on. In three years the railroad sold over a million acres. Hundreds of people bought tracts that averaged about 300 acres each, and everyone raised wheat. As manager of two spreads totaling more than 80,000 acres, Dalrymple ran the world's biggest wheat empire. And the Northern Pacific carried the harvest east. (In 1880 alone, it took 1,440 railroad cars to do it.)

Flourishing fields, phenomenal profits

Ably directing his workers, and using self-binding harvesters and steam-powered threshers as well as draft animals, Dalrymple created a virtual "factory in the field." Each bonanza farm (3,000 acres or more) flourished. Publicity attracted wealthy easterners, and trains routinely stopped near Fargo so that passengers could tour the farms. Even President Rutherford B. Hayes visited Dalrymple's domain, which became a showplace for the latest machinery. The owners of one vast farm even started a telephone network (one of the nation's first) with equipment they bought at the Centennial Exposition.

But by the 1890's, economic crises doomed the huge spreads, and no longer could a farmer "start out in the spring and plow a straight furrow until fall. Then turn around and harvest back."

What Time Is It?

It used to be every town for itself as far as clock-setting was concerned. Whether they called it God's time or sun time, when it was noon in New York it was 11:55 A.M. in Philadelphia. Wisconsin had 38 different local times. Finally in 1883, for the sake of a coherent timetable, the railroads made the nation synchronize its watches by dividing it into four time zones, based on the observatory in Greenwich, England. Initially there was opposition: Bath, Maine, rang its town bell 20 minutes early four times a day, and Augusta, Georgia, pushed its city clock forward 32 minutes at noon to maintain sun time. But the new system won out; the Standard Time Act was finally passed in 1918.

The Year the Horses Died

It was an urban disaster. Cities that depended on horses to pull streetcars, delivery trucks, and other vehicles were swept in 1872 by an epidemic of equine influenza that brought them to a virtual standstill. It started in Canada, spread quickly south to Louisiana, and then west. Few horses died at first, but soon some 200 were dying daily in Philadelphia.

At the height of the Great Epizootic, 18,000 horses were too sick to work in New York City, and in Rochester, New York, not a horse was to be seen in the streets. Horsecar service came to a halt. Some cities tried using oxen to pull the cars, but they were too slow and their hooves too tender. In New York, gangs of unemployed men were put to work (right). Construction sites shut down for lack of materials; food stores and restaurants had to be supplied by men lugging sacks and cans. Fire departments were immobilized, and so the Great Boston Fire burned out of control, completely destroying a 67-acre swath of the downtown area.

There were probably as many theories about the cause of the disease as there were sick horses. Some said it was what the animals had eaten; others said they were breathing poisonous gas. The epidemic ran its course in a few months, but by then streetcar officials had begun looking for alternatives to the horse.

The Start of the Seventh Inning Stretch

It happened in 1882 during a baseball game between New York's Manhattan College and the semi-pro Metropolitans: Brother Jasper (left), the college athletic director, took pity on fidgety students and, calling a time-out during the seventh inning, told them to stand up and stretch for a couple of minutes. The practice was copied by New York Giants fans during an exhibition game against the college team at the Polo Grounds (below), and has since become a baseball tradition.

The man who invented the seventh inning stretch has been honored by the college: Manhattan's team is called the Jaspers.

Emperor Norton I

"At the peremptory request and desire of a large majority of the citizens of the United States, I, Joshua Norton . . . declare and proclaim myself Emperor." After a San Francisco paper ran this notice in 1859, the city took its emperor (below), a businessman who'd fallen on hard times, to heart. A chair was reserved for him in the state legislature; he ate free at fine restaurants. When one citizen tried to have him committed, the judge dismissed the case, noting that Norton was "just about the best going in the king line." A monument in his honor bore the words: Norton I, Emperor of the United States, Protector of Mexico, Joshua A. Norton 1819–1880.

La Belle Siffleuse

Alice Shaw delighted audiences by whistling—with trills, grace notes, and perfect pitch—everything from operatic arias to popular ballads. Ironically, as a child she had so tormented her parents with her singular talent that they forbade her to whistle. But years later, left to support four young daughters, Alice built a career on her unusual skill. At her first recital, a New York charity ball in 1886, she was a sensation; with her good looks and elegant breeding, she soon became known as La Belle Siffleuse *("the beautiful whistler"). Doctors decided that the high, narrow roof of Alice's mouth produced her dazzling tones, but she credited her virtuosity to hours of practice. And the hard work produced results beyond music. Noted one journalist: "Her bust is a beautiful one and this she attributes entirely to whistling."*

Shy and quiet Elizabeth Tilton was convinced that her affair with her pastor, Henry Ward Beecher, "had never proceeded from low or vulgar thoughts . . . but always from pure affection and a high religious love." Her husband saw it differently and sued Beecher for $100,000 for alienating his wife's affection. At left, Beecher and Mrs. Tilton shake hands in court as Mrs. Beecher looks on.

Fallen Angel *An 1870's sex scandal rocked a religious giant*

In 1874 Henry Ward Beecher was not only the most famous and highly paid preacher in America, he was a national symbol of morality and virtue. When civil charges were filed alleging that the pastor of Brooklyn's Plymouth Church had seduced the wife of one of his best friends, supporters across the country cried slander. But the facts of the case and the sensational trial that followed reveal the pathetic hypocrisy of the Gilded Age.

Better paid than the president

Beecher had risen to prominence through his passionate espousal of abolition. Aided by the public relations genius of publisher Henry Bowen and editor Theodore Tilton, the preacher was big business. Pew rentals and contributions from his affluent Brooklyn Heights congregation amounted to $100,000 a year. His popular writings and lecture tours extended his pastoral influence across the country and netted him a neat $15,000 annually beyond his $20,000 salary—which meant that in the early 1870's he earned nearly one and a half times as much as the president of the United States. So popular were his energetic sermons that the Sunday morning ferries crossing New York Harbor to Brooklyn were called Beecher Boats.

But the private Beecher could not measure up to the public image. Burdened with a severe and sexless wife, he sought release in the arms of other women. In 1868 the corpulent cleric began an affair with Elizabeth Tilton, the attractive but somewhat naive wife of his editor.

Two years later Elizabeth, no longer able to contain her guilt, confessed to her husband. Outraged, Tilton confronted his former friend and threatened public revelation; then, for the good of all, he decided to keep things quiet.

Tilton's folly, Woodhull's revenge

But Tilton made a mistake. He confided his frustrations to Elizabeth Cady Stanton, a prominent suffragist and something of a gossip. Stanton let the story slip to, of all people, Victoria Woodhull, a fiery feminist, outspoken leader of the free love movement, and co-editor of *Woodhull and Claflin's Weekly*. Woodhull's views had been attacked by Beecher's sister, Harriet Beecher Stowe (author of *Uncle Tom's Cabin*); in retaliation, Woodhull went public in 1872 with Beecher's steamy story as an example of free love among the mighty. The preacher, to the disappointment of his advocates, answered her allegations only with stony silence.

But in Brooklyn the silence was broken by clumsy cover-ups and scathing whispers. Finally the cuckolded Tilton could stand it no more, and in 1874 he sued Beecher. The heavily publicized trial produced damning evidence, but the all-male jury was unable—or unwilling—to reach a verdict.

Exonerated by a council of Congregational churches, Beecher survived the stain on his reputation and remained at Plymouth Church until his death in 1887. Theodore Tilton died in self-imposed exile in Paris. Elizabeth also remained in Brooklyn, living with her mother. She died in 1897 and was buried in the same Brooklyn cemetery as Henry Ward Beecher.

The President's Desk *Made from the wood of a British ship*

In May 1845 British explorer John Franklin led 128 men into the Arctic to search for the Northwest Passage. None of them ever returned. Rescue parties were launched as early as 1848. Four years later Edward Belcher set out with five ships, among them the sturdy 600-ton H.M.S. *Resolute.*

Belcher searched for the Franklin party for two years. Then, in the spring of 1854, he ordered all his men into one ship and abandoned his other four vessels as they lay trapped in ice. The order was foolish: the ships were sound, supplies were plentiful, and the thaw was near. Returning to England, Belcher was court-martialed for his decision and only narrowly escaped condemnation. But at the time he issued the command, his men had little choice but to obey.

Sixteen months later, in September 1855, American whalers spotted the *Resolute* floating freely more than a thousand miles from where she had been abandoned. By right of salvage the ship now belonged to the whalers, who sailed her into port at New London, Connecticut, just before Christmas. Belcher's other three ships were never found.

The U.S. government bought the *Resolute* from the whalers for $40,000—no small catch—had her refitted, and returned her to the British as a symbol of friendship. She continued to serve for more than 20 years.

When the *Resolute* finally was scrapped, Queen Victoria ordered an oak desk—six feet long and four feet wide—made from her timbers. The desk was presented to President Rutherford B. Hayes in 1880 as a memorial to American courtesy in returning the ship. Every president from Hayes to Kennedy worked at the desk, and in 1977 President Carter had it returned to the Oval Office.

Can You Type and Take Shorthand?

The YWCA began a revolution in woman's work

If there had been a National Secretaries' Week back in 1879, the boss probably would not have brought a dozen roses to the office. In those days, secretaries were almost always men. But the Young Women's Christian Association was about to change all that.

America's YWCA was founded in February 1870 by Georgianna Ballard and 30 other privileged young New York ladies to assist working-class girls who came to the city seeking education and jobs. In its very first year the organization took a radical step toward fulfilling its goal: it established a public library. This may seem demure today, but the 500-volume collection was the first free library in New York that would lend books to women.

The group was no less daring when it came to employment. At a time when most of New York's working girls held tedious, low-paying jobs as servants and factory workers, the YWCA's directors did a survey of work opportunities and discovered that "stenography is the most lucrative of all professions, the demand for stenographers being in large excess of the supply."

To fill that demand, they offered shorthand classes for women in 1879, thereby starting a revolution in the American conception of woman's work. So quickly did successful graduates find jobs that the following year a typing course was added. Although the typewriter was still a newfangled gadget, the farsighted directors of the YWCA thought that it might catch on. Unorthodox as the idea must have seemed, "some businessmen preferred to have their letters done on the typewriter."

In the 1870's people thought that typing was physically too strenuous and intellectually too complicated for women. Early typists, such as the woman above, proved them wrong.

The Naughty Nineties

"She Wiggles, She Jiggles . . ." *But did Little Egypt exist?*

Once upon a time there was a big fair in Chicago, celebrating the 400th anniversary of Columbus's voyage. The fair had astounding scientific exhibits, but it also had trouble paying its bills. Then Little Egypt arrived. She danced nude, drew huge crowds, and saved the fair from financial ruin. . . . Sound like a fairy tale?

Thousands later claimed to remember Little Egypt, but historians have been unable to find any mention of such a dancer at the World's Columbian Exposition of 1893. To be sure, there were "belly dancers" on the midway. But these modest maidens' gyrations were fully covered by long ethnic costumes. A bored observer recalled "inordinately thick ankles and large, voluptuous feet."

Seeley's dinner guest

In his autobiography, Sol Bloom, the man who managed the midway, denied that Little Egypt was there. He said the dancer first appeared at Coney Island, where "she acquired great renown for her actual or reputed stage appearances in the nude. A couple of years after the fair a young woman identified in the papers simply as Little Egypt became famous when she rose unclad out of an enormous pie served in the Waldorf-Astoria at the stag affair that is still so felicitously called the Awful Seeley Dinner." Following this, Little Egypts burst out all over America, and presumably this is the source of the myth of Chicago's nude dancer.

Amid all the confusion, of course, several former Exposition performers claimed to be Chicago's own Little Egypt. One was a midway belly dancer who, in 1936, sued Metro-Goldwyn-Mayer over a movie. Another was a camel, also named Little Egypt, who gave rides to midway tourists. One thing, however, is certain: the camel is not the Little Egypt who popped so memorably out of Mr. Seeley's pie.

Little Egypt (left) wasn't at the fair. The midway's biggest draw, G. W. G. Ferris's giant wheel, was 264 feet high; its 36 cars each held 60 riders.

The UFO's of 1896

Still an unsolved mystery

A WINGED SHIP IN THE SKY.

It Cleaves the Air With Pinions Like a Huge Condor.

ALL SACRAMENTO SEES THE NEW WONDER.

The Inventor's Lawyer Describes the Machine and Says It Is Genuine.

IT WAS SEEN SOARING NEAR SAN JOSE AT MIDNIGHT.

"The Call's" Exclusive Account of the Greatest Invention of the Age Is Now Corroborated by Thousands.

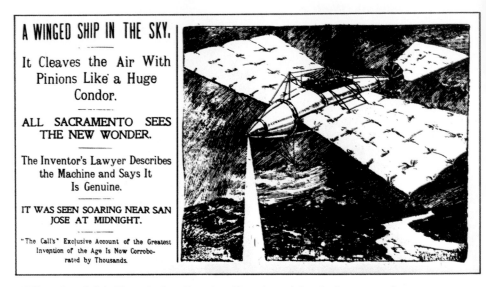

William Randolph Hearst's San Francisco Examiner *debunked reports of the mysterious airship as "The Result of Beer." Its rival, the* Call, *eager to boost circulation, played up the story with hysterical headlines (above).*

A former Sacramento street railway employee was among the first to see it: "Two men seated as though on bicycle frames" below a balloon. Five days later Sacramento's district attorney saw it, and so did the mayor's daughter. It was even seen as far away as San Francisco. Soon sightings were being reported from Canada to Los Angeles. Two fishermen claimed to have talked to the crew.

People skeptical of invaders from outer space stepped forward claiming to know the craft's earthly origin. Among them was a former California attorney general, who claimed acquaintance with the ship's inventor and declared that it could carry half a ton of dynamite, with which it would soon bomb Havana.

The craze faded on the Pacific Coast, only to bloom all over the Midwest. A Kansas farmer claimed a heifer had been cow-napped, and the distinguished St. Louis *Post-Dispatch* reported that "an Elderly Christian Gentleman" had come upon a 20-foot-long vessel on four legs, in front of which sat a "majestic" bearded man and a beautiful golden-haired girl "in nature's garb."

Predictably, messages from the ship began to appear; the most sensational of them was addressed to Thomas A. Edison. Signed "C. L. Harris, electrician, airship N.3," it was indecipherable. Edison declared it a hoax. Airships would be invented someday, he predicted, but "at best" they "would be only toys."

The ship supposedly crashed near Dallas, and the pilot, identified as "not an inhabitant of this world," was buried in the local cemetery. Meanwhile, in Yonkers, New York, the craft was seen heading out to sea.

Scientists suggest that people were merely seeing Venus or some other planet. Or perhaps it was just one more of the hoaxes that were popular in the period. Whatever the source, it's a story that's hard to kill: in 1973 someone made news by stealing the Texas "spaceman's" tombstone.

Hopping Out of Harvard *The first gold medalist in the modern Olympics*

James Brendan Connolly was the son of Irish immigrants to the tough South End of Boston. Forced to leave school in the early grades, he worked at various jobs, educated himself, and was admitted to Harvard in 1895—at the age of 27. Determined to compete the following year in the Olympics (the first since the Romans abolished the Games in A.D. 394), he asked Harvard for a leave of absence. When the college refused, he packed his bags and left for Athens anyway, paying his own expenses.

Connolly's event was the triple jump—or hop, step, and jump, as it was called then. Its final, set for the Games's opening day, was the first on the Olympic schedule. This gave Connolly real problems. The Americans hadn't realized that the Greeks used the Hellenic calendar; so instead of arriving 12 days before the Games, the team arrived just hours before the opening ceremony.

Connolly, tired and 12 pounds overweight, still longed for the first Olympic prize to be awarded in more than 1,500 years. The last to jump, he cleared 45 feet, outdistancing his closest competitor by more than a yard.

Later in life, Connolly went to sea and became a prolific journalist and author, writing 25 novels. The gold medalist never returned to Harvard as a student and rejected its offer of an honorary degree. He did, however, accept an invitation to lecture on literature. At his 50th class reunion the college awarded him a Harvard *H* in track.

Bicycle Bonkers

The leap onto a high-wheeler (bottom, right) was too much for most Americans. But when the "safety" bike was introduced, even the unathletic got rolling. Actress Lillian Russell had a special seat made from a clay mold of her delicate posterior, and the wealthy Goulds and Vanderbilts cycled at exclusive clubs to the music of live bands. Advertisements (below) made it plain that young ladies who lit up men's hearts had their own lamps lit already. A penchant for speed led to the ten-seater (center), and a passion for prizes produced the beaming hero at right, who had just taken first place in a costume parade. There were 100,000 cyclists in America in 1890; by 1896, the height of the craze, there were 4 million. Not bad, considering that brakes weren't introduced until two years later.

DEDICATED TO THE "SEARCH-LIGHT LANTERN."
THE HIT OF THE SEASON!

'GET YOUR LAMPS LIT!'

SONG POLKA

Published by
THEO. A. METZ

NEW YORK.
REMOVED TO, NEAR BROADWAY
1335 Broadway Copyright 1895 by THEO. A. METZ. Entered Stationers' Hall

LONDON.
192 HIGH HOLBORN. W.C.

BY PERMISSION OF NEW YORK HERALD.

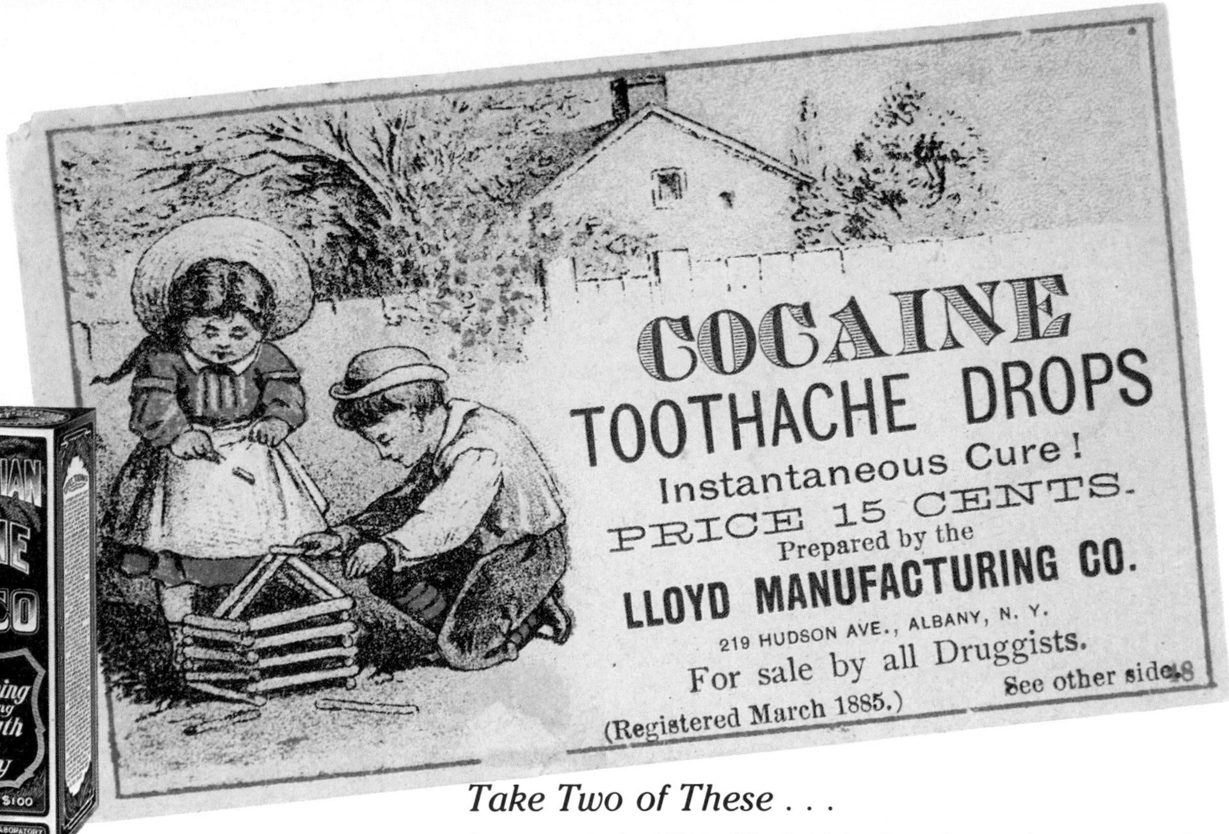

Take Two of These . . .

Drugstores in the 1890's did a brisk business in over-the-counter medicines that contained dangerous narcotics. Not only cocaine but opium derivatives, such as laudanum and morphine, were common remedies for ailments from toothache (above) to insomnia. And it wasn't just at the medicine counter that drugstores helped you get high. In 1886 an Atlanta soda fountain started serving a beverage laced with coca, from which cocaine is derived—hence the drink's name: Coca-Cola. (Coke's formula has changed since.) Sears, Roebuck and Co. even offered a mail-order coca wine (above, left). With the Pure Food and Drug Act of 1906, Congress finally moved to regulate the corner drugstore.

Quickstep's Revenge

The horse-drawn trolley ride from Denver to suburban Cherrelyn was a 15-minute uphill pull. The return trip, by contrast, was a breezy three-minute coast, during which the horse who'd done the work joined the passengers (right). One cunning old steed—aptly named Quickstep—especially enjoyed his work. While pulling with a new horse, he nudged the would-be usurper, entangling him under the trolley and thus ensuring his own job security. The line, known as the Gravity & Bronco street railroad, operated from 1892 to 1910.

Getting on a Roll

George Loher's transcontinental bike ride

Filet mignon was nice, but butcher George Loher wanted a larger slice of life. So in 1895 he decided to bicycle from his hometown of Oakland, California, to New York, a trip of more than 4,300 miles.

Straddling his Stearns Yellow Fellow, Loher looked as if he couldn't move an inch. Fully loaded, the bike weighed 53½ pounds: a saddlebag was strapped to the frame, a bedroll to the handlebars, and a suit of clothes was stuffed under the seat. Nonetheless, Loher lacked some things that most of us would consider necessities—maps and brakes. When he wanted to slow the bike on a downhill run, he "displayed a wheelman's ingenuity by tying a quantity of brush together and trailing it through the dust."

Certainly Loher saw the country. He almost ran into a train in Oregon, broke a wheel in Montana, and was sworn at in Swedish in North Dakota. A typical tourist, he took in all the sights. At the Sing Sing penitentiary outside New York City, he was invited by the warden to sit in the electric chair. "I found it a comfortable piece of furniture (that is, when the dynamo is not running)," he wrote.

Loher completed his odyssey in 80 days. His wanderlust satisfied, he returned to the Oakland butcher shop. By train.

But Can You Do It Without Looking?

The chess champ who played 22 games simultaneously

To play 22 games of chess at the same time is hard enough, but Harry Nelson Pillsbury did it without even looking at the boards. It was easy. He just remembered all the moves everybody made.

Born in Massachusetts in 1872, Pillsbury began playing chess at age 15. Only seven years later he became U.S. representative to Britain's prestigious Hastings Tournament. The older, more temperamental players resented his calm demeanor and ever-present, odorous black cigars. But by the time the last king had been tipped in checkmate, Pillsbury was in first place.

He financed his passion for chess by giving public performances that combined the game with his prodigious powers of memory. During a day off at a German tournament, he took on 21 acknowledged masters simultaneously without seeing a move. Although Pillsbury won only 3 games in this elite field, he did manage 11 draws. Later, playing 22 "blindfold" matches against less awesome opponents, he lost only 1.

At another performance, a pair of educated scamps gave Pillsbury a diabolical test. They supplied a 29-word list containing such tongue-twisters as Oomisillecootsi, madjesoomaloops, Piet Polgelter's Rost, and antiphlogistine. The master mnemonist merely glanced at the list, then started his chess show. A day later Pillsbury recited the list perfectly to the flabbergasted challengers; then he playfully reeled the whole thing off again—backward.

Potato Envy Inspired the First Pro Rodeo

Legend has it that Col. E. A. Slack was in a dark mood as he rode back to Wyoming from the Potato Day festivities in Greeley, Colorado. Why couldn't his hometown of Cheyenne celebrate its heritage with a special event? At about the same time, railroad agent F. W. Angier was watching cowboys break broncos. This work, Angier thought, would make a fascinating show.

Cheyenne citizens got together, raised $562, and on September 23, 1897, launched America's first organized rodeo. It was a natural, since it built on the town's tradition as a cattle center and enabled local cowboys to do for sport what they did for a living. People flocked to the show from as far away as Denver.

Of the 11 events that filled the bill, 5 are still part of the standard rodeo program. But one unusual twist has changed over the years: prizes used to be awarded not only for the best bronc rider but for the horse that bucked the best (both prizewinners are shown above). Oddly enough, the winning rider got a mere $25, while the owner of the meanest horse got a cool $100. Which wasn't small potatoes.

The Cheyenne Frontier Days Rodeo, "The Daddy of 'Em All," is still held every summer.

Greed in the Golden West

The Gay Nineties were brutal in Johnson County, Wyoming

By the late 1880's ranching in the West was monopolized by companies headquartered in New York and London. These cattle barons controlled the Wyoming Stock Growers Association and illegally grazed thousands of cattle on government land, crowding out small ranchers and homesteaders. The small-timers were especially angered by the maverick law, which had been passed by the Wyoming legislature at the barons' urging. It declared that all mavericks (unbranded cattle) were the property of the Stock Growers Association. Since the small ranchers were barred from membership, this meant that their unmarked cattle could be seized by the barons. In retaliation, they started rustling the barons' cattle. Many of these small operators homesteaded in Johnson County.

After an especially severe winter, during which cattle died by the hundreds, the barons took drastic measures to rebuild their dwindling herds. Hiring "cattle detectives," they murdered anyone suspected of rustling. Finally, in 1892, full-scale war broke out. Backed by a few dozen Texas gunmen, the barons headed north from Cheyenne to "exterminate" the "rustlers." Wyoming's acting governor and both U.S. senators condoned the invasion of Johnson County.

The first stop was the cabin of Nate Champion, who had organized a homesteaders' roundup of mavericks. After witnessing the murder of his friend Nick Ray, Champion held the marauders off for hours, until they sent a burning wagon hurtling into his cabin. Trying to break out to freedom, he was cut down in a barrage of bullets.

The barons continued on toward Buffalo, the Johnson County seat. By then, Sheriff "Red" Angus had been alerted to the invasion. Raising a posse, he forced the barons to hole up at the TA ranch, where they threw together a makeshift fort. Local settlers continued to reinforce Angus until some 300 men surrounded the barons' stronghold.

But then word reached Washington about the barons' predicament. Wyoming's senators roused President Benjamin Harrison from bed and persuaded him to send cavalry to the invaders' aid. The troops arrived just as the homesteaders were advancing on the fortification with dynamite.

The barons and the gunmen were imprisoned briefly, but money and power told. Their trial was moved to Cheyenne. Witnesses to Ray and Champion's murders were spirited out of the state. Johnson County went broke paying for the barons' detention and finally dropped the charges.

Exuding smug satisfaction, the cattlemen and gunslingers who invaded Johnson County posed for this photograph shortly after their arrest in 1892.

A New Century

To Save Men From a Drunkard's Fate

Carry Nation's "hatchetations" started a trend

The drinkers in Dobson's Saloon on June 7, 1900, hardly had time to duck as Carry Nation entered, shouting: "I have come to save you from a drunkard's fate!" Although she became famous for battering barrooms with a hatchet, on this first foray in Kiowa, Kansas, she was armed with rocks, and she aimed her missiles with force and accuracy. Soon the place was a sea of broken bottles and shattered mirrors. Surveying her work with pride, Carry admonished the startled barkeep: "Now, Mr. Dobson, I have finished. God be with you."

But the job was *not* done. With her buggyload of rocks, Carry wrecked two more bars, then demanded that the local sheriff arrest her. Startled officials, however, asked only that she leave town.

Carry, president of the local Women's Christian Temperance Union chapter, had heard a voice whisper after a prayer session: "Take something in your hands and throw it at those places and smash them." She didn't question whose voice it was. Loading a wagon with rocks, she drove 20 miles from her home in Medicine Lodge to Kiowa, a town noted for its illegal taprooms (Kansas was dry).

Tracing her views on alcohol to her first husband's death of drink, Carry launched a series of well-publicized raids in Wichita and Topeka, where she first used her famous hatchet. Conservative prohibitionists looked askance at her tactics, but soon many hatchet-wielding women were wrecking saloons all across the country.

Carry also went on the lecture circuit, warning audiences in America and Britain about the dreaded evils of alcohol. Still, nothing gave her more satisfaction than "hatchetation." On one occasion a policeman tried to restrain her: "I must arrest you for defacing property," he said. "I am defacing nothing," cried Carry indignantly. "I am destroying!"

An imposing figure, 6-foot, 175-pound Carry Nation championed the cause of prohibition with her Bible—and her hatchet.

Deadly Influenza

A virulent worldwide plague

In August 1918 the Norwegian liner *Bergensfjord* arrived in Brooklyn. During her transatlantic voyage, 100 passengers had fallen ill and 4 had died. A fifth succumbed just after docking, the first U.S. victim of a deadly form of influenza that was raging across Europe. The disease soon became the scourge of America, recalling the Black Death of the European Middle Ages.

At the peak of the pandemic, more than 100 people died in one day in New York and Boston. In Philadelphia, where there were 528 victims in one 24-hour period, bodies were collected in horse-drawn carts. On Black Thursday in Chicago, almost 400 died. Schools and theaters were closed in many cities (idle chorus girls from Washington's National Burlesque worked as hospital volunteers), and face masks were everywhere.

People in the prime of life were hardest hit. One in three American soldiers who caught the disease died. With flu rampant on troopships, President Woodrow Wilson considered suspending further sailings to Europe, but was persuaded that they were essential to seal the Allied victory. Worldwide, some 27 million people died in the brief course of the pandemic—more than were killed in all of World War I.

Where did it all begin? Ironically, investigators now think that it probably started in the United States. They cite a March 1918 flu outbreak at an army camp in Kansas, followed by similar cases in France soon after the Kansas-based soldiers arrived there. Wartime troop movements hastened the spread of the disease, and measures taken by health authorities seem to have had no effect.

Fearing flu, Seattle's finest (above) wore masks. In one week in 1918, a record 21,000 Americans died.

Mysteriously, the pandemic ended in early 1919. And no one yet knows why, in 1918, a mild germ turned so deadly.

A Short Zoo Story ***The pygmy who went to the Bronx***

For a brief time in the early part of this century, the Bronx Zoo seems to have kept a pygmy on exhibit in a cage. His name was Ota Benga (later Americanized to Otto Bingo), and he was one of a number of pygmies brought from Africa to be in a freak show at the 1904 St. Louis Exposition.

There are conflicting versions of his life. The man who brought him here, Samuel Verner, said that Benga had been rescued from headhunters and had chosen to accept Verner's offer of a trip to America. Benga himself reportedly said that he had been kidnapped. Verner claimed Benga didn't want to go back to Africa after the exposition, so he gave the young pygmy—whose front teeth had been filed down to points—to William Hornaday, the director of the Bronx Zoo. There, billed as a cannibal, Benga was on display in a cage, where he lived along with an orangutan and a parrot.

This spectacle caused a public furor. Blacks campaigned for Benga's release; white clergymen, fearing that he might be used to prove Darwin's theory of evolution, raised a storm of their own. Faced with legal action, Hornaday released Benga, who strolled the zoo grounds, followed by crowds. *(The New York Times* later claimed that Benga had been employed only to feed the apes.)

A group of sympathetic New Jersey clergymen eventually arranged for Benga to attend college, after which he lived with a Virginia family and worked in a nearby factory. When he committed suicide in 1916, it was generally acknowleged that he had never adjusted to life in America. But a cynical Hornaday saw it differently. "Evidently he felt that he would rather die than work for a living," he snorted.

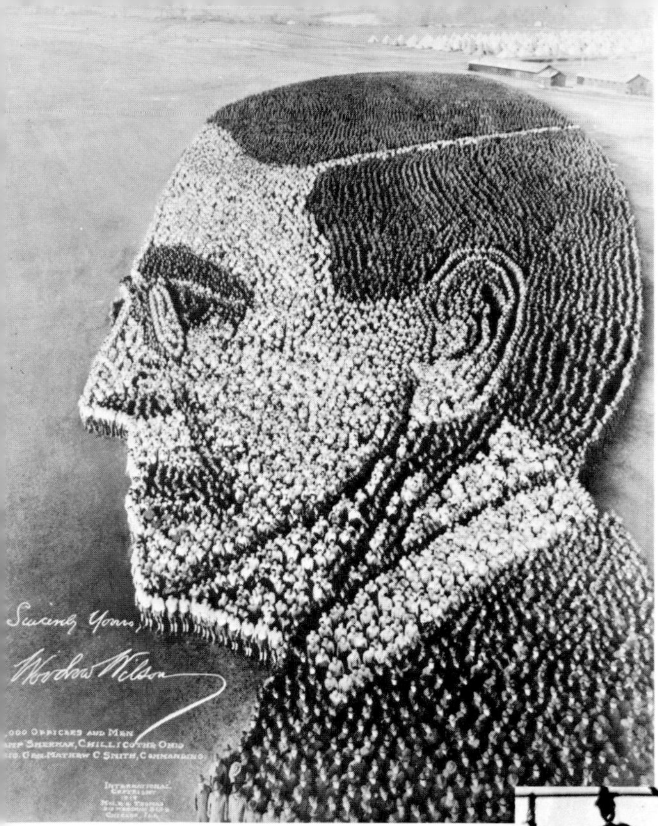

21,000 People = 1 President's Portrait

When photographer Arthur Mole assembled thousands of officers and enlisted men at Camp Sherman in Chillicothe, Ohio, in 1918, he had no ordinary group portrait in mind. Instead, by arranging and rearranging 21,000 soldiers, he formed one of his most famous "living pictures," a huge portrait of President Woodrow Wilson (left). To shoot the picture, he had to climb a 70-foot-high tower. Then, using a megaphone to shout instructions, Mole had the men fill in a detailed outline he had created on the ground. The picture captured the patriotic fancy of America, as did many other efforts of this innovative photographer. Mole arranged thousands of troops into pictures during his career: 10,000 men into a rippling American flag, 19,000 into a profile of Uncle Sam, and 25,000 into the shape of the Liberty Bell. Some 18,000 formed the Statue of Liberty; and his biggest, the living U.S. Shield, used 30,000 people. Servicemen seemed to enjoy it; in a letter home, one of them bragged, "Hey, Mom, I was part of President Wilson's left eyebrow today."

Polar Pose

A "chorus line" of Eskimos (right) was photographed by Robert Peary during one of his Arctic expeditions. The explorer and his longtime black associate, Matthew Henson, reached the North Pole together in 1909. Both men fathered Eskimo children, and a joyous gathering of the clans united many of their descendants for the first time in Boston in 1987.

Back to Nature for Fun and Profit

"I shall be entirely independent of the rest of humanity," Joe Knowles declared on a rainy August morning in 1913. With this, he stripped down to a loincloth and moved into the Maine woods (right, starting a fire without a match). Urban life had spawned a strong back-to-nature movement, and Joe decided to spend two months alone to prove that man could still survive the simple life. His notes to the outside world, written on bark with burnt sticks, were picked up by a Boston Post *reporter. Circulation soared as readers followed Joe's progress. Despite certain discrepancies in his back-to-nature tales—was his fur cloak actually a bearskin he'd purchased for $12?—when he emerged thousands cheered this "modern primitive man." As it turned out, Joe's survival skills in the business world were just as keen as in the wild: his book* Alone in the Wilderness *became an instant best-seller.*

Yes, We Do Have Bananas

In 1900, to convince a somewhat skeptical public that bananas were not poisonous, a grocer in Stillwater asked students at Oklahoma A&M to eat some before a camera (left). (The exotic tropical fruits had first been served in 1875 at an elegant Boston dinner party, where they were eaten daintily with knives and forks.) The grocer's advertising gimmick worked, and sweet, tasty yellow bananas—originally imported from the West Indies—have been an American favorite ever since.

Roots

Money may be the root of all evil, but as former newspaperman John Albert Krohn noted, "Most of us need the 'root.' " So Krohn decided to take a walk—around the perimeter of the United States. He figured he could sell the rights to the story.

Krohn set out from Portland, Maine, on June 1, 1908, his gear in a pyramid-shaped box atop a wheelbarrow. His route led west to Washington, south along the Pacific Coast, east to the Gulf, and then up the Atlantic—9,024 miles in all. Wearing out 11 pairs of shoes, 121 pairs of socks, and 3 rubber tires (one of which was bitten through by a giant snapping turtle), he defrayed expenses by selling souvenir aluminum medals along the way. Response to his mission was keen. Cards and mementoes were attached to his wheelbarrow (right). Frequently Krohn was "arrested" and sentenced to a meal and bed at the best hotel in town.

Returning home after the 357-day trip, he wrote a book and settled into gardening—a fine activity for a man who was already familiar with wheelbarrows and liked to get down to the root.

According to one story, publicist Harry Reichenbach tricked Comstock into attacking Paul Chabas's painting "September Morn" (left). Reichenbach had an art dealer display a print of the painting in his shop window, paid some street kids to stand gawking in front of it—and then called Comstock. Of course the uproar created by morality's champion made the painting a national rage. Not only were millions of prints sold, there were "September Morn" dolls, calendars, cane heads, and even tattoos.

Comstock's Cover-up

America's greatest bluenose devoted his life to protecting us all from nudity

It was an age when bulls were called "gentlemen cows" and delicate ladies ordered turkey "bosom" for dinner. The paragon of this late-Victorian prudery was plump, pompous Anthony Comstock, a professional enemy of sin. As secretary of New York's Society for the Suppression of Vice, he devoted 42 years to purifying the country of everything from rum to church raffles. But his specialty was anti-lewdness, and he was proud of his work. "I have convicted persons enough to fill a passenger train of sixty-one coaches," he boasted in 1913, toward the end of his career. "I have destroyed 160 tons of obscene literature." And he didn't stop at dirty books. According to a YMCA report, in little more than a year he confiscated 60,300 otherwise undefined "articles made of rubber for immoral purposes."

Comstock's campaign often exposed him to danger. Once he narrowly escaped death from a mail bomb; another time, he received a package infected with smallpox. No one can doubt his courage and effectiveness. But, unfortunately, the same zeal that helped him rid America of some of its most vicious pornographers also made him a self-righteous buffoon. He prosecuted a 19-year-old girl for distributing pamphlets for the Art Students' League and attacked demure artworks, such as Paul Chabas's "September Morn" (above). Apparently he once confused paintings from the prestigious French Académie des Beaux-Arts salon with paintings "exhibited in the *Saloons* of Paris."

In a disgusting display of callous arrogance, Comstock publicly expressed satisfaction at having driven 15 people to suicide. Only the 16th gave him pause. She was a deranged woman, who believed she had married an angel of God. Comstock had had her arrested when she published a book of advice for newlyweds.

No wonder this bluenose reformer was vilified and lampooned in the press. One cartoon showed him in court complaining, "Your Honor, this woman gave birth to a naked child." There is, after all, something suspicious about a man whose passion for purity drives him to devote a lifetime to perusing smut.

The Naked and the Dead

An earthquake gave the Bride of Christ Church a big break

Edmund Franz Creffield's Bride of Christ Church brought new meaning to the term *Holy Roller.* Preaching to his female flock in the homes of Corvallis, Oregon, Creffield (who called himself Joshua II) would close the shutters, extol the innocence of the Garden of Eden, and shout, "Vile clothes, begone!" Off came dresses, petticoats, and corsets, and the whole group would roll on the floor, stark naked. Joshua was looking for the girl who would become the "Second Mother of Christ," and so greater excesses followed. After a few such "services," comely 17-year-old Esther Mitchell got the job.

Eventually, irate husbands tarred and feathered Joshua and drove him out of town. Released from prison after doing time for adultery, he reassembled a small band of followers, among them Esther Mitchell. On April 17, 1906, he cursed Corvallis, Portland, Seattle, and San Francisco; the next day San Francisco collapsed in an earthquake. Fearing for Corvallis, some 50 women rushed to join Joshua.

Esther Mitchell's brother tracked the group to Seattle, where he shot the prophet. Tried for murder and acquitted, he was shot by his sister behind the left ear—the exact spot where he had shot Joshua. Esther, who never did bear the "Second Christ," was committed to a state insane asylum.

Charged with adultery in Portland, Joshua II hid out for months under his legal wife's front porch. He is pictured at right shortly after his discovery.

Creffield as he appeared when dug out from under O. V. Hurt's house. An enterprising Corvallis resident has issued postcards bearing this photo of the Holy Roller prophet.

Good-bye, Columbus

There was no room for Santa Claus on Wilbur Glenn Voliva's flat earth

Things started out oddly in Zion City and when Wilbur Glenn Voliva took control of this Illinois utopia, they got a good bit odder.

The town was founded by Alexander Dowie, an Australian faith healer who, having tangled with Chicago's health department, decided to move his operation elsewhere. Blessed with a flowing beard and a charismatic personality, Dowie set himself up as Zion's Grand Overseer. From this exalted position he raised money to build factories and houses and forbade liquor, tobacco, doctors, morticians, pork—and any derogatory or untoward comments about Zion's Grand Overseer.

Then in 1905 Dowie suffered a stroke and gave legal control of the community to his trusted lieutenant, Wilbur Glenn Voliva. So much for trust. While Dowie was recuperating abroad, Voliva expropriated his assets and spread rumors about his fiscal and marital sins. After a rancorous struggle, Voliva emerged as the new Grand Overseer. Like all good usurpers, he imposed an even stricter regime. In addition to Dowie's prohibitions, Voliva frowned on dancing, tan shoes, and the eating of oysters. Three girls were banished for chewing gum, and Santa Claus was outlawed as a fraud.

Most famously, Voliva proclaimed that the earth was flat—a pancake-shaped disc surrounded by a wall of ice. He offered $5,000 to anyone who could disprove it. He also objected to the notion that the earth revolved around the sun and that the sun was millions of miles away. "God made the sun to light the earth," he thundered, "and therefore must have placed it close to the task it was designed to do. What would you think of a man who built a house in Zion and put the lamp to light it in Kenosha, Wisconsin?"

Bathtub Gin and All That Jazz

Tough Times for Temperance

The 18th Amendment made buying booze illegal, so Ma and Pa made it at home

When Representative Andrew Joseph Volstead of Minnesota pushed through the legislation that replaced bartenders with bootleggers, he sparked, quite unintentionally, the Roaring Twenties. It was a time when temperance advocates celebrated their greatest triumph, while the rest of the country seemed to go wild ignoring them.

During Prohibition—which started with the enactment of the 18th Amendment on January 16, 1920, and ended with its repeal 13 years later—you couldn't make liquor, you couldn't sell liquor, and you couldn't transport liquor within America's borders. But that didn't stop many people from drinking liquor, for drinking in itself was not illegal. Indeed, many Americans not only made the easy move from saloon to speakeasy, they developed an almost entirely new national habit—drinking at home. Nothing prevented the trip from cup to lip; the trick was to fill the cup in the first place.

California vintners, with a little guidance from a former assistant attorney general, produced and marketed a perfectly legal grape juice, which after 60 days of loving home fermentation became a tasty wine with a 15-percent alcohol content. The winemakers were so successful that grape acreage in America increased sevenfold, from less than 100,000 acres in 1919 to nearly 700,000 by 1926. Before Prohibition ended, grape growing expanded even further, spurred by government loans.

Not to be outdone, beer barons offered wort, a half-brewed beer that contained no alcohol. With a little yeast and patience, the beverage could be nursed into producing its other, better half.

And the fun wasn't just in the drinking, it was in the fixing. For about $7 and a trip to the local hardware store, anyone with technological imagination could become the proud possessor of a personal still. Information on how to use the devices abounded in books and magazines; there was even a handy government pamphlet. Then, with a few potatoes, or some apples, barley, or oats, the do-it-yourselfer was ready to engage in one of our forefathers' most dearly cherished traditions—breaking a silly law. Bottoms up!

The hefty matron above is just reaching for her medicine. During Prohibition more than a million gallons of alcohol were prescribed annually for "medicinal purposes."

When the smirking smuggler at left lifts her skirt (above), it's easy to see she's taken bootlegging to new heights.

Monkey Business

Teacher John Scopes was recruited for the famous trial

Twenty-four-year-old John Scopes, above (who coincidentally had attended the same Illinois high school as his prosecutor, William Jennings Bryan), had only substituted in the biology class at Dayton's high school. He later told *Life* magazine: "I doubt very much that I taught... evolution. ... I never took the stand... because I really didn't know very much about evolution."

It began on a May afternoon in 1925 in Robinson's Drugstore in Dayton, Tennessee. Local businessman George Rappelyea argued that the state's new law—which made it a crime to teach Darwin's theory of evolution in the public schools because it challenged the biblical account of creation—offered Dayton a rare opportunity. The American Civil Liberties Union (ACLU) had offered to defend anyone willing to be prosecuted to test the law's violation of freedom of speech. Why shouldn't Dayton profit from the publicity? The drugstore group asked John Scopes, a science teacher in the local high school, to become the defendant. Dayton and Darwin were about to get their day in court.

The "Monkey Trial" captured the public's imagination, as reports were flashed across the country in the first-ever radio broadcast of a trial. The prosecution team, gathered by the World's Christian Fundamentals Association, was headed by William Jennings Bryan, three-time presidential candidate, former secretary of state, and outspoken advocate of fundamentalist teachings. For the defense, the ACLU had retained Clarence Darrow, one of the century's outstanding legal minds and a self-confessed agnostic. In the press, it was a clash of titans; in reality, it was a contest between aging crusaders who had often championed the same liberal causes. Darrow had supported Bryan for president, and their mutual respect was deep.

The judge ruled that evolution was not on trial; the question was simply whether Scopes had broken the law by *teaching* evolution. Unable to call scientists as witnesses, a frustrated Darrow called Bryan himself, citing him as an authority on the Bible. At first Bryan parried eloquently, but as Darrow pressed, Bryan became increasingly confused and finally drew laughter from the largely fundamentalist audience.

In the end Scopes was fined $100. The ACLU received national publicity, but failed to get a clear victory; even when the Tennessee Supreme Court overturned the conviction on a technicality, it upheld the anti-evolution law. William Jennings Bryan never left Dayton. Five days after the trial, he took a nap and didn't wake up.

Little Orphan Otto

In 1924 an aspiring cartoonist named Harold Gray took an idea for a new comic strip to Capt. J. M. Patterson, founder of the New York Daily News. *Gray called the strip "Little Orphan Otto." But 40 other strips of the time starred boys, and besides, Patterson thought Otto looked a little effeminate. The paper often reprinted a poem by James Whitcomb Riley called "Little Orphan Annie." "Put skirts on the kid and call her Orphan Annie," Patterson reputedly said. Gray did, and a classic comic strip was born. Gray drew the strip personally until his death 44 years later.*

Here She Is—The First Miss America!

Margaret Gorman, a 16-year-old schoolgirl, was the first to win the title that American beauties still dream of. Merchants started the pageant in 1921 to keep tourists in Atlantic City after Labor Day, and a local reporter coined the magic phrase Miss America. As Miss Washington, D.C., Margaret vied with other "civic beauties"—all clad in short wool bathing dresses—for the newly created crown. Her trophy was a golden statue of a mermaid. Returning as Queen of the Pageant (left) to compete in the even bigger 1922 contest, she lost to Miss Columbus, Ohio. In 1923 she tried again, this time wearing a tank suit. Then she went home and married a real estate agent.

Edifice Complex

The world's tallest building! In the 1920's, as modern skyscrapers began to dominate the silhouette of urban America, the race was on. By 1930 New York could boast of the sleek 1,046-foot Chrysler Building. Its ornamental spire atop an art deco dome made it the record-breaker—but not for long. Not far away, the Empire State Building was rising at the astounding rate of 4½ stories a week. Though originally planned for 1,050 feet, a 200-foot mooring mast was added for dirigibles (right). But the builders soon recognized its disaster potential, and the mast gave way to a tower with a second observation deck. Completed in 1931, the 102-story edifice truly scraped the sky, for at 1,250 feet it was the tallest building in the world—and remained so for 42 years.

The Stained Glass Glory of Sport

The world's largest Gothic cathedral, St. John the Divine in New York City, boasts a stained glass window (panels above and right) featuring a baseball player, a bowler, a cyclist, and many other sports figures. The intricately crafted display was the inspiration of the daughter of the Episcopal bishop of New York. Fascinated by the 1924 Olympic Games, she persuaded her father to devote an entire window to the "glory of sport." To help raise funds, famed sportswriter Grantland Rice wrote: "One of the main objects of both [sports and religion] is to build up the spirit of fair play, square dealing, and clean living." The original secular design was later changed: modern sports figures were relegated to a small area, and such biblical athletes as Samson and Elijah took center stage. The window, dedicated to Saint Hubert, the patron of hunting, was finally installed in 1951.

"What—Me Worry?"

An ad for a Topeka clinic that employed an army of itinerant toothpullers (above) was familiar to Kansans of the 1920's, for the grinning lad had appeared in other ads as a cowboy and as a salesman for shoes and soft drinks. Rediscovered after years of obscurity, he became known far and wide as Alfred E. Neuman, Mad *magazine's cover boy. By 1956 the monthly was touting him as a write-in presidential candidate. He lost.*

Deathwatch Carnival, 1925

Slowly freezing to death in a Kentucky cave, Floyd Collins inspired a media circus

A carnival mood surrounded attempts to free Floyd Collins, pictured at top exploring a different cave.

"Maddox, get me out. . . . Why don't you take me out? . . . Kiss me good-bye, I'm going." Floyd Collins was delirious. For five days he'd been trapped 125 feet underground in a space 8 inches high and 12 feet long. The temperature was 16°F, and water from melting mud and slime dripped constantly on his head. Up above, a raucous crowd of curiosity seekers made for a circus atmosphere.

This wasn't Collins's first trip into a cave. Eight years earlier he had found a cavern beneath his family's farm and had turned it into a tourist attraction. Now he was in Sand Cave, on another farmer's land, hoping to make his fortune. He would get half the rights to anything he found.

Collins was headed back out when his lantern failed. As he crawled on in the darkness, his foot hit a seven-ton boulder. It fell on his left leg. He was trapped, unable to turn or move in the "coffin-like straitjacket" of a dank subterranean hell.

Tourist attraction

Collins's brothers and friends tried to rescue him, but couldn't. Then an eager 19-year-old reporter named "Skeets" Miller crawled into the cave for an interview; he didn't help the trapped spelunker, but a Louisville newspaper picked up the dramatic story (Miller later won the Pulitzer Prize for it), and a national obsession was born. Fifty reporters from 16 cities converged on Sand Cave, along with film crews from six studios. Regular bulletins on the new medium of radio kept the nation apprised of rescue efforts. Over the next two weeks, some 50,000 tourists bought hot dogs, balloons, and soft drinks from vendors around the cave mouth. One weekend 4,500 cars from 20 states transformed the road to the cave into an eight-mile traffic jam. Con men and concessionaires began working the crowd. Women sent letters proposing marriage; one offered to crawl into the cave for the ceremony. Agents tried to book Collins for vaudeville tours.

Meanwhile Floyd Collins was dying, and rescue attempts were in chaos. A fireman proposed pulling his leg off. A college president offered to send in the school's basketball team. On the sixth day, Collins's old business partner led 10 men into the cave, among them Everett Maddox, a tough young miner, who gave Collins his last meal.

When the entrance passage collapsed, experts began tunneling down from above. On February 16 they found Collins's corpse. Doctors estimated that he had died one to three days earlier, after two weeks of pain, terror, and freezing cold.

Collins's body was put on display in a partially glass coffin at the cave on his father's land. In 1929 the corpse was stolen. When it was found nearby, one of the legs was missing.

Celebrating a Bright Idea

The Golden Jubilee of Edison's most famous invention had its problems

It was half a century since Thomas Edison had changed the world's night life by inventing the light bulb, and America wanted to honor the grand old man. General Electric Company officials, seeing a golden opportunity for corporate image-building, hired Edward Bernays, a pioneer of public relations, to create a gala anniversary celebration at their headquarters.

Edison was hesitant; he didn't want to be exploited by the company. Word reached Henry Ford, one of Edison's biggest fans, and a battle for control erupted, with Ford vowing to stop the "shameful action." Finally, they reached a compromise: GE would take part in the venture, scheduled for October 21, 1929, but it would be held at Ford's Michigan reconstruction of Menlo Park, the New Jersey village where Edison had invented the incandescent bulb.

The birth of public relations

Then Edward Bernays got down to work: George M. Cohan composed a theme song, "Thomas Edison, Miracle Man"; the U.S. government issued a commemorative stamp; prominent figures, including President Herbert Hoover, were invited to take part.

Ford had his own grandiose ideas. Deciding that Independence Hall would be a fine setting for the ceremony, he tried to buy the historic building from Philadelphia and move it to Michigan. The city fathers wouldn't sell, so he commissioned a replica. Inside he built an Industrial Museum, filled with memorabilia from the age that Edison's invention had brought to an end. Arriving for the observance, the frail 82-year-old inventor was impressed, but his wife dismissed the project as a "plaything for Mr. Ford."

The bubble bursts

That evening 144 radio stations, the largest hookup in history, broadcast the reenactment of the moment of invention. Later that night, after giving a short speech, Edison collapsed from exhaustion. Within a week, the stock market crash smothered Bernays's carefully crafted public euphoria.

Bernays recalled the event as a boon for public relations, when "ballyhoo artists" gained new stature. It's difficult to separate fact from fabrication here—but isn't that what public relations is about?

Wrong date

Recent studies of notes from Edison's lab reveal that October 21, 1879, was relatively uneventful. It was the *next* day that Edison managed to get an incandescent bulb to burn for 13½ hours. Nonetheless, ever since the Golden Jubilee of Light, the 21st has been regarded as the landmark date. Edison died on October 18, 1931, and was buried on the 21st, exactly two years after the jubilee. At 9:59 P.M. lights all over America were extinguished in a one-minute memorial.

Thomas Edison (right) and his assistant Francis Jehl reenacted the invention of the incandescent bulb.

Hard Times and Wartime

The Battle of Anacostia Flats *The Bonus March on Washington ended in violence*

June 17, 1932, was, according to one Washington newspaper, "the tensest day in the capital since the War." It was the depths of the Depression, and some 10,000 desperate World War I veterans were massed on the Capitol grounds. Across the Anacostia River, living in huts made of materials "dragged out of the big junk pile on the hill above the camp," were another 10,000, including wives and children. The Senate was voting on a bill, already passed by the House, to give every vet his war bonus. The bonus ($1.25 for each day overseas and $1 for every stateside day) had been awarded in 1924 but was not to be paid until 1945. The vets needed it *now* and had swarmed to Washington to demand it.

It was after dark when Walter Waters, leader of the so-called Bonus Expeditionary Force, emerged from the Capitol. "Prepare yourselves for a disappointment, men," he said. "The bonus has been defeated, 62 to 18." Stunned, the ragged throng stood silent.

"Sing 'America,' " Waters shouted, "and go back to your billets!" Heads bared, the men sang out.

Few left Washington. They'd already been in the city nearly three weeks, camped at some 20 different sites, including half-demolished government buildings, and they planned to stay. President Hoover refused to meet with them. Congress set aside $100,000 to transport them anywhere they wished to go. Some 500 left; 1,000 more arrived. A silent, single-file "death march" began in front of the Capitol and lasted until July 16, when 17,000 gathered to watch Congress adjourn.

Still the bonus marchers stayed on, and the authorities grew increasingly nervous. Finally, at 1:45 P.M. on July 28—two full months after the peaceful demonstration had begun—the spark of violence was struck. The police, ordered to clear the government buildings, met with resistance. Two of them opened fire, killing two men. By 4:45 P.M. an infantry battalion, a tank platoon, and a squadron of cavalry were on the scene. In charge was Gen. Douglas MacArthur; his liaison with the police was Maj. Dwight D. Eisenhower; commanding the cavalry was Maj. George S. Patton, Jr.

Militarily speaking, the operation was clean and swift. The infantry fixed bayonets. The cavalry, deployed along the north side of Pennsylvania Avenue, drew their sabers and charged the crowd. "Men, women and children fled shrieking across the broken ground," reported the United Press, "falling into excavations as they strove to avoid the rearing hoofs and saber points. Meantime, infantry on the south side had adjusted gas masks and were hurling tear gas bombs into the block into which they had just driven the veterans."

Within four hours, most bonus camps had been set afire, and the veterans had been driven across the 11th Street Bridge to the huge camp on the Anacostia Flats. By midnight those hovels, too, were ablaze. Around 4 A.M., as a light rain fell, the bonus marchers were forced across the Maryland border. They were told to keep moving to Pennsylvania.

Attorney General William Mitchell called the bonus marchers (left) "the largest aggregation of criminals ever assembled in the city at one time." In fact, Washington's crime rate dropped during their two-month encampment.

Shipwreck Kelly

A flagpole sitter's comedown

"Flagpole sitting ain't what it used to be," lamented Shipwreck Kelly, the master of the craft. "I thought I had a Depression-proof business, but I know better now."

Shipwreck had climbed his first pole for pay in 1924, to publicize a movie. He was soon a star. In 1930, after spending 49 days atop a pole at the Steel Pier in Atlantic City, he descended to the cheers of some 20,000 admirers.

But the rage faded as the Depression settled in. By 1934 Shipwreck was reduced to such stunts as trying to plunge off the George Washington Bridge on a greased rope (the police stopped him). When he died broke on the street in 1952, he was identified by the faded press clippings in his coat.

Defying superstition, Alvin "Shipwreck" Kelly spent Friday, the 13th of October, 1939, eating doughnuts while standing on his head on a plank atop New York City's 56-story Chanin Building. He was probably 54 but claimed to be younger.

Star Light, Star Bright

Lighting up two world's fairs

They called it the Century of Progress Exposition. The 1933 world's fair, marking Chicago's 100th birthday, was supposed to brighten the gloom of the Depression, and its organizers needed a spectacular opening.

They looked to the stars. Arcturus, one of the closest, was 40 light-years away. Thus light that had left it during the first Chicago exposition in 1893 would shine on the new fair. They would use that light!

The world's largest refracting telescope, at Yerkes Observatory in Wisconsin, caught the ray of starlight and focused it onto a photoelectric cell, which measured its energy and transformed it into the current needed to throw a switch at the fairgrounds. As a huge crowd watched, a red glow ran across an illuminated map high above the rostrum in the Hall of Science. Reaching Chicago, it burst into a flashing star. The switch was tripped and a great white beam shot out from a searchlight atop the hall. As it touched one exposition building after another, they were thrown into brilliant light. And the fair was on.

The power of Electra the Eel (above) was harnessed to open the 1939 world's fair in Flushing Meadows, New York.

Hobo Nickels

It was a unique American folk art. Using a knife and chisel, a hobo would rework the Indian's profile on a nickel into the portrait of a clown, a famous figure, a customer, or another hobo; then he'd trade the medallions (right) for food, clothing, or tobacco. In election years, nickel carvers did well turning the buffalo on the back of the coin into an elephant or a donkey. The most prolific of these craftsmen, George Washington "Bo" Hughes, turned out thousands of hobo nickels, including self-portraits and portraits of his lover, Monique (center, bottom).

A Modest Beginning

Happy to have jobs in 1931, New York City workmen put up a 12-foot Christmas tree amid the rubble of demolished brownstones on the future site of Rockefeller Center (right; St. Patrick's Cathedral is in the background). For decorations they used tin cans, paper, and tinsel. Two years later the first official tree was festooned with 700 blue and white lights. The tradition, now grown to a nationally televised spectacular, has been observed ever since.

War Fare

Minnesota meatpacker George Hormel perfected a new product in 1937. Made of pork shoulder, ham, salt, water, sugar, and sodium nitrate, it needed a name. George offered a $100 reward. The winner was the brother of a company executive, and with the help of a high-powered ad campaign (left), an American phenomenon was born.

But it was during World War II that Spam really came into its own. "Without Spam," Nikita Khrushchev later wrote, "we wouldn't have been able to feed our army."

"I ate my share of Spam along with millions of other soldiers," Dwight D. Eisenhower once said. "I will even confess to a few unkind words about it."

Round-trip or One-way?

Sell shaving cream with little roadside signs? Ad men scoffed, but Leonard Odell did it anyway. And so generations of Americans spent happy hours watching for such lighthearted jingles as the 1930 rhyme above. In 1936 a set of signs offered FREE! FREE! / A TRIP / TO MARS / FOR 900 / EMPTY JARS. Supermarket manager Arliss French collected jars from customers and demanded his trip. After lengthy, well-publicized negotiations, conducted in rhyming telegrams, the company sent him—wearing a bubble helmet and a silvery spacesuit—to Moers (pronounced "mars"), a tiny town near Düsseldorf, Germany.

Rosie the Riveter

To ease the labor shortage created by World War II, the U.S. Office of War Information encouraged housewives to don overalls and snoods and go to work in factories. Norman Rockwell's Rosie the Riveter became the symbol of the home front. Rosie's face was female: the model who sat for Rockwell was telephone operator Mary Doyle of Arlington, Vermont. But her husky body was decidedly male—the artist based it on Michelangelo's "Isaiah the Prophet." After the war, although surveys showed that up to 80 percent of the Rosies wanted to keep their jobs, they were nudged back home.

The photograph at left was taken in Oklahoma in the mid-1930's by Arthur Rothstein as part of a Farm Security Administration project. Despite the hardship such photos depicted, they reminded project director Roy Stryker of the courageous words from John Steinbeck's The Grapes of Wrath: *"We ain't gonna die out. People is goin' on."*

Black Blizzards *In the dark days of the Depression, nature dealt a savage blow*

Sunday, April 14, 1935, started as a beautiful day on the southern plains. From southeastern Colorado clear across the Oklahoma panhandle, farm families enjoyed the fresh spring air as they went hopefully to church, praying for rain for their parched land. They had no idea that a windstorm was moving in from the Dakotas, lifting the powdery soil and swirling it into a 1,000-foot-high cloud—a blizzard of black dust and muddy rain hundreds of miles wide.

Suffocation

With winds of 60 m.p.h., the storm moved quickly, engulfing whole towns in total darkness by early afternoon. Motorists were stranded on highways; farmers were unable to find their way home across familiar fields; families cowered in houses, watching the dust pack so thickly against windows it seemed that they were being entombed. People caught outside covered their faces with cloth, terrified that the air would become too thick to breathe. Just a year earlier, a small boy had suffocated in a Kansas dust storm on his way home from school, and such deaths were only slightly more gruesome than those from "dust pneumonia," the slow accumulation of particles in the lungs caused by months of breathing the dusty air.

Not the first

Though probably the worst storm to sweep the Dust Bowl—an area more than twice the size of Pennsylvania, roughly centered where Colorado, New Mexico, Texas, Oklahoma, and Kansas meet—it certainly wasn't the first. Cycles of severe drought had ravaged the region since the end of the Ice Age some 10,000 years ago. The dry spells of the 19th and early 20th centuries had ruined farms and driven settlers from the area. But back then farms were small and not much land was cultivated. Consequently, the dust storms were limited. The 1920's, however, had brought rain, new farming technology, and an influx of investors. Millions upon millions of acres of sod were plowed and planted. When the drought returned in 1931, crops failed and there was nothing to hold the vast expanses of loose soil against the blowing winds. The result was disaster, as nature added her own plague to the despair and financial failure of the Great Depression.

500 miles at sea

On January 21, 1933, the first great cloud of dust swept across the treeless plains, seeming to swallow up the sun itself. Drifting dust from one storm even settled on the president's desk in Washington and was reported by ships 500 miles out to sea. In 1935 alone the winds took an estimated 850 million tons of topsoil. And dust wasn't the only problem. Hailstones the size of baseballs rained down so hard that they killed livestock and smashed through the hoods of cars.

By the time the drought ended in 1940, the Dust Bowl had lost one-third of its population. Only concern for the land's needs and careful soil management keep disaster from happening again.

"Some May Say That I Couldn't Sing, But No One Can Say That I Didn't"

Her voice was ghastly, her self-designed costumes outrageous, and her concerts ridiculous. But Florence Foster Jenkins (left) made audiences cheer. The wealthy heiress was 75 years old when she rented Carnegie Hall for a concert on October 25, 1944. The sold-out performance climaxed in a lively Spanish melody, during which she coyly threw flowers to the audience. The crowd demanded an encore. Out of flowers, she sent her accompanist, Cosme McMoon, to retrieve them, and did it all over again. "She only thought of making other people happy," according to a friend—and she succeeded magnificently. The wild applause that greeted her performances was genuine, and her record album is today a collector's item.

The Voice of the Men Who Do the Dying *Ernie Pyle, the GI's reporter*

During the battle for Cherbourg in World War II, the crew of an American tank, hit by a German shell, scrambled to a nearby doorway for cover. There they met a small, balding man with sad eyes, who was also ducking bullets. They asked for his autograph.

That wasn't unusual. The man was Ernie Pyle, the GI's reporter. He shared the fears, the pain, and the suffering of the men "who do the dying." And in his column, which ran in 700 publications with a combined circulation of 14 million, he made sure that the folks back home knew exactly what their fighting men were really going through.

Pyle, who described himself as a "talker to obscure people," took no notes for his stories—except the names and addresses of the men he spoke with. By 1945 he was earning a six-figure income. But he couldn't desert the men whose stories needed telling; so he headed to the Pacific for the invasion of Okinawa. On April 18, hit by Japanese machine-gun fire on Ie Shima, he died instantly. He was 44.

Ernie Pyle (third from left, with a patrol on Okinawa) wrote with the poignant, personal immediacy of letters home: "It's the perpetual choking dust, the muscle-racking hard ground, the snatched food sitting ill on the stomach, and heat and flies and dirty feet and the constant roar of engines and the perpetual moving and the never settling down and the go, go, go, night and day, and on through the night again. Eventually it all works itself into an emotional tapestry of one dull, dead patter—yesterday is tomorrow and Troina is Randazzo and when will we ever stop and, God, I'm so tired."

Bombshells

The birth of the bikini and the end of the world

This is no cover-up, just the bare facts in brief. Two-piece bathing suits started appearing on the French Riviera in 1945. These weren't true bikinis, simply trunks and tops that left a band of midriff revealed. Some GI's brought the suits home to their wives and girlfriends, who were promptly thrown off local beaches. It wasn't until the summers of 1947 and 1948 that the two-piece style, even in this more modest version, caught on in the United States.

The true bikini—two tiny cloth triangles joined at the hips, and a bra too brief to bear much more than description—was designed by French couturier Jacques Heim, a pioneer in bare-midriff fashions in the 1930's, who based his styles on the sultry wear of Polynesian maidens. He revealed his new revealer amid great media hoopla at a Parisian swimming pool on July 5, 1946, and called it "*atome*—the world's smallest bathing suit."

Bikini Atoll

Just four days earlier, the United States had exploded an atomic bomb over a tiny Pacific island called Bikini Atoll. Throughout the early summer there had been rumors in Paris that this would be a "superbomb," and hostesses started throwing "end-of-the-world" and "Bikini" parties; so Heim's own explosive little atom came quite naturally to be dubbed a bikini by his competitors.

Modest as that first bikini seems today, it must have been pretty skimpy by 1940's standards. Micheline Bernardini, the young woman who modeled the suit, was an experienced stage performer; but she admitted being nervous about wearing the bikini "out in the open" that July day at the pool. "All I remember are the hundreds of journalists all around me, the photographers and flashbulbs," she reminisced in 1970. "I didn't know anymore where I was. I was swimming in the air."

Despite the suit's explosive reception, it certainly wasn't new. Mosaics from the third and fourth centuries depict woman gymnasts in Roman Sicily wearing garments of much the same style.

The bikini was an immediate craze in Europe. But the suit was frowned on in America until well into the 1960's; it wasn't even manufactured in this country until 1959. Perhaps the reason was the same that *Webster's Third New International Dictionary* gives for the name of the suit: "from the comparision of the effects wrought by a scantily clad woman to the effects of an atomic bomb."

Sputtering Before Sputnik

The space age began on October 4, 1957, when the Soviet Union blasted a 184-pound artificial satellite called Sputnik *into orbit. Foremost among those singed by the rocket's afterburners was Dr. Wernher von Braun, a German scientist who had immigrated to the United States after World War II. He could have been first.*

For three years before Sputnik, *Von Braun had tried to convince the Eisenhower administration that his research team's* Redstone *missile could put a satellite into orbit. In 1956 he had even demonstrated its potential, blasting a* Redstone *some 3,000 miles out over the Atlantic to a height of 600 miles. Had the rocket carried additional fuel instead of sand in its upper stages, it could have achieved orbit. But Von Braun's pleas for space exploration were ignored by Washington budget makers, lost amid demands for military rockets. Then came* Sputnik*—and the space race was on.*

Eerie Evenings

Did UFO's buzz HST?

Twice in the summer of 1952, UFO's were picked up on radar screens at Washington's National Airport and Andrews Air Force Base. They seemed to be buzzing the White House and the Capitol.

Near midnight on July 19, flight controllers at National saw "seven pips" clustered together in one corner of the radar screen. They would "loaf along" at 100 to 130 m.p.h., then suddenly accelerate

On July 1, 1946, the United States dropped a 20-kiloton atomic bomb on the deserted Bikini Atoll in the Marshall Islands in the Pacific. The huge blast (above), part of a test of nuclear weapons, blew the socks off Pentagon brass and—as revealed by model Micheline Bernardini (above, left)—had an even more devastating effect on fashion in Paris.

to fantastic speeds—as much as 7,200 m.p.h.—before vanishing. Andrews radar technicians observed blips too, and airline pilots saw bright lights in the sky. But when air force jets investigated at dawn, the lights had disappeared.

The press swarmed the Pentagon. Intelligence officers blamed temperature inversions, but experienced air traffic controllers asserted that the blips represented substantial objects. How else could radar have detected them?

Later that week amber lights were seen elsewhere in the sky, including over the Guided Missile Long-Range Proving Ground in Florida. Then on the 26th more blips appeared on a Washington radar screen. A jet sent in pursuit couldn't even get close. Three days later the air force called a press conference, its "largest and longest" since World War II. Officially, the UFO's were debunked as a weather phenomenon. Nonetheless, the eerie sightings remained a mystery to many.

Flying saucers were reported over the White House during Harry S Truman's last year of occupancy.

Birth of the Frisbee

A champion's collection (left) pays homage to the space-age toy for all ages that owes its discovery to the West Coast and its name to the East Coast. The California-based Wham-O Company liked Frederick Morrison's Flying Saucer, struck a deal, and in 1957 started mass-producing the plastic disc. On a cross-country promotion trip, a Wham-O executive discovered that truck drivers for the Frisbie Pie Company of Connecticut had inspired Yale students to twirl pie tins (above) through the air. He adapted the name for the plastic version, and the updated 19th-century pie tin whirled into the 20th century.

Atomic Age Hits the Fairway

In 1950 scientists perfected a product with the new-age sportsman in mind: a golf ball containing radioactive material. With a small Geiger counter even a pint-size caddy could carry, any duffer could find his atomic golf ball, no matter how far into the rough it had disappeared. (The investment would pay for itself in retrieved balls.) B. F. Goodrich Co. demonstrated this peacetime use of atomic energy (right), but did not go into production. And no other company picked up the ball.

Contest-Winning Columnist

How did Esther Lederer become Ann Landers? A newspaper ran a contest in 1955, and the Chicago housewife won. Her snappy writing and down-to-earth personal advice soon became a favorite of more than 85 million readers. Once she asked readers if they'd be content to forgo sex in favor of cuddling and tender treatment. An avalanche of replies (below) gave her the answer: a resounding yes!

CINZANO
DRAMATIC EDSEL STYLING leads the way
—in distinction, in beauty, in value!
Less than fifty dollars between Edsel and V-8's of the major low-priced makes

The Day They Shook the Lemon Tree

When Vice President Richard Nixon used an Edsel on a visit to Peru in 1958 (left), his diplomatic mission shared a dubious distinction with the car he rode in: both failed.

"Retail sales have been particularly disappointing, and continued production of the Edsel is not justified." With these words, the Ford Motor Company announced in 1959 that, after two dismal years, it would stop making the car with the distinctive grill. Thus the full-size Edsel, which had cost $250 million to produce and had been launched (inset) with great fanfare—just when the public was clamoring for smaller cars—became the automotive industry's most famous lemon.

A Splice of Life

Each spring La Crosse, Kansas, becomes a carnival as contestants vie to be named the world's best barbed wire splicer. There, in the Barbed Wire Capital of the World, enthusiasts gather to swap wire, to admire the 500-plus varieties displayed at the local Barbed Wire Museum, and, of course, to enter the splicing competition. When the first barbed wire appeared in 1873, it solved a major problem for farmers and cattlemen: animal breakthroughs. But even barbed wire snaps, and a new piece has to be spliced into the gap. The contest highlights the annual get-together: an entrant (right) wears gloves, uses no tools, and races against the clock. The finished splice is tested for strength and sag, and the winner garners a cherished title: Champion Splicer of the World.

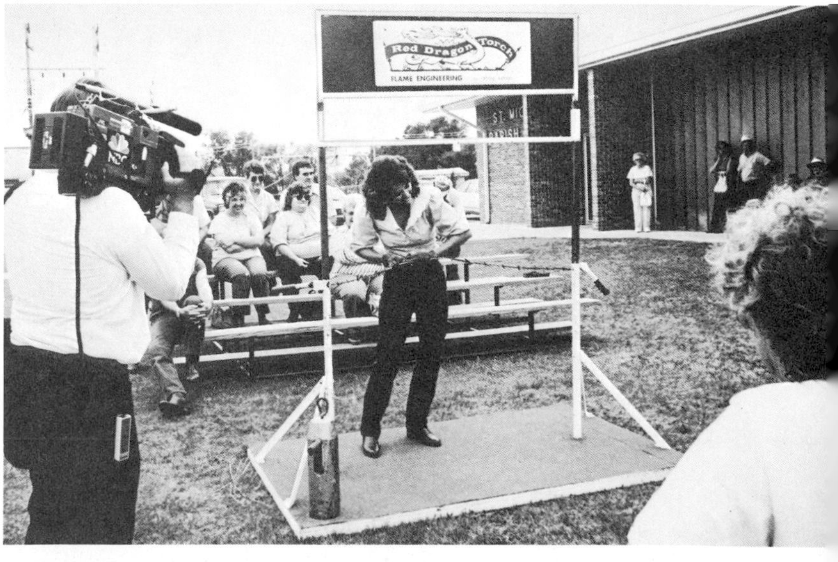
Red Dragon Torch
FLAME ENGINEERING

Animal Decency

A well-dressed horse? Of course!

"Naked animals everywhere! They are on the streets and sidewalks—a public disgrace to our children—and along the highways, causing accidents as motorists take their eyes off the road to watch nude cows and bulls. And these animals are not grazing—they are hanging their heads in shame!"

So proclaimed G. Clifford Prout, Jr., president of the Society for Indecency to Naked Animals (SINA). "It should have been the Society Against Indecency to Naked Animals," he noted, but his father was "not quite of sound mind when he drew up the will." That document bequeathed $400,000 for the purpose of clothing animals everywhere, a longtime family cause. (Prout's grandfather, who fought in the Civil War "against the North *and* the South," had delayed Pickett's Charge as he tried to convince officers to clothe their horses.)

Clifford Prout publicized his cause on television and in newspaper articles featuring photos of well-clad animals. By 1963 the four-year-old SINA claimed a membership of 50,000, and its telephone (the number was MOrality 1-1963) rang constantly. Critics, of course, abounded. Wrote one: "Imagine the dog who couldn't scratch his fleas or the cat that wished to bathe herself."

It was an activist crusade. SINA supplied sympathizers with "summonses" to be issued "for appearing in public with a naked dog, cat, horse, cow, or any domestic animal." The Greyhound Bus Lines was threatened with a boycott for firing a SINA member who painted trousers on the corporate symbol. And Prout demanded that RCA's trademark dog, famous for listening to His Master's Voice, be decently covered.

Not even the First Lady was exempt from SINA's campaign. Demonstrators picketed the White House, insisting that Mrs. Kennedy clothe her horse before riding it.

But then, during a television interview, a CBS employee recognized the SINA leader as Buck Henry, a comedy writer. The truth was revealed: SINA was a hoax, the brainchild of social satirist and professional put-on artist Alan Abel. Henry would go on to stage, screen, and television fame, and Abel to such hoaxes as promoting the Sex Olympics, landing a Martian on Long Island, and writing his own premature obituary (printed in *The New York Times*). But he will probably be best remembered for getting people to put pants on pets.

The First Presidential UFO Sighting

Just after dark on a clear evening in January 1969, several members of the Lions Club of Leary, Georgia, had gathered outdoors before a meeting. Suddenly, a UFO appeared on the horizon. What was unusual about this sighting was that one of the witnesses was a future president: Jimmy Carter.

Carter, the scheduled speaker, wrote in his official report that an object "at one time, as bright as the moon" was sighted in the western sky. The men watched the phenomenon for about 10 minutes. It "seemed to move toward us from a distance," Carter continued, then it eventually departed. He described it as "bluish at first, then reddish, luminous, not solid."

Although later investigation concluded that it was probably the planet Venus (a common mistake in UFO sightings), Carter subsequently declared: "I'll never make fun of people who say they've seen unidentified objects in the sky."

Striding Into the Future *Man walks on the moon*

While some 500 million people watched breathlessly, Neil Armstrong stepped out of his lunar module on July 20, 1969, at 10:56 P.M. EDT. Taking man's first moon walk, he said: "That's one small step for a man, one giant leap for mankind." (Static rendered the word *a* practically inaudible.)

Although Armstrong was the first man to *walk* on the moon, *two* astronauts landed in the module—the other was Buzz Aldrin. He said he was enraptured by the moon's "magnificent desolation."

As Aldrin and Armstrong prepared for the long voyage home, one of their backpacks broke the switch that controlled their module's ascent to the *Apollo 11.* Without some old-fashioned ingenuity, they'd have been stuck there. Inserting a specially designed zero-gravity pen into the broken switch, they managed to flip it—and came back alive!

Future moon walkers will find some mementos left by the astronauts: a piece of the *Kitty Hawk,* flown by the Wright brothers in 1903; a disc with messages from 73 important earthlings; and a memorial honoring the three Americans and two Russians who lost their lives in the space race.

The astronauts' return was "the strangest hero's welcome ever." Since no one knew if they were contaminated, they were relegated to a quarantine trailer for 21 days. To add insult to injury, not only did they fail to receive hugs and handshakes when they arrived on the U.S.S. *Hornet,* but a man followed them around with a spray can of bug-killer.

One of the most unassuming reactions came from Michael Collins, young son of the astronaut who stayed in the spacecraft while the others landed on the moon. When asked what he thought of his father's place in history, he considered it for a moment and asked: "What is history, anyway?"

Fact (left) and fantasy (below): Astonishing similarities abound between Apollo 11*'s 1969 moon mission and Jules Verne's 1865 novel* From the Earth to the Moon. *Like the modern* Columbia, *Verne's spaceship, the* Columbiad, *blasted off from central Florida with a three-man crew, used retro-rockets for descent to the moon, and returned with a splash in the Pacific.*

CHAPTER SEVEN

The Long Frontier

It began when the first European landed on the shore of a wilderness continent, and it continues to this day—part and parcel of our national heritage. It is the adventure of exploring new territory; of blazing a trail and braving the unknown; of being the first to navigate a river, to cross a desert, to climb a mountain, to till a plot of land, to settle a town, to fly the ocean . . . to walk on the moon. It is the frontier, always and still the driving pulse of America.

Posing for a prairie photographer (Custer County, Nebraska, 1886)

The Vikings: Norse sagas tell of Leif Erikson's voyage in A.D. 1000 to a place he called Vinland. There he and his men built houses and spent a winter, but further settlement ran afoul of fierce Indians. Not until 1961 was evidence unearthed proving that these Norsemen did settle in Newfoundland. Though other tales persist, it is generally accepted as the only site of pre-Columbian European contact with the New World.

The First Explorers

A tantalizing tangle of hints, but few solid answers

Who got to the New World first? The Irish? The Welsh? The Phoenicians? The Vikings? Or some other group, as yet unidentified?

In the hills of southern West Virginia are petroglyphs (rock carvings) that were long considered the work of local Indians. But lately, experts have made a convincing case that they are ancient Irish writing which could date from A.D. 500. And in New Hampshire, underground passages, stone chambers, and monoliths quarried by methods predating metal tools have led others to speculate that the Celts (or perhaps the Phoenicians) visited there an incredible 3,000 years ago. No wonder the site is called Mystery Hill.

Welsh-speaking Indians?

A frontier tale at one time gained great popularity. In 1170, so the story goes, Prince Madoc ab Owain Gwynedd sailed west with 120 settlers, landing in Mobile Bay, Alabama. The fact that Madoc *could* have made the trip—Welsh ships of the time were seaworthy—was reinforced by a 17th-century clergyman who claimed to have preached in Welsh to Tuscarora Indians. But many years later, in 1792, another clergyman was sent from Wales to investigate the legends. He found no Welsh-speaking Indians, nor did Lewis and Clark.

Yet sentimental support for the story (backed by the discovery of forts in Tennessee, Georgia, and Alabama that resemble ancient Welsh construction) is strong. In 1953 a plaque was dedicated at Fort Morgan on Mobile Bay. Its inscription: "In memory of Prince Madoc, a Welsh explorer, who landed on the shores of Mobile Bay in 1170 and left behind, with the Indians, the Welsh language."

Columbus at Sea

Things you didn't know about the great discoverer

In 1492 Columbus sailed the ocean blue in the *Pinta,* the *Niña,* and the *Santa Maria.* Everyone knows that. But everyone may be wrong.

Saucy Mary

The year is right, of course, and the *Pinta* and the *Niña* were there. But throughout his journal Columbus never called his flagship *Santa Maria,* referring to her simply as *La Capitana* ("The Flagship"). The sailors called her *La Gallega* ("The Galician") for Galicia, where she was built, but there's evidence that her real name may have been the *Mariagalante* ("saucy, or flirtatious, Mary")—later deemed unsuitable for the voyage's great achievement. (On his second trip to the New World, Columbus's flagship *was* called the *Santa Maria*, but he nicknamed her the *Mariagalante*.)

More important than the flagship's name was its maneuverability. The captains of the *Niña* and the *Pinta* often sailed ahead of the admiral, then waited for an embarrassed Columbus to catch up.

A lawsuit

One of them, Martín Alonso Pinzón, commander of the *Pinta* and a master mariner in his own right, also had dreams of being the discoverer of fabulous new lands. He died two weeks after his return, but his memory was kept alive by relatives, who maintained—in a lawsuit that dragged on until long after Columbus's death in 1506—that only Pinzón's influence, determination, and seamanship had made the discovery possible.

Columbus had come to Pinzón for help, they testified, and the two had struck a deal: everything earned by the voyage would be equally divided. It was Pinzón who replaced two of Columbus's ships with the more seaworthy *Niña* and *Pinta,* and it was he who had habitually taken the lead. Had he not encouraged Columbus with the famous *Adelante!* ("Sail on!"), the disheartened admiral would have turned back. And it was Pinzón's course correction, they insisted, that led to the first landfall.

Columbus's champions argued that it was really Pinzón who wanted to turn back: "Martín Alonso, do me this favor," Columbus begged. "Stay with me this day and night, and if I don't bring you to land before day . . . cut off my head and you shall return." Luckily, land was sighted the next day.

Competition

After the first Caribbean landfall, it had become clear that the fleet wasn't big enough for two ambitious men. While the others searched the islands for gold, Pinzón and the *Pinta* vanished for six weeks. The wayward captain later explained that he had been lured to an island called Babeque by an Indian's talk of gold. He had found none, but the side trip gave him the distinction of being the first European to sail along the shores of modern-day Haiti.

On the return voyage, Pinzón and his ship again disappeared. The admiral feared that the wanderer would return ahead of him and announce the discovery of the New World as his own, but Columbus beat him to port.

The fraudulent log

Columbus kept two logbooks, one public, the other private. Fearing the crew would panic if they knew how far they'd sailed, he entered reduced distances in the public log; but he overestimated his speed, so the phony log was actually more accurate than his own.

Columbus *was* a master sailor. Modern yachtsmen are still challenged by his times. Equally impressive was his ability to locate the same islands each time he crossed 2,500 miles of ocean.

New World Guidebook: Columbus's Journal

Much has been gleaned about Columbus's voyages from Bartolomé de Las Casas, the 16th-century priest who chronicled Spanish exploration. He told the world about hammocks ("very restful to sleep in") and tobacco. But it was the admiral himself who recorded the most vivid impressions of his surroundings on these shores so far from home. "Here the fishes are so unlike ours that it is marvellous," he wrote. "And all the trees . . . as different from ours as day from night, and so the fruits, the herbage, the rocks, and all things." His detailed descriptions set European naturalists aquiver. Among his discoveries was the delicious "pine of the Indies"—the pineapple.

Columbus's third voyage to the New World ended in disgrace. Accused of mishandling the affairs of Hispaniola, the admiral—who by this time also claimed the title of viceroy—was sent back to Spain in 1500, chained in leg irons (right) for the long trip home. Although the sovereigns did not prosecute him, it was two years before he could make his fourth and final voyage to America.

The swine De Soto took on his expedition as an ambulatory larder may also have served to protect his men from poisonous reptiles. Hogs are efficient snake killers.

A Celebration of Roast Pork

De Soto leads hogs on a wild goose chase

Power, glory, and fabulous wealth all seemed within reach for the conquistador Hernando de Soto when the king of Spain offered him the governorship of Florida (the southeastern part of the present United States) in 1537. All he had to do was to explore and settle the land—completely at his own expense. Aware that others had failed in this undertaking, he spent a year in Cuba making preparations.

In May 1539, when De Soto landed at Tampa Bay, Florida, he had with him an expeditionary force of 622 men (cavalry, footmen, and artisans), plus horses, dogs, and—as insurance against starvation—13 Spanish hogs to breed along the way.

Heading north, the Spaniards filed through a land of plenty, but they lacked skills in foraging, hunting, and fishing, and when they couldn't get food from the Indians, they were often hungry. Nevertheless De Soto, fearful of more extreme emergencies ahead, refused to allow the slaughter of pigs. When there was nothing else, the men ate dogs. In less than a year there were 300 swine, and they continued to multiply.

The expedition straggled on, periodically making month-long stops that gave piglets time to grow so they could hoof it with the rest. The squealing hogs had to be coaxed and herded through forests to keep them from straying to grub for nuts and roots. They were driven through bayous and canebrakes, hauled by block-and-tackle across streams, and transported across rivers on crude rafts.

Coming upon the Mississippi in May 1541, De Soto (the first white man to behold the great river) had the hogs ferried across. The swine traveled on to Oklahoma and then started back, as the explorer, who had found no treasure during his 4,000-mile march, bitterly acknowledged failure. In May 1542 he died, probably of malaria, and was interred in the river he had discovered. The hogs—numbering 700—were quickly auctioned off, and his men feasted on roast pork.

The Reluctant Faith Healer

How Cabeza de Vaca survived eight years in the wilderness

Knife in hand, Álvar Núñez Cabeza de Vaca knelt by the prostrate Indian and felt around his heart, where an arrowhead had lodged long ago, causing him constant suffering. Then, intoning a prayer, he made a deep cut, probed with the flint blade, removed the foreign object, and took two stitches. The "whole town came to look" at the arrowhead, and celebrations were held, recorded the Spaniard. "The next day I cut the two stitches and the Indian was well. . . . This cure gave us control throughout the country."

Cabeza de Vaca and his three companions had become medicine men out of necessity. The sole survivors of the 300-man expedition of Pánfilo de Narváez, shipwrecked off the east Texas coast in the spring of 1528, they had been wandering through a strange, unexplored land for seven years, desperately hoping to reach a Spanish outpost. They were alive only because the Indians were convinced they were sorcerers, with the ability to heal or destroy.

At first, when the Indians demanded that the four Spaniards perform as healers, they had ridiculed the idea; but when the Indians withheld food, they quickly reconsidered. "Our method was to bless the sick, breathing upon them, and recite a Pater-noster and an Ave Maria," wrote Cabeza de Vaca. They also applied whatever they knew of European medicine. Apparently the poseurs were quite successful. Grateful, the Indians treated them well, giving them food when they had scarcely enough for themselves.

As they struggled through the Southwest, trying to find their way to Mexico, news of Cabeza de Vaca's surgical feat preceded them and they were received everywhere with showers of presents: 600 hearts of deer, cotton shawls, ceremonial gourd rattles, and in the Sonora River valley, coral beads and 5 ceremonial arrowheads of emerald (probably malachite). "Whence do these come?" asked Cabeza de Vaca. "From the high mountains to the north, where are great populous cities and tall houses," the Indians replied, referring to the pueblos of the Zunis.

In the spring of 1536, the four men, who had trudged 6,000 miles, wept with joy on reaching Culiacán, a Spanish outpost in Mexico, and told their tale. Greed for gold fired the imagination of the Spaniards at Cabeza de Vaca's mention of the great cities to the north. For years to come, Coronado and others would search in vain for the Seven Cities of Cíbola, fabled for their streets of gold.

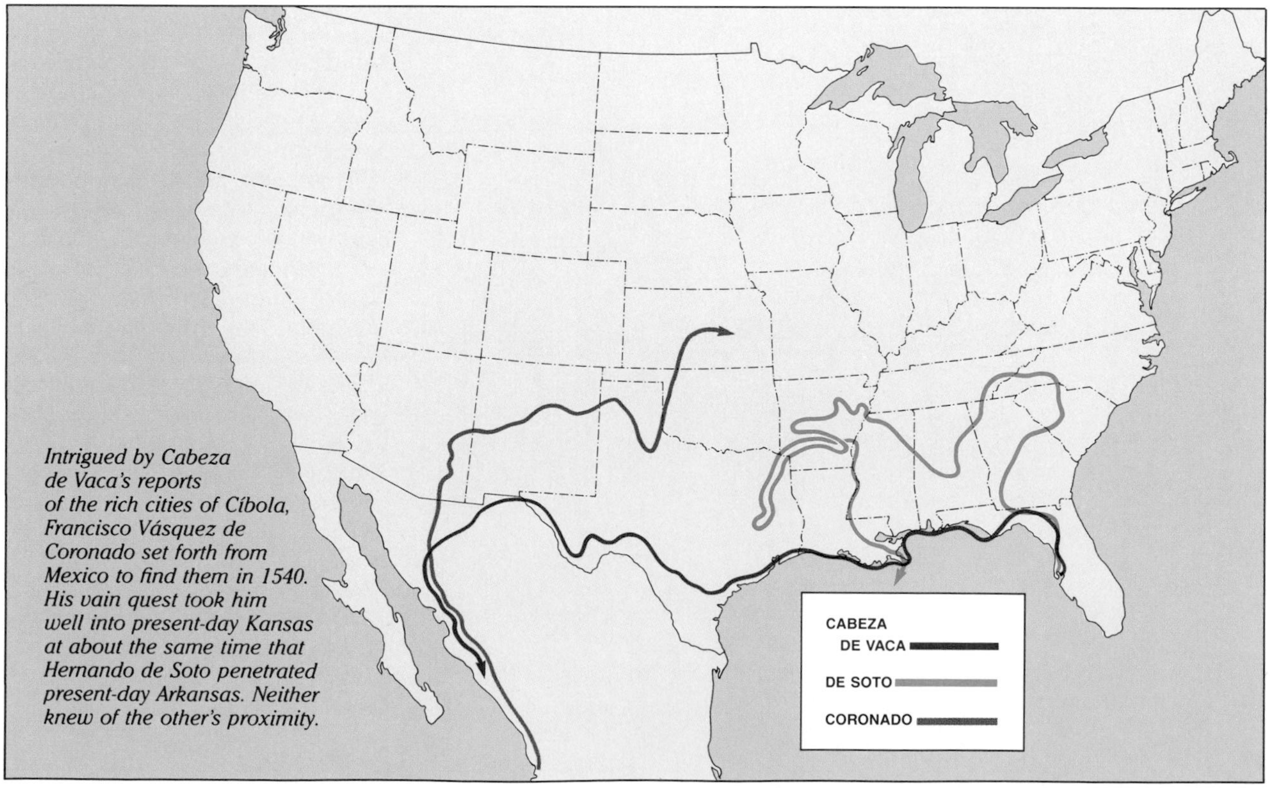

Intrigued by Cabeza de Vaca's reports of the rich cities of Cíbola, Francisco Vásquez de Coronado set forth from Mexico to find them in 1540. His vain quest took him well into present-day Kansas at about the same time that Hernando de Soto penetrated present-day Arkansas. Neither knew of the other's proximity.

The Lost Colony

They vanished in a land they hoped to conquer

One of the first serious attempts to colonize North America resulted in one of its oldest mysteries when an entire colony of 114 men, women, and children disappeared without a trace.

In midsummer 1587 the expedition, financed by Sir Walter Raleigh and led by John White, landed at Roanoke Island near Virginia on a tide of trouble. A year earlier Raleigh had established an English garrison there to protect his title to the region; the only signs of it the colonists could find were a ruined settlement and a single human skeleton. And, ominously, one man who strayed from the camp was found dead, his body abristle with 16 arrows.

Nevertheless, the new settlers remained optimistic. On August 18, 1587, Virginia Dare, White's granddaughter, became the first English child born in America. But with winter approaching and no time for planting, the colony was running out of supplies. Despite protests, White was chosen to return to England for help.

He arrived as the English were busy repelling the Spanish Armada, and was unable to return to Roanoke until 1591. There was no sign of the colonists he'd left except, carved on a tree, the letters CRO, and on a palisade post, the word CROATOAN—the name of another island where the Indians were known to be friendly. Thinking that his group had relocated there, White set out to find them, but he never did. Finally, his ship nearly destroyed by bad weather, he was forced to return to England.

Over the centuries, searches for the lost colony of Roanoke have yielded nothing but theories. Indians probably destroyed it. But what Indians, when, and how will forever remain a mystery.

John White painted birds, animals, and humans native to the New World. At left is an Indian village near Roanoke Island.

This Cruise Was No Pleasure

It set tourism back 200 years

The New World was still very new indeed when, in 1536, sea captain Richard Hore organized the first "pleasure cruise" to its shores. Tourist cruises to the Mediterranean and other warm climes were not uncommon then, though they were often disguised as pilgrimages. Hore was the first to see potential profit in the exciting prospect of visiting the newly discovered continent. Hiring two ships, he announced a sightseeing tour across the ocean. Some 120 people, including 30 gentlemen, signed on at prices designed to make Hore a rich man.

In Newfoundland one of the ships ran out of provisions, and the passengers and crew began to starve. They tried to live off the land, scavenging herbs and roots. Then one man killed another and feasted on him. Soon others began to disappear. Informed of the shocking new development, Captain Hore preached a sermon deploring cannibalism and asking everyone please to abstain from it in the future.

That night, a French ship made the mistake of wandering into the harbor; the ravenous Englishmen commandeered it for their trip home. (Henry VIII later compensated the French for the hijacked vessel.) None of the survivors was ever punished, nor did they explain why, in midsummer, they couldn't have subsisted on Newfoundland's abundant fish and game instead of each other.

Morton and His Maypole

The Puritans were not amused

Thomas Morton, an English lawyer, arrived in Massachusetts in 1625 as part of a group that settled near present-day Quincy, some 25 miles from Plymouth, where the Puritan Saints had landed five years earlier. But whereas those stern souls considered New England a "hideous and desolate wilderness, full of wild beasts and wild men," Morton saw it as a "paradise," and in his opinion the Indians were "more full of humanity than the Christians" who had preceded him.

After the leader and much of the group took off for the milder climate of Virginia, Morton and about a dozen others threw out the lieutenant in charge, released the indentured servants, and set about the enjoyment of paradise. They renamed the plantation Ma-Re-Mount, based on the original Indian name; it soon became Merry Mount, based on their joyous way of life.

In the spring of 1627 Merry Mount instituted "revels & merriment after the old English custom." Up went an 80-foot maypole, decked out with ribbons and flowers; atop it was nailed a pair of antlers. Inviting the Indians to join in, the colonists held a days-long fertility rite, with plenty of beer, dancing, and erotic amenities.

The Merry Mount fur trade flourished, to the detriment of the Saints, who offered the "Savages" disapproval, prayer, and violence. Fearing as they did that contact with the natives' sensual "wickedness" might undermine their own rigid resolve—which prohibited unseemly laughter, let alone revelry—the Saints could not tolerate a neighbor like Morton.

Myles Standish and his Puritan soldiers watch the revelers of Merry Mount celebrate with the Indians around their maypole. The Saints, unwilling to share the wilderness with such licentiousness, hounded Thomas Morton to his death.

In the spring of 1628 Capt. Myles Standish invaded Merry Mount with eight armed men. They captured Morton and left him on a deserted island with nothing but his bare hands and "the thin suit" on his back to await an outbound boat to England. He was charged with selling guns and spirits to the Indians; but the English refused to prosecute, and in 1629 he returned to his "old nest" to resume his fur trade.

This time Puritans John Endicott and John Winthrop of the Massachusetts Bay Colony took up the cudgel. Endicott, "a great swelling fellow," cut down the infamous maypole. Governor Winthrop hauled Morton into court, where he was sentenced to the stocks, stripped of all property, imprisoned, and finally exiled to England. As he sailed, his house was burned down.

Again the English freed Morton. He sought legal revenge against his persecutors and almost succeeded in getting their royal charter revoked. But when he returned to Massachusetts in 1643, he was thrown into jail and kept in irons, without fire or blankets, through the harsh winter. At last, his health broken—"old and crazy," according to Winthrop—Morton was released. By 1646 he was dead.

The First Polish Immigrants *They were here before the Pilgrims*

By the time the *Mayflower* landed at Plymouth, Massachusetts, a group of Polish artisans had been hard at work in Jamestown, Virginia, for more than 12 years. And a full year before the Puritans' arrival, the Poles had helped to establish the democratic process in the New World by staging America's first labor strike.

Capt. John Smith, the colony's leader, saw early on that in order to survive, Jamestown had to do more than just feed itself. It needed to produce goods that could be exported and sold at a profit.

The new land had an abundance of pine trees whose sap could be tapped to produce valuable pitch, tar, resin, and turpentine. And Smith knew exactly where to find men skilled in the manufacture of these commodities. The captain had spent some time in Poland and was familiar with the flourishing pitch, tar, and glass industries there. So it was to Poland that he sent his request for artisans.

The first Polish immigrants arrived in 1608. They were probably indentured workers, which meant that in return for their passage to America, the men had agreed to work for the colony for a certain number of years.

Smith praised the Poles as hard workers and took note of the fact that two of them had saved his life when he was attacked by Indians. The doughty captain was probably thoroughly surprised, then, when the Poles went on strike.

In 1619, as the colonists were preparing to elect members of the Virginia Assembly, the new governor announced that only men of English origin would be allowed to vote. The Poles, having already repaid their debt of indenture, responded to this announcement by laying down their tools. If they couldn't vote, they said, they wouldn't work. This refusal to work was the first such action in the English colonies and a bona fide American milestone.

Their startling demand was quickly met, and a democratic precedent was set. The court record of the Virginia Company for July 21, 1619, puts it best: "Upon some dispute of the Polonians resident in Virginia, it was now agreed . . . they shall be enfranchised and made as free as any inhabitant there whatsoever."

Which Way to Hong Kong?

When the French explorer Samuel de Champlain sent his scout, Jean Nicolet, to find a shortcut to Asia in 1635, he gave him a fine damask robe to impress the Orientals. Nicolet paddled across Lake Michigan and—thinking he'd found China—donned his robe to scramble up the cliffs of Green Bay, Wisconsin. The Winnebago Indians who met him were disappointing, but they mentioned a "great water" (the Mississippi) to the west. And so Nicolet hurried back to Quebec to herald it as the Northwest Passage to Asia.

As a fur trader, La Salle spent years exploring in the Great Lakes area. Given to thinking big, he soon envisioned a grand commercial empire with cargo vessels plying the Great Lakes chain and the Mississippi River down to the Gulf of Mexico. With that still in mind in 1682, he paddled down the great river (left) to locate its delta. The first white man to follow the Mississippi to its mouth, he laid claim to the land bounding it (the Louisiana Territory) for France.

Death in the Wilderness

The explorer was murdered by his own men

Robert Cavelier, sieur de La Salle, had a talent for winning the friendship of the Indians he dealt with, and another for alienating his own men, who found him haughty, rigid, and erratic. Their hatred eventually cost the French explorer his life.

The aristocratic La Salle, who had arrived in Canada in 1666 at the age of 23, had voyaged down the Mississippi River in 1682 and claimed the Louisiana Territory for France.

As a reward, Louis XIV granted him permission in 1684 to establish a trading colony at the mouth of the Mississippi, on condition that he lead an assault against the Spanish colonies in Mexico. (France was at war with Spain then.) Accepting the proviso, he set out with four ships and 300 soldiers and colonists. For some reason (possibly to carry out some secret plan or orders), La Salle sailed past the river's entrance and landed about 500 miles to the west at Matagorda Bay in present-day Texas, where he built a fort in early 1685.

During the next 20 months La Salle made two forays—the first seeking Spanish silver mines in northern Mexico, the second to locate the Mississippi. In the meantime, his colonists, marooned on an inhospitable coast and dying from disease, became distrustful and mutinous.

Finally, on January 7, 1687, La Salle set out for Canada to get help, taking 16 men, among them his nephew Moranget, his footman, two priests (one of whom was La Salle's brother), a surgeon, a loyal Indian, and his trusted aide, Henri Joutel. Left at the fort were 20 or 25 men, women, and children.

On March 15, after a toilsome journey through thickets and woods, the party neared a spot where La Salle had once stashed some wheat and beans. He dispatched a few men to find the grain. It was spoiled, but the Indian did manage to kill two bison. Stopping to smoke the flesh, they sent a man back to La Salle to ask for horses to carry it. He sent them in Moranget's care. Finding that the men had set aside the marrow bones for themselves, a usual practice, Moranget flew into a rage and seized both the meat and the bones, leaving them nothing. Wild with anger, several of the men conspired to murder the loathsome Moranget, as well as La Salle's Indian and footman. In the night, while four kept guard, the surgeon battered all three to death with an ax.

Meanwhile, La Salle, becoming impatient, resolved to find his men. Approaching their campsite, he saw eagles fluttering about. Assuming they had found carrion, he fired a shot. At the sound of his musket, two of the assassins set an ambush. One hid in the weeds, and when La Salle, coming upon the other, asked after his nephew, the hidden traitor shot him dead.

According to Joutel, the conspirators stripped the body "and vented their Malice in vile and opprobrious Language." Kicking him, the surgeon muttered in derision, "There thou liest, Great Bassa, there thou liest." The corpse was dragged through the bushes and left to the beasts.

One of the murderers immediately usurped command, but two months later both he and the surgeon were killed by their followers. Only seven of the party continued on to Canada.

In the years that followed, the Spanish found and rescued several members of La Salle's colony.

Francis Drake Claims California

And sails home circling the globe—the second man to do so

Two centuries before the Spanish began to settle in California, an Englishman landed in a "convenient and fit harbor" along the Pacific Coast and claimed the territory for Queen Elizabeth I.

In 1577 Francis Drake, a master mariner, trader, and privateer, outfitted five ships and set out, apparently with the secret backing of the queen. His mission: to venture into the Pacific, then virtually Spain's domain, via the Strait of Magellan (named for the leader of the first globe-circling expedition). Once there, Drake turned north, plundering Spanish ships and settlements on the South American coast and filling his holds with treasure. He sailed as far as present-day Oregon, no doubt seeking the fabled Northwest Passage as a shortcut home.

Three of Drake's ships were lost in storms, and a fourth turned back. Only his flagship, the 100-ton *Golden Hind,* remained, and she was leaking badly when Drake headed south again, seeking a safe harbor for repairs. On June 17, 1579, after struggling through bitter cold and "stinking fogs," he found his harbor. He spent five weeks there, on the northern California coast, while his ship lay on the beach being caulked.

The shore resembled his native coast, so Drake named the area Nova Albion, "that it might have some affinity . . . with our own country, which was sometimes so called." The Indians greeted the white men with friendly amazement, dubbing Drake their *hyoh* (king). He accepted the title as Elizabeth's envoy and on a brass plate nailed to a post noted "the free giving up of the province and kingdom . . . into her Majestie's hands." Then, his ship repaired, Drake sailed off across the Pacific, returning home to glory—and a knighthood. From then on, though the Spanish continued to call him *El Dragón,* Englishmen forever called him Sir.

Although unfailingly charming in social settings, the elegant Sir Francis Drake (right) was a stern captain who once beheaded an officer for inciting mutiny. When he landed on the coast of northern California (below)—at a spot still disputed by historians—he was warmly greeted by the Indians.

1776: A Banner Year, Coast to Coast

On June 29, 1776, Spain's flag was unfurled on the West Coast in what was to become San Francisco. The ceremony marked the founding by Father Junípero Serra of a Franciscan mission, the northernmost of a chain extending south to San Diego. That same week, on the East Coast, America's independence was proclaimed by the Founding Fathers.

On July 4, as Thomas Jefferson's well-crafted declaration was accepted in Philadelphia, some 3,000 miles away the first mass was celebrated at the newly established mission. Although it was a moment of great bicoastal rejoicing, it would be many challenging years before Americans could claim the land from sea to shining sea.

Founding a mission in early California: The state traces its name to an island in a 16th-century novel, on which a tribe of exotic women lived surrounded by gold treasures.

Fourth of July—Western Style

A booming celebration with political overtones

Nothing was more gratifying to the citizens of the newly formed United States of America than lording their independence over their former British masters. And nobody succeeded in doing so better than two American sea captains, Robert Gray and John Kendrick—even though, at the time, they were a continent away from their countrymen.

In 1789 Gray and Kendrick, who had anchored their ships in scenic Nootka Sound off present-day Vancouver, British Columbia, organized the first Independence Day celebration held anywhere on the West Coast. And their patriotic display had a pointed objective: to humiliate the British ship *Argonaut,* which had dropped anchor nearby.

The Fourth of July celebration was actually the second humiliation in as many days for the British seamen. Only the day before, the *Argonaut* had been captured by two Spanish ships that were also moored in Nootka Sound. The Spanish were trying to prevent the British from laying claim to the area, valuable both for its fine natural harbor and for its profitable fur trade.

Welcome aboard!

Although the Americans themselves were trading for furs, they tried to maintain their neutrality as the ships of the two rival nations faced off. But the *Argonaut*'s capture gave the Yankees an unexpected chance to add to British embarrassment, and they made the most of it. Booming salvos from the guns of the two American ships, the *Columbia Rediviva* and the *Lady Washington,* awoke the British on the morning of July 4. After the cannonade was over, the Americans invited both the British and the Spanish to a gala Independence Day dinner aboard the *Columbia,* followed by a 13-gun salute that was returned by the Spanish ships.

Not surprisingly, the British declined to join in the merrymaking, but the intent of the day's events was certainly not lost on them. "To aggravate the insult to the British nation, the anniversary of the American independence was commemorated with every demonstration of joy," one sailor complained.

A Stars and Stripes record

The British got some measure of revenge the following year, when the disputed territory was awarded to them by treaty. By then, however, the American sailors aboard the *Columbia* had already set another patriotic record. From Nootka Sound, the *Columbia* sailed to China before returning to its home port of Boston by way of the Cape of Good Hope. The globe-circling journey made it the first vessel to carry the new American flag all the way around the world.

Two years later, on another fur-trading expedition, Captain Gray discovered the rushing waters of a spectacular river in the Pacific Northwest and, in honor of his history-making ship, named it the Columbia River.

The "Lost" State

Symbol of the enduring spirit of independence

They called the new state Franklin, but the gentleman from Philadelphia for whom it was named declined to visit. And because of its shaky currency, officials were paid in hides (the governor received 1,000 deerskins as his annual salary). Yet Franklin survived—albeit precariously—for four years before it disappeared from the ever-changing map that traced the nation's growing pains.

As early as 1673, explorers had traveled over the Appalachian Mountains (where Daniel Boone later roamed) to a fertile plain crisscrossed by rivers—what is now eastern Tennessee. A ragtag assortment of colonists later moved west from Virginia and North Carolina to the banks of the Watauga and Nolichucky rivers, where they eked out an existence by growing corn and hunting wild game. But they met opposition from rival claimants to the territory: the Cherokee Indians, the governor of North Carolina, and the British Crown.

"The divine right of the frontier"

A royal proclamation issued in 1763 forbade settlements west of the mountains and reserved for the Crown the right to make treaties with the Indians. But the frontiersmen—who soon numbered in the thousands—refused to abandon their outposts. In 1772 they banded together into the Watauga Association, which established courts of justice and a militia to fend off the Indians. One Tory leader called the Wataugans "backwater men . . . the dregs of mankind"; a later historian referred to their Articles of Association as a declaration of "the divine right of the frontier."

The Revolution found many Wataugans eager to fight the British, especially when Lord Cornwallis sent troops in the direction of the western lands. In a showdown at King's Mountain, South Carolina, mounted Watauga militiamen yelled savage war cries as they took expert aim with their trusty long rifles, and the British were defeated. The victory made heroes of the settlers, particularly John "Nolichucky Jack" Sevier. After independence, however, the "overmountain men" got little support from their parent state, North Carolina. As under the British, they were "grievously taxed without enjoying the blessings of it."

The 14th state?

Then, in 1784, North Carolina offered to cede its Tennessee lands to the central government. Feeling abandoned, the Wataugans held a convention and voted to found Franklin. They adopted a state constitution, elected legislators and a governor—John Sevier—and petitioned for recognition as the 14th state. Thomas Jefferson, who had drawn up a plan for carving new states out of the western territories, backed their request. But the support of 9 of the original 13 states was required, and only 7 voted for approval. Meanwhile, the North Carolina government reclaimed its western lands and tried Sevier as a traitor. The state survived until North Carolina relented, forgave the settlers' back taxes, and pardoned Sevier.

Franklin became part of the Tennessee Territory, and when that state was admitted to the Union in 1796, the citizens elected Sevier as their first governor.

Dig We Must—For a Growing America

From canal to Constitution, via Mount Vernon

"The Western settlers," George Washington wrote, "stand as it were upon a pivot; the touch of a feather would turn them any way." He was referring to the pioneers who had poured into the wilderness of the post-Revolution frontier territory—that vast expanse between the well-populated Atlantic seaboard corridor and the Mississippi River.

What Washington feared was that the isolation of the new settlers from the original 13 states might persuade them to direct their loyalty elsewhere. Using the Mississippi to ship their farm products and fur pelts, they could easily form alliances with the French in New Orleans or with the British along the Great Lakes.

Navigating a canal system

Washington believed he had found a means to turn them the right way—*and* improve his own fortunes. He envisioned a canal system that would make the turbulent Potomac River navigable to within a short portage of the Ohio River, the main route to the new territory.

This would be a viable alternative to the Mississippi and would make it easy to move goods eastward. (And as the barges headed for Georgetown, Maryland—the port at the mouth of the river—they would pass right by Mount Vernon, the general's lovely estate on the bank of the Potomac.)

"Bind those people to us"

Washington foresaw "an amazing increase of our exports, while we bind those people to us by a chain which never can be broken." He was not alone in seeing a need for this waterway; Thomas Jefferson wrote to him urging haste, lest New York State, planning its own canal, steal a march on the western trade. If Washington—who, in the belief that his service to the nation was done, had retired to his estate—could complete the waterway, Jefferson wrote, "What a monument to your retirement it would become!"

The task of the Patowmack Company, chartered in 1785 with Washington as its head, proved daunting. Despite the general's view that navigation of the Potomac was "equal, if not superior, to any in the Union," its foaming rapids and cascading waterfalls challenged early engineering talents; it had always been a boatman's nightmare. Laborers, using powerful black powder, had to blast passages through rock walls. "We had our Blowers, One Run off the other Blown up," noted the first project superintendent, James Rumsey.

When the work was finished, the Potomac was still so unpredictable that the waterway was open to boats only 30 to 45 days a year. Yet the impact of the canal on America's history was staggering.

Under the loose union provided by the Articles of Confederation, the fledgling national government found it hard to make feuding states agree on anything. But under Washington's leadership, the delegates from Maryland and Virginia came to terms in 1785 on a way to proceed with work on the canal. The meeting was so successful that a second session was held to deal with trade problems. Representatives from five states attended, and at Alexander Hamilton's suggestion, they voted to call a convention in Philadelphia "to render the constitution of the Federal Government adequate to the exigencies of the Union."

Today the Patowmack Canal is just a weed-covered ribbon of land. But the document that delegates to the Philadelphia Convention shaped in 1787—the U.S. Constitution—is still very much alive.

Last Days of a Legendary Hero

In his long and active life, Daniel Boone achieved worldwide fame as America's quintessential frontiersman. He was so beloved that in his final years admirers commissioned a portrait of him. Artist Chester Harding—one of his last visitors—found the old man in his small cabin deep in the Missouri woods roasting venison, spitted on the ramrod of his rifle, over a fire. He persuaded Boone to don a fringed buckskin coat for the painting (right), but not the coonskin cap in which he is usually portrayed. The grandson of an English Quaker, Ole Dan'l never wore a coonskin, preferring the broad-brimmed beaver hat that was a family tradition.

Boone was a man for whom the rigors of field and forest outweighed the pleasures of home and hearth. Yet it wasn't the great outdoors that did him in. In 1820, at the age of 85, it seems he overindulged in one of his favorite dishes, baked sweet potatoes, and died of indigestion.

Boone was laid to rest in Missouri beside his wife, Rebecca. But in 1845 Kentucky reclaimed its famous son, and the bodies were reburied there. Modern research suggests, however, that the grave next to Rebecca's may contain the remains of a slave originally buried beside her, and that Boone still rests on a scenic hilltop in Missouri.

Left: Sacagawea converses in sign language with a party of Chinook Indians canoeing near the mouth of the Columbia River. Lewis, his gun at the ready, stands beside her, while Clark, wearing a cocked hat, sits next to York, his slave. The canvas is one of several illustrating the Lewis and Clark expedition by Charles M. Russell, a great painter of the American West.

A Tale of Two Graves

The unknown fate of an American heroine

In a cemetery on the Wind River Indian Reservation near Fort Washakie, Wyoming, stands a prominent tombstone marking the grave of Sacagawea, the young Shoshoni woman who served heroically with the Lewis and Clark expedition in 1805–06. An inscription on the stone, erected by the Wyoming chapter of the Daughters of the American Revolution in 1963, states that she died in 1884 and that the Reverend J. Roberts, who officiated at her burial, identified her original grave site in 1907.

A few years later Dr. Charles Eastman, a Sioux scholar commissioned by the Bureau of Indian Affairs to trace Sacagawea's life, found many who claimed to remember her as an old woman. According to them, she left her husband, the trapper Charbonneau, after he took another wife. She then married a Comanche and, following his death, rejoined the Shoshonis in Wyoming. There she was reunited with Baptiste, the son born to her on the expedition.

But others contend that Sacagawea died at Fort Manuel, South Dakota, when she was only about 25, and was buried in an unmarked grave. On December 20, 1812, a clerk at the fort noted in his journal: "This Evening the Wife of Charbonneau a Snake [Shoshoni] Squaw, died of a putrid fever." Unfortunately, he failed to mention which wife. A dozen years later, however, William Clark (who had provided for the education of Baptiste) listed expedition members and their fates in a notebook; next to "Secarjaweau," he wrote, "Dead." Oddly enough, the complete story of one of America's most celebrated women may never be known.

York, the Goodwill Ambassador

One goal of Lewis and Clark on their westward trek was to establish friendly relations with the various tribes they encountered. Their best ambassador was York, William Clark's slave; the Indians had never seen a black man before.

When the warriors returned to camp, explained a Flathead Indian: "Those who had been brave and fearless, the victorious ones in battle, painted themselves in charcoal. So the black man, they thought, had been the bravest of his party." The Indians would rub York's skin with a wet finger to see whether his color would come off. Its permanence, combined with his feats of strength and agile dancing, led the Indians to regard him as "Great Medicine." Legend has it that when Clark freed York after the expedition, he headed west to become chief of an Indian tribe.

One Night at Grinder's Stand *The mysterious death of Meriwether Lewis*

Toward sunset on October 10, 1809, Meriwether Lewis rode up to Grinder's Stand, a lonely inn 60 miles from Nashville, on the Natchez Trace, a blazed wilderness trail. Dismounting, he asked to stay the night. A few hours later he died of gunshot wounds. Was it suicide? Or murder? To this day no one knows.

Lewis, whom Thomas Jefferson had appointed governor of Upper Louisiana Territory following his expedition with William Clark, was on his way to Washington, D.C., carrying his journals of their trip, which he hoped to have published. He also planned to see the new president, James Madison, to seek reimbursement for his official expenditures. Lewis was seriously in debt.

He and his servant, John Pernier, had left his headquarters in St. Louis by boat on September 4, 1809. Feeling ill (possibly with malaria), Lewis made a two-week stop at Fort Pickering (present-day Memphis) and then set out on horseback to cross Chickasaw territory to the Natchez Trace. James Neeley, agent for the Chickasaw Indians, whom Lewis had met at the fort, accompanied him. On the night of October 9, two horses strayed from camp. The next morning Neeley went to look for them while Lewis rode on with their two servants.

There were no eyewitnesses to what happened at the inn. Mrs. Grinder, whose husband was reportedly away, told Neeley that the 35-year-old explorer was deranged. Neeley wrote to Jefferson: "The woman reports that about three o'clock she heard two pistols fire off in the Governors Room; . . . He had shot himself in the head with one pistol and a little below the breast with the other—when his servant came in he says; I have done the business my good Servant give me some water."

In letters to Jefferson, both Neeley and the officer in command of Fort Pickering said that Lewis was "in a state of mental derangement" while at the fort. And yet twice during that stay the explorer had written entirely lucid letters to President Madison. Jefferson accepted the verdict of suicide, however.

But could Lewis have been murdered? Local tradition holds that Grinder did the job. Two years later Mrs. Grinder changed part of her story; and a full 30 years later she gave a totally new version, saying that the wounded Lewis had crawled off into the woods and that Pernier had appeared the next morning wearing his master's clothes. Was she covering up for her husband?

The $120 Lewis had with him was never recovered. Neeley, who buried him, had no money at the outset of the trip, and yet he was able to give Pernier $15 to travel to Virginia to report to Jefferson. Seven months later Pernier himself died suddenly. Was it mere coincidence?

In 1848 an unfinished column was put up to mark Lewis's grave and signify his untimely death.

Searching for the Red River, Pike (right) veered south into New Mexico, where a Spanish patrol took him into custody and led him to Santa Fe.

Move West? Forget It!

Zebulon Pike's dim prediction

"These vast plains of the western hemisphere may become in time as celebrated as the sandy deserts of Africa," observed Lt. Zebulon M. Pike in 1810, describing the expanses of sand dunes and grasslands he had found. The young explorer, sent west by President Jefferson in 1806, went on to predict:

"But from these immense prairies may arise one great advantage to the United States, viz: The restriction of our population to some certain limits. . . . Our citizens being so prone to rambling . . . will, through necessity, be constrained to limit their extent on the west to the borders of the Missouri and Mississippi, while they leave prairies incapable of cultivation to the wandering and uncivilized aborigines of the country."

Outrunning death: John Colter flees his captors—and begins an amazing trip through hostile country without clothing, food, or a gun to protect himself.

Race for Life

John Colter's incredible 300-mile journey

Trapper, adventurer, woodsman, explorer, and the first of this nation's great mountain men, John Colter was one of the West's mythic figures. And, in the fall of 1808, his fame was assured by a daring and near-miraculous run from the Blackfoot Indians.

Following three years of hazardous duty as a member of Lewis and Clark's expedition along the western frontier, Colter turned to trapping beaver in the Three Forks area of the Missouri River, deep in Blackfoot Indian territory.

Indian attack

One day Colter was inspecting traps by canoe with another veteran of the Lewis and Clark expedition, John Potts. Suddenly the two men found themselves flanked on both banks by Blackfoot braves. Potts was killed as he tried to escape, but Colter was captured and became sport for the Indians. Stripped of all his clothing, including his shoes, the adventurer was led 400 yards out onto the prairie; then the chief let out a war whoop and sent several hundred braves in hot pursuit.

Sprinting painfully across the prickly brush, Colter headed for the Jefferson Fork, some six miles away. He outdistanced all but one spear-carrying Blackfoot, whom he finally turned to face. He managed to kill the pursuer with his own spear. On the verge of collapse, Colter dove into the bitterly cold Jefferson River, where he hid under a pile of timbers until nightfall. He then swam away, drifted downstream, and stumbled ashore.

Astounding arrival

What followed was a legendary 11-day overland trek. Traveling day and night—without a stitch of clothing—Colter climbed mountains, scurried across fields, and tramped through woods, covering an unbelievable 300 miles. When he reached Manuel's Fort on the Big Horn River, he was bearded, bleeding, and barely recognizable. His astonishing journey has guaranteed him a place forever in the pantheon of America's frontier heroes.

The Day the Grizzly Mauled Jed Smith

Hardly a typical mountain man, Jedediah Smith was a teetotaler who traveled "with a Bible in his hand." A stalwart transcontinental explorer who was the first American to reach California by land, he truly showed his mettle when a bear attacked him in 1823.

Smith was leading trappers in the Black Hills when suddenly the bear appeared, sprang, and sent him sprawling. Before the grizzly was killed, it took Smith's head in its mouth. The victim was in terrible shape. A witness, Jim Clyman, wrote that his skull had been cut "to near the crown of his head, leaving a white streak whare [the bear's] teeth passed."

Though torn and bloody, Smith calmly gave orders on how to sew up his wounds. When Clyman said he couldn't save one ear, Smith told him he "must try to stitch it up some way or other." Clyman, a master of understatement, observed of the violent attack: "This gave us a lesson on the character of the grizzly bear which we did not forget."

Lacerations from a fierce encounter with a bear left Jed Smith scarred for life. Long hair hid his mutilated ear.

Sacrificial Rites

Bloody rituals of fire, torture—and death

At one time human sacrifice was quite common in Nebraska. A local Indian tribe, the Skidi Pawnee, believed that if an occasional human were offered up to a deity called the Morning Star, crops would be abundant, hunting good, and the general well-being of the community assured. In 1827 Indian agent John Dougherty acted to put an end to the practice.

Dougherty had been alerted by white fur traders who did business in the area that a Pawnee raiding party had captured a Cheyenne woman, intending to offer her as a sacrifice—although the tribe had promised years before to give up the custom. Now he resolved to visit the Indian chiefs and try to hold them to their word. Fort Atkinson at Council Bluffs, where his agency was located, was about to be abandoned and the garrison was greatly reduced. Nonetheless, the agent put together a small party of soldiers and on April 4 set out for a chat with the chiefs.

The Morning Star ceremony

When the band arrived at the Pawnee village, the five-day ritual was already under way. One of the tribal chiefs asked Dougherty and his group to dine with him. But, since there were six chiefs altogether, so as not to insult anyone at the start of delicate negotiations, the white men devoured half a dozen meals before the evening was over. Afterward, the ceremony of the sacred Morning Star sacrifice was described to them: The victim would be tied to a scaffold and offered to the Morning Star; after torture by fire she would die from an arrow through the heart. Then the victim's chest would be cut open and the blood smeared on one of the Indian priests. After further ritual and celebration, her body was to be left on the open plain, an offering to the animals and the elements.

The next day Dougherty made an eloquent plea for the woman's life, implying that trade items such as gunpowder and flints could be withheld by the government. Then an Indian priest consulted *Tirawahat*, the Master of Life who brought the Skidi universe into existence, and announced that there was no need for a sacrifice. Finally the chiefs agreed to release the Cheyenne woman to Dougherty.

The Indian agent and his party hoped to leave early the next morning, while the village was asleep. But by the time they were ready to go, the entire population was awake and waiting. Some wanted to see them off safely, but others had different intentions.

"A horrid sight"

A Skidi faction believed that to rob the Morning Star of its sacrifice would be to bring ruin to the village, and vowed that the prisoner would never leave alive. As the Cheyenne woman rode her horse past the assemblage, a warrior shot her with an arrow. The crowd went wild, and a heated battle erupted. Dougherty tried desperately to restore order, but by the time he did, it was too late. The woman was dead, her corpse hacked to pieces—"a horrid sight," the agent later reported. But he found some consolation in the fact that the small band of soldiers had "prevented her being tortured to death with firebrands . . . [an] abominable custom."

How a Whale Destroyed the *Essex*

And inspired one of the nation's favorite sea stories

For hardy whalers, no ocean was too wide to cross in pursuit of their mighty prizes. In 1819 more than a dozen ships were launched from Nantucket, all headed for distant hunting grounds in the Pacific. One, the three-masted *Essex,* was to suffer a calamity so dramatic that its fate inspired a classic American novel.

For months the ship survived the hazards of rounding Cape Horn and taking its prey. On November 20, 1820, however, a mammoth sperm whale turned the tables on the *Essex,* ramming it head on. Then the leviathan passed under the vessel, turned, and attacked again. He hit, as first mate Owen Chase recalled, "with ten-fold fury and vengeance." The crew abandoned ship, and from their whaleboats watched in horror as the *Essex* slid into the sea.

A month went by before the survivors—in three small boats, far from land—were roused from their stupor by the sight of a South Pacific islet (known today as Henderson Island). But after six days there, lack of food drove them back to the sea. Death was a constant companion; as one crew member after another lost his life, a decision was made to eat the remains of the dead.

After 83 desperate days at sea, Chase and two companions were rescued by a British brig. Two others were soon found in another whaleboat, and three castaways were picked up from the islet. All returned to Nantucket, Chase forever haunted by the "horrid aspect and malignancy of the whale." The terrible memory—indeed, the entire harrowing experience—inspired Herman Melville's *Moby-Dick.* It was, as Melville himself described it, a "wondrous story."

The Colonel's Runaway Daughter

Help aboard ship was scarce during the Civil War, so John Luce, captain of the whaler America, *felt lucky to add a newcomer to his crew, a sailor who signed on as George Weldon. Here was someone who could pull an oar, climb the rigging, and dance a jig with the best of them.*

But when flogging was ordered because the new sailor had attacked the second mate, all were astonished to find bound breasts beneath "his" shirt. The "sailor" was a Confederate cavalry colonel's missing child, one Georgiana Leonard, and the punishment was never carried out.

In an entry in his log, the captain noted: "This day found out George Weldon to be a woman, the first I ever suspected of such a thing."

The sea, a vast frontier: An angry sperm whale easily destroys a boat manned by those stalwart 19th-century seamen, Nantucket whalers. The Essex *was the first whaling ship sunk by one of these leviathans.*

"New Harmony— All Owin' and No Payin' " was the title of this drawing. A pun on the name of Robert Owen, it caricatured his poor attempts at organization and leadership. His predecessor in New Harmony, Father Rapp, had been much more successful at creating his utopian society of Harmonists.

Creating a Utopia

Harmony, New Harmony, Economy—each had its heyday

Dreaming of a perfect society, religious leader George Rapp and, later, industrialist Robert Owen founded frontier communities that mirrored their ideals.

Rapp arrived from Germany in 1803 and, with his flock, settled near Pittsburgh. In 1807 he decreed that his group become celibate. Later, seeking new horizons, he founded Harmony in Indiana. He sold that town in 1825, moving back to Pennsylvania, where he established Economy. The Harmonists flourished financially and spiritually, although Rapp's teachings, from time to time, were a bit eccentric. When his prediction of the second coming of Christ in 1829 did not materialize, he merely announced a postponement. The Rappites survived 51 years after the death of their leader, finally dissolving in 1898.

Owen, an idealistic Englishman who believed that people were formed by their environment, bought Harmony, Indiana, from Rapp, renamed it New Harmony, and tried to turn it into a perfect environment. About 1,000 people joined his paradise. He promised equality to all (except "persons of color") and exhorted them to strive for "universal happiness." But from the start, there were rumbles of discontent. "The idle and industrious are neither of them satisfied," one resident wrote of the communal life that Owen proposed.

Splinter groups formed and, finances strained, Owen acquired a partner, William Maclure. He arrived aboard the "Boatload of Knowledge" with scientists and educators who brought their own ideas of paradise. The town prospered, but Owen's two-year social experiment collapsed.

New Harmony, now restored, has become a popular tourist attraction. It is also a living legacy of the people who came to these shores to make their dreams of paradise come true.

Would You Move to Ipba Venul?

Stedman Whitwell, an English architect and social reformer, went to New Harmony on the "Boatload of Knowledge."

Scornful of those who named one town for another—Washington, for example, or Springfield—Whitwell had a novel idea: Give each locality a name in which the letters stood for the numbers in its latitude and longitude, all keyed to a complex code of vowels and consonants. Using this method, he reasoned, every town would have a unique name and could be instantly located on any map. Applying his revolutionary system, he christened one of the New Harmony splinter communities Feiba Peveli.

Had Whitwell prevailed, Pittsburgh would be Otfu Veitoup; New York would be Otke Notive; the nation's capital, Feili Nyvul. And Ipba Venul would identify New Harmony.

Zachary Taylor's Dead Letter

Postal problems practically prevented his presidency

The view that "the mail must get through" had, it seems, a rather shaky start. True, the Constitution empowered Congress to "establish Post Offices and Post Roads." But as a practical matter, for 50 years after the document was ratified, to send a letter you just folded it over, sealed it with wax, and gave it to a stagecoach driver. To receive the letter, the addressee had to go to his local post office and pay the charges. When some local letter carriers started working in 1825, their wages were the fees received from addressees; so if you weren't home to pay, you didn't get your letter.

An "odious monopoly"
Although envelopes first appeared in 1839, the stamp problem remained. So did the delivery problem. Roads were often impassable for weeks at a time, holding up all mail. As railroads began to snake across the land in the 1830's and 1840's, delivery in a few areas improved, but overall service was so expensive and haphazard that many people wanted to abolish that "odious monopoly," the post office.

In 1845 Congress legislated cheaper postage. At first postmasters printed their own stamps and cancellations, adding to the general chaos. Finally, a couple of years later, the Post Office Department came through with official postage; the first stamps bore portraits of George Washington and Benjamin Franklin.

Economical, comical Zach
But paying postage still got a letter only as far as the addressee's post office, and he was obliged to bail out his mail with his own cash. Zachary "Old Rough-and-Ready" Taylor, popular hero of the Mexican War, received pounds of mail but wouldn't spend the money to get it out of the Baton Rouge post office; so he had the postmaster send all collect letters to the dead letter office. When the Whig Party nominated Taylor for president in 1848, officials wrote to tell him so. The announcement also landed in the dead letter office—with 10 cents postage due.

It was weeks before the worried Whigs discovered what had happened. They sent another missive (prepaid, this time) and Taylor's acceptance arrived by return mail. The incident provided fodder for campaign claims: the Whigs cited it as a model of frugality, while the Democrats made fun of "economical, comical old Zach." But Taylor won, the last Whig ever elected.

Even when post office mailmen started getting paid in 1863, mail was still delivered only in cities. It was 1896 before farmers enjoyed the "luxury" of Rural Free Delivery.

The 19th-century artist David Gilmour Blythe takes a satirical view of a race to get the mail. In his day there was no home delivery, and letters were held at the post office. The pickpocket at the left is one of the artist's typically sardonic touches.

Sam Houston's Fateful First Marriage

But for Eliza Allen, he just might have been president of the United States

A hero of the War of 1812, a congressman, and governor of Tennessee—all before his 35th birthday—Sam Houston seemed destined for the White House. And although he was 17 years older than his bride when he married the 18-year-old socialite Eliza Allen in 1829, it appeared to be the perfect match for an up-and-coming politician.

Instead, after less than three months, Eliza fled back to her childhood home. Neither spouse would reveal why. There were hints of unfaithfulness, but the only tantalizing glimpse of their marital problems is a letter Houston sent Eliza's father, begging for her return. "She was cold to me and I thought did not love me," he confessed, insisting that "I . . . do love Eliza."

But there was no reply, and rumors that Houston had mistreated his bride were rampant. So hostile was public opinion that when the distraught governor sought religious solace, a minister refused to baptize him—his reputation, it seems, was too tarnished.

Only a week after the scandal erupted, Houston resigned the governorship and left for Arkansas, seeking out the Cherokee Indian tribe with whom he had spent three years as a teenager. Without divorcing Eliza, Houston took an Indian wife—but he continued to wear Eliza's engagement ring in a pouch around his neck. And he drowned his misery in alcohol with such regularity that the Indians called him the Big Drunk.

Not until 1833, after leaving the tribe and settling in Texas, did Houston divorce Eliza. And in 1840, at the age of 47, he wooed and won 21-year-old Margaret Lea. This happy union produced eight children and lasted until Houston's death at the age of 70.

Not even wedded bliss, however, could make Houston break his silence. Once, when he arrived in his cups at a friend's home, his host thought Houston's condition would make it easy to pry the truth out of him. But when he asked what had happened with Eliza, Houston simply jumped on his horse and rode off into the night.

Eliza, who also remarried, was no more forthcoming, though various relatives have claimed to know the truth. One story was that Eliza loved another man, but her parents, blinded by Houston's great reputation, forced her to marry him. Others reported that a jealous Houston locked Eliza in her room when he left her alone, while some maintained that an unhealed wound he had received in combat so revolted the sensitive young woman that she refused all physical contact. (Houston's relatives, citing a medical history compiled during his lifetime, denied this.)

Whatever the cause of the couple's unhappiness, it may well have been on Eliza's mind as she lay dying. She ordered that all pictures of her be burned; and so no image remains of the fair-haired girl who changed Sam Houston's life.

Lt. Sam Houston bravely ignored an arrow wound as he led his men (below) at the 1814 Battle of Horseshoe Bend. Some said the wound never healed. Despite personal woes, he became the first president of the Texas Republic and later was elected to the U.S. Senate when Texas joined the Union in 1845.

The Father of Western Botany

Thomas "Old Curious" Nuttall expanded science's frontier

Many explorers went west before Thomas Nuttall set out in April 1810, but none of them really saw it—at least not the way he did. Arriving in America from his native England at age 22, he got his big break two years later when Dr. Benjamin Smith Barton, a prominent Philadelphia academic, offered to outfit him for a one-man scientific wilderness expedition. Certainly the kind doctor, who fiercely desired scientific acclaim for himself, understood the dangers and the way he was exploiting Nuttall's youthful enthusiasm. "Should his life be spared," wrote Barton with astounding smugness, "he will add much to our knowledge."

Nuttall not only survived, he throve on the two-year trek that took him as far west as the upper Missouri. The Indians, deeming him insane for his fanatic devotion to collecting plant specimens, treated him as a holy man. And indeed, his behavior became bizarre. Once, enraptured by nature's bounty, he wandered 100 miles, finally collapsing from exhaustion. An Indian found him and saved his life.

After several more trips to the Southwest, Nuttall became curator of the Harvard Botanical Garden. The reclusive botanist had a trapdoor built in his boardinghouse living quarters, to avoid encountering other residents. In 1834 he decided that Harvard was wasting his time, so along with a protégé, ornithologist John K. Townsend, he joined a fur-trading expedition to the Pacific Coast. Their collection of western wildlife became a landmark of 19th-century research. Sailing home, Nuttall was nicknamed Old Curious by the ship's crew. When he went to the shipowner's Boston office to pay his bill, the tough-minded merchant told him the passage was free, since he had traveled "not for his own amusement, but for the benefit of mankind."

Birdbrained About Business, Audubon Went to Jail

Naturalist John James Audubon is world-famous for the realism of his bird portraits; but when it came to business, the budding artist's grasp of reality was much more tenuous.

While in his early thirties, Audubon and his brother-in-law built a steam grist and lumber mill in Henderson, Kentucky. "Up went the mill at an enormous expense in a country then as unfit for such a thing as it would be now for me to attempt to settle on the moon," he wrote years later. The enterprise failed in 1819, and Audubon was jailed in Louisville for debt. He was released only after he had declared bankruptcy. "I parted with every particle of property to my creditors and kept only the clothes I wore, my original drawings, and my gun."

"With nothing left to me but my humble talents," Audubon supported his family as a portraitist and pursued his passion to observe and record the birds of America's wilderness. His endeavor eventually took flight into a profitable enterprise. In 1827 the first folios of his famous Birds of America *were published.*

Brotherhood of Blood and Light

Penance in the Southwest

Christians? Or devils? The Penitentes have been called both, for they create a hell on earth by pursuing the quest for absolution to the limits of life and death.

Abandoned believers

It is the week before Easter in the remote mountain valleys of New Mexico and southern Colorado, and the world is preparing for rebirth. This is the holiest season for Los Hermanos Penitentes, the Penitent Brothers, a centuries-old cult whose obscure roots trace back through the Spanish conquistadors and Franciscan missionaries to the fervent Christians of medieval Europe.

Believing that man is innately evil and that this evil can be purged only through punishment, the Penitentes have made Good Friday their most sacred holiday. The bloody rituals with which they observe this day may have developed from more benign practices introduced by the Spanish Franciscan missionaries, who occasionally practiced self-flagellation for the purification of the soul.

About 1800 the Penitentes organized into a formal fraternity with a constitution and officers. Originally their rituals were held in village churches. But when the Spanish were expelled, after Mexico won its independence in 1821, remote villages were abandoned by the church. Though they had no priests, the isolated parishioners tried to maintain the faith, and in the process they developed extreme practices.

In 1833 the bishop of Durango, Mexico, issued an edict condemning the brotherhood. By the middle of the 19th century their ceremonies were banned from church

The figure of death (below) presides over the Penitentes' rituals (left). Often made of wood, sometimes a human skeleton, the macabre image is a reminder of the irredeemable death the brothers hope to avoid by their tortured search for earthly atonement.

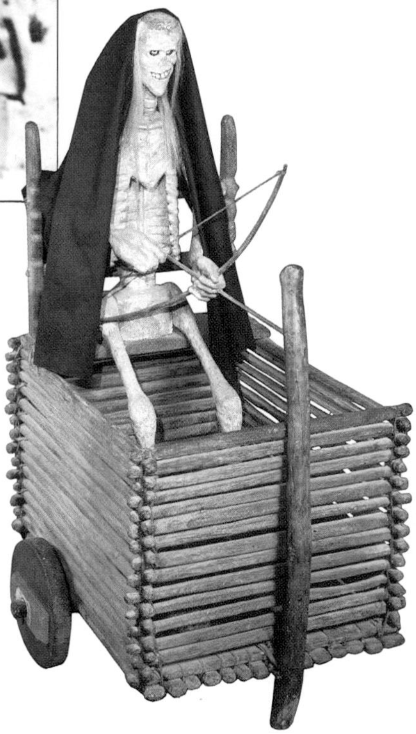

grounds and they were forced to meet secretly outside the villages.

Procession of blood

Charles F. Lummis, a writer and ethnologist, became the first outsider to photograph the Penitentes' Easter week celebration in 1888. His record of the event remains a classic to this day.

Easter Thursday was the culmination of preparations under way since the beginning of Lent. A flute player, his plantive song drifting eerily over the hushed crowd, led a chorus of women in a slow and painful procession. Many of the women were hobbled by cactus stuffed tightly into their shoes.

Behind the women staggered the Brothers of Blood, each man wearing only the white pants of a penitent and a crown of thorns pressed tightly around a black cloth bag shrouding his head. These bags were worn not to conceal the brothers' identities but to protect them from the sin of vanity—from glorying in their suffering before the crowd. As they walked, they lashed their own backs with whips of braided yucca studded with cactus. Their skin was beaten raw and bloody.

Then came three men, bowed under the weight of huge wooden crosses. As they struggled forward, they were viciously whipped by the Brothers of Light, the inner elite of the cult.

Atonement

The next morning, Good Friday, Lummis watched in awe as a black-hooded young man, blood pouring from a wound in his right side, accepted the honor of portraying Christ. Seeing that he was to be bound to the cross, he begged for nails. But too many Christ-actors had died in that way; he was bound by ropes—so tightly that his arms turned black.

Two other brothers with large bundles of cactus strapped to their backs made their way to the base of the cross. Rolling to the ground, they asked that stones be placed to drive the cactus spines more deeply into their flesh. Motionless, but in clear agony, the sufferers remained in their desperate torments for 31 minutes.

Overlooking the entire scene was a Death Cart, a two-wheeled vehicle on which sat a skeleton draped in black and lace, clutching a bow and arrow, the symbol of sudden death.

Presumably, the brotherhood's practices have become less brutal since highways opened the area in the 1920's and its residents became less isolated. In 1947 the bishop of Santa Fe declared that the Penitentes were "a pious association of men joined in charity to commemorate the Passion and death of the Redeemer" and decreed that they were part of the church. But easier access to the broader world also brought Penitente hunters and camera-wielding curiosity seekers. As a result, the order has been driven into an even deeper secrecy.

The First White Women to Cross the Continent

Narcissa Whitman and Eliza Spalding went west, spurred on by missionary zeal

A tale about Northwest Coast Indians seeking the white men's Book of Heaven—the Bible—inspired Narcissa Prentiss, a 16-year-old New Yorker, to become a missionary. However, despite her fine education and deep religious commitment, her request for work in the West was turned down: No single women were needed in Oregon, she was told.

Westbound caravan

When she was in her mid-twenties, Narcissa met Dr. Marcus Whitman. He shared her religious zeal, and *his* application to work as a medical missionary in Oregon was accepted. They married on February 18, 1836, and, along with an agent for the Oregon mission, Rev. Henry Spalding and his wife, Eliza, they joined a caravan heading west. Narcissa (who called Marcus "one of the kindest husbands") described the trek in her spirited journal: "Our fuel for cooking has been dried buffalo dung. Harriet [a sister left behind] will make a face at this, but she would be glad to have her supper cooked." The caravan crossed the Continental Divide on July 4 and soon came upon an annual rendezvous of Indians and fur trappers. The Indians looked "with wonder and astonishment" upon Narcissa and Eliza, the first white women they had ever seen.

The mountainous trail from here on was barely passable. But fortunately for Narcissa, who was now pregnant, Spalding had brought a wagon for the women. (The vehicle was left at Fort Boise, farther west than a wagon had ever been.)

The Whitmans arrived at Fort Walla Walla on September 1, and on March 14, 1837, Narcissa gave birth to the first child born to white parents in the Northwest. A local Indian chief welcomed the baby as a "Cayuse girl."

Fulfillment and tragedy

The missionaries spent 11 years with the Cayuses—some happy, others not. The Whitmans' first misfortune was their daughter's accidental drowning. Although Narcissa was never to have another child, she was soon raising 11 adopted youngsters. Then relations with the people they had come to serve deteriorated—Indian pride made the Cayuses slow to accept the white men's ways and Christianity. As more settlers arrived, the tribe saw its freedom and traditions endangered. Even medicines were suspect. When an epidemic of measles struck and Whitman was unable to save the lives of many tribe members, rumors circulated that he was poisoning his Indian patients.

Suddenly one day a group of firebrands, led by the chief who had welcomed Narcissa's baby, attacked the Whitmans' house. When the smoke cleared, 13 people had been massacred, among them Marcus and Narcissa. Sadly, the dream of Christian service had ended in martyrdom.

Narcissa (above) and Marcus Whitman settled 110 miles from the Spaldings. For more than a decade the Whitmans lived among the Cayuse Indians, only to perish in a bloody massacre (left) on a foggy November day in 1847.

A Promised Land?

The Mormon dream of Deseret

The Deseret alphabet, used to unify the nation (and simplify spelling) for some 20 years, all but disappeared after Brigham Young's death in 1877.

Based on the visions of Joseph Smith, the Church of Jesus Christ of Latter-day Saints (the Mormons) was founded in 1830 in New York, but soon moved to Ohio. That was never considered the promised land, however, and Prophet Smith decreed that the city of God lay in Missouri. Converts flocked to Independence, their new Jerusalem, in the early 1830's, but skirmishes broke out wherever the Mormons settled in Missouri. In 1838 the governor told the state that all Mormons "must be exterminated or driven from the state." Finally, in 1839, the Saints—as they called themselves—retreated from Missouri, leaving a bloody trail of murdered martyrs behind.

The group next chose a bog on the Mississippi River in Illinois. Though it was still not Zion, they thought no one would push them off this mosquito-infested land. Their numbers grew, and the city of Nauvoo soon rivaled Chicago. But resentment against the Mormons flared again, fanned by their practice of polygamy. In 1844, when the city council banned an anti-Mormon newspaper and Smith decreed the destruction of the paper's presses, the governor of Illinois ordered Smith's arrest. Joseph and his brother Hyrum turned themselves in, and an angry mob shot them dead.

Six months later Illinois revoked Nauvoo's charter and the new leader, Brigham Young, declared that the Mormons would move farther west. In 1846 the Saints, forced from their homes, made for Nebraska, where their winter encampment has been compared to Valley Forge. In the spring they moved on, and after much hardship and suffering they reached the Salt Lake Valley in Utah, where Young planned a separate Mormon nation, Deseret.

Salt Lake City and its environs grew quickly. From across the country and around the world—for missionaries worked far afield—Mormons moved to the new land. Farms and mines were started, the terrain was mapped, and Las Vegas (among other outlying communities) was founded as a Mormon colony. But the great Deseret dream faded when Congress declared Utah a U.S. territory. There would be other problems, including court fights that eventually ended the practice of polygamy; but this time the Saints had found their Zion, and remain there to this day.

Mormon Monarchy

An island fit for a king

On his 19th birthday, a New York farm boy confided an extraordinary dream to his diary: he hoped "to rival Cesar [*sic*] or Napoleon." James Jesse Strang got closer to that dream than might have seemed possible when he wrote those words in 1832. From 1850 to 1856 he *was* the monarch of 13-mile-long Beaver Island in Lake Michigan. His subjects? Over 2,500 fellow Mormons who believed that he, not Brigham Young, was the true head of their church.

When Young led the faithful to Utah, Strang's group went to Wisconsin. But in the face of growing hostility, they retreated to Beaver Island. It proved an ideal site on which to establish the kingdom that had been revealed to Strang on sacred brass tablets (claimed by Young's supporters to be the melted remains of a kettle). By the time Strang was crowned in 1850, he had created his own nobility, anointing followers with dabs of oil that produced an eerie glow. (Phosphoresence, it seems, had been added to the oil.)

The puritanical king opposed the practice of polygamy, endorsed by Young—until he met 18-year-old Elvira Eliza Field. Though he already had a wife and four children, he took Elvira as his second bride, persuading the starry-eyed woman to dress as his nephew. After declaring polygamy acceptable, he took four more brides; all four of his new wives were pregnant when, on June 16, 1856, Strang was shot to death by disillusioned former supporters.

Following his death, mainland mobs chased the colonists away. But Beaver Island still bears a trace of its regal past. The chief thoroughfare is called by the name Strang gave it: King's Highway.

First Wagon Train to California

According to one pioneer, "Our ignorance of the route was complete"

The Western Immigration Society. It was a pretentious name for a group who, like most Americans, knew little about the far side of an untamed continent. But in the winter of 1840 California was described as a paradise to Missourian John Bidwell, who, along with 500 families, promptly signed up for a westward trek. By spring, however, enthusiasm had waned, and on departure day, May 9, 1841, only one wagon—and Bidwell—showed up. Undaunted, he waited until 68 people had straggled in.

Because he had a crude map and a letter from a Dr. Marsh in California that contained the only clues to the path they were to follow (and because he showed up with eight men in tow), John Bartleson was elected captain. Talbot Green (carrying a cache of lead bars) was named president. Bidwell was made secretary, and soon they were off. They slowed only to allow a party of missionaries to catch up, because they had with them a guide, Thomas "Broken Hand" Fitzpatrick, a mountain man who knew the route—at least as far as his destination, Soda Springs, Idaho.

Finally, after encountering endless herds of buffalo and a near-catastrophic twisterlike waterspout, they reached Soda Springs, and a parting of the ways. California was to the west; even Fitzpatrick knew little more than that. By now, only 32 people retained their resolve to continue.

While some men rode on in search of a new guide, the rest of the group headed for the Great Salt Lake. But before they reached it, their scouts returned. They could find no guide, but they'd been given advice: not to venture south into the desert, nor too far north, lest they get lost amid steep canyons.

As the wagon train pushed west, the way became increasingly impassable. No longer able to carry sufficient food, they traded with local Indians for berries and a sweet honey ball they favored until they realized that its main ingredient was mashed insects. In the toughest part of the journey, the emigrants virtually clawed their way across the Sierras. Before they reached the other side, Indians had stolen their remaining mounts. Along the way, they were forced to eat crows, wildcats, and whatever else they could find.

And then they came to a valley ripe with wild grapes and deer and antelope. Astonishingly, at the end of that valley lay the farm of Dr. Marsh, whose letter they carried. It was November 4, 1841, and they'd arrived in California's San Joaquin Valley.

In a trek marked by dogged determination and incredible good luck, 1 woman and 31 men had made the historic journey to "paradise."

Epilogue: Bartleson faded into the haze of history. Bidwell made a fortune in the '49 gold rush and even ran for president. And Green turned out to be an embezzler; his lead bars were really gold.

Land Sailors: Trying to Harness the Wind

In 1830 a wind-driven car set sail on the Baltimore & Ohio Railroad. Doomed to failure, the Aeolus *proved how difficult it was to handle when it sailed off the end of the track smack into an embankment.*

In 1853 Tom "Windwagon" Smith was confident that his vehicle could "fly over the plains." But his enormous Conestoga-style wagon, complete with a 20-foot mast flying a huge sail, got caught in a crosswind and careened in a circle—and his investors abandoned ship.

On a sunny spring day in 1860, as a windwagon sailed into Denver, "everyone crossed the street to get a sight of this new-fangled frigate."

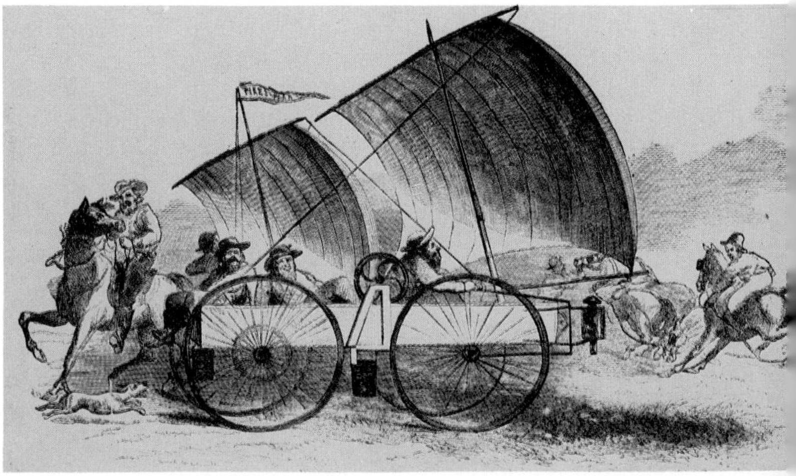

Father of the Oregon Trail

Regarding the Oregon Trail as "sacred to the memories of the pioneers," Ezra Meeker retraced his travels along the famous route four times—the first at age 75.

In 1852 he had gone west with his family, settling in Washington, where he lived for the next 53 years. Then, "to mark it for all time for the children of the pioneers who blazed it," he returned to the trail in 1906 and 1910 by wagon. In 1915 he went by car. And in 1924, at the age of 93, he got a bird's-eye view, following its course for 1,300 miles by plane.

When he died just before his 98th birthday, Ezra Meeker (above) was preparing for another trip on the well-worn pioneer route—in an auto reminiscent of a prairie schooner.

The Wagon Train Led by a Dead Man

A devoted father kept his promise to the end

To William Keil a promise was a sacred thing. In 1855 he promised his 19-year-old son, Willie, that he could lead their wagon train west. Not even Willie's sudden death could prevent him from honoring his word; he had his son's body placed in a lead-lined casket and preserved in alcohol. And when the wagons started rolling westward, Willie led the way.

Decision

Keil, a German immigrant, was a tailor, a medical practitioner, and a Methodist-turned-mystic. His powerful personality and strong religious conviction readily attracted followers. Though he was barely literate, Keil succeeded in establishing a colony in 1844 at Bethel, Missouri. He was, of course, its leader.

Comprising mostly German immigrants, the Bethel Colony had distinguished itself from most other utopian experiments by its relative success. Despite this, Keil felt crowded by secular society. After sending scouts to the Washington Territory to stake out claims, he decided to move part of the colony there.

Departure

The group intended to set out in May 1855. Willie's death from malaria delayed those plans, but not for long. Though deeply saddened, Keil did not preserve and transport the body because of sentiment. He carried the corpse across a continent solely to prove to his followers how strong was the bond of a man's word.

The expedition must have been a bizarre sight: Keil, a bearded, heavy-set man, would give a blast on a trumpet to signal the start of each day's march. Willie's coffin led the cortege. The colonists followed, singing German funeral hymns. And the Indians, respectful, fearful, and at least a little awed, left them alone.

Arrival

Upon reaching the Willapa Valley in October, Keil was disappointed to find the site unsuitable for settlement. Short of money but not of spunk, he resolved to push farther north into the Oregon Territory, where he eventually founded the colony of Aurora.

But first his group took time out for a long overdue ceremony—Willie's burial. Willapa was their original destination and only 20 miles from the Pacific Ocean. Keil had kept his promise: Willie had led them across the continent.

"I, Only an Indian Woman"

Sarah Winnemucca, fighter for Indian survival

Stunned at the poverty and degradation of her people, the Paiutes, in the mid-1860's, Sarah Winnemucca delivered a stiff message: become like the white people and learn to work for a living!

Sarah, about 21 years old, was impressed by the whites. She had been living with them in California and had attended a convent school at the insistence of her grandfather, Chief Truckee. Guide for the explorer John C. Frémont in the 1840's, he had great admiration for the palefaces.

But her people were learning bitterness. After the great silver strike of 1859, whites had swarmed into western Nevada, the Paiutes' territory, grabbing their land and depriving them of a livelihood. In 1860 a war blazed between whites and Indians; afterward, the Paiutes were driven onto Pyramid Lake Reservation, where they could find little food. Starving, many crept back to the white settlements to accept handouts or take menial jobs—or to steal.

Polite indifference

A high-spirited, precocious young woman, Sarah was proud of being a Paiute. Her father, Chief Winnemucca, was too mild and ineffectual to lead, so she stepped forward to spur her people on and to solicit the help of white officials. Soon becoming exasperated by their polite indifference, she joined her brother Natchez on the reservation.

There she was outraged by the corruption of the Indian agent in charge, who leased reservation land to white ranchers and sold government provisions that were intended for the Paiutes, leaving them to starve. After the Indians retaliated for the killing of one of their own, the agent asked the commander of Fort McDermitt to send troops to punish them. Instead, he summoned Sarah and Natchez to hear *their* side.

"We went like the wind," she recalled. Impassioned and eloquent, she described the Paiutes' plight. At once the commander dispatched supplies and canvas tents. He even offered the Paiutes the fort as a refuge from the whites! Before long, 900 Paiutes were living there, and Sarah was earning $65 a month as camp interpreter.

Cruel treatment

All went well until the sympathetic commander was transferred; his replacement cut off the Indians' food rations, and the hungry Paiutes returned to Pyramid Lake Reservation. Realizing that her people needed a permanent home and farming skills, Sarah repeatedly asked the commissioner of Indian Affairs in Washington, D.C., for assistance. She was considered a troublemaker.

In 1875 Sarah led many Paiutes north to the Malheur Reservation in Oregon, where she was hired as interpreter for agent Sam Parrish. Unlike most Indian agents—virtual tyrants who had bought their posts—he did all he could for the Indians. But he was replaced by a man named William Rinehart. Under his cruel administration, the Indians suffered helplessly. When Sarah protested to Washington, Rinehart attacked her character.

In 1878 the desperate Paiutes collected $29.65 to send Sarah to the nation's capital to plead their case. She started out on June 8 with her team of horses and a buckboard, carrying three white passengers bound for Silver City, Idaho. From there she planned to take the Union Pacific Railroad.

A dangerous mission

As they rumbled toward Silver City, a U.S. Army detachment halted them and Sarah learned that the Bannocks, an Idaho tribe, were leading a great Indian uprising and had kidnapped part of her peace-loving tribe, including her father. The army, worried that the Paiutes might join forces with the Bannocks, needed someone to steal into the enemy encampment and help them to escape to Fort Lyon. Sarah undertook the dangerous mission. Riding day and night, she covered 223 miles, accompanied by two Paiute men. "Yes, I went for the Government when the officers could not get an Indian man or a white man to go for love or money," she declared. "I, only an Indian woman, went and saved my father and his people."

During the three-month Bannock War, Sarah, as interpreter for Gen. O. O. Howard, fearlessly galloped back and forth with dispatches and read the Indian smoke signals. At the end of the war, the Paiutes named her a chief, an honor never before accorded a woman. The federal government awarded Sarah $500, but ignored a promise to her that the Paiutes could return to their ancestral lands.

Instead, the tribe was force-marched in the dead of winter over two mountain ranges to a desolate reservation in Yakima, Washington. After more than a month's trek, during which many froze to death, 543 Snake and Paiute Indians arrived at Yakima and were herded into a long, unheated shed. The Paiutes accused Sarah of having been duped by the white men she had trusted. She was devastated. "I wish this was my last day in this cruel world," she wrote.

The spurned order

Chief Sarah made a bold move: she went to San Francisco to give lectures on the plight of her tribe. "If your people will help us . . . I will promise to educate my people and make them law-abiding citizens of the United States," she told applauding audiences.

Alarmed by the surge of sympathy for Sarah, the Bureau of Indian Affairs invited her to Washington to talk with Secretary of the Interior Carl Schurz and meet President Rutherford B. Hayes. Schurz issued an order freeing the Paiutes from the reservation and guaranteeing them land allotments. But when Sarah triumphantly presented the order to the Indian agent at Yakima, he ignored it. It was not, he said, addressed to him.

In 1883 Sarah turned again to the lecture platform, traveling this time to Boston and other eastern cities. She gained further attention for her cause by writing her autobiography, *Life among the Paiutes: Their Wrongs and Claims* (the first book in English by an Indian). The next year Sarah was invited to testify before a congressional committee, and Congress quickly passed a bill allowing the Paiutes to leave Yakima. This time it was Secretary Schurz who ignored it.

His betrayal was a blow from which Sarah never recovered. Returning to Nevada, she opened a school for Indian children. In 1887, after the death of her husband (her second white spouse), she grew despondent and went to visit her sister in Montana. There she died in 1891, apparently of tuberculosis.

Wearing a beaded buckskin tunic and red leather leggings, Chief Sarah Winnemucca was a knockout in Boston lecture halls. Speaking from the heart, she moved audiences to tears.

Beyond the Shirt Off His Back

How long underwear saved John Wesley Powell

Explorer John Wesley Powell lost his right arm in the Battle of Shiloh. Almost seven years later, that loss nearly cost him his life. The near-fatal mishap occurred in 1869, while he was scaling a sheer rock wall that towered more than 800 feet above the Green River in Utah.

Powell, a largely self-trained geologist and naturalist, was leading a nine-man party down the Colorado River and its tributaries—they would be the first to travel through the Grand Canyon. As he and a companion, George Bradley, inched along a treacherous rock face, he saw a promising foothold, made a short leap—and found himself trapped. He was what rock climbers call "rimmed," unable to move without risk of falling.

Powell's diary, as illustrated above, never explained how Bradley shed his long johns while remaining clothed.

Powell shouted to Bradley, who was able to climb to a ledge above him but was still too far away to reach his arm. Bradley searched for a branch to stretch down; finding none, he tried the barometer case they carried for scientific observations. But the case was too thick for Powell to grasp securely with his one hand.

By this time, Powell's legs were about to give out. "My muscles begin to tremble," he recalled in his diary. "If I lose my hold, I shall fall to the bottom." Just then Bradley had an inspiration. He quickly stripped off his long underwear and extended the dangling legs down toward Powell. With his heart in his throat, the trapped explorer loosed his grip on the rock and made a life-or-death grab for the waving cloth. It worked. The underwear held, and Bradley was able to lift Powell high enough to grasp his wrist and pull him to safety.

Bradley's inspired use of his own underwear proved a boon to American science. Powell went on to chart the Grand Canyon and head both the U.S. Geological Survey and the Bureau of American Ethnology. In his day, he was America's most important scientific administrator and a strong advocate of government-funded research.

Mercer's Maidens

Rounding the Horn with a boatload of brides

Asa Shinn Mercer knew exactly what Washington Territory needed most: Women!

The adventurous men who had migrated to the Pacific Northwest in the mid-19th century were so lonely that stories circulated of miners traveling the entire day simply to gaze from afar at a female face. To young Mercer, already a founder and the first president of the territory's new university by his mid-twenties, the solution to the problem seemed clear, if a continent away. New England, its male population decimated by the Civil War, had a surplus of young women. The task was simply to bring the supply to the demand.

Early in 1865 Mercer placed an advertisement in a Seattle newspaper, promising to find a wife for every man who subscribed $300 toward the cost of bringing her from the East. Reaction was predictably enthusiastic. Seattle even held a band concert in Mercer's honor the day he left on his cross-country connubial campaign.

Although one New York magazine approvingly wrote of him as a modern Moses leading an exodus to the West, hoots of disbelief greeted his assurances that the girls would be employed only as schoolmistresses of the greatest propriety. Skeptics wondered how there could be any children to teach in Washington if so few women resided there. Rumors arose of more tainted intentions, and Mercer was accused of "seeking to carry off young girls for the benefit of miserable old bachelors." Nonetheless, plenty of adventuresome young women saw the logic of his transcontinental plan, and he jubilantly wrote home to Seattle that he had 300 recruits.

Then his troubles began. By the time he was able to get passage for the "Mercer girls" on January 16, 1866, his flock had dwindled to a mere 100. The four-month trip around Cape Horn took a further toll—not in seasickness but in lovesickness. Predictably, despite warnings from both Mercer and the captain, romance blossomed between the ship's passengers and its crew.

But even shipboard dalliance paled when compared with the enthusiastic welcome the ladies found in Lota, Chile, where they were courted by that outpost's military officers. One of Mercer's belles rode a spirited horse with such style that she received 17 proposals on the spot. Many others wanted to stay with their Chilean suitors, forcing the ship's captain to sneak out of port at night to prevent his precious cargo from escaping. Later, 11 *did* stay behind in San Francisco.

Excitement ran so high as the ship docked at Seattle that Mercer had to go ashore first to warn eager swains to mind their manners if they wanted a bride.

Subscribers to the original fund soon discovered that their $300 outlay gave them no added advantage in securing a wife. One man, who had given Mercer money to bring back a particular lady with whom he had corresponded, found instead a different woman of the same name. Making the best of it, he gallantly proposed: "All I want is a wife, and if you are willin' I would as soon take you as the other woman." But this Mercer girl had not come so far to be second best. "I do not wish to marry, sir," came the reply.

Not all the newcomers were so unyielding. Among the first marriages after the long-awaited ship reached Seattle was that of Miss Annie Stephens, formerly of Baltimore, to Asa Shinn Mercer.

The courage and grit of the female voyagers who Asa Shinn Mercer led around Cape Horn to Seattle are undeniable. Nonetheless, the illustrator of this sketch, for the January 6, 1866, issue of Harper's Weekly, *depicted the women demurely posed on the deck of the steamship* Continental, *as if they were setting out on an afternoon excursion.*

Putting a Lid on the Casket Girls Myth

There are still families in New Orleans who believe that they are descended from a 1728 shipload of French women called the Casket Girls. They were given the name not for any morbid reason but because the French government, which sponsored them, gave each one an outfit of clothes in a small trunk—a cassette *in French. Hence, they were known as* filles de la cassette, *or "casket girls." Religious orphans, they had been raised at a Parisian hospital and were (at least socially) a good deal more desirable than the region's earlier influx of femininity: women who had been forcibly exported to America from French prisons or from careers as prostitutes.*

But this page in the family genealogy is a myth. The Casket Girls never reached New Orleans. They debarked in 1721 at Old Biloxi (now Ocean Springs, Mississippi)—81 pristine young ladies overseen by a trio of nuns. Old Biloxi's males wasted no time getting them to the altar; 70 weddings took place between February and August. As for New Orleans, it got a boatload of Ursuline nuns in August 1727.

Writing Was the Easy Part *The mail makes its way west*

Shortly after gold was discovered in California in 1848, the Post Office awarded a contract to the Pacific Mail Steamship Company. Eastern mail took a month to reach San Francisco by way of Panama, where it crossed the isthmus by rail. Mail was left unsorted, and miners had to paw through mountains of letters once they arrived at the post office. In typical gold-rush spirit, entrepreneurs quickly took advantage of this chaos: for an ounce of gold ($16), Alexander Todd would find and deliver a letter. By 1852 Wells Fargo & Company had begun private mail delivery.

Overland routes and the Pony Express

In 1856 more than 75,000 Californians petitioned for overland transcontinental delivery. The postmaster general awarded the $600,000 annual contract to John Butterfield's 2,800-mile Oxbow Route through the Southwest. Butterfield promised delivery in 25 days and, to the astonishment of skeptics, he did it. On September 16, 1858, a coach left Tipton, Missouri, reaching San Francisco only 23 days, 23 hours later. "A glorious triumph for civilization and the Union," gushed President James Buchanan.

In April 1860 the Pony Express cut the time to 10 days or less. Its founder, William H. Russell, won the federal contract by recruiting the right kind of riders: "Wanted: Young, skinny, wiry fellows not over 18. Must be expert riders willing to risk death daily. Orphans preferred." Although it lasted less than 19 months, the Pony Express carried 34,753 pieces of mail over the 1,966 miles between St. Joseph, Missouri, and Sacramento, California, losing only one mail sack. The record time of 7 days, 17 hours was set getting Lincoln's 1861 inaugural address to California. But in October of that year, when the transcontinental telegraph line was completed, the Pony Express became an anachronism.

End of an era

The death knell of horse and wagon delivery was struck by the hammers that drove the golden spike to complete the transcontinental railway on May 10, 1869. Mail had been sorted in railroad cars since 1862 on runs between Hannibal and St. Joseph, Missouri, where it was shifted to westbound stagecoaches. In 1864 the railroad post office began, and with transcontinental railroads, mail arrived in California presorted. By 1930 the railway mail service, a branch of the U.S. Post Office, was using more than 10,000 trains to deliver mail to every crossroads town in the country.

Fenton Whiting, pictured at left in an 1861 engraving, proved that many modern mail carriers are wrong: a dog can be the postman's best friend. In the winter of 1858 he hitched some mongrels to a $75 sled and brought the mail through California's deep Sierra Nevada snow by dog team. His canine couriers lasted until 1865, when sleigh runners were put on stagecoaches and horses were fitted with snowshoes for the winter runs.

Clothes Don't Make the Man

The stagecoach driver had a secret

Charlie Parkhurst, a hard-drinking tobacco chewer, went west from New England during the California gold rush. Finding work as a stagecoach driver, he promptly became a legend for bringing runs in on time. So obsessive was Charlie about schedules that he once raced his coach across a bridge as it was collapsing beneath him.

The first time Charlie was held up, he shot two of the bandits dead. But despite this bravado, Charlie was strangely shy and fastidious. He insisted on sleeping away from other drivers, and he was always clean shaven.

When Charlie died in 1879, his neighbors finally discovered his secret—"he" was a woman. As Charlotte Parkhurst, she had first worn men's clothes to escape from an orphanage. The clothes also got her by an election board at Soquel, California. In November 1868 she was the first woman to vote in a presidential election.

William Hamilton, the first Pony Express rider to reach San Francisco, actually arrived by steamboat from Sacramento. Amid great ceremony (left), he and his horse debarked at 12:38 A.M. on April 14, 1860. Later deliveries were made by the boat's captain.

Short of U.S. troops, Maj. Frank North and his brother Luther led Pawnees (above) against Sioux and Cheyenne raiders.

Protecting the Iron Horse

"Bareback" Pawnee riders aided the Union Pacific

As the Union Pacific workers on the transcontinental railroad moved west from Omaha, they quickly found themselves attacked by Sioux and Cheyennes, whose hunting grounds they had invaded. The army was supposed to provide protection, but post–Civil War budget cuts had thinned its ranks. Only about 200 cavalrymen and 600 infantrymen were on duty between Omaha and the Colorado border some 500 miles away. Fort Kearny, Nebraska, for example, had a garrison of 12 infantrymen and a small marching band.

The railroad finally got able defenders when Maj. Frank North recruited Pawnee Indians to patrol the tracks. The Pawnees had been farmers in Texas until the Spanish introduced horses; then they became nomads whose buffalo hunts made them enemies of the Sioux and Cheyennes. Outfitted with regulation uniforms, the Pawnee scouts outraged spit-and-polish officers by cutting the seats from their trousers and riding barebottomed into action.

Their effectiveness, however, was undeniable. When Chief Turkey Leg's Cheyennes derailed a freight train near Plum Creek, Nebraska, in 1867, North's Pawnees were more than 200 miles away. They reached Plum Creek the next day and, without a pause, took after the Cheyennes, killing 17 of them. There were no more Indian raids in Nebraska that year.

A Hair-raising Case

The man who was scalped and left for dead

A doctor practicing medicine on the nation's western frontier in the mid-1800's had to be prepared for almost anything. Yet in August 1867, when Dr. Richard Moore of Omaha was confronted by a man carrying his scalp in a bucket of water, all of his medical talents—as well as his constitution—were put to the test. For here on his doorstep was a patient who had barely escaped with his life, let alone his hair.

Ambush!

The victim of the scalping was William Thompson, a repairman for the Union Pacific Railroad who had been sent out to fix a break in a telegraph line. On the way, he was set upon by a band of Cheyenne Indians in a sudden, vicious attack. They took his scalp, but an Indian accidentally dropped it as he mounted his steed. Though, as he later said, "it just felt as if the whole head was taken right off," Thompson managed to retrieve the scalp.

After struggling some 15 miles to the nearest railway station, the victim was taken to Omaha, where Dr. Moore assessed his pitiful pate. "The scalp was entirely removed from a space measuring nine inches by seven," he later reported. "The denuded surface extended from one inch above the left eyebrow backwards." Thompson's hope of having his scalp restored was dashed when he was told it simply could not be sewn back in place. With time and care, however, his head healed.

Before returning to his native England, Thompson gave the scalp, now tanned and preserved, to Dr. Moore, who eventually presented it to the Omaha Public Library Museum for display. It was, assuredly, a grisly memento of savage times in the Old West.

William Thompson, after he was treated for the terrible wounds suffered in an Indian attack. In addition to being scalped, he was also the victim of a tomahawk wound to his head and a gunshot wound in the arm.

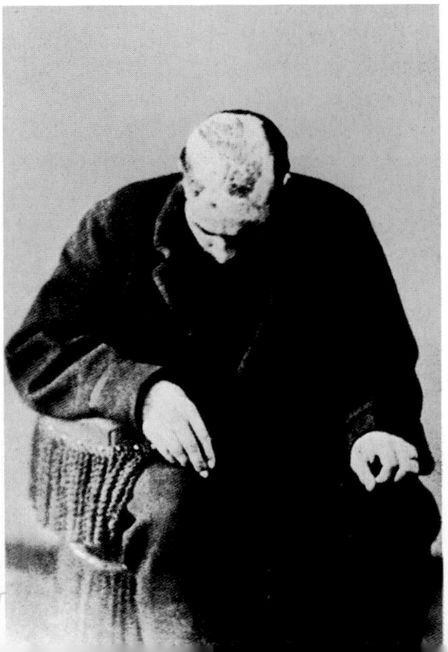

Calamity Jane

A foul-mouthed frontier-style Florence Nightingale

While drinking in a Montana bar near the end of her life, the notorious Calamity Jane turned to her friend, a cowhand named Teddy Blue, and remarked: "I want to be left alone to go to Hell in my own way. I want to be with you boys, that's the only life I know." They were drinking on money Blue had paid back for a kindness she had done him years before.

Much maligned by a host of tall tales and long-remembered legends, Calamity Jane was basically a loner, given to bragging and brawling and hanging around with some pretty rough varmints. But, as it turns out, she was also a woman of great compassion who gave money to hungry cowhands, treated children gently, and tended the sick wherever she happened to be.

Smallpox strikes

The two sides of her character were never more evident than in Deadwood, South Dakota, during the smallpox epidemic of 1878.

The smallpox victims, relegated by terrified residents to a little shack outside town, were cared for by Deadwood's lone physician, Dr. Babcock. One day he was startled to find Calamity waiting for him in front of the modest cabin. When he asked her what she was doing there, the tall, scruffy-looking woman replied, "Well, Doc, somebody's got to take care of them."

Calamity's humanity

After entering the shack, she ordered the doctor to tell her just what to do. And then she proceeded to do it. Her nursing abilities had already been praised in a newspaper account: "There's a lot of humanity in Calamity."

Plucky Pioneer Midwife

When Minnie Melton arrived in Pine, Idaho, in the early 1880's, she was the closest thing the community had to a doctor. Not only did she deliver babies, but she ministered to the citizenry with sage tea, cocklebur syrup, and other remedies that she always carried. Wearing a handmade shawl and a bonnet, her trademarks, she became a familiar sight in and around the little gold-mining town.

When called out during fierce winter weather, Minnie was carried by the "human chair brigade" (right) through snow that was often over the head of this tiny (four-foot six-inch) good samaritan.

Jane stayed at the remote pesthouse (as it was called) caring for patients until the epidemic finally ended. C. H. Robinson, who was a small boy at the time, recalled "Old Calam" as a devoted nurse who was given to growling orders like, "Here, you little bastard, drink this soup."

A story that some view as doubtful, but that might just be typical, has Jane taking sacks of groceries out of a Deadwood store. When the owner pointed out that she had failed to pay the two ounces of gold dust he had charged her for the purchases, she drew her six-gun and said, "Don't worry about your damned bill. I'll pay for it when the boys get better."

Whether Calamity Jane was the romantic figure of western legend or a violent, hard-drinking slattern, it is clear she could be counted on to pitch in when help was needed. The only time she was ever tried for a crime, it turned out that the money she had stolen had been contributed to a hospital for the care of a sick prostitute.

Calamity Jane died in 1903 and was buried in Deadwood. The undertaker, who had been one of her smallpox patients, donated a coffin. And the rector of the cemetery, who sealed her coffin and lowered her into the grave, was none other than C. H. Robinson, who had been so gruffly and lovingly nursed back to health by Calamity Jane in the sad little pesthouse during the terrible epidemic of '78.

Flamboyant figure with a heart of gold: "Hellcat" Calamity Jane—born Martha Jane Canary—shows her sentimental side as she visits the grave of her good friend Wild Bill Hickok, murdered by cowardly Jack McCall while playing poker in 1876. At her request, she was buried beside Hickok after her death in 1903.

A Plague Like Those of Biblical Times

The hideous swarms ate everything but the rocks

In 1874 locusts ravaged parts of South Dakota, Minnesota, Nebraska, Kansas, Missouri, and Iowa. Burning off the pests—even using guns—proved futile. By 1902 the species was extinct; nobody knows why.

The suddenness of the onslaught was astounding. Farm families would first notice a thick gray cloud approaching. Then they would hear the beating of wings, a sound not unlike that of a cascading waterfall. All at once there would descend a swarm of 120 billion grasshoppers—a mile high, 100 miles wide, and up to 300 miles long.

The hoppers plunged down, and the munching noises of their feasting echoed across the land. First they'd devour the crops, then go after the tools and harnesses. Desperately, people hit at the greedy insects—sometimes four deep on the ground—with whatever they could wield. But no matter how many were killed, others took their places. They ate through cloth hastily thrown over crops, survived fires, and ignored smudge pots. (One farmer claimed that hoppers would warm their legs by his fire.) "Hopperdozers" were used; the insects were forced into a pan of sticky tar, then thrown into a fire.

The ravenous creatures also invaded homes and stores, consuming clothing, curtains, and of course food. Then, after a few days, they went on to ruin some other area, leaving wells and streams polluted with their corpses. People whose existences were already spare were reduced to destitution.

The insects were actually Rocky Mountain locusts. They normally bred in the foothills of Montana and Wyoming, but in dry weather, such as the summers from 1874 to 1878, they swarmed to more fertile lands.

Frontier farmers were a hearty lot, but this plague discouraged hundreds of them; giving up the fight, they went back east. Others hung on. They appointed committees to go east for supplies, some counties voted relief bonds to aid the destitute, and affected states also provided aid. In 1875 Congress appropriated $30,000 for seeds. Meanwhile, settlers continued to be lured west by free or cheap land. They knew they faced the risk of being wiped out by storms, drought, or locusts, but these optimists contended that "things will be better this year." And, for some, they were.

From Russia, With Know-how

The immigrants who brought winter wheat to Kansas

Before Kansas became America's Breadbasket, corn was king. But when the Mennonites arrived in 1874 with bushels of hardy winter wheat seed, an agricultural explosion was touched off.

The pacifist Mennonites, a sect that had, over generations, been cast out of one country after another, had come to America by way of the Ukraine in Russia. Kansas, seeking a population that could farm efficiently, wooed them and welcomed them. Settling in, they built communities that have survived to this day, and in a real sense they brought stability to the Sunflower State.

Both drought and a plague of locusts greeted the first Mennonites. Unfazed, the practical, hardworking immigrants built houses and planted their winter wheat. The plague had wiped out the corn and the soft spring wheat, but winter wheat, sown the previous fall and cut before the insect attack, had turned a profit. That did it. Winter wheat became Kansas's main crop, and the new pioneers tamed the plains.

Though the newcomers were welcomed for their agricultural acumen, local newspapers at first mocked their odd clothing and different ways. But when the Mennonites paid their debts in gold, scorn turned to praise, for members of the sect certainly refilled the depleted state coffers.

Ultimately the wheat yields increased to such an extent that—just to complete the circle—in this century Kansas and neighboring states have shipped wheat to Russia, the country to which the bountiful fields of grain can easily be traced.

The "Kansas Fever" Exodus

In a phenomenal migration, thousands of blacks—called Exodusters—streamed west seeking a better life

Eager to escape laws requiring passes, harsh sharecropper contracts, imprisonment, and murder, thousands of blacks were beset with "Kansas fever," and in 1879 they set off for the promised land, where slavery had never existed. Many who poured off southern plantations onto steamboats were nearly destitute, few knew anything about Kansas, and most had been duped by promises of free transportation and land.

The first boatload landed in St. Louis in "utter want." Local blacks opened their churches as dormitories and collected money to send the throngs on to Kansas. But Kansas City refused to allow blacks to settle there, so they moved to tiny Wyandotte, which shortly "looked like the almshouses of the Mississippi Valley had been searched to get them together."

Southern whites blamed the exodus on fraudulent handbills and railroad promotions. But blacks had been leaving the South for years—ever since it became clear that Reconstruction promises would not be fulfilled. The National Colonization Council had plans to send émigrés to Liberia, but in 1879 Kansas fever even overshadowed the attractions of Africa.

A steamboat strike, though finally settled, slowed the migration, and by 1881 the flood of Exodusters was reduced to a trickle.

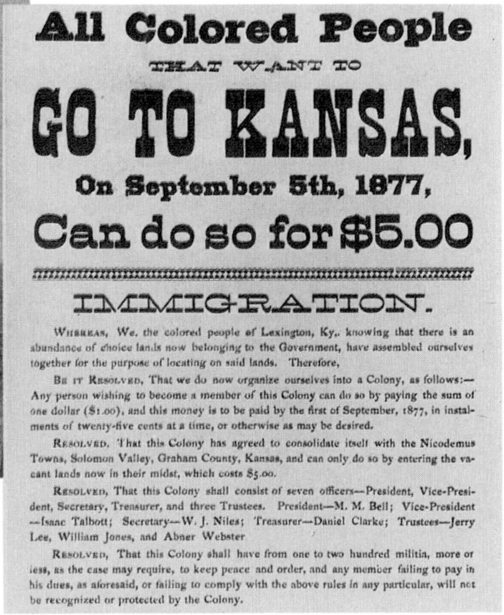

All Colored People

THAT WANT TO

GO TO KANSAS,

On September 5th, 1877,

Can do so for $5.00

IMMIGRATION.

WHEREAS, We, the colored people of Lexington, Ky., knowing that there is an abundance of choice lands now belonging to the Government, have assembled ourselves together for the purpose of locating on said lands. Therefore,

BE IT RESOLVED, That we do now organize ourselves into a Colony, as follows:—Any person wishing to become a member of this Colony can do so by paying the sum of one dollar ($1.00), and this money is to be paid by the first of September, 1877, in instalments of twenty-five cents at a time, or otherwise as may be desired.

RESOLVED, That this Colony has agreed to consolidate itself with the Nicodemus Towns, Solomon Valley, Graham County, Kansas, and can only do so by entering the vacant lands now in their midst, which costs $5.00.

RESOLVED, That this Colony shall consist of seven officers—President, Vice-President, Secretary, Treasurer, and three Trustees. President—M. M. Bell; Vice-President—Isaac Talbott; Secretary—W. J. Niles; Treasurer—Daniel Clarke; Trustees—Jerry Lee, William Jones, and Abner Webster

RESOLVED, That this Colony shall have from one to two hundred militia, more or less, as the case may require, to keep peace and order, and any member failing to pay in his dues, as aforesaid, or failing to comply with the above rules in any particular, will not be recognized or protected by the Colony.

A Tennessee cabinetmaker claimed to be the Father of the Colored Exodus. "Pap" Singleton's handbills encouraged emigration, and in 1879 Singleton Colony was incorporated near present-day Emporia, Kansas.

The Hard Drive West

Goodnight and Loving's cattle herds blazed a new route

A great cattle baron in his later years, with a herd of 100,000, Charlie Goodnight (above) did much to establish respect for the law among ranchers who saw nothing wrong with stealing unbranded stock.

Most Texas cattlemen drove their great herds of longhorns north to the stockyards in Missouri or Kansas, but not Charlie Goodnight. In the spring of 1866 he planned to blaze a new *westward* trail to Colorado. There was plenty of good range there, and lots of money because of the new silver mines.

Outfitting for his first drive, the 30-year-old Goodnight, a former Texas ranger and an experienced woodsman, bought a government wagon with strong iron axles, equipped it with a chuckbox, and stocked it with sourdough starter and other provisions—thus creating the first chuck wagon. He was nearly ready to depart when he met Oliver Loving, another pioneer cattleman, and they agreed to join forces. They set out with 2,000 longhorns and 18 cowboys.

Goodnight's route went through New Mexico to avoid dangerous Comanche country, but encountered a host of new problems. From Fort Belknap in the Texas panhandle they would take the old stagecoach-rutted Butterfield Mail Route to the Middle Concho River and follow it to its headwaters; from there they would have to cross 80 miles of waterless plain to the Pecos River. Continuing up the Pecos, their course would parallel the Rockies north to Denver.

On June 6 Goodnight and Loving pointed their cattle westward. Reaching the headwaters of the Concho, they filled their water barrels and let the cattle drink. Then they headed into the setting sun to cross the dreaded plain. By the end of the second day, the cattle were too thirsty to bed down, and so they stumbled on. For three days and nights the men rode without sleep, driving cattle that bawled constantly for water. More than 300 animals died, their carcasses left to mark the trail.

Smelling water when it was still miles away, the crazed beasts made a mad dash and, at the end of the stampede, catapulted over the river's steep banks. Many drowned. Others were mired in quicksand. Some drank from alkali holes (pools of water with a poisonous concentration of alkaline salt scoured up by the river) and dropped dead in their tracks.

Rounding up the survivors, Goodnight and Loving pushed north along the Pecos through desolate rattlesnake country. By then many cows were dropping calves. Hundreds of newborns had to be shot while the cows, bawling until they were hoarse, milled about trying to find their offspring.

About July 1 they reached Fort Sumner, where the army had in its charge several thousand starving Indians. The military bought part of the herd for eight cents a pound on the hoof—a total of $12,000 in gold. Overjoyed, Loving pressed on to Colorado to sell the rest while Goodnight backtracked to Texas to bring up a second herd before winter set in.

This time, crossing the arid plain, Goodnight let the cattle graze at sunup and sundown and trailed them in between. Using this system, he never lost another head. In years to follow, millions of hoofs would pound the Goodnight-Loving Trail.

Gobbling Up America

How else could you get the birds to market?

In the 1860's, after a fire had destroyed Henry Hooker's store in Hangtown, California, he bought a big flock of turkeys for $1.50 apiece and, with the help of two dogs, set out for Carson City, Nevada. At the edge of a precipice high in the Sierras, the birds balked. Nagged by the dogs, they flew off the cliff and vanished. After a desperate scramble down, Hooker found his turkeys in the trees and gathered them together. He finally sold them to hungry silver miners for $5 each and built a ranch.

Turkey drives had long been common. Fast runners, the big birds can briefly outstrip a pony, and so when an Arkansas farmer once bet that his ducks could beat a flock of turkeys to market 60 miles away, the bet was accepted. The turkeys left the ducks far behind but then stopped to roost. The ducks walked all night and won. A turkey's habit of roosting whenever and wherever it chooses caused other problems: on a Vermont-to-Boston drive a flock once alighted on a schoolhouse, stoving in the roof and nearly killing the schoolmaster.

Code of the Range

Texan Sam Maverick refused to brand his cattle back in the 1840's. Some said it was so he could round up his neighbors' unbranded stock along with his own. Others claimed Sam himself was the victim of rustlers because his livestock was unmarked. In any event, an unbranded cow came to be called a maverick.

On the open range, where many herds mingled, branding was essential for identifying an owner. A good cowhand knew all the variations of the elements combined in a brand: letters, numerals, geometric designs, and pictorial symbols. Brands are read from left to right, from top to bottom, and from the outside in. Ranchers often personalized their brands. The symbol $\overline{\text{yy}}$, for example, belonged to one Mr. Barwise.

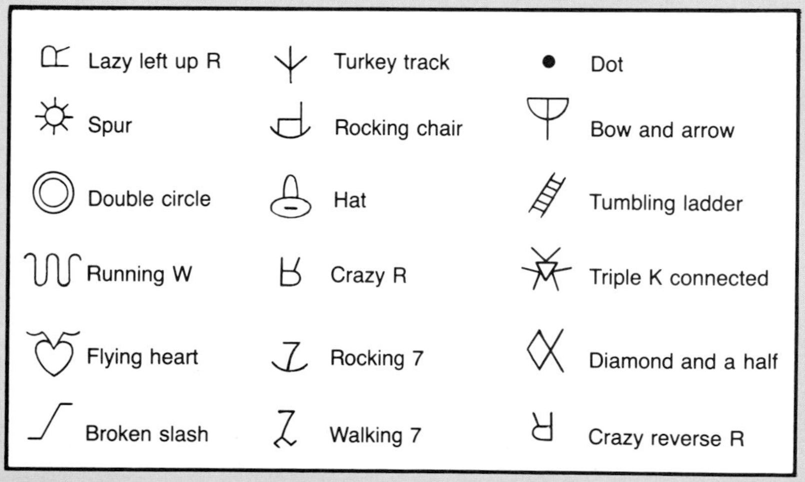
Lazy left up R
Spur
Double circle
Running W
Flying heart
Broken slash
Turkey track
Rocking chair
Hat
Crazy R
Rocking 7
Walking 7
Dot
Bow and arrow
Tumbling ladder
Triple K connected
Diamond and a half
Crazy reverse R

The brand at left expressed the view of Texas rancher T. J. Walker: "A man's a fool to raise cattle." Cowhands occasionally used their branding irons to change the F to B as a joke.

Three street arabs (left) asleep in the only home they know—a filthy New York alley. This photograph was taken by Jacob Riis, the journalist whose book How the Other Half Lives *starkly portrayed the conditions from which the Children's Aid Society eventually rescued some 100,000 unwanted boys and girls by finding them new homes.*

From Eastern Slums to Western Farms

Charles Brace's orphan trains gave homeless children a break

They were called street arabs—ragged children who roamed the streets of New York City. By day they were newsboys, bootblacks, beggars, and thieves; by night they slept in barges on the river or in alleyways. In 19th-century New York only a few overcrowded orphanages offered any alternative. That is until 1854, when Charles Brace founded the Children's Aid Society and proposed a novel plan: remove these children from the filthy slums and send them west, to the wholesome atmosphere of America's heartland.

From 1854 to 1929 the Children's Aid Society gathered up tens of thousands of unwanted children. They came from various institutions and even from parents who could not afford to keep them. Each child was given a bath and fresh clothes, and put on an orphan train to find a new home with a family in the West.

The orphan train's arrival was an event as exciting as any fair or traveling show. The train would pull into a small farming community, where hundreds of couples from miles around waited anxiously in a church or the town hall. The children were brought in to be perused by the locals, who, after making a selection, would arrange things with the society's agent, help their new offspring into the family buggy, and go home.

By modern standards such methods seem primitive, even cruel. But life in the city streets offered nothing better, and though not every story had a happy ending, the society did have some striking successes. A 1917 study showed that thousands of farmers, merchants, doctors, and lawyers had gotten their start on orphan trains. Even two future governors—Andrew Burke of North Dakota and John Brady of the Alaska Territory—were taken from a Randall's Island orphanage and sent west on the same train.

Early in this century social workers began finding ways to keep families together; foster homes and modern methods of adoption brought an end to the orphan trains. But while they lasted, they offered a practical solution to an urgent problem.

Clifford Griffin's Lonely Death

Monument to a lost love

High on Brown Mountain, near the town of Silver Plume in the Colorado Rockies, stands a 15-foot granite obelisk with an unlikely inscription: "Clifford Griffin . . . of Brand Hall, Shropshire, England . . . buried near this spot."

The brothers Heneage and Clifford Griffin immigrated to America and became miners. But though they grew rich on silver and gold, Clifford remained disconsolate. He was said to be grieving for his fiancée, who had died just before their wedding. Every evening he would stand by his lonely mountain cabin and play his violin, while other miners listened, far below.

Legend has it that Griffin gouged out a grave from the solid rock and that one June evening in 1887 he finished playing, walked to his tomb, and shot himself. Heneage left money for the care of the grave and returned to England. Mysteriously, although 100 years have passed, the remote mountain obelisk is still scrupulously kept up.

The Miners' Angel

Nellie Cashman did good wherever she could

At 16, Nellie Cashman, a tiny, dark-eyed brunette with a brogue and a hearty laugh, came from Ireland with her sister Fannie and settled in San Francisco. Fannie married and had seven children, but times were hard, and in 1877 Nellie set out for Alaska, where gold had been discovered near Juneau.

According to Nellie, she journeyed north with a party of 200 miners, then "alternately mined and kept a boardinghouse." That fall, when an outbreak of scurvy threatened health and lives in the camp, she traveled 77 days in arctic weather with six men to bring in 1,500 pounds of vegetables and other supplies from Victoria; although they were literally worth their weight in gold, she gave potatoes away to anyone who needed them.

Nellie next tried Virginia City and Tucson, Arizona, where she opened the first of her many restaurants. But brand-new Tombstone, the site of huge silver strikes, beckoned. In 1880 she opened the Nevada Cash Store, selling fruit, provisions, gents' furnishings, dry goods, and children's shoes. Then came the Russ House, a hotel and restaurant. Miners flocked there. "If a fellow has no money, Miss Nellie gives him board and lodging until he makes a stake," one of them wrote.

Tombstone was a boomtown, full of gamblers, prostitutes, and such legendary gunfighters as Wyatt Earp and Doc Holliday. Nellie went calmly about, doing good. She built a Catholic church and was treasurer of the Irish National Land League. She wrote an eloquent newspaper plea for aid for "our less favored kindred in the unequal contest they are waging against . . . want."

In 1884 five men were to be hanged for murder. They were upset because bleachers were being built to make their execution a public spectacle, and because their bodies were to be denied burial and given to medical students for dissection. The night before the execution, Nellie led a midnight party of miners to destroy the bleachers. Then, for 10 nights afterward, two prospectors guarded the murderers' graves.

After 20 years in Tombstone, interspersed by mining expeditions to Baja California, New Mexico, and the Arizona Territory, Nellie returned to Alaska, where she mined and ran a store for the next quarter-century. She ignored friends' requests that she slow down. "I've suffered trials and hardships in the frozen plains of Alaska, and on the deserts of Arizona . . . but I have been happy and healthy," she declared. Her last mining camp was inside the Arctic Circle. She died at 73, in Victoria, from double pneumonia she had contracted after flying in a mail plane.

Premature Landowners

When large parts of the Oklahoma district were opened for free settlement in 1889, tens of thousands thronged to the borders to await the starting gun at noon on April 22 (left). But some sneaked in sooner to stake their claims, even lathering their horses with soap to make them look as if they had just arrived. They were derisively called Sooners, but the term later became respectable; today Oklahoma's nickname is the Sooner State.

On the island of Kauai, 19th-century Hawaiian cowboys (left) bravely straddle some wild descendants of the cattle sent as a gift by Great Britain. The unruly animals sometimes tried to kill men by charging and goring them with their long horns.

The Tropical Cowboy

Polynesian lassos and orchid sombreros

The people of Hawaii had never seen anything quite like these beasts. First, longhorn cattle were brought to the islands in 1793 by British navigator George Vancouver as a gift for King Kamehameha I. Released to roam the lava slopes of unfenced pastures and the forests of pungent eucalyptus, camphor, and sandalwood trees, the tiny herd multiplied rapidly. Then—not to be outdone by the British—the United States shipped a gift of California mustangs to Hawaii in 1803. They too were allowed to run wild.

Within a few decades, the tropical landscape was being transformed by vast foraging herds of cattle and horses. Lush forests were becoming dry, barren plains, and agriculture suffered. Seeing the need for control, King Kamehameha II dispatched agents to California in 1832 to fetch Mexican, Indian, and Spanish vaqueros to teach his people how to domesticate the horses and use them to control the cattle.

The new arrivals made a striking picture in their brightly colored wool ponchos and sashes, and their dashing brimmed sombreros. In time they imparted their cowpunching skills to the Hawaiians, who called themselves *paniolos,* from the word *espanoles* ("Spaniards"). The Hawaiian cowboys added their own flamboyant touches to their outfits: wreaths of orchids on their hats, wooden saddles carved in the likeness of gods, and lariats woven with Polynesian symbols. A few—notably Ikua Purdy, Eben Low, and Archie Kaaua—became top-class rodeo performers in Hawaii and on the mainland.

In effect, the Old West had crossed the seas to the islands. Giant cattle ranches were established on Hawaii and Maui. But cattle roundups had one distinctly local feature: the *paniolos* would lead the bellowing longhorns out from shore through shark-infested waters to be hoisted aboard waiting boats that took them to market in Honolulu.

As on the mainland, there are far fewer ranches today. But the *paniolo* remains a symbol of Hawaii—as the cowboy is of the Old West—a romantic figure holding a revered place in island culture.

A Cloak Fit for a King

When King Kamehameha I wanted a garment that would express the grandeur of his monarchy, he ordered the completion of an unfinished ancestral cloak that ordinary mortals could never duplicate. It was made solely from the feathers of the rare mamo bird; since each bird yielded only six or seven yellow feathers, some 80,000 had to die to provide the 450,000 needed. Ironically, the magnificent garment could not be completed during the king's lifetime; it was later valued at more than $1 million.

Charles Francis Hall—An Unlikely Explorer

His fascination with a lost expedition led to a mystery within a mystery

"I am on a mission of love . . . ready to do or die," Charles Hall rhapsodized in his diary. The former blacksmith and engraver had never before been north of Vermont. But when he first read of the disappearance in 1847 of the renowned English explorer Sir John Franklin on his third Arctic expedition, Hall suddenly saw his mission in life: he too would be an explorer, and he would find out what had happened to Franklin and his men.

The novice sailor set out in May 1860 aboard a whaling ship with a pitiful $980 worth of supplies. He reached Frobisher Bay, where he settled down to live with the Eskimos for the next two years. Hall learned the Eskimo dialects, ate the local food (including seal's blood), and allowed the shamans to treat his maladies.

Although he gleaned no information about the Franklin expedition, Hall returned to the United States rich in experience and, with his usual determination, began raising funds for another Arctic journey. This time, he *did* find relics of the Franklin voyage. And although Hall's bullying and inability to pay his crew almost caused a mutiny, the second expedition established his reputation as an explorer. In 1871 Congress appropriated $50,000 to fund what Hall regarded as his ultimate mission: to sail to the North Pole.

In July, Hall set out from New London on the steamer/sailing ship *Polaris*. Always single-minded, he paid no attention to the simmering stockpot of personalities he'd thrown together. The chief scientific officer, Dr. Emil Bessels, showed open contempt for Hall's scientific qualifications. The sailing master, Sidney Budington, constantly raided the ship's alcohol supply. And ethnic tensions flared among the crew.

But for a while the men made progress, reaching a point of 82°11′—the farthest north a ship had ever sailed. Then winds and ice-clogged seas pushed the *Polaris* south. Hall decided to take refuge for the winter in an inlet he dubbed Thank God Bay, ignoring vehement objections from Bessels and Budington.

The days turned colder, became months. Rations dwindled. Hall set out for a two-week probe of the area. When he returned, he asked for a cup of coffee. Shortly after drinking it, he complained of "a foul stomach." A few days later he was delirious. Sure that Bessels was poisoning him, Hall refused the doctor's medication. Finally, he died. Dr. Bessels's diagnosis: "Apoplexy."

A naval commission later exonerated Bessels and Budington of murder. But in 1968 two scholars exhumed Hall's frozen body. Analysis of hair and fingernails confirmed their suspicions: Hall had been poisoned with arsenic. But the murderers would never be found. Hall, who tried so hard to solve the mystery of an explorer's death, is now himself a murder mystery.

Almost a century after the sudden death of Charles Hall (below), Dr. Chauncey Loomis and Dr. Franklin Paddock traveled to Greenland, found his frozen grave, and exhumed his body (bottom), wrapped in an American flag. Arsenic poisoning was revealed after Hall's hair and nails were treated in a nuclear reactor in Toronto.

Charles Wilkes's sketch of man's first landing on the Antarctic continent was later made into a painting (left), and illustrates that the voyage was a feat not only of exploration and navigation but of survival. The men's clothes, as Wilkes wrote, were "entirely unworthy in the service, and inferior in every way."

Chaos at the Bottom of the World

Charles Wilkes charted an unknown continent

The expedition was controversial from the start. Fishing interests lobbied the government for accurate charts of the lucrative but dangerous Antarctic waters, while other powerful factions opposed public funding. After $30,000 was finally appropriated, several politically astute naval officers declined to command the expedition. But Charles Wilkes, never one to let caution stand in the way of duty, accepted; and in August 1838 his six wooden ships began what would be a four-year journey to the bottom of the world.

It seemed as if everything conceivable was against them. On the first foray into far southern waters, beset by pack ice and racked by gales, one ship sank with all hands. Denying defeat, Wilkes sailed into the South Pacific and spent several months mapping the islands of Hawaii, Tahiti, and Samoa. After putting into Sydney, Australia, for repairs, Wilkes sailed south once more on December 26, 1839, leading the way in his ship, the *Vincennes.* A month later he sighted an Antarctic continent. Wilkes sailed along the unknown coast for hundreds of miles, making charts as he went. In February he rendezvoused with his other ships and led them home.

Upon his return in 1842, Wilkes was outraged that other explorers had challenged his findings. Englishman James Ross, sailing by charts Wilkes had sent him in Australia, claimed to have sailed across areas Wilkes had marked as land. A French captain, Dumont d'Urville, claimed to have sighted Antarctica a day before Wilkes.

Later studies did reveal some inaccuracies in Wilkes's charts—probably because the reflective qualities of the Antarctic atmosphere can distort the proximity of land—but most were astonishingly accurate. D'Urville's ship's log showed that he had failed to allow for the international dateline; Wilkes's sighting had preceded the Frenchman's by 10 hours. Today a vast expanse of the continent he explored at such risk honors the intrepid American's achievement: Wilkes Land's 1,500-mile coastline is about one-fifth of Antarctica's shore.

Holes in the Poles?

"I ask 100 brave companions . . . to start from Siberia . . . I engage we find a warm and rich land, stocked with thrifty vegetables and animals . . . northward of latitude 82." John Symmes, a hero of the War of 1812, was convinced that he could easily sail over the curved rim of a polar hole and into a hollow earth. Attempts by likeminded congressmen to fund Symmes's journey failed in 1823, but public lectures by a Hollow Earth disciple, Jeremiah Reynolds, stressed the commercial potential of the bizarre crusade and helped win support for the Wilkes expedition 15 years later.

The Wrong Stuff

The fabrications of Frederick Cook

Frederick Cook dramatically surveys an Arctic horizon in one of the faked photographs that dazzled the public.

On September 6, 1909, a weary, triumphant Robert Peary wired from Labrador: "Stars and Stripes nailed to the pole—Peary." The 53-year-old explorer had spent nearly 23 years pursuing his goal, but his cable was too late. Five days earlier Dr. Frederick Cook had wired from the Shetland Islands that he had beaten Peary by a year. Commander Peary, a proud and forthright man, told the press that Cook was a liar: It was impossible to reach the pole with only two Eskimos and two sledges. Cook may have been away from his Greenland base for 14 months, but he'd either been hunting or gotten lost.

The controversy was among the most vicious in the history of exploration. Peary spoke to Cook's Eskimo companions, who said that they had gone "no distance north and not out of sight of land." Peary's own claim was supported by Matthew Henson, his longtime aide. But Henson was black, and many people would not take his word. Instead, they believed the handsome and charming Dr. Cook; a bona fide explorer, he had scaled Denali (Mount McKinley), Alaska's highest peak, and brought back a photograph of the view.

But on the day Cook received the keys to New York City, the man who had climbed McKinley with him said they had never been near the 20,320-foot peak. The Explorer's Club investigated and found that the "summit" picture had been taken from a 5,300-foot ridge. Next, an astronomer proved that Cook had fabricated the date and latitude on which he claimed to have seen the midnight sun.

Nevertheless, much of the public still found Cook too charming to disbelieve, and Peary grew increasingly bitter; after he retired from the navy in 1911, he often refused to discuss the North Pole. In 1918, two years before Peary's death, Cook's "North Pole" photographs were discredited. The plausible doctor later served four years in Fort Leavenworth for promoting stock in a company owning oil he had "discovered" in Wyoming.

The Real Thing *Sourdoughs climb McKinley*

One day in 1909 a group of Alaskan miners, popularly called Sourdoughs, were sitting in a saloon in Fairbanks talking about outsiders, like Dr. Frederick Cook, climbing "their" Mount McKinley. Convinced that Cook's ascent had never been made, some of the boys decided to prove it the only way they knew how: by doing it themselves. Enthusiasm in Fairbanks ran high. "Our boys will . . . show up Dr. Cook and other 'outside' doctors and expeditions," the Fairbanks *Times* declared.

Four Sourdoughs—Tom Lloyd, Billy Taylor, Pete Anderson, and Charlie McGonagall—set out in December 1909. For climbing shoes, they strapped spikes on their moccasins. They used hooked poles to balance themselves. In March they reached a ridge 11,000 feet up, and on April 3, carrying a 14-foot wooden flagpole, some doughnuts, and thermoses of hot chocolate, three miners raced for the North Peak. Taylor and Anderson won.

Just as simply as they had gone up, the Sourdoughs returned to camp, in an incredible 18 hours (the ascent would later take professional climbers two weeks). But when Lloyd got back to Fairbanks, few believed his outrageous story, and nobody could see the flagpole.

The first professional climbers to scale Mount McKinley reached the South Peak in June 1913. To their complete amazement, standing proudly on the North Peak, only 850 feet below, was the flagpole left by the Sourdoughs.

Pioneer in the Sky

The first to fly across the Continental Divide

As a child in Ohio, Cromwell Dixon dreamed of flying to Mars. He even drew blueprints for a manned rocket—quite a feat for a boy born in 1892. At 14 he designed a "sky bicycle," a 32-foot silk hot-air balloon on a wooden frame connected to a propeller driven by bicycle pedals and a rudder. Dixon persuaded his mother to sell some jewelry to raise $500 to build it, and for the next three years the boy pedaled his contraption at county fairs. By 1911 Dixon was ready for bigger things. After only three days at the Curtiss Aviation School in Hammondsport, New York, he soloed in a biplane, and when the Aero Club of America gave him pilot's license No. 43, he was, at 19, the youngest pilot in the country.

Ever supportive, Dixon's mother signed a contract with Curtiss so that the underage boy could fly in air shows. After he developed the Dixon corkscrew dive, a spiral from 8,000 feet that leveled off just above the ground, his weekly pay jumped from $1,500 to $2,000.

Then Dixon decided to be first to fly over the Rocky Mountains. Little was known of mountain flying; several previous attempts had been ended by treacherous downdrafts. To encourage the feat, a consortium that included showman John Ringling and the president of the Great Northern Railway had put up a $10,000 purse.

On September 30, 1911, Dixon took off from the Montana state fairgrounds in Helena. He spent 15 minutes reaching an altitude of 7,000 feet—only 800 feet higher than the mountains he intended to cross—then headed for Blossburg, just over the Continental Divide. To provide a landmark, his friends lit a bonfire on a high peak near the town. When Dixon landed, he said, "Boys, I knew I could do it," and wired Curtiss. Tragically, a few days later, Dixon was killed at Spokane, Washington, when a sudden air current slammed his plane into the ground, crushing him under the engine.

Cromwell Dixon's biplane (below) was little more than a bamboo framework. One newspaper referred to it as a "motor kite."

Harriet Quimby

First American aviatrix

The first woman in America—and the second in the world—to earn a pilot's license was Harriet Quimby. A successful journalist in New York City, Harriet became intrigued by airplanes after covering a flying meet in 1910. When reporters quizzed her about taking flying lessons, Harriet replied, "There is no more risk in an airplane than a high-speed automobile, and a lot more fun. Why shouldn't we have some good American women pilots?"

Harriet passed the test for her pilot's license in a Blériot monoplane. America was flying-crazy, and there was good money in air shows. Harriet toured the East and Mexico with the Moisant International Aviators troupe. Then she decided she would be the first woman to fly across the English Channel.

She took off in a biplane on April 16, 1912, sitting in a wicker basket seat in the open fuselage and keeping her bearings in dense fog with only a compass. Finally she risked dropping to 1,000 feet—and emerged into bright sunlight over a French beach. Alas, the sinking of the *Titanic* robbed the pilot of her headlines; and a *New York Times* editorial huffed that her feat "proves ability and capacity, but it doesn't prove equality."

In July, Harriet went to attack the world speed record at the Harvard-Boston Aviation Meet. Although the Blériot was thought to be unstable with a passenger, she took the air-show manager for a spin over Boston Harbor. Suddenly the plane's nose dropped sharply. Harriet managed to right it but, as horrified spectators watched, the plane flipped into another nosedive and crashed into the harbor. Harriet Quimby was dead at 37.

Before the first airmail flight, a road map was strapped to George Boyle's knee (left) to help him navigate 140 miles to Philadelphia. In a later U.S. Post Office test (below), mail was picked up at Mitchel Field, N.Y. William "Wild Bill" Hopson (bottom) was one of the crack civilian pilots who died trying to fly through bad weather.

Airmail or Groundmail?

Ups and downs in the U.S. Postal Service

May 15, 1918, simply wasn't Lt. George Boyle's day. He had been chosen to pilot the first leg of the first scheduled airmail flight, from Washington, D.C., to New York City; curious spectators, among them President Woodrow Wilson, were gathered to witness the historic takeoff of the modified JN-4H biplane, the flying Jenny. But the Jenny seemed to be rooted to the ground, its 150-h.p. Hispano-Suiza engine silent. Boyle sat in the cockpit shouting "Contact" while mechanics desperately spun the propeller—until the awful truth struck them: the plane's gas tank was empty.

Fueled at last, the Jenny rose skyward. But instead of heading north, Boyle circled the field and flew south. An hour later Capt. Benjamin Lipsner, coordinator of the U.S. Post Office's new airmail service, got a phone call from the embarrassed pilot. Explaining that his "compass had gotten a little mixed up," Boyle confessed he had just crashed, and his plane was upside-down in a Maryland cornfield. Lipsner sent a car to recover the pilot and the three sacks of mail.

Some months later military fliers were replaced by a small corps of intrepid airmen, whose skills became legendary. Without cockpit navigational aids, they kept on course by following highways, railroad tracks, and riverbeds. For the first nighttime transcontinental mail flight, residents of small Nebraska towns lit bonfires to help pilot Jack Knight find his way.

Not all the pilots made it. Of the original 50 fliers, 32 died in crashes. And others had so many near misses, they lost count. One young pilot on the St. Louis-to-Chicago run twice bailed out of his crippled plane safely, earning the nickname Lucky Lindy; Charles Lindbergh, who joined the service in 1926, was on leave of absence when he made his historic transatlantic flight the following year. Before he realized that fame would make a return to his old job impossible, Lindbergh confidently told reporters: "I am an airmail pilot and expect to fly the mail again."

A Stroll Through Space

The astronaut who really didn't want to come in from the cold

It was the longest space mission up to that time: a mind-boggling 66 orbits around 1,906,684 miles of the earth. But what captured the imagination of people all over the world—and caused quite a bit of concern for the National Aeronautics and Space Administration (NASA)—was the first American to walk in space.

On June 3, 1965, astronaut Ed White, wearing a 31¼-pound space suit that cost $26,000, opened the hatch of the *Gemini 4* space capsule at 3:41 P.M. EDT and floated out. He was 135 miles above the earth, a slender 30-foot lifeline his only link to the rest of humanity.

The mission plan called for a 12-minute space walk. But White started having so much fun "walking" on top of the world while traveling at 17,500 miles an hour that he decided not to come in.

"They [the earthbound controllers at NASA] want you to get back in now," Jim McDivitt, White's partner back inside *Gemini 4,* told him at the appropriate moment.

"I'm not coming in . . . this is fun," the space walker responded.

"Come in," McDivitt ordered.

Ground control soon informed the astronauts that they had about four more minutes until they reached Bermuda—and darkness on the other side of the earth. But White was still happily afloat at the end of his tether.

"Come on. Let's get back in here before it gets dark," McDivitt pleaded.

"It's the saddest moment of my life," said White.

"Well, you're going to find that it's sadder when we have to come down with this thing."

A golden lifeline tethered astronaut Ed White to Gemini 4 *during one phase of the four-day flight. When the compressed gas in his guidance gun ran out, he instantly became the first self-propelled man in space.*

At this point an exasperated ground control still couldn't believe that White wasn't back inside. "*Gemini 4. Gemini 4.* Get back in. . . . You getting him back in?"

McDivitt answered: "He's standing in the seat now and his legs are below the instrument panel." A sigh of relief went up all along the NASA control panel at Houston. "Okay," NASA said. "Get him back in. You're going to have Bermuda in about 20 seconds."

White had set a record by walking through space for a very long 21 minutes. He had strolled across 6,000 miles of the earth before giving in to the more routine (but no less spectacular) experience of whizzing around the planet in a space capsule.

An Astronomical Rate of Pay for Astronauts?

Michael Collins got the chance to walk in space twice during the Gemini 10 *mission in 1966. After returning to Earth, the astronaut put in his travel voucher for the flight. At $8 per day, the total for three days came to $24 (as much of a bargain for NASA, no doubt, as Manhattan Island had been for Peter Minuit more than three centuries earlier).*

Some eight years after his mission, Collins acknowledged in his autobiography that he should have claimed seven cents a mile on that voucher, which would have entitled him to $80,000 for the trip. He didn't attempt it, though, because one of the original Mercury *astronauts had already tried that stunt and in return had received a bill "for a couple of million dollars" for the nonreusable rocket that had catapulted him into space.*

Beyond the Terrestrial Frontier

Speeding toward the mysterious world of distant stars and galaxies

Hurtling out of our solar system, the appropriately named *Pioneer* spacecraft are carrying America's exploration to incredibly distant frontiers.

The primary mission of *Pioneer 10* was an encounter with Jupiter in December 1973, 21 months after its launch from Cape Canaveral. As fascinated earthlings looked on, *Pioneer*'s equipment sent back photographic transmissions of Jupiter's amazing Great Red Spot and detailed images of its satellites. The spacecraft also discovered that Jupiter is a mammoth liquid hydrogen planet with no solid surface beneath the thick clouds that envelop it.

The record-setting *Pioneer 10* was the first man-made object to navigate the main asteroid belt (discovering that it presents no great hazard to spacecraft), the first to confront Jupiter and its powerful radiation belts, and the first to cross the orbits of Uranus, Pluto, and Neptune. Since moving beyond the solar system, the craft has investigated the mysteries of the sun's atmosphere, the heliosphere.

Launched more than a year after its sister spacecraft, *Pioneer 11* provided the first close-up observations of Saturn's stupendous network of rings as well as its magnetic field, satellites, radiation belts, and atmosphere. It also paved the way for the more sophisticated *Voyager* probe four years later. (The two *Voyager* spacecraft transmitted the spectacular photos showing details of Saturn's fabled rings.)

As both *Pioneer* craft wander into unknown interstellar regions, they carry identical six- by nine-inch plaques. Each plaque, created to show any intelligent aliens who might intercept it where it comes from and who sent it, bears a simple diagram of the earth and the solar system, a drawing of a woman and a man, and some basic scientific symbols. Scientists have noted that the *Pioneer* plaques represent "a mark of humanity which might survive . . . the Solar System itself!" Surely the plaques, and the vehicles that carry them, push America's frontiers beyond the wildest imaginings of those who struggled across the continent in covered wagons not much more than a century ago.

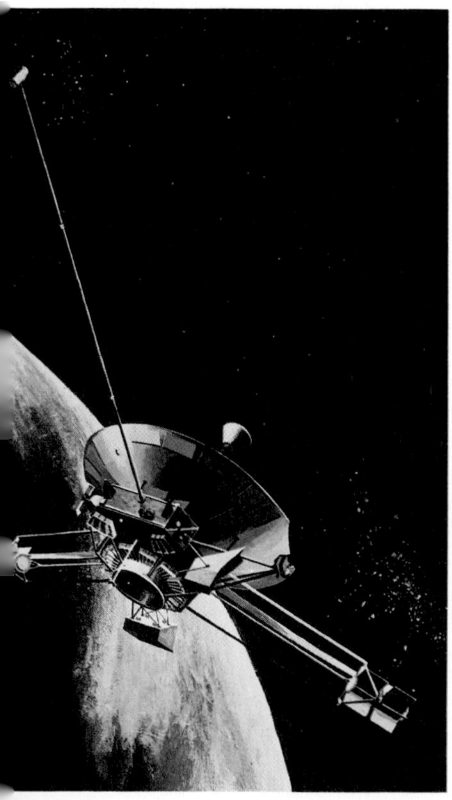

The first unmanned spacecraft fully powered by nuclear energy, Pioneer 10 *sped past Jupiter (left) on its interstellar flight. On June 13, 1983, it became the first probe to leave the solar system. Dramatic photographs of Saturn's rings (above) were transmitted by both* Voyager *spacecraft in 1980.*

CHAPTER EIGHT

Brainstorms and Boondoggles

Call it American ingenuity, Yankee know-how, or just plain inventiveness. The fact is that American thinkers and tinkers have been in the forefront of science, medicine, and technology since before our nation existed. Such creative geniuses as Franklin, Fulton, Whitney, Morse, Bell, Edison, Ford, and the Wright brothers have led the way—along with a host of other Americans whose names aren't so well known. But of course not all the bright ideas in the files of the U.S. Patent Office are works of genius.

A 16-disc "helicopter" (Clearing, Illinois, 1910)

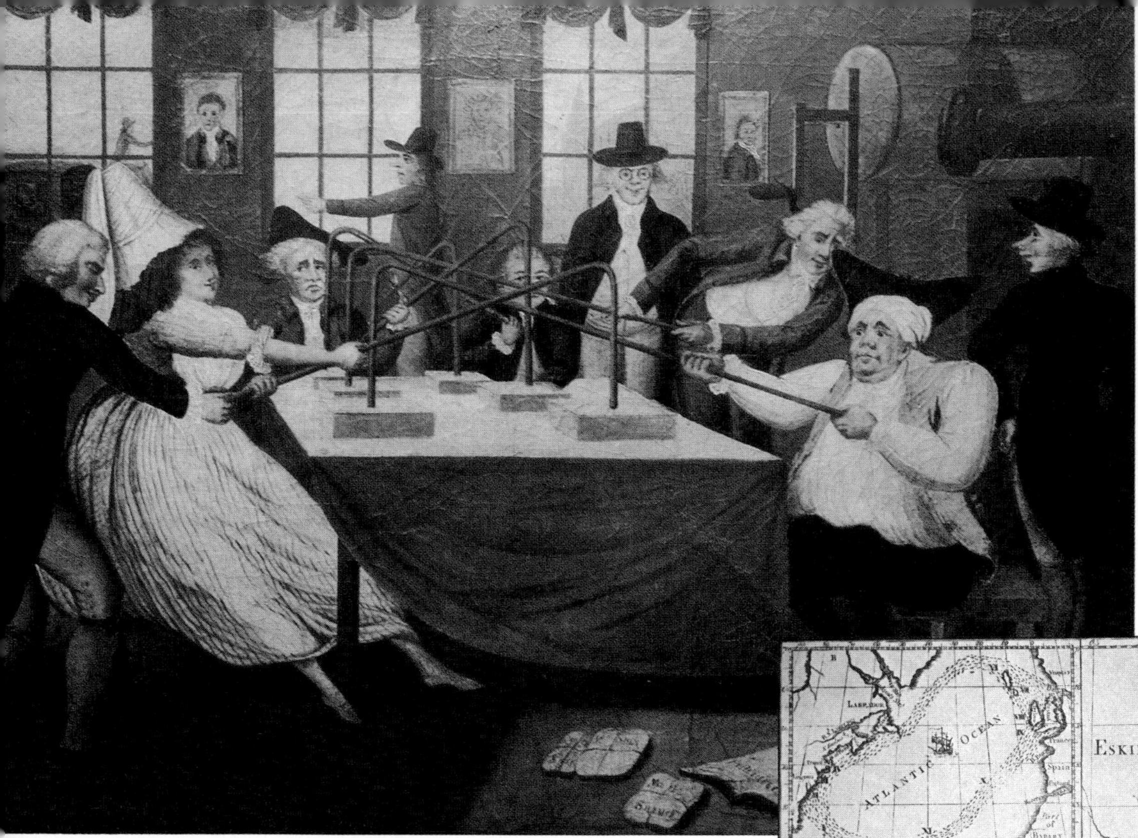

A novel party game came from Franklin's electrical experiments: people rubbed charged rods (left) for a thrill. Below: Using notes made during transatlantic trips, he was the first to chart the Gulf Stream.

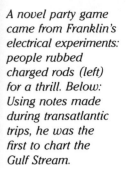

An Authentic American Genius

Benjamin Franklin "snatched the lightning from heaven and the sceptre from tyrants"

Printer, author, scientist, diplomat, statesman, "damned revolutionary" (according to George III), and a framer of the Constitution—Benjamin Franklin was all of these and more. Yet throughout his long and busy life he never ceased to pursue his passion for invention. Fed by an insatiable curiosity and a fertile imagination, his restless mind ranged far and wide in search of solutions to common and complex problems. And if one wasn't there, he'd invent it.

In 1723, when he was 17, Franklin left Boston for a career as a printer in Philadelphia. Eventually he published *Poor Richard's Almanack,* the book of wit and wisdom that included many of his maxims, among them "God helps those who help themselves."

Later he became intrigued with a budding discipline, science, which led to some of his best-known inventions. One of his first innovations was the Pennsylvania fireplace (known today as the Franklin stove). It would, its inventor claimed, make a room "twice as warm with a quarter the wood."

What really captivated Franklin was an electrical demonstration he witnessed in 1746. Acquiring apparatus, he promptly began to experiment and came up with the concept of positive and negative charges. He showed that electricity could be stored in a device he called an electrical battery. When his published conclusions were read before the Royal Society in England, Franklin's scientific reputation was assured.

Then, in 1752, came his most fabled experiment, proving that lightning is an electrical phenomenon. While there is some debate as to whether Franklin participated in the experiment, his description of drawing electricity from lightning with a metal-pointed kite—"to be raised when a thunder-gust appears"—is definitive. And there is no doubt that Franklin *was* responsible for the lightning rod. (Even the British royal palace installed this safety device!)

Franklin's inventiveness was not limited to electricity. He perfected the rocking chair, and at the age of 77, troubled by failing eyesight, he took time out from negotiating

With the ingenious use of common items (including knitting needle tips), Franklin devised a generator.

the Treaty of Paris that ended the Revolutionary War to design the first bifocals. For his own enjoyment he devised the armonica, a musical instrument played by rubbing fingers against rotating glass globes. Franklin called its tones "incomparably sweet," and Mozart and Beethoven evidently agreed; both of them composed for it.

Always busy, Franklin created an odometer; attached to a carriage axle, it recorded the number of miles driven. He also conceived of a clock that told the hours, minutes, *and* seconds by means of a simple movement. And generations of students can trace their school desk, a combined chair and table, to Franklin's 1800 design.

Typically, he never patented his brainstorms. Expressing his firm belief in the free exchange of ideas, Franklin wrote: "As we enjoy great advantages from the inventions of others, we should be glad of an opportunity to serve others by an invention of ours."

The Count and the Coffeepot

The American nobleman who invented the kitchen

Benjamin Thompson was born in Massachusetts in 1753 and developed an early interest in science. A Loyalist during the Revolution, he fled the country under threat of tar and feathers and wound up in Europe, where he spent most of his adult life as a scientist, inventor, and international adventurer with the reputation of a scoundrel. In 1795, having already been knighted in England and Germany, he became a Bavarian nobleman, giving himself the title Count Rumford. (The name came from the small New Hampshire town where he had taught school—later Concord, the state capital.)

In England and on the Continent, Rumford pursued his lifelong interest in the properties of heat. From his researches came an invention that revolutionized the world's kitchens: the cook stove.

He continued to experiment with ways of enclosing stoves and with cooking equipment in the House of Industry in Munich. There he came up with "a new Contrivance for roasting Meat," and so the roaster entered the kitchen. Flushed with success, he wrote to his dear friend Lady Palmerston: "I lately roasted 100 lb. of Veal in six large pieces at once through and through . . . several persons . . . declared they never tasted roasted meat more delicately done."

Along the way Rumford also devised an improved coffeepot, a photometer to test the intensity of various sources of light, a calorimeter to measure the heat of various fuels, and a portable lamp to which he gave his name. All in all, this early expatriate achieved his self-proclaimed goal: "To increase the enjoyment and comforts of life."

Count Rumford posed as a colonel in the King's American Dragoons (right) for portraitist Thomas Gainsborough. Below: By enclosing a fire and providing an opening at the top, the count produced the innovative Rumford stove. He also designed kettles to be used on it and, to the delight of coffee lovers everywhere, a portable coffee maker.

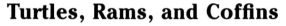

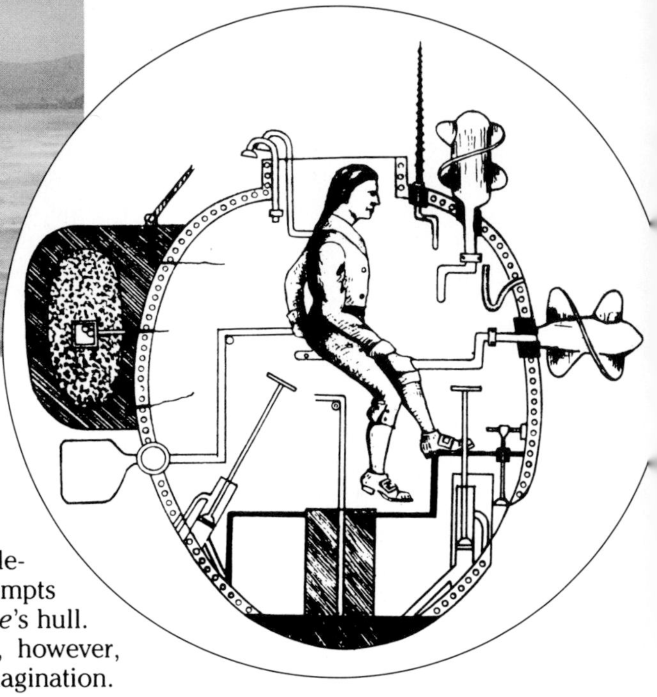

Turtles, Rams, and Coffins

The long, costly birth of the submarine

It was after midnight on a September evening in 1776. The powerful British fleet was anchored off Staten Island, poised to attack Gen. George Washington's beleaguered army on Manhattan. Confident of their superiority, they were unaware that a deadly new weapon was aimed at their admiral's flagship, the *Eagle.*

Bobbing just beneath the choppy waves, an odd, egg-shaped craft proceeded ponderously but steadily, powered by the furious cranking and peddling of Sgt. Ezra Lee, Connecticut Militia. His mission: to float under the *Eagle,* attach a mine, and blow the British vessel to smithereens.

Lee's assault, the first submarine attack in naval history, was the brainchild of David Bushnell. Four years earlier, while spending his inheritance to attend Yale as a 30-year-old undergraduate, Bushnell had shown that gunpowder could be ignited underwater in a sealed container. He developed the submarine as a stealthy means of attaching these submerged bombs to their targets.

The attack by the *Turtle* (as the world's first workable sub was called) failed because Sergeant Lee was unable to screw the bomb onto her target, despite three dogged attempts directly below the *Eagle*'s hull. The new weapon did, however, capture the military imagination.

Above, left: Early in the American Revolution, David Bushnell's Turtle *made its way across New York Harbor on history's first submarine attack. The hand- and foot-powered vessel (above) may have been primitive, but it had a propeller for forward motion, water tanks for ballast, and a conning tower for vision, all of which are used in modern submarines.*

The Peripatetic Coffin

It was not until the Civil War that a submarine succeeded in battle. Desperate for a way to break the Union Navy's blockade of Southern ports, the Confederacy developed the *Hunley,* a sub made from a boiler tank about 25 feet long, propelled by eight men pumping a hand crank. Three crews drowned during tests, and the ship was morbidly nicknamed the Peripatetic Coffin. Nonetheless, on the evening of February 17, 1864, the *Hunley* rammed and sank the Union sloop *Housatonic* in Charleston Harbor. It was a Pyrrhic victory; the *Hunley*'s entire crew drowned.

The first modern subs

The modern submarine was made possible by two key inventions: the electric engine for submerged cruising and the self-propelled torpedo. Among the first to use them successfully was John P. Holland. After the U.S. Navy rejected his submarine in 1875, Holland threw in with the Fenian Society, a group of Irish radicals committed to their country's independence. Although this association was short-lived, Holland's *Fenian Ram* presaged the design of submarines used until the advent of nuclear power.

The *Holland VI,* purchased by the U.S. Navy in 1900, beat out a submarine designed by another American, Simon Lake, who is noted for his work on the development of periscopes. Lake had proposed a sub that crept along the ocean floor on wheels. Undaunted by rejection, he went on to sell the craft to the Russians.

Twenty Years Before Fulton

John Fitch and James Rumsey pioneered the steamboat

The Constitution wasn't the only American institution launched in Philadelphia in 1787. On August 22, members of the federal convention gathered at the Delaware River to witness a voyage of the nation's first practical steamboat. Designed by John Fitch, an itinerant brass worker from New Jersey, the ship was propelled by 12 steam-driven paddles, 6 to a side. To some observers it looked like a giant bug walking across the water.

Inspired by the publicity surrounding Fitch's vessel, Virginian James Rumsey launched a steamboat on the Potomac River three months later. Rumsey's craft—which he had been working on secretly for two years—was a kind of jet boat, propelled by streams of water forced out through the stern by a steam-driven pump.

Neither Fitch nor Rumsey was financially successful; America wasn't ready for steam travel. In later years Fitch wrote: "The day will come when some more powerful man will get fame and riches from my invention." That man was to be Robert Fulton, whose *Clermont* churned up and down the Hudson River on August 17, 1807.

John Fitch had wanted to design a steam wagon, but a look at American roads quickly convinced him that steamboating was more sensible. His first craft (above, left) was launched on July 26, 1786. Later Fitch's vessels achieved speeds of eight m.p.h. James Rumsey's jet boat (above) was powered by a water-tube steam boiler, the model for the efficient boilers that power much of modern industry.

Fulton Hoped to Sell Submarines to Napoleon

Before his steamboat made him famous, Robert Fulton experimented with submarines and tried to sell them to Napoleon as the antidote to Britain's bullying dominance of the seas. The emperor was intrigued by the prototype in 1801 and proposed to test the weapon by offering its inventor up to 400,000 francs for any British vessels he sank. But despite a summer of eager hunting, Fulton and his two-man crew were unable to bomb any ships, and the French lost interest. Ever the entrepreneur, Fulton then offered his craft to the British, but they too let the project sink.

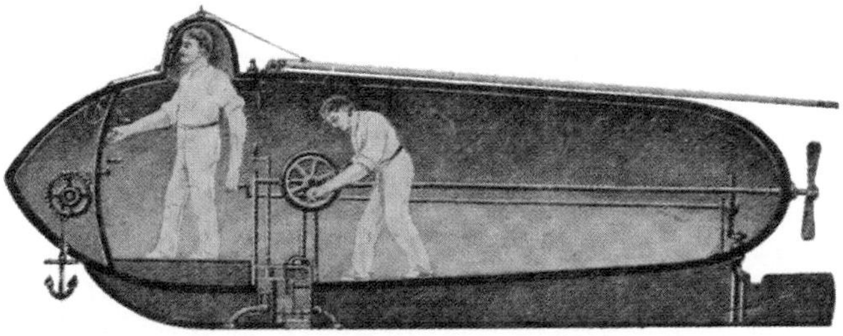

Fulton's 21-foot submarine Nautilus *was driven by sails on the surface and a hand-cranked propeller underwater. It introduced horizontal rudders for depth control, a feature that became standard on modern subs.*

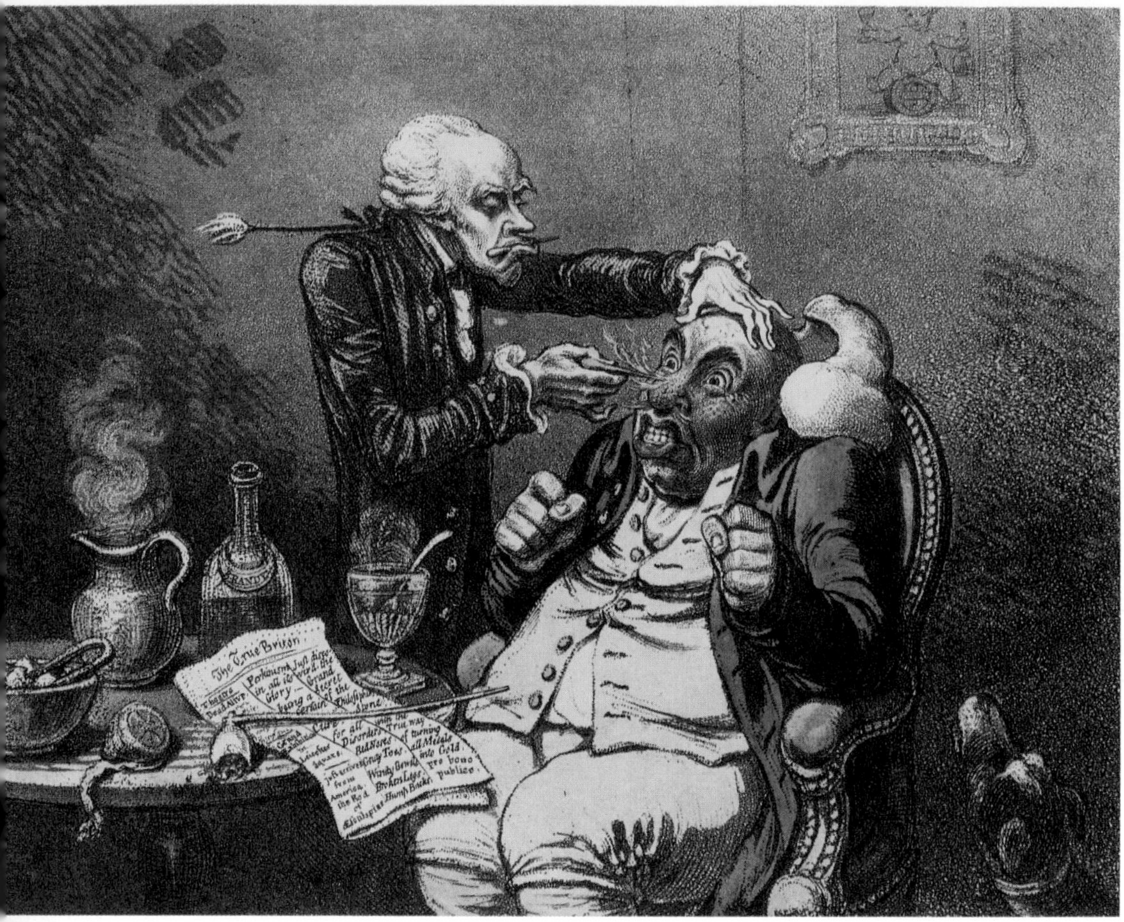

Dr. Elisha Perkins created (from a "secret alloy") three-inch-long Metallic Tractors that he sold in pairs, claiming they pulled illness out of the body magnetically. He turned a profit on this dubious medical product—and became a source of inspiration for contemporary cartoonists (left). Perkins acquired quite a following despite the fact that he was dubbed America's first medical quack.

The Doctor's Sure Cure

Was it a medical marvel, a magic wand, or merely a set of useless metal rods?

Born in 1741 to a distinguished physician and his wife in Norwich, Connecticut, Elisha Perkins started his career honorably enough. He became a doctor, built a decent practice, and was a founding member of the state medical society.

But to support his wife and 10 children, Dr. Perkins badly needed a supplemental income. And so—inspired by the new theory of animal electricity—he began selling pairs of metal rods; drawn across an afflicted area of the body, he claimed, they would relieve pain or any other ill.

Dr. Perkins took out a patent on these amazing Metallic Tractors and marketed them for a whopping $25 a pair. The Connecticut Medical Society promptly expelled him, but many distinguished patients, including Chief Justice Oliver Ellsworth, several congressmen, and, it is said, George Washington, continued to use the magic wands.

Though often called a quack (his "treatment" was the subject of a scathing poem entitled "Terrible Tractoration!!"), Perkins believed firmly in his invention. In 1799 the good doctor went to New York to "venture his life" during a yellow fever epidemic. Neither his Tractors nor his highly touted antiseptic (made of vinegar and sodium chloride) worked; Perkins himself caught the fever and died.

But the Metallic Tractors continued to sell. In Denmark a scientific committee pronounced them highly effective, and in London there flourished a Perkinean Institution, (formed by Perkins's son Benjamin, who proceeded to get rich selling his father's devices). Only after a test proved that wooden bars apparently worked just as well—a triumph of the power of suggestion—were Perkins's Tractors finally discarded.

America's First Automobile

It was a four-wheeled amphibian

Oliver Evans's cumbersome hybrid was a 30-foot barge with dredging equipment at one end and a steam engine at the other, all supported by four sturdy wheels.

When the Philadelphia Board of Health hired Oliver Evans to dredge the Schuylkill, its members got more than they bargained for. Evans not only built the first steam-driven dredge ever used in this country, he also built America's first automobile. And what's more, the dredge and the automobile were the very same machine. Christening it the Orukter Amphibolos (Amphibious Digger), he drove it from his workshop to the river in 1805.

Evans was only 17 when James Watt's steam engine came along. A gifted mechanical engineer, the youth began dreaming and working on a way to use steam in building "land carriages without animal power." But he had little money, and his ideas were constantly met with public ridicule. He was 40 before he could prove his point.

Evans had already invented a high-pressure steam engine that was used for running everything from marble saws to flour mills. But when he proposed to build a fleet of steam-powered land carriages for carrying grain across Pennsylvania cheaper than it could be done by horse-drawn wagons, he was turned down flat by the Lancaster Turnpike Company.

To convince the public that his engine "could propel both land and water carriages," Evans added wheels to the board of health's dredging scow. With everything ready, he printed handbills inviting the populace, for a fee of 25 cents, "to come and see America's First Automobile Built and Driven by America's First Automobile Driver." And the audience got their quarter's worth: the prototype Orukter steamed through the heart of Philadelphia before plunging into the Schuykill; once in the water, it easily outdistanced all other river craft.

Sadly, this impressive debut failed to earn Evans enough financial backing to go on producing his land carriages. But he remained confident that the automobile would prevail one day. "The time will come," he wrote, "when people will travel in stages [coaches] moved by steam engines from one city to another almost as fast as birds can fly—15 to 20 miles an hour."

The Only Written Language Ever Invented by Just One Man

Though he never learned to read and write English, Sequoyah singlehandedly brought literacy to the Cherokees. Fascinated by white men's books, this son of an Indian woman and a white trader dreamed of creating a written language. His breakthrough came when he divided all Cherokee sounds into 86 syllables, devising a symbol to represent each one. Inspired by the script in missionary Bibles, Sequoyah used it as the basis for his new alphabet, turning letters upside down or on their sides, sometimes adding curlicues. However intricate the designs, their function was simple, and Sequoyah taught his five-year-old daughter to read in less than a week. In 1821 a group of skeptical tribal chiefs also mastered the alphabet in seven days, then gave Sequoyah permission to teach the language to the whole tribe.

After his death in 1843, this Cherokee chieftain was honored in a way that made his name known far and wide: the towering redwood trees of California were named Sequoias.

Success in the Studio—and the Laboratory

In 1843, as Samuel F. B. Morse was stringing wires in the Capitol basement to prepare a demonstration of his telegraph for Congress, he came across his statue of Hercules, a memento of his days as an art student. This chance encounter brought together the two phases of his life, for while he is best recalled as the inventor of the telegraph and of the code bearing his name, in his long, eclectic life he also won praise as one of the finest artists of his generation.

After graduating from Yale in 1810, Morse went to England to study art. His major accomplishments were a huge painting and a small sculpture, both entitled "The Dying Hercules." Returning home, Morse took up portraiture to support himself. His outstanding works included a dramatic portrait of Lafayette and several large pictures acclaimed for their meticulous detail and portrayal of historic figures. He produced a number of successful portraits of famous people, among them inventor Eli Whitney (left). Gaining a large reputation but a small income, Morse had gradually withdrawn from artistic pursuits by 1837, the year he patented what was later hailed as "the greatest wonder and the greatest benefit of the age," the telegraph.

A Famous Inventor Was His Own Best Salesman

How Eli Whitney garnered a government contract—and avoided bankruptcy

Playing fast and loose with defense contracts is nothing new. Eli Whitney was doing it back in 1798. And instead of disgracing him, the scam enhanced his reputation by creating the legend that he pioneered the use of interchangeable parts in manufacturing, the very basis of modern industrial technology.

From his invention of the cotton gin—developed with the inspiration, ingenuity, and financial backing of his patron, Catherine Littlefield Greene—Whitney had hoped to grow rich, but loopholes in the patent law robbed him of his profits. Faced with bankruptcy, he learned that Congress, fearing an attack by France, was awarding contracts for the manufacture of muskets. Whitney had no experience making armaments, but he saw the $5,000 advance payment as a way to bolster his battered finances, and so, convincing federal authorities that he could complete 10,000 muskets in just two years, he signed on.

To produce such a huge quantity in so short a time he would, he said, use a new method he had developed "to form tools so the tools themselves shall . . . give to every part its just proportion." In other words, he would make guns with interchangeable parts.

Congress was so impressed by Whitney's reputation that it awarded him *double* the usual advance. The money "saved me from ruin," Whitney triumphantly wrote to a friend.

In his jubilation, the inventor neglected to mention that he had neither the machinery nor the skilled workmen at his New Haven, Connecticut, factory to produce the parts he had so glowingly promised. But the U.S. Armory in Springfield, Massachusetts, had both. "I might bribe workmen from Springfield to come to make me such tools," Whitney confessed, acknowledging for the first time that the radical new technique was not his own invention.

Evidently Whitney was not able to hire any Springfield workers, for his guns had no interchangeable parts. In fact, some musket pieces had identifying marks showing they could be used only with similarly marked parts. Moreover, the inventor never delivered any of the weapons on time.

Although the contract deadline was 1800, by 1801 Whitney had finished only 500 guns. The entire order was completed *nine years late,* by which time the French threat had disappeared. But by then, so had the threat to Whitney's finances.

He Took a Chance— and Saved a Life

The doctor who solved a surgical dilemma

At a time when scarcely one American doctor in ten had formal training, Ephraim McDowell was unusual: apprenticed to a doctor in Virginia, he had pursued further study in surgery in Scotland. No wonder that in 1809 two local practitioners summoned him from his office in Danville, Kentucky, to assist with the delivery of overdue twins. But when Dr. McDowell arrived at the backwoods cabin of Jane Crawford, his examination showed that she was not in labor at all; she was suffering from a massive ovarian tumor.

The doctor's diagnosis presented a dilemma: without surgery to remove the growth, the patient would die. But according to prevailing wisdom, the operation itself would surely kill her. Still, Dr. McDowell held out a slim chance. Mrs. Crawford understood the odds, and chose to risk it.

On the day of the surgery, local citizens, outraged at the proposed operation, surrounded the doctor's office trying to beat down the door.

It was much calmer inside. Mrs. Crawford, her senses perhaps dulled somewhat by the standard tranquillizers of the period—alcohol or opium—sang hymns to take her mind off the pain while McDowell removed a 22½-pound tumor. The operation was a complete success; 25 days after the surgery, the doctor pronounced the patient "perfectly well." And so she was: Jane Crawford lived another 32 years.

As Ephraim McDowell performed the first ovariotomy in 1809, an angry mob besieged his office. Dr. McDowell is honored today as the pioneer of abdominal surgery.

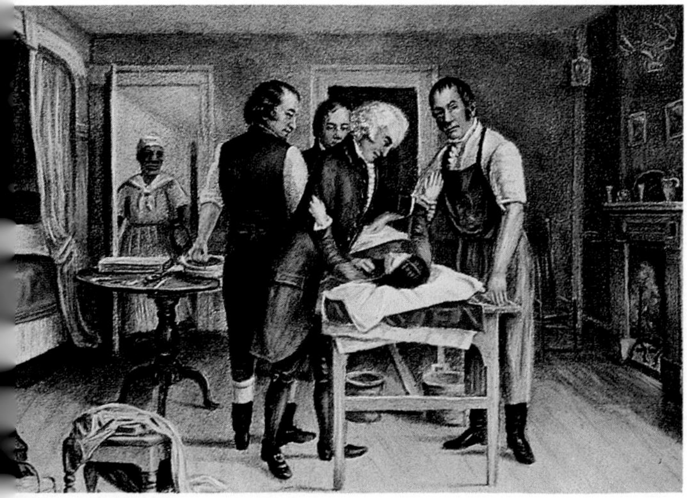

Bright Ideas

(from the files of the U.S. Patent Office)

Improved Rocking Chair
Patent No. 92,379 (July 6, 1869)
Inventor: Charles Singer
South Bend, Ind.

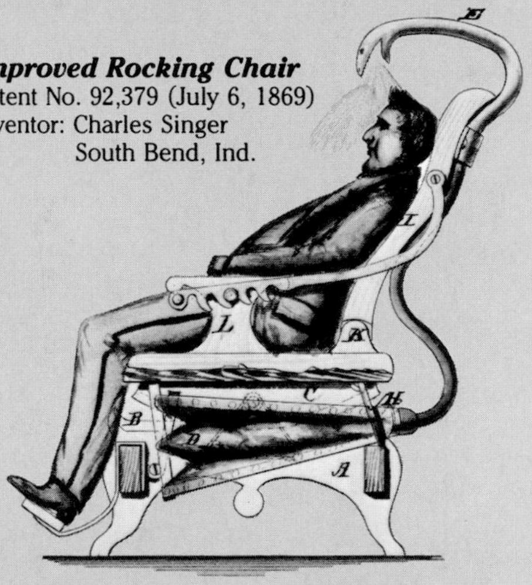

A form of personal air conditioning was provided by an "improvement in the construction of rocking chairs, with air blowing attachments, having . . . the support of a bellows . . . on which the rockers, which are fixed close to the seat, may work, instead of on the floor." A tube connected to the bellows could be directed anywhere the sitter chose.

Rocking-Chair Churn
Patent No. 1,051,684 (Jan. 28, 1913)
Inventor: Alfred Clark
East Corinth, Me.

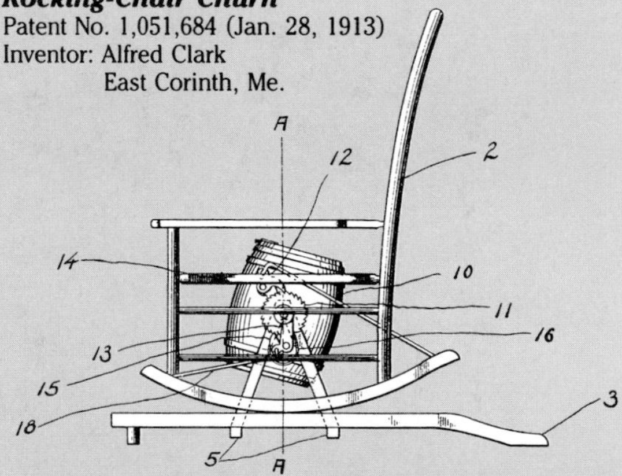

"This invention relates to improvements in churns and especially with reference to improvements in means, actuated by a rocking chair . . . so that a churn may be operated by a person seated and rocking in a rocking chair, the invention consisting in the construction, combination and arrangement of devices."

Vacuumed, Not Burned

How the Shakers helped Gail Borden develop condensed milk

For Texan Gail Borden, preserving food wasn't a pastime, it was a passion. He'd seen children die from drinking spoiled milk.

The great-great-great-grandson of Roger Williams (the religious reformer who had founded Rhode Island), Borden moved to Texas, took part in the revolution against Mexico, and then settled down to experiment with condensed food. At one memorable dinner party he served concentrated soup and fruit, testing both the palates and the politeness of his guests.

Later, Borden developed the "meat biscuit," a dried meat extract much like Indian pemmican. Returning from London in 1851, where he received an award for the biscuits, he had the experience that shaped the rest of his life.

Sick cows, suffering children

Cows, taken on ship to provide food, sickened during the voyage; children either went hungry or became ill from tainted milk. Some babies died. In an age before refrigeration, Borden vowed to find some way of keeping milk fresh.

At first he tried boiling the milk, but this left an offensive burnt taste. Then he remembered the Shakers of New Lebanon, New York; after his wife died in 1844, Borden, like many widowers of the period, had placed his children with the Shakers to be raised. While visiting the children, he saw the Shakers concentrating fruit juice with vacuum pans they had developed. The pans sealed out air, thus allowing the liquid to evaporate at a lower temperature.

Moving to the Shaker village, Borden experimented for months, finally finding a method that left condensed milk tasty and unspoiled for more than two days.

Purity before Pasteur

But as a business venture, his idea failed. Customers in New York City preferred the taste they were used to: watered "swill milk," which contained chalk to make it white and molasses to make it creamy. Borden tried again in 1858, with better marketing and financial backing. This time his condensed milk caught on, especially after a newspaper revealed the foulness of the swill.

In fact, what Borden had developed was a way of purifying milk, 11 years before Louis Pasteur revolutionized biology with his discovery of germs.

Alonzo Holister, who assisted Borden in his experiments, stands next to one of the vacuum pans used to condense milk.

Shaking Out the Wash

When David Parker, a Shaker from Canterbury, New Hampshire, saw how much energy went into doing laundry, he created a new washing machine. Shaker sisters were jubilant, and the washers, patented in 1858, made a splash in the commercial market as well. Hotels from the Parker House in Boston to the Tremont in Chicago clamored for them; one Philadelphia hotel fired 14 laundresses after the machines took over their work.

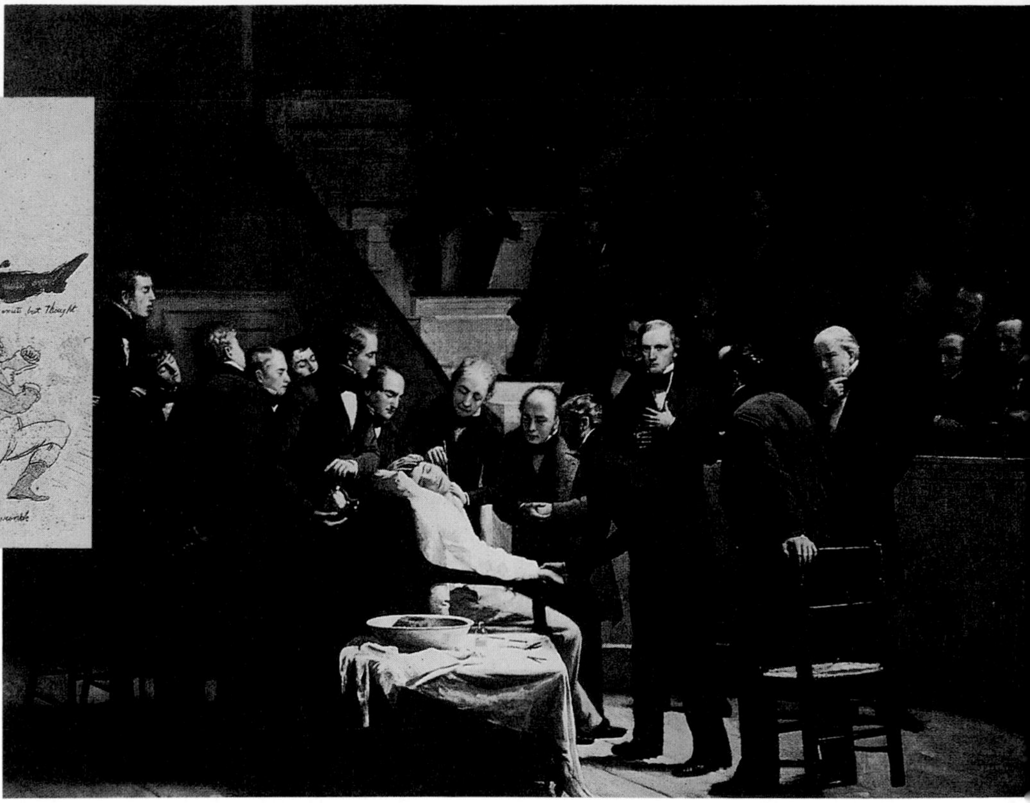

First used as a "genteel way of getting drunk" (above), anesthesia became a medicinal boon. Right: In 1846 Dr. William Morton administered ether as Dr. John Warren performed a history-making demonstration of painless surgery.

The Laughter and the Pain *An 1840's party game led to the first anesthetic*

Well into the 19th century, surgery was crude and painful, a last resort for those in unbearable agony. Only the swiftness of the surgeon's hand limited the torture the patient had to endure. Then in 1842 Crawford Long, a physician in rural Jefferson, Georgia, attended an "ether party."

In those days itinerant performers toured America demonstrating the silly side effects of nitrous oxide, or laughing gas. Approached by friends to make the stuff for their own frolic, Dr. Long suggested that they try sulfuric ether instead, a compound he himself had found suitably diverting. Thus began a series of parties where the Georgians chuckled in blissful oblivion at their own bruising stumbles and falls.

Intrigued that the merrymakers felt no pain, Dr. Long convinced fellow partygoer James Venable to sniff ether before having a tumor removed—and on March 30, 1842, the operation was performed painlessly. The world, however, would have to wait for this breakthrough; not fully convinced, the doctor delayed publishing his findings.

Two years later Horace Wells, a dentist in Hartford, Connecticut, attended a laughing gas show, recognized nitrous oxide's anesthetic potential, and took his discovery to Massachusetts General Hospital in Boston. But when the demonstration went awry, Wells was ridiculed and dismissed as a fraud.

It was left to Dr. William Morton, who had once practiced dentistry with Wells, to bring anesthesia to the world. Morton learned of ether's numbing properties from Dr. Charles Jackson, a Boston chemist, and soon he was trying it on patients himself. Then, disguising the common chemical with aromatic oils and a new name, he too approached Massachusetts General as the creator of a wonder drug. In the fall of 1846 the hospital's chief of surgery used ether in the removal of a huge neck tumor and in a leg amputation. The age of anesthetics had begun.

Years of bitter controversy followed concerning who actually made the discovery. The loudest voice belonged to Dr. Morton, who patented his compound and hoped to make a fortune. Visiting New York in 1868 to defend his position against supporters of Dr. Jackson, Morton had a seizure and died. Jackson fared little better. After seeing the tombstone that gave the credit to Morton, Jackson went insane; he spent the rest of his life in an asylum.

Saddest of all was Dr. Wells, who became addicted to chloroform and slowly destroyed his mind. Confined to a New York City jail, he soaked a cloth in the drug, painlessly severed an artery, and bled to death.

Dr. Long, who'd been too timid to publish, continued as a successful general practitioner in Georgia until 1878, when he died while making a house call.

A Medical Breakthrough

The wound with a view

By using an open wound in a man's abdomen as a unique peephole to knowledge, a pioneering medical researcher, Dr. William A. Beaumont, discovered much of what we know about the human digestive system.

It started in 1822, when Beaumont was an army surgeon in Michigan. A young Canadian trapper, Alexis St. Martin, was accidentally shot in the side. Dr. Beaumont thought St. Martin was a goner; his wound was so large that a man could put his hand through it. But the doctor treated him, and St. Martin survived. The hole in his side, however, never closed. A 2½-inch opening remained, and a skin flap formed that could be lifted to inspect the man's insides.

"I can look directly into the cavity of the Stomach," Beaumont wrote, "observe its motion, and almost see the process of digestion." As a result, the doctor found out a great deal more about how the digestive tract works than anyone had ever known before. His book on the subject, published in 1833, put Beaumont in the scientific spotlight—and he'd never gone to medical school. Incredibly, 90 percent of his observations are *still* valid.

Beaumont had taken the pauperized St. Martin in, and despite spats and quarrels, for about a decade he saw to it that his experimental subject was well taken care of.

When St. Martin died—he outlived his doctor by 20 years—he was buried eight feet below ground to ensure that no scientific curiosity-seekers would try to dig him up.

Basic Training

Getting railroads on the right track

Trains averaged only 10 miles per hour in the early days of railroading. There were no brakes, no lights, and no whistles. Engineers had to stop to chase animals off the tracks, and derailments were commonplace. To improve the lives of trainmen and passengers alike, a lot of inventing needed to be done, and American ingenuity rose to the challenge.

Avoiding accidents

The first rails were L-shaped iron strips bolted to wooden planks. Too much speed on a curve, a stone on the track, or a broken rail—and the train derailed.

In 1830 Robert Stevens and his brother, sons of famed inventor-engineer John Stevens, founded New Jersey's Camden & Amboy Railroad. The next year, on his way to England to buy an engine, Robert whittled a model of a T-shaped track that could be spiked to a wooden crosstie on both sides. Upon his arrival, he persuaded skeptical ironmongers to cast his "utterly insane" designs. (The T-rail is *still* standard worldwide.)

When Stevens's new locomotive, the *John Bull,* arrived in Philadelphia in pieces, Isaac Dripps (who'd never seen one before) put it together. To enable it to navigate curves more easily, he replaced the huge front wheels with two small ones that held a V-shaped shield—the first cowcatcher.

Moving right along

John Jervis improved Dripps's design with a swiveling, four-wheeled truck on his engine's front end. With it, the boiler became a counterweight on curves. Meanwhile, Matthias Baldwin designed a steam-tight high-pressure boiler that enabled his train to reach an unheard-of 80 miles an hour!

High speed spawned numerous safety devices. The first locomotive headlight was an enlarged oil-burning ship's lantern mounted above the cowcatcher. With a series of reflectors behind its foot-high lens, it could beam a light as far as 100 feet ahead. And, as an

Bright Ideas *(from the files of the U.S. Patent Office)*

"By means of the rod I the stop-cock F may be opened, thus permitting the water to escape from the boiler through the nozzle D . . . with a great degree of force, and to a considerable distance . . . frightening horses and cattle off the track."

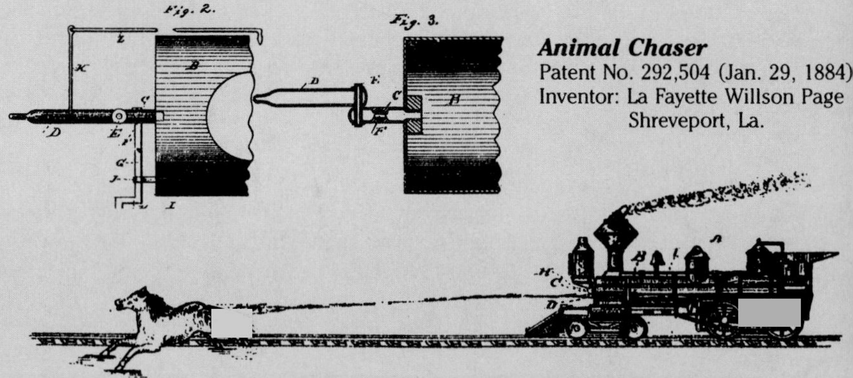

Animal Chaser
Patent No. 292,504 (Jan. 29, 1884)
Inventor: La Fayette Willson Page
Shreveport, La.

Left: An 1860 locomotive boasted many improvements, among them a bright headlight, a steam whistle, a flexible front section that helped it cling to curves, and a new cowcatcher. (Sharp prongs on the old design impaled livestock. The improved version no longer gored animals; it merely tossed them off the tracks.) Below: In 1868 Eli Janney patented the automatic "knuckle coupler." Resembling curled fingers, it replaced the hand operation performed by brakemen, who were often crushed fastening cars together.

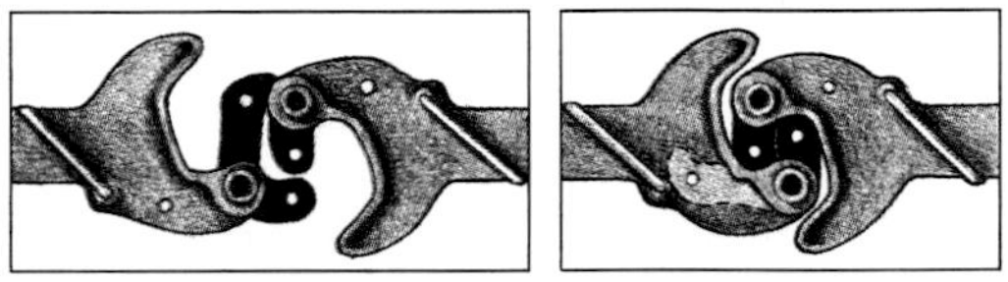

engineer pulled a cord to open a valve, the first locomotive steam whistle wailed across the land.

Reporting by wire

After the dizzying decade of the 1830's, the pace of invention abated a bit. The telegraph was first used on the Erie Railroad in 1851, when the superintendent of the line took the throttle from a nervous engineer and chugged west on a single track, relying on telegraphed reports that the eastbound train was delayed. As late as 1871, though, an express plowed into a local in Massachusetts because the line still depended on railroad timetables.

The air brake was a boon to the perilous life of brakemen. Patented by George Westinghouse in 1869, it meant that there was no longer any need to crawl atop moving cars to stop each one by hand, or worry about collisions when trains *couldn't* stop.

Cutting casualties

Still, it took a 20-year crusade to force railroads to adopt the system. Not until 1893 did President Benjamin Harrison sign a bill requiring air brakes (and automatic couplers) on all locomotives. By 1894, casualties had dropped 60 percent.

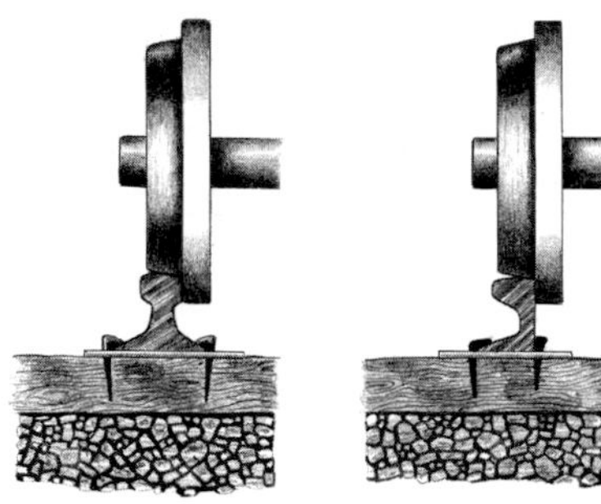

A flanged wheel rides the sturdier T-shaped track (left) that replaced the L-rail (right) in the 1830's.

"This invention . . . consists in the novel construction and combination of the parts . . . whereby one train may pass over another train which it meets or overtakes upon the same track. . . .

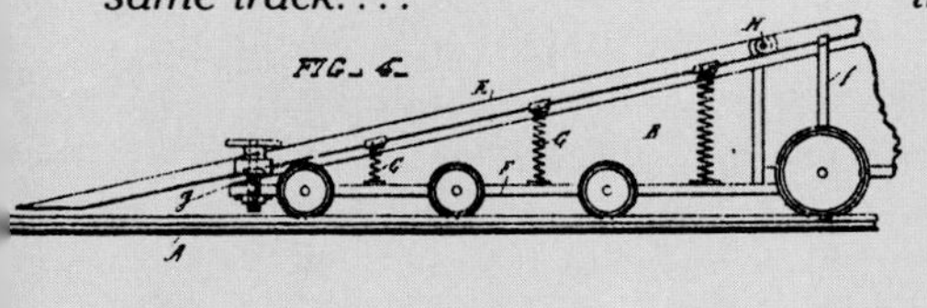

"When one train meets or overtakes another train, one train will run up the rails E carried by the other train, and will run along the rails E and descend onto the rails A at the other end of the lower train, as shown in Fig. 1.

"The trains have the inclined lower ends of their rails E adjusted at different distances from the rails A in a prearranged manner. . . . The train having the ends of its rails E higher above the rails A than those of the train it meets will rise and run up on the rails E of the other train."

New, Useful Railroad-Trains
Patent No. 536,360 (Mar. 26, 1895)
Inventor: Henry Latimer Simmons
Wickes, Mont.

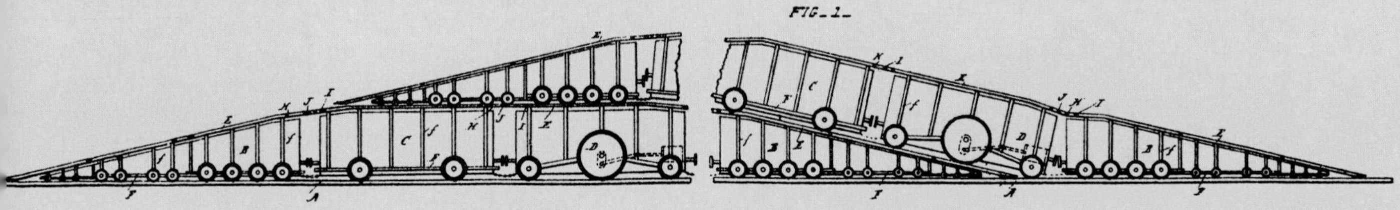

"The Vertical Railway"

Mr. Otis's safety elevator changed the skyline of urban America forever

The setting was the dazzling 1854 Crystal Palace Exposition in New York City. On display was one of the mechanical marvels of America's first world's fair. It was an intriguing sight: On a hoist platform, surrounded by barrels and packing cases, stood a handsome gentleman in his early forties; he was lifted to the hoist's highest point, some 30 feet above the assembled spectators. Then Elisha Graves Otis, the man on the platform, gave orders to cut the hoisting rope. The crowd gasped, but Otis calmly doffed his elegant top hat, bowed from the waist, and said: "All safe, gentlemen, all safe!" For the motionless platform and its inventor were in absolutely no danger.

Hoists had been used since antiquity. Otis's insight wasn't in how to get things up, but in how to keep them from falling down unexpectedly.

Teeth

Thus was born the modern elevator, a hoist safe enough for people to ride in. Otis had built his first lift in 1852, to carry bedsteads to the second story of the New York factory where he worked. Such machines were relatively common, but none could boast Otis's safety device—two metal hooks at the sides of the car, attached by a springline to the hoist cable. If the cable broke or tension was released, the hooks immediately sprang out, catching in teeth that were cut into the guide rails in the elevator shaft. Descent was stopped at once.

At first Otis didn't think his invention was worth much; he dreamed of going to California to try his luck at panning gold. Then he received two orders for his safety lift, and suddenly it seemed wiser to seek his fortune at home.

The New York *Tribune* called Otis's Crystal Palace feat "daring" and "sensational," but it would be three years before a New York department store took a gamble and installed an Otis elevator to lift its passengers five stories at a speed of 40 feet per minute, hardly faster than walking the stairs. (By way of comparison, at that speed it would take an elevator 36 minutes to reach the top of the world's tallest building, the Sears Tower in Chicago.)

Architecture looks up

By the early 1870's the elevator had begun to change skylines all across America. Architects started looking up, rather than out. From a limit of 5 stories (the most that people could reasonably be expected to climb), buildings soon grew to 12 stories tall.

Elisha Otis lifted the world into the age of the high-rise. His elevators were safe, even if their pulley ropes broke; so they were trusted to carry passengers.

In 1904 the Otis Company, then directed by Elisha's two sons, pioneered the gearless traction elevator. An innovative element in the creation of the skyscraper, it was used in New York's 41-story Singer Building in 1907 and again, in 1932, in the 102-story Empire State Building.

Today, thanks to Elisha Otis, elevators speed passengers to the top of tall buildings at rates of up to 1,800 feet per minute (about 20.5 m.p.h.).

"Zip 'Er Up! Zip 'Er Down!"

Either way, the slide fastener got off to a shaky start

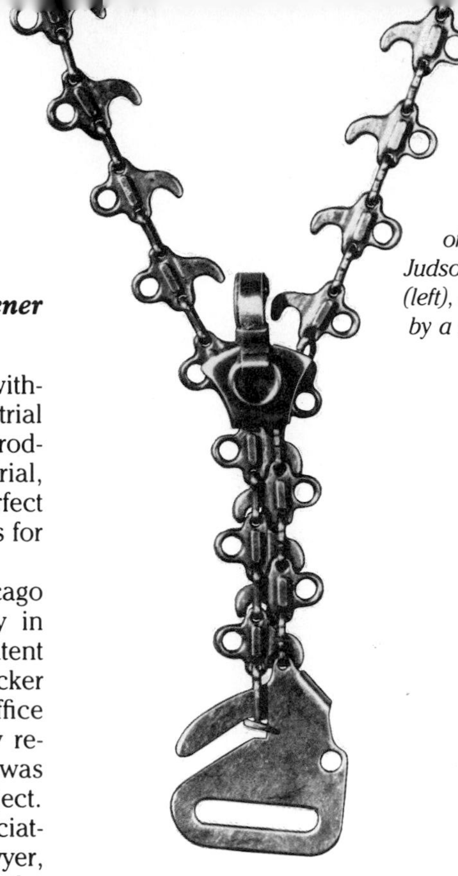

To eliminate the time-consuming job of lacing up boots and clothing, Whitcomb Judson invented the zipper. The first prototype (left), a combination of hooks and eyes closed by a slide fastener, looked as cumbersome as the job it was designed to replace.

Where would the world be without zippers? One of industrial America's most successful products, it took two decades of trial, error, and frustration to perfect the marvel that everyone takes for granted today.

Whitcomb Judson of Chicago assured his place in history in 1891 when he applied for a patent on a "Clasp Locker or Unlocker for Shoes." Since the patent office had nothing on file remotely resembling Judson's device, he was free to go ahead with his project.

The only person who appreciated the slide fastener was a lawyer, Col. Lewis Walker, who set up the Universal Fastener Company in 1894 to manufacture it. He and Judson then put fasteners on their shoes to advertise their practicality, but they still needed a machine for quantity production. Finally, one was successfully tested in 1905. To celebrate, Walker ordered a keg of beer and scheduled a demonstration, but nothing happened. The machine had quit.

Still, Walker's faith was unbounded. Reorganizing the company, he had Judson simplify his invention; the result was called the C-Curity fastener. Ads proclaimed: "A Pull and It's Done! No More Open Skirts. . . . Ask the Girl."

That last sentence proved to be the company's undoing, for the fasteners, with a tendency to pop open at inopportune moments, soon became a joke.

This humiliation was too much for Judson, but Walker continued to work on the device, although the company was so broke that he returned to his law practice to survive. (He was once forced to settle a grocery bill with worthless shares of stock; eventually, the grocer made a fortune.) Walker's faith finally paid off when the prototype for the modern zipper was perfected in 1913.

But people hadn't forgotten the C-Curity fiasco. For years the new fasteners were considered mere novelty items; only actors used them regularly—to make quick costume changes. It wasn't until 1917, when an itinerant tailor used the fasteners on money belts for sailors, that Walker's company took off.

The name *zipper* was first used when B. F. Goodrich Co. put fasteners on galoshes in 1923. The company president himself promoted the product, urging people to "Zip 'er up! Zip 'er down!" Zippers was the trademark for the galoshes. But the public remembered zippers long after the overshoes were forgotten.

Walker laughed all the way to the bank. He was the president of his original company—later renamed Talon—until his death at age 83 in 1938.

Bright Ideas (from the files of the U.S. Patent Office)

"This . . . improved fire-escape or safety device, by which a person may safely jump out of the window of a burning building . . . consists of a parachute attached . . . to the upper part of the body, in combination with over-shoes having elastic bottom pads of suitable thickness to take up the concussion with the ground. . . . The parachute serves the purpose of buoying the body in the air . . . while the padded shoes secure the safe landing on the ground."

Improvement in Fire Escapes
Patent No. 221,855 (Nov. 18, 1879)
Inventor: Benjamin Oppenheimer
Trenton, Tenn.

Curious whales, like the one above, threatened to sever the transatlantic cable even as Cyrus Field's ships were laying it.

Suddenly the World Shrank

Cyrus Field's race to bridge the Atlantic

By 1854 a message could be sent from Maine to New Orleans in minutes. But 2,000 miles of storm-tossed ocean separated American cities from the capitals of Europe, and so the same message might take two weeks to reach London. To shorten the time would require laying a cable across the Atlantic, a feat that everyone knew was impossible—everyone, that is, except Cyrus Field.

Short-lived triumph

Field, a New York paper merchant, had already retired with a fortune at the age of 34, when he conceived the plan of a transatlantic cable. The idea was feasible: the wire could rest on a submerged plateau between Newfoundland and Ireland. Encouraged, Field formed the Atlantic Telegraph Company in 1856. Soon ideas from the public began flooding in. One proposed suspending the cable by underwater balloons; another suggested floating call boxes for the benefit of passing ships.

Fancy schemes, however, soon gave way to harsh realities. The technical problems were mammoth; the open ocean was brutal to both men and equipment. Although the 2,500-mile-long cable weighed a ton per mile, it snapped in the rolling sea. Storms, cable partings, and other setbacks led to two years of delays. It was not until August 1858 that a cable was successfully laid and the continents were electronically connected.

But the triumph was short-lived. Following an inaugural greeting from Queen Victoria to President Buchanan, the cable went dead—much to the delight of Perry McDonough Collins.

The Pacific connection

Collins had a different plan. Approaching Western Union, he proposed to run a cable north to Alaska, under the narrow Bering Strait, and then across Siberia to the wires of Europe. In 1864 Western Union agreed. Meanwhile, Field had secured backing for a second transatlantic attempt—and the race was on.

On July 27, 1866, despite serious setbacks along the way, Field's ship steamed into Heart's Content, Newfoundland, trailing her massive cable behind her. This time, the cable worked perfectly; 12 years after he had begun the project, the Atlantic was bridged. Although it was the death knell for the Siberian route, communications were so bad that it took almost a year before crews in Alaska learned of the Atlantic success.

Collins's effort was abandoned; but all was not for naught. The *diplomatic* connections that had been developed with Russia bore fruit a year later, when America bought Alaska from the Russians for the bargain price of $7.2 million.

Rains of Terror

Two brothers changed the way the South fought the Civil War

The Confederate Army couldn't have waged war without the Rains brothers, Gabriel and George. Little ammunition had been manufactured in the South since the early 1800's, and there was barely enough gunpowder in reserve for one month of fighting—until the Rainses took the reins.

Gunpowder George

Brother George turned his background in chemistry, geology, and mineralogy to the gunpowder crisis. Although he'd never set foot in a powder mill, he quickly found ways to ease the shortage.

In those days, the main ingredient of gunpowder was potassium nitrate, better known as saltpeter. Through diligent exploration, George found huge deposits of the stuff in the limestone caves of Tennessee, Arkansas, Alabama, and Georgia. He was so thorough that he even set crews to mining the nitrate from outhouses. Within four months the South was manufacturing 3,000 pounds of gunpowder a day. By war's end, the main factory at Augusta, Georgia, had produced nearly 1.4 million tons.

The weapons of retreat

It was older brother Gabriel, a brigadier general, who actually changed the way the Civil War was fought, however. In 1862 he halted a Union advance on his retreating forces at Yorktown, Virginia, by using a new weapon of his own design—the land mine. Complete with conical tin coverings to protect them from rain, these deadly devices were detonated by pressure from horses' hooves. As the Yankee pursuers were thrown into disarray, their casualties were many.

Spurred by this success, Confederate units set mines anyplace Yankees might touch—in bags of flour, around telegraph poles, and inside wells. The use of these weapons provoked moral outrage on both sides of the Mason-Dixon Line. Even the Confederate commander Lt. Gen. James Longstreet was horrified; he forbade further deployment of the mines. But Gabriel went over Longstreet's head to Secretary of War George Randolph, who endorsed their use for defensive purposes.

Floating torpedoes

Gabriel didn't stop at dry land. Soon the Federals were encountering mines in the James River. Detonated by wire from the riverbanks, some of these submerged bombs weighed 1,950 pounds. When wire became scarce, Rains sent women agents behind enemy lines to steal some.

The ingenious weaponeer also sent floating torpedoes, propelled by a river's current, to greet Union ships; in all, 58 vessels were damaged. One bomb blew a steamship some 50 feet high, killing all but 3 of its 150-man crew.

Coal bombs

But Gabriel's masterpiece was a bomb designed to look like a lump of coal. The unassuming explosive would be tossed on a coal barge; when it was eventually shoveled into a ship's boiler, the explosion was catastrophic. Among early victims was the *Greyhound,* a blockade runner that had been captured by the Union Navy. Admiral David Porter, who survived the devastation, immediately ordered that any Confederate found with imitation coal was to be shot.

Needless to say, the power of Brother Gabriel's deadly inventions came from the gunpowder made by Brother George.

Bright Ideas

(from the files of the U.S. Patent Office)

Tapeworm Trap

Patent No. 11,942 (Nov. 14, 1854)
Inventor: Alpheus Myers
Logansport, Ind.

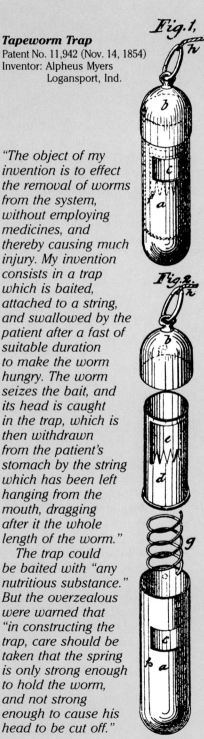

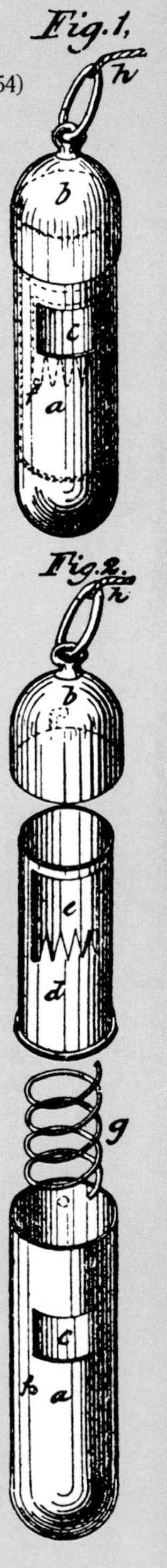

"The object of my invention is to effect the removal of worms from the system, without employing medicines, and thereby causing much injury. My invention consists in a trap which is baited, attached to a string, and swallowed by the patient after a fast of suitable duration to make the worm hungry. The worm seizes the bait, and its head is caught in the trap, which is then withdrawn from the patient's stomach by the string which has been left hanging from the mouth, dragging after it the whole length of the worm."

The trap could be baited with "any nutritious substance." But the overzealous were warned that "in constructing the trap, care should be taken that the spring is only strong enough to hold the worm, and not strong enough to cause his head to be cut off."

Machine-Gun Maxim's Peaceful Inventions

Curlers, coffee substitutes, a better mousetrap . . . and the filament for Edison's bulb

In 1883 Hiram Maxim changed warfare forever by inventing the first truly automatic machine gun. Although his fame rests almost entirely on that weapon, from which all modern automatic firearms descend, the Maine-born inventor was also one of Thomas A. Edison's most prolific rivals in the development of electricity. Maxim held 122 patents in the United States and 149 in England.

First inventions

Born in 1840 in tiny Sangerville, Maine, Maxim had had only five years of school when, at 14, he was apprenticed to a carriage maker. Soon after, he produced his first invention, an automatic mousetrap designed to be reset by the struggles of the dying mouse. Moving on to better jobs, he received his first patent in 1866, for a hair-curling iron.

Electricity

After settling in New York City, Maxim invented a locomotive headlight and machines for generating illuminating gas. While employed as chief engineer of the United States Electric Lighting Company, which made the country's earliest attempt to provide public electricity, he invented and installed New York's first electric arc lights in the headquarters of the Equitable Insurance Company.

His method of standardizing carbon filaments made Edison's incandescent light bulb marketable on a large scale, but Maxim lost this potentially lucrative patent because his company failed to pay the required fees.

Nonetheless, his electrical genius was celebrated. In 1881 he received the French Légion d'Honneur for an automatic regulator that maintained a constant charge in an electrical circuit, no matter how many lamps it lit.

Ten shots a second

The next year, in Vienna, an American told Maxim, "Hang your chemistry and electricity! If you want to make a pile of money, invent something that will enable these Europeans to cut each others' throats with greater facility." Maxim went to London and invented a gun that used the energy of the recoil to load the next bullet and eject the spent shell. By holding down the trigger, a gunner could fire 10 shots per second through the single barrel.

Patented Cures for War

Dr. McLean thought he'd devised the ultimate deterrents

Pharmaceutical tycoon J. H. McLean made his money in patent medicines with overblown names like McLean's Strengthening Cordial and Blood Purifier. But treating the ailing individual wasn't enough. He longed to cure the world of war; so he devised a wild array of weapons and fortifications and presented them in 1880 in an illustrated volume: *Dr. J. H. McLean's Peace Makers.*

Among McLean's deterrents was a sort of PT boat, equipped with the sonarlike Dr. McLean's Wonderful Hydrophone, which would detect the sounds of an unseen enemy. He claimed that his Annihilator, a four-wheeled cannon, could fire 60 shots a minute. And this was just the economy model. The mightier Lady McLean—chivalrously named for his wife (it looked like a giant mouth organ on a wheeled platform)—was supposedly "Capable of Throwing 1,584 to 2,000 shots in a Minute!" Not overlooking the soldiers' domestic needs, McLean was especially proud of his Iron Forms, portable bulwarks that could be converted into feed boxes or cooking ranges. Unfortunately, none of the doctor's weapons was ever manufactured, although a Turkish sultan *did* try to order a few.

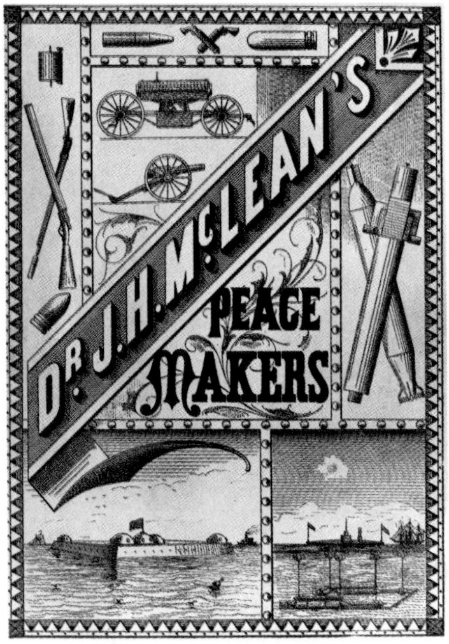

The inventor's catalog (above) offered weapons so horrible that they would make war unthinkable.

It was a big improvement over the Civil War's hand-cranked, multi-barrel Gatling gun—and it initiated devastating slaughter.

Prostituted talent?

About 1889 Maxim decided that "if a domestic goose can fly, so can a man," so he invented a steam-powered flying machine that in 1894 actually got off the ground. He also dabbled with bulletproof vests (an ironic counterpoint to the machine gun) and such benign domestic products as coffee substitutes, vacuum cleaners, tires, and fuel pumps.

A chronic bronchitis sufferer, he invented a steam inhaler, only to be accused of "prostituting my talents on quack nostrums." With bitterness the inventor concluded: "It is a very creditable thing to invent a killing machine, and nothing less than a disgrace to invent an apparatus to prevent human suffering."

Hiram Maxim (above) invented a weapon that made the solitary soldier the equal of armies. In 1893 four Maxim machine guns killed 3,000 Zulus in an hour and a half. During World War I, 21,000 British troops were slaughtered at the Somme in a single day by the German version of the weapon.

Bright Ideas *(from the files of the U.S. Patent Office)*

Combined Helmet, Gun, Cooking Pan
Patent No. 1,183,492 (May 16, 1916)
Inventor: Albert B. Pratt
Lyndon, Vt.

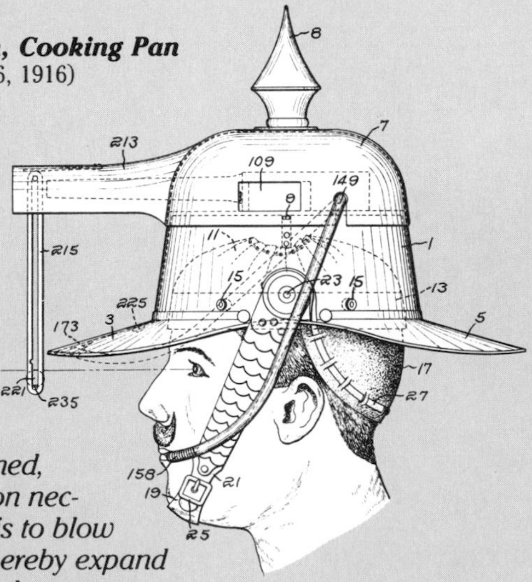

"A gun adapted to be mounted on and fired from the head . . . is automatically aimed unconsciously and incidentally to the turning of the head of the marksman. . . . With the gun thus aimed, the only further operation necessary to fire the same is to blow through the tube and thereby expand the [inflatable] bulb and operate the trigger. . . . The crown of the helmet . . . may be inverted and used as a cooking utensil. . . . The spike may be stuck in the ground to support the utensil."

Combined Plow and Gun
Patent No. 35,600 (June 17, 1862)
Inventors: C. M. French and W. H. Fancher
Waterloo, N.Y.

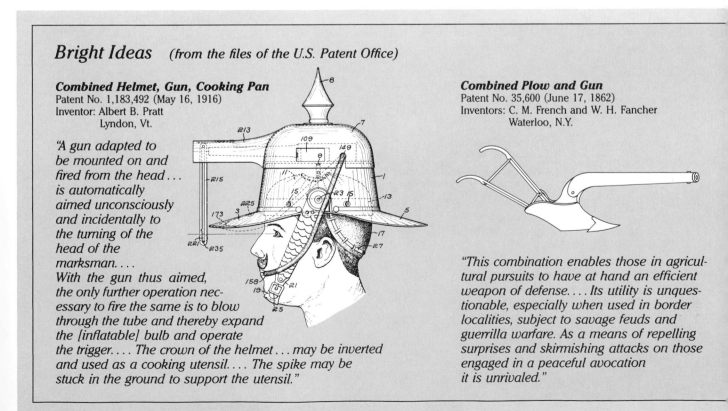

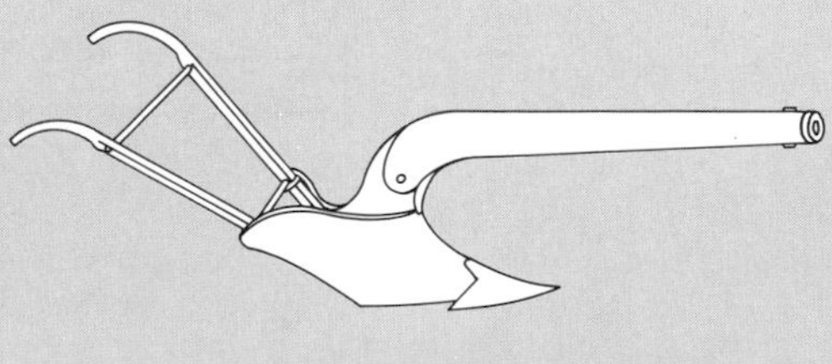

"This combination enables those in agricultural pursuits to have at hand an efficient weapon of defense. . . . Its utility is unquestionable, especially when used in border localities, subject to savage feuds and guerrilla warfare. As a means of repelling surprises and skirmishing attacks on those engaged in a peaceful avocation it is unrivaled."

Populating Mars

Percival Lowell thought he saw canals on the Red Planet

Many of his scientific contemporaries would have been surprised at the thought that Percival Lowell's ideas would one day help to carry man into space—they considered his notions outrageous.

Lowell, a Boston blueblood, was fascinated by the work of Italian astronomer Giovanni Schiaparelli, who in 1877 observed that Mars's surface is marked by *canali.* The word simply means "channels"; but it was regularly translated as "canals," suggesting to Lowell that the intriguing trenches were the work of an advanced civilization that was dying from lack of water and had constructed an elaborate irrigation system to tap the planet's melting polar ice cap. In 1894 the wealthy visionary built an observatory in the clear air of Arizona to get a better look.

Newspaper accounts of Lowell's views created a Mars craze among the public, but most scientists were unimpressed. Even so, the notion of canals was not put to rest until 1965, when *Mariner 4* sent back pictures of a frozen, lifeless wasteland.

Lowell *did* make major contributions to science, including his work toward the discovery of Pluto. In fact, by inspiring a young boy to choose a career, one of his lectures led directly to space exploration. The boy was Robert Goddard, the father of American rocketry.

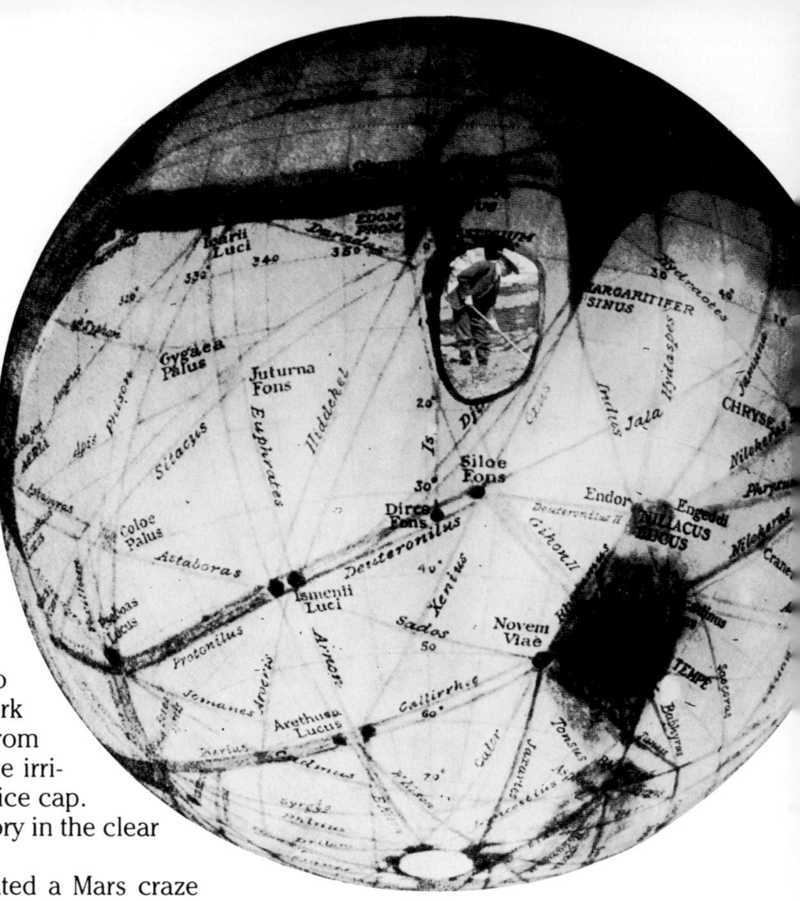

In 1905 astronomer Percival Lowell received a birthday card from the workers at his observatory in Flagstaff, Arizona. On it they pictured their boss gardening among the canals he had mapped on Mars.

Bright Ideas *(from the files of the U.S. Patent Office)*

"In some rural districts, where, from the primitive habits of the people, there is but little call for a privy, except for an occasional visitor, and where a hole in the ground serves as a privy-vault... to meet the requirements for a generation or two, there would be but little call for my valuable improvement.... [However] in the larger towns and cities... perhaps half of the expense and much of the annoyance [of cleaning privy vaults] may be saved."

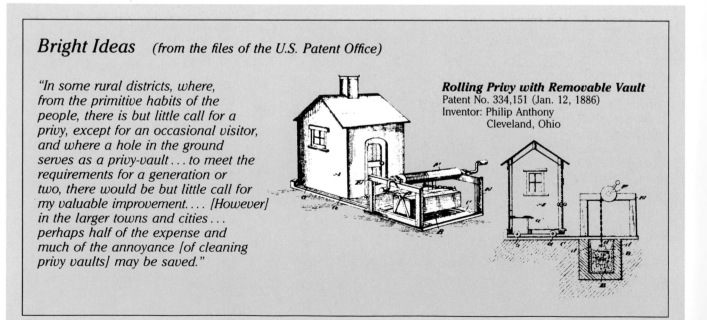

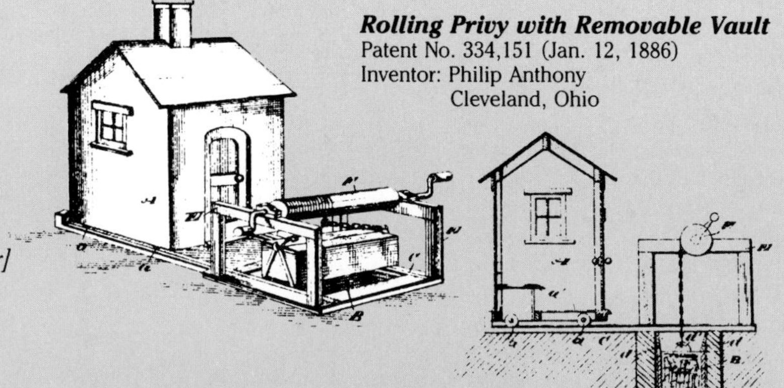

Rolling Privy with Removable Vault
Patent No. 334,151 (Jan. 12, 1886)
Inventor: Philip Anthony
Cleveland, Ohio

Ringing the Wrong Bell *Antonio Meucci, a father of the telephone*

Before 1876 few people shared Alexander Graham Bell's vision of the awesome power of the telephone as vividly as a man Bell didn't even know: a theatrical set designer from Staten Island, New York, named Antonio Meucci. Born in Florence, Italy, in 1808, Meucci had studied drawing and mechanical engineering before becoming a set designer for the theater and opera in Florence. Moving to Cuba, he became superintendent of mechanics at Havana's Tacon Opera House.

A voice through the wire

Simultaneously, Meucci pursued experiments with electricity, established his own electroplating business, and used electrotherapy to treat rheumatism. During one of these treatments he heard, over the wires he was using, the voice of a speaker three rooms away. He later learned how to amplify voices by attaching a paper cone to the wires.

When he left Cuba in 1850 and settled on Staten Island, he continued his experiments with the *teletrofono,* and by the mid-1850's was using it to speak to his wife on the third floor from his basement workshop. By 1857 Meucci had developed a working model; but when he demonstrated it to potential investors three years later, he failed to get their backing.

Bad luck

It marked the beginning of a long series of disappointments. Over the next 10 years, Meucci worked on other inventions and obtained patents for a canal steamer, a marine telegraph, and a device that measured humidity. Unfortunately, the patents were registered under the names of his investors, and Meucci did not share in the financial rewards.

Seriously injured in an explosion on a New York Harbor ferryboat, Meucci was bedridden for five months, and his wife was forced to sell his best telephone models to a junkman to raise desperately needed cash.

Patents before Bell

But the inventor remained determined to produce a telephone. He took drawings and a detailed description to the patent office and received a caveat, or temporary patent, in December 1871, a full five years before Bell was to receive a patent for his own telephone. Meucci renewed the caveat the following two years but let it lapse in 1874 because he couldn't afford the fees.

In desperation, Meucci offered his telephone plans to a local Western Union official, who held the designs and models for almost two years and then lost them. A few months later Bell received his patent, a process that took only three weeks. Subsequent legal appeals by Meucci failed. He died in 1889, a poor and heartbroken man.

Mark Twain Dialed the Wrong Number

America's foremost humorist was a bit of a sucker for investing in other people's inventions, but he somehow managed to turn down a stock offering in the telephone from Alexander Graham Bell. Twain wrote: "I said I didn't want anything more to do with wildcat speculation. Then he (Bell) offered the stock to me at twenty-five. I said I didn't want it at any price. He became eager; insisted that I take five hundred dollars' worth. He said he would sell me as much as I wanted for five-hundred dollars. . . . But I was the burnt child, and I resisted all those temptations—resisted them easily; went off with my check intact, and next day lent five thousand of it, on an unendorsed note, to a friend who was going to go bankrupt three days later." The small investment Bell was seeking would have earned Twain $190,000. The author had better luck with his own creation, however. The self-pasting scrapbook he patented (right)—which he called a "great humanizing and civilizing invention"—made a tidy profit.

Alexander Graham Bell's HD–4 *hydrofoil (left) set a marine speed record of 70.86 m.p.h. in 1919. His telephone (below) won first prize at the Centennial Exhibition in 1876.*

Gray Versus Bell

Taking credit for the telephone

As Thomas Nast's 1886 cartoon shows, Elisha Gray and Alexander Graham Bell were not the only claimants to the telephone. Many patents, including some by Thomas A. Edison, went into the design. Over several decades, some 600 lawsuits were litigated before Bell's patent was finally upheld.

As an inventor, Elisha Gray was a consummate professional. He got his first patent—for an automatic telegraph relay—in 1867, at the age of 32. Later, when Western Union bought his printer (it translated Morse code into type), he used the profit to form Gray & Barton, a partnership that was to become Western Electric.

In the early 1870's Gray turned his attention to an urgent problem: how to send several simultaneous signals over one telegraph wire. Whoever created such a "multiplex" system would reap a rich reward. Gray's idea, to use a different musical tone for each message, was fairly simple in terms of transmission; the difficulty lay in creating a receiver capable of sorting out the tones. Attacking the challenge in his usual methodical way, Gray designed prototype after prototype and then tinkered with them, learning from each mistake.

An odd side effect

In the process, it became clear that such a receiver could also reproduce the tones of the human voice, if an adequate transmitter could be developed. Gray thought he knew how to do that, but the multiplex telegraph took priority.

Meanwhile a young amateur named Alexander Graham Bell was working on the same problem, and competition between the two grew fierce. A teacher of speech to the deaf, Bell understood the mechanics of speech and was trying to apply similar principles to a multiplex telegraph. He, too, realized the potential for sending speech over a wire.

"Bell seems to be spending all his energies in [the] talking telegraph," Gray wrote to his attorney. "While this is very interesting scientifically, it has no commercial value. . . . I don't want at present to spend my time and money for that which will bring no reward."

Nonetheless, on Valentine's Day 1876, Gray filed a caveat (a description of a new device, not yet perfected) with the U.S. Patent Office for a talking telegraph. He was too late. A few hours earlier Bell had applied for a patent on *his* telephone, even though it, too, was not yet perfected. Gray's lawyer said that he could block Bell's patent by filing a full application, but Gray saw no reason to waste time and money on a "toy." He wanted to display a working model of his

Bell's work with giant kites (left; the pilot was to ride in the center) led to the development of tetrahedral cells. His wife, Mabel Hubbard (inset, carrying a tetrahedral structure), worked closely with him throughout 45 years of marriage.

multiplex at the Centennial Exhibition in Philadelphia that summer.

Bell knew the telephone was no toy. "*The whole thing is mine—*" he wrote his father, "and I am sure of fame, fortune, and success."

Historic accident

On March 10, 1876, Bell accidentally spilled acid on his clothes and shouted to his assistant, "Mr. Watson, come here. I want you!" Watson, in another room, heard the words over the telephone.

Both Gray and Bell displayed their inventions at the Centennial Exhibition in June. The judges were amazed when Gray's multiplex received eight messages at once from New York, but they awarded first prize for scientific achievement to Bell.

Bell offered to sell his patents to Western Union for $100,000 and was turned down. Instead, the company bought Gray's patents and sued Bell for infringement. The case was finally settled in the courts, leaving Bell in sole possession of the telephone.

Elisha Gray was not satisfied. He spent the rest of his life trying to prove that he, not his younger rival, had invented the telephone.

Meanwhile, Bell went on teaching the deaf (Helen Keller became a close friend). In 1879 he created the audiometer to detect hearing loss. As a result of his work, degrees of loudness came to be measured in bels or decibels.

An eclectic genius

Bell's imagination knew few limits. After his newborn son died of respiratory failure in 1881, he developed a "vacuum jacket," a forerunner of the iron lung. His graphophone improved on Edison's phonograph by recording on wax cylinders rather than tinfoil. His solar still used the sun to condense pure water from saltwater.

In the 1890's, fascinated by the prospect of manned flight, Bell experimented with rockets, rotors, aerofoils, and huge kites. After the Wright brothers flew, he organized the Aerial Experiment Association to further the development of controlled, powered flight.

He experimented in genetics, trying to develop four-nippled sheep that would bear twins and give enough milk to feed them.

During World War I, Bell worked on "water ears," an early form of submarine detection, and developed a hydrofoil craft to serve as a high-speed submarine chaser.

Strowger's Revenge

Almon Brown Strowger, a Kansas City undertaker, was losing business—and he blamed the local switchboard operator. Whether through sloppiness or duplicity, she had failed to notify him of the death of a close friend, and his competitor got the work. So he decided to create a telephone system that didn't rely on an operator.

Strowger made a rough model from a paper-collar box, 100 straight pins, and a pencil. Then, with the help of his nephew Walter and a Wichita jeweler, he designed a more sophisticated model and on March 12, 1889, filed for a patent on his Automatic Telephone Exchange. Further refinements earned more patents.

In November 1892 La Porte, Indiana, became the first city to replace operators with automation. During the introductory ceremonies, Strowger—forever free of the funeral business—noted that under his system "the telephone girl would have to go, but she would only be following in the footsteps of the messenger boy whose services were dispensed with by the invention of the telephone."

The tinfoil phonograph (below) created a new career for Thomas Edison, who went into the recording business, often auditioning performers at his lab in West Orange, New Jersey. It's lucky the cheery singer at left couldn't see the impresario's face.

The Sound Writer

Edison expected the phonograph to serve the telephone

Since the dawn of time, sounds have been as fleetingly ephemeral as dreams; even the most exquisite vanish as they occur, leaving only a memory. Then in 1877 Thomas Edison captured this elusive element, finally giving it a permanence that art and writing had achieved millennia earlier.

So new was his invention, so different from anything anyone had ever conceived, that the patent was approved in just seven weeks. But at first no one, not even Edison, foresaw the revolution the phonograph would create.

The idea for recording the human voice came to Edison while he worked on a new telephone transmitter, which used a needle instead of a tuning fork to pick up sound vibrations. "I was singing to the mouthpiece of a telephone when the vibrations of the voice sent the fine steel point into my finger," he wrote. "If I could record the actions of the point . . . I saw no reason why the thing would not talk."

A friend bet him a barrel of apples that he'd never get his talking machine to work. But within weeks Edison had developed a device with which the voice literally drew a picture of itself: a stylus, jiggled by sound vibrations, inscribed a pattern on a sheet of tinfoil as it rotated on a metal cylinder. Aptly, he named the invention the phonograph, or sound writer. And he won the apples.

Originally little more than a novelty, the phonograph caused a sensation everywhere it was demonstrated. In one week in Boston people paid more than $1,800 in admissions to hear it cough, bark, crow, and speak French.

Now that the phonograph existed, the question was how to use it. Edison thought it would serve the telephone, which he believed would be too expensive for most Americans to own. As a former telegraph operator, the inventor foresaw central stations at which people would record their messages on his "telephone repeater." The messages would then be transmitted over phone lines to another office at which recipients could listen to them in the senders' own voices.

It took more than a decade for the phonograph to emerge as a machine for home entertainment. By then it had become one of Edison's favorite inventions, and he went on to a 40-year career as a recording producer.

Although partially deaf, Edison had perfect pitch; he personally supervised auditions, and he certainly knew what he liked. In the early 1920's the Russian composer Sergei Rachmaninoff came to his studio to make a trial record. After only a few bars, Edison interrupted with: "Who told you you're a piano player? You're a pounder—that's what you are, a pounder!" Rachmaninoff put on his hat and walked out.

Edison's fascination with the sound machine lasted a lifetime. In 1927, at the age of 80, he developed a double-sided, 80-r.p.m., 10-inch LP that played for 40 minutes. Ahead of its time, the record was a commercial failure; nonetheless, the phonograph was already creating one of the world's most prosperous industries.

Edison's Greatest Achievement

The "invention factory" at Menlo Park

Thomas Edison had no formal scientific training and no time for "theo-retical scientists." He thought of himself as an entrepreneur who was in "the invention business"; only projects with a marketable outcome interested him. It was typical, therefore, that in 1876 he created perhaps his greatest invention—the world's first "invention factory." Moving his staff of some 15 people to a large new clapboard building packed with scientific paraphernalia and malodorous chemicals in rural Menlo Park, New Jersey, he established an industrial research laboratory and boldly proclaimed it would produce "a minor invention every ten days and a big thing every six months or so." The prediction seemed preposterous. But just 10 years later the research facility had grown into a full-fledged village, and Edison had been granted 420 patents, including those for the phonograph and the incandescent light bulb.

These achievements earned the inventor the sobriquet Wizard of Menlo Park. But Edison knew there was no magic to it. "Genius," he said, "is two percent inspiration and ninety-eight percent perspiration"—and his appetite for work was unmatched. The town of Menlo Park reflected his philosophy, offering few diversions to fill leisure time. One day, to help alleviate Mrs. Edison's boredom, her husband converted a telephone receiver into a loudspeaker and, by means of his private phone line to Western Union headquarters in New York City, let her listen to a concert taking place 23 miles away.

Edison abandoned Menlo Park in 1886 for larger facilities in West Orange. But the work in that New Jersey pasture signaled the end to an age when "pure" scientists looked down on such "practical" scientists as Edison, who invented for money, and it laid the foundation for the great industrial think tanks of today.

Mind-Reading Machine

Thomas Edison gave mysticism and paranormal phenomena a distinctly scientific twist: he theorized that memory was composed of electronlike particles hurtling through space (even through outer space), bringing otherworldly knowledge to certain people. Furthermore, he believed the particles never died; they simply left the body of the dying to search for another friendly human host.

Henry Ford introduced the inventor to a medium, Bert Reese, whose telepathic experiments Edison tried to duplicate by using electric coils wound around the head. "Four of us gathered at one time in four different rooms, each wearing the apparatus." But, the inventor admitted, "we achieved no results in mind reading."

Despite the failure, and even after Reese was accused of fakery in 1926, Edison vouched for him to another genius obsessed with the paranormal—magician Harry Houdini.

Posing in the Menlo Park lab for this 1880 photograph, Edison (seated center, wearing a kerchief) and his staff reveal little of the energy that made this one of history's most prolific "invention factories" and the first true industrial research lab.

The Executioner's Choice

The electric chair became a grisly showcase in the rivalry between Edison and Westinghouse

From its inception in 1886, the competition between Thomas Edison's direct current (DC) and George Westinghouse's alternating current (AC) was fierce. AC was cheaper to transmit, but DC was thought to be safer. When Harold P. Brown, a self-taught electrical consultant, joined this "battle of the currents" two years later, the business rivalry took on a cruelly macabre twist.

Brown, an advocate of Edison's DC because of its safety, tortured animals to determine how much of each current they could survive. At a public demonstration at Columbia University, he exposed a caged dog to 300 volts of DC (about the level of AC the animal could withstand). Then, as the dog howled in agony, he increased the charge to 400, 500, and finally 1,000 volts.

Observers were sickened and outraged, but Brown's timing was perfect. New York State had recently formed a commission to investigate alternatives to hanging as a method of capital punishment. Electrocution had been considered, and now the commissioners asked Edison for his opinion. The great inventor was opposed to execution; but if it must take place, he said, an application of his rival Westinghouse's lethal AC would be the most humane way.

On January 1, 1889, New York became the first state to adopt electrical execution. Needing an expert to manage the project, officials hired none other than Harold P. Brown—who proceeded to invent the electric chair. Although the law did not specify the type of current to be used, Brown powered his device with a Westinghouse dynamo, hoping to malign AC as the "executioner's current."

Despite the publicity, Brown's scheme to discredit alternating current failed, and AC eventually triumphed in the marketplace because of its lower distribution costs. Properly insulated and applied, it soon became the national standard.

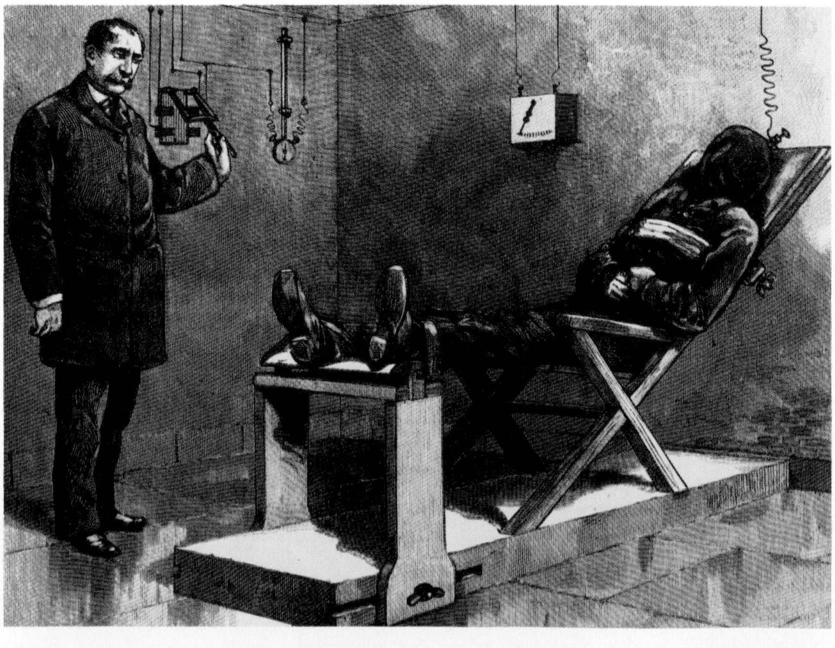

On August 6, 1890, William Kemmler, convicted of "chopping his wife to bits with an axe," became the first person to be executed in the electric chair. The switch at New York's Auburn Prison was closed for 17 seconds, and Kemmler appeared to be dead. Then his body started to twitch. Believing he was still alive, prison officials decided to administer another charge, but took a full two minutes to reattach Kemmler to the chair. The next blast lasted 70 seconds, during which the corpse started to burn. Gruesome engravings, such as the one at left, fueled moral debate over the execution.

Edison's Blunder

"It's all gone, but we had a hell of a time spending it"

By the age of 43, Thomas Edison was wealthy, free of business burdens, and restless. "I'm going to do something now," he told a friend, "so different and so much bigger than anything I've ever done before that people will forget that my name ever was connected with anything electrical!"

The scheme was a new kind of iron mining, and the time was ripe. In the early 1890's the price of iron ore had skyrocketed. Edison purchased 19,000 acres near Ogdensburg, New Jersey, that had been mined of the richest deposits but still contained an estimated 2 billion tons of low-grade iron ore. There he built an entire village, complete with a mammoth stone quarry, rock-crushing machines, and a seven-story ore separator of his own design—at its heart were 480 magnets to remove the ore from the pulverized stone.

The machines were a marvel,

but from the beginning there were major problems. Equipment often broke down and the work was dangerous. Edison was forced to rebuild the entire plant when its foundations began to crumble. Nor were the financial returns cheery: the Depression of 1893 stilled production as new orders ceased to come in. When rich iron deposits were discovered in the Mesabi Range in Minnesota, the price of ore plummeted from $7.50 a ton to $2.65.

With more than $2 million of his own and his associates' money invested in the project, Edison was nearly bankrupt by 1899. Still, he had a long and productive career ahead of him, and in his usual fashion he did not take the failure to heart. "Well, it's all gone," he said, "but we had a hell of a time spending it."

Edison's venture into iron mining was prompted by a fishing trip. Noticing rich ore deposits mixed with a beach's sand, he hit upon the idea of using magnets to remove ore from pulverized rock. But by 1899 the technologically wondrous quarry and factory he had built (above) were closing, the inventor had lost a fortune, and the whole enterprise was being ridiculed as "Edison's folly."

Bright Ideas *(from the files of the U.S. Patent Office)*

"This invention . . . consists of electrical devices applied to bedsteads in such a manner that currents of electricity will be sent through the bodies of the bugs, which will either kill them or startle them, so that they will leave the bedstead. . . . I place pairs of metallic contacts . . . so close together that an insect in passing from one to the other must necessarily . . . close the circuit through its own body, and thus receive a current of electricity . . . which will either terminate its career at once or make it seek other locations. In like manner contact-strips . . . may be located . . . on the bedstead or on the bedsprings, which will so harass the bugs as to cause them to shun the bed entirely."

Electrical Bedbug Exterminator
Patent No. 616,049 (Dec. 13, 1898)
Inventor: Frank M. Archer
New York, N.Y.

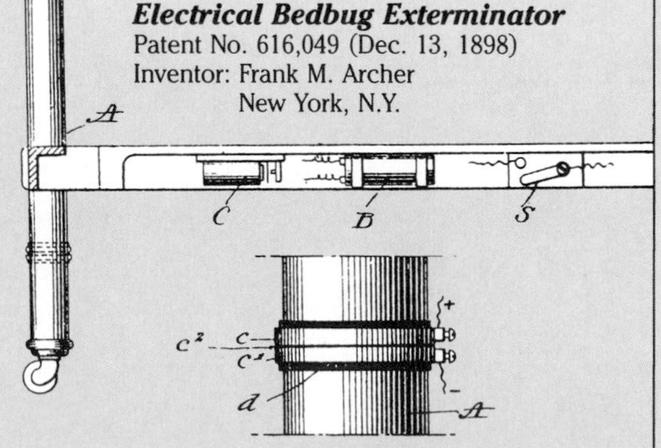

A 19th-Century Computer

The gifted young inventor said it all began with chicken salad

As rows of primly dressed young women tabulated the U.S. population for the 1890 census by pounding away on "statistical pianos," they were marking the start of a new era. For the machines they operated were calculators invented by Herman Hollerith, a young man just 30 years old, and his new devices heralded the dawn of the computer age.

When Hollerith was asked how he came to invent his machines, his reply was: "Chicken salad." A dance partner had invited him to her home to enjoy his favorite dish. There he met her father, head of the Division of Vital Statistics for the 1880 census, who suggested that a machine using notched cards could tabulate census statistics, which were still counted by hand.

Intrigued, Hollerith recalled a train ticket with his description punched out in a "punch photograph." With this as the starting point, he devised a machine that used the punch card to record information and other machinery to electrically "read" and tabulate it.

In a test against two hand methods, the machines proved twice as fast, and Hollerith won the contract for the 1890 census. (Alexander Graham Bell, who had invented another card-sorting machine, abandoned his project.)

The census office rented 56 of Hollerith's machines. They were powered by batteries recharged from the brand-new Edison electrical circuits. Wires ran to an airy room where "nice-looking girls in cool white dresses" sat at what looked like upright pianos, punching hundreds of cards a day. "Women are better adapted for this particular work than men," wrote the New York *Sun.* (A night shift of men confused the system and was soon eliminated, but while it lasted, the two shifts exchanged flirtatious notes.)

Since one operator could count some 80,000 people a day, the entire population—62,622,250—was added up in only six weeks. The census superintendent was delighted. "The bright young women and the sturdy young men of our Population Division," he enthused, "could run through the entire population of the earth . . . estimated at 1,300,000,000, in less than 200 days."

A newspaper observed that the inventor of the statistical piano (above) "will not likely get very rich." But in 1924 Herman Hollerith's Tabulating Machine Co. became IBM.

One Kitchen Gadget That Does It All

Electricity caught up with creativity in the late 1880's when the first small motor was introduced. It wasn't very long before kitchen appliances abounded: toasters and roasters, hot plates and coffee grinders—no device was neglected for long. But the super-gadget at left, envisioned by one clever cartoonist, never made it off the drawing board.

Bright Ideas

(from the files of the U.S. Patent Office)

Method of Preserving the Dead
Patent No. 748,284 (Dec. 29, 1903)
Inventor: Joseph Karwowski
Herkimer, N.Y.

"I . . . a subject of the Czar of Russia, residing at Herkimer . . . have invented certain new and useful Improvements in Methods of Preserving the Dead . . . whereby a corpse may be hermetically incased within a block of transparent glass [and] maintained for an indefinite period in a perfect and life-like condition.

"I first surround the corpse 1 with a thick layer 2 of sodium silicate or water-glass. After the corpse has been thus inclosed . . . it is allowed to remain for a short time within a compartment or chamber having a dry heated temperature . . . to evaporate the water from this incasing layer, after which molten glass is applied to the desired thickness. . . . Cylindrical or other forms may be substituted for the rectangular block. . . . The head alone may be preserved in this manner, if preferred. It will be at once noted that a body preserved in this way may be kept indefinitely. . . . The glass surrounding the corpse being transparent, the body will be at all times visible."

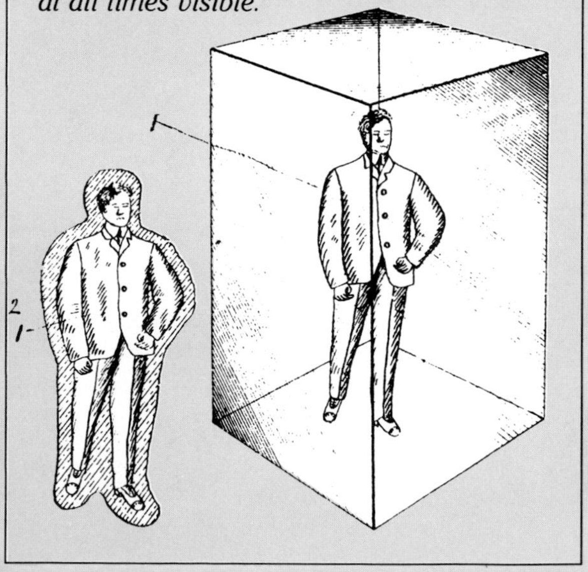

An early advertisement for the soap that Harley Procter was inspired to name after Psalms 45:8: "All thy garments smell of myrrh, and aloes, and cassia, out of the ivory palaces, whereby they have made thee glad."

It Floats!

The true story of Ivory is no soap opera

Harley Procter was proud. In 1878 his company had come up with a soap bar as fine as the finest imported castile soaps, but much less expensive. Indeed, a chemist's report confirmed the fact that Procter & Gamble's White Soap (Ivory's original name) was 99 and 44/100 percent pure. Then, by sheer accident, the soap acquired a new asset.

One day a worker forgot to shut off the soap-making machine when he went out to lunch. The mixture had turned frothy when he returned, but the soap was shipped out anyway. After all, the ingredients were the same. Who'd notice?

Well, *customers* did—and deluged the company with requests for its unique "soap that floats." After some hasty detective work, Procter found out that P&G had inadvertently created a floating gold mine.

The soap boasted of its purity and lightness well into the 20th century with the familiar slogan "Ivory: 99 and 44/100% pure—it floats."

Ether . . . Or? *The experiment failed—and posed a question for Einstein*

Until 1887 most scientists held that the universe and everything in it was permeated by a mysterious substance called ether. Odorless, tasteless, and invisible, it was presumed to be the necessary constant by which to measure the speed and position of all things, including the earth itself.

The problem was that no one could prove ether existed.

In 1887 a pair of Cleveland scientists, Albert A. Michelson and Edward W. Morley, devised an apparatus to do so. An arrangement of glass plates and mirrors, it split light into two beams and sent them the same distance in perpendicular directions. Reflected back to the center by mirrors, the beams met to form a pattern of light and dark bands.

The idea was that the earth, as it moved through the ether, must buck an "ether wind," just as a bicyclist faces air resistance. A beam of light moving in the same direction as the earth must be slowed by this wind. If it turned out that one of the two beams *was* slowed in this way, the pattern would change and the existence of ether would be proved.

But the pattern didn't change.

Physicists were appalled; without ether, the concept of a clockwork universe—based on Sir Isaac Newton's 200-year-old principles of mechanics—was shattered. Not until 1905, when the young Albert Einstein ignored ether and boldly announced the theory of relativity and the constancy of the speed of light, was the problem resolved.

In 1907 Michelson became the first American scientist to win the Nobel Prize, for his development of optical precision instruments.

The First Assembly Line *It disassembled pigs in Cincinnati*

Henry Ford, credited with creating the modern assembly line, said that the "idea came in a general way from the overhead trolley that the Chicago packers use in dressing beef." That may be where *he* got the idea, but the Chicagoans got it from Cincinnati.

By the 1850's, some 400,000 pigs per year were being herded through Cincinnati's streets. The city was, said a British visitor, "a monster piggery. . . . Alive and dead, whole and divided into portions, their outsides and their insides, their grunts and their squeals, meet you at every moment."

The scene inside a slaughterhouse was, according to landscape architect Frederick L. Olmsted, "a sort of human chopping machine. . . . By a skilled sleight-of-hand, hams, shoulders, clear, mess and prime fly off. . . . Amazed, we took out our watches and counted thirty-five seconds, from the moment when one hog touched the table until the next occupied its place." In the 1860's Wilson, Eggleston & Company installed an overhead track to speed things up even more.

Meanwhile, the meat-packing industry was centralizing in Chicago. The pork business left Cincinnati to join it, taking along the idea and technology of the overhead conveyor. And so, when Henry Ford needed inspiration, he got it in Chicago, not Cincinnati, where the disassembly line was born.

After a dip in boiling water (left) each carcass was scraped clean, then hooked to an overhead track (right) to be moved from worker to worker.

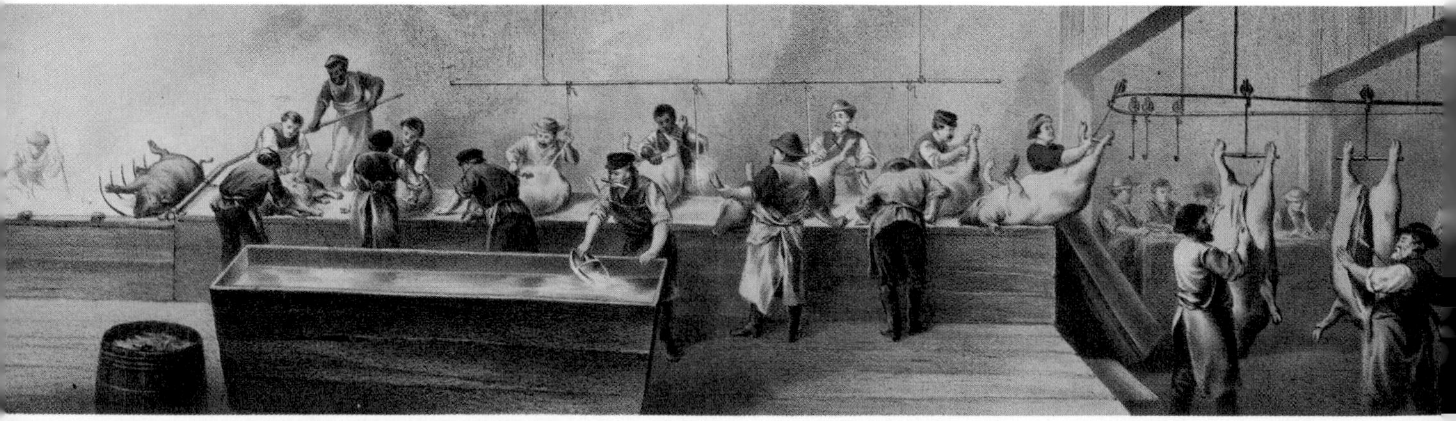

Nathan Stubblefield, Lost Genius

Radio's true inventor had no head for business

Nathan Stubblefield posed at home with his family and equipment in 1902. His son Bernard (far left) had already become the world's first radio musician.

He was a lonely, impoverished hermit when he was found starved to death in a shack near his hometown of Murray, Kentucky, in 1928. His body went into an unmarked grave. The world had forgotten Nathan B. Stubblefield, who had invented radio.

It was about 1890, when the Italian wizard Guglielmo Marconi was still in his teens, that Stubblefield demonstrated his wireless telephone for a few friends on his farm. He filed no patent then, just went on tinkering. Finally, on January 1, 1902 (less than a month after Marconi had transmitted the letter *S* across the Atlantic in Morse code), the Kentuckian got around to a public demonstration. About 1,000 friends and neighbors watched in amazement as, speaking softly into a two-foot-square box, he was heard at half a dozen listening posts around town. Then his 14-year-old son, Bernard, whistled and played the harmonica. Later that year Stubblefield gave a more impressive and better publicized demonstration in Washington, D.C., from a steam launch on the Potomac River.

At this point, the inventor should have capitalized on his ingenuity. He *did* patent his wireless telephone and form a company to promote it, but it never did anything more than sell stock.

Marconi, known today as the father of radio, actually pioneered wireless telegraphy, the transmission of Morse code. Stubblefield sent *voices* and *music* over the air. In a 1908 patent he described how to put radios in horseless carriages, making him the father of the car radio—another invention that did not make him rich. In fact, none of his inventions, including a battery devised for radios, made much money.

His marriage later broke up, his house burned down, and his spirit withered. Still, he continued to work on new inventions. But shortly before his death he destroyed them all and burned their plans.

Bright Ideas (*from the files of the U.S. Patent Office*)

This "hollow decoy animal [consists] of hide, canvas, or the equivalent thereof, exteriorly decorated or marked to represent the animal in imitation of which the decoy is constructed.... Arranged on the framework [are] hooks adapted to engage the upper edges of the belts of the hunters, whereby the weight of the decoy is supported thereby without interfering with the movements of the hunters, either in walking, as in approaching their game, or in discharging their pieces.... The neck portion... is hinged at its lower edge... to swing downwardly, and thereby allow the hunter occupying the front portion of the shell to discharge his piece over the neck portion.... Whether the decoy is made in the shape of a cow or other animal is immaterial."

Hunting Decoy
Patent No. 586,145 (July 13, 1897)
Inventor: John Sievers, Jr.
Ames, Neb.

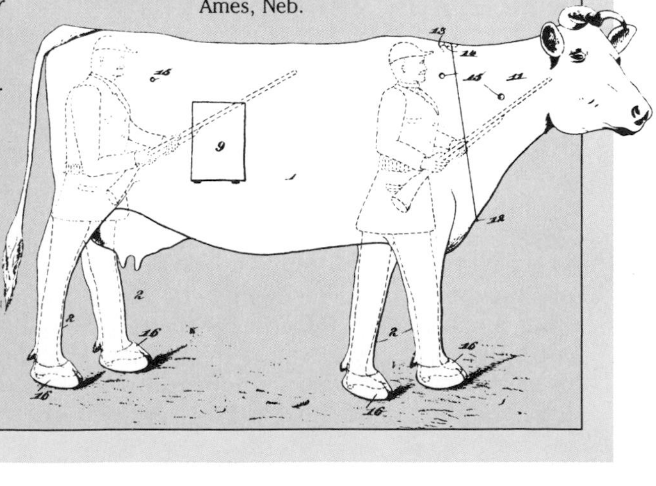

The failure of Langley's Great Aerodrome *(above) was seen as proof that manned flight was impossible. Hence, few believed in the Wrights' success nine days later.*

Langley's Folly *And the Wrights' stuff*

"Will man ever fly?" The debate raged into the 20th century, with scientists arrayed on both sides of the question. The highly respected Simon Newcomb of Johns Hopkins University wrote articles proving definitively that the thing was impossible. And even if a man managed to get a machine in the air, he wrote in 1903, "once he slackens his speed, down he begins to fall . . . a dead mass. How shall he reach the ground without destroying his delicate machinery?"

Meanwhile, Samuel Pierpont Langley, secretary of the Smithsonian Institution and the nation's unofficial chief scientist, had staked his reputation on proving that it *could* be done. He was already a celebrity because of two unmanned steam-powered models that had flown as far as 4,200 feet in 1896. When the Spanish-American War broke out in 1898, the War Department gave him $50,000 to develop a manned motor-driven flying machine. He added another $20,000 of Smithsonian funds, and on December 8, 1903, he was ready.

His machine, the *Great Aerodrome,* was mounted atop a houseboat anchored in Washington's Potomac River. Charles Manly, the Smithsonian's chief aeronautical assistant, stripped to his union suit, twisted himself into the cockpit, and was catapulted down a 60-foot track. A large group of news reporters watched as the *Great Aerodrome* turned an awkward flip and splashed down—flat on its back. Manly and a workman who plunged in to rescue him were fished out, shivering.

Newspapers had a field day ridiculing "Langley's Folly." The public was outraged, the House of Representatives debated the foolish expenditure of government funds, and the Senate threatened an investigation.

The next day a young bicycle mechanic, Orville Wright, left Dayton, Ohio, on a train bound for Kitty Hawk, a remote fishing village in North Carolina. Eight days later, on December 17, he and his brother, Wilbur, after three years of work at their own expense, became the first to achieve powered flight.

Although the Wrights had notified newspapers of their plans, no reporters came to watch. The New York *Daily Tribune* noted the flight with a short item—on the sports page. "Dayton Boys Fly Airship," bragged the Dayton *Evening Herald*. But there was no fanfare when the "Dayton boys" came home. For one thing,

The First Fatal Air Crash

As 2,000 people watched, Orville Wright and Lt. Thomas E. Selfridge (above) soared 150 feet over Fort Myer, Virginia. It was September 17, 1908. Wright was demonstrating his latest airplane for the army as Selfridge, cofounder of the Aerial Experiment Association, assessed its military value. During the fourth and final lap, a guy wire broke loose and fouled a propeller. The plane, said one eyewitness, "came down like a bird shot dead in full flight." Orville's left leg and hip were smashed; Selfridge, his skull fractured, died that night.

nobody understood what they'd done; an "airship" could be a balloon. Nor was the rest of America impressed. The great Langley had failed; how could two bicycle mechanics do it? The first magazine to tell the story was *Gleanings in Bee Culture,* in March 1904.

The Wrights began sustaining flight by making wide circles over a pasture near Dayton. Again, no one paid any attention. One farmer saw the machine fly 24 miles in 38 minutes, but kept right on plowing.

Ultimately the Wrights offered their patents to the U.S. government. But, still smarting over the Langley affair, the War Department would take no action until a machine "by actual operation is shown to be able to produce horizontal flight and to carry an operator."

Meanwhile, Langley's successor at the Smithsonian spearheaded efforts to prove that the *Great Aerodrome* had really been the first airplane. The machine was later put on exhibit there; miffed, Orville Wright sent the original *Wright Flyer* to the Science Museum in London. Not until December 17, 1948—11 months after Orville's death—did this priceless American treasure receive its place of honor in the Smithsonian.

Bright Ideas

(from the files of the U.S. Patent Office)

"This invention relates to a new apparatus for enabling men to fly with the use of side and dorsal wings, which are connected with the extremities for operation.

"The chief object of the present invention is to support the flying apparatus entirely on the trunk of the operator, and remove all weight from the arms and legs, so that they will be free to give their entire strength to the operation.... The weight of the whole machine need not exceed 15 pounds. It is constructed inside of a semicircle, all the points touching the periphery.

"In order to make a beginning one foot is disengaged from the stirrup, when, by raising the other foot and pushing the hands upward and forward . . . the wings are raised.... The actions are intended to be natural, resembling those of swimming in water."

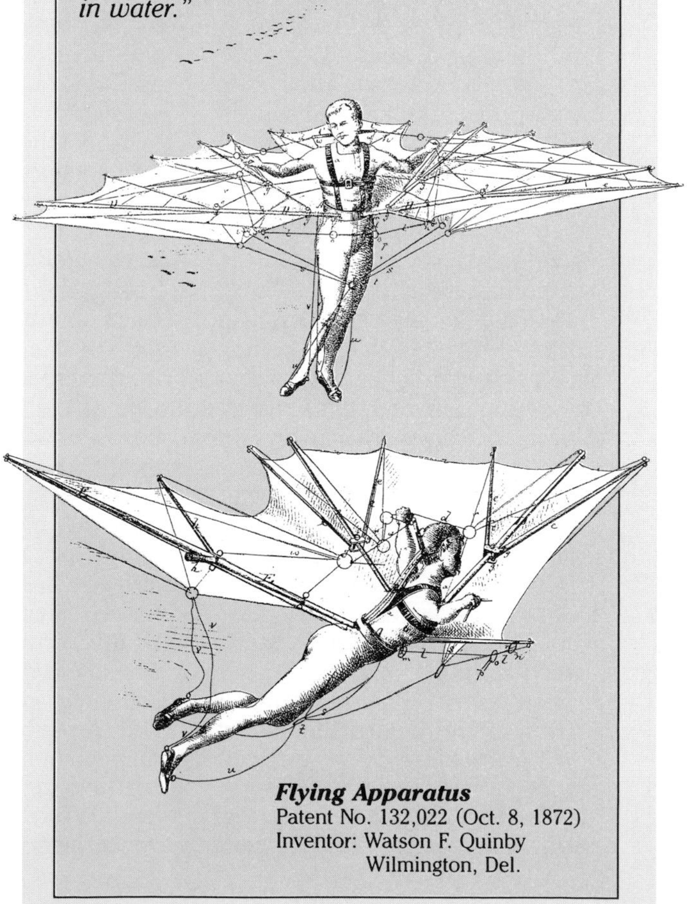

Flying Apparatus
Patent No. 132,022 (Oct. 8, 1872)
Inventor: Watson F. Quinby
Wilmington, Del.

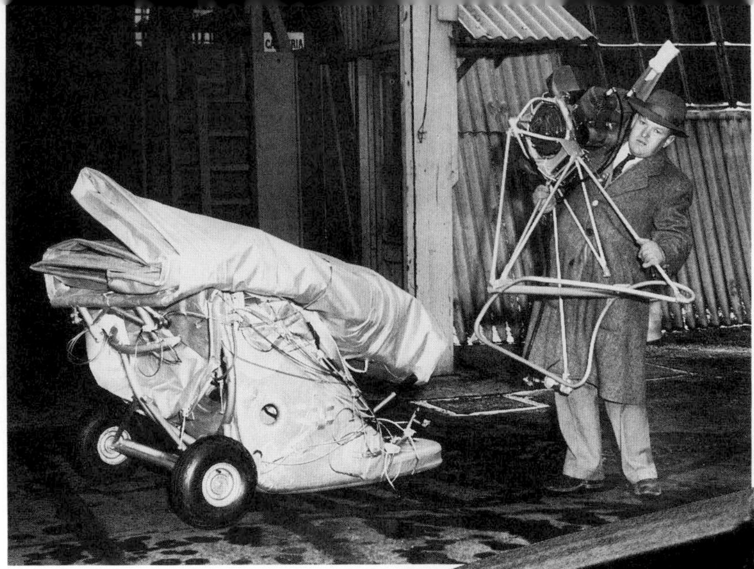

Hopes were high in the late 1950's for inflatable planes. Originally developed for the military, one Goodyear product weighed only 290 pounds. Inflated (below), it had a 28-foot wingspan. Folded (like the plane at left), it fit into a station wagon.

Flights of Fancy

High tech and hoopla in pursuit of the personal plane

Thousands of planes zoom over a city, piloted by shoppers going to the mall, businesspeople headed for three-martini lunches, and car pool members getting their kids from school. An air controller's nightmare? On the contrary, this astounding prospect—the dream of the personal plane—was an American fantasy even before the Wright brothers got us off the ground in 1903.

Within a decade of that historic flight the dream was real for a few wealthy daredevils, who used seaplanes to commute from country estates to waterfront hangars in downtown New York and Chicago. But these audacious aircraft were dangerous and expensive: far from personal planes for Everyman. At a time when a car cost $500—more than most workers made in a year—these planes sold for $7,000.

Then Henry Ford, the man who made a fortune democratizing the roads with his modestly priced Model T, had visions of doing it all over again in the sky. The experiments he started in 1926 ended in disaster two years later when a friend crashed Ford's prototype plane at Miami Beach and was killed. By 1930 the auto magnate was out of the airplane business completely.

Others, however, were eager to take his place, especially after the federal government began supporting the quest for a "poor man's plane" that would be both as safe and as cheap as the family car. Some of the backyard inventors of these "foolproof" flying machines showed real genius. One of them, Fred Weick, developed the anti-tailspin design and three-wheel landing gear that are standard on modern planes.

By the mid-1930's combination car-planes, suitable for both the skyways and the highways, were making their way off the drawing boards, down the road, and into the air. In August 1936 test pilot John Ray astonished Washington, D.C., as he landed a forerunner of the helicopter in a city park. Folding the gangling overhead blades, he then drove the prototype to the Department of Commerce, where he presented it to government officials. When the ceremony was over, Ray took off again; but in midflight his craft's oil pressure suddenly dropped dangerously. Spotting a near-empty roadway, the pilot landed, pulled into a gas station, and replenished his oil supply. Within minutes, he was back in the air.

After World War II, people expected the personal plane to really take off. Towns built airfields, high schools offered flying lessons, and car dealers prepared to add aircraft to their showrooms. Even Macy's department store was selling planes. A small flock of flying cars again fluttered across technology's horizon. One, the *Airphibian,* was featured in *Life* magazine when its inventor piloted it to New York to enjoy an evening at the theater. But these hybrids neither flew as well as a sleek small plane nor cruised the highways with the ease and comfort of the family car. Eventually they all failed to fly in the marketplace—long before they could cause traffic jams in the sky.

The first successful person-powered plane was launched in 1977. Two years later the pedal-driven Gossamer Albatross *(above) successfully flew 22 miles to cross the English Channel. Although the plane weighs only 55 pounds, its 94 foot wingspan (right) is longer than that of a DC-9.*

The Convair Stinson Aircar *(below) is an ironically apt symbol for the plane-car dream of the 1950's. On the* Aircar*'s third trip aloft it ran out of gas and crashed (left). The pilot was unharmed, but the project never recovered.*

"Nothing Has Come Along to Beat the Horse"

As far as J. P. Morgan was concerned, the automobile had no future

As the 19th century gave way to the 20th, many investors shared the opinion of Senator Chauncey Depew, whose faith in four-footed transportation was unshakable. "Nothing has come along to beat the horse," he counseled. "Keep your money." And no one agreed with him more than J. P. Morgan, who had made millions by shrewd investments in industry. But when it came to gauging the potential of the vehicle that would change American life, he was way off base.

The first auto companies

Morgan's opportunity to get into the automobile business came in 1908, when William Crapo Durant approached him for a loan. Durant and Benjamin Briscoe proposed a merger with two other auto manufacturers, Henry Ford and Ransom Olds; but Ford (who was just about to introduce the Model T) wanted a total of $3 million, making the deal much too expensive. Now the pair were seeking Morgan's capital to combine their own firms, Buick and Maxwell-Briscoe.

When Durant confidently predicted that annual auto sales would someday reach 500,000, he was laughed out of the room. "If he has any sense," snorted one of Morgan's partners, "he'll keep such notions to himself."

A familiar name

Briscoe went out on his own, but his company failed. Durant, meanwhile, without the backing of the financiers, went ahead and formed a holding company with $2,000. He named it General Motors.

By 1910 Durant was faltering and received help from some of Morgan's competitors. A decade later, however, the House of Morgan had another chance to get into the car business.

Brink of bankruptcy

With a total of $30 million in debts, General Motors was in deep trouble. To forestall bankruptcy, Durant turned to two financial giants: J. P. Morgan and Co. and Pierre du Pont. They saved the company, but at a tremendous cost. Du Pont took over as president—and Durant was out.

Help Stamp Out Pollution! *Use Horseless Transportation!*

By the turn of the century, urban Americans were drowning in pollution. Tons of it. There were 150,000 horses in New York City alone, each one producing an average of 22 pounds of manure a day. By contrast, Rochester, New York, had a mere 15,000 horses. But collectively they produced enough manure in 1900 to cover one acre to the astounding depth of 175 feet.

Health hazards

The stench was appalling, and at its worst, horse manure was a serious health hazard. Authorities in Rochester calculated that their acre of manure would breed 16 billion flies—and flies carried all kinds of diseases, including cholera, typhoid fever, and dysentery. Insurance actuaries found that people working in or living near livery stables had a higher rate of these infectious diseases than did the general public. And there was a livery stable on every block.

When dry weather persisted, it turned manure into dust that would "cover our clothes, ruin our furniture, and blow up into our nostrils." On the other hand, when rain fell on uncollected manure, the streets turned into cesspools. Women wearing long gowns were forced to raise their skirts as they crossed the streets, or risk hemlines filled with filth. (America's cities did not boast the amenities that London supplied: crossing sweepers, who cleared the pedestrians' paths at intersections.)

Street sounds

Noise pollution from the din of iron wheels and horseshoes on cobblestones recalled Benjamin Franklin's early-18th-century lament about the "thundering of coaches, chariots, chaises, waggons, drays and the whole fraternity of noise" in his beloved Philadelphia. As time went by, the noise was blamed for creating a variety of nervous disorders.

With the early years of the 20th century came automobiles, vying with horses along the nation's increasingly crowded streets and highways. Meantime, magazines were filled with articles urging the banning of horses. Writers asserted that horseless vehicles were cleaner, quieter, cheaper, and faster. And, for a while, they were.

Bright Ideas *(from the files of the U.S. Patent Office)*

"This invention relates to an attachment for automobiles and more especially for closed vehicles . . . to provide a simple and efficient device by means of which the driver of the vehicle can speak to persons in front thereof, thereby to facilitate traffic.

"Referring to the figures by character of reference 1 designates a tube arranged longitudinally of the hood of a vehicle. This tube is provided at one end with a small megaphone which can consist of a flared extension 2 of the tube. The other end of the tube is extended into the vehicle to a point close to the driver where it is provided with a mouth-piece into which the driver can easily speak."

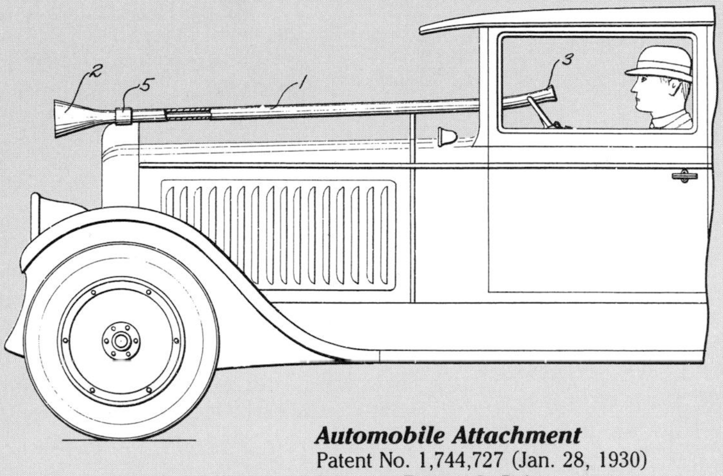

Automobile Attachment
Patent No. 1,744,727 (Jan. 28, 1930)
Inventor: Eugene L. Baker
Taunton, Mass.

As horseless vehicles appeared on city thoroughfares, this steam-driven streetcar was one ingenious solution to a new problem—frightened horses on busy streets.

Was Henry Ford Taken for a Ride?

Cheap, efficient, and readily available, it was a gasoline substitute that could transform the automobile industry. At least this was the claim of Louis Enricht in 1916, when he insisted that his chemical mixture would run any car for about a penny a gallon. Always ready to prove his point, he'd brandish a vial of green liquid, mix it with water, and pour it in the dry gas tank of any car handy. The engine would promptly start up.

Seeking cheaper fuel for his Tin Lizzies, Henry Ford felt that there was substance to the claim. Even after Enricht's participation in shady land deals and questionable stock transactions was revealed, the auto pioneer gave the con man $1,000 in cash and a car on which he could continue to test the amazing elixir.

When the rights to Enricht's discovery were apparently sold to another company for $1 million, Ford canceled the deal, suing Enricht for the return of his Model T. In a comedy of errors, the auto was returned without the motor. So by the time Ford pulled out, he'd lost $1,000 and his car engine.

While no one ever discovered what Enricht's potion was, experts theorize that he used acetone. Added to water, it could indeed run a car. But the subsequent corrosion would ruin the motor.

A Concrete Look at the Garden of Eden

Watch Eve hand Adam an apple! Recoil from Satan's pitchfork! See snakes slither around grapevines! Enjoy it all at the Garden of Eden in Lucas, Kansas (below), where a free-wheeling interpretation of the Book of Genesis features intertwined trees and figures made entirely of concrete—113 tons of it, fashioned into 29 unusual trees and 150 unique sculptures.

Civil War veteran S. P. Dinsmoor was 64 years old when he started sculpting his Garden in 1907; it took him 22 years to finish it. After his death, he was laid to rest in a glass-topped coffin (which is also on view) so that on resurrection day, he said, the lid would "fly open, and I will sail out."

Bright Ideas

(from the files of the U.S. Patent Office)

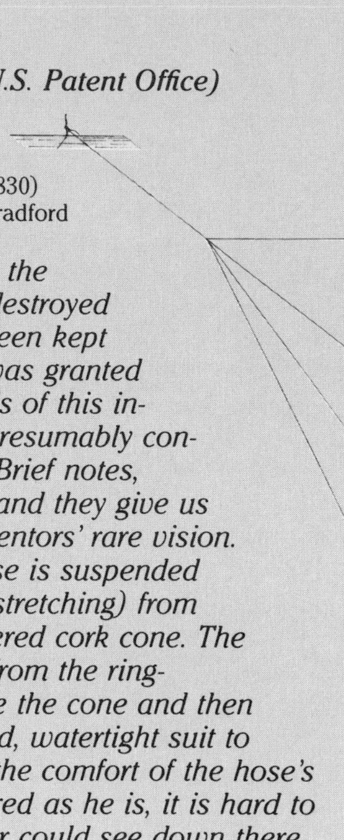

Submarine Explorer
Patent No. 5,834 (Feb. 18, 1830)
Inventors: S. Short and N. Bradford

Unfortunately, a fire in the Patent Office in 1836 destroyed the records that had been kept since the first patent was granted in 1790, and the details of this ingenious device were presumably consumed by the flames. Brief notes, however, did survive, and they give us a glimpse of these inventors' rare vision. A large waterproof hose is suspended by chains (to prevent stretching) from a floating, leather-covered cork cone. The diver enters the hose from the ring-shaped platform inside the cone and then descends in a weighted, watertight suit to explore the depths in the comfort of the hose's airy interior. Encumbered as he is, it is hard to imagine what the diver could see down there.

"Don't pass the babies by!" At the Coney Island display of thriving premature infants, one of the barkers was an unknown English actor, Archibald Leach, who moved on to Hollywood. There he acquired a new name: Cary Grant.

Boardwalk Babies

Making medical history—with a show-biz touch

In the early decades of this century, the best treatment for dangerously frail premature infants could be found on the midway at Coney Island. That's where Dr. Martin Couney demonstrated the life-saving benefits of a device new to—and scorned by—medicine: the infant incubator. Audiences willingly paid admission to marvel at the incredibly tiny babies, each nestled snugly in an incubator in a glass-enclosed nursery. As the tots put on enough weight to leave Couney's pavilion, he would replace them with new preemies struggling for survival.

Couney's show-business career began quite by accident in 1896, when he was a young doctor at the French maternity hospital where incubators were first developed. He was asked to demonstrate the new device at an international exposition in Berlin, and the exhibit, complete with premature babies who had been supplied by German hospitals, was such a success (as was the technology) that Couney followed with exhibitions in London and Paris.

Hope for American preemies

In 1901 Couney brought his touring incubator show to the United States for the Pan-American Exposition in Buffalo; the preemies proved to be such a popular attraction that the doctor decided to remain in America. Two years later he built an ornate baby palace on the boardwalk at Coney Island in New York and hired handsome young barkers to hustle the crowd through the turnstiles. Once inside, the spectators were often given a vivid demonstration of just how small the preemies were: Couney's chief nurse (there was a full professional staff in attendance at all times) would remove a ring from her finger and easily slip it over the wrist of one of the tiny tots.

The good doctor profited from the demonstrations, taking in $72,000 for a 10-month stay at a San Francisco exposition alone. At the Chicago World's Fair in 1933–34, Couney's pavilion was next to fan dancer Sally Rand's; when police came to arrest the stripper, she protested that at least she wore more clothes than her tiny neighbors.

Belated recognition

Remarkably, it took the medical profession decades to catch on: for nearly 40 years Couney toured the country, publicizing incubators. Then, in belated recognition of his work, the New York Medical Society presented him with a platinum watch in 1937. Ironically, acceptance by his fellow doctors spelled the end for Couney's sideshow. As hospitals finally began to establish units to treat premature babies, attendance at his exhibits declined. In the mid-1940's, almost half a century after he had begun his combined career as a neonatal pediatrician and show-business entrepreneur, Couney closed the Coney Island pavilion for good.

Of the 8,000 premature babies he had treated, Couney maintained that an astonishing 6,500 had survived. "I made my propaganda for the preemie," he explained. "My work is done."

Max's Magic

He invented glamour

Max Factor was often seen on movie sets applying his makeup to such beautiful stars as Clara Bow (above).

Makeup is always the stuff of make-believe, and that may be what Max Factor understood best. He started as a makeup artist for the theater and movies, and went on to virtually create the modern cosmetics industry by putting the glamour of the stage and screen within easy reach of every American woman. His role was so fundamental, he even popularized the word *makeup.*

After working as a makeup artist for the Russian Royal Ballet, Factor came to America in 1904. He settled in St. Louis and opened a concession selling beauty aids at that year's world's fair. Within four years he had started a theatrical makeup store in Los Angeles. There he found that traditional stick greasepaint was too thick and garish for use in the movies; so in 1914 he introduced a thinner cream greasepaint in more precise skin tones.

It wasn't his last contribution to movie magic. Later he created the first human-hair wig used in a movie, and in 1918 he made the first false eyelashes, for actress Phyllis Haver. Lip gloss, developed in 1930 for use under film lights, was also one of his ideas.

But it was the special requirements of color film that led to Factor's best-known invention—pancake makeup. The flat cake of transparent makeup in its little pan, applied with a sponge, was introduced in 1938 and was soon used off the screen by models and actresses, because of the natural-looking sheen it gave their faces. Women everywhere quickly followed suit. When Factor started his business, few American women used makeup; today many don't leave home without it.

The Birth of the Bra *Mary Jacob broke the binds of womanhood*

"When I made my debut, girlish figures were being enclosed in a sort of boxlike armor of whalebone and pink cordage. This contraption ran upward from the knee to under the armpit. . . . They were hellishly binding." So wrote Mary Phelps Jacob, a free-spirited American socialite who was never one to be tightly bound. In her late twenties, Jacob fled her proper marriage for a European tryst with playboy Harry Crosby, then changed her first name to Caresse, rode an elephant naked through the Parisian streets, and founded an avant-garde publishing house that brought out works by such "pornographers" as James Joyce, D. H. Lawrence, and Ezra Pound.

Years earlier, as a teenager in 1913, Jacob had for all intents and purposes invented the bra. One evening she wanted to wear a rose-garlanded dress to a party but was concerned by the way her corset cover "kept peeping through the roses around my bosom." So she ordered her maid to bring her two handkerchiefs, pinned them together, and tied the ends behind her back. "The result was delicious," she wrote. "I could move much more freely, a nearly naked feeling."

Jacob sold the patent for her "backless brassiere" to the Warner Brothers Corset Company of Bridgeport, Connecticut, for $1,500. And the bra as we know it was born. (The term *brassiere* had been introduced more than a decade earlier, in 1902, by Charles DeBevoise, who used the French word for "arm protector" to name his corset covers with padded shoulder straps.)

Bright Ideas *(from the files of the U.S. Patent Office)*

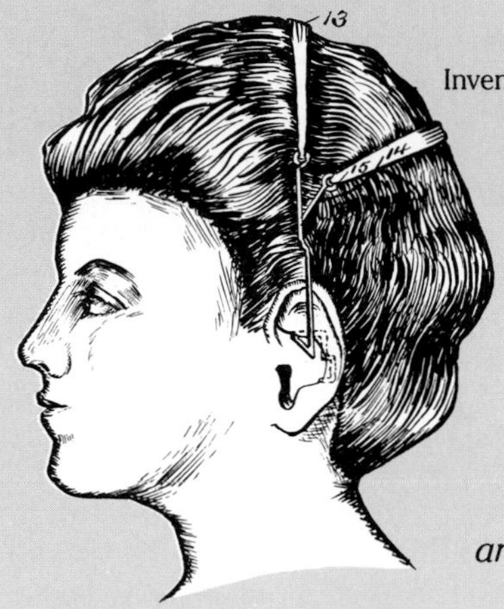

Wrinkle Remover
Patent No. 1,062,399 (May 20, 1913)
Inventors: Abbie Hess and Alfred Lee Tibbals
Kansas City, Kans.

"A pair of engaging members may be inserted in the ears of a wearer for exerting an upward and rearward pull thereon. [The device] prevents contraction [of the ears] so as to relieve partial deafness, and . . . so as to prevent the forming of wrinkles in the skin, and the growth of a double-chin."

Dimple Maker
Patent No. 560,351 (May 19, 1896)
Inventor: Martin Goetze
Berlin, Germany

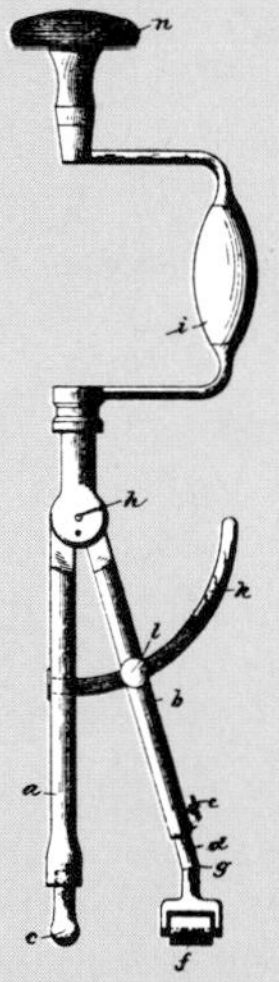

"In order to make the body susceptible to the production of artistic dimples, it is necessary . . . that the cellular tissues surrounding the spot . . . should be made susceptible to its production by means of massage. . . . The knob [of the device's] arm must be set on the selected spot. . . . The cylinder serves to mass and make the spot where the dimple is to be produced malleable."

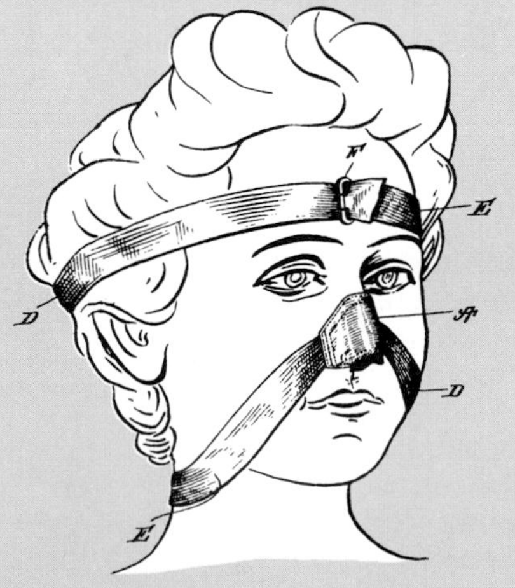

Nose Shaper
Patent No. 850,978 (Apr. 23, 1907)
Inventor: Ignatius Nathaniel Soares
Framingham, Mass.

"The noses of a great many persons are slightly deformed and therefore . . . the appearance of the face is more or less disfigured. Such deformity can frequently be remedied by a gentle but continuous pressure . . . in a way that shall be painless to the individual."

Inside Jobs

A new route for rhinoplasty

It sounds like torture, but it was a major medical advance. Prior to 1887, "nose jobs" were performed by cutting through the skin on the outside of the nose to get at the bony deformities and excessive tissue below. But this method left hideous scars, which often were greater psychological burdens than the embarrassing proboscis had been in the first place.

Then Dr. John Orlando Roe, a nose and throat specialist from Rochester, New York, invented a new approach. Using cocaine as an anesthetic, he cut the flesh *inside* the nose and pried the skin back from the underlying bone. This allowed him to insert a tiny saw he had designed for sculpting the distorted cartilage without scarring the face. As primitive as the procedure was, Roe's results were miraculous, and his intranasal surgery became the basis for modern rhinoplasty.

Roe's method was especially useful for whittling boney humps, such as that on the woman's nose at right. His success is apparent below.

A Deluge of Rainmakers

The heyday of the men they called pluviculturists

Back in 1839 Pennsylvanian James Espy claimed that rain could easily be produced by heating the air. But his plan to saturate parched farmland by building great log fires across vast stretches of the West never materialized.

A new theory emerged in the late 19th century: loud noises could make rain. It was put to the test in Texas, where Robert Dyrenforth piled up enough munitions for a small war. He blasted the skies and "made rain," but subsequent battles with the skies failed. Noted one editor: "He attacked front and rear, by the right and left flank. But the sky remained clear as the complexion of a Saxon maid."

Daniel Ruggles patented the first explosive rainmaking device in 1880. It was a cartridge-laden balloon.

In California, Charles Mallory Hatfield explained: "I do not make rain. I merely attract the clouds and they do the rest." Mixing an evil-smelling concoction of 23 chemicals in a huge pan, he took credit for an 18-inch rainfall in Los Angeles and was handsomely paid. Both the weather bureau and the press attacked him, but the public adored him and his fees soared.

Then in 1916 drought-stricken San Diego sought his services. He obliged, and the rains came—indeed, it was a veritable deluge that killed people and ruined crops. Not only didn't Hatfield get paid, but he was run out of town by an army of pitchfork-wielding farmers.

The Father of Television

An unknown young scientist was once told to do "something more useful"

If it weren't for a Russian engineer who immigrated to America, the world might not be watching television today. Yet Vladimir Zworykin is certainly not a household name.

Zworykin's lifelong interest in electronics began when he pushed a buzzer on his father's steamboat; a sailor responded promptly, and the five-year-old was hooked. He became an electrical engineer, and by 1919 he had moved to the United States, landing a job as a research engineer at the Westinghouse Electric Corporation.

Working in the company's Pittsburgh laboratory, Zworykin invented the iconoscope (electronic camera) and the kinescope (picture tube). Then, in 1923, he proudly demonstrated his most enduring invention: television—in this case, a cloudy image of boats on the river outside his lab appeared on the screen. His employers, however, were not impressed. Zworykin was urged, he later said, "to spend my time on something more useful."

But by 1929 Zworykin had obtained the first patent for color television. David Sarnoff, founder of the Radio Corporation of America (RCA), asked what it would take to develop TV for commercial use. Zworykin, who really had no idea, answered with assurance: a year and a half, and $100,000. Sarnoff hired him and later delighted in pointing out that in the end it took 20 years and $50 million.

Zworykin worked on many other inventions while at RCA, among them the electron microscope (developed in an amazing three months, before the company's budget office even knew about it) and "electric eye" infrared tubes, the first sniperscopes in World War II.

But despite the fact that he lived to see his most famous invention flourish—he died in 1982 at age 92—Zworykin rejected what TV had become. As he told a reporter: "The technique is wonderful. It is beyond my expectation. But the programs! I would never let my children even come close to this thing."

Nylon stockings were first publicly displayed by a quartette of stylish models who wore them at the 1939 New York World's Fair (left). They were an instant hit, and sales soared: 64 million pairs of the "run-resistant" stockings were sold during the first year they were on the market.

The Brilliant Creator of Nylon *He didn't live to see its astonishing success*

A distinguished chemistry professor at Harvard University, Wallace H. Carothers was hired by Du Pont in 1928 to head a laboratory research team. The offer was especially attractive to the 31-year-old scientist because, as he wrote to a friend: "Nobody asks any questions as to how I am spending my time." It was a situation a researcher dreams of: being paid to do his work unfettered by commercial concerns.

He specialized in synthetic materials, and in 1930 he and his team invented neoprene, a synthetic rubber that brought Du Pont healthy profits. But Carothers's professional paradise was not to last; it came to an end when the Great Depression caused Du Pont to change its research policy. Profit now took precedence over pure science, and the dedicated chemist despaired at the loss of his integrity. Although he and his team *did* perfect a synthetic fiber—nylon—he saw himself as a failed scientist.

Carothers became severely depressed. Alone in a hotel room on April 29, 1937, just three weeks after he had been awarded the patent for nylon, he swallowed a fatal dose of cyanide. He was 41.

Bright Ideas (from the files of the U.S. Patent Office)

Fly Swatting Device
Patent No. 1,468,373 (Sept. 18, 1923)
Inventor: George W. Blake
Wyandotte, Mich.

"This invention aims to provide a fly swatting device . . . which will afford considerable amusement to juveniles and at the same time contribute to the extermination of flies and similar insects. The device is made to represent a fire arm having a projectile provided with a swatting or imprisoning member [which can be concave so that it] may more or less accommodate itself to surfaces of various contours in order to swat, imprison or kill the fly or insect toward which said member is projected."

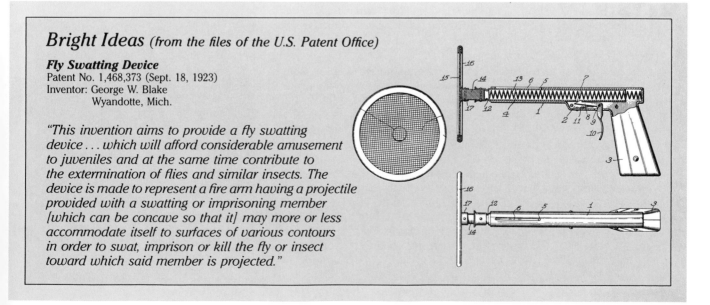

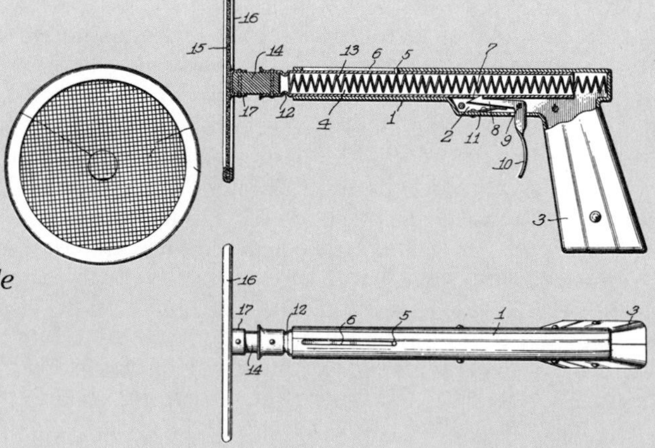

One of two silk purses created by chemist Arthur Little, in the style of the Middle Ages, is displayed at the Smithsonian Institution; the other (left) is on permanent exhibit at his company's headquarters.

A Chemist's Triumph

He proved that you* can *make a silk purse out of a sow's ear

A consulting chemist with his own firm in 1921, Arthur D. Little wanted to demonstrate to skeptical industrialists that chemistry was a tool for creating ingenious solutions to old problems. More than pure science was at stake: Little wanted to produce rayon, the first synthetic silklike fabric, but he needed financing for the enterprise.

In an attempt to attract business, Little had a Chicago slaughterhouse boil down 100 pounds of sows' ears to 10 pounds of glue. The concoction was sent to his company's Massachusetts headquarters, where chemicals were added to turn it into a jelly that was forced through tiny holes in a cylinder. The resulting threads were treated to give them strength and flexibility, then the ersatz silk was dyed and woven into cloth from which two purses were made. The result, Little wrote, was "one of which both Her Serene and Royal Highness, the Queen of the Burgundians, in her palace, and the lowly Sukie in her sty, might well have been proud."

Little died 14 years after the well-publicized silk-purse affair, but the debunking of clichés remained a tradition at his firm. In 1977 employees took aim at the old saw "going over like a lead balloon." Three balloons, each sheathed in a very thin layer of lead foil, were filled with helium. The first, behaving like a traditional lead balloon, failed to rise. The second stayed aloft briefly. But the third one, its design just right, gave new meaning to the phrase. Seemingly light as a feather, the lead balloon soared high into the sky, and when last seen it was majestically floating out over the Atlantic Ocean.

The Birth of Silly Putty

It began as a fad, but it stuck around

During World War II General Electric engineer James Wright was trying to develop a rubber substitute when he came up with some gooey stuff that, to his surprise, bounced when he dropped it. Although it had no practical use, everyone found it fascinating. It stretched, it snapped, it shattered when hit with a hammer, and when pressed against newsprint (right) it picked up the ink, colors and all. Not practical, but certainly fun to have around.

It owes its name and fame, however, to Peter Hodgson, who dubbed it Silly Putty, included it in the 1949 catalog of the toy store owner who'd told him about it—and created a best-seller.

Hodgson (who thought it was more than just a passing fancy) borrowed $147, packed Silly Putty into egg cartons from a local poultry association, went on the road, and proved its continuing popularity. After more than 40 years, it's a fad that definitely hasn't gone away.

Silly Putty (above) can be serious stuff: it's been used for strengthening hands, taking lint off clothes, and fastening down weightless tools on space missions.

Brain Drain?

Einstein's gray matter came to rest in a carton in Kansas

The brain of Albert Einstein (above) has been preserved for decades in formaldehyde (top). His cerebellum is in the Mason jar in the center.

When a knotty problem comes up, wouldn't it be nice to have Albert Einstein's brain? Well, you can't, because Dr. Thomas Harvey has it. And the story of how a little-known pathologist came to possess the brain of a world-famous genius is almost as amazing as Einstein's theory of relativity.

When he died on April 18, 1955, Einstein's remains were cremated—except for his brain. It was announced by Princeton Hospital, where he expired, that a study would be made to see if the scientist's genius was the result of any unusual brain features. But nothing more was heard about the matter until 1978, when a reporter painstakingly traced the brain to Dr. Harvey, who had performed the autopsy.

When interviewed, Dr. Harvey (who had long since moved to Wichita) was storing Einstein's brain in jars in a cardboard box marked "Costa Cider." It was hidden behind a beer cooler in his cluttered office. He explained that Einstein's son had let him keep the brain for the study, believing that his father wanted it. But people who knew the unassuming Einstein doubted that he would have countenanced such a thing.

Ironically, Dr. Harvey's secretiveness may well have guaranteed Einstein the privacy he sought. Though he has now had the brain for decades, the doctor has yet to publish the results of any study.

So far, all that is known has come from a California researcher named Marian Diamond, who had to negotiate for some three years before Dr. Harvey would agree to part with four small samples of the precious material. Diamond discovered that Einstein had measurably more glial cells, which supply nourishment to the brain, than the average person. But she emphasized that this overabundance alone could not account for Einstein's genius.

Modern scientists aren't sure that a study of Einstein's brain would help explain his extraordinary intelligence. In fact, they believe that the great man's gray matter has been afloat in chemicals for so long that neither Dr. Harvey nor other researchers will ever learn very much from it.

What Has Five Wheels and Practically Parks Itself?

The Parccar! Invented by San Francisco lumberman Brooks Walker in the early 1950's, the Parccar featured a fifth wheel that occupied most of the trunk of a Cadillac. To park Walker's car (right), the driver simply put the front wheels into the curb, lowered the fifth wheel to the ground (raising the two rear wheels), and then swung the back end of the car into the parking space. With this device, a 12-foot car could park in a 13-foot space in nine seconds.

CHAPTER NINE

The Call to Arms

*The names ring out:
Bunker Hill, Tippecanoe,
The Alamo, Bull Run,
Gettysburg, San Juan Hill,
The Argonne, Midway,
Omaha Beach, Inchon . . .
These are just a few of the
places where generation
after generation of
Americans have served and
sacrificed. Here are stories
of courage and terror,
cunning and foolishness,
heroism and ignominy;
of great leaders and some
who were not so great;
and especially of the
unsung men and women
who have had to put aside
their daily lives to answer
their nation's call.*

Behind the lines (outside Richmond, Virginia, 1862)

Half-breed

Pocahontas's son went to war against his mother's people

Thomas Rolfe could have been an Indian chief. Instead, the son of Princess Pocahontas and Jamestown planter John Rolfe became a wealthy landowner, inheriting his father's 400-acre plantation and thousands of acres from his grandfather, Chief Powhatan. And when push came to shove, he donned an English uniform and helped to wipe out his mother's tribe.

Raised by an uncle in England after Pocahontas died there in 1617, the young half-breed returned to his Virginia birthplace about 1635. Relations had been tense between colonists and Indians since 1622, when the Powhatan tribe—led by Pocahontas's uncle, the war chief Opechancanough—had massacred 347 people, including John Rolfe.

Colonists were forbidden to "speak or parley" with the Indians, but young Rolfe petitioned the governor in 1641 "to let him go to see *Opachankeno* to whom he is allied and *Cleopatra,* his mother's sister." No record of the meeting exists; we must imagine the confrontation between the Anglicized 26-year-old, hearing his mother's tongue spoken for the first time in his adult life, and the Indians, gazing at the face that bore a striking resemblance to that of their beloved lost princess.

In 1644 Opechancanough, said to be over 100 years old, mounted another assault. Carried on a litter, he led his warriors in raids that killed more than 400 Virginians. The colonists, among them Lt. Thomas Rolfe, fought back. Opechancanough was captured and killed. By 1646 the General Assembly reported that the Indians were "so routed and dispersed they are no longer a nation."

King Philip's War *Puritans versus Indians*

Metacom, also known as Philip, was only 24 when he became chief, or king, of the Wampanoags in 1662, succeeding his brother Alexander. (Chief Massasoit, who had befriended the Pilgrims in 1621, gave *all* his sons English names.) Claiming that an English doctor had poisoned his brother, King Philip vowed vengeance.

For 13 years Philip swallowed his hatred. Meanwhile the Puritans, favoring so-called praying, or converted, Indians, took more and more land from his people; they even confiscated the tribe's guns, forcing them to relearn how to hunt with bows and arrows.

In 1675, after the Puritans tried and executed three Indians who, on Philip's orders, had killed a Harvard-educated praying Indian as an English spy, the Wampanoags and some allied tribes began to raid villages, burning and killing. They were opposed by a mixed troop of whites and Indians led by a 35-year-old carpenter named Benjamin Church. As expert a swamp fighter as Philip himself, Church tracked his quarry relentlessly, but the elusive Philip reveled in a prophecy that he would never die at English hands. After one bloody battle, Church *did* capture Philip's wife and son, who wound up among the many Indians sold into slavery by the Puritans. Philip's hatred burned brighter.

One day Philip killed one of his own warriors with a tomahawk—for merely suggesting that the chief consider peace. The man's brother, Alderman, defected and led Church to Philip's camp. That night, August 12, 1676, Philip woke once, saying that he had dreamed of being captured. Aroused at dawn by shots, he leapt from the flat rock that had been his bed and, gun in hand, fled into the swamp. There he was shot through the heart by Alderman. His head was impaled on a pole, his body quartered and hung from trees. One hand went to Alderman, who kept it in a bucket of rum, exhibiting it for money.

For 25 years after King Philip's death, his head was displayed on a pole in Plymouth, the original Pilgrim settlement befriended by his father.

The hallucinogenic alkaloids contained in the plant's leaves turned a group of English soldiers into a troop of buffoons.

How Jimsonweed Got Its Name

The poisonous plant packed a potent punch

The English troops were bored. A thousand of them had crossed the Atlantic to suppress a rebellion in Jamestown, but by the time they arrived in 1677, the action was all over. The rebel leader, Nathaniel Bacon—who had driven the royal governor, Sir William Berkeley, to the Eastern Shore and then burned Jamestown—had died of a fever the previous October, and Berkeley was in the midst of taking reprisals against the insurgents. Setting up camps around the burned-out settlement, the troops cooled their heels while the governor tried and executed 23 of Bacon's followers.

One group of soldiers, foraging for food, came upon a leafy plant called the thorn apple (for its spiny fruit) and decided to cook up its foliage as a mess of greens. It was a bad mistake, but it could have been worse: if they hadn't overcooked the stuff, it would almost surely have killed them.

What actually happened was set down by Robert Beverly in his 1705 *History and Present State of Virginia:* "Some of them eat plentifully of it, the Effect of which was a very pleasant Comedy; for they turn'd natural Fools upon it for several Days: One would blow up a Feather in the Air; another would dart Straws at it with much Fury; another stark naked was sitting up in a Corner, like a Monkey, grinning and making mows at them; a Fourth would fondly kiss and paw his Companions and snear in their Faces with a Countenance more antick than any in a Dutch Droll. In this Frantick Condition they were confined, lest they should in their Folly destroy themselves, though it was observed, that all their Actions were full of Innocence and good Nature. . . . A Thousand such simple Tricks they play'd, and after Eleven Days, return'd to themselves again, not remembring any thing that had pass'd."

As a result of this incident the extremely poisonous thorn apple, *Datura stramonium,* came to be called Jamestown weed, a name that was eventually slurred to jimsonweed. Much later the same name was applied to the plant's equally toxic western cousin, *Datura meteloides*.

Oglethorpe's Deception *The War of Jenkins' Ear in Georgia*

In 1739 a shaky peace between England and Spain flared into war. Commercial interests in the West Indies lay at the heart of the dispute, but Robert Jenkins' ear touched the thing off.

Jenkins had been master of the English merchant ship *Rebecca* in 1731, when she was stopped and boarded by a Spanish coast guard vessel—whose captain not only stripped the *Rebecca* of her cargo but cut off Jenkins' ear. Seven years later, when the English Parliament felt that Spanish depredations had gone too far, someone remembered Jenkins and called him to testify. The mariner not only told the story of his capture and mutilation, but produced his mummified ear. The ghoulish symbol became the rallying point for war.

Among the most enthusiastic hawks was James Oglethorpe, a veteran soldier and philanthropist who in 1732 had founded the colony of Georgia as a place where debtors released from prison could start new lives. Oglethorpe had lobbied Parliament long and hard for help in containing attacks on Georgia from Spanish Florida. Now he saw an opportunity to do something about the situation.

In the spring of 1740 he led a combined group of Georgians, South Carolinians, and friendly Indians in a successful attack on several Spanish outposts near St. Augustine. But an ensuing assault on the Spanish stronghold itself failed, and Oglethorpe was forced to retreat with his fever-ridden army to the strategic border town of Frederica.

There, in July 1742, the Spanish made a play for English Georgia by attacking Frederica with a large sea and land force. Oglethorpe had been expecting them. Though his troops were severely outnumbered, they ambushed the invaders in a battle so fierce it earned the name Bloody Marsh.

The Spanish were about to retreat when a Frenchman who'd been fighting with Oglethorpe deserted and revealed how weak the colonists' forces really were. Heartened, the Spanish prepared a counterattack—then fell prey to an ingenious bit of deception. Upon hearing of the Frenchman's treachery, Oglethorpe released one of his Spanish prisoners and sent him back to the enemy with a "secret" message for the deserter, designed to make him look like a double agent: he was to go ahead with the prearranged plan to lure the Spaniards into a trap.

The Spanish commander packed up his men and ships and sailed away. The War of Jenkins' Ear and the battle of Bloody Marsh ended forever the Spanish threat against England's southern colonies.

Germ Warfare—Colonial Style

Two blankets and a handkerchief

Lord Jeffrey Amherst was a seasoned soldier, the shining hero of the French and Indian War, and the commander in chief of British troops in North America. Despite this, he had little personal experience fighting Indians, and some of the tales he heard about Indian battle made him sick. Supposedly one captured British officer had been boiled and eaten. Another officer had been killed while on a peace mission; it was said the Indians mutilated his body and ate his heart.

Amherst was getting mad, and in his anger he himself resorted to some pretty barbaric tactics.

"I wish to hear of no prisoners," he wrote to Col. Henry Bouquet, the man he put in charge of rescuing beleaguered Fort Pitt, on the site of modern Pittsburgh. "Could it not be contrived to send the smallpox among those disaffected tribes of Indians?" Bouquet replied that he would try.

A few months later, on June 24, 1763, Capt. Simeon Ecuyer, the commander at Fort Pitt, wrote in his diary of a meeting with Turtle's Heart, a leader of the attacking Delaware Indians. It seems that Turtle's Heart had come to the fort to try his hand at a little psychological warfare.

Expressing concern for the defenders' safety, he told them that a vast army of six united tribes had already overwhelmed the entire countryside, but the Delawares could offer protection if the settlers would give up the fort at once and flee. Captain Ecuyer thanked the Indians profusely for their concern; then "out of our regard to them we gave them two blankets and an handkerchief out of the Small Pox Hospital. I hope it will have the desired effect."

It did. Before long, a lethal smallpox epidemic raged through the Indian camps, killing warriors and their families alike.

Double-cross Lacrosse

The Chippewa birthday bash for King George

What's the difference between Englishmen and Frenchmen? Ask any Chippewa warrior, for when they started bashing heads at Fort Michilimackinac in 1763, it was quite clear that they knew.

After their victory in the French and Indian War, the British took control of America's interior and immediately inaugurated humiliating trade and settlement policies that infuriated the Indians. Soon many Native Americans had had enough. Pontiac, the great Ottawa chief, declared war and found support from the Hurons, Chippewas, and other tribes. Their goal was to seize all 11 British forts around the Great Lakes.

On June 2, 1763, King George III's 25th birthday, local Chippewas honored him with a game of *baggatiway* (the precursor of modern lacrosse) outside Fort Michilimackinac, the site of present-day Mackinaw City, Michigan. The fort's haughty commander and most of his 35 soldiers watched the game with bemused interest from outside the open gate, until one player threw the ball over the stockade and all the Indians rushed inside after it. There they slaughtered 16 British defenders and took the rest prisoner. French fur traders looked on in terror, but hardly a Frenchman was harmed.

Chippewas, like the chief at right, were only one of many tribes who played lacrosse at celebrations. Sometimes fields were a mile long and hundreds of braves took part.

Mama's Boy

If the Father of Our Country hadn't had a possessive mother, America's history might have been different.

Mary Ball Washington was a strong-willed orphan who married late; when her husband died, she transferred all her passion to young George. He escaped her overbearing devotion by fleeing to Mount Vernon, a family estate owned by his older half-brother, Lawrence, who had sailed with the Royal Navy. When George was 14 years old, Lawrence suggested that the restless boy go to sea. But Mom was not enthusiastic, especially after her brother in England wrote that the navy would "cut him and staple him and use him like a Negro, or rather, like a dog." So Washington, his bags packed, had to abandon his dreams of being a British sailor and settle for growing up to lead his nation against Britain.

Even after George was grown, Mary felt miffed that he neglected her for public affairs. And her complaints weren't discreet. Despite the fact that he supported her Fredericksburg home, she petitioned the Virginia Assembly for a pension, claiming destitution.

Finally George could bear no more. He wrote to her that she had made the world see him as an "unjust and undutiful son," and suggested that she rent her farms, hire out her servants, and live with one of her children—but not with him. She never took his advice, but she did leave him most of her sizable estate when she died.

Upstarts Go to War *"Yankee Doodle" changes sides*

Boston was a powder keg in April 1775. But Gen. Thomas Gage and his seasoned British regulars were confident they could put down any uprising of farmers and shopkeepers. And the redcoats didn't keep their disdain to themselves. As they marched, they sang a sarcastic song that mocked Americans as rustic buffoons. The song was "Yankee Doodle."

On the night of April 18, however, the British weren't singing. They were marching stealthily westward to destroy a rebel arsenal at Concord and arrest John Adams and John Hancock. Outside Lexington they captured a night rider named Paul Revere. But they didn't consider him worth arresting; they just took his horse and set him free. Revere walked to where Adams and Hancock were staying and helped them escape. Other riders made for Concord.

The cocky British were met the next morning at Concord's North Bridge by militia from all the surrounding towns—and the farmers routed them.

Big guns

As the New England patriots plotted their next moves, one thing was certain: they would need cannon. Capt. Benedict Arnold of the Connecticut Militia knew where to get them. British-held Fort Ticonderoga in upstate New York had plenty, he said, and only a token force to guard it. Arnold himself offered to lead the attack. But en route he ran into Col. Ethan Allen and his Green Mountain Boys, who had the same idea. The backwoods Vermonters, who had been formed into a crack guerrilla unit five years earlier—not to fight the British but to settle a land dispute with neighboring New York—proved too much even for Arnold's ego, and the outraged future traitor was forced to take a backseat to Allen's rowdy troops.

Fort Ticonderoga and its vital supply of cannon were captured on May 10, without a single casualty. Allen, with Arnold at his side, rapped on the fort's main door at dawn and demanded the garrison's immediate surrender. The British officer who answered the knock had his pants draped over his arm. He listened politely to the Americans, then decided they really would have to speak to Ticonderoga's commander. Allen did, and the fort surrendered.

Wrong hill, right spirit

Once the colonials had cannon, General Gage knew his position in Boston was vulnerable, for if the rebels could occupy the strategic heights outside the city, their big guns would control the harbor. Even though Ticonderoga was 300 miles away and the Americans would have to wait until winter before they could transport the heavy cannon by sled through the rugged backcountry, the general resolved to strike quickly.

Colonial spies learned his plans and the Americans moved into action. Rebel leaders ordered the militia to occupy Bunker Hill above Charlestown; but the militia's own commanders, Gen. Israel Putnam and Col. William Prescott, occupied Breed's Hill some 2,000 feet away instead. The reasons for the confused orders still baffle historians, but the fact is that the famous Battle of Bunker Hill took place on Breed's.

Gage, eager to show what trained infantry could do, played right into the colonials' hands by ordering a frontal assault. Instead of fleeing as expected, the Americans cut the enemy down with disciplined fire from behind hastily constructed bulwarks. More than half of the 2,000 redcoats were killed or wounded; the Americans suffered some 450 casualties.

Nonetheless, the British technically won the battle, but only because the undersupplied rebels ran out of ammunition. British Gen. Henry Clinton said of the victory: "Another such would have ruined us."

After these hard-fought conflicts, the British started singing a different tune, and the patriots took up choruses of "Yankee Doodle" with an inspired sarcasm the redcoats had never imagined.

This British matron sports an outrageous hairpiece modeled on the Battle of Bunker Hill. Entitled Bunker Hill or America's Head Dress *and dated 1776, the engraving satirized both the fashions of the period and the Americans' pride in their courageous stand.*

Washington's Crossing

The painting and the attack

Only a second version of Leutze's painting (above) made it to the United States. The original, which had been damaged by fire at his studio, hung in Bremen, Germany, until September 5, 1942, when it was destroyed in an Allied bombing raid.

The famous depiction of George Washington crossing the Delaware was actually painted in Germany in 1851 by Emanuel Leutze, who used American tourists as models but patterned the river on the Rhine. The boats, the flag, the dress, and the ice are inaccurate; nonetheless, Leutze vividly captured the drama of the assault.

On Christmas night 1776, Hessian troops at Trenton, New Jersey, had been convinced by an American spy that the colonials were too disorganized to attack. Meanwhile, 2,400 men and 18 cannon were ferried across the freezing river by a regiment of Massachusetts fishermen. The daring offensive was a complete surprise; a Tory *tried* to alert the Hessians, but their drunken commander refused to interrupt a card game to receive the message. More than 100 Hessians were killed or wounded; nearly 1,000 were taken prisoner. No American lives were lost.

Spreading the Word *Riders of the American Revolution*

The poet Longfellow invited readers: "Listen, my children, and you shall hear of the midnight ride of Paul Revere." But who ever heard of Jack Jouett, or Tench Tilghman, or Israel Bissel? These heroes also leaped to their saddles for American liberty.

Jefferson's close call

On the night of June 3–4, 1781, Jouett, a captain in the Virginia Militia, saved Thomas Jefferson and the entire Virginia Assembly from 250 British troops who had been sent to Charlottesville to capture them. The 27-year-old colonial spied the redcoated dragoons at Cuckoo Tavern in Louisa County and took off into the night.

Unlike Revere's ride along well-traveled roads, Jouett's 40-mile trek took him through wilderness, where riding was slow by day and potentially deadly in darkness. When the captain reached Jefferson's home at dawn, his face was swollen and bleeding from being lashed by branches. By the time the British arrived, the Americans had fled.

Tench Tilghman made his trip four months later, this time bearing good news rather than warnings. As General Washington's aide-de-camp, he sped to Philadelphia to announce to Congress the British surrender at Yorktown. Traveling from Virginia by boat and horseback, it took him five days to complete the journey of some 200 miles.

The longest ride

But no messenger can match Israel Bissel, a humble post rider on the Boston–New York route. After the Battle of Lexington and Concord on April 19, 1775, Bissel was ordered to raise the alarm by carrying the news to New Haven, Connecticut. He reached Worcester, Massachusetts, normally a day's ride, in two hours—then, according to tradition, his horse promptly dropped dead. Pausing only to get another mount, Bissel pressed on and by April 22 had reached New Haven. In two more days he was in New York; by April 25, Philadelphia. His 125-hour, 345-mile ride sparked anti-British riots and signaled American militia units throughout the Northeast to mobilize for war.

Lord Dunmore's Little War

When the shooting started, not everyone was ready to rebel

The rumbles of the Revolution were not looked upon favorably by the British governor of Virginia, John Murray, earl of Dunmore. Originally a popular governor, Dunmore definitely misread the rebels' cause, responding with force and tyranny where political persuasion might have worked.

As early as 1773, in an attempt to crush revolutionary sentiments, he dissolved the House of Burgesses. Later, with skirmishes breaking out, he forced Norfolk residents to sign an oath of loyalty to the Crown; those who refused had to go into hiding. And lest anyone's identity remain in question, Loyalists had to wear a strip of red cloth.

Then, in a bold move—one that lost him precious support among the white population—he freed all able-bodied slaves who agreed to side with the Loyalists. Many blacks flocked to him, serving under white officers in Lord Dunmore's Ethiopian Regiment. Battle lines were forming, and open hostility flared.

Finally forced to leave Virginia and direct the Loyalists from the safety of a ship, Dunmore sent his troops into their only major battle, at Great Bridge. The result was a resounding defeat. Within months, the Britishers and their slave armies were fatally weakened.

In 1776 Dunmore fled back to England, where he was returned to Parliament, representing the Scots. Later, in recognition of his loyalty, the king appointed him governor of the Bahamas.

Not a Shot Was Fired

How crafty George Rogers Clark occupied the Illinois country

At dawn on July 4, 1778, the inhabitants of Kaskaskia, near the Mississippi River in present-day southern Illinois, awoke to find the streets guarded by 178 ragged, bearded men who ordered them to stay in their homes. George Rogers Clark, commander of this motley force, made the villagers sit indoors for hours. Although the westerners were only halfhearted Loyalists, their militia had vowed to resist the Revolutionaries. But while the militia was belligerent, it certainly wasn't alert, for under cover of darkness Clark's men had surrounded Kaskaskia without firing a single shot. When one resident finally ventured out, Clark assured him that the Americans were friends, and soon the streets were full of celebrating people. They also helped persuade the inhabitants of Cahokia and Vincennes to welcome Clark and his men.

But Clark was in a tight spot. Almost half of his troops insisted on going home, so his men were outnumbered 25 to 1 by the Indian allies of the British. Clark decided to call a peace conference. Bluffing all the way, he offered the Indians a peace belt and a war belt, claiming that he didn't care which one they chose. His audacity so impressed the Indians that they took the peace belt, and within five weeks Clark had won pledges of good behavior from almost a dozen tribes.

A bold, shrewd strategist, Clark had succeeded in securing America's frontier territory. And all without bloodshed.

"Behind Every Great Man Is a Woman"

And, possibly, her ex-escort

Benedict Arnold is America's most famous traitor. But did he win that dubious distinction on his own? Probably not, because he was married to the indomitable Peggy, who dreamed that her husband's treason would enable her to return one day to the subdued colonies as Lady Arnold. And they were but two corners of a treacherous triangle that included Maj. John André, adjutant general of the British Army in North America—and Peggy's ex-boyfriend.

Arnold had his own reasons to defect. Despite the fact that he was a great general and a hero on the field of battle, a cloud hung over him: word of shady financial dealings had led to a court-martial, and although he was found innocent of some charges, the military court insisted that Washington reprimand him.

Arnold's bitterness against the Revolutionary government was deeply ingrained by the time he met 18-year-old Peggy Shippen, his future second wife, in Philadelphia in 1778. Before Arnold arrived there, Peggy had been the life of the British social scene, often seen in the company of the dashing Major André.

When Arnold started negotiating the sale of West Point, he dealt with André in New York. Using the code name Monk, Arnold sent secret messages and pleas for money to André. Peggy, too, corresponded with her old flame, attempting to ease the difficult negotiations.

Then, on the morning of September 25, 1780, Washington stopped to have breakfast with the Arnolds on his way to West Point. Upon his arrival he was disappointed to discover that Ar-

In his captors' grasp (above), Maj. John André offered his watch as a bribe for his release. On October 2, 1780, he was hanged "as a Spy from the Enemy." André's capture had revealed the treason of Benedict Arnold, and he and his family eventually fled to London. There, the glamorous Peggy (left, with one of the five Arnold children) posed for a portrait.

nold had just rushed to the fort and that Mrs. Arnold was ill. Washington became even more annoyed when he arrived at West Point to learn that Arnold hadn't even shown up there that morning. A stickler for protocol, he was deeply offended that one of his favorite generals would so rudely snub him.

The reason for the snub was soon clear: That very morning, after his first face-to-face meeting with Arnold, André had been arrested on his way back to British lines. Even though he was wearing a disguise, he had been picked up—and evidence of the plot was found in his stocking. Just before Washington showed up, word of the arrest reached Arnold and he barely escaped.

Peggy remained behind in her room and, at about the time that the stunned Washington heard the report of Arnold's treason, she conveniently went mad. "As the lovely lady raved and gestured," one historian later observed of Peggy's dramatic command performance before the general, "her clothes sometimes parted to reveal charms that should have been hidden."

The act worked. Washington refused to believe that Peggy—described by Alexander Hamilton as possessing "all the sweetness of beauty, all the loveliness of innocence"—could be involved in such a heinous crime.

Peggy's old friend André, caught red-handed, was hanged as a spy eight days later. (Washington suggested "a handsome gratuity" for André's captors, John Paulding, Isaac Van Wert, and David Williams. Congress voted each of them a lifetime pension and had medallions struck in their honor.)

Recovering in remarkably short order, Peggy was reunited with her husband. Ultimately, after Arnold had led a force of Loyalists and deserters in a series of raids against American troops in Virgina, the two moved to England where, comfortably supported by pensions, they spent most of the rest of their lives.

To Catch a Spy

On October 20, 1780, Sgt. Maj. John Champe outraged his friends by fleeing the Continental Army to join the Tories and deserters being organized by Benedict Arnold. In fact, Gen. George Washington had ordered Champe to bring Arnold back for trial and hanging as a lesson to other would-be traitors. Boldly, Champe planned to grab the traitor during his usual after-dinner stroll in New York. But before the deed could be done, Champe found himself embarking for Virginia with Arnold's legion. He escaped to his own regiment and, when his story was told, was cheered by his old comrades.

In 1798 President Washington wanted to make Champe a captain. But by then Champe had died, never having achieved the rank he had so desired.

Larger Than Life *The tale of a forgotten hero*

As dawn broke over Camden, South Carolina, on August 16, 1780, General Cornwallis's seasoned British troops launched a sudden bayonet attack on an American force of largely inexperienced Virginia and North Carolina militiamen. It quickly became a rout. Weapons were abandoned as officers and men alike fled the field; the American commander, Gen. Horatio Gates, didn't rein in his horse for 60 miles.

But amid the terror and confusion, at least one Virginian acted like a hero that day. They say that Pvt. Peter Francisco lifted a 1,100-pound cannon and *carried* it to the rear. Then he shot a grenadier threatening his commanding officer, Col. William Mayo. Ordered by a British cavalryman to drop his musket, he used the bayonet to lift the hapless horseman from the saddle and, wearing his victim's headgear, rode among the enemy yelling, "Yonder go the damned rebels!" When he saw Mayo being led away, a prisoner, he cut the British captor down, gave the officer the horse, and saw him safely on his way.

It was all in a day's work for Peter Francisco. The 19-year-old giant, said to be the strongest man in the colonies, was already a veteran of three years' warfare. He was wounded at Brandywine in 1777, at Monmouth in 1778, and at Stony Point in 1779—where he first wielded a five-foot broadsword made for him at the order of General Washington. At Guilford Courthouse in 1781, his thigh laid open by a bayonet, Francisco chopped down 11 British troops before collapsing.

After each battle the legend of the American Samson grew. His exploits were recounted for years; he was called "the most famous private soldier of the Revolutionary War." Yet today—as seems to be the fate of privates everywhere—his name is all but forgotten.

In 1823 the massive Peter Francisco became sergeant at arms for the Virginia House of Delegates. The only time he had to restore order, he simply carried the offending legislator out by the scruff of his neck and the seat of his pants.

The Private Private *Robert Shurtleff's secret*

During a skirmish at East Chester, New York, Pvt. Robert Shurtleff took a musket ball in the thigh. Rejecting medical help, the young soldier crawled into the woods and hid until the wound healed over. Then, rejoining the 4th Massachusetts Regiment, Shurtleff marched into the Adirondack Mountains to battle Mohawk Indians.

Later, serving as a clerk to Gen. John Paterson in Philadelphia, Shurtleff fell ill with "malignant fever" (probably influenza) and was taken to a hospital. This time there was no escape; Dr. Barnabas Binney was amazed to discover that his delirious patient was a woman!

Deborah Sampson, descended from Pilgrims, had first enlisted under the name Timothy Thayer. But using her bounty money to celebrate at a local tavern, she all too clearly revealed her identity. Her church excommunicated her for wearing men's clothes and behaving "very loose and un-Christianlike." The army bounced her.

Walking 75 miles to Worcester, Deborah enlisted again as Robert Shurtleff. This was in May 1782, six months after the surrender at Yorktown, but there was still plenty of fighting. Guerrilla bands, known as "cowboys," raped and pillaged at will in a no-man's-land between the British lines at Yonkers, New York, and the American lines at Peekskill; Deborah's regiment was sent to fight them.

In her first skirmish, Deborah took a saber slash to the left cheek. Recovering with only a scar, she wrote home that she was working in a "large but well-regulated family." It was in her next battle that she got the musket wound.

The kindly Dr. Binney kept Deborah's secret for a time. But when his niece fell in love with the "handsome young soldier," he told General Paterson, who told George Washington. On October 23, 1783, Deborah was honorably discharged. When, clad in a dress, she watched her old regiment pass in review, no one recognized her.

Surrender at Yorktown

A victory marked by subterfuge and a breach of etiquette

During the summer of 1781 Gen. George Washington was undecided whether to mount an all-out attack against the British garrison in New York City or against the troops of Gen. Charles Cornwallis in the South. As a result, his English counterpart, Sir Henry Clinton, was kept guessing. And after Col. Alexander Hamilton—while telling a known British double agent that the target would be Virginia—let the man catch sight of a marked map of New York, Clinton was sure that the northern city was the real objective.

Meanwhile a French fleet, under the Comte de Grasse, drove British warships from the Virginia coast. American and French troops, meeting near New York, started south. On September 28 more than 16,000 of them laid siege to Cornwallis's stronghold at Yorktown. For about a week, beginning on October 9, as De Grasse prevented escape or reinforcement by sea, the Virginia town was pounded by artillery, in the heaviest barrage laid down to that time in the Western Hemisphere. Cornwallis, expecting a fleet from the north, held on.

American victory seemed assured until October 16, when De Grasse told Washington that the French fleet must leave within 48 hours. A ruse was needed, or the siege would have to be lifted. Again, Hamilton played a gambit superbly: under a flag of truce, he let it be known that an assault was imminent and that American troops were "so exasperated at the Conduct of the British to the Southward, that they could not . . . be restrained by authority and Discipline." An immediate surrender, he suggested, would save much bloodshed.

The next morning a message from Cornwallis asked for "a cessation of hostilities for twenty-four hours" while terms of surrender were discussed. Washington, with an anxious eye toward the sea, agreed to only *two* hours. Terms were arrived at, and at 2:00 P.M. on October 19, 1781, in a formal ceremony that Cornwallis boycotted, the last major battle of the American Revolution came to an official end.

"For Military Merit"

The Purple Heart was the first medal "for military merit" ever given to enlisted men. Created in 1782 by George Washington, it lapsed into disuse for 150 years. Reinstated to honor Washington's 200th birthday, it is today given to anyone wounded in action.

For the formal surrender, Gen. Charles Cornwallis, feigning illness, sent a subordinate. Washington, rather than deal with an officer of lesser rank, had his second in command, Gen. Benjamin Lincoln (center in this John Turner painting), receive the ceremonial sword.

The Indian They Called the Prophet

He claimed to "cause the sun to stand still"

His was a dissolute, misspent youth: Laulewasika, the younger brother of the great Shawnee leader Tecumseh, even lost an eye during one of his drunken brawls. Then one day, while casually lighting his pipe, he suddenly collapsed—apparently dead. Tribe members were astonished when, as they were making burial arrangements, he awoke and calmly announced that he had returned from the Master of Life and was now a prophet named Tenskwatawa.

The message the Prophet preached was really an Indian version of fundamentalism he'd probably adapted from sermons he heard at a nearby Shaker community. Indians, he insisted, had to return to the ancient ways of the Master of Life and renounce all influences and customs of the white man—particularly religion and liquor. In addition, Tenskwatawa claimed to have received the power to heal all diseases and to stop the white man's bullets.

This religious message fit in perfectly with his brother's plans to create a confederation of all Indian tribes to fight white settlers in the Old Northwest. Indeed, the two brothers often traveled together to various tribes. Tecumseh would galvanize the crowd with his eloquent political appeal, then Tenskwatawa would finish them off with his missionary revivalism. The brothers eventually set up headquarters for their new Indian nation at a town they called Tippecanoe, or Prophetstown.

The combination alarmed the territorial governor of Indiana, William Henry Harrison, who challenged Tenskwatawa to perform a miracle. "If he is really a prophet," the governor declared, "ask him to cause the sun to stand still, the moon to alter its course, the rivers to cease to flow. . . . If he does these things, you may then believe he has been sent from God."

As if in reply to this challenge, at 11:30 on the morning of June 16, 1806, the Prophet arrived at an Indian gathering in a long black robe and headdress of raven's feathers and pointed his finger at the sun, which obediently began to disappear. As darkness fell, the Indians cowered in terror. Tenskwatawa asked the Master of Life to bring back the sun, and it reappeared. There was no doubt that Tenskwatawa had the crowd completely under his spell. (As it turns out, it was not the Prophet's magic, but an eclipse he knew was coming that caused the sudden darkness at noon.)

The self-proclaimed prophet Tenskwatawa ("The Open Door") was disgraced by the defeat at Tippecanoe and retired to present-day Kansas where, for his loyalty during the War of 1812, he lived on a British pension.

Harrison had the last laugh, though—and laughed all the way to the White House 35 years later. While Tecumseh was assembling an army to battle the Americans, he left Tenskwatawa in charge of Tippecanoe with specific instructions not to get into a fight until he returned.

But Tenskwatawa, a better prophet than politician, bowed to the demands of the militant Indians who wanted to attack Harrison immediately. First he had the warriors touch his "bean belt" to make them immune to bullets, then dip their weapons in his "magic bowl" to ensure victory.

Neither belt nor bowl was effective. The Indians were routed at the Battle of Tippecanoe, and the town was burned to the ground. The surviving warriors were so incensed at being duped by Tenskwatawa that they were ready to kill him on the spot. But glib as ever, he was able to talk them out of it by claiming that the presence of his squaw at the magic bowl had ruined all the spells.

Tecumseh returned home to find Tenskwatawa's credibility demolished, Prophetstown lost, and his grand plans for a unified resistance destroyed. He fought on gallantly against the invaders, joining the British during the War of 1812, but was shot dead on the battlefield in 1813.

The Shores of Tripoli *An ill-assorted army fought America's first foreign war*

The Barbary Coast of North Africa was dangerous territory in 1802. Pirates plied the Mediterranean waters, preying on ships of all nations. There were two ways to prevent attack: either pay off the ruling potentates, or declare war.

For a time the young American republic paid, much to the disgust of its consul in Tunis, William Eaton, who once described a local ruler as "a huge, shaggy beast, sitting [on a] cushion of embroidered velvet." Thus Eaton was pleased when the United States went to war with the Principality of Tripoli (in present-day Libya) and its ruler, the "Bashaw" Yusuf Karamanli.

But the American navy did such a poor job that Eaton fired off a note saying that the nation "may as well send out *Quaker meeting houses* to float about this sea." Then he came up with a plan. The Bashaw Yusuf had taken power by forcing his father and his brother Hamet into exile. Eaton proposed to offer Hamet help in regaining his rightful throne. By 1804 Eaton, accompanied by Marine Lt. Presley O'Bannon, six marines, and two naval midshipmen, met with Hamet in Egypt and persuaded him to go along with the plan.

A ragtag army was assembled, and a strange procession began its trek across the Libyan desert: "General" Eaton (technically a civilian), in full-dress uniform, was followed by O'Bannon and his marines, the midshipmen, some Greek mercenaries, a Tyrolean soldier of fortune, 25 Christian artillerymen, one cannon, Prince Hamet with a guard of 90 colorfully garbed Bedouin cavalrymen, and a camel train. Thus equipped, the United States was off to fight its first foreign war.

The object was to capture Derna, a Tripolitan coastal town. After wandering from well to well, paying bribes, and coping with a mutiny, Eaton and his hordes—their ranks swollen by hundreds of Bedouin warriors accompanied by all their wives and children—finally rendezvoused with the navy.

Eaton resupplied his army from American ships, and in short order the battle was on. The ships rained fire on the fortifications while Hamet's cavalry guarded against an attack by Yusuf's legion. Finally Eaton, along with O'Bannon and his troops, led the irregulars in a daring assault. Two marines fell dead, and Eaton was shot in the arm. But the town was theirs. It had been a heroic struggle, one in which Eaton had demonstrated exceptional leadership.

Yusuf's forces were then easily defeated, but as the shots died out, Eaton received shocking news: while he had been marching wearily and battling fiercely, American diplomats had been negotiating with Yusuf. A peace treaty had been hammered out, and Eaton and his troops were ordered to withdraw.

Eaton returned to America a bitter man. But the short war was not a total waste—the arduous march "to the shores of Tripoli" is immortalized in the opening lines of the Marine Hymn.

Along the Barbary Coast: A seaman deflects a scimitar blow aimed at naval hero Stephen Decatur (right, above). Amazingly, both survived. Even greater heroism followed. In an attempt to destroy Tripoli's fleet, Richard Somers sailed into the harbor aboard an explosives-laden ship (right). Discovered before completing the mission, he and his crew blew up their own vessel, choosing "death and destruction of the enemy to captivity and torturing slavery."

Miracle at the Capital *A hurricane saved Washington from the British*

"Clear out, clear out!" President James Madison's servant galloped to the Executive Mansion with frightening news of the battle at Bladensburg, Maryland. American militia were in disarray. Madison himself had witnessed the debacle and now sent word to his wife, Dolley, to flee. The fall of the nation's capital was imminent.

Just eight days earlier some 4,000 British troops, well-seasoned from fighting Napoleon, had begun a whirlwind sweep through the Chesapeake Capes. The Americans, ill-led and ill-trained, could muster little effective defense. Now, on August 24, 1814, civilians and soldiers alike were fleeing Washington in a panicked melee. It was the beginning of a national humiliation that would become surreal even for the conquerors.

When the British marched into the city that evening, it was nearly deserted. The only resistance they encountered was a single volley of musket fire—but that killed one redcoat, wounded three others, and shot the horse from under their commander, Maj. Gen. Robert Ross.

The invaders moved quickly to the Capitol, where they feared the Americans might make a defiant last stand. After shooting rockets through the windows, an assault party stormed the entrance, broke down the door—and was greeted by silence. Soon both the Senate and House chambers were ablaze. Before the night was over the White House and Treasury were also in flames.

Yet the soldiers roamed the city like tourists. At the abandoned office of the *National Intelligencer,* General Ross picked up a copy of the newspaper's last issue, the one that had assured Washingtonians their city was safe. He tried to stuff it into his coat, but failed. "Damn it," he cried, "my pocket is full of old Madison's love letters." The British general had taken them earlier as souvenirs of the White House.

The next morning Ross's troops were charged by a solitary horseman firing wildly. The rider—John Lewis, a grandnephew of George Washington—sought revenge for his suffering during impressment in the Royal Navy, a practice that had helped start the war. The redcoats shot him dead.

Dr. William Thornton, superintendent of the Patent Office, was a more effective defender. Returning to his office to retrieve a violin, he found British soldiers preparing to burn the building. If they did so, he scolded, they would be equated with the barbarians who had destroyed the ancient library at Alexandria. The argument worked; the Patent Office was spared.

Then the British encountered their first setback. While they were destroying 150 barrels of gunpowder at a deserted American fort, the barrels exploded. Some 30 redcoats died from the blast; 44 were wounded. Shortly thereafter, the storm clouds that had threatened all day released a torrential hurricane. Ross's troops and lines of communication were thrown into confusion; the general ordered a retreat to the ships. It was as if nature had saved the city in the absence of human defenders.

Ironically, although the hurricane quenched many of the fires the British had set, it blew the roof off the Patent Office, which Dr. Thornton just that morning had so eloquently preserved.

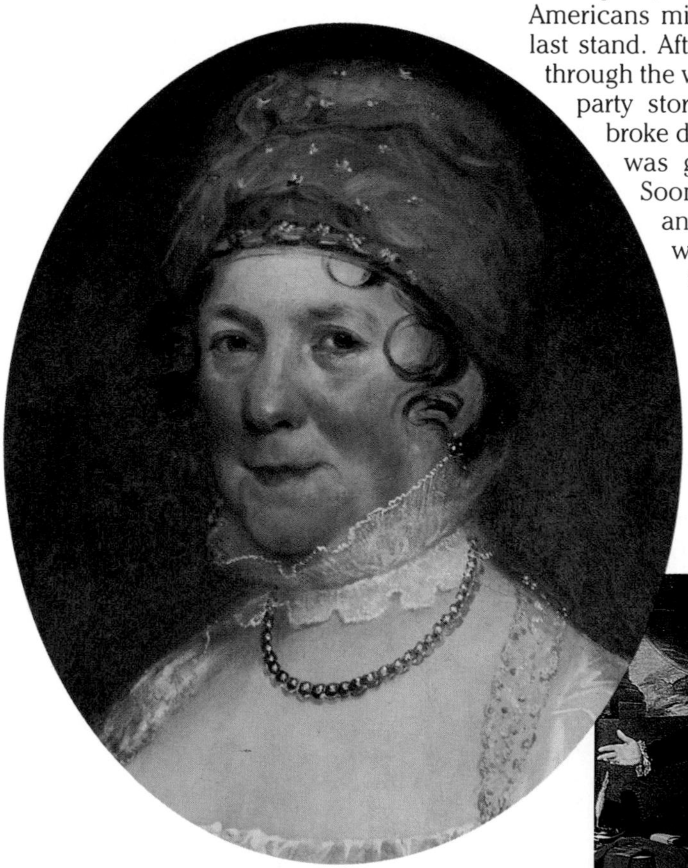

Dolley Madison (above) refused to flee the White House without Gilbert Stuart's portrait of George Washington (right). Workmen finally had to break the frame, which was screwed to the wall.

Tenant farmers in New York State had to take up arms to win the fundamental right to own their own land. Calling themselves "Indians" (their chief was known as Big Thunder), they donned war paint or hoods and robes of calico and challenged the patroon system. At the approach of the patroon's men, the sound of tin horns—until then the usual call to mealtime—echoed through the hills.

The Fight to Free America's Serfs

A guerrilla uprising ended feudalism along the Hudson

The buildings, the harvests, the livestock, and the health of the land were the result of tenant farmers' labor and investment. But the land itself, nearly 2 million acres of it, belonged to the patroon landlords *forever*—their ancestors had been granted it by Dutch trading companies in return for colonizing the Hudson River valley in the 1600's. When the English took over from the Dutch, they did nothing to disrupt the system. Some tenant families had worked their plots for generations; yet still the patroon was like their feudal lord, and they owed him annual tribute in the form of wagonloads of firewood and a share of their crops, delivered to his estate.

This form of feudalism even survived the struggle for liberty and equality that climaxed in the American Revolution and led to our Constitution—Alexander Hamilton helped by drawing up clever leases for his in-law, Stephen Van Rensselaer III, converting the annual tribute to rent.

Van Rensselaer, known as the Good Patroon, was a benevolent lord; in bad years, he often let rent from the poorest of his 60,000 to 100,000 tenants go unpaid. But when he died in January 1839, he left a will stipulating that his estate's $400,000 worth of debts were to be paid by collecting all back rents.

His sons ruthlessly pushed to collect, and the tenants organized to resist them, proclaiming their own declaration of independence on July 4, 1839. A 500-man posse sent to evict the tenant leaders was met by 2,400 hostile farmers. New York Gov. William Seward had to send the state militia to put down the rebellion. But tenant resistance spread. Inspired by the Boston Tea Party, bands of "Indians" disguised in war paint or calico hoods prevented the auctioning of farmers' property and drove off sheriffs who tried to serve eviction notices.

In 1842 the state legislature's judiciary committee reported that the rents were unjust, but—pressured by the patroons—it also held that the state was powerless to prevent them. Clearly, the legal route to redress was closed, and the ranks of the Calico Indians swelled to a peak of 10,000 members, organized for the sake of secrecy into cells of 10 to 15. Their chief was Smith Boughton, a doctor in Stephentown, New York, who took the name Big Thunder.

When a bystander was accidentally killed during a tenants' rally in December 1844, Boughton, who was merely speaking at the rally, was arrested for manslaughter. Seven months later a bullying sheriff was killed during a confrontation at a farm auction. Hundreds of farmers were jailed, and the Hudson Valley was virtually placed under martial law. But the vindictive bias of the trials that followed actually helped the tenants' cause. Their political base grew, and they triumphed at the polls in 1845 and 1846, electing legislators and a governor favorable to their cause. Political prisoners, including Smith Boughton, were freed, and a new state constitution prohibited new feudal leases and reformed existing ones. Two centuries of injustice were ending.

The Alamo

It gave Texas a battle cry that fired its fight for independence

While his bands blared the barbaric "no quarter" command, Mexico's Antonio López de Santa Anna threw thousands against 189 defenders of the Alamo at dawn. And because Col. William Travis disobeyed Gen. Sam Houston's orders to destroy the crumbling mission-fortress, the Alamo won its indelible place in history. For Travis saw the Alamo as the key to Texas, and he swore to hold out till help arrived—or to die. Jim Bowie and a sharpshooting ex-congressman named Davy Crockett were among those heroes who stood by him.

The siege began February 23, 1836. The Texans and the American volunteers, armed with long rifles, were crack shots, and the Mexicans' muskets were woefully inaccurate. But the attackers' bayonets took a bloody toll when, after suffering heavy losses on March 6, they swarmed over the thinly manned walls surrounding the Alamo chapel. Travis and his men died fighting. The desperately ill Bowie, his pistol in hand and his bowie knife at his side, was killed in his bed.

To the last man, the 189 were slaughtered. But they'd killed more than 600 Mexicans and become an inspiration to Houston's little army. "Remember the Alamo!" was the cry on April 21, as the general's troops shattered the Mexican army at San Jacinto—and wrested Texas's independence from Mexico.

The Original Yellow Rose of Texas

A heroine who did much more than "sparkle like the dew"

She was certainly not a typical 19th-century Southern belle, for the real Yellow Rose of Texas was a slave named Emily Morgan. Celebrated in the original version of the famous song as "the sweetest rose of color," she kept Mexico's President-General Antonio López de Santa Anna dallying on his silken sheets while the Texans surprised his army, thereby becoming the heroine of the Battle of San Jacinto, at which Texas won its independence.

Emily Morgan, 20 years old, was a lovely mulatto with a "high-yellow" complexion—which no doubt accounts for the flower's color in the song, since there is *no* yellow rose native to Texas. Santa Anna, the self-acclaimed Napoleon of the West, was a notorious womanizer who traveled in style with a three-room carpeted silk tent. He picked up Emily during the sacking of New Washington, Texas, where her owner, Col. James Morgan, had his plantation.

Escape—and capture

When Santa Anna sent a slave on a reconnaisance mission, Emily Morgan told the man where Gen. Sam Houston was so he could warn the Texans of the Mexicans' whereabouts. Meanwhile, Santa Anna and his men set up camp on the plains of San Jacinto. While the president-general spent the fateful day of April 21, 1836, with his beautiful companion, the Texans crept up and charged the startled troops in full battle cry. Santa Anna, exotically (but scantily) clad in silk drawers and bright red morocco slippers, rushed from his candy-striped tent and leapt on a Texas horse to escape. But the horse ran straight to its ranch nearby, and Santa Anna was handily captured the next morning.

The furious battle was over in a mere 20 minutes. And Emily Morgan, who survived to tell her story to the colonel, was freed.

Although Santa Anna was victorious at the Alamo, he was defeated at San Jacinto and again, in 1847, at Cerro Gordo. It was during the latter rout that he (near right) became fair game for one cartoonist.

Regiment of Heroes

The great (and grueling) march to Mexico

They traveled 3,600 miles by land and 2,000 miles by water. They had no orders from Washington, no supplies, and no pay, so they lived off the land, fought with ammunition captured from the enemy—and left a trail of victories. That's what made this trek the greatest long march in U.S. military history.

The commander of the 1st Regiment of Missouri Mounted Volunteers was a redheaded 6-foot 4-inch lawyer, Col. Alexander Doniphan. When the Mexican War broke out in 1846, he organized a force, mostly of spirited farm boys, and joined Gen. Stephen Kearny's victorious expedition to New Mexico.

From Santa Fe, Doniphan prepared to join Gen. J. E. Wool's men, who were headed south for Chihuahua, 600 miles away. Christmas found the volunteers 30 miles from El Paso at Brazito, where a Mexican force ambushed them and demanded surrender. Doniphan promptly attacked; in half an hour the Mexicans fled.

Word reached Doniphan in El Paso that General Wool's orders had been changed; he was to join Gen. Zachary Taylor. With no instructions from his superiors, Doniphan decided to continue on to Chihuahua. At Rio Sacramento (18 miles from their destination) his troops confronted a Mexican army of 4,000. Doniphan had fewer than 900 men, but they overran the fortifications, and the enemy scattered. When the tattered Missourians finally swarmed into Chihuahua, they looked more like bandits than the conquerors they were.

From Chihuahua, the men marched an amazing 700 miles to join General Taylor at Saltillo, where victory again was theirs. Continuing to the Rio Grande, they set sail, adding 2,000 water miles as they headed for New Orleans. There the men were greeted as heroes, fed well, paid for their exemplary service, and sent home. The Show-Me State gave them another rousing welcome, as cheering crowds, parades, and fireworks honored the incredible trek of these men from Missouri.

Doniphan's men never wore the elegant uniforms shown on this song sheet. They arrived with their buckskins in shreds.

A Long, Fast Ride—California Style

When 600 well-armed Mexican troops surrounded an ill-equipped band of 50 Americans in Los Angeles in 1846, it was Juan Flaco who volunteered (for $500) to make a daring 500-mile dash on horseback to get help. Carrying messages written on cigarette papers inscribed with Capt. Archibald Gillespie's seal and the words "Believe the bearer," Flaco sped north to Monterey to seek out Commodore Robert Stockton.

The ride was harrowing. At one point Flaco, whose first horse was shot out from under him by pursuing Mexicans, was forced to run 27 miles. Then, on a horse supplied by a rancher, he negotiated treacherous mountains, dense brush, and a rugged coastline. Incredibly, he reached Monterey in four days—only to find that Stockton was anchored in San Francisco harbor. So Flaco pressed on.

Responding to the desperate plea, Stockton dispatched his ship and its 350-man crew to southern California. Unfortunately, rough weather delayed the vessel.

Ultimately Flaco's heroic ride did not prevent surrender. But it did lead to the recapture of Los Angeles and, according to one reporter, to the rescue of U.S. forces "from utter destruction."

Trist's Treaty *The man who really won the West got fired*

Nicholas P. Trist negotiated the treaty that ended the Mexican War and added California, Nevada, Arizona, New Mexico, Utah, and parts of Colorado and Wyoming to America's expanding territory, finally stretching the nation from sea to sea. It was the most bizarre diplomatic achievement in U.S. history. And it ruined his life.

Trist arrived in Mexico in May 1847 as a special envoy from President James K. Polk. His job was to offer the Mexicans, who were being badly beaten, terms for surrender. But blunders and bickering led to confusion. Polk lost faith in his emissary and in October had him recalled.

Defying the president's order, Trist stayed on and continued his negotiations without official authority. He was finally making progress. By January 25, 1848, he had an agreement: Mexico would accept $15 million for the land it ceded to the United States. The treaty was signed a week later, and in the spring the Senate approved it. But Polk remained furious about Trist's insubordination and fired him in disgrace.

The diplomat spent much of the rest of his life working as a menial clerk for a railroad. Not until 1870, 23 years after his success in Mexico, was he officially recognized for his achievement. By then, of course, the West was a thriving part of the United States, due largely to the discovery of gold in California on January 24, 1848—just one day before Trist had persuaded the Mexicans to sell the territory.

The U.S. Army's Camel Corps *And the ravages of the Red Ghost*

If you believe the records, colonial Virginia considered using camels for transportation in the 1700's. By 1836 the beasts were seriously recommended to the army for exploration of the Southwest. But it wasn't until 19 years later that U.S. Secretary of War Jefferson Davis (later president of the Confederacy) pushed through an appropriation of $30,000 for the experiment. Within a year 32 full-grown camels arrived at the harbor in Indianola, Texas, after a three-month ocean voyage from Egypt. The stench, according to local reports, was horrendous. But the officer in charge was so impressed by the animals that he immediately sent back to the Middle East for more.

Lt. Edward Beale, a former naval officer, used 25 of the camels to survey a route from Fort Defiance, New Mexico, to eastern California, trailblazing part of what became the famous U.S. Highway 66. He too was impressed. Three camels could carry on their backs as much as six mules could pull in a wagon—and move nearly twice as fast. Beale's enthusiasm led the War Department to request 1,000 more camels in 1858. But by then Congress had more pressing business to contend with: the impending Civil War.

Apart from Beale, most people found the camels hard to handle, and in 1863 the army project was ended. The animals were auctioned, many of them ending up in circuses or carrying freight for mining companies. Others "escaped" (or were driven) into the wild and became legends—like the Red Ghost.

This red-furred giant first appeared in the Arizona Territory in 1883, when he trampled a woman to death outside her cabin. Only later was the source of the animal's fear of people discovered: a human corpse was lashed to his back. It was never learned whether the person had died before or after being tied to the camel. The Red Ghost raged through Arizona for a decade until he was shot. Reports of wild camels continued in the West as late as 1941.

As transportation for the military, camels proved disastrous. Rebellious by nature and difficult to train, the dromedaries enraged the army's mule skinners, who not only despised their ornery dispositions but resented their foreign origin as well.

Gray-Eyed Man of Destiny

William Walker in Nicaragua

Only one native-born American has ever become president of another sovereign nation. His name was William Walker. At various times in his life he'd been a doctor, a lawyer, a newspaperman, and a hypnotist. But it was as a *filibuster* (from a Dutch word meaning freebooter or soldier of fortune) that he seized the presidency of Nicaragua in 1856.

Walker had been approached two years earlier by an American investor, who had cut a deal with one of Nicaragua's warring factions to provide a mercenary army. After carefully wording his contract so as not to run afoul of U.S. neutrality laws, the 31-year-old adventurer took the job. He landed in Nicaragua on June 16, 1855, at the head of a tough band of 58 fighting men drawn from daredevils and soldiers-for-hire. They called themselves the Immortals.

The country they found was in perpetual revolution; there had been 15 presidents in six years. Its chief importance, as far as most North Americans were concerned, was that it was the site of Commodore Cornelius Vanderbilt's Accessory Transit Company, which carried passengers and freight across the Isthmus of Panama in the era before the canal was built.

William Walker (top) was an unlikely swashbuckler. He was short and slight and had a squeaky voice. But he was also brilliant, having graduated summa cum laude *from the University of Nashville at the age of 14. The mercenaries Walker led to Nicaragua relaxed in a convent (above) after capturing the capital at Granada.*

The Nicaraguans quickly realized that Walker was a dangerous man. There were fierce early battles, and the daredevil invaders once had to make a life-or-death dash for freedom after being surrounded. But in less than five months Walker's growing band of mercenaries captured the enemy faction's capital of Granada in a surprise attack.

From that point Walker was the power in Nicaragua. The newspaper he founded touted him as "the gray-eyed man of destiny," foretold by Indian legends, who would lead the nation. It was an easy myth to embrace, for Walker, although he weighed barely 120 pounds, had piercing gray eyes that seemed like windows on a will of steel. After ruling through a puppet government, he himself took the oath as president on July 12, 1856.

But amid these moves to consolidate his empire, the filibuster had made one fatal mistake: he had crossed Cornelius Vanderbilt. Soon after seizing power, Walker had conspired with the men who headed Vanderbilt's transit company to squeeze the Commodore out. In response, the powerful American shipping magnate financed an invasion of Nicaragua by Costa Rica; he even managed to enlist the aid of the British and American navies. Walker held on until May 1, 1857, before surrendering and being sent back to the United States.

Continuing to claim the presidency of Nicaragua, Walker tried several times to return. He was executed in Honduras in September 1860. To this day he is remembered by Latin Americans as a hated symbol of Yankee imperialism.

Bleeding Kansas *Where battles and bloodshed foreshadowed the Civil War*

For Senator Stephen A. Douglas, slavery was nothing to get excited about. What really excited him was his plan to organize the sprawling Nebraska Territory so that a railroad could be built through it from Chicago to the Pacific. And if, in so doing, he upset the razor-thin balance between the nation's pro- and anti-slavery forces—well, he could ride out the storm. It would blow over in time, he was sure. He was tragically mistaken.

Southerners in Congress, fearing a new Northern state, had defeated every bill to organize the territory, in which slavery was barred by the long-revered Missouri Compromise. To win them over, Douglas proposed dividing the territory into Kansas and Nebraska and letting the settlers of each decide upon the issue of slavery or freedom.

His Kansas-Nebraska Act of 1854 repealed the Missouri Compromise. And the storm it brewed not only wrecked Douglas's chances of ever becoming president but pushed the nation a bloody step toward civil war.

Determined to control Kansas, proslavers poured in to build the towns of Leavenworth and Atchison. Free-staters challenged them by founding Lawrence and Topeka. Guerrilla warfare flashed across the land, fueled by such supporters as the abolitionist minister Henry Ward Beecher, whose Brooklyn congregation sent crates of Sharps rifles marked "Farming Implements." (The weapons were soon known as Beecher's Bibles.) Livestock was stolen or slaughtered, crops and homes were burned, and captives were shot dead.

In a year's time, at least 200 people were killed and many more were wounded. Raiders from Missouri gutted Lawrence in 1856; John Brown and his followers struck back by murdering five proslavers at Pottawatomie, Kansas. One abolitionist minister, facing a noose for his views, was spared when a proslaver argued that the cause would be sullied by hanging a man of the cloth. He was tarred and feathered instead.

When an election was called to choose a territorial legislature, Senator David Rice Atchison of Missouri sent hundreds of proslavers into Kansas to intimidate voters and stuff ballot boxes for "a dollar a day and free whiskey." Their side won, and wrote a constitution in 1857. It was voted down in an 1858 referendum.

The next year, another convention adopted a new constitution flatly barring slavery; and in 1861, after 11 Southern states had seceded from the Union, a free Kansas became the 34th state. But history will long remember its violent beginnings as Bleeding Kansas—the first unofficial battlefield of the Civil War.

Victims are scalped, corpses robbed, and Miss Liberty pleads her case in a cartoon attacking pro- and anti-slavery forces alike.

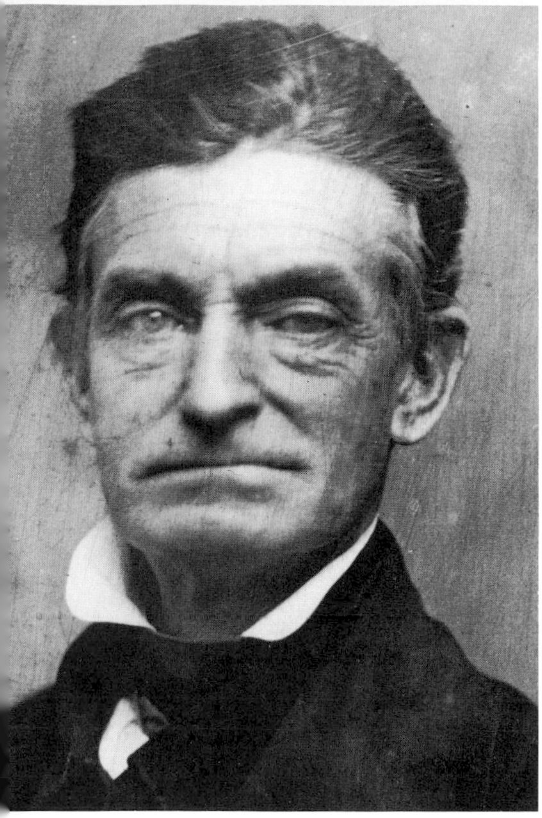

John Brown

He had "a little touch of insanity about his glittering gray-blue eyes," and he hacked five proslavers to death in Kansas. He seized a federal arsenal at Harpers Ferry, Virginia, in 1859, taking George Washington's great-grandnephew hostage. Robert E. Lee captured him. Stonewall Jackson and John Wilkes Booth watched him hang. But, oddly enough, the song "John Brown's Body" had nothing to do with him. The men of a Massachusetts volunteer regiment first sang it in 1861, to taunt a messmate, Sgt. John Brown.

The Pig War of San Juan Island

Britain and America almost came to blows over a dead porker

According to the Oregon Treaty of 1846, the strait between Vancouver Island and the mainland was the boundary between British and American territories. But there were *two* straits, and San Juan Island was between them. Britain and America both claimed it, and settlers from each country quickly took up residence.

When America tried to tax British produce, farmer Charles John Griffin refused to pay, insisting that he was not subject to American taxation. Then in 1859 one of his pigs got loose and began rooting around in the potato patch of American Lyman Cutlar, who promptly shot it. Livid, Griffin went to the local British magistrate, demanding a payment of $100 for the pig. Cutlar refused to pay, insisting that *he* was not subject to *British* law. Tempers flared.

Americans petitioned their government for protection. Soon Capt. George Pickett—later to lead a famous charge at Gettysburg—arrived with troops. British Columbia sent warships to rout them. But each side waited for the other to fire the first shot. Finally, Gen. Winfield Scott came from Washington to propose that the standoff be institutionalized: each country would station 100 men on San Juan Island until an accord could be reached. The British accepted.

Meanwhile the Civil War occurred, and it was 12 years before the matter was submitted to German emperor Wilhelm I for binding abitration. He ruled in favor of America in 1872.

Sunrise at Fort Sumter

The opening shots

Early in 1861 all eyes were on Charleston, South Carolina, where the Civil War was sure to begin—if it was to begin at all.

U.S. troops held the "impregnable" Fort Sumter, at the entrance to Charleston Harbor, and the Confederacy, deeming them a foreign force, wanted them out. President Lincoln promised to "hold, occupy, and possess" the fort no matter what. But if it came to war, he was determined that the U.S. not fire the first shot.

"Under no circumstances," President Jefferson Davis wired Gen. P.G.T. Beauregard, "are you to allow provisions to be sent to Fort Sumter." On April 10 another wire ordered him to ensure the fort's evacuation or "reduce it."

And so, at 4:30 A.M. on April 12, Lt. Henry S. Farley lobbed a signal shell that burst 100 feet above the fort, and firing began. In his diary, 67-year-old Edmund Ruffin wrote that "by order of General Beauregard" he'd been given the "compliment" of firing the first shot, and his *was* the first shell to hit the fort. An ardent secessionist whose teachings on crop rotation had virtually saved the Southern economy decades before, Ruffin again became the hero of the day.

Not until 7:00 A.M. did Capt. Abner Doubleday order a reply. The first Union shot "bounded off the sloping roof of the battery opposite without producing any apparent effect," he later recalled.

Ruffin survived the war but, mourning the demise of his beloved South, committed suicide on June 18, 1865. Doubleday, who lived till 1893, mentioned Fort Sumter in his memoirs, but made no reference to ever having invented the game of baseball.

Civil War Firsts

The Civil War is called the first modern war because of the forward-looking (and sometimes outlandish) military innovations it spawned, among them:

Conscription. *America's first draftees fought this war.*
Fork-barreled cannon. *They fired two balls connected by a chain, for mowing down whole lines of the attacking enemy.*
Aircraft carriers. *Barges transported and moored reconnaissance balloons.*
Water walkers. *Reportedly, Union soldiers were to wear tiny canoes as boots and propel themselves over the water with paddles.*

"The Most Shot-at Man of the Civil War"

Thaddeus Lowe and the U.S. Army's balloon corps

At 3:30 A.M. on April 20, 1861, Thaddeus Lowe set out from Cincinnati on a test flight of his 20,000-cubic-foot balloon *Enterprise.* After traveling at more than 100 m.p.h., he was deflected from his course by crosswinds. He landed in South Carolina, expecting a hero's welcome. But Fort Sumter had fallen just six days earlier, and Lowe was arrested as a Federal spy. Only after local professors vouched for his purely scientific interests was he released. The audacious aeronaut simply hadn't realized how close America was to civil war.

Heading north, Lowe became leader of the Aeronautic Corps of the Army of the Potomac, a group composed primarily of civilian balloonists who made more than 3,000 flights during the war's first two years. Most of these were reconnaissance missions from moored balloons carrying up to five miles of telegraph wire, so that the aeronauts could direct ground artillery and transmit information about enemy troop movements. Once Lowe was brought down behind Confederate lines. His wife, who had witnessed the crash, led the nighttime commandos who came to his rescue.

Poet and historian Carl Sandburg called Thaddeus Lowe (feeling the gas bag at the far right) "the most shot-at man of the Civil War."

Although no laughing matter to the president, Lincoln's difficulty finding generals inspired Confederate levity. This 1863 cartoon appeared in the Southern Illustrated News.

General Problems

Lee went South, and Lincoln looked to Europe

When Abraham Lincoln became president, one of his greatest challenges in preserving the Union was finding a general competent enough to do it. His only authentic military star at the onset of war was 75-year-old Gen. Winfield Scott, hero of the War of 1812 and the Mexican War, who became the first commander of the Union Army. Declining health and the fatigue of old age forced the diligent general into retirement within months.

Lee's crisis of conscience

Before the war broke out, General Scott reportedly pleaded with Lt. Col. Robert E. Lee not to join the secession. Scott hinted that Lee, while nominally serving under him, would in fact command the Union armies in the field, since Scott himself was too old. Soon the offer was official. But Lee declined, not because he supported slavery, but because of loyalty to Virginia, whose history had been shaped by his ancestors for generations.

When Lee informed Scott of his decision, the aged general remarked, "Lee, you have made the greatest

mistake of your life; but I feared it would be so." Virginia officially proposed secession on April 17, 1861. On the 20th Lee resigned from the U.S. Army. Three days later he was named commander of Virginia's armed forces.

McClellan's cigars

From there the Union course was downhill. Gen. George McClellan, who virtually built the Union Army from scratch, saw himself as a young Napoleon and referred to Lincoln as "the Gorilla." Despite his arrogance, McClellan, and most other Union generals, suffered from what Lincoln called "the slows."

In September 1862 Lee invaded Maryland and split his army into two sections in order to secure his supply routes. McClellan is said to have received advance word of Lee's plans when a Union soldier in Frederick, Maryland, stooped to pick up three Virginia cigars that had dropped in the street. The cigars were wrapped in a copy of the Southern general's orders to his field commanders. McClellan was ecstatic; his larger army now had a perfect opportunity to surprise and overwhelm the divided Confederate troops. But McClellan's advance was so slow that Lee was able to regroup his army at Antietam. The battle there on September 17 was one of the bloodiest of the war. Although McClellan reported it as a great victory, it is often cited as one of his major blunders. He outnumbered Lee's force almost two-to-one; but indecisiveness prevented him from destroying the Southern army and ending the war. Lee escaped with his forces intact as McClellan found excuses to delay pursuit.

Another Union general, Fighting Joe Hooker, was infamous for his bizarre attitudes and behavior. Allegedly, his camp was so filled with prostitutes that the ladies acquired a new name: "hookers."

Garibaldi

The paucity of Northern leadership had been apparent from the beginning. It drove Lincoln to attempt to enlist Giuseppe Garibaldi, the hero of Italian unification, as early as 1861. But talks broke down when Garibaldi, who had fought against slavery in South America, wanted a promise that American slaves would be freed. Even well into the war, Lincoln doubted that he could make this commitment and still preserve the Union.

The president's problem would continue until Lt. Gen. Ulysses S. Grant forcefully took control of both the army and the war in March 1864.

Ulysses S. Grant

The paradoxical warrior

It isn't unusual for a soldier to be superstitious. But the weird habits of Hiram Ulysses Grant (who changed his name at West Point to avoid the initials *HUG*) became a military legend.

Grant had a phobia about retracing his steps. If he went past a place he was looking for, he would never turn back—he'd just keep walking until he could work his way around again. When he became a general, this strange habit was manifested as a refusal to retreat. Supporters praised his toughness. But detractors, even in the North, were horrified by the resultant bloodshed and called him the Butcher.

Yet this man, who unflinchingly sent thousands of soldiers to their deaths, had an acute aversion to killing animals, so much so that before the Mexican War he was teased by fellow army officers who liked to hunt. They called him Little Beauty.

Grant's respect for animals influenced his diet. He would eat only charred meat, and he rejected fowl absolutely, saying that he would never eat anything that walked on two legs. The mere sight of bloody meat was enough to drive him from the table.

Nor was Grant oblivious to the suffering of his men. After the Battle of Shiloh, he spent an entire night beneath a tree in the pouring rain rather than take the only cover available—an improvised hospital. The blood and screams of the wounded were more than "the Butcher" could bear.

Grant's love of horses is apparent in this sketch he drew in 1842 while a cadet at West Point. As a Civil War general he became furious at a teamster for beating a mare; he had the man tied to a post for six hours.

Battlefield Bands *Music in the Civil War*

Requisite for a good battle in the Civil War were opposing soldiers, sufficient weapons, and at least two brass bands. During nearly every major battle, music urged the troops onward, and military units hotly competed for talented musicians. At Fort Sumter, a Federal band mournfully accompanied the surrender. Selections from *Il Trovatore* were stirringly played at Shiloh by a band stationed right at the front. During the Battle of Gettysburg, the musical aggregations of the 11th and 26th North Carolina regiments got so loud they were shot at by irked Union soldiers.

By the summer of 1862 there were an estimated 618 bands in the service of the Union, at a cost of $4 million. This averaged out to 1 musician for every 41 soldiers. The underfunded Confederacy had fewer and smaller musical ensembles. The 2nd Virginia Regiment, however, did manage to form a band—with instruments taken from a New York unit after a battle.

During the siege of Atlanta, a Georgia cornet player gave suppertime concerts at the front. One night the fighting was so heavy he didn't show up, and there was a flood of protest—from angry *Northern* soldiers who had looked forward to his performance. A short cease-fire was worked out so that the cornetist's melodies could drift through the evening. After each selection both sides applauded wildly. But as soon as his concert had ended, the bloody shooting resumed.

Stonewall Jackson's Other Grave *He was shot by his own men*

Thomas Jonathan Jackson had been a professor of philosophy and artillery tactics at Virginia Military Institute in 1861. As a Confederate officer in the Civil War, he practiced what he preached.

Jackson distinguished himself early in the war. At the First Battle of Bull Run, in July 1861, Union troops had shattered the Confederate line until the men under his command shored the breach. "See, there is Jackson standing like a stone wall!" cried Gen. Bernard E. Bee. Bee soon fell in the fighting, but the nickname stuck to Jackson.

His severe but inspiring military bearing may have been caused by a touch of hypochondria. Jackson never ate pepper, claiming it weakened his left leg; raspberries, bread, and milk were his preferred meal. He was comfortable only in a stiff, upright position, with his organs set "naturally" on top of each other. In this erect posture astride his mount, one arm outstretched, he led his men to combat.

Jackson took a bullet in his upraised hand at Bull Run. The examining doctor insisted that an injured finger be amputated, but as he turned to fetch his instruments, the general got up and quickly rode away. It was one of the few times Jackson—who often exhorted his troops, "The Stonewall Brigade never retreats"—took to his heels himself.

Victory followed victory, until Jackson's greatest triumph turned out to be his last. In the spring of 1863 his troops soundly thrashed the Union forces of Gen. Joseph Hooker at Chancellorsville, Virginia, forcing them into retreat. The next evening, as Jackson returned from a risky scouting mission, he was fired upon by his own troops, who in the darkness were unaware of his identity. Two bullets shattered his left arm, and this time he could not escape the surgeon. The arm was immediately amputated. Jackson might have recovered had he not ordered a servant to place cold towels on his body to lower his fever. The general contracted pneumonia and died a week later.

The amputated arm was given its own formal military burial near Chancellorsville in a properly marked grave. The inscription reads simply: "Arm of Stonewall Jackson. May 3, 1863." The rest of the general is buried more than 100 miles away at Lexington, Virginia.

Posing at left are some of the Confederate heroes of the Battle of Gettysburg. These members of the 26th North Carolina Regimental Band played so loudly to inspire their warriors that Yankee troops fired on them. Confederate Gen. Robert E. Lee once said, "It's impossible to have an army without music."

A Rainbow Array

We think of the Civil War as being fought by men in blue and gray, but in fact soldiers on both sides marched to battle with flair in a variety of colorful uniforms. Before the war began there were only some 15,000 full-time soldiers in the U.S. regular army. Most of the military was in volunteer militias. After the Confederates attacked Fort Sumter on April 12, 1861, these local units were mobilized, and many enticed recruits by offering fancy uniforms that added panache to local pride.

It led to a dizzying array of finery. One New York regiment wore plaid kilts. At the other extreme of elegance, a Confederate unit that included former convicts wore striped pants presumably made of bed ticking. The pantaloons of French Zouaves were popular on both sides because of their romantic association with the Crimean War. An Indiana regiment went to battle in gray, but had to abandon it to avoid being taken for the enemy.

Finely bedecked Yankee troops included (from left to right): a sergeant of the 79th Regiment, New York State Militia; a musician from the 114th Pennsylvania Volunteer Infantry (also called Collis Zouaves, in honor of their commander); a rifleman from the 1st Regiment U.S. Sharpshooters; and a foot soldier in Zouave attire from the 146th New York Volunteer Infantry.

Heroines of Espionage *Female spies served both sides bravely*

The First Battle of Bull Run might not have been such a smashing Confederate victory without the flowing curls of a blushing Southern belle. On July 9, 1861, Rose Greenhow hid a ciphered message in the tresses of one of her lovely couriers. When the girl combed out her hair for Rebel officers, they learned that Union troops were about to march on Richmond. A second message a week later contained the invaders' exact strength and marching orders.

"Within rifle range of the White House"
The victorious Confederate general, P.G.T. Beauregard, later noted with pride that the woman who provided this crucial intelligence "lived in a house within rifle range of the White House." That house on 16th Street became the heart of a Rebel spy network as Greenhow took full advantage of her position as one of Washington's most alluring hostesses. At the height of her activities, she directed more than 50 agents—48 of them women—who worked in five states, including far-off Texas. Many an official panicked when detective Allan Pinkerton arrested her for espionage in August 1861.

Even while jailed, Greenhow somehow managed to smuggle secrets about the Union Army to Richmond. A loyal Southerner to the end, she died while trying to run a Federal blockade off the North Carolina coast in 1864.

Crazy Bet
Greenhow may have lived near the White House, but Union spy Elizabeth Van Lew placed a servant

right in the home of Jefferson Davis, president of the Confederacy. Although Van Lew came from one of Richmond's wealthiest families, her Northern schooling had made her a fervent abolitionist. Dressing in rags and feigning madness, she visited captured Union soldiers at Libby Prison to gather and disperse information. Neighbors in the Confederate capital dismissed her as Crazy Bet. But as she observed, "It helps me in my work."

Van Lew was anything but crazy. Not only did she provide military intelligence, she also hid Union soldiers who had escaped from Confederate prisons in a secret room in her house. Once she even masterminded a scheme to smuggle the corpse of a Union officer through Confederate lines to a decent burial.

More prudent than Greenhow, Van Lew was a Union agent in the heart of Dixie for the entire war. As Richmond fell, she raised the first Stars and Stripes over the city. Later, Gen. Ulysses S. Grant visited her personally; he considered Crazy Bet one of his most valuable spies.

Belle Boyd (left) was no beauty, but the notorious Confederate agent captivated men. Actress Pauline Cushman (below), born in New Orleans, was arrested as a Union spy in Tennessee. Sentenced to death, she escaped when Federal troops overran the town in which she was being held prisoner. After the war she toured the country, continuing her theatrical career.

The Joan of Arc of the Confederacy

Belle Boyd was only 17 years old on July 4, 1861, when Federal soldiers, a little drunk from celebrating, began looting houses and insulting residents in her hometown of Martinsburg (in present-day West Virginia). One tipsy soldier threatened to raise a Union flag over the Boyds' house. When Belle's mother protested, the soldier responded abusively—and Belle shot him dead.

Soon she was riding all over the Shenandoah Valley gathering information for the Confederacy. Her most daring exploit took place at Front Royal, Virginia, where, as she told it, she learned that retreating Yankee soldiers planned to burn the town's bridges as they fled. Taking off at a run down the street, she dashed past Union pickets, dodging their rifle fire as she sped across the open field to Gen. Stonewall Jackson and his attacking Southern troops. Jackson quickly moved to take the bridges before they could be destroyed.

Often arrested, Boyd was just as often released, sometimes in prisoner exchanges, until she became famous as the Joan of Arc of the Confederacy. On her last mission in 1864 she was carrying letters from Jefferson Davis to agents in England when the blockade runner on which she traveled was seized by a Union warship. Once again her charm and spunk didn't fail her. The Yankee commander asked her to marry him. She was not yet 20 years old.

The Northernmost Rebel Raid

How the Civil War came to Vermont

They swooped down out of Canada—20 cavalrymen organized by Confederate agent George Sanders and led by Lt. Bennett Young—and laid siege to St. Albans, Vermont. With his gun drawn, Young mounted the steps of a hotel and shouted: "This city is now in the possession of the Confederate States of America."

It was October 19, 1864, and the Civil War battlefields suddenly didn't seem so far from this village that hugs the scenic Lake Champlain shoreline. For the citizens of the tiny town near the Canadian border had become victims of a Rebel raid.

Shock and confusion followed as gun-toting horsemen galloped down Main Street, herding terrorized townfolk onto the village green. The raiders then turned their attention to robbing the local banks. Even though the Confederates dropped much of their loot in the confusion of escape, they still managed to make off with some $200,000. As a final humiliation, they tried to burn down the town. But success eluded them; only a woodshed was destroyed by the flames.

It was as long as half an hour before St. Albans residents could organize a pursuit party, and by that time the Rebel-yelling marauders were well on their way back toward the Canadian border. The hit-and-run raid had lasted about 30 minutes.

Bank tellers in St. Albans, Vermont, were forced to pledge allegiance to the Confederacy as Rebels robbed them.

Burning New York

The incendiary plot was not a blazing success

The Confederacy was at a low ebb in November 1864. General Sherman was marching through Georgia, and Southern troops were on the defensive everywhere. In a desperate attempt to force the North to negotiate, Confederate agents based in Canada devised a fantastic scheme: they would burn the entire city of New York.

The agents had been assured that the city was ripe for rebellion. They were wrong, but the Southerners opted for arson anyway to show the Yankees, firsthand, the horror of war. On November 25 they struck.

Carrying small glass bombs of an incendiary fluid called Greek fire in a valise, an agent would check into a hotel, set his room ablaze, and leave. The city was soon in a panic; alarms sounded, firemen sped through the streets, and rumors were rife.

But the Greek fire didn't work very well, and the fire department acted quickly. And so, although flames broke out in 12 hotels, there was no serious damage. Two arsonists were captured, including Capt. Robert Cobb Kennedy, who became the last Confederate soldier to be hanged before the Civil War ended.

An arsonist at work in the Tammany Hotel.

The $275,000 Sack of Flour

A bagful of benefits for Union troops

The end of the bloody conflict was a year away, and soldiers were suffering on Civil War battlefields up and down the eastern seaboard. Meanwhile, far removed from the action—in the little town of Austin, Nevada—a local election turned into a bonanza for the fighting men of the Union Army.

It all began in 1864 when Reuel Colt Gridley, the Democratic candidate for mayor, proposed a friendly wager to the Republican, Dr. H. S. Herrick. If Herrick lost the election he would carry a sack of flour from Clifton to Austin, marching to the tune of "Dixie," and present it to Gridley. If Gridley lost *he* would carry the flour in the opposite direction, to the tune of "John Brown's Body," and turn it over to Herrick.

Gridley lost and, true to his word, he made the mile-and-a-quarter trek carrying a 50-pound sack of flour decorated with red, white, and blue ribbons and flags. He was accompanied by his 13-year-old son holding an American flag proudly aloft, a band playing the required music, and a joyous procession of townspeople intent on participating in the celebration that was sure to follow. At the presentation ceremony Gridley handed over to Dr. (now also Mayor) Herrick the flour and the flag, along with a broom (to signify that the winning party had made a clean sweep) and a sponge (to signify that it was entitled to absorb all the places of profit in town).

Reuel Colt Gridley traveled from coast to coast with his fund-raising flour sack. His old friend Mark Twain (whom he had known since their boyhood days in Hannibal, Missouri) told the story of the peripatetic philanthropist in his 1872 book Roughing It.

The first auction

Herrick didn't need or want the flour, so Gridley suggested they auction it off and send the proceeds to the U.S. Sanitary Commission fund. (The commission, set up at the beginning of the Civil War to provide aid and relief to Union soldiers and their dependent families, was the forerunner of the American Red Cross.)

In 1864 Nevada was in the midst of a silver-mining boom and "money was wonderfully plentiful. The trouble was not how to get it, but how . . . to get rid of it." There was fierce competition among the miners to display generosity and loyalty to the Union cause. So, after Gridley himself bought the sack of flour for $300, he returned it to be auctioned off again. And so it went, with miner after miner bidding outrageous sums and then redonating his prize for another sale. Before the day was over, the sack of flour had brought in some $5,000.

When the residents of neighboring Virginia City heard about the round-robin auction, civic pride demanded that they bid for the sack of flour, too—and outdo those upstarts in Austin. Thus began the remarkable odyssey that took Reuel Gridley all over Washoe County, Nevada; to Sacramento, San Francisco, and Stockton in California; across the country to New York City; and finally to a Sanitary Commission fair in St. Louis, where the flour was used to bake small cakes that were sold for a dollar apiece. At all of these stops, and at many others in between, this same sack of flour was auctioned off again and again. In the end, an astonishing $275,000 had been raised.

Famous last words

The president of the Sanitary Commission proclaimed that Gridley's sack "promised to become more renowned than any other in history since the sack of Troy." It is now in the collection of the Nevada Historical Society. And at his gravesite a monument erected in Gridley's honor is inscribed with an appropriate epitaph: "The Soldiers' Friend."

Victories at Sea

Not every Civil War battle was a landlocked encounter

Skeptics called it Ericsson's Folly (after its stubborn Swedish inventor) or the "cheesebox on a raft." But its real name was the *Monitor,* for the large revolving gun turret, or monitor, atop its flat deck. It was the Union's representative in the world's first battle between ironclad warships.

The Confederacy had rescued the Union frigate *Merrimack* from the bottom of Norfolk harbor and plated it with iron to serve as a ram. It was rechristened the *Virginia,* but the old name stuck. When the two met head-on it was the beginning of the end for the proud reign of wooden warships.

Clangorous confrontation

On March 8, 1862, the *Merrimack* sank one Union sloop and crippled a frigate, part of a blockading squadron at Hampton Roads, Virginia. But when she returned on March 9 to finish the job, her captain was astonished to see the Yankee cheesebox come at him out of the mist. A clangorous four-hour slugging match ensued.

Like two cautious heavyweights, the ships circled each other. The *Monitor*'s turret was hard to control, so its crew just let it revolve; but then messengers had to tell the gunners if they'd hit anything. As shot upon shot bounced noisily off iron plating, the metal monsters bumped at least five times.

When the *Monitor* backed off because her captain was blinded by a powder burst, the *Merrimack*'s captain apparently thought his adversary was retreating. His ship had sprung a leak anyway, so he left. Both sides claimed victory.

Far-ranging fighter

Not all sea combat took place close to home. In 1865 a Confederate captain sailed his armored clipper ship on a mission all the way to the Pacific Ocean!

The *Shenandoah*'s assignment was to cripple the Northern economy by attacking whaling ships. The vessel reached Australia, then headed north, with Capt. James Waddell and his crew burning or scuttling ships as they went. The startled skipper of one whaler, brandishing a newspaper account of the surrender at Appomattox Court House, told Waddell that the war was over. Undeterred, the captain fought on. In the ice-clogged Bering Strait off the coast of Siberia, he came upon a cluster of American whalers. He burned eight of them.

A full four months after the surrender, Waddell asked a passing British ship for news of the war. "What war?" came the reply. Convinced at last, the Confederate raider set sail for England.

In her 13-month, 60,000-mile globe-circling trip, the *Shenandoah* had seized 38 ships. And the shot that she had fired at the whalers in the Bering Strait was the last one of the Civil War.

Thousands of Frenchmen watched from the shore as the Union sloop-of-war Kearsarge *battled the Confederate marauder* Alabama *just off Cherbourg, France, on June 19, 1864. The* Alabama, *which had roamed the seas at will, challenging and sinking Union vessels, went down stern first, in clouds of smoke. Among the spectators was the famed impressionist artist Edouard Manet, who painted the dramatic scene below.*

Enemies No More

The gallantry of Joshua Chamberlain

On the morning of April 12, 1865—exactly four years after the Civil War had begun at Fort Sumter—Maj. Gen. John Gordon paraded his men down the main street of Appomattox Court House. Robert E. Lee had chosen him, because of his unswerving valor, to make the formal surrender of the Army of Northern Virginia.

Union soldiers lined the street, commanded by Maj. Gen. Joshua Chamberlain. As the Confederate troops came abreast, Chamberlain, in an unheard-of show of respect, ordered his men to salute. At first Gordon was too dejected to be aware of the tribute; but when he heard the Union troops shifting their guns, he responded in kind. Wheeling to face Chamberlain, he spurred his horse to its hind legs, raised his sword, and lowered it to his toe. Then, head held high, he ordered his men to return the Union salute. In silence, Americans who had fought and suffered bitterly now honored each other's courage.

General Gordon later described Chamberlain as "one of the knightliest soldiers of the Federal army." But not all Southerners appreciated the knightly gesture. "You may forgive us," Gen. Henry Wise berated Chamberlain, "but we won't be forgiven. There is a rancor in our hearts. . . . We hate you, sir."

After the war, Chamberlain, awarded the Medal of Honor for his heroism at Gettysburg, was elected governor of Maine. He later became president of Bowdoin College. For the rest of his life, he carried a souvenir of the Civil War—a silver tube in his abdomen to drain a wound that never healed and eventually killed him.

"He was a man of much dignity," Ulysses S. Grant later wrote of Robert E. Lee (above, leaving the McLean House). "I felt like anything rather than rejoicing at the downfall of a foe who had fought so long and valiantly and had suffered so much."

McLean's Real Estate

The peace was almost as destructive as the war

Wilmer McLean, a Virginia grocer, had a nose for history—if not for real estate. During the First Battle of Bull Run (the first major conflict of the Civil War) Confederate Gen. P.G.T. Beauregard commandeered McLean's house for his headquarters. A Union cannonball crashed through the kitchen. A year later, after the Second Battle of Bull Run once more ravaged his land, McLean decided to move on.

He settled his family in a brick farmhouse in the backwater town of Appomattox Court House, Virginia. But the war followed him. On April 9, 1865, Robert E. Lee sent Col. Charles Marshall to find an appropriate site for a conference with Ulysses S. Grant. The first person Marshall asked about possible places was Wilmer McLean, who took him to a deserted house without furniture. Marshall rejected it, and history caught up with McLean again. Sensing the inevitable, he offered his own home for the meeting.

The surrender, signed by Lee and Grant that afternoon in McLean's front parlor, ended the war—and ravaged McLean's home. Gen. Edward O. C. Ord paid him $40 for the table at which Grant had sat, and another Union general (either Philip Sheridan or George A. Custer) got Lee's table for $25. McLean refused to sell the rest of his furniture, but other souvenir hunters were less scrupulous. Chairs were broken up, upholstery ripped to shreds, and the parlor reduced to shambles in the rush for mementos.

Prints like this one by Currier and Ives vilified Davis, who was accused of plotting Lincoln's murder.

The Capture of Jefferson Davis

It's a lie that he wore his wife's dress

"He slipped into his wife's petticoats, crinoline, and dress, but in his hurry he forgot to put on her stockings and shoes." So ran a report in the New York *Herald* on May 16, 1865, purporting to describe Confederate President Jefferson Davis's attempt to elude Union troops. None of it was true.

Certainly Davis had tried to escape. Even after General Lee surrendered, the Southern president had refused to concede defeat and had headed for Texas to make a final stand. But at dawn on May 10 his camp near Irwinville, Georgia, was surprised by troops from the 4th Michigan Cavalry. He later said that, as he bolted from the dark tent in his gray suit and boots, he grabbed his wife's cloak by mistake instead of his own; she threw a shawl over his shoulders.

Rumors that Davis had dressed as a woman became vicious headlines after Secretary of War Edwin M. Stanton released them to the press. But when the War Department asked that Davis's "dress" be turned over to Stanton, all he received were the cloak and shawl. They were locked away in an office safe, where they stayed until 1945.

Chief Cochise and His White "Brother"

Two courageous leaders forged a unique frontier friendship

In the 1860's settlers in the Southwest were terrorized by the formidable Chiricahua Apache chief Cochise and his warriors. Wrongfully arrested for kidnapping a white child in 1861, Cochise escaped and went on the warpath, triggering a savage hit-and-run war that lasted more than 10 years and cost at least 1,000 lives.

Then Thomas Jefferson Jeffords appeared on the scene. Formerly a ship captain, Indian trader, and army scout, he was now a Tucson-based mail contractor. Distressed by the loss of 14 of his couriers, Jeffords rode alone into Cochise's camp and offered to lay down his arms as a token of good faith. He met "a man of great natural ability, a splendid specimen of physical manhood. . . . His religion was truth and loyalty." Cochise in turn admired the courage of tall, red-bearded Jeffords, calling him *chickasaw* ("brother"). Their meeting lasted for several days, and a legendary friendship grew out of it.

Although the war went on, Jeffords's mail riders were never attacked again. Jeffords was often scorned as an "Indian-lover," but when President Grant sought peace with the Apaches, he was asked to help. At a historic meeting in 1872, Cochise agreed to a treaty ending his raids in exchange for a reservation in his tribe's homeland. He laid down one condition: that Tom Jeffords was to be Indian agent for the reservation. The appointment was made, and peace was achieved—for nearly four years.

After Cochise died in 1874, the hard-won trust began to erode. Jeffords was replaced in 1876, and—faced with the threat of moving to a distant reservation—some Chiricahua Apaches rebelled under a new leader, as tough as Cochise and destined to become even more legendary. His name was Geronimo.

In 1892 ex-Indian agent Tom Jeffords (below) became a recluse near Tucson. A tough, hard-drinking bachelor, he was the unlikely model for the romantic figure played by Jimmy Stewart in the 1950 film Broken Arrow.

Slaughter on the Plains

Under the terms of the Medicine Lodge Treaty of 1867, the government agreed to protect the Indians on the reservations set aside for them. Since the millions of bison that roamed the southwestern plains provided the tribes with food, shelter, and other necessities, the treaty also called for the army to prosecute buffalo hunters for poaching on Indian territory. But when white marksmen had exhausted the herds in Kansas, Maj. Richard Dodge made it clear that his soldiers wouldn't stop them.

"Boys," he said, "if I were a buffalo hunter, I would hunt where the buffaloes are."

And that's what they did.

In a desperate attempt to save a vanishing way of life, the Buffalo War erupted in 1874. Hundreds of braves attacked a hunter's outpost in the Texas panhandle. They were badly beaten by 28 men armed with Sharps rifles.

By annihilating the bison, hunters kept their pockets well lined—and helped the army to keep the Plains tribes dependent on supplies doled out by federal agents.

Regret was rare. In later years a white hunter bragged: "If it had not been for the accomplishment of the buffalo hunters, the wild bison would still graze where Amarillo now is, and the red man would still reign supreme over the pampas of the Panhandle."

April Fool

Among the 16,000 identical government-issue headstones in the Santa Fe National Cemetery is a single life-size statue of a reclining soldier in his army uniform, complete with ammunition. Its inscription is simple: "Dennis O'Leary, Pvt., Co 1, 23 Infty, died Apl 1, 1901, Age 23 yrs & 9 mo."

According to a legend, (unconfirmed by official army records), Private O'Leary killed himself while serving with 76 other men at the remote frontier outpost of Fort Wingate, New Mexico. The soldier, somewhat of a loner, had been sentenced to the guardhouse for going AWOL for several weeks. He dutifully served his time, but his dereliction was never explained until the day he shot himself. His suicide note gave the location of a "memento" he had left in the mountains: the elaborately carved sandstone statue with the April 1 date of his death already inscribed.

Indian Messiah

The Ghost Dancers' hope ended in tragedy

Although it lasted only two years, by the time the Ghost Dance movement was over, Sitting Bull was dead and more than 200 Sioux (mostly women and children) and 25 U.S. soldiers had been killed at Wounded Knee Creek. Yet the Ghost Dance began as a kind of Christianity that expressed the Indians' longing to return to their vanished past.

Ghost Dancing had occurred before among the Plains tribes. But it emerged anew early in 1889 when a Nevada Paiute holy man named Wovoka—who had been raised by a white family after his father's death—had a vision. In it God assured him that Christ's second coming was at hand, and the prophet learned a sacred dance, which the Indians should perform to hasten the new age. When the messiah came, the dancers would be lifted into the air as a bountiful land slid into place beneath them, burying the old corrupt world. Indians who had died would be resurrected to join their descendants on earth—which may be why the dance was called the Ghost Dance.

Although the peaceful message encouraged only trancelike dancing, white Indian agents were frightened. They feared they were losing control of the tribes. Reports of Ghost Shirts, which the Indians believed to be impervious to bullets, only heightened their alarm.

In December 1890 the government tried to arrest Sitting Bull, whom they thought was inciting the Ghost Dancers. He resisted and was murdered. A few days later Big Foot, another Sioux chief, learned that his own arrest had been ordered. When he and his people slipped away, the 7th Cavalry—General Custer's old regiment, which the Sioux had massacred at the Little Bighorn—was sent to bring them back.

On December 28 the soldiers intercepted Big Foot, who was dying of pneumonia, and about 350 of his followers. The Indians were moved out peacefully to a camp at Wounded Knee Creek, where the braves were told to surrender their weapons. Reports vary, but it's certain that someone fired a shot, and the nervous, tired, and freezing troops who surrounded the camp opened fire.

The terrified Indians discovered that their Ghost Shirts were worthless. Some fought back, but many of the women, children, and elderly fled—and as they ran they were slaughtered. Corpses were recovered miles from the camp. One baby, half frozen, was found sheltered desperately in its dead mother's arms, still nursing at her breast.

This was the last "battle" the army fought against the Indians. It ended forever the Ghost Dance and the dream of an Indian messiah.

The Ghost Dance (above) was not a war dance. But most whites didn't understand this and were frightened by the Indians' belief that their Ghost Shirts, like the Pawnee one at right, could not be penetrated by bullets.

Sitting Bull's Murder

As the winter dawn broke over South Dakota on Monday, December 15, 1890, 43 blue-uniformed Indian policemen crossed the Standing Rock Reservation toward the house of the powerful Hunkpapa Sioux medicine man Sitting Bull. They were there to arrest him. As they dragged the Sioux leader from his cabin, his teenage son Crowfoot awoke and joined some 150 Hunkpapas who had gathered outside. Now Sitting Bull refused to go. One of his supporters fired at the policemen, hitting their leader, Lt. Bull Head. As the lieutenant fell, he fired into Sitting Bull's chest. Another policeman shot him in the back of the head, killing him instantly. Pandemonium erupted. Shouts and bullets sounded everywhere. Crowfoot was killed. Cued by the gunshots, Sitting Bull's trained horse, whom he had ridden in Buffalo Bill Cody's Wild West Show, started his trick routine; to him the bloodbath—in which 15 people died—was just one more show. But to the awestruck Indians it was as if Sitting Bull's spirit had entered the horse, who now danced to hasten the coming messiah.

Only Congress Can Declare War

But one aggressive newspaper owner had other ideas

They say that soon after illustrator Frederic Remington arrived in Cuba to cover the revolution against Spain for the New York *Journal,* he asked to return home because there was no war. But his boss, press lord William Randolph Hearst, fired off a message: "Please remain," he wired. "You furnish the pictures; I'll furnish the war."

The story may be apocryphal, but it could have happened. Hearst needed a war in the worst way. He was embroiled in a circulation battle with Joseph Pulitzer's mighty New York *World,* and he knew that there was nothing like a war to grab the readers' attention.

The only problem was getting hostilities cranked up. A tiny band of Cubans were in rebellion against the autocratic Spanish rule, but the "unkempt mob of brave but disorganized bushwhackers" (according to one Hearst biographer) didn't stand a chance unless they could get American troops to do their fighting for them.

This was where Hearst cheerfully stepped in, printing any item of rebel propaganda as gospel truth. Remington's graphic drawings helped too. Once, Spanish police boarded an American steamship and searched three young Cuban women suspected of carrying rebel messages. "DOES OUR FLAG PROTECT WOMEN?" the *Journal*'s headline demanded. Beneath it was a Remington sketch of a quite naked lady being thoroughly searched by three leering Spaniards. But when the woman in question showed up in New York, she explained that *women* had searched her in privacy—a fact the rival *World* was quick to headline.

Getting caught by the truth was merely a temporary setback for Hearst. When Evangelina Cosio y Cisneros was arrested for trying to help her rebel father break out of jail, Hearst's imaginative reporters claimed that her only crime had been defending her chastity against a lustful Spanish colonel. "We've got Spain now," Hearst boasted. He managed to have "the Cuban Joan of Arc" liberated in a dramatic prison break, then brought her to New York for a tumultuous heroine's welcome, and a new round of hysterical headlines.

Remember the *Maine*!

The deception was so great that Spain began to fear America's newspapers more than its government. Unable to stand up to the more powerful nation, Spain did everything to soothe the situation, even granting autonomy to Cuba.

Then on February 15, 1898, the U.S. battleship *Maine* blew up in Havana harbor (from causes unknown to this day), and Hearst finally got his war. "THE WHOLE COUNTRY THRILLS WITH WAR FEVER," the *Journal* declared on February 18, blaming the explosion on Spain. Hearst even offered readers a card game called "War With Spain."

President McKinley opposed the war—according to Teddy Roosevelt, he had "no more backbone than a chocolate eclair"—but was swept along and asked Congress to declare war on Spain. And Hearst wouldn't let anybody forget who had started it all. "HOW DO YOU LIKE THE JOURNAL'S WAR?" a headline immodestly asked. Then Hearst offered readers a $1,000 prize for the best idea on how to get the conflict off to a good start.

The Hero of Kettle Hill

Didn't TR deserve a medal?

In the sweltering Cuban heat of July 1898, Lt. Col. Theodore Roosevelt, commander of a volunteer cavalry regiment called the Rough Riders, was ready for the most crucial battle of the Spanish-American War: the attack on heavily fortified San Juan Heights. But the orders never arrived. Illness had intervened, and while the American chain of command stumbled, Roosevelt fumed.

It was bad enough his cavalrymen had to fight on foot, for all horses except officers' mounts had been ordered left in Florida. Now, as they moved to the right of the attack line and waited, they found a hill laced with Spanish gunmen who cut them to shreds with deadly accurate rifle fire.

"Let my men through!"

Finally, Roosevelt advanced his troops to the foot of the hill (called Kettle Hill, for a huge caldron on top that was used to process sugar cane). There he encountered elements of the 9th U.S. Cavalry (Colored) and ordered their white captain to charge the hill. When the officer refused, questioning TR's authority to give such a command, the future president bellowed: "Then let my men through!"

The black soldiers, despite their officer, stood up against the killing fusillade, flattened a barbed wire fence with their bodies, and joined in the heroic charge. Astride his horse Little Texas, TR ignored the bullets that flew past with a sound "like the ripping of a silk dress."

They took the hill and, seeing that the main attack had begun on San Juan Hill some 700 yards away, set up a fusillade of their own against the defending Spaniards. Then TR decided to join the attack, but forgot to order his men to follow. Finding himself almost alone partway down the far slope of Kettle Hill, he ran back, yelled, "Forward, march!" and made it to the top of San Juan Hill in time to participate in the final victory.

Alger's revenge
TR was recommended for the Medal of Honor, but because of politics he never got it. At the end of the three-month war, the Americans who remained in Cuba were being decimated by malaria, but Secretary of War Russell Alger failed to move them to a healthier climate. Roosevelt and other senior officers sent a letter to the press describing the emergency. The outcry was a factor in Alger's forced resignation, and there is evidence that before leaving office Alger saw to it that TR's medal would be denied. Roosevelt was crushed.

Bittersweet justice
During TR's presidency an act was passed listing the rules that make the Medal of Honor a true symbol of heroism. And it was Franklin Delano Roosevelt (a cousin) who bestowed the medal posthumously on Theodore Roosevelt, Jr., during World War II. "His father would have been the proudest," he declared. He certainly would have.

Cuba, 1898: Theodore Roosevelt posed with his Rough Riders after the stunning victory at San Juan Hill.

Medal of Honor

Gen. John J. Pershing said he'd trade his stars for it. Harry Truman said he'd rather have one than be president. They were referring to the Medal of Honor, the highest U.S. military decoration, awarded for acts of heroism on the battlefield "above and beyond the call of duty."

The medal was established during the Civil War, when Dr. Mary Walker (above) served as the army's first female assistant surgeon. She also became the only woman ever to win the medal. After the war she was a famous curmudgeon, wearing men's clothes (with her medal always on the lapel) and fighting for women's rights. Dr. Walker's medal was among those revoked in 1917, but it was finally reinstated—half a century later.

TR and the Barbary Pirate

"Perdicaris alive or Raisuli dead"

President Theodore Roosevelt's rough and ready response to the kidnapping of Ion Perdicaris by Barbary pirates became a permanent part of the folklore surrounding his public image. The cartoon at left was drawn in 1906, two years after the incident.

In 1904 a Berber chieftain named Mubu Ahmed er Raisuli provided the perfect target for Teddy Roosevelt to shake his big stick at—and without much need to speak softly. Raisuli was disgusted with Morocco's weak-willed young sultan, Abdul-Aziz, who under the Svengali-like sway of his advisers allowed the French free reign in his country as long as they provided him with extravagant Western gadgets: an assortment of bicycles, cameras (600 of them), grand pianos (25), and a gold automobile, which couldn't be used much, since Morocco had no roads.

As a step toward overthrowing the government, the audacious pirate decided to embarrass the bumbling sultan. Leading a flurry of cutlass-waving Berbers, he snatched wealthy American Ion Perdicaris and his stepson from a pleasant terrace dinner at the family's ostentatious Tangier villa. Although the ransom note and demands were addressed solely to the Moroccan government, Raisuli hoped to involve the United States, whose volatile president would certainly draw worldwide attention to the incident.

The Arab's dreams couldn't have been more fully realized. The kidnapping, tailor-made for TR's style of rough-rider politics, was just what the president needed to rescue his sagging bid for election to a second term. The American consul in Tangier, Samuel Gummeré, had requested a warship as a show of force. TR sent four of them. And even though Raisuli had a reputation for returning messengers with their throats cut (or just sending back their decapitated heads in melon baskets), TR dispatched negotiators to the terrorist's camp. American newspapers played up the story with blaring headlines.

But as negotiations dragged on for more than a month, Roosevelt got a surprise: Perdicaris might not be an American citizen after all. During the Civil War he had registered as a Greek citizen in an attempt to protect his landholdings in the Confederacy, which otherwise would have been confiscated when he failed to answer a draft call. The president and his aides decided to keep mum. Roosevelt was busting to send in the troops.

Raisuli finally agreed to free his hostages for certain political concessions and $70,000 in ransom from the Moroccan government. However, on the day before the scheduled release, he called the deal off. Consul Gummeré shot off a telegram to TR, stressing the potential humiliation for the United States and asking for an ultimatum. Secretary of State John Hay provided it, at Roosevelt's order. His telegram back to Gummeré read: "This Government wants Perdicaris alive or Raisuli dead." Although the message also urged the envoy to proceed cautiously and await further orders, only the section with the demand was released to the American press. When it was read to the Republican convention—which, while endorsing Roosevelt unanimously, had been lackadaisical—the delegates went wild. The old Rough Rider's presidential campaign was off to a thrilling start.

But the telegram had little effect. By the time it reached Morocco, Raisuli had changed his mind again. The matter was settled, the ransom paid, and the hostages freed. Perdicaris publicly praised his captor's civility and also admitted privately to Gummeré that he had never reinstated his American citizenship—a fact that was covered up for nearly 40 years, until it was revealed in a biography of Hay.

As for Raisuli's political goals, they fell victim to his own success. He had made the sultan's incompetence so obvious that the ruler was overthrown by his brother, whose firm administration curtailed the pirate's activities. In addition, the French were so angered by the kidnapping that they strove to exert even greater influence in Morocco.

The 1975 movie based on the incident, *The Wind and the Lion,* gave the twisted tale yet another fictional turn: it changed Perdicaris into a woman (played by Candice Bergen) so that there could be a love story. Sean Connery was Raisuli.

"Shoot Him Again, Tougher . . ."

How Pancho Villa held up Hollywood

Mexican bandit and revolutionary Pancho Villa became the Robin Hood of his country when his well-armed men defeated Mexico's federal troops in 1913. But perhaps his greatest scheme for robbing the rich to pay the poor was the deal he cut with a Hollywood studio to star in a movie about his exploits.

On January 3, 1914, Villa signed a contract with the Mutual Film Corporation giving him a $25,000 advance and 50 percent of all profits. In return, if Villa was victorious in a battle, Mutual would own the right to show the film of the fighting in the areas his troops had conquered and throughout the United States and Canada. Camera crews were invited to join Villa's army as it swept across Mexico, and the fiery revolutionary agreed to stage his raids during daylight hours to facilitate filming. In fact, the contract even required Villa to reenact battles for the cameramen if the footage they had shot wasn't sufficiently "realistic."

The resulting film—*The Life of General Villa*—was a military voyeur's delight. On May 5, 1914, a critic from the New York *World* stated: "There is thunder and gore from beginning to end. Marvelous pictures of the fighting at Torreón are woven clearly into the drama of Villa's life. . . . The whole is so realistic that it is almost as good as being on the scene, and far much safer."

Mexican revolutionary Francisco "Pancho" Villa (below) was just as shrewd about politics as battle. Well aware of the value of propaganda, he used films of his army's triumphs as an effective psychological weapon.

Allen Dulles's Date

Lenin's lesson for the CIA

Allen Dulles was looking forward to the night of April 11, 1917, because he had a date with Helene Herzog, whom he'd been wild about since he was 15 years old, when he studied French with her family. Helene had spurned his schoolboy advances. But now he was 24, World War I was raging, and he worked in the American legation in Berne, Switzerland. He figured his chances were better.

Although the office was closed, Dulles was working late that afternoon when the phone rang. His heart sank. The caller was a Russian revolutionary living in exile in Switzerland. He declared that he was coming to Berne with important information and needed to talk with someone in the American legation immediately.

Since nobody else was around, that meant Dulles. But Dulles had a date, so he told his caller that he would have to come by the next morning. The man was adamant that tomorrow would be too late—and Dulles was just as adamant about Helene.

History doesn't tell us how the date went, but it does record that later that evening Vladimir Ilyich Lenin boarded a train in Switzerland and was allowed passage across Germany to Sweden. Within days he was in Moscow, the revolution had started, and Russia was pulling out of the war with Germany, abandoning the Allied cause. Apparently, Lenin had been trying to alert President Woodrow Wilson to the scheme in advance. But Wilson learned the news with the rest of the world—because Dulles had a date.

After becoming head of the CIA 36 years later, Dulles repeated the story as a warning to every class of new agents.

Minister Without Portfolio *The case of the spy on the train*

World War I was raging in Europe, but the United States kept its distance. Even after 124 Americans went down with the torpedoed *Lusitania* in May 1915, isolationist sentiment remained strong. An absentminded German spy master helped change that.

Heinrich Albert, officially a commercial attaché at the German Embassy, kept meticulous records on his highly sophisticated espionage ring, operating all across America. And these details were in his briefcase when he boarded the Sixth Avenue el in New York City on July 24, 1915. But he forgot his precious cargo on the el, and Secret Service Agent Frank Burke, who was tailing him, pounced on it, ran off the train, and dashed down to the street. With Albert in hot pursuit, Burke hopped on a streetcar and told the conductor that he was being chased by a madman. To avoid a scene, the motorman bypassed the next stop—leaving the panting, half-crazed German stranded.

In Albert's briefcase, officials found schemes for buying all of America's chlorine (used in poison gas) and toluol (for TNT) to prevent their sale to Britain and France. But in their most enterprising plot, the Germans had set up a munitions factory, planning to take huge orders from Britain and France—and never to deliver them. They also hoped to buy so much incendiary powder that it would be impossible for other companies to fill orders.

U.S. authorities made the skulduggery public (without admitting the briefcase theft) by leaking the story to the New York *World* on the promise that the paper would not reveal its source. The ensuing hue and cry helped persuade Americans that Germany was a menace. And the escapade gave Albert a new title; he became known as Minister Without Portfolio.

Breaking the Code

A crucial cable finally fanned the winds of war

It was not on the field of battle that the Germans committed their worst blunder during World War I. The site was, instead, a Western Union telegraph office.

In 1917 Germany's submarine fleet was capable of cutting Britain's lifeline to the world. The only hope for the British seemed to lie with the United States; but President Woodrow Wilson refused to abandon his neutral position, declaring that to enter the war would be a "crime against civilization." His stand led Germany to resume submarine warfare against all vessels bound for Britain.

Even so, on January 16, German foreign secretary Arthur Zimmermann sent an odd cable to his minister in Washington, by way of the U.S. diplomatic line—which Wilson allowed Germany to use to send peace proposals to Britain. Western Union relayed the message to the German legation in Mexico, and from there it was delivered to Mexico's president.

The carefully coded message proposed that if U.S. neutrality could not be maintained, Mexico should enter the war on the side of Germany in exchange for "generous financial support" and reclamation of "lost territory" in the Southwest. To make sure the message got through, it was also sent by wireless and through a Swedish diplomatic channel.

Indomitable as ever, British intelligence intercepted all three messages and broke the "unbreakable" German code. One problem remained: how to use the information without revealing the decoding. First the British waited to see if renewed submarine warfare would push Wilson into the war.

It didn't. Finally, they gave him the message—with the cover story that one of their spies had stolen it from the Germans in Mexico.

Wilson was livid; Germany had used America's own cable against her. But many citizens believed the message was fake. How could its authenticity be proven without jeopardizing the code breakers?

Remarkably, Western Union resolved the dilemma. Breaking its own rules, it released a copy of the telegram. Zimmermann then admitted sending it. With America itself a target, all chances for neutrality were gone, and on April 6 the United States entered the war.

Arthur Zimmermann's proposal of a German-Mexican alliance pushed America into World War I.

1918: A war-weary doughboy (left) in the Argonne Forest, where the Lost Battalion fought. Cher Ami ("Dear Friend"), the pigeon that carried the battalion's desperate message, arrived minus an eye and a leg. The fine feathered hero won a Distinguished Service Cross, and was later stuffed (below) and displayed at the Smithsonian Institution.

The Lost Battalion

Doomed heroes in a bleak and brutal war

Neither lost nor a battalion, they were 550 stalwart soldiers—the tattered remnants of New York's famed 77th "Statue of Liberty" Division—fighting their way through France. Commanding them was a bespectacled Wall Street lawyer, Maj. Charles Whittlesey, who won the Medal of Honor for his deeds.

When Allied forces began the 1918 drive that would end World War I, the 77th faced the Argonne Forest, a formidable German stronghold. Whittlesey's exhausted troops had been fighting steadily for weeks; nonetheless, Gen. John J. "Black Jack" Pershing ordered the Americans to advance "without regard of losses." When the major's protest was refused, he responded: "I'll attack, but whether you'll hear from me again, I don't know."

Surrounded by the enemy

On October 2 Whittlesey led his men through a steep ravine dotted with enemy gunners. Withering fire came from the left side, but the troops managed to make it up and over the right side of the ravine. They reached the high ground easily, but they were alone. Certain that the group was spearheading a massive attack, the Germans rushed reinforcements into the area—and the major and his men were cut off. A few carrier pigeons brought along in a cage were their only means of communication. Of the four companies sent as reinforcements, just one got through. "Our mission is to hold this position at all costs," the steadfast Whittlesey told his men. "No falling back."

A third of the force became casualties of an attack the next day—and there was neither food nor medical supplies. On October 4 a misguided Allied artillery barrage hit Whittlesey's men. The major wrote a message pinpointing their position and pleading: "For heaven's sake, stop it." His last pigeon, Cher Ami, flew through enemy fire to deliver it, and two hours later the shelling stopped.

After an airlift failed (the hungry men watched supplies fall behind German lines), the "Lost Battalion" became nationwide news. Embarrassed, General Pershing ordered a rescue effort. It too failed.

So few survivors

Although Whittlesey's force was too weak to bury its dead, when the Germans suggested surrender the major didn't even reply. Not until five harrowing days had passed did relief get through. Only 190 Americans survived the living nightmare.

Three years later the highly decorated Whittlesey also became a casualty. Unable to come to terms with the disparity between his celebrity and the ordeal of his men, he committed suicide.

Premature Peace

The anticlimactic armistice

Just before noon on November 7, 1918, the New York headquarters of United Press received a cable from its president, Roy Howard. It read: "Urgent. Armistice allies Germans signed 11 smorning hostilities ceased two safternoon."

The news, which bannered the nation's midday papers, set off celebrations across America. Everywhere people poured into the streets, laughing and crying; in New York City delirious crowds cheered one of the largest tickertape parades in history.

Howard was thrilled with his scoop. Through a series of coincidences, he had gotten the armistice report from none other than the American naval commander in French waters, Adm. Henry B. Wilson. Rushing to the offices of a Brest newspaper and using its machinery, he had managed to slip his wire past French censorship and through to UP headquarters in New York. At the same time, Admiral Wilson had released the joyous news in Brest.

That evening Howard went with a few friends to a bar in town to celebrate. In the midst of the uproar a coded message was quietly delivered to an officer in his party. Deciphering it, he handed it to Howard: "Armistice report untrue. War Ministry issues absolute denial and declares enemy plenipotentiaries to be still on way through lines. . . . Wire full details of local hoax immediately."

The celebration came to a halt and Howard turned white. Clearly, he and the United Press were doomed. Admiral Wilson exonerated him, however, by publicly taking the blame for the false news, apparently the work of German spies. Four days later peace was *officially* declared.

How Not to Kidnap a Kaiser

Luke Lea's self-assigned mission was really impossible

After Germany's defeat in 1918, Kaiser Wilhelm took refuge at the castle of a friend in Amerongen, Holland. This outraged Col. Luke Lea, who believed the German ruler should be tried as a war criminal. So Lea, who was stationed in Luxembourg, concocted a plan to kidnap the kaiser and "present him as a New Year's gift to President Wilson" at the Paris peace conference. To assist him, he recruited seven fellow Tennesseans. Surreptitiously they acquired passes, commandeered two army cars, and set off for Amerongen.

Reaching the castle, the men bluffed their way past the guards, demanding to see the kaiser. They were led to a large, elegantly furnished library. A man dressed in tails appeared, introduced himself as Count von Bentinck, and asked the purpose of the visit. Lea replied, "I can reveal that only to the kaiser."

But the kaiser refused to see Lea unless he first stated his reasons for coming, and Lea refused to comply. After the stalemate had dragged on for an hour, Lea decided to leave. Bowing to their confused host, the Tennesseans made a polite exit. By then a crowd of soldiers had gathered outside, and so the Americans sped away.

Narrowly escaping a court-martial, Lea was instead reprimanded by Gen. John J. Pershing. Later, the general confessed that he would have given "a year's pay" to have gone along on Lea's adventure.

This 1916 cartoon by Kirby, which ran in the New York World, *showed Kaiser Wilhelm II in a typical propaganda pose, "restoring" Serbia and Belgium. When the hated German ruler was later given asylum by neutral Holland, the Allies, who blamed him for the Great War, were outraged.*

The conductorettes "have proven remarkably steady and honest," said an official of the New York and Queens Railroad shortly after World War I ended. "They have been courteous to our patrons and we have had very few complaints." Nevertheless, the women were soon sacked.

Promises, Promises *Conductorettes lose their jobs*

When the draft created a manpower shortage in 1917, the New York and Queens Railroad began hiring women to run its trolley cars. Within a year 25 conductorettes were working on the Queens lines. A local paper enthusiastically reported that the women "have made such a success of the work that some of them have been appointed inspectors."

The railroad was so satisfied with the conductorettes that it supplied them with khaki-colored winter overcoats (at $17 apiece), doubled their pay to $25 a week, and made a commitment to their permanent employment at the war's end. "The women conductors have come to stay on our lines just as long as they want to continue in their present jobs," an official promised. "We now have about 50 and are taking more on as fast as they apply for positions."

But alas, this pledge didn't last as long as the winter coats.

In May 1919 Gov. Al Smith signed a bill to "better the conditions of women" by limiting them to only 54 working hours a week. Maybe it really was too difficult to accommodate the new law; at any rate, in September the company fired all of the women in favor of returning men.

"Known but to God" *Choosing the anonymous hero to honor all war dead*

On October 22, 1921, four bodies were exhumed at four different cemeteries in France, near sites where American soldiers were known to have fallen in the War to End All Wars.

Those given the grim assignment of selecting the remains had to make sure they were indeed Americans but were otherwise truly unidentifiable, with no clues as to name, rank, or service. For evidence they relied upon the location of the original burial, gunshot wounds, and fragments of uniform. The bodies were embalmed, placed in similar coffins, and taken to the city hall at Chalons-sur-Marne, where a small chapel had been arranged.

In a simple ceremony on the morning of October 24, Sgt. Edward S. Younger, a soldier decorated for heroism in the war, entered the chapel, circled the four caskets, and—choosing at random—placed a spray of white roses on the second from the right. The chosen soldier was interred at Arlington National Cemetery on Armistice Day. On his white marble tomb appears this inscription: "Here Rests in Honored Glory an American Soldier Known but to God."

In the 1920's Hector C. Bywater (above) predicted that a sneak Japanese aerial attack on a major U.S. base in the Pacific would launch a great war. Bywater died 16 months before the drama he so vividly portrayed was acted out at Pearl Harbor. His book may well have served as a blueprint for Japan.

The Surprise at Pearl Harbor *The "day of infamy" was foretold years earlier*

The surprise attack on Pearl Harbor should not have been a surprise to U.S. military officials! At least, not if they had paid attention—as the Japanese had—to a book published in America in 1925. Its title: *The Great Pacific War.* Written by Hector C. Bywater, a British naval intelligence agent and military correspondent, it vividly foretold the strategy the Japanese would employ in a war against America.

The Japanese ambition, Bywater wrote, was to conquer China and Korea for raw materials. But to achieve her goal, Japan would first have to cripple American forces in the Pacific. She would do so in a series of precision strikes, Bywater said; he went on to predict that the war would begin with a devastating sneak air attack on U.S. naval forces. The first target, he thought, would be Manila Bay. He was wrong about the target, but uncannily accurate otherwise.

Did the Japanese in fact use Bywater's book as a blueprint for their assault? At the time it was published, Isoroku Yamamoto, Japan's brilliant commander in World War II, was stationed in Washington, D.C., as naval attaché. Fluent in English, he could hardly have missed the book—it was featured on the front page of *The New York Times Book Review.*

Also, both *The Great Pacific War* and Bywater's 1921 study, *Sea Power in the Pacific*, were pirated in Japan and circulated among its officers. Years later Mitsuo Fuchida, a prominent Japanese military historian, admitted that when he attended the Japanese Naval War College in 1936, both works were studied.

By then students taking final exams at the Japanese naval academy were routinely asked: "How would you attack Pearl Harbor?" America may have helped answer that question too! War games conducted by Adm. Harry Yarnell in Hawaiian waters in 1932 revealed the vulnerability of Pearl Harbor to a surprise predawn aerial attack launched from aircraft carriers. The results of the games were widely publicized.

Yet to what extent, if any, Admiral Yamamoto was seriously influenced by Bywater is hard to say. Bywater had also predicted the ultimate destruction of the Imperial Navy and the bombing of Tokyo.

A Close Squeak

The Battle of Midway, the decisive turning point of World War II in the Pacific, would have been a disaster had it not been for Comdr. Joseph J. Rochefort, Jr., who in 1940 had helped break the top Japanese naval code known as the JN-25.

Following the Pearl Harbor disaster, America anxiously wondered where and when the Japanese would strike again. (Knowing the code had done no good on December 7, 1941, because the Japanese had maintained radio silence prior to the attack.) Then, in the spring of 1942, Rochefort's intelligence unit in Hawaii started picking up an unusual volume of coded radio traffic from the Japanese fleet. What they read was ominous. Adm. Isoroku Yamamoto was pulling together a huge fleet for an assault on a target called "AF." It was believed the letters were coded map coordinates for Midway, but Adm. Chester Nimitz could take no chances. He had to be sure.

Rochefort proposed a ruse. He sent a coded message to Midway telling the Americans to return a bogus message, uncoded, that the island's water distillation system had broken down. The trick worked. A few days later the Japanese code reported that "AF" was short on water.

With this information, Nimitz rushed to position the U.S. fleet on the flank of the Japanese, who thought it was 1,300 miles away in Hawaii. When the Japanese launched their attack, they were dumbfounded by an American counterattack that sank four of their aircraft carriers and ended their ability to take the offensive. "In attempting surprise," said Nimitz, "the Japanese were themselves surprised."

Kamikaze Bats and Balloon Bombs

Both sides had secret weapons that fizzled

A Pennsylvania dentist, Lytle S. Adams, was driving home from Carlsbad Caverns in New Mexico when he heard about Pearl Harbor. Remembering the millions of bats in the caverns, Adams wondered why they couldn't be armed with tiny incendiary bombs. He sent his idea to President Roosevelt, who agreed to give it a shot. The army and the navy spent 27 months of research and $2 million on what came to be called Operation X-ray.

The plan was simple enough. Hundreds of thousands of bats would be captured and stored, asleep, in freezers. A one-ounce bomb would be attached to the loose skin on each one's chest. The bats were to be dropped from a plane over Japan in containers that would open at 1,000 feet. Startled, the bats would head for the nearest cracks and crevices of buildings and chew off the bombs, which would explode, shooting a two-foot-high flame into the air for eight minutes.

Early testing at an army air force base in California had mixed results: some bats slept through free fall and dropped like rocks; others escaped and set the entire base on fire, including a general's car. The army then passed Operation X-ray on to the navy. But the project came to an abrupt halt in 1944, as the military worked on a bomb far more powerful than anything a bat could deliver.

Cranes and sympathy

Meanwhile, the Japanese were working on Operation Fu-Go—a plan to wreak havoc in America with balloons towing incendiary bombs. Made of rice paper and inflated with hydrogen, the balloons measured 33 feet in diameter. Toward the end of 1944 more than 300 of them sailed the jet stream across the Pacific to the West Coast.

In May 1945 one of the balloon bombs exploded in Oregon, killing a woman and five children on a picnic—the war's only casualties in continental America. In 1987 several of the Japanese women who had made that balloon sent notes of sympathy to the victims' families, along with 1,000 folded paper cranes, a Japanese symbol of peace.

Left: A bat bomber takes a snooze. Below: A balloon and its bomb drape a California telephone wire.

Dummy tanks had to be pumped up under cover of darkness because they squirmed wildly while inflating.

Phantoms of the Army

Their deception deflated—and defeated—the enemy

The 603rd Engineer Camouflage Battalion almost blew its cover one morning in 1944 when a couple of French cyclists watched four soldiers pick up a huge tank and turn it around. The tank was inflated rubber, and the 603rd was just doing its job: fooling the Germans.

Deception has been part of warfare at least since the Trojan horse; during World War II it became high art. In fact, the members of the 603rd *were* artists. They included fashion designer Bill Blass and painter Ellsworth Kelly, as well as a Hollywood set designer and assorted illustrators and photographers.

The special weapons of the battalion (which belonged to the 23rd Headquarters Special Troops) were dummy planes, tanks, and antiaircraft guns; amplified recordings that created war sounds; flash canisters for gunfire; and fake shoulder patches. To enable a combat unit to change positions or to attack while the Germans thought it hadn't moved at all, the 1,800 men of the 23rd impersonated entire divisions. They would move in at night, change insignias, and inflate their rubber dummies. Meanwhile, the troops they were replacing sneaked away. Though inflated tanks and planes might suddenly spring leaks or burst when the sun expanded the pumped-in air, by and large the artifice worked. Their impersonation of tank and field artillery battalions once fooled not only the 38,000 Germans holding the French port of Brest, but nearby Allied troops as well.

The 23rd hit the beaches at Normandy a few days after D-Day, an invasion that itself was made possible, in part, by an entire ghost army—the First United States Army Group (FUSAG)—that helped divert enemy troops before, during, and after the onslaught. Supposedly stationed in England, FUSAG faked radio communications and planted intelligence messages with double agents to convince the Germans that it was going to attack at Pas de Calais and that the Normandy invasion was a mere diversion. A series of distinguished real generals, including George S. Patton, did stints as FUSAG commanders.

When the 9th Army was trying to cross the Rhine in March 1945, the 23rd created the illusion of a huge buildup at Viersen; "divisions" paraded about, hundreds of rubber vehicles and planes and elaborate bridging equipment were displayed, and entire field hospitals were built. The real crossing took the Germans completely by surprise.

It was the 23rd's last work of artifice. In May the hostilities in Europe ended, and in September the battalion was sent home.

Eisenhower at Ease

Why Ike gave up poker—in his own words: "One man who appeared every night [for the poker game] was uniquely unskilled. The young man came to me and asked whether I would take government bonds to pay for his losses. It turned out that these were 'Baby Bonds,' saved by his wife during the years he had been away to war. I went to my other friends in the game, and we agreed to let him get his money back.

"This was not achieved easily. One of the hardest things known to man is to make a fellow win in poker who plays as if bent on losing every nickel. At one point my adjutant found himself with a good hand. The only way to disqualify himself was to have too many cards. While the others were picking up their hands, he dropped his cards on one lying in front of him, and then said: 'I'm sorry. I called for two cards and wanted only one. Now I have six cards. My hand is dead.' But it took until nearly midnight to get the job done.

"I decided that I had to quit playing poker. Most losers were bound to be spending not only their own money but their families'. If we had stayed with our original intention of playing only with bachelors, perhaps this could have been all right. But now I felt that it was a bad idea—and from then on I did not play with anybody in the army."

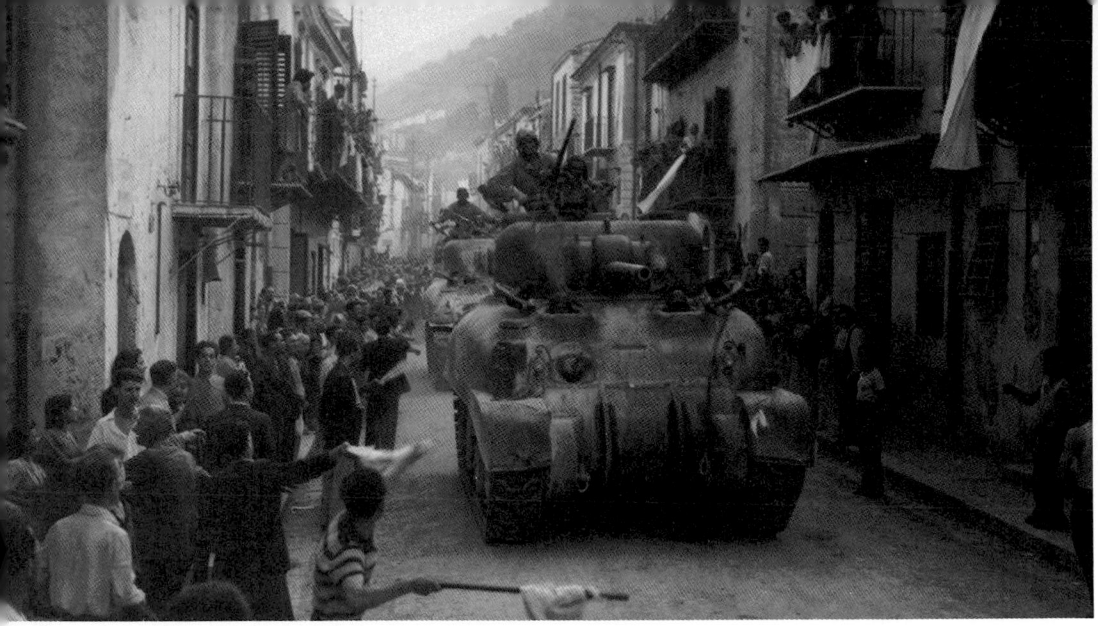

July 22, 1943: Cheering residents greeted the men of Gen. George S. Patton's forces (left) as they rolled through the streets of Palermo, Sicily's capital. It was just 12 days after the Allies had landed on the beaches of the big island off the toe of Italy's boot.

Sicilian Strategy *The Mafia connection*

Treacherously mined harbors. Booby-trapped beaches. Rocky terrain. More than 400,000 enemy troops. As the Allies zeroed in on Sicily in 1943, the strategic island threatened to be a costly prize. Yet casualties were remarkably light, and Sicily was captured in 39 days.

A growing enmity between the Germans and Italians was partly responsible for the swiftness of the victory. But there were other factors, for the U.S. Navy had solicited help from a most unlikely source—the American underworld.

The navy lacked an effective intelligence network in Sicily. As part of its jury-rigged effort to gather information—it even checked tourists' snapshots of ports—it turned to Charles "Lucky" Luciano, the Mafia chieftain and big-time purveyor of prostitutes who was serving a 30- to 50-year prison sentence.

Luciano, a poor Sicilian immigrant turned organized crime kingpin, was reluctant at first, but finally agreed to lend the navy his Mafia contacts. Lucky (so called because he'd survived a vicious murder attempt) was a powerful crime leader both in the United States and in Sicily, where the organization controlled most local governments. His influence (combined with an ongoing feud between the Mafia and Mussolini's Fascists) attracted hundreds of informants. With their help, intelligence officers penetrated Italian naval headquarters, filching vital maps and documents. Mafia members even acted as guides for advance units and "persuaded" Italian soldiers not to fight.

After the war the navy moved quickly to cover up its Mafia connections. And although Luciano had not been promised any deal for his cooperation, the gangster *was* released from prison and deported to Italy in 1946, after serving only 10 years of his sentence.

Four Chaplains, Four Heroes *The greatest sermon ever preached*

"We'll be stowed away like a bunch of sardines in a tin can," said one of the 903 GI's boarding the S.S. *Dorchester* on a dreary January day in 1943.

Also boarding the "tin can" were four chaplains: Protestants George Fox (winner of a Silver Star for bravery) and Clark Poling; Alexander Goode, a witty rabbi; and a high-spirited priest named Johnny Washington. As they headed across the icy North Atlantic, where German U-boats lurked, the clergy offered solace to the fearful soldiers.

At 1:00 A.M. on February 3 a German torpedo ripped into the ship. "She's going down!" the men cried, scrambling for lifeboats.

A young GI crept up to one of the clergymen. "Padre," he whispered, "I've lost my life jacket." "Take this," the chaplain said, handing the soldier his own jacket. "I'm staying. I won't need it."

One by one, the other three also gave up their life jackets. Then the chaplains, arms linked and heads raised in prayer, stood on deck as the *Dorchester* slipped beneath the waves. They were among 678 men lost that night.

President Harry Truman later praised the four: "I don't think in the history of the world that there has been anything in heroism equal to this. It was the greatest sermon that was ever preached."

D-Day's Disastrous DD Tanks

The Allies' new secret weapons sank like stones

Sherman tanks fitted with flotation collars seemed like wonder weapons on English lakes, but they failed tragically in the Normandy invasion.

This was the weapon that would win the war: a 32-ton Sherman tank with a 7-foot canvas collar folded accordionlike against its sides. The brainchild of Nicholas Straussler, a Hungarian immigrant in England, the "bloomers" could float the tank on water, where it was driven by two rear-mounted propellers powered by the same engine that drove it on land. Hence the invention's name, the Duplex Drive (DD) Tank.

Developed by the British, the tanks quickly gained enthusiastic support. Gen. George C. Marshall, the U.S. Army's chief of staff, had already approved their use, and British prime minister Winston Churchill predicted they would have an integral role in any assault on the Continent.

The DD's were first demonstrated to Allied supreme commander Gen. Dwight D. Eisenhower on a small English lake. Ike, an experienced tank commander himself, was so taken with the amphibian that he took one out for a spin. This was the perfect weapon for a European invasion. Drop these tanks in the water, have them scurry up the beach, clearing out machine-gun nests, and the infantry would march in behind them. The few reservations the generals heard about the tanks' seaworthiness were lost in the euphoria.

Unfortunately, the English Channel around Normandy on June 6, 1944, was nothing like that quiet lake. It was still wild from the storm that had forced cancellation of an invasion attempt just the day before. To make matters worse, the DD crews had had little more than a month of training.

At Utah Beach, navy officers tried to launch the DD's in rough water 5,000 yards from shore. But the army commander of the 70th Tank Battalion demanded to be ferried closer to the beachhead, despite danger from submerged mines. One landing craft struck a mine and was blown up. But all 28 of the DD's actually put in the water at Utah made it ashore, guns blazing. This was the floating tank's greatest success.

Omaha Beach, however, was a tragedy. The seas were rougher there, but the 741st Tank Battalion in the eastern sector dutifully persisted in its mission. Without consulting the chief naval officer, army captains decided to launch the DD's from their transports some 6,000 yards offshore. As the canvas flotation "bloomers" collapsed in the choppy seas, the DD's sank, one after another, like stones. The men atop the tanks struggled to break through the seven-foot collars. But the soldiers inside never had a chance. Only 2 of the 29 DD's the 741st put in the water made it ashore. The skipper of one transport lifted his ramp as soon as he saw the first tank sink, thus saving three more, which were landed later.

Not only did the infantry at Omaha lose the DD tank cover, but the Allied air attack overshot the beach and the naval bombardment undershot it. German defenses were intact and waiting when the landing parties hit the shore. The GI's were sitting ducks. Only at the cost of thousands of American lives was a beachhold secured.

The last battle

The Normandy invasion wasn't the last conflict for the 741st Battalion. In 1979 the mayor of St.-Laurent-sur-Mer announced that the tanks, still offshore, were tangling the nets of local fishermen. The army sent a diver to look briefly. But then one of the officers responsible for recovering the bodies of fallen soldiers halted the search, stating that funds were "not available to finance the salvage of the tanks. The army's responsibility begins when the tanks are out of the water."

So the army and navy are still bickering about control off Omaha Beach, and the brave men of the 741st remain at the bottom of the Atlantic, having yet to reach the coastline they died so courageously trying to secure.

The Ordeal of the *Indianapolis* ***Nobody knew it was there***

A little before midnight on Sunday, July 29, 1945, the heavy cruiser *Indianapolis* was returning from a secret mission to the Pacific atoll of Tinian. She had delivered parts for the atomic bomb that would be dropped on Hiroshima eight days later. Headed toward Leyte in the Philippines, the vessel was ripped by torpedoes from a Japanese submarine. Within 15 minutes she had vanished beneath the surface, the last American ship sunk by the enemy in World War II. For her survivors, the most desperate days of the war were about to begin.

The ship sank so quickly that of the 1,199 crewmen, only some 850, including Capt. Charles McVay, escaped. In the confusion, they had released a mere dozen life rafts and six flotation nets, and the captain had been unable to send an SOS. But the survivors weren't even aware of their greatest catastrophe. An earlier message giving the ship's estimated arrival time had been so garbled in transmission that it couldn't be decoded, and no one at Leyte had asked for a retransmission. The terrifying truth was that it would take days for the U.S. naval command to discover that the *Indianapolis* was missing. Her survivors were alone and unnoticed—except by the sharks.

As morning dawned on Monday, July 30, ominous fins sliced the water: 88 men were attacked and killed in the largest group of survivors; 25 more in another. One sailor had his legs bitten off; becoming top-heavy in his life vest, he tipped upside down and drowned. The sharks continued to feed intermittently for days.

The effects of exposure and lack of fresh water were less gruesome but even more deadly. Sunburn became lethal; men went blind. Those who drank seawater got salt poisoning; those who abstained, succumbed to dehydration. Sailors started hallucinating. After 48 hours in the sea, the kapok life jackets became waterlogged and began dragging men under.

But, extraordinarily, many of the survivors maintained hope, even when planes flew overhead without seeing them. Finally, at five minutes past noon on Thursday, August 2, they were spotted. Lt. W. Charles Gwinn, a navy pilot on a routine flight, had given in to mild curiosity and dipped his PV-1 Ventura aircraft to inspect what he thought was an oil slick.

Rescue ships arrived around midnight. By then the crew of the *Indianapolis* had been in the water for four full days—96 desperately terrifying hours. Only 316 men survived, and for one of them, Captain McVay, the ordeal was not yet over.

In a move apparently aimed at appeasing public outrage, McVay was court-martialed, the only U.S. Navy captain in World War II to face trial for losing a ship. Many of his crew believed he had been made a scapegoat for naval brass, who by failing to keep track of the ship's location had botched the rescue. As expected, the captain was found guilty—but within a year the navy remitted his sentence.

Rescuers were aghast at the suffering. Holding a sailor who didn't make it, one seaman wept, "Mac, if we had've known you were out here like this, we'd have come sooner."

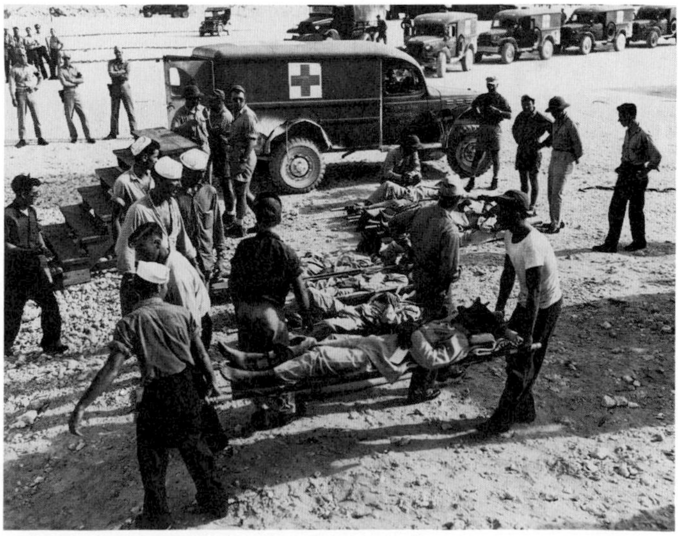

D-Day Crossword Puzzles

In the five weeks prior to the invasion of Normandy, London's Daily Telegraph *published five crossword puzzles containing top-secret D-Day code words. "Utah," "Omaha," "Mulberry," and "Neptune" appeared as solutions during May. But the biggest blow came on June 2, just four days before the invasion, when "Overlord," the code name for the entire operation, was given as the answer to 11 across.*

Soon, Leonard Dawe, the bespectacled 54-year-old physics teacher who had compiled the Daily Telegraph *puzzles for more than 20 years, found himself being grilled by Scotland Yard. But it was all just an amazing coincidence. The suspicious crosswords were not a double-cross, and the Germans remained puzzled about the time and location of the D-Day invasion.*

The Power of Words, the Passion of Victims *Atoms at Hiroshima*

The age of atomic warfare may have been started by a confusing translation from the Japanese.

Mokusatsu

Daily air raids were taking a heavy toll on Japan during the summer of 1945; defeat seemed imminent. On July 26, Allied leaders issued the Potsdam Agreement: "We call upon the government of Japan to proclaim now the unconditional surrender of all Japanese armed forces. . . . The alternative for Japan is prompt and utter destruction." But the offer was also in some ways generous; it allowed Japanese soldiers to return home without imprisonment.

Emperor Hirohito believed the Potsdam peace terms "were the most reasonable to be expected." But Prime Minister Kantaro Suzuki disagreed; he felt Japan still had some negotiating leverage with the Russians. Soon, Suzuki was telling reporters that Japan must *mokusatsu* the Allied offer.

Mokusatsu literally means "to kill with silence." Suzuki later claimed he had meant "no comment." But the Japanese news agency, Domei, quickly translated the word as "ignore." With this, the bombing of Hiroshima and Nagasaki was virtually inevitable.

The other victims

Just a week later, on August 6, 1945, the *Enola Gay* took off on its fateful mission. At 8:15 A.M. bombadier Maj. Thomas Ferebee had his target in his sights: the Aioi Bridge crossing the Ota River in Hiroshima.

About half a mile from his target the crew of the *Lonesome Lady,* which had been shot down just 10 days earlier, were being held as war prisoners along with fliers from two other American planes—at least 10 GI's in all.

Although the solid brick of their cells managed to withstand the awesome initial blast, only three of these prisoners are known to have survived the explosion. Navy pilot Normand Brissette and the *Lonesome Lady*'s gunner, Ralph Neal, stayed nose-deep in a cesspool until the flames died down. As soon as they emerged, they were recaptured by the Japanese. During the next days each suffered acutely with oozing sores and constant vomiting, the result of radiation exposure. Both men died slow and horrible deaths.

The third American who survived the explosion died as a scapegoat for the bombing. History doesn't record his name, but an eyewitness called him "the handsomest boy I ever saw." He was tied to the remains of the Aioi Bridge with a placard that said: "Beat This American Soldier Before You Pass."

Besides these military prisoners, more than 3,000 Japanese-American civilians were stranded in Hiroshima when the war began. Of those who survived the blast, perhaps 1,000 returned to the United States.

The story of any single person who endured the atomic attack on Japan is appalling. If we then consider statistics in light of these scenes of individual agony, the extent of human suffering begins to stagger the mind: the two bomb blasts at Hiroshima and Nagasaki killed 300,000 people.

One second after the atomic bomb's explosion at Hiroshima, a fireball 650 feet wide scorched everything in its path. Shock waves destroyed brick buildings within a mile of the bomb site; wooden buildings were simply obliterated. Half an hour later a firestorm was sweeping the city. This was followed by a muddy, chilling rain, which poured radioactivity. Some 80,000 people were dead by mid-afternoon; another 120,000 were dying. For more than a mile from the bomb's point of impact the once thriving city was ashes.

"Old Soldiers Never Die . . ."

MacArthur got the news from a radio report

Gen. Douglas MacArthur had brilliantly routed the North Koreans at Inchon in September 1950 and pursued them into North Korea. But the offensive backfired. MacArthur's soldiers were ambushed by Chinese Communists, and the general pressed President Truman for permission to attack inside China. But Truman refused, loath to start a major conflict so soon after World War II.

MacArthur found Truman's position incomprehensible and repeatedly made his unhappiness known to the press. The president saw this as gross insubordination for which there was only one solution: MacArthur must go—and Truman wanted the satisfaction of firing him.

To forestall the great general's resignation, the White House announced his dismissal in a hastily called press conference at 1:00 A.M. on April 11, 1951. Halfway around the world an officer at MacArthur's headquarters informed the 71-year-old general that he'd been dumped. The officer had heard the news on the radio.

MacArthur's firing created a predictable uproar, and everywhere he went well-wishers greeted him. Jokes ridiculing the president became popular, among them one about a Truman beer: just like any other beer—but without a head.

A replica of the 24½-foot H-bomb that fell on New Mexico from a B-36 in 1957 is displayed at the National Atomic Museum in Albuquerque.

Bombs Over Albuquerque

The day they nearly nuked New Mexico

It weighed 42,000 pounds, it was one of the nation's most powerful hydrogen bombs, and in May 1957 it fell on New Mexico.

The Mark 17, as this monster armament was called, is cited in the *Nuclear Weapons Databook* as "the first droppable thermonuclear bomb to be tested." But this "test" most definitely went awry. A safety-release lever was in the wrong position, causing the Mark 17 to rip away the bomb-bay door and fall from the plane. Although its nonnuclear explosives blasted a 25-foot-wide crater in the desert, its 10-megaton nuclear charge miraculously wasn't set off, narrowly averting horror for New Mexico: the bomb was hundreds of times more powerful than the one that had leveled Hiroshima.

In 1981 the government issued a noncommital report about the accident. Five years later the Albuquerque *Journal* used the Freedom of Information Act to dig up further documentation. When the truth came out, a Defense Department spokesman tried hard to look on the bright side: the nuclear bomb's failure to explode, he pointed out, "confirms the efficacy of the safety devices."

ACKNOWLEDGMENTS

The editors wish to express special appreciation to the following individuals and organizations for their generous assistance with the research for this book:

Carol L. Bagley and Jo Ann Ruckman, Idaho State University. Philip Vanderbilt Brady, Vanderbilt Family Historian. Barnaby Bullard, Loudonville, N.Y. Theodore Chase, Dover, Mass. Sue Collins, Stillwater Public Library, Stillwater, Minn. Hollis N. Cook, Tombstone, Ariz. J. Cooper, University of Wisconsin, Department of History. David J. Frent, Political Americana Historian. Albert E. Grollin, New York. Helen Harrison, Guest Curator, Queens Museum. Illustrious Lester J. Harrison, Brooklyn Masonic Temple. Kenneth Jessen, Loveland, Colo. Donald E. Loker, Niagara Falls Public Library, Niagara Falls, N.Y. Oscar Mastin, Patent and Trademark Office, U.S. Department of Commerce. Dan Morgan, Cincinnati, for information on Private O'Leary. Douglas C. Moul, *Civil War Times Illustrated.* Dr. Charles E. Nolan, Archdiocese of New Orleans. Colleen Phillips, Cincinnati, Ohio. Marcia C. Stein, March of Dimes. Jane Sumpter, Virginia State Library. Bernard Titowsky, Austin Book Shop. Alan D. Weiner, Richmond, Va., for the story on D-Day tanks.

Alabama Department of Archives and History, Reference Division. Alabama Historical Association. Alaska Department of Natural Resources. Alexander Graham Bell National Historic Park. American Bowling Congress. *American History Illustrated.* Appomattox Court House National Historical Park. Arizona Historical Society. Arkansas Historical Association. AT&T Company Historical Archives. Avon Products, Inc. Baseball Hall of Fame. Basketball Hall of Fame. Baylor University, The Texas Collection. Beersheba Springs Historical Society, Beersheba Springs, Tenn. Berkeley Plantation. Berkshire Athenaeum. Bishop Museum. Booker T. Washington National Monument. Borden, Inc. *The Boston Globe.* Brooklyn Historic Railway Association. California Historical Society. California State Archives. The Chapel of Four Chaplains. Chesebrough-Pond's, Inc. Chicago Historical Society. The Church of Jesus Christ of Latter-day Saints, Historical Department. Cincinnati Historical Society. City of New York, Police Department, Youth Services Division. *Civil War Times Illustrated.* Colorado Division of Archives and Public Records. Colorado Historical Society. Comstock Historic House. Connecticut Historical Society. Connecticut State Library. Cornell University, New York Historical Resources Center. Delaware Bureau of Archives and Records Management. Department of the Navy, Naval Historical Center. Department of the Treasury, U.S. Mint. The Dirksen Congressional Center. Dover Public Library, Dover, Del. Dr Pepper Company. Dwight D. Eisenhower Library. *Early American Life.* Essex Institute. F & F Laboratories, Inc. Federal Bureau of Investigation. Fitchburg Public Library, Fitchburg, Mass. The Florida State Museum. Fort Boonesboro State Park. Fort Clatsop National Memorial. Franklin D. Roosevelt Library. Frederick Law Olmsted National Historic Site. Fredericksburg National Military Park. The Garibaldi and Meucci Memorial Museum. Georgia Department of Archives and History. Gerald R. Ford Library. Governor Hogg Shrine State Historical Park. Henry Ford Museum and Greenfield Village. Herbert Hoover National Historic Site. The Hideout Inc. The Historical Society of Delaware. The Historical Society of Pennsylvania. Historical Society of Western Pennsylvania. Hubbell Trading Post National Historic Site. Idaho State Historical Society. Illinois Historic Preservation Agency, Galena State Historic Sites. January 12th, 1888 Blizzard Club. Jedediah Smith Society. Jimmy Carter Library. John Brown Historical Association, Inc. John Muir National Historic Site. John Wesley Powell Memorial Museum. Jones Memorial Library, Lynchburg, Va. Judah L. Magnes Memorial Museum, Western Jewish History Center. Kansas State Historical Society. Kentucky Historical Society. La Crosse Chamber of Commerce, La Crosse, Kans. Lindbergh Historic Site. Longfellow National Historic Site. Louisiana State Museum. MacArthur Memorial. Maine Historical Society. Manhattan College, College Relations Office. Marshall Gold Discovery State Park. Martin Van Buren National Historic Site. Massachusetts Historical Society. Max Factor & Co. Melrose Plantation. Mississippi Department of Archives and History. Missouri Historical Society. Montana Historical Society. Montgomery Ward & Co., Inc. Monticello. Morton Thiokol, Inc. Mount Holyoke College. Museum of New Mexico. Natchez Trace Parkway. National Soft Drink Association. Nebraska State Historical Society. Nevada Historical Society. North Carolina Department of Cultural Resources, Division of Archives and History. The Northeastern Nevada Museum. Oklahoma Historical Society. Omaha Public Library. Orange County Historical Society, Va. Oregon State University, Kerr Library. Phillips Petroleum Company. Plimoth Plantation, Inc. Polish Historical Commission of the Central Council of Polish Organizations of Pittsburgh. The Procter & Gamble Co. Pro Football Hall of Fame. Queensboro Public Library, Long Island Division. R. E. Olds Transportation Museum. Republican National Committee. Robert E. Lee Memorial Association, Inc., Stratford Hall Plantation. Rosenberg Library. Rough Riders Memorial and City Museum. Rutherford B. Hayes Presidential Center. Rutledge Hill Press. Salem Public Library, Salem, Mass. The Sam Rayburn Library. San Luis Obispo County Historical Society, Calif. Scholl, Inc. Sears, Roebuck and Co. Shelby County Historical Society, Tex. Shell Oil Company. Smithsonian Institution, National Air and Space Museum. South Carolina Department of Archives and History. Southern Jewish Historical Society. St. Francis de Sales Church, Cincinnati. State Historical Society of Missouri. State Historical Society of North Dakota. State Library of Massachusetts. Stephentown Historical Society, N.Y. Supreme Court Historical Society. Swiss Mennonite Cultural & Historical Association. Tennessee Historical Society. Texas Historical Commission. Texas State Library. Thomas Jefferson Memorial Foundation, Inc. Tubac Presidio State Historic Park. Union Pacific Railroad. U.S. Chess Federation. U.S. Postal Service, History Department. U.S. Senate Historical Office. University of Akron, Bierce Library. Utah Division of State History. Uvalde, Tex., City Manager's Office. Virginia Department of Conservation and Historic Resources, Division of Historic Landmarks. Virginia Historical Society. The Washington State Historical Society. Weaverville Joss House Association. Western Postal History Museum. The White House, Office of Correspondence. Will Rogers Memorial. Wyoming State Archives, Museums & Historical Department. Yankee Publications, Inc. Yonkers Public Library, Yonkers, N.Y. YWCA of the City of New York. Zion Evangelical Lutheran Church, Manheim, Pa.

Special appreciation is extended to the following individuals for their valuable assistance in picture research:

American Antiquarian Society, Georgia Barnhill. Brown Brothers, Meredith Collins. Chicago Historical Society, Linda Ziemer. Denver Public Library, Eleanor Gehres. Eastern National Park and Monument Association, Patricia Mallory. Edison Historic Site, Eric Olsen. Florida State Archives, Joan Morris. George Eastman House, Barbara Galasso. Harvard College Library, Wallace F. Dailey. Harvard Theatre Collection, Jeanne Newlin. Henry Ford Museum, Cynthia Read Miller. Kansas State Historical Society, Tom Norris. Library of Congress, Jerry Kearns. Metropolitan Museum of Art, Deanna Cross. Museum of the City of New York, Ellen Wallenstein. National Air and Space Museum, Rita Cipalla. National Archives, James Trimble. National Museum of American History, David Haberstick. National Portrait Gallery, Will Staff. New Hampshire Historical Society, William Copeley. New-York Historical Society, Wendy Shadwell. New York Public Library, Francis Mattson, Roberta Waddell. New York Public Library, Schomburg Center for Research in Black Culture, Betty Odabashian. Oklahoma Historical Society, Robert Nespor. Peabody Museum of Salem, Mark Sexton. Yale University Art Gallery, William Cuffe.

Picture Credits

5 The Bettmann Archive. ***8–9*** Manchester (N.H.) Historic Association Photo Archives/Photography by Harlan A. Marshall. ***10*** *top* Courtesy, Museum of Fine Arts, Boston; *bottom* Courtesy, American Antiquarian Society. ***11*** The Bostonian Society/Old State House. ***12*** *top* Courtesy of The Cincinnati Historical Society; *bottom* AP/Wide World Photos. ***13*** Foxborough Historical Commission. ***14*** UPI/Bettmann Newsphotos. ***15*** Culver Pictures. ***16*** Maryland Historical Society, Baltimore. ***17*** *top* The New York Public Library; *lower* The New Haven Colony Historical Society. ***18*** International Museum of Photography at George Eastman House. ***19*** *top* Courtesy, American Antiquarian Society; *bottom* The New York Public Library, Picture Collection. ***20–21*** Library of Congress. ***22*** *left* Library of Congress; *right* Harvard Theatre Collection. ***23*** National Philatelic Collection, Smithsonian Institution. ***24*** Photo courtesy of Abbeville Press, Inc. ***25*** Yankee Publishing Incorporated. ***26*** Reproduced with permission of AT&T Corporate Archive. ***27*** Courtesy of The New-York Historical Society, New York City. ***28*** The Metropolitan Museum of Art, The Edward W. C. Arnold Collection of New York Prints, Maps and Pictures; Bequest of Edward W. C. Arnold, 1954. ***29*** The Schlesinger Library, Radcliffe College. ***30*** Culver Pictures. ***31*** *left* Jackson County Historical Society; *right* The Denver Public Library, Western History Department. ***32*** Courtesy of the New York Society Library. ***33*** *top* The Bettmann Archive; *bottom* Frank Driggs Collection. ***34*** *left* Texas Historical Commission; *right* The Bettmann Archive. ***35*** *upper* The Bettmann Archive; *bottom* Private Collection. ***36*** *left* Rutherford B. Hayes Presidential Center; *right* North Carolina Division of Archives and History. ***37*** The Kansas State Historical Society, Topeka. ***38*** The New York Public Library. ***39*** *top* Culver Pictures; *bottom* Circus World Museum. ***40*** Photograph courtesy of New York State Historical Association, Special Collections, Cooperstown. ***41*** Courtesy, Colorado Historical Society. ***42*** *top* Courtesy of Capt. Joseph F. Enright; *bottom* Library of Congress. ***44*** Foxborough Historical Commission. ***45*** *left* Culver Pictures; *right* National Baseball Library, Cooperstown, N.Y. ***46–47*** Connecticut State Library/Photography by Gus Johnson. ***49*** *left* Liberty Bell Slot Collection; *right* Courtesy of The New-York Historical Society, New York City. ***50*** *top* The original painting hangs in the Selectmen's Meeting Room, Abbot Hall, Marblehead, Massachusetts. ***51*** Smithsonian Institution/NMAH. ***53*** *top* Yale University Art Gallery; *inset* Library of Congress. ***54*** The Metropolitan Museum of Art, Bequest of Adele S. Colgate, 1962. ***55*** The Imogen Cunningham Trust. ***56*** *bottom left & center* The New York Public Library, U.S. History, Local History & Genealogy Division; *bottom right* National Archives. ***58*** Mount Rushmore National Memorial, National Park Service. ***59*** Courtesy of the Chicago Historical Society. ***60*** *top* Library of Congress; *bottom* Maryland Historical Society, Baltimore. ***61*** *upper* Nawrocki Stock Photo Inc.; *bottom* James A. McInnis. ***62*** Christian Kempf/Bibliothèque de la Ville de Colmar. ***63*** *center* Courtesy of The New-York Historical Society, New York City; *remainder* National Archives. ***65*** Library of Congress. ***66*** National Gallery of Art, Washington, Gift of Mrs. Robert Homans. ***67*** *top* Wyoming State Archives, Museums and Historical Department; *bottom* The New York Public Library, Picture Collection. ***68–69*** AP/Wide World Photos. ***70*** Independence National Historical Park Collection. ***71*** Library of Congress. ***72*** Courtesy of The New-York Historical Society, New York City. ***74*** *top* Langdon Clay; *remainder* Monticello. ***75*** Monticello. ***79 & 80*** Library of Congress. ***81*** *left* Library of Congress; *right* The Pierce Brigade. ***82*** *left* Independence National Historical Park Collection; *right* Chicago Historical Society. ***84*** *top* The National Portrait

Gallery, Smithsonian Institution; *lower left* The New York Public Library, Print Collection, Miriam and Ira D. Wallach Division of Art, Prints and Photographs; *bottom right* The Harry T. Peters Collection, Museum of the City of New York. ***85*** The National Portrait Gallery, Smithsonian Institution. ***86*** Culver Pictures. ***88 & 89*** Culver Pictures. ***90*** The Rutherford B. Hayes Presidential Center. ***91*** Library of Congress. ***92 & 93*** Culver Pictures. ***94*** Library of Congress. ***95*** *left* Smithsonian Institution, Division of Political History; *right* Theodore Roosevelt Collection, Harvard College Library. ***96*** *top* Brown Brothers. ***96–97*** *bottom* Culver Pictures. ***97*** *top* Courtesy, American Antiquarian Society; *lower right* Library of Congress. ***98*** *left* AP/Wide World Photos; *right* The New York Public Library, Picture Collection. ***99*** Library of Congress. ***100*** *top* Brown Brothers; *lower* UPI/Bettmann Newsphotos. ***101*** *top* Culver Pictures; *bottom* UPI/Bettmann Newsphotos. ***102*** *left* Louisiana State Museum; *right* Library of Congress. ***103*** AP/Wide World Photos. ***104*** The Kansas State Historical Society, Topeka. ***105*** UPI/Bettmann Newsphotos. ***107*** Franklin D. Roosevelt Library. ***108*** *top* AP/Wide World Photos; *bottom* Harry S. Truman Library. ***109*** *left* UPI/Bettmann Newsphotos; *right* The New York Public Library. ***110*** © 1952 Walt Kelly, courtesy of Selby Kelly. ***111*** Drawing by David Levine, reprinted with permission from *The New York Review of Books* © 1966. ***112*** *left Look* Magazine Collection, Library of Congress; *right* UPI/Bettmann Newsphotos. ***113*** AP/Wide World Photos. ***114–115*** Museum of the City of New York/The Byron Collection. ***116*** (detail) The National Portrait Gallery, Smithsonian Institution, Transfer from the National Gallery of Art, Gift of Andrew W. Mellon, 1942. ***117*** Library of Congress. ***118*** Collections of the Maine Historical Society. ***119*** Courtesy of Morton Salt Division, Morton Thiokol, Inc. ***120*** Missouri Historical Society. ***121*** *bottom* The New York Public Library, Rare Book Division; *inset* The New York Public Library. ***122*** Peabody Museum of Salem, Photography by Mark Sexton. ***123*** *left* The New York Public Library, Picture Collection; *right* UPI/Bettmann Newsphotos. ***124*** The National Portrait Gallery, Smithsonian Institution. ***125*** Culver Pictures. ***126*** California Historical Society, San Francisco. ***127*** *left* Arizona Historical Foundation; *right* Richard Crandall. ***128*** Library of Congress. ***129*** Drake Well Museum. ***130*** Brown Brothers. ***132*** *top* Culver Pictures; *inset* The Denver Public Library, Western History Department. ***133*** *left* UPI/Bettmann Newsphotos; *right* The Bettmann Archive. ***134*** Collection, The Museum of Modern Art, New York, Gift of A. Conger Goodyear. ***135*** Brown Brothers. ***136*** Union Pacific Railroad Museum Collection. ***138*** *bottom* Culver Pictures; *inset* Brown Brothers. ***139*** Brown Brothers. ***140*** Museum of the City of New York. ***141*** Montgomery Ward. ***142*** Culver Pictures. ***143*** *top* UPI/Bettmann Newsphotos; *inset* Culver Pictures. ***144*** *bottom* J. R. Monaco; *inset* Culver Pictures. ***145*** Alton H. Blackington Collection. ***146*** *left* UPI/Bettmann Newsphotos; *right* AP/Wide World Photos. ***147*** *left* Culver Pictures. ***148*** *top left* Courtesy of the Florida State Archives; *top right* Motor Vehicle Manufacturers Association of the United States, Inc.; *lower* Courtesy of the National Automotive History Collection of the Detroit Public Library. ***150*** The New York Public Library, Schomburg Center for Research in Black Culture. ***151*** The Kobal Collection. ***153*** *left* UPI/Bettmann Newsphotos; *right* McDonald's. ***154–155*** The Bettmann Archive. ***156*** Courtesy of The New-York Historical Society, New York City. ***158*** *top* Library of Congress; *bottom* The New York Public Library, Rare Book Division. ***159*** The New York Public Library, Rare Book Division. ***161*** Yale University Art Gallery. ***162*** *top* Brown Brothers; *inset* Courtesy of Chase Manhattan Archives. ***164*** Library of Congress. ***165*** The New York Public Library. ***166*** Courtesy, Colorado Historical Society. ***167*** Pinkerton's, Inc. ***168*** Library of Congress. ***169*** National Archives. ***170*** The Kansas State Historical Society, Topeka. ***171*** *left* The Denver Public Library, Western History Department; *right* The New York Public Library. ***172*** Nez Perce County Historical Society, Inc., Lewiston, Idaho. ***173*** Barker Texas History Center, University of Texas at Austin. ***174*** Wells Fargo Bank. ***175*** *top* The New York Public Library, Picture Collection; *bottom* Federal Bureau of Investigation. ***176*** Western History Collections, University of Oklahoma Library. ***177*** *top* Archives and Manuscripts Division of the Oklahoma Historical Society. ***178*** Courtesy of The New-York Historical Society, New York City. ***179*** *left* Bicycle Federation of America; *right* The New York Public Library, Picture Collection. ***180*** The Denver Public Library, Western History Department. ***181*** The New York Public Library, Picture Collection. ***182*** National Archives. ***184*** Courtesy of George Mills. ***186*** National Archives. ***187*** Union Pacific Railroad Museum Collection. ***188*** St. Louis Mercantile Library Association. ***189*** *left* The Kobal Collection; *right* From "The World Encyclopedia of Comics," edited by Maurice Horn, Chelsea House Publishers. ***190*** *bottom* From the Collection of The Public Library of Cincinnati and Hamilton County; *inset* UPI/Bettmann Newsphotos. ***191*** The Bettmann Archive. ***192*** AP/Wide World Photos. ***193*** UPI/Bettmann Newsphotos. ***194*** *left* Brown Brothers; *right* Courtesy of Contrac, Controlled Activities Corporation. ***195*** Movie Star News. ***196–197*** Culver Pictures. ***198 & 199*** The New York Public Library, Rare Book Division. ***200*** *top* Library of Congress; *bottom* Courtesy of the Essex Institute, Salem, Massachusetts. ***201*** *top* Culver Pictures; (wampum) New York State Museum, State Education Department; *inset* The New York Public Library, Rare Book Division. ***203*** Culver Pictures. ***205*** The New York Public Library, Picture Collection. ***206*** *left* Harvard Theatre Collection; *top right* National Archives; *bottom* Courtesy of the John Carter Brown Library at Brown University. ***207*** Philadelphia Museum of Art, The George W. Elkins Collection. ***209*** The New York Public Library, Print Collection, Miriam and Ira D. Wallach Division of Art, Prints and Photographs. ***210*** *bottom* Courtesy of The New-York Historical Society, New York City. ***212*** The New York Public Library, Picture Collection. ***213*** *lower right* California Department of Transportation; *bottom* Illustration by Carl Rakeman. ***214*** Fruitlands Museum, Harvard, Massachusetts. ***215*** *bottom* Oneida Community Historical Committee; *inset* Culver Pictures. ***216*** *upper* The New York Public Library, Picture Collection; *bottom* Archives Center, National Museum of American History, Smithsonian Institution. ***217*** The Metropolitan Museum of Art, Gift of I. N. Phelps Stokes, Edward S. Hawes, Alice Mary Hawes, Marion Augusta Hawes, 1937. ***218*** *left* National Portrait Gallery, Smithsonian Institution; *right* Lester S. Levy Collection of Sheet Music, Special Collections, Milton S. Eisenhower Library, The Johns Hopkins University. ***219*** *top* Courtesy of the Strong Museum, Rochester, New York; *upper right* Collection of Mrs. Marshall F. Driggs; *bottom* The New York Public Library, Theatre Collection. ***220*** *left* National Baseball Library, Cooperstown, New York; *bottom* The Bettmann Archive; *inset* Courtesy, American Antiquarian Society. ***221*** Culver Pictures. ***222*** The Bettmann Archive. ***223*** Haynes Foundation Collection, Montana Historical Society, Helena, Montana. ***224*** *left* Courtesy of Manhattan College; *bottom* Library of Congress. ***224–225*** *top* Courtesy of Mrs. Frank Rowsome, Jr., from *Trolley Car Treasury* by Frank Rowsome, Jr., McGraw-Hill Book Company, Inc. © 1956 by Frank Rowsome, Jr. ***225*** *bottom left* The New York Public Library, Music Division; *right* AP/Wide World Photos. ***226*** Culver Pictures. ***227*** The Bettmann Archive. ***228*** Culver Pictures. ***229*** The New York Public Library, Picture Collection. ***230*** *top* Museum of the City of New York/The Byron Collection; *bottom left* Lester S. Levy Collection of Sheet Music, Special Collections, Milton S. Eisenhower Library, The Johns Hopkins University; *bottom right* Courtesy of the Florida State Archives. ***230–231*** *center* Culver Pictures. ***231*** *upper left* William H. Helfand Collection; *top right* William H. Helfand Collection/Photography by Al Freni; *bottom* The Denver Public Library, Western History Department. ***232*** Courtesy of J. S. Palen, Cheyenne, Wyoming. ***233*** Photograph courtesy American Heritage Center, University of Wyoming. ***234*** Brown Brothers. ***235*** Culver Pictures. ***236*** *top* Courtesy of the Chicago Historical Society; *middle* By Admiral Robert E. Peary, Courtesy of the Peary Family; *bottom* The New York Public Library. ***237*** *top* The Cunningham Collection; *bottom* Collections of the Maine Historical Society. ***238*** The Metropolitan Museum of Art, Purchase, Mr. and Mrs. William Coxe Wright Gift, 1957. ***239*** Collection of Dick Pintarich. ***240*** *top* Library of Congress; *remainder* The Bettmann Archive. ***241*** *right* Reprinted by permission: Tribune Media; *left* The Bettmann Archive. ***242*** *left* UPI/Bettmann Newsphotos; *right* U.S. Navy Photo. ***243*** *lower left* John W. Ripley; *remainder* Gregory Thorp. ***244*** *top* UPI/Bettmann Newsphotos; *inset* AP/Wide World Photos. ***245*** From the collections of Henry Ford Museum & Greenfield Village. ***246*** Library of Congress. ***247*** UPI/Bettmann Newsphotos. ***248*** *bottom* The Rockefeller Group; *remainder* Bill Fivaz. ***249*** *top left* Geo. A. Hormel & Co.; *bottom* Reprinted by permission of the Norman Rockwell Estate. ***250*** Library of Congress. ***251*** *top* Culver Pictures; *inset* BMG Music; *bottom* AP/Wide World Photos. ***252*** Dominique Berretty. ***253*** *top* National Archives. ***254*** *top left* Courtesy of Ron Widel; *bottom left & right* UPI/Bettmann Newsphotos. ***255*** *upper left* UPI/Bettmann Newsphotos; *inset* From the collections of Henry Ford Museum & Greenfield Village; *bottom* Rush County News, La Crosse, Kansas. ***256*** UPI/Bettmann Newsphotos. ***257*** *left* NASA; *right* The New York Public Library. ***258–259*** Solomon D. Butcher Collection, Nebraska State Historical Society. ***260*** The Pierpont Morgan Library. ***261*** Library of Congress. ***264*** Reproduced by courtesy of the Trustees of the British Museum. ***266*** The State Historical Society of Wisconsin. ***267*** National Gallery of Art, Washington, D.C. ***268*** *bottom* The New York Public Library, Rare Book Division; *inset* Library of Congress. ***269*** The New York Public Library. ***271*** The Filson Club. ***272*** Amon Carter Museum, Fort Worth. ***273*** *bottom* The New York Public Library; *inset* Independence National Park Collection, Philadelphia. ***275*** The Kansas State Historical Society, Topeka. ***276*** The Kendall Whaling Museum, Sharon, Massachusetts. ***277*** Indiana Historical Society. ***278*** The Carnegie Museum of Art, Pittsburgh, Museum purchase, 1942. ***279*** *bottom* National Archives; *inset* International Museum of Photography at George Eastman House. ***281*** Courtesy of the Southwest Museum, Los Angeles, California. ***282*** *left* Reproduced by permission of the Caxton Printers, Ltd., Caldwell, Idaho; *right* Culver Pictures. ***283*** The New York Public Library. ***284*** The Bettmann Archive. ***285*** Washington State Historical Society, Tacoma, Washington. ***287*** Nevada Historical Society. ***288*** The New York Public Library, American History Division. ***289*** Courtesy of The New-York Historical Society, New York City. ***290*** *left* Wells Fargo Bank History Room; *right* The New York Public Library, Picture Collection. ***291 & 292*** Nebraska State Historical Society. ***293*** *top* Courtesy of Don O'Neill; *bottom* Library of Congress. ***294*** *top* Courtesy of The New-York Historical Society, New York City. ***295*** The Kansas State Historical Society, Topeka. ***296*** *top* Courtesy of the Buffalo Bill Historical Center, Cody, Wyoming; *inset* Colorado Historical Society. ***298*** Photograph by Jacob A. Riis, Jacob A. Riis Collection, Museum of the City of New York. ***299*** Oklahoma Historical Society. ***300*** *top* Bishop Museum/A. F. Mitchell. ***301*** Courtesy of Chauncey C. Loomis. ***302*** *top* The Beinecke Rare Book and Manuscript Library, Yale University; *bottom* Special Collections Division, University of Washington Libraries. ***303*** Culver Pictures. ***304*** Montana Historical Society, Helena. ***305*** *upper right* UPI/Bettmann Newsphotos; *remainder* National Air and Space Museum, Smithsonian Institution. ***306*** NASA. ***307*** *top* Photri; *bottom* NASA. ***308–309*** Courtesy of the Chicago Historical Society. ***310*** *top* Library Company of Philadelphia; *inset* American Philosophical Society. ***311*** *top* Courtesy of The Franklin Institute Science Museum, Philadelphia, Pennsylvania; *lower right* (portrait) Independence National Historical Park Collection; *bottom left & upper & lower center* The New York Public Library. ***312*** *left* Official U.S. Navy Photograph; *right* General Dynamics Photo. ***313*** *top* Eric Sloane; *inset* Smithsonian Institution. ***314*** National Library of Medicine. ***315*** The Bettmann Archive. ***316*** Yale University Art Gallery, Gift of George

Hoadley, B.A., 1801. ***317*** *left* The Bettmann Archive; *top right* National Archives; *lower right* The New York Public Library. ***318*** *left* The Shaker Museum; *right* Borden, Inc. ***319*** *left* Library Company of Philadelphia; *right* Boston Medical Library in The Francis A. Countway Library of Medicine. ***320*** The New York Public Library. ***321*** *top* The New York Public Library, Picture Collection; *bottom* The New York Public Library. ***322*** Otis Elevator Company/United Technologies Corporation. ***323*** The New York Public Library. ***324*** The Metropolitan Museum of Art, Gift of Cyrus W. Field, 1892. ***325*** Reproduced from "Absolutely Mad Inventions" published by Dover Publications, Inc., in 1970. ***326*** The New York Public Library. ***327*** *top* The Bettmann Archive; *bottom right* The New York Public Library. ***328*** *top* Lowell Observatory Photograph; *bottom* The New York Public Library. ***329*** Mark Twain Memorial, Hartford, Connecticut. ***330*** *left* Library of Congress; *top right* Michael Freeman; *center* Culver Pictures. ***331*** Library of Congress. ***332 & 333*** U.S. Department of the Interior, National Park Service, Edison National Historic Site. ***334*** Culver Pictures. ***335*** *top* U.S. Department of the Interior, National Park Service, Edison National Historic Site; *bottom* The New York Public Library. ***336*** *left* The Picture Magazine; *right* Smithsonian Institution. ***337*** *left* The New York Public Library; *right* Smithsonian Institution. ***338*** Library of Congress. ***339*** *top* Courtesy of L. J. Hortin; *bottom* The New York Public Library. ***340*** National Air and Space Museum, Smithsonian Institution. ***341*** *left* Smithsonian Institution; *right* The New York Public Library. ***342*** AP/Wide World Photos. ***343*** *lower left* General Dynamics; *bottom* The New York Public Library; *remainder* AP/Wide World Photos. ***345*** *top* The New York Public Library; *bottom* The Bettmann Archive. ***346*** *top* National Archives; *bottom* Taro Yamasaki/*People* Weekly © 1987 Time, Inc. ***347*** Frederick Fried Archives. ***348*** Culver Pictures. ***349*** *bottom right* The New York Academy of Medicine; *remainder* The New York Public Library. ***350*** Culver Pictures. ***351*** *top* UPI/Bettmann Newsphotos; *bottom* The New York Public Library. ***352*** *top* Courtesy of Arthur D. Little; *bottom* Reprinted with special permission of King Features Syndicate, Inc./Photography by James A. McInnis. ***353*** *top* David Hutson; *middle* The Bettmann Archive; *bottom* Fred Lyon/Rapho/Photo Researchers. ***354–355*** Library of Congress. ***356*** The New York Public Library. ***359*** *upper* The State Historical Society of Wisconsin; *bottom* The New York Public Library, Rare Book Division. ***360*** Colonial Williamsburg Foundation. ***361*** The Metropolitan Museum of Art, Gift of John Stewart Kennedy, 1897. ***363*** *left* The Historical Society of Pennsylvania; *right* Courtesy, The Henry Francis du Pont Winterthur Museum. ***364*** Virginia State Library and Archives. ***365*** *left* Yale University Art Gallery; *right* James A. McInnis. ***366*** Library of Congress. ***367*** *bottom* Courtesy of The New-York Historical Society, New York City; *inset* Culver Pictures. ***368*** *left* Courtesy of The New-York Historical Society, New York City; *right* National Portrait Gallery, Smithsonian Institution. ***369*** The New York Public Library. ***370*** Library of Congress. ***371*** Beinecke Rare Book and Manuscript Library, Yale University. ***373*** *top* The Bettmann Archive; *lower* Culver Pictures. ***374*** The New York Public Library, Print Collection, Miriam and Ira D. Wallach Division of Art, Prints and Photographs. ***375*** Boston Athenaeum. ***376 & 377*** Library of Congress. ***378*** *top* Courtesy of Mrs. Philip D. Sang. ***378–379*** *bottom* The Moravian Music Foundation. ***380*** Courtesy of the Company of Military Historians. ***381*** *top* The Bettmann Archive; *bottom* Library of Congress. ***382*** *left* The Granger Collection, New York; *right* Culver Pictures. ***383*** *left* The Nevada Historical Society. ***384*** Philadelphia Museum of Art, The John G. Johnson Collection of Philadelphia. ***385*** Culver Pictures. ***386*** The Bettmann Archive. ***387*** Arizona Historical Society. ***388*** *left* Tom Conroy. ***388–389*** *top* Smithsonian Institution. ***389*** *lower right* The Museum of the American Indian, Heye Foundation; *bottom* The Denver Public Library, Western History Department. ***391*** *left* Library of Congress; *right* The Bettmann Archive. ***392 & 393*** Library of Congress. ***394*** Culver Pictures. ***395*** *left* National Archives; *right* The New York Public Library. ***396*** Culver Pictures. ***397*** Queens Library, L.I. Collection, Weber Collection. ***398*** *left* U.S. Army Photograph; *right* Courtesy of the Rev. Hector W. Bywater. ***399*** *left* The New York Public Library; *right* Bert Webber. ***400*** *bottom* UPI/Bettmann Newsphotos. ***401*** National Archives. ***402*** Imperial War Museum. ***403*** AP/Wide World Photos. ***404*** UPI/Bettmann Newsphotos. ***405*** *left* Richard Pipes; *right* UPI/Bettmann Newsphotos.

Efforts have been made to contact the holder of the copyright for each picture. In several cases these sources have been untraceable, for which we offer our apologies.

Several of the black and white pictures obtained for this book have been hand colored by Kenneth Chaya and Nancy Mace.

Illustration Credits

2–3 Peter De Sève. ***43*** Gregg Hinlicky. ***50*** *bottom* Bill Shortridge. ***56*** Nick Calabrese. ***77*** *top* Michael Conway; *bottom* Gerry Gersten. ***78*** Gil Eisner. ***83*** Gil Eisner. ***131*** Bill Shortridge. ***149*** Gregg Hinlicky. ***157*** Richard Williams. ***160*** Gil Eisner. ***177*** *bottom* Gregg Hinlicky. ***183*** Bill Shortridge. ***185*** Victor Lazzaro. ***195*** *top* Nancy Mace. ***204*** Steve Gray. ***210*** *inset* Bill Shortridge. ***213*** *top* Steve Gray. ***249*** *top right* Nancy Mace. ***253*** *bottom* Nancy Mace. ***254*** *top right* Bill Shortridge. ***262*** Ed Vebell. ***265*** Richard Williams. ***274*** Richard Williams. ***297*** *top* Steve Gray. ***297*** *center and bottom* Bill Shortridge. ***311*** *bottom right* Bill Shortridge. ***321*** *center* Bill Shortridge. ***327*** *bottom right* Bill Shortridge. ***357*** Peter De Sève. ***372*** Rick McCollum. ***400*** *top* Steve Gray.

INDEX

A

D

E

I

J

K

L

M

N

O

P

Q

R